CAMBRIDGE I

Books of enduring scholarly value

Literary studies

This series provides a high-quality selection of early printings of literary works, textual editions, anthologies and literary criticism which are of lasting scholarly interest. Ranging from Old English to Shakespeare to early twentieth-century work from around the world, these books offer a valuable resource for scholars in reception history, textual editing, and literary studies.

The Girlhood of Shakespeare's Heroines

Mary Cowden Clarke (1809-98) was the daughter of the publisher Vincent Novello. She was a noted Shakespearian scholar who produced a complete concordance to his works in 1845, and her fascination with the plays led to her publishing in 1850 a series of imaginative accounts of the girlhood of some of his heroines. Her motive was 'to imagine the possible circumstances and influences of scene, event, and associate, surrounding the infant life of his heroines, which might have conduced to originate and foster those germs of character recognized in their maturity as by him developed; to conjecture what might have been the first imperfect dawnings of that which he has shown us in the meridian blaze of perfection'. These 'prequels' offer a back-story which is surprising in its subversive interpretation of the plays and especially of the role of the 'hero'. This volume contains the stories of Beatrice and Hero, Olivia, Hermione, Viola and Imogen.

Cambridge University Press has long been a pioneer in the reissuing of out-of-print titles from its own backlist, producing digital reprints of books that are still sought after by scholars and students but could not be reprinted economically using traditional technology. The Cambridge Library Collection extends this activity to a wider range of books which are still of importance to researchers and professionals, either for the source material they contain, or as landmarks in the history of their academic discipline.

Drawing from the world-renowned collections in the Cambridge University Library, and guided by the advice of experts in each subject area, Cambridge University Press is using state-of-the-art scanning machines in its own Printing House to capture the content of each book selected for inclusion. The files are processed to give a consistently clear, crisp image, and the books finished to the high quality standard for which the Press is recognised around the world. The latest print-on-demand technology ensures that the books will remain available indefinitely, and that orders for single or multiple copies can quickly be supplied.

The Cambridge Library Collection will bring back to life books of enduring scholarly value (including out-of-copyright works originally issued by other publishers) across a wide range of disciplines in the humanities and social sciences and in science and technology.

The Girlhood of Shakespeare's Heroines

In a Series of Fifteen Tales

VOLUME 3

MARY COWDEN CLARKE

CAMBRIDGE
UNIVERSITY PRESS

CAMBRIDGE UNIVERSITY PRESS

Cambridge, New York, Melbourne, Madrid, Cape Town, Singapore,
São Paolo, Delhi, Dubai, Tokyo

Published in the United States of America by Cambridge University Press, New York

www.cambridge.org
Information on this title: www.cambridge.org/9781108001281

© in this compilation Cambridge University Press 2009

This edition first published 1851
This digitally printed version 2009

ISBN 978-1-108-00128-1 Paperback

THE

GIRLHOOD

OF

SHAKESPEARE'S HEROINES;

IN

A SERIES OF FIFTEEN TALES,

BY

MARY COWDEN CLARKE,

Author of the Concordance to Shakespeare.

"as petty to his ends,
As is the morn-dew on the myrtle leaf
To his grand sea."
Shakespeare.

TALE XI.

BEATRICE AND HERO; THE COUSINS.

LONDON:

W. H. SMITH & SON, 136, STRAND; AND SIMPKIN, MARSHALL, & CO.,
STATIONERS' HALL COURT.

1851.

TO

CHARLES ROBERT LESLIE, Esq., R.A.,

IN ADMIRATION OF HIS PICTURE OF

SHAKESPEARE'S "BEATRICE;"

AND OF HIS UNIFORM MASTERY IN

THE POET'S SUBJECTS;

THIS TALE IS DEDICATED

BY

MARY COWDEN CLARKE.

BEATRICE AND HERO; THE COUSINS.

"A pleasant-spirited lady. There's little of the melancholy element in her."

"Is she not a modest young lady? * * she is the sweetest lady that ever I looked on."

Much ado about nothing.

A sound cuff.

"What do you hit me for?"

Another. "Give it up! Will you give it up?"

"No!"

Another cuff. And a box on the ear. "Give it up, I say!"

Another "No" was about to be bawled; and a look in the lout's eye gave token that it would probably be accompanied by a return of the blows he had received; but suddenly he seemed to think better of it. Muttering something about being "too near master constable's house, or he'd ha' kept it as sure as he was alive," the boy flung down the demanded toy, turned on his heel, and made off.

The little girl who was thus left victress of the field, picked up the doll, brushed the dust off its smart skirts, arranged its rumpled head-dress, ascertained that its nose was neither cracked nor flattened, nor its eyes damaged, and then triumphantly walked up to another little girl, who had stood aloof during the affray, and restored the plundered favorite to her arms.

"Oh, I'm so glad to have her back! My beautiful new doll that my father gave me only yesterday!" exclaimed the child, hugging it to her, and smiling through the tears that still glittered on her cheeks.

"Why did you let him snatch it from you?" said the other little girl. "Why didn't you run after him, and force him to give it up?"

"He was such a great fierce lad—I couldn't—I didn't dare;" replied she.

"Why didn't your sister run after him, then, for you, and thump him, till he gave it up?" persisted the first little girl, looking towards a young boy who stood by, rubbing his knees, his back, and his elbows alternately; looking very scared, and very disconsolate; with a few big tears rolling down his face; and evidently in all the discomfiture of having only just recovered his legs.

"I'm not a girl, miss!" he blurted out, with a half shame-faced, half indignant glance at the beautiful, spirited face that was eyeing him. "What made you take me for a girl? Don't you see my dress?" And he cast a look of sheepish pride at his legs, which certainly were cased in masculine fashion.

"Don't I see your tears? What's crying but the trick of a girl?" said she, with a motion of her lips that made him wince. "Why didn't you fly after the fellow, instead of standing blubbering there?"

"He knocked me down!" said the boy. "He took good care to make sure of me, before he snatched at Hero's doll. How could I fly, miss, when he knocked me down? It's not so easy to fly, let me tell you, when a fellow sends you sprawling."

"But I suppose you could have scrambled up again, couldn't you? Unless you thought it more prudent to lie still. But for the sake of your sister's doll, you might have——"

"She isn't my sister,—she's my cousin!" interrupted the boy, glad to seize upon any point of defence, that he could safely maintain.

"Never mind, Gaetano, I have my doll again;" said its owner; and then, with her kind sweet tone, she turned to the little girl who had so bravely rescued it for her, and thanked her, in a manner so pretty and earnest, as to bespeak her unmistakeably the young lady born and bred.

The children fell into talk; and began to question each other how it was they happened to be out alone, how they had met, who they were, and so forth.

It appeared that the little girl, Hero, was the governor of Messina's daughter, his sole child and heiress; that the young boy, Gaetano, was the son of her uncle, Antonio. That they had left the palace in the morning, for a walk, attended by a servant; but that some show, or public procession, had suddenly attracted a crowd, in which they had been separated from their attendant. The other little girl, when she learned their names, uttered an exclamation of surprise. She told them that she was their cousin; that her name was Beatrice. That she was bound to their house, at the very time she encountered them; and that, singularly enough, the circumstance which had occasioned Hero and Gaetano to lose sight of their attendant, had also separated her from the person who was entrusted with the charge of bringing her from her native place to Messina.

Beatrice was an orphan. Her mother had married a poor lieutenant, contrary to the will of a rich maiden aunt; and, in consequence, had been cast off, disavowed, denounced. She had lived in seclusion, in a distant part of the island, enjoying the society of her husband, when the intervals of his military duties allowed him to be with her; and finding her chief happiness in the cultivation of her child's mind and disposition. While her husband lived, she had little missed the family ties she had broken for his sake; but he fell in battle; and then, beneath the stroke of this sudden affliction, her heart learned to acknowledge that she had been unfeeling and ungrateful, in not having better striven to soften the resentment of one who had brought her up, and centred all her hopes in the niece who so cruelly disappointed her; it learned to feel that she had been unmindful of the affectionate bonds in which she had once lived with her brothers, Leonato and Antonio; it learned to perceive that she had suffered pride and un-relenting—with their ever-strengthening, ever-hardening barriers,—to in-terpose between her aunt and herself, and that she had allowed coldness, and indifference, to estrange her from her best friends. She felt that it was now too late to attempt the recovery of her aunt's favor; but, on her death-bed, she bequeathed her little girl to the guardianship of Leonato, beseech-ing him to be a father to her orphan child.

It was on her way to her future home, that Beatrice happened to witness the incident which brought her so unexpectedly acquainted with her young relations. She saw the ruffianly lad snatch the child's doll; she saw neither the little girl nor her companion make any attempt at resistance; and her own immediate impulse was to force him to yield his prey. How she suc-ceeded has been seen.

"But what shall we do? We none of us know our way? I don't—

you don't, Hero ; and of course you don't, miss ?—Beatrice, I mean. Of
course, cousin Beatrice, you can't be expected to know the streets here in
Messina, or the way to the governor's palace (that's my uncle),—you, who
have never lived here;" said Gaetano. "Oh dear, oh dear, how provoking
it is of Matteo to have let us stray so ! Where can he be, I wonder ? You
don't see him anywhere, do you, cousin Hero ? "

"No, cousin ;" she replied.

" Oh dear, how could he be so careless of us ? " repeated Gaetano, with
a look deplorably helpless.

Beatrice took her handkerchief out of her pocket, and held it towards him.

" What's this for ? " he said.

" I thought you might be going to cry again, and would want it to wipe
your tears ;" replied Beatrice. " With that rueful look and tone, what but
weeping should follow ? "

" Ah, it's all very well ;" said the boy; " but we're very young, and
oughtn't to be left alone. My father and my uncle will both be rarely
angry with Matteo, when they hear how he lost us, staring about him."

" But how are they to hear ? " returned she. " You are no tale-bearer,
sure, to bring a poor serving-man into disgrace ? "

" Why, when a servant neglects his duty, what are we to do, miss ? "
said Gaetano.

" Not tell tales, miss; certainly not tell tales ;" replied she.

" Why do you call me ' miss,' cousin Beatrice ? I've told you already,
I'm no girl. If it's because you are displeased at my calling you miss,
now that I know you for my cousin ; you should recollect that it isn't so
easy all of a sudden to get into the way of calling a strange little girl by
her name. It seems so familiar ; and I don't know how it is, but you're
not one to be familiar with, I think."

. She laughed. " And you should recollect that it isn't so easy to treat
you as a boy, when I see you behave like a girl. But, come, I'll forgive
your calling me ' miss,' if you'll let me call you so."

" No, no ;" he said ; " I'd rather not. I won't be called so; and I'm sure
I don't wish to call you ' miss." Nay, I like calling you Beatrice, much
better. Only, let me get accustomed to it, cousin."

" Very well, cousin. Meantime, cheer up, put on a bold face, and enquire our way for us, at some house ;" she said.

" I don't know—I never did—I'm not accustomed to speak to strangers ;"
hesitated he.

" And if you never begin, you certainly never will be accustomed. Are
you afraid of getting bad habits ? Or do you intend to go through the
world without speaking to any but your intimates ? " she said.

" I don't know what you mean ;" said he, with a puzzled look. The boy
stood gazing in her face for a moment or two ; but there was something in
that clear eye, and in the turn of that lip, that made him cast down his
eyes, and bite his lip.

" Shall we try if this way will lead us right ? " said Hero, pointing down
a street that looked invitingly cool ; there was a fountain in the centre,
shaded by a broad-spreading chesnut-tree ; round which stood a group of
women, washing, and filling pitchers ; some men watering their mules ;
the animals whisking away the flies with their tails, shaking their long
ears, and drawing refreshing draughts from the marble basin, through their
bright and tasseled head-gear.

" Stay, suppose I just ask that lad, who is lounging in yonder door-way,
whether this turning will do ;" said Beatrice, stepping forward as she
spoke, and addressing her enquiry to a sturdy hobbedehoy, who was idly
chipping splinters off the door-post with the end of a bill he poised in his
hand.

" Thou know'st not whom thou'rt questioning, little girl ;" he said, looking over his shoulder at her in a lordly manner ; " 'twere a pity of thy life,
an' thou were't to question me too closely, seeing that I am the constable's
eldest son ; and seeing moreover, that thou art, or I'm much mista'en, no
better than thou shouldst be. 'Tis my father's calling to apprehend all
aspicious people, and vagroms ; and .were I to tell him that I have seen
you three chits loitering about here for some time past, he'd charge you be
accused in no time. I've had my eye on you, I promise ye ; and think
not over well of your looks, I tell ye honestly."

" What dost thou see in our looks, that hits not thy taste, fellow ? " said
Beatrice.

" Nay, ' fellow' not me, little girl, nor ' thou' not me, if thou be'st wise. 'Tis not for mendicomes and vagabonds to make too familiar with a limb of the law,—a limb, a very member,—being as I am, constable's son, and likely to be constable myself, one of these days."

" We are neither beggars nor thieves, law-limb ;" she replied ; " we but seek to know our way ; we only ask——"

" You only ' ask ! ' What is asking but begging, I should like to know ? What is wandering, but going astray ; what is going astray, but erring ; what is erring, but wickedness ; and what is wickedness, but the high-road to thieving ? Trust me, I think you're no more virtuous than you should be."

" Who is, Jack ? Let us all try and be as good as we may, we can scarce hope to be more good than we should and ought to be."

" What mean you, by calling me ' Jack,' little girl ? 'Tis none of my name. Another proof of error, in thee, thou see'st."

" No error—nor proof of error—but a plain truth, as I will prove. I call thee Jack ; for art thou not Jack—in office ? "

" I am not in office yet ; though 'tis not to be doubted there's a goodly dearth of brains here, to make me exceed to my father's office hereafter. The meritless sire makes the meritless son ; and my father has long been known for the most meritless man to be constable in Messina. So, thou see'st, Jack-in-office is not my title now, whatever it may be by-and-by ; and thou only commit'st thyself more and more, each word thou speak'st, little girl ; and will force me to commit thee to my father's comprehension, if thou have not a care."

" Heaven deliver us from any of the family comprehension, which I think is none of the most promising, to judge by the sample. It sufficeth not, even to direct us the right road ;" said Beatrice, turning away, with Hero and Gaetano, who had been for the last few minutes plucking at her skirts to prevent her from getting them into trouble with this foolish lad.

They instinctively turned down the inviting-looking street ; and when they reached the spot where the fountain stood, Hero said she should like to sit down and rest, under the shady tree. There was a wooden bench, ran round its trunk ; and here the three children seated themselves, watching the good-humoured women, as they laughed and talked over their splashing task, with the muleteers, and the rest of the men grouped around.

"How pleasant the water looks! How it sparkles, and plashes down from the dolphins' mouths! The sound is as welcome as the sight!" said Hero. "How delicious a draught of it would be."

"I'm so thirsty!" said Gaetano, in his lackadaisical tone of lament.

"Why don't you drink, then?" said Beatrice.

"I can't;" said he. "I can't drink from the basin, where the mules are dipping their noses in, and fouling the water; and where the women are muddling it with their linen."

"We might perhaps find a reason why you should drink with mules; but as for your making a wash-tub serve you for the nonce, that might be an unfitting utensil, for such a lady-like boy as my cousin Gaetano;" said Beatrice. "Why can't you make a drinking-cup of your hand, and hold it beneath one of the fresh streams from the dolphin-mouths?"

"It'd splash so;" said Gaetano.

"And signorina Gaetano would be wet through, and mayhap, take cold!" laughed Beatrice. "I suppose, too, she is too modest,—too timid in speaking to strangers, to ask one of these good people to help her. But you are tired, Hero, and would be glad of a draught from the fountain. I'll try what can be done."

Beatrice advanced among the men and women, and said in a frank, raised voice :—"Is there any one here, who will lend a horn, or a cup of any kind, to a little girl who is thirsty?"

For a moment, there was a look of wonder at the beautiful child who stood thus amidst them, with her clear eyes, and fearless voice; the next, several pocket drinking-cups of horn, leather, or wood, with which most of them were provided, were heartily proffered.

After they had all three partaken of the welcome refreshment, Beatrice said, in her firm ringing tone :—"If any one of you will show us the way to the governor's palace, signor Leonato will join his thanks to ours, for the kindness his daughter has received at your hands, good friends."

There was a murmur of surprise ran through the crowd; and then there was a loud shout :—"Evviva signor Leonato! Long live our noble governor!"

Beatrice was warmly welcomed to her new home, by all its inmates. Her uncle Leonato grew to love her no less proudly and fondly than his own child ; her uncle Antonio was entertained with her sprightliness and confirmed bearing, so different from his own boy's ill-assured ways ; Hero felt as if a sister had been suddenly vouchsafed to her ; and Gaetano was perplexed, pleased, vexed, and interested with her, all at once. He had been a sickly infant, was still a delicate child, and was therefore petted, humoured, and indulged in all his whims and whinings, his fears and his fancies, until he was the spoiled boy,—the half-girl,—that so amazed and amused Beatrice, when she first saw him.

Like all cowardly children, he was always getting into hurts and accidents ; like all over-cautious children, he was always getting into scrapes ; like all self-pitying children, he was always getting into trouble. He was ever dreading something about to happen, or lamenting over something that had happened. He was in a perpetual state of uneasiness and fret. His face was always lengthened ; his air discomfited ; his lips ready to quiver, and his eyes ready to fill,—or rather to brim over ; for they were generally moistened, and glistening, preparatory to a shower, at the least word or event.

"Hark ! There's that unhappy boy ! Howling again, I declare !" said Beatrice to Hero, as sounds of lamentation reached them, in an alley of the garden, where the two little girls were walking together. "What can be the matter now, I wonder ? Some portentous trifle, or terrible nothing, I suppose, as usual. He certainly is the most unhappy of children ! Unhappy in the misfortunes that befal him, unhappy in his sense of them. Poor Gaetano ! 'Gaetano, the infelicitous,' I call him."

"You should not nick-name him, coz ;" said little Hero ; "I don't think he likes it. He has been accustomed to have his own way, and he won't choose to be laughed at."

"I shall give him no choice ; I shall try and laugh him out of some of his whimsies, whether he will or no ;" answered Beatrice.

"But do it by degrees, then ; be very gentle with him ; for he's not strong, poor little fellow ;" said tender-hearted Hero.

"His pate's not strong, assuredly. Pooh ! It'll do him good to be bantered; he must learn to bear a joke, or he'll never be worth anything. A boy that can't take a joke, will never be able to defend himself against a blow. Coolness and fortitude are main things in both cases, for victory."

"You ought to have been a boy yourself, cousin Beatrice, you are so fearless and so firm; and know so well what a boy ought to be;" said Hero.

"I like courage, in boy or girl;" said Beatrice. "A girl needn't be unseemly bold, or forward, for having a strong heart; any more than a boy need be an unfeeling brute for knowing how to face danger. But here comes infelicitous Gaetano."

He was making his way hastily towards them, when a large hornet happening to fly close by his ear, made him start aside; his foot tripped, he stumbled, and fell headlong; his face flat upon the gravel-path. He cried lustily. The girls both ran to pick him up.

"His nose bleeds!" exclaimed Hero.

"Oh, the blood!" he said, turning pale; and my hands are grazed! See here! Oh dear! oh dear!" and he burst out a-crying afresh.

"Dear little cherub!" said Beatrice.

"Are you pitying me, or are you laughing at me?" he said. "What do you mean by cherub? I'm no cherub, cousin Beatrice."

"No? Don't you 'continually cry?' You are ever proclaiming your right to the title. Here, let me wipe away the marks, and when you don't see them, perhaps you'll forget the wounds; they're not very deep; only a scratch or two."

"But they smart so, you can't think. And my nose, oh, my nose! See how it keeps bleeding!"

"Stay, I'll run into the house for something to stop it;" said Beatrice; "and when the blood has done flowing, you can dry up your tears, you know, at the same time."

"Are you angry with her, Gaetano?" said his cousin Hero, peeping into his face; as Beatrice flew away to bring sponge and water, and to get help.

"Oh, no! I'm never angry with cousin Beatrice, tease me as much as she will;" said he, his tears subsiding into sobs; "she never seems to do it from malice—but as if she couldn't help the fun of it. I suppose it's

funny to her, though it's not so to me." And he sighed in his lachrymose
style.

" If it's not pleasant to you, what if we beg her not to tease you any
more ? " said Hero.

" No, no ; I don't wish her to give up teasing me. I don't know how
it is, but somehow, though I'm provoked with her, I rather like it. She
looks so bright with good-humour, while she's joking me, that I feel
pleased, even though I'm teased. Did you ever notice, cousin Hero, how
her eyes sparkle, and how her lip curls, when she's rating me ? I look at
her face, and then I can't feel angry. It's very odd ; but I can't."

" I'm glad of it ; for that shows you have a good temper of your own,
dear Gaetano ;" said Hero ; " and so, I know, you have. But so has
Beatrice too, for all she loves to plague and torment you a little. See how
good-naturedly she helped you up, and now runs off to fetch something
that'll cure you. Let us go and meet her."

Some few years had gone by without incident, after Beatrice's domes-
tication at her uncle Leonato's house ; when, unexpectedly, he received a
message from the countess Giustina, his aunt, to say, that now his young
daughter was beyond babyhood, she wished to see her, and make acquaintance with her, as the individual in whose person would eventually centre
the honors of their house. This countess Giustina, was an old lady of very
dignified notions. She was proud of her patrician blood, proud of her
relations : proud of their independent position, yet proud of the added importance they derived from their connection with her. This countess
Giustina, was the aunt whom the mother of Beatrice had mortally offended
by her marriage ; as an alliance far beneath that which her niece had a
right to form. The old lady was a strict disciplinarian ; she thought that
it was her pride, her sense of honor, her idea of what was due, which were
wounded by this match. They were, but not solely. Her affections had
received a stab deeper than all the rest. Her heart had been more warmly
fixed upon this girl,—whom she had brought up, and fostered from the
very hour which orphaned the little creature and its brothers,—than she

herself knew; and when she vowed never to forgive her, never more to look upon her face, she little imagined that the bitter regret of love, no less than resentment, dictated the denunciation. In the pang of finding that she was not all-in-all to this beloved niece, as her niece was to her, she cast from her all compromise of comfort, by resolving never more to communicate with, or behold her. She remained shut up in her castle, with a few faithful retainers; held little intercourse with the world; none, save an occasional interchange of messengers, bearing greetings between her two nephews and herself. She never lost the habit of authority with them, which she had acquired during the years when they were boys, left to her care; and now, when she wrote to her nephew Leonato, bidding him give her the pleasure of seeing his daughter, to spend a few months with her, she dictated entirely the conditions of the visit. She told him neither his brother Antonio, nor himself, were to come this time, as she wished to judge his little girl, uncontrolled by the presence of father or uncle. She forbade the attendance of any hand-maidens; saying, that her own woman should wait upon the young ladies. She begged that Hero might be accompanied by her female cousin only. This was the sole allusion made to Beatrice throughout the letter; but Leonato knew enough of his aunt, to understand, that this signified his niece was to be included in the invitation.

He rejoiced that the lady Giustina should have wished their visit, as it showed her interest in his child; he remembered that in his boyhood he had himself received nothing but kindness and sensible indulgence from his aunt, notwithstanding the rigid discipline she maintained, and he was well-pleased that his own daughter should now enjoy the same treatment; he was glad, too, that the young girls should have the pleasant change of a country holiday. The old lady's castle lay up among the mountains, a long day's journey from Messina, in a wild, picturesque solitude; and the fresh breezes of the high ground, would form a healthful contrast with the heat of the plains.

"Will it not be charming?" said Beatrice to her cousin, as the two girls paced up and down the orchard-path, together; soon after Leonato had announced to them the intended visit.

"Ye—yes ;" murmured Hero.

"Only think, Hero! A delicious journey—a fine old castle—noble grounds—a grand view—with glorious rambles among the mountains. Will it not be charming—most charming ? "

"Well, I suppose so—most charming ;" repeated Hero ; but in a tone anything but the echo of her cousin's eager delight.

"Why, thou say'st 'charming' in a most lugubrious voice ; worthy to be that of infelicitous Gaetano himself!" said the laughing Beatrice. "Dost thou really not enjoy the thoughts of this charming holiday ? "

Hero did not immediately answer ; and Beatrice after observing her for a moment, went on :—" Why, thou look'st as scared and as helpless as our doughty cousin, when I smother him with impossible propositions. Come, tell me, Hero ; dost thou, in faith, dislike it ? "

"N—o ;" said Hero.

"Or dread it ? " said Beatrice, eyeing her closely.

"No ;" repeated Hero. But it was more hesitatingly uttered than before ; and she glanced disturbedly in her cousin's face, and then threw an uneasy look behind her.

"Thou dost, Hero. Tell me, now, like the honest girl thou art, what it is thou fear'st."

"Well then, how can you like the thoughts of the journey, when we may be waylaid by robbers ? They say, that in those mountain roads, they lurk about, and hide behind rocks, and watch their opportunity, and then suddenly start out, and pounce upon unwary passengers, and rob and murder them. Oh, Beatrice ! "

"And, oh, Hero !—They may waylay grown people, but why should they attack little girls ? We're safe from the signori masnadieri, depend on't. Forget the unlikely terrors of the journey, and think of nothing but the positive delights of the visit."

"Worse, worse, Beatrice ! I could tell you such things I have heard, of the strictness of our great-aunt, lady Giustina. She never forgives the smallest fault, or overlooks the slightest misbehaviour. Think what it will be to live all day long, and for many weeks and months together, beneath her severe eye. I fancy I feel it upon me now ;" said Hero, shivering ;

" even your courage would quail beneath that severe eye, I think, Beatrice. Ursula has told me such things of the countess Giustina's tasking eye. She says no one was ever known to meet it steadily."

" When they felt they deserved its reproof, I suppose ;" said Beatrice. " But how came your maid Ursula to know anything about the lady Giustina ? She is too young, surely, ever to have been at Montaspro ? "

" Her mother lived in the castle, many years ago. She was in the countess's service ; and when my father was appointed governor of Messina, lady Giustina sent him Ursula's mother as a clever housekeeper. Old Ursula has often made her daughter and me shudder with her stories of Montaspro, and its imperious mistress. By day, lady Giustina's terrible eye ; and by night,——"

Hero broke off. Beatrice could see her actually tremble.

" Well ; by night——? " urged Beatrice.

" Oh, I can't repeat it,—I can't tell you,—we shall see, all too surely, when we go to Montaspro ;" whispered Hero. " Now you know why I did not think of my visit there with any great delight."

" But if you dread it, why not ask my uncle to allow you to give it up ?" said Beatrice.

" O, I would not on any account object to going ;" said Hero. " My father respects our aunt. I have heard him say, he owes her a large debt of gratitude : she was a friend to him in his boyhood ; she was like a mother to him and his brother and sister,—uncle Antonio, and aunt Beatrice,—when they were all three left orphans. She is very, very good. although so strict, I know."

" If she be good and just, we have nothing to fear ;" said Beatrice.

" I was too young when my mother died," she went on, gravely, " to understand much of what she felt and thought ; but I think I can make out, from what I remember of words she dropped, at the time, that she reproached herself with ingratitude towards one who, with all her severity, had been bountiful in goodness and care. If lady Giustina was harsh and unforgiving in the hour of her anger, she was at any rate generous and kind before offence had been given. We'll try and think of this, when we see her, if she should chance to be very severe with us."

VOL. III.   B

" One comfort, we shall go together ;" said Hero ; " and you will help
me to bear difficulties cheerfully, and teach me to meet them bravely.
With you, Beatrice, I shall be ashamed to be a coward ; and with you time
must always pass happily."

There was a handsome retinue appointed, to conduct the two young
ladies to their destination ; for Leonato knew, that although his aunt had
thought proper to forbid the attendance of women-servants, yet that she
would be displeased, were her grand-nieces not to travel in a style befitting
their rank. Their journey was to be performed in a kind of coach', or
litter, drawn by mules, well-suited to the rugged mountain-paths they
would have to traverse.

Their way lay through scenery of the most picturesque beauty. It
almost immediately arose from the plains ; and wound among the uplands ;
commanding a grand view of sea and land. Beneath them lay the city,
with its amphitheatre of palaces ; beyond it stretched its sickle-shaped harbour, bearing stately vessels within its bosom, at safe anchorage. Still
farther might be seen the sparkling waters of the Faro di Messina, bounded
by the opposite Calabrian coast, with the cliffs of Scylla ; whose frowning
aspect, and baying of her ever-threatening rock-dogs, were softened by
distance.

The early morning sun shone brilliantly, and as yet, temperately, upon
all ; for they had commenced their journey with the dawn, and were to
halt at noon-tide, in order to avoid the greatest heat of the day, and that
they might reach Montaspro before night-fall. The fervid blue of the
cloudless sky, arched above ; while around them, was the welcome verdure
of trees, and pasture,—at that altitude fresh and unscorched. The luxuriant foliage of the chesnut-tree, the walnut, the fig, the almond, and of the
graceful ash, which yields its rich tribute in shape of manna ; alternated
with the soberer hues of olive and cork trees ; impervious hedges of spine-
leaved aloes, intermingled with the Indian fig, or prickly pear, flanking the
way-side, together presented variety in profusion.

The novelty, the beauty, the delightful sense of open air and motion, had
their effect upon Hero. She had forgotten her apprehensions, in the present
pleasure. She enjoyed the journey to the full as much as her cousin ; and

it was not until the sun was sinking towards the west, that she began to exhibit symptoms of an abated satisfaction. The path became wilder and wilder, as they penetrated farther up among the mountain solitudes; the purple glow of evening threw a less brilliant light upon all around; the shadows deepened and lengthened among the rocks; there were fewer trees, and barer and more rugged crags on every side. Her animated tone subsided; her admiring exclamations became fewer and fewer, and at length sank into silence.

Beatrice at first did not heed the change; then, when she remarked it, she thought it proceeded from weariness, and she let the conversation drop, that Hero might have quiet, and rest. But she soon saw that so far from resting, her cousin grew less and less tranquil; and at length her uneasiness was so visible, that Beatrice thought the best way would be to notice it, and try to cheer her with sprightly talk, and an encouraging tone.

"Are you looking out for Montaspro, Hero? We cannot be far from it, I should think. We shall soon be there, I dare say; and then for a hearty supper, and a good long rest. This mountain air sharpens the appetite to an edge as keen,—nay, keener,—than itself. If it wear out the spirits, at length, with its delicious excitement, and weary the limbs, with many hours of it, yet it bountifully repairs the mischief, by supplying the means of restoring both spirit and strength. Your mountaineers eat well, and sleep well, whereby they are ever fresh and ready for the morrow. How we shall enjoy to-morrow morning, Hero!"

"Shall we?" said Hero, abstractedly. She could hardly follow Beatrice's words, so engaged was she in peering out.

"Have you caught a glimpse of the castle yet?" asked Beatrice.

"No; I am not watching for the castle. I was looking yonder. Don't you see something brindled, crouching over there? If it should be a wolf! They say, that there are wolves among these mountains; and snakes, Beatrice."

"Well, they won't hurt us; they can't glide up into the coach, and bite our heads off, unaware, can they, Hero?" laughed her cousin.

"Hush! What's that?—Hark! don't you hear a noise? If it should be banditti!"

" It sounds to me, like the rush of waters ;" said Beatrice. She paused
to listen. Then, she pointed through the curtains on her side. " Look!
is not that a grand sight ? " she said.

Through an opening in the rocks, appeared the castle of Montaspro. It
stood perched, as it were, mid-air, on the summit of a precipitous crag, that
beetled up in solitary preeminence from amid the surrounding heights. It
seemed standing aloof, in sullen majesty, austere and repulsive. Its walls,
rough and solid, looked part of the rock from which it reared its frowning
crest. No shrubs, or trees, feathered the sides of the yawning chasm beneath ; no draping ivy, or vine, hung its festoons amid the rifts, to grace
and conceal the stony bareness ; but abrupt and jagged points ; shelving
ledges, and sheer depths, among which leaped, and tore, and boiled, a fierce
mountain torrent, were the environments that aided the effect of haughty
and almost hostile seclusion, which the castle presented.

" And that is Montaspro ? " whispered Hero. " It looks a fit residence
for our stern grand-aunt, the severe-eyed lady Giustina. How shall we
ever venture to encounter her ? I know I shall never dare look her in the
face ; so I shall never know whether she is pleased or angry with me.
I may go on offending her, from want of courage to meet her eye. I wish
I hadn't heard about that terrible eye of hers. It haunts me. I feel as if
it were watching us all the way up this glen to her castle."

" Think of it but as a fable—such as the eye of our Ætna Polyphemus
of old ;" said Beatrice. " Scorn it, like the sea-nymph Galatea ; defy it,
and outwit it, like the brave Ulysses."

" I have not a spark of bravery in me, when I think of being so near ;"
said the trembling Hero.

" We are yet some distance ; the road winds ;" answered Beatrice.
" Come, call thy courage to thee. Remember, she's no ogress ; she will
neither eat thee, nor murder thee. Let her looks be never so terrible, she
will not harm thee, believe it."

" If Gaetano were but here ! " murmured Hero.

" What ! Gaetano, the infelicitous ? How should he aid us, in the name
of all that's impossible ? How should he be a champion, who cannot help
himself ? How should he be a stay, who can't hold up against the least

wind of mischance. What should make thee wish for him, Hero? Why, thine own name were of more avail in a difficulty, than his whole strength. 'Tis the very unhopefullest thing thou couldst have hit upon, to wish him here. Why, he would bring us into more trouble with his whimpering, and hamper us more with his terrors, in a single hour, than we could suffer trouble and terror from aunt Giustina in a week. Of all wretchedness, desire not infelicitous Gaetano were with us. What could make you wish for him?"

"He would be one more, at any rate;" said Hero; "one more, on our side, to face the lady Giustina."

"One more to quail before her, you mean;" replied Beatrice; "his only help, would be helping to dishearten us; his only aid, assisting us to bewail ourselves; his only support, supporting us in our fears, which ten to one, are but groundless fears, after all. Best think so, till we're sure they have some foundation; and best save up our courage till we actually need it, instead of spending its strength beforehand, running to meet disagreeables half-way, that may never be there, at all, to meet us."

They had yet a considerable space to traverse, ere they reached Mortaspro; the road went far round; the commanding situation of the castle rendered it visible long before it was reached; and thus, Hero, instead of gathering courage, had time to confirm herself in her alarms, as is mostly the case in such periods of protracted expectation. The evening glow faded, leaving the rocky solitude more chill and blank than ever; each succeeding view they obained of the castle, it showed more and more gloomy; and by the time they arrived at its portals, night had thrown its dark pall over the scene, heightening the mysterious solemnity of the approach, and exciting Hero's agitation to an almost unbearable degree.

As the litter proceeded across the drawbridge, and beneath the massive gateway, and they entered a spacious courtyard, where a body of the lady Giustina's retainers received them by torch-light, the scene was so strange, so impressive, that it might well have struck more self-possessed and more experienced travellers than the two young cousins, with awe.

They were assisted to alight, with much ceremonial deference. They found stationed in the great hall, a grey-headed old man, very stately and upright,—the countess's seneschal, or steward; and a grey-headed old dame, also very stately and upright, and very angular,—the countess's own woman, or duenna. By these two personages, they were accosted in a grave manner, and begged to state which of their two young ladyships was his lordship the governor's daughter. Hero got out a word or two, announcing herself; and then the two stately personages, giving her the preference, led the cousins in a silent and stately manner into a spacious apartment, where sat the lady of Montaspro. She occupied an easy chair by the hearth ; but she sat perfectly erect. She was surrounded by all the tokens of wealth and of a magnificent taste ; but her own person was simply attired, to an almost ostentatious plainness. She was entirely in black—her gown of a homely stuff, her head-gear a plain coif ; but there was that in herself, which denoted her, unmistakeably, the gentlewoman. She needed no richness of dress to set forth her claims to high rank, no jewels to declare her illustrious name,—her pride of birth, or dignity. She sat there, a noblewoman, in her whole aspect ; in her very look, in the slightest turn of her head, in the least motion of her hand. She had marked features, but her complexion retained its delicacy ; that, and the silver-white of her hair, made her face and hands show in almost snowy contrast with her swart garments. There were two points of color in her countenance. Her eyes were jet-black, of piercing brilliancy, with an alert and observant motion, rather belonging to youth, or maturity, than to such advanced years ; and her lips were of a vivid red, no less remarkable at her age.

"And you are Hero ?" she said, taking a hand of her young grand-niece in hers.

" Yes, madam ;" replied Hero; "and here is Beatrice ;" she added, looking towards her cousin, who had followed her up to the countess's chair.

But the lady Giustina kept her eyes fixed upon Hero's face, saying :— "I see your father in your look, maiden. How is he ? How doth my good nephew Leonato ? "

" My father is well, madam, and bade me present his dutiful greetings to your ladyship. My cousin is charged with them, no less than myself." And again she turned to where Beatrice stood waiting to pay her respects.

But the countess went on :—" And how doth my worthy nephew

Antonio ? He hath a son, I hear. Doth he give promise of being as hasty as his sire could be, when a boy ? "

" My cousin Gaetano is the most gentle creature living, madam ; and Beatrice will tell you, that——"

Again Hero moved towards Beatrice ; and again, lady Giustina took no notice of the reference.

" Too gentle, is scarce commendable in a boy, whatever it may be in a girl ;" she said ; " and when thou talk'st of the most gentle of living creatures, what can a young thing like you, know of degrees of gentleness in so large a range of beings ? Speak ever within bounds, little maiden, lest thou chance to out-state fact, and so prove thyself either ignorant or false."

Abashed at having already incurred her aunt's rebuke, Hero had no voice for a reply. There was a pause. And then the countess put her two hands upon the arms of her chair, and turning her face in the direction of Beatrice, said in a suppressed voice :—" Come hither, child."

Beatrice advanced a step, and stood immediately before her. The old lady's eyes were fixed upon her own lap, for another instant ; then raised as if by an effort of will, and directed full upon the face of the young girl.

The keen black eyes never wavered ; their lids never stirred ; the muscles of the mouth never altered ; but the red lips waned in color, until they blanched to the whiteness of the pale face itself.

Beatrice, while the countess thus continued to gaze upon her, had it in her heart to say that she had no greetings to bring from a living parent, but that her mother's parting hour had been embittered by the thought of dying unforgiven of one, who had been deeply beloved, though so un-relenting ; but there was something arose within her, to check the re-proachful speech.

The lady Giustina raised her hand, as if to screen her eyes from the glare of light. " Remove that lamp farther back ;" she said to one of the attendants ; then, turning again to Beatrice, she said :—" Welcome to Montaspro, child ; I am well pleased that you should have accompanied Hero ; well pleased to have both my young cousins to spend some time with me ; and trust they are well-pleased to come."

" I have rejoiced, ever since I learned we were to visit the castle, madam ;" replied Beatrice.

" And now, Prisca," said the lady Giustina, addressing her stately gentle-woman, " these young ladies will doubtless be glad to see their rooms. Lead them thither, and assist them with what change of apparel they think fit and refreshing, ere they return to take some refection with me. They must need some, after their long day's journey."

The ancient handmaiden performed her mistress's bidding, by beckoning an attendant to precede them with lights. She led the way up a flight of stairs, wide enough to have admitted the two girls being carried up them in the litter in which they had travelled,—mules and all ; it was of wood, so dark with age, as to look like ebony, and so bright with polishing, as to reflect the lights the attendant carried, like a mirror. They passed on into a corridor so lofty, and so long, that it looked like the aisle of a cathedral ; it opened by side doors, into different chambers. One of these doors, the stately gentlewoman threw open ; while she looked at Hero, and said :— " Yours, young lady ! "

As Hero peeped into its depths, she thought it looked like a chill cavern ; but the stately gentlewoman did not tarry for her to examine it, or to enter, but led the way straight on, to the end of the corridor, till she came to another flight of stairs, as wide, as dark, as polished as the other. At the top, they found themselves in a narrow gallery, which seemed to lead somewhere out upon the ramparts of the castle ; certainly, into the open air ; for there was a strong draught, which threatened to extinguish the lights. After traversing this gallery, they came to another long and lofty corridor ; at one of the doors in which, the ancient duenna stopped, and throwing it open in like manner as before, she looked at Beatrice, and said :—" Yours, young lady ! "

The two girls exchanged a dismayed glance ; they had always, since their living together, been accustomed to occupy the same sleeping-room, and Beatrice knew her cousin would not like this solitary arrangement,— especially so far distant from each other.

Hero stood aghast, and said nothing. But Beatrice said :—" We are in the habit of having but one room between us, mistress Prisca ; either of these we have seen, will serve for us both."

" My lady ordered separate chambers ;" said the ancient gentlewoman, with the sententiousness of an oracle.

" Can we not have rooms nearer together, then, mistress Prisca ? " persisted Beatrice.

"These are the appointed chambers ;" rejoined the gentlewoman, as if uttering an irrevocable fiat.

" Why not dis-appoint them ? Better they be disappointed, surely, than we, of sleeping near each other, when we desire it ;" replied Beatrice.

" If you wish alteration, you must ask my lady ;" said the duenna.

" No, no ; pray, Beatrice, no, no ;" eagerly whispered Hero ; then she added aloud :—" Let it be as it is ; since it is my aunt's wish, we are satisfied."

The cousins hastily performed such toilette evolutions, as would enable them to meet their grand-aunt in requisite order for supper ; while the grim mistress Prisca officiated as tire-woman. She was a gaunt, bony person, looking mightily like a veteran man-at-arms dressed in a coif and pinners, and petticoats. She had angular features, pointed elbows, a flat chest ; and her skirts hung so lank, as to look as if they wrapped a couple of vine-props. She was habitually silent ; never spoke, but in reply ; and when she did open her lips, she used the fewest possible words, and spoke in the dryest possible voice. She glided about the gloomy apartment, hovering round the two girls, supplying them with what they needed ; looking like a ghostly skeleton, doomed to walk the earth in the garb of a waiting-woman, abiding until she should be accosted, according to the invariable usage of ghosts, ere she could speak to these inhabitants of earth.

During the meal, lady Giustina was very gracious to her young cousins ; and afterwards dismissed them to their night's rest with words of hospitable courtesy.

At the door of Hero's cavernous room the cousins parted for the night. Mistress Prisca being present, they only exchanged a good-night kiss, and a silent squeeze of the hand ; but Beatrice, as she took her way on to her own chill cavern, thought of Hero's white cheeks, and could not get to sleep for some time, from sympathy with the discomfort she knew her cousin was suffering.

Next morning, the first glimpse she had of them, showed how accurately she had guessed; they were still more wan, and poor Hero had evidently had little or no rest.

There was no time for question or sympathy, however; for mistress Prisca told them her lady was already in the breakfast-room expecting them. Beatrice, who had hastened to Hero's room, now helped her cousin to get ready; and, after as speedy dressing as might be, the two girls hurried down.

The lady Giustina was seated at the breakfast-table, when Beatrice and Hero approached to pay her their morning respects.

"Your journey somewhat excuses your late-rising, maidens;" said the countess; "but remember, for the future, my breakfast-hour is earlier; and it is but fitting respect, that youth should not keep age waiting."

There was no want of color in Hero's cheeks now; but as she took her seat at the breakfast-table, she found courage to say :—" Beatrice would have been ready, madam, but that she waited for me."

This vindication of her cousin, at her own expense, pleased the old lady; and she said :—" Perhaps you slept badly, and that made you late. How did you rest?"

Unfortunately, Hero, anxious to conciliate her aunt, answered :—" Thank you, madam ; quite well."

The countess had noticed the pale young cheeks, and in surmising their cause, had half resolved to indulge Hero,—who she at once saw was a gentle, timid child,—with companionship at night; but this denial of having rested ill, she deemed a deviation from truth, and as such, resolved to punish it, by taking no farther notice of her tremors. At any rate, she resolved that the little girl should herself ask for what she desired, before help was proffered.

"In future, then, let me find you with your cousin, here, in the breakfast-room when I come down. As I said before, better youth should wait for age, than age for youth."

"And yet age would be glad sometimes to wait for youth, if it could hope to be overtaken by it again, would it not, aunt?" said Beatrice. "It would be pleasant to keep people older than ourselves, waiting, if we could hope to make them as young as.ourselves; for then we might hope to keep them the longer with us, you know."

"So, so, saucy child, thou hast a rogue's tongue of thine own, hast thou?" said the countess, with a smiling tone, that showed her anything but displeased by the sally.

"I have a heart that beats so merry a tune, aunt, it sets my tongue dancing, whether I will or no; will you pardon it, if it caper unseasonably?"

"Not if it cut unseasonable or unreasonable capers;" answered the old lady. "But provided it do not exceed a discreet gaiety, I shall be glad to let it dance to the bidding of its heart's tune of content."

"And that is to the tune of I know not how much,—a measureless measure!" said Beatrice, in great glee to find the formidable aunt encourage her in rattling on gaily, as she was wont. "I am in higher than tip-topmost spirits, this morning, at the thought of the delightful mountain ramble you are going to allow us to take, madam."

"Am I, child? No, not a mountain ramble; these wild passes might not be so safe for you. Montaspro hath not a neighbour roof within many miles of it; and the rocks and caverns harbour gentry, they say, who are not pleasant to meet with. What makes you tremble, Hero?" said lady Giustina, interrupting herself, and fixing her jet eyes upon the young girl's face. "There is no fear of these lawless people, while you are within the walls of Montaspro. I hope you do not give way to idle fears. I despise a dastardly spirit! Your father's child should be no coward."

"My cousin belies neither her father's name, nor her own, madam;" said Beatrice. "Hero is no coward."

"She seems no great heroine;" said lady Giustina. "How wouldst thou be able to meet a real danger, maiden, if thou quak'st now at the mere mention of one? Keep thy heart brave, and thy spirit strong, and then they will serve thee in time of need."

"Hero hath a tender heart, and a gentle spirit, madam, but they neither of them want for courage when occasion calls for it;" said Beatrice. "She hath stood between me and disgrace many a time, when my giddy spirits had well-nigh got me into scrapes; and as for poor Gaetano,—she hath been a very Ægis 'twixt him and disaster. But shall we not, indeed, be allowed to enjoy a ramble among this fine scenery ? "

" Beyond the demesnes, you must not go ;" said the countess. " But the castle-grounds are extensive, and command several fine points of view. You shall walk abroad, attended by my gentlewoman, after breakfast."

Beatrice felt disposed to have uttered a remark as to the abatement their delight in the ramble would suffer, if accompanie l by mistress Prisca ; but she prudently suppressed it.

The grounds belonging to castle Montaspro were indeed, as their mistress had described them, both fine and extensive. They were magnificent in their wild luxuriance ; grand in their uncultivated beauty. Notwithstanding the presence of the angular duenna, Beatrice enjoyed her walk intensely ; but she could perceive that her cousin was constrained, abstracted, joyless. She longed for an opportunity of speaking unreservedly with Hero, that she might endeavour to reason her out of her uneasiness, and to cheer her into better spirits. She felt there was no chance of it, so long as that lank shadow, that ghostly silence, stalked beside them ; so she resolved to get rid of the restraint. Beatrice knew it was of no use to appeal to mistress Prisca herself, who would be sure to reply :—" My lady bade me accompany you ;" or, " The countess desired I should attend you ;" so she hit upon a device to distance her without her concurrence.

" Come, Hero ! Let you and me have a good race together, as far as yonder pine-clump ! " exclaimed she, with a glance at her cousin ; and in another moment the two girls had set off at a rate of speed, that quickly left mistress Prisca far in the rear. By dint of appointing fresh goals, as often as the duenna gained upon them, Beatrice and Hero contrived to get some snatches of talk together.

" Dear Hero, you are unhappy, I fear ; tell me what grieves you."

" Not unhappy, Beatrice ; but I wish we were at home. This wild place—this gloomy old castle—my terrible aunt,——"

" Nay, she is not so terrible, surely, as we had pictured to ourselves. Though she can look seriously enough when she chooses, yet she can also look pleasantly. Did you see ?—She all but smiled this morning."

" But how sternly her face settles into an immovable expression some-times. Oh, how she looked at you last night, Beatrice ! My blood boiled, when I saw that hard unkind gaze fixed upon you,—you who had never— who could never have done anything to offend her."

" You forget that she saw in me the daughter of my mother ;" said Beatrice, in a low voice. " She had offended her."

" How cruel, how unjust, to resent your mother's offences upon you !" exclaimed Hero. " And then how coldly she received you ! Hardly deigned to look at you ! Never called you by your name ! Never said ' Beatrice,' but ' child.' Never even took you by the hand. Oh, she is a hard, unfeeling, terrible woman !"

" Do you know, Hero," said Beatrice, " I have a notion those very things you have instanced, prove her not to be the cold hard woman you take her to be. I can't help fancying that it was not that she disdained, but that she dreaded, to look upon me, lest she should see a face that would remind her of one she remembers but too fondly and sadly. I think that she called me ' child' because her pale lips (did you notice how pale they grew ?) dared not trust themselves to utter the name ' Beatrice '—which was that of my mother,—the niece who was once as dear to her as a child. And I think she grasped the arms of her chair, on purpose that she might not take my hand, lest I should feel hers tremble. As these things came into my head about her, do you know, Hero, I pitied my aunt instead of fearing her."

" I wish I had your courage, Beatrice ;" sighed Hero. " It was very kind of you to say what you did for me, this morning, of my being no coward ; but I fear sometimes that I am a bit of one."

" Then don't let yourself grow into a whole one ;" said Beatrice. " Cast away the rotten morsel of poltroonery, if thou'rt conscious of any such thing in thy composition, and resolve to be a sound and entire brave girl."

Hero smiled ; as she always did at her cousin's attempts to cheer and encourage her ; but the next instant, her face dropped again, as she said :— " Oh, Beatrice ! night will come again !"

" Ay ; or day would never come again. Night must succeed, or we should ne'er have the blessed dawn. If we gave up the dark hours, how could we have the joy of beholding the light break ; eh, Hero ?"

"But when night returns, we shall be sundered again, dear coz!" said Hero. "They will make us sleep in separate rooms; and I don't like to be away from thee. I confess, I dread to be alone in the dark; darkness fills me with I know not what alarms. Especially after what I have heard of Montaspro;" and she visibly shuddered.

"What hast thou heard, dear?" said Beatrice gently.

"A tall figure, dressed in white, and veiled with black, they say, has been seen to wander through the corridors and chambers of the castle; it wrings its hands, and moans sadly,—that it is fearful to see and hear;" whispered Hero.

"Most likely the moonbeams gliding in phantom shapes upon the old walls; and the wind sobbing and sighing as it bears them company;" said Beatrice.

"Oh, indeed, Ursula said,——"

"Ursula has told thee a parcel of fine stories, dear Hero; to see if she could not make thee open thy eyes, and admire at them;" said Beatrice. "Thou see'st, dear girl, we met with no robbers by the way, as she spoke of; and thou saw'st nothing last night, that should make thee believe there is anything more real in her foolish tale of the ghostly figure; didst thou, Hero?"

"I saw nothing, certainly;" said Hero. "But oh, dear Beatrice, if you only knew how I lay and trembled, and could not go to sleep, do all I could; and how my heart beat, and my head ached; and how I longed for your pleasant voice to comfort me; and your kind arms to hug me round, and make me feel safe."

"Dear Hero!" said Beatrice, as the cousins embraced each other affectionately. "We'll get permission to share the same sleeping-room in future; and then thou wilt have thy fair night's rest. How came you to say you slept well, when lady Giustina asked this morning how you rested? You must not let your fancies make you a coward in speech, dearest coz; that is worse than any other cowardice; it leads you to be afraid of the truth."

"I meant not to tell a falsehood;" said Hero; "but I hardly know what I answer my aunt; I stand so in awe of her."

"If you do not like to ask her leave that we have one room, I will;" said Beatrice.

"No, no, Beatrice; if you love me, don't do that. I should rather anything than that! She will think me a coward! She will reproach me with my dastardly spirit. Promise me that you won't speak of it to my aunt. Anything better than that. The very thought of the veiled spirit itself, is less terrible to me than lady Giustina's face of displeasure."

Beatrice had but just time to calm Hero's agitation by the required promise, before the angular mistress Prisca overtook them. . She made no remark, but her looks censured them severely. Of these, however, the cousins took no notice; and they returned, in silence, to the castle.

Day followed day, and week succeeded to week; and yet Hero's awe of the countess Giustina lessened no jot. Her night terrors were as powerful as ever; but they yielded before the greater one of letting her aunt know of them. She resisted all her cousin's persuasions, either to avow them herself, or to suffer them to be avowed for her; and the lady Giustina, who had some notion of what was passing in her timid niece's heart, though not to its full extent, deemed it a point of duty not to foster a weakness, by affording it succour. She erred from a good motive; though she certainly erred, in too great strictness of dealing with a youthful nature. She did not sufficiently allow for involuntary defects; she treated all faults with equal severity; she did not rightly distinguish between the mere failings of inexperience, or of native temperament, and those of wilful dereliction. She was so eager for those she loved, to be perfect, that she was harsher with their imperfections than she would have been with those of persons less dear to her. She conceived it to be so imperatively her duty to consider their good, in preference to their happiness, that she risked rendering miserable those, to secure whose welfare she would have sacrificed her own. She was austere from kindness; and unrelenting from regard. Her affection would not permit her to be fond; and her love forbade her to be indulgent. She put the severest restraint upon her own heart, when she was most rigorous towards her favorites.

Thus, poor Hero was left to struggle, unassisted, with all her contending apprehensions. Beatrice watched her narrowly,—for their opportunities of conversing confidentially were very rare,—and she could perceive that this state of agitation, this alternation of vague night alarms, with daily anxiety, were preying upon her cousin's health and spirits.

One cause of the anxiety, arose from Hero's frequent delinquencies in the matter of early-rising, and her consequent dread of her aunt's displeasure, which never failed to be evinced on every such occasion.

The long wakeful nights—the many hours spent in feverish alarm, in lieu of healthful repose, made the poor young girl heavy to sleep of a morning ; and when the hour came for her to get up, she had often not long sunk into a profound slumber. Then came the late waking, the hurried dressing, the hurry of trepidation, and the hurrying down stairs.

Hero would enter, with trembling steps, beating heart, and contrite deprecation in every conscious look and gesture, as she approached the breakfast-table to pay her morning respects to her awful aunt already seated there. While Beatrice's eyes filled and sparkled with mingled grief and indignation to see her cousin in such evident suffering, lady Giustina would coldly turn her eyes upon the abashed offender, and say :— "Late, as usual, Hero ? I thought I signified my wish that you should be in the breakfast-room, every morning, before I make my appearance."

"Indeed, madam, I meant to be up early ;" Hero would falter ; "but I don't know how it was,—I lay,—I intended,—I,—I suppose I must have dropped asleep again while I was thinking to get up."

" A not unfrequent result of lying intending to get up, instead of jumping up at the first intention ;" said the countess. "At your age, maiden, I was an inveterate slug-a-bed, myself ; but by a little resolution I contrived to break myself of the habit,—a most pernicious one, believe me."

" What a pity so many pleasant things are pronounced pernicious !" exclaimed Beatrice. " Why should lying in bed be pernicious ? It's on the contrary, delicious !"

" Lying late is pernicious to the health—to the energies,—moral, physical, and intellectual ;" said lady Giustina. " Neither man nor woman can hope to be good or great, strong or worthy, who indulges the habit. It enfeebles the frame, impairs the beauty, injures the faculties, and destroys self-respect. For body and soul, alike pernicious. There is scarcely a more unwholesome habit."

"Ay, everybody says so ;" said Beatrice. "But don't you think, aunt, that perhaps it isn't true? Perhaps it has been put about by the grave-diggers for the benefit of their craft."

"Child! child!" said lady Giustina, suppressing the smile she felt stealing upon her; "your sportiveness is not unbecoming at times—and upon proper subjects; but I must caution you not to let it tamper with that which should be gravely considered. Early-rising is momentous to our welfare through life, and should not be lightly spoken of; and more-over, do not encourage your cousin in her foibles, by laughing at them, or by laughing off the reproof that should cure them."

"One happy thing is, aunt, that Hero has so few faults to cure, she will soon get through the task, when she sets about it ; " said Beatrice.

"The fewer faults she has, the more imperative it is that she should set earnestly to work to root them out,—for her own sake, and for that of those who love her;" said lady Giustina. "It is more vexatious to discover blemishes in a fine picture than in an indifferent one ; it is more grievous to find stains, and specks, and flaws upon a goodly mirror, than upon a paltry pocket-glass. Hero is the daughter of my noble nephew, and I would fain have her blameless. She is a gentle, good girl, and I would see her become all that is virtuous and excellent in woman."

At this unexpected praise, from her strict aunt, Hero's cheeks became crimson. She glowed with a strange feeling of encouragement; she felt a pride and gratification in the lady Giustina's approbation, that she might very likely never have experienced from that of any one less habitually severe ; but it could not console her for the want of affectionate ease, and loving freedom in their intercourse. So deeply, by children of Hero's temperament, is kindness of manner felt to be the most winning of all qualities in their elders and associates.

"And was my uncle Leonato always so noble ?" asked Beatrice. "Was he always as grave and good, as decorous and proper-behaved, as kind and condescending, as he is now, aunt ? Children are sometimes rather more faulty than they grow up to be. Who knows? perhaps at her age he

Vol. III.   c

wanted as much of being perfect as his daughter does. What kind of boy
was he?"

The countess looked straight into the smiling eyes, that sparkled and
flashed their sly saucy meaning up into hers; the old lady seemed to find
something very attractive there. That unabashed aspect,—equally remote
from impudent boldness, as from shyness or awkwardness,—that confident
expression of a clear heart and mind, a transparent soul, which belonged
to Beatrice, gave her beautiful features their crowning grace. Lady
Giustina continued to gaze; fascinated, as it were, by what she beheld, and
lost in thought. Suddenly, she covered her eyes with her hands; and
when she withdrew them, her lips were very pale. But she gave no other
token of emotion; and said, in a composed voice:—"You shall see what
kind of boy your uncle was, child. Come with me."

She arose to leave the room; then, turning, and perceiving that Hero
was modestly remaining, she added:—"Come with me, both of you;
you shall both see what a noble boy, my nephew Leonato was. I have
a picture of him, taken when a youth; and though it shows him outwardly
fair, it doth not express him more goodly, than his own merits proclaimed
him to be, in all respects."

The countess led the way across the great hall to a small door, which
led into a long gallery, looking out across the precipitous rock on which
the castle stood, for some distance down the valley. The other end of the
gallery opened into a chamber which formed the base of a turret, that
sprang up, at one end of the castle, from the pleasaunce or garden. This
turret, from its upper windows, commanded the fine wild picturesque view
of the valley, the rocks, and the cascade, on one side; and the prospect of
the wooded castle-grounds on the other. The turret was ascended by
a winding stair; and the chamber on its highest story was the one which
had been selected by the lady of the castle as her own private room. Years
had scarcely rendered the steep and narrow stairs any obstacle to one, who
still retained so much of her youthful erectness, and alert energy; and the
old lady now stepped on before her two grand-nieces, with a pace scarce
less assured than their own.

When they reached the top of the winding stair, the countess opened a door, and raising some hangings that covered it on the inside, bade Hero and Beatrice enter.

They found themselves in a circular room, hung round,—with the exception of the spaces occupied by the three windows,—with dark green tapestry, worked elaborately, representing the story of Proserpine borne away by Dis from the fields of Enna. In one corner stood an ebony cabinet, inlaid with silver ; near to it was a table of green marble, bearing an ivory casket wrought with silver, and crusted with jewels. Above the casket hung three pictures, one of which was covered with a black curtain. Beyond the farther window, was a kneeling-chair, and desk,—the countess's oratory ; and close beside it, stood her bed, hung with dark curtains to match the tapestry.

The lady Giustina led her grand-nieces at once to the pictures ; and pointing to the two uncovered ones, said :—" You see my nephews, Leonato and Antonio, precisely as they looked, when little more than your respective ages, maidens."

And then she went on to tell them of the youths' good qualities, of their promising talents, of their obedience, their docility, their dutiful conduct from childhood to manhood. She told them of Leonato's high sense of honor ; and of Antonio's hasty, but affectionate, and generous temper. She spoke at length, and with all the minutia of pride and affection, of the several peculiarities that distinguished them ; and related many anecdotes of their boyhood, such as age loves to dwell upon, and such as youth interestedly listens to, of the by-gone youthful days and doings of their predecessors.

Beatrice, while the old lady was speaking, felt her curiosity strangely excited respecting the veiled picture that hung between the portraits of her uncles. She could scarcely maintain her attention to the narration, so intently were her thoughts engrossed with the hidden painting. She could not keep her eyes from it. They fastened themselves upon it. The ardour with which she looked, seemed as though capable of raising the black silk veil, or curtain, which concealed it from her gaze. She felt as if she knew what must be beneath, and yet as if she must certify her surmise. This feeling grew ; and when her aunt at length paused, she could no longer

resist its impulse. She advanced, stepped upon a low stool that stood beside
the marble table, and stretching forth her hand towards the black curtain,
to draw it back, said impetuously :—" And this picture, aunt ?"

" Hold !" exclaimed the voice of lady Giustina.

The tone was so piercing, its command so imperative, that Beatrice
dropped her hand, on the instant, and stepped down.

" Rash ! Presumptuous ! You know not what you dare ! You know
not to what peril you expose me—my soul—my vow——"

In great disorder, the countess poured forth these incoherent words.
Her jet eyes flashed fire upon Beatrice ; who trembled,—not from fear—
but to behold the agitation she had caused in one so old, and so habitually
calm.

All self-controul seemed, for the moment, lost. The grey hair was
pushed hurriedly from her temples ; the white face and lips worked con-
vulsively ; the nostrils quivered, and the aged hands were clenched in
spasmodic fixure.

Presently, by an effort, she seemed to recall her composure. She murmured something, in half articulate words ; then went to her oratory, and
knelt there for a space, absorbed in silent prayer.

When she arose from her knees, and returned to the spot where the two
girls stood motionless with concern, she spoke to them with her usual
air,—serious, self-possessed, authoritative. She turned to the cabinet ;
unlocked it, drew forth some of its drawers, containing shells, fossils, and
other natural curiosities, which she showed to them with entertaining comments and instructive explanations. She showed them a fine collection of
medals ; some very costly and beautiful jewels ; which, she told them,
were heir-looms belonging to their ancient house ; and which, some day
or other, would be theirs, in virtue of descent from that noble and honorable
stock to which they belonged. She dwelt with some complacency on this
theme, and seemed to think that family-pride was nowise unbecoming.
She told them the story of the tapestry-hangings ; how that they had been
given to her for the decoration of her favorite apartment, by a venerable
friend of hers, who possessed a castle in the interior of the island, on the
very site, tradition said, of the fields of Enna. She told them many curious

legends of their native Sicily ; evidently exerting herself to efface, by the interest of her present conversation, the remembrance of her temporary emotion, and of the incident which had called it forth ; and when they were all apparently restored to their ordinary mood, she led the way from the turret-chamber, and returned to the usual sitting-rooms of the castle.

But not so easily could the impression be removed. Upon Hero it produced the effect of heightening the awe she already felt of her grand-aunt ; and in Beatrice it excited a strong feeling towards her, compounded of curiosity, liking, provocation, compassion, admiration, sympathy, and interest, all at once. She certainly felt more attracted towards her than ever ; at the same time that she felt less able to venture upon intimacies or familiarities with a being so singular.

But her thoughts, at this period, became centred upon her cousin. She perceived that Hero grew daily more hollow-eyed, more wan, more languid. She noticed that her meals were scarcely touched ; that she started at the most trifling noise ; and that she frequently lapsed into silence and abstraction. Beatrice watched assiduously for an opportunity of speaking in private with her, but none could she obtain.

At last, she determined to take a bold measure, which should secure to them an uninterrupted interview, besides affording the means of remaining with Hero long enough to comfort and reassure her.

She resolved, that when the angular duenna left her for the night, and when a sufficient time should have elapsed to give warrant for supposing that all within the castle had retired to rest,—she would get up, and make her way through the passages and galleries to Hero's room.

That very night she put her plan in execution. She stole through the darkness,—for she would not take the lamp with her, lest it should betray her procedure,—along the corridor, and into the narrow gallery. Midway, she fancied she saw something stir. A fitful light shone from the loopholes in the outer wall ; and she paused, trying to make out what it was she saw. A shiver crept over her, but she resolutely shook it off, with the thought that it was the fresh outer air which made her blood chill. Again she could make out that something moved, in the dim space beyond. She strove to steady her gaze ; and then she smiled, at finding that it was a bat

flitting to and fro, having made its way into the gallery through the loop-
holes. She hastened onward ; glided down the dark staircase, and found
her way into the corridor below. She crept along, carefully counting the
doors as she passed, that she might be sure of the one belonging to Hero's
chamber ; and when she reached it, she opened it softly, and spoke, that
her cousin might at once recognize her voice.

" Is it possible ! Dear, dear Beatrice ! Is that you ? " exclaimed
Hero, starting up at the welcome sound, and clinging to her cousin with
delight.

" To be sure ! to be sure ! It is I ! Who should it it be, you foolish
trembler ? I'll wager now, you have been watching the door, fancying the
veiled spectre would steal in, and make you pop your head under the bed-
clothes, like a goose as you are. But you see it's no ghost ; only your own
sauce-box cousin, come to rate you for scaring yourself out of your wits,
and the roses out of your cheeks, with such idle fancies. Come, confess ;
you have never seen such a thing as the shadow of a shade, the ghost of
a spectre, have you ? Why then should you torment yourself with con-
juring up vain terrors of things that never exist, of appearances that never
appear ? Wait till they show themselves, ere you show you're afraid
of them."

" But I've had such terrible dreams, Beatrice ; whispered Hero. " If
you only knew ! Here, get into bed ; you'll take cold. How good you
are to come to me ! And through those long dark passages, too ! Oh,
how brave of you to venture—and how kind, for my sake ! Dear, dear
Beatrice ! " As Hero hugged her cousin, and nestled close to her, she again
whispered of the fearful dreams she had had.

" One, in particular. I must tell you, Beatrice, how dreadful it was, that
you may own it was enough to make any one a coward, to behold such
fearful things. I thought I had offended aunt Giustina by coming down
very late—so late, that she was sitting at the table, ready for dinner, instead of for breakfast. She spoke to me in her marble way—you know,
Beatrice,—said that I had transgressed beyond the limits of her forbearance,
and that she therefore intended punishing me in so signal a manner, that
I should learn to obey her in future. I saw her sign to Domenico, the old

seneschal, who came towards me, took me by the hand, and led me away. I saw you start up, with your cheeks on fire, to plead for me ; but the door closed upon me, and I heard you no more. The seneschal took me across the hall ; and opened that low door, studded with iron, beneath the great stair-case. I saw dark steep steps leading downwards, under ground ; and thought I remembered having heard it said that they led to some vaulted dungeons beneath the chapel. The seneschal went on in silence, leading me down with him, and I thought I now understood, that I was to be shut up here, in chains and darkness. I was just going to appeal to Domenico, when he seemed to fade away, and instead of him, I saw my father, standing at a little distance, before me. He beckoned to me, looking smiling and happy ; and then I saw that there was a crowd of people standing about him, all very gaily dressed, as if for some festal occasion. I found that the dark steps, the underground vaults, had disappeared ; and that instead, I was in the chapel, brilliantly lighted,—the high altar dressed, —a venerable priest standing near it. I saw you, Beatrice. You were, like my father, smiling, and looking joyfully towards me. I found that I had a long white veil on, which fell all round me ; but I don't think I was going to be a nun. My father took my hand, and kissed my forehead, and led me towards the altar ; but just as I had come within a pace of it, something seemed to rise out of the earth—very ghastly and hideous. I couldn't rightly make it out—what it was—a figure—a shape—I cannot describe it ;—but I felt it to be something monstrous,—revolting, shocking,—unspeakably horrible and loathly. I recoiled ; and turned towards my father, to take refuge in his arms,—and oh, Beatrice ! That was worst of all ! I thought he shrank from me—as if I had somehow acquired part of the loathliness of this thing,—whatever it was,—that had arisen out of the earth to poison all our joy. I cast my eyes towards you, Beatrice. You were looking very sorrowful, and yet angry ; just as you do when you think I am in disgrace, unjustly. Then the whole scene swam before my eyes ; I seemed to be falling, falling, falling, down an immeasurable depth, I knew not whither. I struggled ; and awoke, striving to cry out. My face was covered with tears, and I lay bathed in an agony of terror. Oh, such nights as I have spent in this fearful castle ! "

"You shall spend no more such! At least, if my lying by your side
can prevent your imagination from running wild, and playing you such
painful tricks as these, my poor Hero!" said her cousin. "I will steal
down from my room each night, as soon as dragoness Prisca leaves me;
so, do you keep a brave heart for that short time; and then we'll sleep
cosily together, holding the ghosts at bay till cock-crow; when you know
they take their flight from earth, as I will to my own room again, in time
to dress for breakfast."

"Dear coz! And then you will be sure to call me early, and make me
get up; and then I shall escape the disgrace of being too late, as I so often
am;" said Hero.

As she spoke, Beatrice started up in bed, and remained motionless.

"What? What? Do you see something? Do you hear anything?"
whispered Hero.

"No, no;" replied Beatrice; but Hero felt that she trembled, and was
much agitated.

"I fear I have done very wrong—it is my fault—the lamp!" exclaimed
Beatrice, under her breath. "Do you not perceive a strong smell of burning, Hero?"

"Certainly,—yes,—I surely do!" returned Hero.

"Now there is real danger—true cause for alarm—show yourself a brave
girl, dear coz;" said Beatrice. "You who have owned to being a coward
about ghosts, and that you are afraid of the dark—will yet prove yourself
of good courage in the hour most needful. I fear the castle is on fire.
Get up; dress yourself quickly; make the best of your way down stairs;
across the hall, into the offices, and rouse the household. I will join you,
as soon as possible."

"Are you not going with me?" said Hero, who had sprung out of bed,
and was obeying her cousin's directions with an alacrity that showed she
really had the presence of mind, and self-possession, in this moment of
actual peril, which had failed her under an imaginary fear.

"No; but I shall be below scarcely a moment after you; I must go up-
stairs—I must see whether it be my own folly—my own imprudence——"

Beatrice paused not to explain, but hurried away, wholly possessed with the one thought of ascertaining whether it was owing to her having left the lamp burning, that the fire had broken out. This strange irrational reasoning, this perverse notion of necessity on absurd grounds, is a not unfrequent concomitant of a sudden alarm of fire. People have been known to save the most worthless trifles—to waste their energies upon preserving the veriest rubbish, and committing all kinds of vagaries, both of thought and deed, in the trepidation of such a moment. So it was with Beatrice ; she could not divest herself of the feeling that it was her imperative duty to go back to her room, and see whether it was her carelessness that had caused this calamity. She sped on in all the eagerness, and senseless pertinacity, which such an object, so viewed, inspires ; not perceiving that with each step, the smell of burning, and the suffocating presence of smoke became less perceptible. But when she reached her own room,—and beheld the lamp safely standing where she had left it—and had ejaculated one fervent exclamation of thanksgiving at finding that she had not herself to reproach, as the occasion of the evil,—her next thought was one which filled her anew with agitation. Her aunt ! Lady Giustina,—old—sleeping apart—in that lonely turret—none to warn her—to arouse her !

Beatrice retraced her steps with even more eagerness than she had come. She flew back along the passages ; enabled to use greater speed than before, by the terrible light that now began to glare upon her path. Through the loop-holes in the gallery-wall, she caught glimpses of the red glow that seemed to fill the air outside. As she descended the first flight of stairs, she was conscious that the atmosphere became denser and hotter ; and when she had reached the landing at the end of the lower corridor, and came upon the staircase leading into the hall, she found that she was approaching the seat of the fire itself. Volumes of smoke rolled through the spacious hall, and curled up towards its lofty roof. She could hear the crackling of the flames—and the splitting of timbers. She would not suffer herself to be appalled, but kept steadily on. She made her way straight across the hall, towards the door which she knew opened into the gallery communicating with the turret. As she hurried along, she caught sight,—through the range of windows that looked out across the precipice, down which foamed the cataract and torrent, and on which Montaspro

stood perched,—of the scene of wild and terrific grandeur which the valley
now presented. The rocks and giant cliffs that rose abruptly on every
side, reflected the lurid glare from the burning castle. They could be
tracked far down the valley in strange unnatural vividness. They were
redeemed from the blackness of night by the huge torch that flared its
light upon them ; and the sky was flushed with the broad crimson glow,
flung far and wide. The darkness of the mountain gorge, the savage
desolation of its ravines, showed more than ever gloomy and threatening,
beneath the glare of this dread beacon. The rifts and chasms yawned
around with a more sombre depth, while the salient points and edges of
the crags, caught the unwonted glare. But Beatrice scarce allowed herself
one hasty, awe-stricken glance, at the sublime horror of the scene without.
She steadied her thoughts upon the task she had in hand. She held her
way onwards, resolving to shut out, as much as possible, the sense of
sounds and sights that every moment thickened around her. She had just
attained the entrance to the turret, when a portion of the inner wall of the
gallery gave way, and a volume of flame and smoke came bursting
through into the space she had passed, as if pursuing her. She instinctively closed the door behind her, as if to put a barrier between herself and
the approaching fire ; and then sped up the winding-stair. She reached
the door at the top,—her aunt's chamber-door. She waited for no ceremonial knock ; but opened softly, lifted the tapestry, and entered. The
room was in perfect stillness. Its mistress lay in a deep sleep. The air
of complete repose, of peace, of tranquillity, of utter unconsciousness, that
dwelt within the place, and upon the features of the aged countess, smote
upon the young girl's heart, with almost a feeling of self-reproach, that she
should come to arouse one so calmly at rest, into all the tumult of terror
and danger ; but the next moment, the urgency of the peril pressed upon
her recollection, and she leaned over lady Giustina, whispering:—"Awake,
dear aunt, awake!"

The countess opened her eyes, fixed them on the beautiful young face
hanging over her, and said :—" Already morning, darling ?—And so my
Beatrice is come, as usual, to neip me arise. Methought I dreamed a long
and ugly dream, that you were gone from me, my Beatrice !"

The tenderness in the tone,—the name,—such as never before had the young girl heard from those lips; the fond look, such as never before had she seen in that rigidly-calm face; all told Beatrice that the old countess's thoughts had gone back, in the first confused and imperfect perceptions of awakening, to that period of her life when her other Beatrice, her own child-niece, used daily to awaken her, hanging lovingly over her. The idea of the contrast of the present night, with those quiet happy mornings, the remembrance of her mother, the discovery of the deeply-cherished tenderness in which her mother really survived, within the heart of the externally-austere countess, all combined to overpower Beatrice for a moment; but she recalled her courage, and endeavoured effectually to awaken the lady Giustina to a true sense of what was passing.

"Dear aunt! It is not morning. It is night. But there is danger. You must get up. Let me lead you away."

The old countess passed her hand across her eyes; and seemed struggling to reduce her scattered thoughts to order. Her habit of self-controul prevailed. When she withdrew her hand, her face wore its accustomed calmly-severe aspect; but her lips had turned deathly white.

"How came you here, maiden?" she said sternly. "I know you now! You looked for the moment like one I——you seemed to my scarce-awakened vision, one of the angels from heaven. How came you to venture hither, child? I love not intruders in my room. No one ever enters here unbidden. Begone, child!"

"It is no time to obey you now, aunt. You must rise,—and quickly. You must go with me!"

"You are bold, maiden!——" the countess began.

"Listen, dear aunt; understand me; the castle is on fire, and we shall hardly get forth in time!"

Lady Giustina's habitual self-command again came to her aid. She got up, without a word more; threw on a dressing-gown, put her feet into slippers, and went with a firm unhurried step, towards the door of the apartment, beckoning Beatrice to accompany her, with her usual air of calm authority. But on raising the hangings, and issuing out upon the landing at the head of the winding-stairs, she perceived the smoke rising in volumes, and could hear the roaring of the flames below. Another moment or two, and the door at the foot of the turret, which Beatrice had closed behind her, as she came up,—crashed in, and the flames came pouring through the breach, caught to the first steps of the staircase, and sent their spiral tongues, darting and threatening, up the interior of the turret.

Beatrice cast one look at the impassable gulf beneath them; her tongue clove to the roof of her mouth; her lips seemed suddenly bereft of all moisture, her throat was parched; but she uttered no sound. She fixed her eyes upon her aunt's face, mutely took her hand between both hers, and grasped it very tight.

"Brave wench!" exclaimed the old countess, as she returned the firm pressure; her eye dilating, and her lip regaining its ruddy colour, in the proud delight of noting a fearless spirit, worthy of the noble race from which they sprang. But as she continued to gaze upon that courageous young face, its features once more revived within her the memory of those they so closely resembled; and she ejaculated with an emotion, which the thought of her own danger had never once called forth :—" And must she perish? Is there no way to save her? So young! So brave! So beautiful!" Her voice sank to a whisper as she added :—" *Her* child!"

Beatrice strove in vain to articulate the words that arose in her heart; but she raised the hand she held to her lips; and led her aunt back into the room, and stood opposite to the veiled picture, and pointed up towards it; and then she found voice to say :—" Since we must die, let us look upon her face together. Let the child hear you pardon her mother."

"My vow to Heaven!—I took a vow I would never more behold that face——" murmured the aged countess.

"Heaven absolves you from it by the lips of her child;" said Beatrice, earnestly. "Doubt it not. Bid me draw the curtain. Pronounce her forgiveness. 'Twill give us both courage to meet death." Her tone was low, but clear. It seemed as though the high thoughts that possessed this young creature, in this supreme moment, rendered her collected amidst its terrors. It seemed as though the hope of atoning her dead mother, with one whom she had so loved and offended, raised her above the fear of death itself.

"God of mercy, acquit my soul of wilful sin!" murmured the countess devoutly. "In His name, draw the curtain, my child; and let me look once more upon that beloved face, which I never thought to see, until heaven itself should reveal it to me."

"She blessed you in her parting hour, besought pardon for her errors towards you, and your name was the last word she breathed;" whispered Beatrice, as she unveiled the picture.

The light from the advancing flames shone through the doorway upon the aged form bent in fervent thanksgiving; and upon the youthful face that seemed mirrored in the picture she gazed at in reverent devotion.

At that moment there was a sound at one of the windows,—the window that looked across the castle-grounds. Backed by the red glare outside, Beatrice could perceive the dark figure of a man, attempting to effect an entrance through the casement. It was Pietro, one of the countess's faithful retainers, who had reared a scaling-ladder against the wall of the turret, and had climbed up, to attempt the rescue of his aged mistress.

"See, aunt! There is help at hand! They are coming to save us!" Beatrice sprang to the casement to unfasten it.

"The countess! My lady!—where is she?" shouted the man, as he put the young girl aside, and leaped into the chamber. "Quick, quick, madam! For the love of heaven! Trust yourself in my arms—they are strong and lusty—they will bear you down safe—I will not doubt it—with the help of the Almighty I shall be able to lift you down to earth in safety. Come, madam!"

But lady Giustina drew back. "Her child! Save her! Save Beatrice!" exclaimed the aged countess, pointing to her niece.

"By your leave, my lady, I save none, till I have saved yourself;" said Pietro sturdily. "Deign to throw your arm well over my shoulder, madam, and I'll carry you safely. Fear not—hesitate not—there's no moment to lose."

"Pietro," said his mistress, with that voice of stern decision which none around her dared oppose, "I charge you on your fealty, do as I command. As I have ever found thee a faithful liegeman to our house, perform now the last behest, it may be, that I shall ever enjoin thee. Save her—save the child of one I loved better than myself,—and if it be God's will, that I should also be preserved, return for me!"

"There will be scant time!" muttered Pietro. "But be it as your ladyship wills." And he turned to where the young girl stood.

But Beatrice in her turn refused to be rescued first.

"My child—my Beatrice—obey my wish;" said lady Giustina, in her impressive tone, now rendered more than ever so, by the persuasive tenderness that trembled in its pleading. "Better, if one must perish, the decaying tree, than the young sapling. If Heaven will that both shall survive, be it so. If not, I am content to die thus." And the aged countess pointed with a happy smile to the portrait of her with whom she was now reunited in peace, forgiveness, and love.

Pietro, merely saying, "My lady must not be gainsaid," lifted Beatrice in one of his stalwart arms, bidding her lean her weight as much across his shoulder as might be; climbed the window-sill; firmly planted his foot upon the first rung of the ladder; and commenced his descent.

As the man appeared from the window, with his human burden, there arose an irrepressible shout from those anxiously assembled below; but the next instant, it was hushed; a solemn silence took its place, as breathlessly his progress was watched. Pietro bore her carefully, steadily. They were still some feet from the ground, when Beatrice threw herself out of his arms, exclaiming :—"Return! return! Go up again! Hasten! hasten!"

The man needed no urging; he had scarcely felt himself freed from his load, ere he was re-mounting towards the turret-window. But by this time, the flames had made their way into the chamber. Their dread light could be seen through the casement, flickering, and glaring; now obscured and dulled, anon in a sudden blaze, fitfully revealing the interior of the room to the night-sky.

Intensely the watching eyes beneath, followed Pietro's every movement, as he neared the burning window. They saw him gain it,—boldly step in,—into the very midst of the smoke and flames.

A pause ensued, of unspeakable suspense.

Nothing could be discerned of what passed within the room; but the next moment, a tremendous rushing sound—a crumbling and mighty yielding—and then the floor sank in burning ruins, the roof collapsed, and fell in, leaving the outer walls of the turret, a hollow tower—a mere shell, from which spouted forth a volume of fire, waving and flaming upward in fatal splendour.

A cry of horror burst from the crowd of faithful retainers ; while the two cousins clung to each other, weeping and awe-stricken.

The moment Beatrice reached the ground, she had been clasped in the arms of Hero. When they parted, in the first alarm of fire, Hero had hastened down stairs, across the hall, and towards the quarter of the castle where the servants slept. But it was some time ere she succeeded in finding her way ; and when she had done so, she had great difficulty in rousing them. Then, when they were awakened, they were in such consternation, so scared, so bewildered, that it took some time to make them understand what they had to do. Hero, with a courage and forethought which might hardly have been expected from one of her timid bearing under ordinary circumstances, spoke to them reassuringly, and took a tone of quiet authority that more than anything recalled them to their duty. She showed in this moment of terror and confusion, the fortitude that gentle natures frequently possess ; a fortitude that gives way under threats of the imagination, while it stands firm in real calamity. The first thing of course, was to warn the lady Giustina ; but when they would have gone to her apartments, they found the access already in flames. The gallery that led to the turret, was even then filled with smoke, and burning rapidly. To get to her window, was the next thought that struck them ; and all hurried round to the foot of the turret outside. This wing of the castle arose from the commencement of the pleasaunce and grounds, where they adjoined the rocky precipice, on which the front of the edifice was reared. A scaling-ladder was planted against the turret wall ; stout-framed and stout-hearted Pietro volunteered mounting to the rescue of his honored lady ; while the rest watched the result with breathless expectation. Hero had no thought of anxiety but for her aged aunt. She fancied that Beatrice was already in safety ; having left her fully aware of the impending danger, and in a spot from which there was facile escape. What then was her dismay, when she discovered in the person borne down the ladder by Pietro, no other than her beloved cousin. But she had no sooner hugged her in her arms, surely and securely on the earth, than her solicitude again arose for the lady Giustina. Tremblingly the two cousins together watched the attempt made by the faithful servitor; appalled, they together beheld him perish in his heroic effort.

The morning dawned upon the ruins of Montaspro. The old seneschal asked the young ladies if they would not have a messenger despatched to Messina, that the lord governor might be informed of the calamity which had befallen; and that he might come and fetch away his daughter and niece from so melancholy a scene.

"Dear Beatrice," said Hero, "let us leave it at once. We shall arrive at home as soon as the messenger. I cannot endure the thought of remaining here, now that we have lost her, whom I fear I never lovèd so tenderly as she deserved. Besides, we can break the tidings of her fate more gently to my dear father, than he would hear them from another. Let us go home without delay. I sigh to be at home. I pine for home."

"If there were but means——" began Beatrice.

"The litter and mules are safe, young lady;" said Domenico. "The outhouses where they were bestowed, have escaped the fire. There is naught need detain you in this scene of desolation. I will undertake that all diligent search be made for the remains of mine honored mistress, and see that all care be taken to give them reverent obsequy."

"Be it so, good Domenico;" said Hero. "Bid them harness; in less than half an hour, my cousin and I will be ready to set forth."

The sun had scarcely arisen, when the little train wound along the mountain path leading from Montaspro. The blackened, and still-smoking walls, lay a disfigured heap, where late they had stood erect in strength and seeming security; stricken, and prostrate, on the very spot where they had frowned defiant. The bright gilding of the morning beams, the smiling beauty of the azure sky, seemed a mockery, as they hung over the castle ruins smouldering within this gloomy mountain gorge.

The cousins kept their eyes mournfully fixed upon the spot, so long as it remained in view; but when the windings of the road deviated, farther down the valley, and the intervening rocks hid Montaspro from their sight,

Hero, with a deep sigh of suspended breath, sank back among the cushions of the litter.

Worn out with the fatigues and excitement of the past night, the young girl fell asleep; and Beatrice, glad to see her thus, addressed herself to seek a like repose.

Some hours must have elapsed; for when Beatrice awoke, she saw that the sun was high in the heavens. Hero still slept; and her cousin, unwilling to disturb her, watched in silence. The soft regular breathings, the placid expression of countenance, the perfect repose of attitude, all bespoke how sweet, how deep, was this welcome and most salutary sleep. Nothing could so probably restore Hero, after the late exhaustion of spirits she had undergone, as this profound and prolonged rest; and Beatrice remained quite still, that it might not be interrupted. There was ample occupation for her thoughts, in what had so recently occurred; but, willing to divert them from so painful a subject, she allowed them to dwell upon the beauties of the scenery through which the litter was passing. The sterile rocks, and barren crags, that immediately neighboured Montaspro, had given place to less stern features of the picturesque. Rocks still abounded, on either side of the road, but they were covered with verdure; they were less abrupt and angular in their form, sloping and undulating, rather than jutting forth in harsh and pointed outlines. Groups of trees clothed their sides, giving grace and variety to the picture; while beneath their shade, grew luxuriantly green, the corn and grass, which at this altitude flourished, but which, lower down in the valleys, lay brown and scorched. The tall and slender sugar-cane, and the fantastic growth of the prickly pear, or Indian fig, that occurred at intervals, imparted something of an oriental effect to the rich profusion of leaves and plants. Wherever a patch of bare rock appeared, lizards were sure to be basking; revelling in the heat, with outspread limbs embracing the baked stone, and backs dilating beneath the rays of the sun, as if fixed in a transport of burning adoration; but darting away with the speed of light at the approach of intruders. Among the underwood might be seen a stray porcupine huddling to its burrow, or lazily sleeping in the noontide heat. Birds hovered about the trees; and innumerable bees hummed their busy music among the flowery blossoms and weeds that gave out their aroma to the summer air.

The mules were slowly toiling up a long rise; the attendants were strolling on leisurely a-head; when Beatrice, attracted by the leafy coolness of a grove of trees that skirted the road, felt inclined to walk awhile, that she might the more entirely enjoy their shade. She softly unfastened the door of the litter without awakening her cousin, and sprang lightly to the ground. The beauty, the stillness, won upon her. She wandered on among the trees; now gathering wild fruit and berries; now discovering a store of honey in some rocky crevice, or hollow of a tree; now stooping to collect a limpid draught in the palm of her hand from brook or rivulet. On emerging from the grove at the summit, a fine reach of extended landscape met her view. The road wound on, down the mountain, and was lost in the distance among wooded plain and valley, that stretched far away, as far as the eye could reach, until they again rose into upland and hill. A moment she still lingered, to feast her eyes upon the glorious prospect; yet a moment longer she lingered, to gather for Hero a branch of ripe oranges that hung temptingly near, ere she should bound onward to overtake the litter. She had secured the golden fruit, when her attention was caught by a purple cluster of grapes, that nestled amid some vine-leaves, drooping just above her head. The thought of the refreshment they would be to her cousin on awakening from sleep, made her long to add them to the oranges. As she scrambled up the tangled bank where they grew, and reached among the leaves and tendrils for her prize, she became suddenly aware of two strange faces that peered at her from above. They shone like burnished metal,—their deep olive complexion, bronzed by constant exposure to the sun; they were hung about with black elf-locks of matted hair, and had eyes that sparkled with mingled keenness and ferocity. These two faces kept an unwinking gaze fastened upon Beatrice, that made her feel she was the undoubted object of their watch. Her heart beat, as the thought of Hero's tales of banditti crossed her mind; but hastily resolving that her best chance of safety was to behave as if they were harmless peasants, until she found them hostile, said, as she nodded up in their direction :—" Good-day, friends! I suppose this ground is no en-

closed vineyard ; and that it is hardly a theft for a thirsty traveller to help
herself to a handful of fruit ?"

The men came crashing and bursting through the foliage towards her.
They were tall stout fellows, in mountaineer garb, with broad shady hats,
and knives in their girdles ; one had a short spear, or lance, in his hand,
while the other grasped a bow and arrows.

" It's not for us to decide too strictly on what's theft, and what's not,
young lady;" laughed one of them ; " but it's my notion that all things
by the road-side, come fairly to hand, if so be that a man can lay hands on
them.   What say you, Matteo ?"

" Truly, I think that's sound law, brother ;" grinned the other. " The
high-way's free to all men, to pick up whatsoever waifs and strays they
may find there, or the devil's in it. If the high-way and the road-side
an't free, I should like to know where a man is to find freedom, for my
part, that's all !"

" And so you're a traveller, are you, signorina ?" said the first fellow.
" As sure as my name's Filippino, I'd ha' been bound,—no,—I'd ha'
wagered, you didn't belong hereabouts. And yet you're not on foot,
neither ; those little feet would never ha' brought you far. No, no, you
can't be on foot."

" Why, don't you see, I am ?" said Beatrice, as she stooped for her
branch of oranges, which she had laid on the bank while she reached up
to gather the grapes ; " so I'll bid you good-morning ; I must tarry no
longer."

" Ay, you're on foot,—or on your feet,—now ; we see that well enough,
signorina ;" said Filippino, with a wink ; " but it's my opinion that you
have only just stepped out of yonder litter, trotting down hill, there ; and
that it's in that you've been travelling."

" Well guessed ;" said Beatrice ; " and I'll thank you, friend, to add to
your courtesies, by shouting to that same litter, that it may stop for me.
Your voice will carry farther than mine, I fancy."

" It'll outscream an eagle, in general, signorina ; but I'm afeard I've
got a hoarseness, just now ;" said the man, leering facetiously.

" And my throat is well enough in a barcarola, but tells for nothing in a shout;" said his companion. "It's a good singing-voice, but a bad speaking-voice."

"So I hear;" replied Beatrice. "I'll try my own." And she suddenly gave a loud ringing call; but it failed to reach those to whom it was addressed. She could see the litter and the attendant horsemen still plodding on.

One of the men started, half drew his knife, and muttered a curse; but the other laughed, and said :—"Don't be in a hurry to leave us, signorina; we can't part with you yet. It isn't every day we have the honor of seeing the governor of Messina's daughter in our mountain solitudes. You must pay a visit to our captain; he'll be delighted to see you. Ay, you may look at me, young lady; but I know who you are, fast enough. You're not so grown out of knowledge since then, but I can remember you for the little one that bade some of us take you and your cousins home to the governor's house, that he might thank us for his daughter's safety."

Beatrice now recollected the face of the man who spoke, as one of those she had seen among the group, standing by the fountain, on the day she and her cousins lost their way, some years before.

" And now we'll make him not only thank us, but pay us, for returning her to him safely;" said the other. "But come, signorina, you must go see our captain."

"Some other time; I cannot stay now;" said she. "Present my compliments to your chief; and say, that on some fitter opportunity, I shall with all due delight make his acquaintance; but that now, he must excuse me."

"No time like the present, signorina; no excuse will serve; you must come;" said Filippino.

"Since you'll take no denial,—since you're so hospitably pressing,"— said Beatrice; "come, then, lead me to your captain."

She saw that there was no escape from these masnadieri. She saw that she might preserve Hero from the fright and possible peril of capture, if she maintained their delusion with respect to her identity; she therefore resolved to go bravely through with the adventure, gaining spirits from the thought that she had so far rather it had occurred to herself than to her more timid cousin.

The two men walked on either side of her, leading the way through the grove of trees, along the skirts of which she had so lately passed. It thickened into a close wood; but the men threaded their way unhesitatingly, amid all the intricacies of bush and briar, thicket and dell, underwood, overhanging branches, and near-set boles of trees; until at length they came to a comparatively open space, though surrounded on all sides by rock and wood. In the midst, on the margin of a small lake, there stood an old dismantled watch-tower, or stronghold. Its roof was open to the sky; its walls were rent and ruined; and it was covered with ivy and other parasitical plants that flourish on decay.

Beatrice, struck with the romantic beauty of the spot, said :—" If that be your captain's abode, he hath commendable taste in a house, so far as site is concerned; but methinks he might keep it in better repair, with stronger chance of in-door comfort."

" He hath a solider roof than one of masonry, for his abiding-place ;" said Filippino, as he struck three smart blows against a rock near which they stood. A portal, so artificially constructed, that it seemed, when closed, like a portion of the solid crag itself, receded at the signal, and gave entrance to a cavern, part natural, part hewn out. Beatrice, on being led in, found herself in an arched space, that seemed like a vast hall supported by irregular pillars. At the farther end, several men were employed spreading a board with food and wine; while near to them paced a man with folded arms, and lowering brow, as if lost in moody thought. Beatrice's conductors went towards their chief, and exchanged a few hasty words with him. The short colloquy ended by his saying, in a harsh voice, as he flung himself on a kind of settle, spread with the skins of wild animals, " Bring her hither."

The two men returned to where Beatrice stood, and said :—" Our captain desires to speak with you, young lady."

" Is it thus your captain receives his guests ? " said Beatrice. " Scant courtesy, methinks, to loll there, and send a message, instead of stepping forward to greet them himself. The welcome they meet, tempts few to visit here a second time, I imagine."

" Few visit us at all, by their own good will ;" grinned Filippino ;

it taketh some persuasion,—not to say force,—to prevail upon travellers to become our guests."

"Your people lack discipline, signor capitano," said Beatrice, advancing; "you should teach them better manners, than to keep a young lady waiting in the entrance, while they parley with their master; and they would doubtless learn to doff their hats in her presence, were they to see you set them an example;" added she, glancing at the broad beaver which shaded his brow, already darkened by a heavy frown.

Involuntarily,—in his surprise at her coolness,—the man's hand stole to his hat, and lifted it from his head; but he was yet more surprised to see the young girl quietly seat herself beside him upon the settle, saying:— "Well; they told me you wanted to speak to me. What have you to say?"

"I am in the habit of putting questions, not of answering them, young lady;" said the man sternly. "Those who are brought before me, stand there, and reply, in lieu of sitting here, questioning me."

"I sit here from no wish to come so close, believe me;" answered she; "but I saw no other seat at hand, and I am tired with my ramble. If you have not the courtesy to offer me a chair, I must help myself, and take one. That is the mode here, I fancy."

"We have learned to help ourselves, since none will help us;" said the robber-chief, in his harsh voice. "I see you guess our calling. We live upon what we can seize, or extort, from the fears of those who have made us outcasts. Trusty Filippino and Matteo saw the litter approaching this morning; watched; saw that it contained only yourself and your sick cousin,—she is your cousin, is she not?"

"Yes; but I don't see how her being my cousin, gives you a right to way-lay me;" said Beatrice.

"They guessed that to plunder the litter would profit them little;" proceeded the captain; "as it was not probable that two girls travelling alone would carry much worth taking. But on recognizing one of them for the governor of Messina's daughter, they knew that by detaining her, they could secure heavy ransom. This is our object, I tell you honestly."

"Your words are more honest than your deeds, then, signor capitano;" said she.

" Young lady, I'm a plain man, and——"

" I see you are;" interrupted Beatrice.

" I'm a plain man, who speak my plain mind ; and I tell you——"

" If person and mind are both so ill-favored, the less shown of either the better ;" said she.

His lip struggled with a smile, as the captain went on :—" I tell you, young lady, ransom we are determined to have ; and you will be detained here as hostage, until such time as we are in possession of the sum."

" Best send me to fetch it ;" said Beatrice.

" That would show less wit on our part than you have shown on yours, young lady ;" answered the man ; his forbidding look visibly relaxing beneath the sunshine of the young girl's playful manner. There was something, too, in the fearless ease with which this scarcely more than child bore herself beneath his eye, that irresistibly won upon his nature, accustomed, as he was, to see even grown people quail before him. " We will not fail to obtain your ransom ;" he continued. " Concern not yourself as to the measures taken."

" My only concern is that you should get it ;" said Beatrice.

" We shall surely do that ;" he replied. " Meantime, signorina, you must be content to remain here."

" Remain I must ; contentedly, is more than you can compel me to, or I can answer for ;" interrupted she.

" To remain here our prisoner ;" he resumed ; " though you shall have all courteous treatment."

" That is glad hearing ; if it be only as a welcome change from what I have already had ;" said she. " Suppose you begin your courtesy by offering me something to eat and drink ; for I am half-famished. I have had but scant breakfast this morning ; and travelling sharpens the appetite."

" We were about to sit down to our noontide meal, when you entered. Will you share it with us ?" said the brigand.

" It will be the first stolen dinner I ever ate ; it should needs be sweet. I suppose you dispense with grace-saying here, since all your meals are graceless ; being, as they are, the produce not of labour, but of thieving ; not of slavery, but knavery. No offence, I hope, gentlemen ; you cannot

but take pride in hearing your profession named, since you take no shame
to follow it."

"Corpo di Bellona! a spirited young devil she is!" exclaimed one of the
men enthusiastically. "I would thou wert a few years older, little one,
and thou shouldst stay here, and be our queen! 'Tis a million pities thou'rt
not old enough to marry our captain, and share his sway! Corpo di
Bacco! I'll drink your health, young lady!"

"Fill me a cup, and I'll pledge you all, good gentlemen;" said Beatrice.
"But I have no ambition to be your queen. I should soon be an unpopular
monarch among you, for I should begin my rule, by reforming your ways.
No molestation of peaceful travellers—no way-laying of unoffending passengers—no detaining people against their will, and extorting unjust
ransoms from their anxious friends. Liberty, not license, on the road,
should then be your maxim ; and I would make you observe, what now
I only give you as a toast—' Freedom for *all* upon the highway!'"

She nodded gracefully round to them, as she put her lips to the wine-
cup ; and the robbers shouted a loud ' Evviva !' to her honor.

"And now, as I am a prisoner, a dungeon is to be my withdrawing-
room, I presume ;" she said. "Let me begone to it at once, for I am not
accustomed to the prolonged dinner-table you doubtless favor ; and I would
not be the means of curtailing your enjoyments. Use no ceremony with
me, I beg. Pray do not think of rising from table one moment before your
usual time, on my account ; but let me retire."

"If you will pass your word not to attempt escape, young lady," said
the grim captain, "you shall have free range throughout our fastness ;
I think I can trust you."

"If I were so simple as to promise, you might be so simple as to trust
me ; but if I have wit enough to get out, and you skill enough to keep me,
why should we either of us bind ourselves to what we mayn't care to abide
by ? I might repent my promise ; you, your trust. No, no, best be free
altogether, where neither promise nor trust are like to be preserved."

"The strong-room in the tower must be your portion, then, wilful
one ;" said the robber-chief, nodding to Filippino, who led the way with
Beatrice out of the cavern hall. They passed through a long subterranean

passage, at the end of which were some rude steps cut in the rock, that communicated with the basement of the old watch-tower. In one of the upper chambers, her conductor left her, after a somewhat ostentatious drawing of bolts, turning of keys, and fastening of chains on the outside, that she might hear she was securely locked in.

The young girl, the moment she was alone, eagerly inspected her prison. It was a middle-sized room; bare of furniture, with the exception of a pallet-bed, a rough table, a stool, and an iron lamp. There was but one window,—if that might be called a window, which was a mere grated outlet. But it was not very high up in the wall; and the embrasure was so deep, that Beatrice could lean upon it, and look out upon the magnificent view that spread in front of the tower. She remained here for some time, feasting her eyes upon the beauties of rock, lake, and wood, while her thoughts flew to Hero,—to her uncles; to what would be the consternation of the former on waking, and discovering her cousin no longer by her side in the litter; to what would be the anxiety of the latter in learning that she had not returned home. But then came the consoling thought of the promptitude with which they would send to her rescue, when they should learn what had befallen her. As she leaned, musing, her eyes closed, her head dropped upon her arms, and she slept.

It was late in the afternoon, when she was awakened by the unfastening of her prison-door, and the entrance of Filippino.

"I have brought you some supper, young lady;" he said; "and I am but a rough chambermaid, but I'll try and make your bed a bit tidy for you, against you go to rest. You see, the last gentleman that slept here, left his bedclothes rather in a tumble. He was roused up on a sudden,— on particular business,—he couldn't be spared, you see,—but he slept sound ever after. He was never disturbed again,—never wakened no more."

"He was despatched to a better rest than any to be found under this roof, hospitable as it may be, I suppose;" said Beatrice, as she watched the man, smoothing the rags and coarse linen that lay heaped on the pallet.

"You needn't fear resting, mind;" said Filippino, turning to look at her; "nor disturbing neither. You'll not be roused, like the gentleman, nor sent to rest, as he was. You'll not be wanted on the business he was wanted for. You've friends to pay your price for you."

" That's one of the comforts of being a helpless girl ; " said she ;
" I needn't take care of myself. It's almost a pity though, for my friends'
sake, that I'm not a worthless girl, for then they needn't buy me back."

" If they're of my mind, they won't grudge a good round sum, for such a
brave-hearted little creature as you. Per Bacco ! What a glorious robber
you'd make ! "

" Should I ? "

" Yes, that you would. Maledetto ! I could find in my heart to curse
and swear, when I think of such an amazon spirit as that, going back to
be quenched and dulled in a round of stupid fine-lady existence, instead of
staying here to spend a free roving life worthy of it. It's enough to make
a man blaspheme, to think of the crosses of fate ! That you should be
doomed to pass through life a governor's daughter, when you would have
made such a noble masnadiera ! "

" Never mind, Filippino ; " returned she laughing ; " we must be resigned
to things as they are. We can only learn to submit with the best grace
we can muster, and settle them as we best may. Here, accommodate me
by drinking this flagon of wine ; it is a superfluous part of the supper
you have kindly brought, as regards me ; but by taking the disposal of it
on you, you may please both yourself and me."

" There again ! What a hand you'd be at dividing spoil ! Such notions
of justness and fitness as you have, to be wasted on civilized society,—
where everything's adjusted for you ! Now in our way o' life, they'd have
had such fine scope ! Destiny ought to be ashamed of itself, for thwarting
Nature at this rate. Why, you were born for a leader of banditti,—if
you'd only been a boy ; and Fortune's a cross-grained jade, to have made
you a young lady and a governor's daughter."

" Nay, there's a consoling point in most things,—a bright side to almost
everything, good Filippino ; " said Beatrice ; " perhaps, after all, those
very notions of justice and fitness you speak of, might have interfered to
prevent my making so good a bandit-chief as you're pleased to fancy.
I might have some foolish scruples, and troublesome fastidiousnesses touching right and wrong, that would probably have spoiled me for a robber."

" Not a bit of it ; you'd soon have got the better of them. Don't tell
me ; I know you're just the right stuff to make a highwayman of."

" But supposing I had in time overcome early prejudices; learned to see right and wrong in their true light, perceiving that it was right to take from others what I could have by force, and wrong to leave them in possession of what I could extort; that I had acquired wider principles on the subject of property, than the old strict ones in which I was brought up, yet even then, I fear me, I should have made but a sorry bandit. No, no; let me not aspire too high. Disappointed ambition is misery. Since I cannot hope to be a worthy thief, let me rest contented with mine own station."

" Well, you may take it as you will, but I shall never cease to regret that you were born a lady, when you might have been a brigand," said Filippino. " Cospetto! Che vergogna! Che peccato! But it can't be helped! Buona notte, signorina. Felice notte!"

" Felice notte!" echoed Beatrice. " Good night, good Filippino. May thy dreams be undisturbed by regrets for me."

".Felice notte!" repeated Filippino, as he withdrew, muttering, " Ma che peccato!"

When she was again left to herself, Beatrice for the first time felt a little down-hearted. Night was coming on; here, in this wild place, among these wild and lawless men, with no friend at hand to cheer or aid her, a sense of loneliness, of unprotectedness, crept over her; and she sat, for a space, in a pensive attitude, lost in saddened thought. Then she took some of the bread and fruit from the supper Filippino had brought, and took them to her old leaning-place, the deep window-ledge, and eat them there, that her eyes might imbibe comfort and hope, from the view of Nature in her serene aspect. The moon had risen, and the lovely sequestered spot lay steeped in her soft beams. The lake was like a mirror, save where the night breeze from the mountain gently stirred its surface, and caused the planet's rays to be reflected in silvery undulation. Hesperus, and a few attendant stars, peered from the blue firmament, and lent their placid light to the scene. The masses of foliage clothing the well-wooded rocks, looked sombre and embrowned against the radiant Sicilian sky, of a clear and cloudless azure, although deepened by night into intenser colour. As she gazed, the thought of her friends, of what would be her uncle

Leonato's solicitude, her uncle Antonio's uneasiness, her cousin Gaetano's lamentations, and, above all, Hero's misery, at her prolonged absence, made her writhe with impatience at her captivity ; and, in an irresistible impulse of longing to get to them, she clutched at one of the bars of the iron grating before her. To her surprise and delight it moved beneath her grasp. She felt it sensibly give way. She applied all her strength in pulling at it ; and to give still greater purchase, she climbed up into the deep embrasure. It yielded more and more ; and at length she succeeded in wrenching it out of its rusty socket, entirely. Its removal afforded space sufficient for her to pass her body through the opening thus made ; but the difficulty now was, to avail herself of this egress. The bed-clothes torn into lengths, and fastened together, might form a means of letting herself down outside ; but she remembered that the watch-tower stood immediately on the brink of the lake, and she was uncertain whether the walls might not go sheer down into the water. She determined to try, however. She set to work with the energy inspired by a definite object and hope, and at length succeeded in forming her knotted ladder. She fastened one end securely to the loose iron bar, that it might form a steadying weight, and the other end to the grating. She then lowered it out ; and by the tightened strain, found that it could not have reached to the ground. Notwithstanding, she crept through the opening of the grating, and trusted herself to the strength of the new-made rope. Beatrice was a girl of courageous heart, and firm mind ; therefore no nervous terrors added their force to the mere physical effect of her new situation ; but this was sufficient to make her head swim, and her heart beat, as she felt herself suddenly launched mid-air, with nothing but her own hands and feet to depend upon for safety. Luckily, she had been accustomed to active sports, and constant out-of-door exercise, which gave her strength of limb, as well as good command of them. Firmly she clung to her bed-clothes-ladder, carefully letting herself down from knot to knot, until at length she had the joy of feeling that she had arrived at the friendly iron bar. She planted her feet steadily upon it, as it hung crosswise ; and then ventured to look down, which she had refrained from doing till now. She found that she was within a few feet of the bottom of the tower ; but although the rugged walls did not absolutely spring from the water itself, yet the ledge of earth which surrounded them was so narrow, that it could scarcely afford a footing. Still, Beatrice resolved to risk letting herself drop upon it,—the rather, as the light of the moon enabled her to discern that the lake, so far from being deep just there, was shallow and shelving, its pebbly bottom clearly to be seen. With an inward aspiration, therefore, she quitted her hold, slid down, and fell safely to the ground. Before endeavouring to regain her feet, she lay still for a moment, that she might recover from the giddiness that she felt; and then she leaned over the grassy edge, and dipped her hands in the cold water, and laved some on her face; and then the giddiness passed quite off.

With great care she made her way along the grassy ledge that margined the lake; the rugged inequalities of the old stone walls, and the tufts and twigs of lichen, brambles, and tough grass that grew among their interstices, affording her the means of clinging for safety, and helping herself forward. A false step must have plunged her in the water; but she kept steadily on, proceeding cautiously, though unremittingly; until at length she reached a spot where the ground widened, and she could tread with freedom. She had nothing to guide her in the choice of a path; but any direction seemed well, so that it led away from the tower walls. She struck at once across a grassy plain, dotted with trees, that lay stretched before her; the lake abruptly diverging to her right, leaving an onward way open and unimpeded. She kept as much as possible within the shadow of the trees, that her progress might be unnoted, should there be any stragglers of the troop abroad. The moon shone high in the heavens; the warm breath of a Sicilian night was tempered by the freshness of the mountain air; there was the bright silvery dew upon grass and leaf; while thousands of fire-flies floated around her path, like spirits of light, and buoyancy, and winged hope, to cheer her onward. The sense of liberty within, seemed to find tangible expression and response in every object that met her view; and Beatrice walked on at a rapid pace, her frame alert, her soul elate, her heart happy. After a time the way became steeper; it arose from the plain she had passed, among the rocks and higher ground. Gradually it had less and less of tree and vegetation; and

she began to fear that she might be getting back again among the mountain range, from which on the previous day she had journeyed. She had
no means of judging her course ; but she instinctively kept forward, that
she might, at any rate, leave the robber-hold in the rear. The rocks became every moment more cliff-like in their aspect ; and there was now a
certain quality in the air, that seemed to tell her she was approaching the
sea. She had hardly recognised this,—with a feeling of welcome natural
to an islander, and one accustomed to dwell on the sea-shore,—ere she
came upon a sight at once lovely and sublime. Between an arched opening
of the rocks,—forming, as it were, a natural frame to the picture,—she
saw, down, many feet below, the calm blue sea, sleeping beneath the
moonbeams, its broad expanse stretching away, far as eye could reach ; in
the foreground lay the green and sloping shore ; and to the extreme right
arose majestic Ætna, crowned with volcanic fires. Volumes of smoke
curled around its lofty head, mingled with wreaths of flame that spired
upwards, proclaiming to earth, sea, and sky, the might and magnificence
of the Mountain-King.

Beatrice seated herself in a hollow of the rock, that she might rest herself,
and contemplate at ease this superb spectacle ; and when its awful beauty had
impressed itself upon her imagination in characters never to be effaced, she
turned to the tranquil loveliness of ocean, for repose and refreshment of
spirit. The coast immediately beneath, formed one of those exquisite
sequestered bays so numerous on the classic shores of Sicily, such as the
poesy of the Greek creed peopled with Galatea and her train, sea-nymphs
and Tritons gambolling upon the green waves, blowing through pearly
shells and sounding conchs ; and now, as the young girl gazed, she saw a
little fleet of boats, with each its gleaming torch-light. She knew these
craft belonged to poor fishermen, who by night pursue their calling, in
search of tunny and sword-fish ; but they gave a wondrous air of peaceful
animation to the scene, as the distant lights glowed like reflected stars upon
the surface of the water, in contrast with the broad glare of Ætna's consuming fires.

When Beatrice resumed her way, she determined she would endeavour,—by keeping Ætna immediately behind her, and the sea on her

right hand,—to shape her course northward, which she knew would then be the direction of Messina. For some time, she succeeded in her purpose ; but as the track led more and more away from the shore, and the rocks on either side arose higher and higher, she found that both the sea and Ætna were unavoidably lost to her view. She wandered on for some hours ; having lost all trace of whether she were pursuing her homeward way, but resolved nevertheless to persevere ; when, just as day broke, she discovered, to her great mortification, that she was not far from the spot where she had yesterday morning first encountered the two robbers. She could not be mistaken ; there was the road, winding down the declivity, where she had last seen the litter, trotting away in the distance, hopelessly unhearing of her cry to stop ; there was the tangled bank, up which she had scrambled to pluck the fruit for Hero ; there the very spot whence she had beheld the brigands' faces glaring down upon her. The thought that even now they might be watching her, that she had unconsciously returned to the precise place most likely to afford risk of meeting them again, filled her with such alarm and uneasiness, that it sufficed to give her afresh that energy which an instant before had well-nigh failed her, from vexation and fatigue. Notwithstanding that she was by this time much tired with her long night ramble, she walked, or rather ran, with her best speed, down the hill, avoiding the open road, lest she should be seen, but skirting it, to keep it in view, that she might be sure of her way. She had nearly reached the more level ground, at the foot of the descent, when she saw a man with a sickle in his hand ; there was a mule beside him, fastened to a tree, grazing ; and into the large baskets that were slung on either side of the animal, the man was loading the green fodder as he reaped. He was shouting a rustic song, in broad Sicilian dialect, at the full stretch of his lungs. His garb was coarse ; and his look was unmistakeably countrified. "He looks safely a peasant,—a peasant,—a rude peasant—I may surely trust him ;" thought Beatrice, as she eyed the man, who looked up at her approaching step.

"Hallo, little one ! Where did you start from ? From the earth, or from the bole of a tree ? Or did you drop from the clouds ? Out of breath, panting, dusty ! Are you pursued ?"

"Not pursued, but afraid of being pursued,—almost as bad, good friend ;"

she said. " In fear of being affrighted, is the fearfullest of frights. Will
you be my friend, and help me to escape being caught, as well as the dread
of catching ?"

" Who's to catch you, child ? Or perhaps you deserve to catch it, as the
saying is. Have you been doing anything amiss ? Have you run away
from rightful punishment,—from your true friends ?"

" No, no ; they have no right,—they are no friends,—they are enemies;
in one word, I have been seized by the masnadieri,—have made my escape
from them, and fear lest they should discover it, and recover me. Hide me,
good man ; give me rest and shelter for awhile, and then be my guide to
Messina,—to my home,—where you shall have both thanks and reward."

" Softly, softly, little one! how glibly your tongue runs on ;" said
the peasant, who, unlike the generality of his vivacious countrymen, seemed
gifted with peculiar phlegm in his mode of speaking, thinking, and acting.
" Let me understand this matter. You have been taken by the masnadieri.
Good. You call them no friends, but enemies. Good again ; so far as you
are concerned ; but its different in my case. They are no enemies of
mine—but very good friends and neighbours—as friends and neighbours go."

" That's to say, they neither rob nor murder you ;" said Beatrice.

" Exactly ;" assented the peasant. " And it would be a poor return on
my part, if I were to rob them of their hope of gain. They'd think
I joined to defraud them, if they knew I helped you out of their clutches.
They expect ransom for you ; and if their hostage slips away, how are
they to get it, I should like to know ? Be just ; and tell me that. Be
reasonable."

" Just as reasonable as you will ; and no less just than is reason ;"
answered she ; " but in your turn, be honest, and say at once you won't
help me."

" I shall say no such thing, for I mean no such thing ;" said he. " I'll
help you if I can ; but it must be without offence to my excellent friends,
the signori masnadieri. I must keep well with them. Keep clear of
affronts with friends,—'specially powerful ones,—and be kind if ye can to
strangers, is no bad rule. It's mine."

" Well then, now to square your rule between us. I need your kindness ; how do you propose to aid me, and yet keep all smooth with your worthy friends ? "

" Thus. You want to get away from them ; very natural. They want to keep you ; very fair. I want to please both parties ; very right. If I manage your escape, unknown to them, well and good in all ways ; you are saved, and they remain unoffended,—that's the main thing."

" And how is this to be done ? Quick, quick, good man ! They may even now be upon us."

" 'Tis for that very reason, I must contrive a way to take you to my hut unseen, little one ;" said the peasant ; " it is at some distance, and on your way there, we might, as likely as not, stumble upon one or other of the signori briganti. Here, step into this basket ; you will ride softly and easily upon this couch of new-cut grass, and I will cover you lightly over with more, so that no matter whom we meet, I shall be seen in no awkward company, and my mule will seem to carry a no less innocent load than green fodder. Be heedful of suspicious circumstances, and mind your appearances, is another good rule for passing through life safely and well."

" You are full of beneficial rules for self-regulation, good man, or at any rate they are full of selfish benefit ;" said Beatrice laughing, as she stepped into the pannier. " Now, be a little practical in your measures ; put some stones in the opposite basket, that it may weigh down the grave charge you consent to carry in this one ; otherwise you'll be betrayed by a lop-sided appearance. Wear a show of equity, at least, before the world."

" Mayhap you think I ought to beware how I burthen my conscience with a deception ;" grinned the man, as he began to pile the grass over the bright face of the young girl that was smiling up at him from amidst the green heap ; " if so, step out again, and save me from sin."

" 'Tis thy mule bears the burthen, not thy soul, man ;" replied she ; " thou saddl'st the sin,—if sin there be,—not upon thy conscience, but upon thy beast's back, and so shift'st it from thine own shoulders, like the wise man thou hast proclaimed thyself to be, in thy rules for self-government and advantage."

" Be silent, and lie still ;" said the peasant.

Vol. III.   E

"You bid me do the two most difficult things in nature,—at least, feminine nature,—if what slanderers say, be true; a girl is but a woman in the bud; and if full-blown womanhood, with all her practice, finds it so hard to hold her tongue, and keep quiet, how can a young girl expect to succeed? But I'll try, for your sake; since you've agreed to oblige me."

The peasant, after putting the final touch to his arrangements,—duly filling up the green heap, and nicely adjusting the balance of his mule's panniers,—led the animal by the rein; with an easy air full of virtuous unconsciousness, resuming his rustic song, as he went his way.

It was not long ere he had occasion to rejoice at his forethought.

A voice called lustily after him :—"Girolamo! Ohe! Girolamo!"

"Ah, messer Matteo! Bon giorno!" said the peasant, turning to salute the bandit with every appearance of hearty greeting; "you are early abroad this morning. Ah, well, you can't be too early at work. Early industry makes wealth betimes. The ready hand comes soon to gain. Swift to seize is speed to win; eh, messer Matteo? Excellent rules all."

"You're a shrewd dog, master Girolamo;" answered Matteo, with a sly glance, "and know how to match things cunningly; no man better can pass off a queer act with a seemly saying, a wry deed with a strict sentence, or an ugly trick with a pretty speech. 'Tis a commendable art, and helps one through the world, amazingly; but I could never attain it, myself. So, as I couldn't depend upon my tongue to gloze me on, I was fain to have recourse to my hand; a bold snatch for a living, and a bold blow for all defence."

"Boldness in word and deed becomes the honest man;" said peasant Girolamo, in his moralising, sententious style. "Earnest in meaning; sincere in speech; brave in act. You can't do better than follow that rule."

"Let's to business, then;" said the robber. "Our people got hold of a young girl yesterday, whom we've reason to know is none other than the governor of Messina's daughter. It stands to reason that we ought to get a good ransom for such as she, and we took care of her, according. But see the heartlessness of the world! So far from feeling grateful, this young hussy must needs take advantage of our all being peacefully asleep, to steal away in the night, and leave us without so much as good bye t'ye, or thanks for the food and the shelter she had."

" And you are out this morning to look after her, and see if you can reclaim her, messer Matteo ? " said Girolamo.

" Even so ; " answered he. " When Filippino went to look in upon her at day-break, just to see that she was all safe and comfortable, he found the bird flown ; and I was despatched to try and bring her back to cage. You haven't-happened to see her pass by, have you, Girolamo ? " continued Matteo, twitching out one or two of the blades of grass that overhung the basket in which Beatrice lay ensconced. " A little gay-eyed, red-lipped thing, that looks too bright and fearless to mind anything. She seems not to know what tears mean ; and as if neither harm nor sorrow could ever come near her. She speaks up so open, and looks so straight into your face, that you feel as if she must be right and you wrong ; which isn't altogether pleasant, though it isn't altogether unpleasant,—to look at."

" Just such a child as you describe, I saw, this very morning, not half an hour ago ; " said the peasant. " She was wandering about. I questioned her, as in duty bound. She told me she had made her escape from your hands. I washed mine of the concern, as became me. I said you would not approve of my helping her away, if it should come to your ears that I had done so ; and that I liked to live in peace with my neighbours."

" Well said, good Girolamo ; " said Matteo ; " our captain shall know of the good turn you have done him. And so you left the little one to do as well as she could. Quite right. And whereabouts was this ? "

" Close by ; just up there, yonder ; " said the peasant, scrupulously pointing to the spot where the colloquy had taken place between himself and Beatrice.

" And you think I shall find her there still ? " said Matteo.

" She can't have got far ; " replied Girolamo. " I shouldn't wonder, but she's crouching among the long grass ; hiding somewhere quite near, I'll be bound."

" Thanks, good friend, I'll not forget to report you to our captain ; and, in return for your neighbourliness, it shall go hard but we'll spare you a token of our good-will out of the chit's ransom, when it is ours ; " said the robber, as he strode off in the direction pointed out.

" I'm much bounden to you, messer Matteo," said the peasant ; " lest I seem selfish, I'll not say I wish you may get it."

And coolly taking up his song again at the very note, and turn of the tune, where he had been interrupted, the phlegmatic Girolamo jogged on by the side of his mule as before. For some time, they went on thus; Beatrice peering through the wicker frame-work, and getting sufficient air to prevent her smothering in her green nest; which, baked through and through by the sun, now mounted high into the heavens, became somewhat oppressive; but the motion was easy, and she had the pleasant feeling that she was snugly and securely making her way homewards. At length, the mule, of its own accord, turned out of the main path ; the glare of the sun was exchanged for the cool green light of trees overhead ; the dust of the road no longer arose in clouds about them ; there was the loose rich earth of cultivated ground beneath their feet ; and the panniers brushed their way past lines of maize, vines, canes, and waving broom plants. She could discern that they were entering a small 'campagna,' of humble pretensions, but well tilled, and kept in order. There were apple, walnut, and peach trees ; and near the house, she noted the usual broad trays made of canes, on which lay figs spread to dry for winter provision. The house was a mere cottage, built in the rudest form ; but of stone, with thick walls, as a protection against the heat ; while the side trellis, over-run with vine-leaves and drooping clusters, the bunches of bright orange-coloured ears of Indian corn that hung round the windows to ripen and dry, with here and there a long-necked bottle-gourd, and a huge tawny pumpkin, gave a picturesque effect to the spot, which a place of greater elegance and exactness might have lacked.

Peasant Girolamo did the honors of his 'campagna' with much courtesy, after his own phlegmatic fashion ; bidding Beatrice abide beneath the vine-trellis until he should have seen his mule unladen, and comfortably stalled and littered ; observing that "care to his beast, was its master's first duty, to the end it might be ready and able for his next need." He said that his guest was not to scruple helping herself to some of the grapes that hung so temptingly ; remarking that, "when a license was likely to be taken, it was as well to have the credit of granting it." And after he had paid due attention to the mule, he went into the cottage, and spread a table, and set chairs, and made other hospitable preparations in his own orderly, methodical manner. He had an air as if he were discharging a moral duty in all he uttered; and performing a religious ceremony in all he did; so precise, and formal, and completely unnational, was this Sicilian peasant, Girolamo. When he had concluded his arrangements, he went to the door, and beckoned Beatrice in.

He glanced with a sort of meek triumph, a kind of composed pride, upon the repast he had set forth; as though he knew its super-excellence, but that he was capable of the heroism of bestowing it upon his new acquaintance, since he had already done so much for her. It looked certainly very tempting; a crusty loaf of barley-bread upon an olive-wood trencher; cheese made of ewes' milk, embedded in cool green leaves; honey, looking like liquid topaz; and heaps of fruit, golden oranges, burnished pomegranates, rough walnuts, purple grapes, rosy apples, and bloomy peaches, piled into a pyramid that looked as though Amalthea's horn had tumbled its contents upon the board.

The young girl's many hours' fast, and long wanderings in the open air, had given her an appetite which lent the crowning zest to this pleasant meal; and the relish with which she evidently enjoyed, and did justice to his entertainment, was not lost upon her host. He looked on approvingly from time to time, in the intervals of his own eating; cut for her huge corner hunks of bread, and selected for her the choicest fruit. He pledged her in some of the rough new wine which formed his own beverage; but seeing that she merely put her lips to it from courtesy, he went and filled a gourd with water, cold and fresh from the well, for her especial drinking.

"To some palates, water comes more welcome than wine;" he said; "a young lady's mouth hath mostly this delicacy of taste; to please it, I grudge not the trouble of fetching."

"Mine host is as gallant as he is hospitable;" said Beatrice. "In this delicious draught, refreshing and grateful, I drink his health; not coolly,— for all the coldness of the cup,—but thankfully and heartily, in return for his kindness to a strange little girl, a poor unfriended wayfarer."

"Help to others without injury to self, is a debt we all owe; and when we can discharge it, it does us credit;" said the moral Girolamo; "nay, it ought to afford us pleasure, when a convenient opportunity offers; since the acquittal of a duty or a debt is sure to bring ease of conscience; and ease of conscience is happiness,—virtuous happiness."

" 'Tis a kind of ease and delight to you, I doubt not, master Girolamo, to deliver yourself of these goodly sentences, in which you seem to abound ; " said Beatrice, with a merry twinkle in her eyes ; " they seem to rise and mantle as cream, on the rich milk of your brain ; you pour them forth like oil, in such a stream of platitude and plenitude, that it is pity you have not more hearers to be edified by them. You lead a very quiet life, here, I conjecture ? "

" I live quite alone ; but he who hath virtuous thoughts to keep him company, cannot complain of solitude, young lady ; " said Girolamo ; " they are better than visitors ; they never come inopportunely, they never tire ; their very sweets never cloy. Let me give you some of this honey, by-the-by ; it is very fine ; my swarms originally came from thymy Hybla."

" I have already had abundance of good things,—good things to repletion ; " said Beatrice. " But you will not think me wanting in acknowledgment, if I seem eager to quit them, the moment I have had enough. Pity my impatience to reach home, to see my friends, to relieve their anxiety, to embrace them all once more."

" Far be it from me to thwart so natural, so worthy a desire ; " said the peasant. " Orecchiutone, my good mule, will have rested and dined by this time. Let us away, then, in the same order we came."

" Must I become food for asses and mules again ? " said Beatrice.

" No, little one ; " replied Girolamo, with a grim smile ; " like many a better wit than thyself, thou dost but wear the semblance for a time, that thou may'st pass current with the world,—the majority of whom are either foolish or obstinate, and can't or won't relish wit in its true form."

" If one, both ; " said Beatrice ; " asses of men, are mostly mulish ; and mules of men, assish. And so, to force them to swallow unpalateable truth and sense, it is to be offered to them in the guise of unformidable nonsense,—familiar food,—innocent stuff,—green fodder ? I shall try to remember thy precept, good Girolamo."

" Good precepts make good people,—that is if they are taken to heart, as they should be ; " said Girolamo. " It's my opinion, that in good hands you might become anything. Moulded by a master-hand, you'll be a diamond,—a very star among women ; now you're but a lively child, a mere child—hardly better than the green fodder you represent. But by-and-by,—Aha! altra cosa!"

"May you live to see what I shall grow up to be, good friend! I trust I may do honor to your prediction;" said Beatrice.

Through the afternoon, they went jogging on again; until at length, towards evening, they arrived within view of the gates of Messina.

Leonato was perturbedly pacing up and down one of his saloons, anxiously hoping for news of his lost niece, from some one of the several parties he had sent forth in search of her. Ever since the previous evening, the palace had been a scene of distraction. Hero had arrived in the greatest distress, bringing the news of the calamity at Montaspro, and of her cousin's unaccountable disappearance. She herself had slept late into the day, worn out with her previous emotion and fatigue. On awakening, she had missed Beatrice from her side; but at first imagined that she had merely got out to walk for a while. She had caused the litter to halt, hoping every instant to see her cousin come up with it; but after lingering in vain, till there could be no longer any doubt that Beatrice must have lost her way, Hero had hurried home to Messina, that her father might take instant and effectual means for having their dear one sought and recovered.

As yet no intelligence had returned; and Leonato was still in all the newness of his grief for the countess Giustina's untimely fate, divided by his suspense respecting Beatrice, when an attendant hastily entered the saloon, to say, that there was a strange man, a peasant mountaineer, who was in the court-yard, insisting upon seeing his lordship, the lord governor of Messina himself.

"Perchance he brings news of my niece; bring him hither; why did you not admit him at once?"

"My lord, he will neither be brought hither, nor admitted, nor anything else;" said the attendant. "He will not wait upon your lordship; but says forsooth your lordship must come down to him, as he can't leave his mule. We offered to take charge of the beast; he wouldn't hear of it. We proposed to take his message; not a word would he deliver. We questioned

him, we rated him, we even made as if we would have turned him out of
the court-yard, but nothing would bring him to reason,—nothing would
suit him but my lord governor must descend in person, and hear what he
had to say. The rascal rustic ! The pitiful peasant ! Had we not feared
that he might bring news of my young lady Beatrice, which we might lose,
an' we turned him away, he should soon have seen the outside of the
palace-gates."

Half of the attendant's ireful speech at this insult to his master's dignity,
was lost to Leonato, who had hurried out of the saloon, as soon as he had
gathered that the peasant would only tell what he had to say, to himself.

At sight of the lord governor entering the court-yard, the crowd of
lackeys, and guards, and attendants, that had gathered round the stranger,
gave way ; and Leonato advanced to the spot where stood Girolamo holding
his mule by the bridle, with an air perfectly grave and cool. He seemed
not to be disturbed one jot by the hubbub of enquiry, and remonstrance,
and indignation around him ; but to stand there, prepared for the firm
performance of a duty, the carrying through of a momentous act, the consummation of an important deed.

" I am come to offer you a bargain, my lord governor; will you buy
this load of green hay?   Will you give me a fair price for it ? " he said.

" I will give thee thine own price for it, good fellow, if, as I hope, thou
bring'st me news of my dear child, my lost niece, my Beatrice. Tell me
what thou know'st of her. Speak, man ! " said Leonato eagerly.

" If I bring you better than news of her, my lord ? What if I bring you
herself ? " said Girolamo.

" Where is she ? Where have you left her ? " said Leonato.

" What price shall I say for the green hay, my lord governor ? " said
the peasant.   " Any price is no price ; best fix the sum."

" Name it thyself, fellow.   But why keep tormenting me about a paltry
hay-load, when I am dying to hear of my Beatrice."

" Every one for his own pet interest, my lord, as is natural ; your
thought runs all upon your niece, mine all upon the contents of my panniers, quite natural ; " said Girolamo.   " But you bid fairly, you offer mine
own price. If I name a high one,—as I shall,—don't wonder. You'll
think it cheap."

"What thou wilt. But Beatrice—you say you have brought her—where does she tarry—why is not she home? She was ever all impatience to fly to me."

"She has had much ado to restrain it;" said Beatrice, springing up, throwing off the heap of green fodder, and leaping from the midst of it into her uncle's embrace.

"And now, good friend, tell me what I can do for thee, in return for the happiness thou hast bestowed;" said Leonato, turning to peasant Girolamo, after the first transports of finding Beatrice restored; "this purse of gold shall acquit my promise of purchasing the load of hay; but I would have thee tell me if there be anything in which I can farther pleasure thee, as a recompense for the care thou hast taken of my wanderer. Speak frankly."

"Since you bid me, my lord governor, I will honestly tell you, there are three things in which you can mainly oblige me. Firstly, let your treasurer exchange me this purse of gold for the like value in copper coins; secondly, allow it not to get wind how my young lady, your niece, made her way home; and thirdly, give me your lordship's promise that you will not visit their late misdemeanour upon my neighbours."

"Grant him his petition for my sake, dear uncle, and I will explain all;" said Beatrice, observing some surprise, and hesitation in her uncle's look. "I fancy, I have learned enough of mine excellent friend Girolamo's ways of thinking, during the single day I have had the pleasure of his acquaintance, to interpret the grounds of his three requests. Friend Girolamo is of a cautious turn of mind, and would fain not attract the attention of his neighbours, by any ostentatious display of an unwonted kind of metal, when next he hath occasion to disburse coin; which would be the case had he gold pieces to change; therefore he modestly and wisely preferreth copper. Friend Girolamo is of a peaceable turn of mind, and would fain not run the chance of giving offence, by having it known that he aided me to find my way back to Messina, unransomed. And lastly, friend Girolamo is of a generous turn of mind, and therefore speaks a good word on behalf of those who have it in their power to give him a helping hand now and then, as his very good friends and neighbours."

Peasant Girolamo, who had checked off on his fingers each clause of her speech in succession, as they were uttered by Beatrice, at its conclusion, nodded gravely:—"Well set forth, little one; I could hardly have better delivered it, mine own self."

" It shall all be as thou wishest, good fellow;" said Leonato; "but the copper coins will be a heavy burthen for thee to carry."

"Friend Girolamo hath the prudence to let his mule bear all trouble-some charges, for him;" said Beatrice. "The docile beast jogs on, unmindful of risk or weight. A world of mischief in the form of womanhood; or that perilous breed-bate and parent of care, money; all's one, to plodding, patient Orecchiutone." The young girl patted the good animal's neck; and then extended her hand in a kindly farewell to its master; upon which Girolamo made his parting obeisances, and took his departure towards his mountain home.

"And now for uncle Antonio, and my dear Hero, and cousin Gaetano!" exclaimed Beatrice, "Where are they all?"

"Here come my brother, and Hero!" said her uncle. "As for poor Gaetano, he's in bed."

"In bed!"

"Ay; he was so distressed when he found you were missing, that he was obliged to lie down; and he has not been up since. Poor lad! I believe he was really ill; he worked himself into such a fever of inquietude, it was quite pitiable."

"Pitiable, indeed!" exclaimed Beatrice. "To take it to heart, he must take to his bed! Alack, most infelicitous of Gaetanos!"

Time went on. Leonato, as the young people grew up, abated nothing of his indulgence towards them; he loved his daughter Hero tenderly; and her two cousins he treated in every respect like children of his own. There was a strength, a spirited decision of character, belonging to Beatrice, joined to her cheerful-hearted, playful manners, that gained her her uncle's esteem,—almost respect, as well as his fondness. He loved her as a most winning, delightful creature, whilst he entertained for her a regard like that which is felt towards an equal. Many things, which to his daughter, with her more soft and yielding nature, he would not have dreamed of confiding, to Beatrice with her quick intelligence, he imparted, as to a tried and valued friend, upon whose judgment he could rely. He had none of the paltry fear which is apt to beset many of his sex, that to take counsel of a woman, is to give her an opportunity of governing him. He had the sense to perceive native good understanding ; the wisdom to cultivate and strengthen it into future excellence, which might avail both its possessor and her friends ; and the prudence to give it such accompanying principles of morality, and at the same time so much of his own trust and honor, as should teach it to use its power for its fosterer's good, not for his subjugation : and when the result was achieved, he was not afraid of availing himself of the aid such a mind could afford him, because it happened to be a woman's. Between Hero and Beatrice a perfect understanding and affection subsisted. Hero partook too much of her father's candour and generosity of disposition not to appreciate Beatrice's superiority of intellect, and to yield it, in consequence, her entire and unjealous admiration ; while Beatrice on her part, was so passionately attached to Hero's gentle excellence, and so perfectly unvain herself, that no idea but of equality and love could have place between them. There was moreover, just that spice of indolence in Hero's character,—not unfrequently a part of softness and sweetness such as hers,—which made the energy of mind and body that characterized her cousin, peculiarly valuable, as something to be looked up to, and relied upon. Thus, the trust placed in Beatrice by her uncle Leonato, and the active part she took in the household at his request, were regarded by his daughter not only as natural consequence of superior ability, but as tasks which she gladly beheld fulfilled by one more suited to their exigencies than she felt herself to be, either from power or inclination. In a weak girl, such a state of things might have engendered envious misgivings of undue influence ; have inspired jealous fears of a rival in her father's affection ; in a feeble-minded girl, they would most probably have produced lamentations at her own inferiority, and hatred of her cousin's excellence ; but Hero was tender, not weak ; gentle, not feeble. She was of a loving nature, with all the thousand good and generous qualities comprised in that one attribute.

As for Gaetano, he grew up to be, as a young fellow, much what his boyhood had promised.

"Cousin Beatrice," he said to her one day, "my father has been telling me 'tis high time I should be thinking of a profession; what's your opinion?"

"It goes beyond your father's;" said she.

"How?"

"That you should be doing something more than thinking; though it would be well, if you could do that much, to any purpose."

"But Beatrice, I want you to be serious; leave jesting."

"I'm perfectly serious. Want of thought is no jesting matter; though many thoughtless people pass for jesters."

"Do you know, cousin Beatrice, I think I should like to be a soldier; it's a gentlemanly profession."

"Certes, tis a good profession for a thoughtless gentleman; none better. Should his brains chance to get knocked out, there'll be the less to regret."

"Ay, but that chance is just what I don't altogether like;" said Gaetano. "I think I'll change my mind."

"You couldn't do better;" she replied. "You must be a gainer."

"Nay but Beatrice; I am in earnest. I really want to consult you. Listen to me with a sad brow."

"I cannot;" she said. "'Tis not in my face, or my nature. But, look into mine eye, for the picture-in-little of thine own; which is sad enough in all conscience,—sad as an ill-baked cake."

"I wonder whether I could be a statesman;" he said, ponderingly; "'tis an honorable position, and my uncle's influence would not be wanting, I know, to push me forward."

"If you are indeed in earnest, Gaetanino mio," she said, "determine to push youself forward. Make such strength, by work, as shall carry you on of your own force, and not by that of interest or influence; such strength as shall raise you to eminence, and maintain you there, unpushed, unsupported. Learn to rely on yourself."

"Ah, cousin Beatrice, I an't clever."

"Work, then; work hard; work in earnest; and make yourself clever."

"Hard work's so difficult!" sighed Gaetano.

"If it were easy, it wouldn't be hard; and if it were not hard, it wouldn't prevail or endure. I'm afraid there's no choosing any profession, in which hard work isn't a condition,—for success."

"And, of course, I should like to be successful;" said Gaetano ruefully.

"Then be so. Exert yourself;" said his cousin.

"Dear Beatrice, to you,—so full of animation, so full of energy, so quick-witted, so bright,—nothing seems more possible; but to me, who am the reverse of bright,—dull, in fact,—exertion is just the most formidable thing in the world. You see I am not strong; either in health or in spirit. 'Work?' I wish I could work!"

"Don't wish : try. Wishing is wasting time in breath, which should be given to endeavour. 'I wish I could,' mostly means 'I wish somebody else would, for me.'"

"She is hard upon me;" sighed Gaetano, as Beatrice turned away into the next alley to gather some honeysuckles that had just come into bloom, and hung in profusion round a pleached bower there.

"Tell her so, and she will be more forbearing;" said Hero, who was in the garden with them, and overheard his words.

"No; I do not wish her to forbear me. I like her to take me to task; I like to fancy that she interests herself in me sufficiently to rate my faults. I would not have her abate one jot of her lively banter—her vivacity enchants me—but I cannot bear to think she despises me."

"Despise you! The very animation of her rebuke proves her regard. She strives to inspire you with some of her own energy; she would not do that by one she cared nothing for. But she must do it in her own way,—which is raillery; sometimes apt to forget, in its sportive humour, that the spirits of others may not keep pace with its own. When she runs you a little too hard in her playful attacks, you must forgive them for the sake of the kindness and affection they really betoken."

"You think so, cousin Hero!" said poor Gaetano, with sparkling eyes. "If I could believe she cared one straw that I were less of a blockhead than I am, I verily think it would give me strength to work; to strive, to force myself into becoming something better worthy her notice,—her regard. Her 'regard,' you said, cousin Hero, didn't you? But no, it is impossible she can regard so very a dullard as I know myself to be."

"She hath a sincere regard for you, dear cousin;" said Hero. "Believe it, believe that we both love our cousin Gaetano the better for that very modesty of character which will not let him think better of himself than he does; though we could wish that he would not let it hinder him from becoming all that he might be."

" Your gentle nature prompts you to say this, cousin Hero, to comfort me under my sense of defect;" he said.

" You are too despondent, cousin Gaetano;" replied she. " You torment yourself. You make your own misery. You do yourself injustice, every way."

" Of my own deficiency, I am but too sensible. It is the only thing, alas, in which I am sensible;" he added.

" Gaetano complaining of being too sensible!" said Beatrice as she returned towards them. " He is fruitful in complaint I know; but even his ingenuity I should scarce have thought would have discovered that source of lament. Too sensitive, or too full of sensibility, for the bluff dignity of manhood, might afford more legitimate regret, methinks; eh, gentle coz?"

" Sensible of mine own defects,—no more;" he said meekly and deprecatingly.

" No more? What would you more? What could you claim higher? What sense can be better than that which teaches you your own wants? It tells you what you need, it tells you what you should seek, it tells you what you must make your own, to supply that which you lack. Courage, man! If you have got so far as to find out thus much, 'tis your own fault if you do not achieve more,—all."

" When I hear you speak thus, cousin Beatrice, when I see that beaming look, I feel as if I could do, I could be, anything you bid me. But directly I leave you, I feel as if I walked out of the sun into the shade; my fancies cool, my spirits chill, my hopes grow cold; all is dark and sad with me."

" Kindle a fire within, that shall supply the place of the sun's heat, cousin mine;" she said. " Fan the sparks of your own mind into ardour; keep it furnished with plenty of fuel, and a steady warmth shall glow, that will be worth all you can receive from my rays."

" But promise that you will not withdraw their light from me; they do me good, although they sometimes scorch."

" Bravissimo! For the infelicitous, that's not amiss;" she replied.

An attendant coming just then, to summon Gaetano to his father, Hero said to Beatrice :—"'You should be more merciful to him, coz. If he be not so bright as we could all wish,—himself included, for no one is more conscious of his inferiority than he,—you should pity, not taunt him."

" Nay, he cannot be in want of pity from others, who hath so much of his own. He is too much of a self-pitier. The only form of pity I can bestow, is to allow that he is pitiful. I feel so provoked with him, I could scourge him with the feathers of my fan. But that might make the poor dear creature weep. ' Pity him !' Truly he is a most commiserable fellow."

" He hath a fear that you hold him in contempt, cousin ; and that hurts his feelings."

"His feelings are over-tender. They are without their natural skin. They shrink from a touch, like a snail's horns. Why doth he not case-harden himself against the chance of contempt by conduct that shall command respect. A man should be able to protect himself from a woman's scorn. He should be capable of returning her jest-blows with as hard-hitting as her own. He should show that he spares her,—as he would refrain from striking her,—with the forbearance of superior strength."

" But if he hath not that superior strength ? If he acknowledge yours, and defer to it, should not that teach you the very forbearance you speak of, coz ?" replied Hero.

" Let him not yield it slavish deference, and I will not use it tyran-nously ;" said Beatrice. " It is because I think there is more in him than he's aware, that I would teach him not to undervalue himself. A little ill-usage will but make him look about him for his defences, of which, I believe, he hath more than he knows. Once let him find out his own powers, and learn to trust to them, he will leave his sickly fancies, and rouse himself in good earnest to become what mine uncle, his father, could wish."

About this time Leonato set forth on a progress through the island, taking his daughter Hero with him, and leaving Beatrice in Messina, with Antonio and Gaetano, to hold the court during his absence. His reliance on the zeal of his brother, and on the spirit, tact, and discretion of his niece, gave him full security that all would proceed as he could wish. It happened, shortly after the lord governor was gone, that the duchess of Milan, with the prince her son, arrived in Messina, bringing letters to the court. She was travelling, in great state, to visit various cities, and places of note ; it was thought, with a view to choosing a consort for the dukedom's heir.

It so chanced, that upon their first arrival and presentation, the illustrious visitors imagined no other than that Beatrice was the daughter of Leonato ; and it was not until the interview they had with her was wellnigh over, that the fact of her being his niece, and not his only child and heiress, was discovered. But the change this discovery worked upon the haughty duchess, and her insolent son, was too marked to rest unperceived by Beatrice. She saw that the affectionate courtesy, the coaxing flattery, with which the duchess overwhelmed her at first, was soon exchanged for an air of insupportable arrogance and patronage. She saw that the respectful adulation, the deferential observance with which the prince had originally addressed her, suddenly took a turn of familiarity and freedom in its unreserved admiration, the most offensive.

In her quality of hostess, however, and for the sake of her uncle, whose guests they were, she forbore to resent their behaviour ; resolving patiently to endure it for the present.

On their return from the palace, the duchess questioned her son upon the evident impression Beatrice's wit and beauty had made upon his susceptible imagination. " Fear not, madam," he had replied ; " I shall not fail to keep my heart and hand free for the governor's daughter when she makes her appearance ; meanwhile allow me to amuse myself with that charming sparkler, who hath too much discernment to feel otherwise than flattered by the notice of your son."

The duchess, contented with this assurance of his docility in reference to Leonato's heiress, now gave herself up solely to the object of establishing their popularity in a court with which it had long been her project to form an alliance. Their high rank, together with the cajoling condescensions of the worldly mother, and the handsome person, and insinuating manners of the son, failed not to procure them everywhere the reception they sought.

All the world of Messina joined in their laudation, and vied with each other in sounding their praises. Nothing was talked of but the distinguished air of the duchess, and her marvellous kindness; the graces and accomplishments of her son, his amiability, his irresistible fascinations.

"My sister says he is the sweetest prince;" said a rich city lady to Beatrice, upon one occasion. "The most condescending! His highness visits her as unceremoniously, bless you, as though he were a man of no greater consequence than her husband."

"Ay, I have heard that theirs is quite an undress acquaintance; that they are on terms of morning-gown familiarity—I might almost say, of night-cap intimacy. A high honor, truly. But there are not wanting women who find that his grace's graciousness and easy ways amount to freedoms; and who accordingly approve them not,—nay, regard them as dishonor rather than honor;" said Beatrice.

"Such women are mere spiteful prudes; envious because they have not his highness's attentions and society;" replied the lady, tossing her head.

"On the contrary; my informant found he pressed so close a friendship, that she was compelled to decline his acquaintance;" said Beatrice.

"Who are these people that all the world are talking about?" enquired Hero, of her cousin Beatrice, upon her return home; "this duchess of Milan, and her son?"

"Who are they? The duchess of Milan, and her son, the prince;" answered Beatrice. "In these two titles, the good folks of Messina seem to think are comprised all that is great, and good, and charming."

"But what think you of them, coz? Come, describe them to me. First, for the duchess."

"Well, then, to picture her to you morally, she is the sort of woman who comforts her husband in a misfortune, by telling him 'tis his own fault; and to present her to you physically, she hath the face of a parrot; a sharp, smooth beak, a sidelong eye, with a black tongue capable of uttering well-sounding sentences."

"What age?" asked Hero.

F

"There comes a time when the weakness of plucking out grey hairs is mad waste of all we're worth;" replied Beatrice. "The duchess hath reached that period."

- "Do not her white hairs give her a venerable look?" said Hero.

"She forfeits it, by being ashamed of them;" said Beatrice. "Nature sets this snow-wreath upon a woman's brow in requital for the youthful graces of which years rob her, that she may engage reverence where she formerly won admiration; but if she affront Nature with bedizenments of Art, she gains neither reverence nor admiration,—naught save ridicule."

"And the son?"

"You will see him and judge for yourself. He is to be at the court ball my uncle gives this evening, in honor of your return."

"Meantime, tell me how thou hast seen and judged him coz;" insisted Hero.

"Frankly then, he pleases neither my sight nor my judgment. He hath too much license in his regard. His looks hold freer communion with my person than I approve. His eyes are too attentive; they are ever busier with my face, my neck, or my hands, while I speak, than his thoughts with my words; and I like not such mode of converse. And then his insolence to Gaetano. He is as disdainful to him, as he is presuming to me."

"To Gaetano! He is too modest, surely, to provoke insult."

"Modest? Ay; but there are some people who love to kick modesty, for no other reason than that it is modesty,—too modest to kick again."

During the entertainment given at the palace that evening, the prince's manner to Beatrice was totally changed. He affected to neglect her; and to devote himself to her cousin Hero. But he could not avoid allowing his attention to be distracted towards the end of the room where her brilliancy of beauty and manner drew a little crowd around her. He did his utmost to control his thoughts, to concentrate them upon the object he had in view; but they perpetually wandered to that which possessed so potent a spell for him. His jealousy was roused by perceiving her the centre of compliments, and flatteries; incense of mouth, ear, and eye, from gazers

and listeners; while it was in a measure appeased, at the same time that
his admiration was heightened, by the smiling ease with which she parried
the homage, half receiving it as her due, half rejecting it as scarce worthy
of acceptance. Above all, he rejoiced to perceive the absolute indifference
with which she treated every one. He could discern no shadow of preference towards any who addressed her. Vivacity, playfulness, gaiety of
heart, marked her manner; but no symptom of inclination, no token of
superior liking was there.

Presently he saw her led forth to dance by a gentleman of lofty air.
The prince could not help watching her graceful and spirited movements
through the measure. When it ended, he saw her partner draw her arm
through his, and lead her to a cooler portion of the apartment. They came
near to where he sat, trying to entertain Hero in conversation; and he
could overhear part of theirs.

Beatrice appeared to have been pleading some suit with great earnestness,
which seemed to have been withstood; for she rejoined :—" I beg your
pardon, my lord; I was giving you credit for a heart and feelings; I crave
forgiveness for doing a statesman the injustice of believing he possessed
any such unstatesmanlike attributes."

" You urge this young poet's cause, madam, with a warmth that suggests
a very peculiar interest in the subject;" sneered the gentleman.

" The subject is ill-rewarded genius, my lord; it is one that warmly
interests me, I own;" she said.

" And your zeal in the theme is heightened by ardour for the man,
I fear. Lady, you know my own hopes. I cannot relinquish them. This
young poet, tell me,—my mind misgives me,——"

" True, my lord, it does misgive you;" said Beatrice, with sparkling
eyes, and an impetuosity very different from her usual light mood; "let
me tell you it does misgive you; it gives you a multitude of things amiss.
It gives you false views, false impressions, false convictions. It gives you
to draw false conclusions, to act upon false premises; it gives you to make
false judgments, and to deliver false and unjust sentences. Moreover, your
mind—your statesman's mind,—unencumbered by such superfluous ex-
crescences as heart and feelings—unbiassed by such weaknesses as loves

and hatreds, sympathies, affinities, antipathies, and repugnances,—contemplates genius, intellect, and such like gifts, to be the patented right, the exclusive monopoly of you rulers; or that if they dare to exist among the ruled, they are to be considered as so many illegal possessions, and their produce to be fined, taxed, mulcted, drained down to proper dimensions accordingly, for the behoof of the state stock, which cannot be too large, too arrogant in plethoric abundance."

"'Tis not to be doubted, the motive for this vehemence, madam;" said the nobleman, with a deeply offended air. "Your client shall not fail to learn his good fortune;" he added, as he bowed and left her.

Presently, a young man, with an air of intolerable and unmistakeable self-sufficiency, the look of a thorough-paced coxcomb, made his way towards the spot where Beatrice still stood.

He addressed her with a strain of high-flown acknowledgements, in which flattered self-love, and consciousness of desert, mingled in equal measure. It was evident he thought the aspirings of his heart, and the marvels of his brain, were each on the point of receiving their due estimation and reward. He had just been informed by the chagrined and disappointed statesman, of the manner in which the lady Beatrice had betrayed her partiality for the man in pleading the cause of the poet; and he had come to pour forth his conceited complacency of gratitude.

Beatrice heard him to an end; until he had revealed the full extent of his fatuity; and then she merely said :—" I worked for the cause, not for thee, man; for the principle, not for the individual. As one who claims brotherhood with poets, you may conceive me entitled to your thanks, for the love I bear sweet poesy, and for the earnestness with which I pleaded her rights; but in good sooth, I deserve no gratitude of yours."

He looked confounded at this cool reception, where he had evidently been led to expect so different a one; and shortly after, bowed himself from her presence, to go and rail at lady's caprice.

"You dismissed the poor devil with a scorn that will teach him less presumption in future, madam;" said the prince, as Beatrice approached to speak to her cousin.

"Presumption is an inapt pupil, my lord;" replied Beatrice; "it is slow

to take a hint, and dull at learning a lesson; it requires whipping.
I should not have used the rod to yonder puppy, but that he is a pretender
as well as a presumer. A poetaster; no true poet. I had not him in my
thoughts when I urged the cause of poetry and genius erewhile. This man
is a sorry scribbler,—a versifier; one who thinks he writes poetry, because
he puts down his lines all of a length."

"Many lose their way through life, mistaking their right road to Fame;"
said the prince.

"Nay, perish miserably;" she rejoined. "Witness the numskull who
threw himself into the burning mountain, one day, to pick up a name; but
he only calcined himself into an eternal fool, who, knowing his own farthing
value, chucked it into a hole. Or that fellow who set light to the Ephesian
temple, to kindle himself a reputation that should flame down to posterity;
but he did no more than brand himself an ass, in arson immortality.
Goddess Dian was busied elsewhere,—tending the birth of another of
those Famesters, Alexander the great baby, who cried for a second world-
orange,—or she had never suffered her shrine to be scorched to cinder."

"You care not for renown, fair lady?" enquired the prince.

"I care not for too much of a good thing, my lord;" she replied.
"Had I been Eve, I should have asked to be let out of Paradise, long
before she was turned out."

"Indeed! Why?"

"I should have liked to see something of the world;" answered Beatrice.

"And rejoiced the world to see you;" said the prince.

"A vacant compliment, my lord. You forget; the world was empty,
then; of men, at least, whose admiration is supposed to be the one thing
acceptable to us women."

"If the world were empty, you would fill it,—with delight;" said the
prince, forgetting all his resolutions with regard to paying exclusive court
to Hero.

"A delightful world! Pity your highness did not live then, and have
it all to yourself;" said Beatrice. "But here comes cousin Gaetano, to
claim his promised dance with me."

And fair Hero will accord me her hand for this measure?" said the
prince.

Later in the evening, the prince saw Beatrice engaged in lively talk with
a gentleman whom he had not seen before.   The stranger was handsome;
with great spirit and grace in all his movements.   He had an open, animated countenance, with eyes of remarkable brilliancy and intelligence;
a noble, easy air, bespeaking the well-bred man, and distinguished gentleman.   The prince had the curiosity to ask who he was.

"His name is signor Benedick, of Padua;" replied Antonio, of whom
the inquiry was made.   "He is newly arrived in Messina, and hath letters
to my brother Leonato, from his excellent friend don Pedro of Arragon,
who promises soon to be here himself."

"The lady Beatrice grants this stranger much of her attention;"
remarked the prince ; "he hath held her in talk I know not how long."

"She is interested to find one who can retort her own smartness upon
her, I fancy;" said her uncle ; "from what I overheard of their colloquy
but now, I could gather that she hath met with her match.   But yonder
is my old friend, count Gregorio ; I must to him, and ask whether he hath
heard lately of the young soldier, his nephew Claudio."

Antonio hurried away, leaving the prince still moodily watching Beatrice
from a distance.   "I am no longer master of myself;" he muttered.
"To gaze upon her,—to hear her, is to lose all command, all controul.
Why do I trust myself even thus near ?   If my mother's hope is to be
fulfilled, I should shun her.   Where is Hero ?   Let me seek her ; and
keep my thoughts steadily on the end in view."

In pursuance of this purpose, his highness, the next morning, arrived
at the palace, fully determined to dedicate all his attention to Hero, and to
banish Beatrice from his mind.   But, to the utter subversion of all his
prudent resolves, on being ushered into the saloon usually occupied by the
cousins, he found Beatrice sitting alone at her embroidery-frame.   He
approached with involuntary eagerness ; but endeavouring to recover
himself, he made some enquiry respecting the lady Hero.

"My cousin indulges in a late hour this morning, to match her late
hours of last night, my lord;" said Beatrice.   "If you will favor her with
a still later, in your visit, she will probably be pleased to receive your
highness."

"I will await her coming, here, if my presence be not unwelcome to the embroideress;" said the prince.

"So that you come not so near as to hinder the free drawing of my needle, my lord, your presence is no more unwelcome than usual;" said Beatrice, as the prince took a seat close to her elbow.

"Is the progress of your embroidery so important, that you cannot spare a moment from it?" he said.

"'Tis important, in all likelihood, as aught that may claim my attention. Besides, I can talk and work; stitch and listen at the same time; like a thrifty housewife, save the precious moments, by putting them to double use."

"But it is a loss of half the pleasure, conversing with a woman at needle-work; it is to miss the comment of her eye when you speak, and its lustre when she replies;" said the prince.

"Your confidence assumes that you speak to pleasure her, my lord; otherwise, the comment might chance to be so little agreeable that it were better avoided, and the lustre rather fierce than benign."

"I have been so favored hitherto as to have seen few marks of displeasure from fair ladies' eyes;" said the prince; "I will not fear that the lady Beatrice can be less gracious to me than those who were her inferiors in every gracious attribute."

"If you boast their favor, my lord, they must be my superiors in grace;" said Beatrice.

"Can you accord me none, then?" whispered the prince.

"I cannot spare it; I cannot afford to be graceless myself;" she said.

"You will not understand me. So perverse! So chilling!" said the prince. "Why so cold lady?"

"'Tis the winter quarter, my lord. But though the season be unusually severe, yet I care not to be kept warm by such near neighbourhood. Your chair encroaches upon my comfort; give me freer room, my lord."

"I do but admire these beauties of yours;" he said, pointing to the flowers of her embroidery, and bending still more closely over her.

"Your highness's breath flutters the fur on my dress; I neither like the down to be scared, nor my shoulder to be breathed upon; my temper ruffles at both."

"By heaven, the swan-down itself shames not the whiteness of the shoulder 'gainst which it rests." And the prince's lips dared to touch it with a kiss. In an instant, the whiteness of the skin he had at once so lauded and profaned, was lost in the glow that suffused it,—like northern snows encrimsoned by the midnight sun.

Beatrice started up; calling, in her ringing voice :—"Who waits!" There was a pause. One of the attendants from the ante-room, entered. When he appeared, his young mistress said :—"Open the door; and if ever this person comes again, shut it."

Without farther words, she turned away, and left the apartment.

Not long after, her uncle Antonio met her, and with the tremulous motion of the head peculiar to him when he was agitated, or excited, said :—"What is this I hear, niece, that you have dismissed the prince with indignity?"

"He offered me one;" she said quietly.

"Is it possible? A man of his condition? His highness could not surely——"

"His highness was guilty of a baseness, dear uncle; neither you nor uncle Leonato would have had me submit to the affront passed upon me."

"Surely not; yet my brother will be vexed that a man of the prince's rank and influence should quit Messina offended;" said Antonio.

"If he scruple not to give offence, let him e'en take it, an' he will;" returned Beatrice; "and, for his rank, his grace disgraced himself by his own deed."

The expected guest, don Pedro of Aragon, arrives. He is a valued friend of Leonato's; and very different, in all respects, from the prince whom he succeeds as a visitor at the court of Messina. The young duke of Milan was a selfish libertine, with sufficient ambition to wish to controul his passions for the sake of an advantageous match, but not sufficient virtue to subjugate them; while the prince of Arragon is a noble gentleman, full of honor and high principle. He brings with him his brother, don John; a gentleman of temper as unhappy as his origin; for he is an illegitimate son of the late prince their father by a low-bred woman. His tastes are degraded, his habits vicious, his nature crafty, and his manners morose. But don Pedro permits his accompanying him, that a better example may act propitiously; and serve to wean him from the unworthy society he has hitherto frequented.

The brothers were attended, each by their several followers. Don Pedro had a large retinue, as befitted his rank; with one confidential servant, named Balthazar. This Balthazar was a staid, worthy man; he had native good sense, and had had an excellent education; he was much respected by the prince his master, and he possessed one accomplishment which won him his especial liking and favor. Balthazar was an admirable musician; he played on the lute with great skill, and possessed a charming tenor voice.

Don John's attendant was named Borachio; a dashing, dissolute fellow, who passed for very good-looking, among the tribe of susceptible serving-damsels and waiting-gentlewomen.

One of the lady Hero's women, Margaret, a smart, forward girl, was smitten on the spot. The instant she beheld this irresistible gentleman's gentleman, she fell desperately in love. She flirted, she coquetted, she 'kept company with him'; though she held him aloof all the while'; prudently resolving not to give up so good a situation as she enjoyed with her young mistress, the governor of Messina's daughter, either by a loss of reputation, or by a marriage with a roving blade, who might desert her the next week to follow his master's fortunes.

This flirtation cost the sober, serious Balthazar many a pang. With all his sobriety and gravity, he could not resist the captivation of the smart damsel, Margaret. He loved her against his better sense; he loved her in spite of himself; his prudence was not proof against her pretty face, and brisk gaiety. But all his love, strong and involuntary as it was, availed him nothing. It could not win him one smile from her whose whole stock was lavished upon the showy, rakish Borachio.

But the love-affairs of the hall and ante-chamber need be no farther adverted to.

Don Pedro's visit to his old friend at Messina had lasted about a month, when one morning a young gentleman, an officer, arrived at the governor's palace, enquiring for the prince, and announcing that he brought news from the army to his highness.

It happened that don Pedro, with signor Benedick, signor Leonato, signor Antonio, Gaetano, and Beatrice, had ridden forth on a short excursion in the neighbourhood, to visit some classic remains of great beauty, regarding which, the prince had expressed interest and curiosity.

The young soldier,—who had announced his name as count Claudio, saying that he would await the return of don Pedro,—was shown into one of the saloons ; which chanced to be a favorite sitting-room of the two young lady-cousins. It opened into a large conservatory, full of exotics, and the rarer flowers and plants. In this saloon sat the young officer for some time ; listlessly turning over a large portfolio of engravings that lay open on a stand ; examining the various elegancies that profusely adorned the table ; glancing at the embroidery-frame in one window, that announced occasional feminine occupation of the apartment ; looking at the pictures that hung upon the wall ; and varying all these attempts to beguile the time, by a low-whistled tune, or a half-hummed air ; when, of a sudden his attention was attracted by the sound of another voice, also singing a little quiet song, in that sort of busy idleness, and occupied leisure, which employs the fingers, while it leaves the thoughts and voice free to move to music.

He held his breath, and listened. Yes, it was a soft womanly voice, sweet and clear, singing very near to him. It seemed to proceed from the conservatory. He was sitting not far from the open door which led directly into it ; but on raising his eyes, he saw mirrored in a tall Venetian glass that covered a large portion of the wall opposite to him, a complete picture of the interior of the conservatory, which he could contemplate without stirring from the position he occupied.

It presented to him, amid the profusion of foliage and blossoms with which the conservatory was filled, the figure of a young girl ; graceful, beautiful, blooming as themselves. She had a light but capacious basket on one arm ; into which she dropped the flowers as she cut them. She was gathering a large quantity, and culling them with some niceness ; for still she went on cropping flower after flower, now reaching up after some half-blown favorite, now plunging amid a thicket of leaves, now pressing through stem and spray for some choice bud, or selected beauty. And ever as she proceeded in her fragrant task, she murmured her low liquid carol, with tones as sweet and full, as were the perfumes and colors she collected.

The young officer sat entranced, watching her. Count Claudio was not of a disposition to be troubled by any refinement of notion, such as might have prompted a nature of more scrupulous delicacy and generosity than his, to step forward and announce his presence to the young lady. He was a man of the world, a soldier, with certain accomplishments of person and manner that made him pass for a very pleasant, gentlemanly youth ; he thought the young girl made an exceedingly pretty picture, bending among her plants and flowers ; and he had no hesitation in gazing on it as long as he pleased,—which was as long as it continued before him.

At length the basket was filled ; and the young lady advanced towards the door which led into the saloon. As she entered, she perceived the count. A blush of surprise, at seeing a stranger, where she had expected to find no one, crossed her ingenuous face ; but no embarrassment, no confusion, marred the high-bred ease and grace with which she approached him, and paid him the courtesy of reception in her father's absence.

He hastened to explain, that he was the bearer of despatches to don Pedro; which he feared would summon him from the scene of his present enjoyment, as his highness's presence was required at the seat of war.

On the return of the riding party, it was found that it was even so ; and on the very day after, don Pedro and his train bade adieu to Leonato ; not however, without the expression of a hope that when the campaign was over, they should all return to enjoy a renewal of their pleasant visit.

Their departure left quite a void in Leonato's circle. The affability, and kindly feeling of don Pedro ; with the wit and spirit of signor Benedick; were especially missed. The family party were assembled in the saloon, the evening after their friends had left them ; when they fell into the unconscious silence which betokens an unexpressed regret, felt in common ; until Beatrice exclaimed :—

"Come, this is dull work, this sitting doing nothing. Thinking and brooding, is worse than nothing, yet the same,—'tis naught."

" What should we do better, coz ? " said Hero.

" Talk—talk scandal.   Let us amuse ourselves with backbiting our
friends, in revenge for turning their backs upon us."

" What scandal wilt thou invent, niece ?   For sure calumny itself cannot
find aught to report amiss of the noble gentlemen who have just left us ; "
said Leonato.   " There is my esteemed friend, don Pedro ; even thy saucy
tongue will not dare level slander against a gentleman so complete ? "

" He is your dearest friend, uncle mine ; " she said ; " that should exempt
him from censure, even though his own desert did not set slander at defiance.
But there is his brother, don John.   Can charity itself say a word in his
favour, and hope to be thought other than hypocrisy ? "

" He was ever an unhappy gentleman ; " said Antonio ; " his position
and his disposition are both unhappy."

" And, certes, he makes those about him unhappy ; " said Beatrice.
" He is enough to poison bliss itself.   If a woman were to meet him in
Heaven, she'd pray to be delivered thence."

" You allow there's a likelihood of his going thither ? " said her uncle
Leonato, smiling ; " there's a chance yet for my friend's poor brother."

" He is indeed a poor soul !   Yet he hath the pride of the prince of
fallen angels,—Lucifer himself."

" Do you think he's proud ? " asked Leonato.

" ' Proud ? '   He's too proud to say his prayers ; " she answered.

" How like you count Claudio, the young soldier, my friend Gregorio's
nephew ? " asked Antonio.

" I saw him but yesterday for the first time ; " she replied ; 'tis hard to
judge a man by a few hours' knowledge, when whole years scarce suffice
a woman to get all her husband's foibles by heart ; but a soldier's character
is seldom so deep but it may be seen through, as you look into a stream,—
down to the very bottom at once."

" Pure, and transparent ; " said Hero.

" Cry you mercy, sweet coz ! " said Beatrice.   " What say you to
shallow, and nothing but gay babble ? "

" Claudio hath more in him than belongs to a mere soldier ; " said
Leonato ; " he is a young gentleman of good discretion, good breeding, and
good birth."

" With a good pair of eyes, uncle, a good leg, a good hand, and an excellent good opinion of himself altogether ; " said Beatrice.

" Nay, you cannot call him vain, cousin ; " said Hero ; " he hath a tongue as ready in others' praise, as it is mute upon his own."

" You have haply given more time to the study of this new tongue than I, coz ; " returned Beatrice. " I learned scarce anything of it ; you seem well versed in its subtleties. I give you joy of your proficiency, sweet Hero."

" You have not told us what you think of signor Benedick, of Padua, niece ; " said Leonato.

" I think nothing of him, uncle. Which may mean that I take him to be worthy of no thought ; or that I think him of no worth. The truth is, he hath sunk himself to a cipher in my opinion, since I have found the poor opinion·he hath of women."

" I know signor Benedick stands at low rate with cousin Beatrice ; " said Gaetano ; " for she treats him even more roughly than she does me. She uses little ceremony with us, but still less with him. But I can't wonder at it ; for the gentleman is scarce civil to her. He seizes all occasion to taunt and retort upon her for her just treament of him ; calling her my lady Disdain, and other fine witty names, that I can't see the humour of, for the life of me. If she disdain him, very right ; if she scoff at him, so much the better."

" But what is this poor opinion he entertains of women, niece ? " said Leonato.

" Marry, uncle, this ; he professes to believe that none look on him, but love him."

" He should at least be grateful for their weakness, and hold his tongue about it ; " said her uncle, laughing.

" So far from gratitude, he professes, that, for his part, he can love none in return. ' Bella donna ' is the deadliest of all poisons to him. He desires to keep his heart unscorched ; whereby he thinks he proveth he hath more sense in one of his little toes, than Leander in all his big head,—who, they say, poor youth, was troubled with water on his brain, besides fire in his heart."

"You will allow that signor Benedick hath wit, niece? No one can deny him to have wit;" said Leonato.

"Truly uncle, if Nature hath gifted him with any, 'tis the more shame of him to mislay it as he does. 'Tis ever new moon with him; the best part of his wits are gone wandering; and where he should seek 'em, is in darkness."

"Nay, niece, this is sheer malice. Benedick's wit is ever forcible, lively, and present to the occasion."

"Right uncle, 'tis so ever present, we would fain have the relief of its absence. We rejoice in its absence,—as we are doing now."

But the campaign lasted long; the wars were protracted; and it was more than a twelvemonth ere don Pedro was at liberty to fulfil his promise of returning to Messina. At the end of that period, however, a messenger arrived from his highness; announcing his approach forthwith. Leonato and his family welcomed the tidings with joy; and questioned the bearer eagerly respecting their friends. Beatrice perplexed the man by asking after her old wit-adversary thus:—"*I pray you, is signor Montanto returned from the wars, or no?*"

When Hero rejoined:—"*My cousin means signor Benedick, of Padua.*"

And now, gentle readers, you will rejoice, "when you have seen the sequel."

FINIS.

THE

GIRLHOOD

OF

SHAKESPEARE'S HEROINES;

IN

A SERIES OF FIFTEEN TALES,

BY

MARY COWDEN CLARKE,

Author of the Concordance to Shakespeare.

"as petty to his ends,
As is the morn-dew on the myrtle leaf
To his grand sea."
Shakespeare.

TALE XII.

OLIVIA; THE LADY OF ILLYRIA.

LONDON:

W. H. SMITH & SON, 136, STRAND; AND SIMPKIN, MARSHALL, & CO.,
STATIONERS' HALL COURT.

1851.

TO

KENNY MEADOWS, Esq.,

IN RECOGNITION OF THE

EXQUISITE SPIRIT

OF HIS

SHAKESPEAREAN ILLUSTRATIONS,

THIS TALE IS DEDICATED,

BY

MARY COWDEN CLARKE.

TALE XII.

OLIVIA; THE LADY OF ILLYRIA.

"She that hath a heart of that fine frame,
To pay this debt of love but to a brother,
How will she love, when the rich, golden shaft,
Hath kill'd the flock of all affections else
That live in her! when liver, brain, and heart,
These sovereign thrones, are all supplied, and filled,
(Her sweet perfections) with one self king!"

Twelfth Night.

It was one of those glorious evenings on the Adriatic shores. The sun had set; but the rich orange glow in the west, still marked the gorgeous pomp of his departure; mingling its fervid gold with the intense blue of the southern sky. The vivid glare of light was sobered into a depth of color,—the heat of day was tempered into a soft luxurious warmth, that filled the air with voluptuous beauty. The nearer trees were embrowned in shadow; the mountain horizon lay empurpled in distance. All was steeped in the sumptuous hues, and balmy repose of evening in a meridional clime. The sole enjoyer of the scene, at this hour, was a solitary horseman, pacing slowly along the road; which lay rather inland, the sea-coast screened from view by trees, and broken ground, and such intervening objects. It was scarcely more than a bridle-way; little frequented by travellers, although it led to the principal place in Illyria, where the reigning duke held his court; strangers mostly arriving by ship, and proceeding from the harbour into the capital. The extreme loneliness of the road, together with its picturesque aspect,—the deep and almost solemn beauty of the evening, seemed in perfect harmony with the horseman's mood. He was wrapt in thought, which allowed of just so much perception of external circumstances and influences, as to render him alive to their sympathy with his feelings. These had till now been so full of a recent misery, that they were unable to occupy themselves with aught save their own fruitless, but imperious activity; but this evening, for the first time since his heavy bereavement, they suffered themselves to be soothed into something like calm. His spirit could bear to admit the mysterious consolations of mighty Nature; he could endure to look upon her in her serene aspect, and not feel it a mockery,—a jarring discord, to the tumults within his soul. He yielded his heart to her benign ministry, and felt he could accept her comfort.

He was a native of the south of Germany; a gentleman of birth and fortune. He was the sole surviving representative of an ancient house; but in marriage with a woman whom he passionately loved, he had felt no longer alone in existence. His wife was to him all the world; friends, society, enjoyment, happiness, were all comprised to him in her single self. In her possession he had possessed all. In her loss he had lost all. She had died in giving birth to their first child. He was smitten, in his anguish, with a brain fever, which for a long time threatened both intellect and life; but youth, and a fine constitution, redeemed him from extinction of either; though he was scarce grateful for the boon. Return of reason was return of consciousness in misery; restoration to life, was renewal of unhappy existence. On recovering from his prolonged illness, his old housekeeper,—a faithful creature, but one little skilled in dealing with such profound feelings as his,—had opened all his wounds afresh, by familiar allusions to his loss, commonplace condolences, entreaties that he would see how like his little daughter was to the " dear departed lady," and prosy details of how nicely she had managed to bring up the baby baroness, her-self, by hand, instead of trusting it to " any interested hussy of a wet-nurse." He had borne all patiently; merely begging, in a quiet voice, that she would let him know when the child was asleep, as he chose to trust himself to look upon it first thus.

His wish was obeyed. At night, when the baby was laid in its little bed, the housekeeper summoned him to the room, He entered; his face very pale; his knees trembled, and his hand shook; but there was that in his look, as he pointed to the door, which cut the garrulous housekeeper short in her stream of words, and caused her to walk out in the very midst of her oration. She heard the door locked upon her, as she withdrew.

When she returned,—in some alarm at the length of time that elapsed, ere she was summoned,—she found the door flung wide open, no one in the room, and the litle bed empty. The father, on being left alone, had staggered to where his child lay; but with the first glance at that baby face which had cost life to her whom it innocently resembled, came so overwhelming a rush of emotion, so many wild regrets, so passionate a sense of his misery, that all other wishes were merged in the one distracted desire to fly from any chance of witness to his grief.

' With the desperation of anguish, jealous of its solitary indulgence, he formed his resolve. Hastily but tenderly, he wrapped the sleeping babe in the warm coverlet; crept out of the room; stole down stairs, into his library; furnished himself with money; went straight to the stable; saddled a horse, mounted, and rode fast and far away from his ancestral castle,—from the prying eyes, and prating gossip of officious attachment. He determined to travel; that alone he might wrestle with his sorrow, and try what time and new objects might do towards softening its agony. He journeyed on horseback, carrying his little daughter before him, softly cradled in the quilted coverlet; and so far from finding her presence a burthen or an inconvenience, it was the only thing that afforded a diversion to his misery. The providing for her comfort, the necessary forethought for her accommodation, served to arouse him from the exclusive brooding upon his loss. He proposed to wander along the shores of the Adriatic, through Illyria, and Dalmatia, as lands where he might range uninterruptedly and unobservedly. He had reached Illyria, and was pursuing his solitary way, when the soft glories of that sunset evening first stole upon his wounded spirit, and reawakened it to a sense of peace and calm.

He had, for some miles, not met with a single passer, or a house of any kind, save a straggling cottage or two, mere peasant-huts, or vine-dressers' habitations. But at a bend of the road, he came to a cypress avenue, that led up to a fine old mansion, embowered in trees, and surrounded by extensive grounds. The deep orange glow from the west, still lent its rich hue to the sky, forming a gorgeous back-ground to the picture; while the single lustrous star of evening shone immediately above the house. It looked so quiet, so secluded; all was so still, and suggestive of repose about it, that the horseman could not help pausing to gaze upon this sequestered dwelling. He was irresistibly attracted by its air of unostentatious yet substantial comfort. It looked an embodiment of those qualities which to an English mind are summed in the one word 'home.' It was the recognition of this home-look, that caused the traveller to stop and contemplate the place so attentively.

He rode on with a deep sigh, as he thought how little any dwelling could now be 'home' to him. Then his train of regretful thought branched off into the idea of his child's future home. Would she be doomed to pass her life with so unfit an associate for a young hopeful spirit, as his own? Would it be right to retain her in companionship with a broken-hearted man, a widower-father? What would indeed be her home? He peeped at the close-nestled face of his little one, who lay in a profound slumber, lulled by the open air, and the plodding pace of the horse. There was something in the serene expression of the sleeping babe, that whispered hope to the father's heart,—hope, and a something allied to interest in the future.

At that instant, a sharp pain smote him. He was stabbed in the back, by a coward stroke from a ruffian, who, in company with three others, had sprung from a thicket unperceived, and set upon him. They repeated the blow, and he fell from his horse, pierced and bleeding. They lost no time in rifling his pockets of all they contained; during which process he swooned. With an assurance to each other, that he was safely settled, they were proceeding to ransack the holsters and other cases about the horse's housings, when, one of the brigands remarking that they could do that at their leisure, and had best make off lest they should be surprised, they all plunged into the thicket again, leading the animal with them.

After a space, the pain of his hurts roused the wounded man from his swoon. His first thought was his child. With the instinct that surmounts the pang of death itself, in a parent's heart, he had clutched the babe fast, in falling. This, together with the strange impunity with which infant limbs sustain the roughest shocks, from their unresisting mode of meeting them, had preserved the little creature. It lay,—still close curled up within the quilted coverlet,—near beside him. He strove to raise himself. A vague thought of endeavouring to reach the house he had so lately passed, swam through his brain. But it would not be; the blood oozed fast; no means of staunching it; no help; no hope; he tried to shout, his voice died away; his arms made one effort to grasp her to his heart, and then his head fell back in the dust of the pathway.

Within that house sat a family party. It consisted of a gentleman, who sat in an arm-chair, with one elbow leaning on the table near him, reading,— in a most luxurious state of domestic comfort and ease,—to a lady seated near him, occupied with some kind of light needle-work. As the candle-light fell upon the bent head of the gentleman, and the hand that supported it, there was something in the shape and turn of both, that bespoke the high-bred man; while in the listening countenance of the lady, there was both beauty and intelligence. Near to them stood a cradle; in it lay a heap of snowy clothing, from the midst of which peered a rosy little face, with blue eyes that stared and blinked alternately, as if they were now wondering what could be the meaning of the humming monotony of the reading aloud, now resolving to break it up with a startling roar that should demand summary attention. Close beside the cradle, on a low stool, sat a little girl, who was employed in rocking her baby brother, and watching anxiously the staring eyes, and the several moods they portended; now amusing herself with the grave interest they seemed to be taking in the subject of the book, now all terror lest they should screw up into an in-flexible determination to obtain a hearing for their small owner.

Before this point was settled to the satisfaction of the small mind employed upon it, another interruption to the reading occurred. There was a loud ring at the entrance-bell.

"My brother Toby lets us know of his arrival, this evening, with yet more than his usual energy;" said the lady. "I could wish he would not ring with so imperative a hand. It almost sounds like some dread sum-mons—the hasty announcement of some fearful accident."

"The level murmur of the reading has made it sound more than common

sudden ; " replied the gentleman, with an anxious glance at his wife's face ;
for he knew that her health was not strong, and that her nerves were easily
shaken. " Fear nothing, my love ; 'tis no more than Toby's eagerness to
apprise us of his coming,—which he knows always enlivens and pleasures us."

But the first sight of his brother-in-law's face, as he entered the room,
showed the gentleman that something had indeed happened more than
usual.

In lieu of the hearty, easy, and somewhat boisterous way in which the
new-comer made his nightly entrance among them ; instead of the bright,
good-humoured, jovial look that generally beamed from out his broad and
ruddy countenance ; he came in hurriedly, agitatedly, with pale cheeks, and
with an expression in his eyes, that spoke plainly their having just come
from beholding a sight of horror. In his arms he held an infant covered
with blood.

He hastily told his story. How he was coming as usual, to spend the
evening with his sister and her husband, whistling thoughtlessly as he
lounged along the road, when he had nearly stumbled over the body of a
man, that lay right in his path, pierced through with wounds. How he
had discovered upon leaning down to succour him, that he was quite dead ;
that he must have fallen by the hand of robbers, for that his pockets had
been rifled ; all his money and papers gone. How, upon the dead man's
bosom lay the sleeping babe, steeped in its father's blood. How he had
raised it in his arms, and brought it home to his sister. He ended by
saying that he had taken leave to send some of his good brother's servants
to fetch the body of the poor gentleman out of the road.

" And now, sister mine," added he, " let me have a cup of old Chianti,
to take the taste out of my throat. It still sticks there. Nothing but
wine will wash my palate clean of the queer flavour that came upon it, when
I saw that poor young fellow lying weltering on the ground ; his bright
hair in the dust, his eyes up-staring, his mouth agape, and his little child,
with its head upon his breast, all unconscious of the dreadful sight so near.
Poor innocent ! See it now ! "

The child had awakened ; and was leaping and bounding in his arms towards the shining candle, and crowing with delight at the brilliant object that attracted its gaze.

The eyes of the good-natured sir Toby were moist, as he watched the rapture of the little one, dancing for joy, and thought of how he had found it. He went on tossing it, and indulging it with the gay sight; while both his brother and sister partook of his emotion to see the little creature with its starry eyes, and gleeful crow, and frock bedabbled with the heart-blood of him who gave it life.

"You will let it be our child, my husband; it shall abide with us, shall it not, and be no less our care, than our own two?" whispered the lady.

"Surely;" replied he. "What says my little Olivia, will she have a baby-sister as well as a baby-brother?" And the gentleman turned to his young daughter, who had stolen from the cradle-side, and was peering under his arm at the pretty stranger.

But before she could reply, the small individual in the cradle, having at length come to the conclusion that a yell was advisable, as the only way of making his wrongs known,—wrongs which had lately received a grievous addition to the insult of reading aloud in his presence, by the daring defalcation of his young nurse,—now began to cry lustily. This created an instant diversion in his favour. All eyes were turned from the babe sir Toby was jumping and tossing, to the one that lay roaring in the cradle. For some time every effort to soothe the small gentleman's indignation was unavailing. Just as they began to indulge a too-sanguine belief of a lull, a fresh blare put all their hopes to the route; and no sooner had they succeeded in calming that, and ventured to admit a dawning hope of coming peace, when another, and still another rave burst out. At length his sister hit upon the happy expedient of showing him the new baby. In an instant, the sight of the bright, sparkling, lively little thing, took his attention, and his fancy; he held out his arms towards it, and strained, and kicked, and struggled to get at it.

"Put it in the cradle with him! Let him have it near! Let's see what he'll do with it!" exclaimed the little Olivia, enchanted that her baby-brother should have such a new toy to play with.

Her uncle Toby placed the child gently by the side of the other one;

and there they both lay, crowing, and kicking, and cooing at one another;
partly in play, partly in wonder; but merry, and happy, as could be.

As they stood watching the pretty sight the lady said softly :—"Poor
little creature! I wonder what her name is! Were there no traces,
brother ?—no pocket-book,—no mark by which you could guess who or
what the unhappy traveller was ?"

"None ; but he had the unmistakeable look of a gentleman;" replied
sir Toby. "No matter however, for his, or his child's true name; since
you and my good brother consent to adopt the little one, give her a name
of your own choosing."

"Since she was found by the light of the stars,—or rather of one star;
for, no other than the evening planet is in the sky ; and since her starry
eyes still dance before mine, as they leaped and shone, reflecting the candle
light; and since she comes to us like a little star herself, beaming and
sparkling, to make our evening bright; what say you to calling her
Astrella ?" returned the babe's new father.

And thus it was settled.

The gentleman who adopted the orphan foundling, was count Benucci.
He had married an English lady, who, with her brother, was travelling
on the continent for the sake of her health ; which had never been strong
since the loss of her parents. At Venice, during the carnival, they had
met ; and the Illyrian nobleman, struck with the gentle beauty of the fair
English girl, had ceased not until he had won his way to her heart, and
persuaded her to exchange her native land for his. He had succeeded in
prevailing upon her brother to do the like. Orphans, without kindred, or
ties, to attach them to England, they had felt the less reluctance in resolving
to form a new home abroad, where they might live unseparated from each
other, and with a new friend, who bade fair to replace in his warmth of
regard, the few acquaintances they had possessed in their own country.
The count would fain have induced his wife's brother to take up his abode
with them in their own mansion; but sir Toby, in his sturdy English way,
had preferred an independent bachelor lodging in the suburbs of the capital,

not far from which count Benucci's estate lay. In every way, he said, it would suit him best. He should have the gaieties of a town life, which were a part of his constitutional requirements; he should have freer scope for putting in practice his own peculiar theory of good living, without interfering with his brother and sister's notions—or chance of interference from them; he could have their society whenever he desired it, by taking a walk of less than two miles, which would be of advantage to his health— his temperament more than verging on the florid and the epicurean, not to say, the plethoric; and that thus his pleasure in their company would ever have the zest of novelty, and risk no abatement from a necessitated constancy.

The count liked his good-humoured frankness, his sociality, his heartiness, his easy temper, and enjoying disposition, too well, not to let him bring them in his own way; and his sister was glad to have him with her at any rate, and on any terms, most agreeable to himself.

Thus it came, that no evening passed at Casa Benucci without its inmates seeing the broad good-humoured face, and burly figure of the young English knight, sir Toby Belch, making their way along the avenue; bringing with them an atmosphere of cheerfulness, and mirth, and readiness for any hilarious or convivial proceedings that might be toward. He looked a beaming personification of enjoyment,—a jovial embodying of jollity, and relish for jollification. Capacity for revelling to the utmost lengths of revel, sat upon each feature; a festive expression swam and glistened in his eye; a luxurious fullness rounded his cheeks and lips, giving smoothness, flexibility, ease, to their every line and curve; a lazy richness and repose dwelt in his ample chin; there was a rotund plenitude of plumpness in his person, and a universal air of ruddy ripeness,—of maturity in youth, that made him look the poets' feigned Bacchus in the guise of an Englishman under thirty. In harmony with all these external indications, he had a voice racy, and mellow; a mouth that rolled out its words with a sonorous tone, and unctuous flow, at once recommending and enjoying the good things it uttered; while it conveyed a no less enjoyment of those it swallowed.

The vicinity of Casa Benucci to the capital, enabled the count to draw around him a great deal of society ; and for some time after his marriage, his house was the resort of a large circle of friends,—the learned, the witty, the gay, and the accomplished of both sexes. But after the birth of her first child, the countess's health had relapsed into the delicacy, from which it had been temporarily restored. Her husband's devoted affection for her, and the intellectual resources he possessed within himself, caused the sacrifice of company to be little felt by either of them ; they thenceforward saw few guests, lived a calm retired life, and gave themselves up entirely to domestic pleasures. About four years after their little daughter was born, the countess brought her lord a son. The baby was called Cynthio ; and formed the delight of his young sister Olivia ; as both the children constituted that of their parents, and uncle.

Sir Toby's good-humoured countenance never looked more good-humoured than when it was leaning down to answer some prattled question of the little Olivia's ; or looking laughing up to her as she rode on his shoulder ; or hanging in good-natured giant wonderment over the miniature features of baby Cynthio, as he dandled it in his arms, or watched it in its cradle. With the children, in return, this merry uncle was an especial favorite ; and, from the time he brought the little stranger among them, no less a favorite with her than with the rest.

The hour of the jolly knight's advent, was looked forward to by them all, as the period when sport and mirth of all kinds were to abound, and be at their height. He himself was in general request. Olivia wanted him to look at her pet dove, or her own peculiar garden ; but Cynthio had scrambled up to sit astride on one of his knees, that it might be his ' cavalluccio ; ' and Astrella had seized upon his foot for a see-saw.

It was generally found that in these various struggles for the appropriation of good-humoured sir Toby, the one that prevailed was Astrella. She had a winning little coaxing way with her, that was irresistible ; and then the other two were naturally of so yielding, so generous a disposition, that it came, as a matter of course, they should give up their whims to hers. Olivia gave way to her brother, because he was younger, and because she doted on him, and so that he was happy, she was happy ; and Cynthio gave way to Astrella, because he took more interest in watching her, than in pursuing his own devices. The fascination that this little creature had possessed for his baby eyes the first time she had come within their ken, never lost its power, never abated of its influence. The sight of Astrella, at any moment, sufficed to quiet him, to engage his whole attention. In the midst of a roar blatant, the vision of the little Astrella held up before him, would act as a sedative, and change his cries of wrath into cries of pleasure ; and as he advanced from babyhood into boyhood, it was still the same ; were he in ever so obstreperous a fit of contumacy, bring Astrella where he was, and his perverseness would become playfulness, his rashness and violence turn to gladness. Her presence was a delight to him, that seemed to swallow up and absorb all others. He would forget his own plays to watch hers, or to join in them ; he would neglect his own pursuits, to help her in hers ; he would at any time leave what he was about, to look for her, and see what she was doing.

A boy among girls is apt to become exacting,—an unconscious tyrant ; making them minister to his whims, and yield in all things to his will and fantasy. But Cynthio, in his worship of Astrella, not only bent his own humours and tastes to her likings, and devoted himself to her service ; he also caused his sister's inclinations to become ancillary to those of his little idol. Olivia's pleasure was to please Cynthio ; and since his happiness consisted in seeing Astrella happy, it followed, as a matter of course, that all which could tend to make her happy was done by both loving sister and loving brother. It must be confessed that, thus, the felicity of all three was attained ; for Astrella was just one of those sweet natures that are not spoiled by indulgence. She was affectionate ; therefore so much love made her loving in return. She was gentle, and modest ; therefore so much yielding made her grateful, not encroaching or imperious. She was a warm-hearted, charming child ; as apt to gladden others by her joyful but unselfish acceptance of kindness, as she was alive to its gladdening reception herself. She was very beautiful ; one of those clear brown beauties, that are designated by a single word in French. She was a ' brunette.' She had soft, brown eyes, capable of expressing deepest feeling, yet sparkling with intelligence. Her hair was brown, with a bright golden light upon it. Her skin was one of those complexions that cannot be called fair, yet are well-nigh more lustrous than the most dazzling whiteness ; a transparent surface, that shows every slender blue vein, every varying glow of emotion, each rosy blush, or timid pallor. And she possessed sensibility to exhibit such a complexion in its highest perfection. While yet a mere child, the thought of earning the commendation of the count, of displeasing the countess, or of making sir Toby laugh, would heighten her color, or blanche her cheek, or flush it into brightness, as either of the fancies possessed her.

Olivia was no less beautiful ; but hers was a beauty of a totally different character. She was a dark beauty. She had dark hair, like a raven's wing—as glossy, as smooth as its plumage. She had dark eyes, large, liquid, and full ; with that peculiar transparency, which seems to admit of penetration into their very depths. Her skin was of that tint known as an olive complexion ; a pure, even tint, exquisitely calculated to show to advantage the pencilled eye-brows, and long lashes. Scarcely any color tinged the cheek ; but its absence was not felt as a defect, in that delicate, waxen, uniform hue, with oval shapeliness, belonging to an Italian face.

Her little brother, Cynthio, was even radiantly fair. He had one of those seraph heads, which the painters of old loved to multiply in their beatific subjects. Locks of light golden hair hung around a face beaming with roseate beauty. His eyes were like sapphires ; so clear, so gem-like an azure was theirs. His throat and forehead were white and polished as sculptured marble ; and his lips were coral-red. His beauty was almost feminine in its extreme fairness ; a complexion so delicate, features so regular, limbs so symmetrically formed, seemed rather those of a girl than a boy. But his countenance had spirit, as well as delicacy ; and his limbs energy, as well as grace.

They were still, all three, mere children, when Astrella was attacked by a violent fever. The countess left the sick-room to hear the opinion of the physician who was called in. She did not perceive that her little son, Cynthio, was within hearing ; who, after the doctor's first few words, crept out of the room, in search of Olivia. The young boy was accustomed to refer to his sister all questions that puzzled or interested him.

" Olivia, what did the doctor mean by saying :—' I will not conceal from you, madam, that there is danger,—great danger.' Did he mean danger to Astrella? Danger! What danger?"

"Did he say so?" asked Olivia, her eyes filling with tears. "Poor Astrella! I did not know she was so ill; last night she was quite well. And now——"

"Then the danger is to her! What danger? Tell me, tell me, Olivia!" said Cynthio, impatiently, and with the same marks of emotion as his sister.

"Danger that she will die!" wept Olivia.

"'Die!' what is 'die,' sister? What do you mean?"

"She will leave us—be taken from us for ever—we shall never see her again!" said Olivia; and she tried to explain to her innocent young brother the terrible mystery of death, as well as her simple, child-like conceptions of it would permit.

As she proceeded, Cynthio fixed his eyes upon her face, and drank in her words with a kind of breathless wonderment and horror; then burst into a passion of tears, exclaiming "Astrella! Dear Astrella! Ah, Astrella mia!"

His sister attempted to soothe him; but he broke away from her, and ran out of the room even more hurriedly than he had entered.

She was about to follow him, when her mother came in, looking anxious and pale, but as if with a resolution to speak calmly and with patience.

"Listen to what I have to say to you, Olivia mia;" she said. "Do not come to me; stay where you are, dear child;" as her daughter would have run towards her. "Show me that you can behave like a little woman, my Olivia; be brave and steady in affliction,—the courage mostly needed from a woman. The physician has pronounced Astrella's disorder to be a fever of the most virulent kind. He does not conceal from me that he fears the worst for the dear child. But he tells me that if I would save my other darlings, I must keep them from entering her room—nay, send them from the house. The disorder is infectious. Go therefore to your father, and beg him from me——"

"But yourself, dear mamma——" interrupted Olivia.

"I do not fear contagion;" said her mother; "besides, whatever may

VOL. III.   H be the risk for me, it is already encountered; I have been all night in the sick-room with her. To none other than myself will I yield the charge of watching my Astrella; whom I love not less than my own dear ones. Go, my dear child, as I bid thee, to thy father, and tell him all this. Tell him I entreat that he will lose no time in taking Cynthio and yourself to a place of safety; when this is done, I shall be relieved of the only anxiety which might give force to the fever to take effect upon myself; and thus we shall have the better chance for the happy result which I hope may attend my careful nursing."

"Dear mamma——" still hesitated Olivia.

"Lose no time; do as I would have thee, dear child;" urged the countess, as she prepared to return to her little patient. "I may not embrace thee, lest harm should already dwell in my touch; but I fold thee to my heart in spirit, and bid Heaven's blessing and a mother's be with thee."

But on re-entering the sick-room, what was this tender mother's dismay at seeing her young son stretched upon the bed by the side of Astrella, sobbing as if his little heart would break.

His head was buried in the bed-clothes, as he yielded to this overpowering fit of grief; then he started up, and resumed hanging over her, kissing her flushed cheeks, and parched lips, flooding them with his tears, and snatching her burning hands in his.

"Cynthio mio, how came you here? Listen to me, dear boy;" said his mother, bending over him, and whispering in her gentle voice. "Do not cry so bitterly; hear what I have to say. You will disturb poor Astrella by this violence of grief; be still, be quiet, lest you make her worse."

The sobs were checked, the cries stifled, the tears held back, as well as he could.

"Oh she is very ill, mamma! Very ill!" he faltered. "See how she lies, taking no notice of anything; and just now, her poor head was turning from side to side, backwards and forwards, backwards and forwards,—and she was talking—O so fast!—and without any meaning—and she didn't seem to hear, or make out what I said, when I spoke to her. O she's very ill! And that cruel doctor said,—I heard him,—that there was danger; and now I know what that means."

He buried his face once more in the bed-clothes that he might smother lamentations which would not be restrained.

"How came you to overhear what was said? I did not see you,—I did not know you were in the room;" said his mother. "But cease crying, dear Cynthio; be more of a man; you will not only hurt Astrella by it, but you will make yourself ill."

"I am not afraid of being ill; I came here on purpose to be ill,—to be ill with Astrella;" replied Cynthio. "I heard him say that first; I heard the doctor say, 'I would advise you, madam, to forbid any one to enter the little girl's room,—they might take the fever of her; it is of a very infectious kind. I will not deceive you; there is danger,—great danger.'

"How could you come hither, then, without my leave, Cynthio?" said his mother; "since you heard what the doctor said."

"I heard him advise you to forbid our coming;" said Cynthio; "that was only his advice; you had not said you forbade it, and lest you should, I left the room directly; for I thought it very hard Astrella should have the fever all by herself,—quite alone,—no one to keep her company, to amuse her, to play with her; so I determined I would come and be ill here too. In my way, I asked Olivia, what the doctor meant by 'danger,— great danger.' And oh, she told me! Dear, dear Astrella!" His sobs breaking forth afresh.

"You learned the danger, yet you still came! Ah, my dear boy!" involuntarily exclaimed the countess.

"You would not have had me stay away for that, mother?" said he, his blue eyes flashing through their tears. "You have always said boys should be brave, and learn to face danger. There was the more need for me to come and help her, if there was danger to be met. Why should Astrella meet it alone? Oh, Astrella! Astrella!"

And the little fellow again flung himself down, his cheek close against hers.

"The mischief is incurred, alas!" murmured the mother. "Heaven avert its worst consequence!" And now, since it was too late to hope that by sending him from the room, the chance of infection could be avoided, she, with the wisdom taught by a mother's love, turned the very strength of his affection,—which had brought him into peril,—to a means of advantage. She availed herself of his passionate fondness for the little Astrella, by urging him to subdue his grief for her sake ; that he might keep well in order to help nurse the patient through her illness. This thought did more to rouse him from his grief than anything else. The idea that he might contribute to her comfort, the hope that he might help to make her well, were the happiest suggestions that could have been devised.

"And do you think she will be saved from dying, if we nurse her carefully, mamma ? Do you think she will recover, if we take pains ? " he asked, almost joyfully.

"We will try our utmost in that hope ; " said the mother ; "and for the rest, we must have faith in Heaven's mercy. In the worst evils that befal, there are two chief resources ; which bring their own comfort. Do our best, and trust in God." And soon, the strength of these consolations was tested by the poor mother herself ; she had need of all their aid beneath the trial that awaited her ; of all the fortitude they could lend, when she beheld her young boy languish, and sicken, and fall ill of the same raging fever that burned in the veins of Astrella. His noble, unselfish love, his affectionate sympathy for his little play-fellow, rendered it only the more heart-breaking to see him the victim of his generous impulse. And yet, in the very hour when her fears were at their highest,—when she thought there was no chance but she must lose him,—the mother felt that she could not wish him one jot less noble, less excellent. A mother's heart cannot afford to abate a single trait of goodness in her child ; she will rather yield him up the harder sacrifice, with all his perfections, than consent to own in him one virtue, one merit the less.

"My Cynthio is but worthier of Heaven ; " sighed the mother, as she strove to school her murmuring heart into submission.

But she was not doomed to endure this bitter extremity. Her son was spared to her. Both he and Astrella struggled through their peril, and survived.

The fever left them weak, and singularly altered in person. Astrella had shot up into a tall thin girl, looking three or four years older than she really was ; while the boy Cynthio seemed to have shrunk into the dimensions of a baby. His fair face had become wan; his active limbs had shrivelled into skin and bone; he had wasted away to a mere skeleton of what he once was; and he had so little strength left, that he could only move about wheeled in a garden-chair.

Change of air,—especially sea air, being recommended, the count removed his family to one of his tenant's houses, that stood on the extremest verge of the estate, and was situated down on the very beach.

This place, though humble, and possessing none of the conveniences of their own luxurious mansion, yet found favor with the invalids. Here, they could be out-of-doors as long as they pleased. The cool hours of morning and evening,—at earliest dawn, and by latest sun-down,—they spent close on the margin of the sea; watching the calm blue expanse, with its scarce-varying tide; wooing the light breeze that occasionally played upon its surface; gathering shells upon the smooth brown sand, and bringing them to the side of Cynthio's chair. He would lie there patiently, watching his sister and Astrella, as they flitted to and fro, never once uttering a repining word that he could not run about with them. He seemed to find pleasure enough in following every active movement of the latter, as her agile figure moved hither and thither; and his words, his manner, showed never-failing interest and delight when she brought her collected treasures, or hovered about him to help arrange them. Near them would sit the count and countess, reading, or noting the pastimes of their children, happy in their happiness. The countess's health, never strong, had suffered much from the anxiety and confinement consequent upon the children's illness; and her husband was as glad for her sake as for theirs, of this sea-side sojourn.

The children had two new companions, also, who helped to make the time pass gaily. Their uncle, sir Toby, had been absent for some time, on a visit of several months, at a friend's house in Venice. Their two new play-fellows were more of their own age. One was a brisk, lively girl, daughter to the count's tenant, in whose house they were at present lodging. With the ease of southern manners,—which admits a freedom of intercourse between persons of unequal rank, unknown to the stiffer northerns, and yet which nowise extinguishes the real respect of dependants towards their

superiors in station,—this tenant's daughter could join in the sports of the
children of a count, her father's landlord, without a notion of presumption on
her part, or derogation on theirs.   She was a few years older than Olivia ;
had a comely face, a smart person, high spirits, and a paramount turn for
waggery and drollery.   Her name was Maria.   The other, was a young
lad, who was said to be the orphan son of a poor fisherman, drowned on
that coast.   The boy had strayed from a neighbouring hamlet ; and this
was all that could be gathered from the rambling story he had told of his
origin.   He was reputed an oddity ; but his light-hearted frolic, fun, and
inexhaustible good-temper, made him a great favorite with those among
whom he had come to dwell.   There was not a cottage round about but
gladly afforded a meal or a shelter for as long as he chose to remain, to
whimsical Feste, as they called him.

" 'Tis a strange name, they have given thee, my lad ; " said the count to
him, one day.   " And yet I know not, but it suits thee as well as another."

" Nay, better, my lord count ; better than a better name could fit one
that hath nothing good about him, save a good heart, good sight, and
a good voice.   A good name is somewhat of a burthen, too, to him that is
gifted with other good gifts—as modesty, for instance.   Best rest contented
without it, believe me."

" How, boy ?   Methinks the modestest of men aspires to stand well with
his fellows ; the meekest ambition would fain have a good name ;" said
count Benucci ; for he had taken a fancy to this youth, for his merry
humour, and loved to encourage its sallies.

" Troth, my lord, thus may a good name be a burden to a modest man ;
it weighs him down with a heavy sense of his own lack of merit ; besides
pressing upon him the necessity of living up to itself.   A thousand things
that a man unshackled by it might permit himself, may never be indulged
in by one that hath the ill luck to get a good name.   No, I'll none of it.
Give me an indifferent name, and free leave to do what odd things
I please,—it may be, among them, a few better ones than I'm given
credit for."

" What kind of name dost call thine own, boy ?   Is that an indifferent
one ?"

" 'Tis indifferent, in so far, as, 'tis indifferent to me how I'm called, so that it be not too late for meals or good fortune, my lord ;" replied he. " But, in truth, it cannot well be called indifferent, in so much as it was given me as a token of liking, rather than of indifference ; nor can it be called a bad name, since the good folks hereabouts gave it me in no ill-will. They first named me Festeggiante, as signifying that joyous spirit, that festive disposition they were pleased to ascribe to me, or rather, to discover in me ; and afterwards it dwindled into Feste, as being the more familiar, as well as more festinate designation."

" Well then, Feste, thou shalt e'en go with me, an' thou wilt, when we return home to Casa Benucci, and be henceforth one of its inmates ; since I think thou hast no particular dwelling of thine own, nor no more pressing engagement elsewhere ;" said the count.

" I know not what accomplishments I may boast that should entitle me to such good service as yours, my lord ;" said the lad, carrying off a certain choking sensation that came into his throat, with an attempt to retain his usual careless gaiety ; " but among them is not the art of making professions ; otherwise I might protest gratitude and ever faithful loyalty in return for your lordship's goodness ; but though I proclaim not these, they are none the less living in my heart."

" Let them rest there, good lad ; and let me know of them but through thine own happy looks, and blythe words. I love a mirthful speech, and a gay song, both which I know thou canst give me ; so I shall be the gainer by having thee with me at Casa Benucci."

There was but one person who objected to this addition to the household. That one, was an individual accustomed to pretty much authority in the dispensation of its affairs,—the count's steward, Malvolio. He was a grave personage ; had an exalted opinion of what was due to the dignity and honor of the house of Benucci, and the most precise notions of honor and dignity generally. He was exact in etiquette ; strict in punctilio. He was a great observer of forms himself ; and demanded the most formal observance from others. He had a serious stateliness of deportment that is seldom seen but in middle age ; and bore himself with all the staid importance of advanced life, when still quite a young man. His

demeanour was that of a man fully possessed with the innate consciousness
of merit. He stalked about with an air of proud self-content, of serenely
triumphant interior approval. He held himself very loftily; as if his
erect body were a type of his upright soul. On his countenance sat an
unruffled composure, as of a conscience on good terms with itself; a perpetual complacency, the reflection of a heart incessantly occupied with its
own worth. He looked as though he knew of powers and goodnesses
within, which cast a perpetual shine outwards; and that his greatness of
spirit bade him permit some of this light to fall upon others for whose
inferiority he could make allowance; although for their benefit, he would
not suffer either their defects or errors to pass without the assistance of
his admonition, reprobation, and censure. In his manners there was
condescension,—a kind of patronising affability, as of superiority extending
generous encouragement to less perfect humanity; but withal a reservation
of rectitude which would take the earliest needful occasion of asserting
itself. He had an implicit faith in his own judgment; a firm conviction
of his supreme excellence. He believed his counsel invaluable; his
opinions unimpeachable, as they were infallible. He had the count's confidence, for he was a man of integrity; no less honest and trustworthy than
fastidious, ceremonious, and pompous; no less sincerely attached to the
true welfare of the house of Benucci, than zealous for its repute and nice
conduct. His foibles were tolerated, for the sake of the sterling qualities
he really possessed.

When this grave steward first heard his lord's intention of admitting the
boy Feste among his retainers, as a kind of privileged fool, half jester, half
minstrel, he failed not to remonstrate with the count on the uselessness such
an appendage would be to the household; setting forth, in his own didactic
style, arguments against the measure; saying that he knew it was a fashion
that had much obtained among families of distinction, though he could not
but consider it an absurd, a worthless amusement,—if amusement it could
be called, to entertain oneself with the follies and futilities that issued from
the mouth of ignorance; that it was affording a licence to folly to utter
its nonsense, in lieu of encouraging wisdom to profit the world by the
utterance of its axioms; that it was a piece of extravagance to have such

another eater of bread in the house, who could contribute nothing in return,—no service, no help,—naught save emptiness and vain laughter; that though the honorable house of Benucci had a right to its fashionable extravagances as well as any other; yet he thought it behoved this family in particular to set an example of higher tastes, by refusing to harbour folly, and by resolving to surround themselves with none other than persons of decorum and discretion.

"Good Malvolio," answered the count; "in thine own person we have decorum and discretion enow to suffice the entire household. Content thyself that it controls and supervises the whole; that it secures for us the comfort and well-being a household so directed enjoys. Let me indulge myself with this one freak of folly,—idle and vain, if thou·wilt, yet pleasant withal,—and do thou continue to give me the countervailing benefit of thy sageness and solidity. They must ever have their weight with me, for their true poise and value."

Satisfied by this concession, the grave steward gave his sanction to his master's wish.

The sojourn at the sea-side had produced its hoped-for effect. When the family returned home to their own mansion, it was with renovated health and·strength. The countess seemed less delicate than she had been for some years; and her young son was restored from the state of helplessness to which his illness had reduced him. But though Cynthio recovered the use of his limbs, was able·to dispense entirely with that of his garden-chair, and could run about as freely as ever; yet his growth was irretrievably stinted. He remained a very little fellow; and seemed a mere child, for some years to come. On the contrary, Astrella's sudden increase of stature after the fever, went on. She not only outstripped Cynthio, but she grew still taller than Olivia; who, though nearly four years her senior, was frequently taken for the younger girl.

Cynthio's devotion to Astrella continued the same. His deference to her lightest word, his delight in procuring her joy, his happiness in her presence, the fondness with which he watched her every look and movement, the assiduity with which he studied her tastes, complied with her likings, and prevented her wishes, were singular, in one so young. He seemed to have no will but hers; and to have as much pleasure in yielding his, when it chanced to differ, as most children find in getting their own way. He was so attentive to her, so careful of her, that it became matter of remark; he was called Astrella's 'little husband.'

He took much pride in the title; and spoke of her as 'my wife,' with great complacency. He said it as if it gave him a sort of property in her, a right of guarding her, which evidently delighted himself, while it amusingly contrasted with his childish looks and slight proportions. It gratified him to call this tall girl 'my wife,' as bringing her more on a level with himself by the air of authority and protection it enabled him to put on. It was the only air of the kind he ever cared to assume towards her; whom he treated more as an idol, than an equal; one to be worshipped, rather than loved. Olivia, he held in tender regard; and behaved to her with the easy, familiar confidence of brother towards sister; but for Astrella, the affection he testified, had the fond reverence, the devoted attachment, the passionate intensity, which, in one of elder years would have formed the preference of a lover.

Soon after their re-establishment at Casa Benucci, sir Toby returned from Venice. He brought with him a young Frenchman, whom he had met there; and to whose society he had taken a great fancy. As the knight's bachelor lodgings, in the capital, afforded no accommodation for visitors, he begged his brother-in-law, the count, to invite the young gentleman to his own house.

The chevalier Dorfaux was welcomed by the count and countess with all the cordiality that his introduction by their brother, sir Toby, ensured. The young Frenchman's lively manners and companionable qualities soon won him the favor of the count; but from the first there was something—to which she could have scarce given a name, a something rather felt than understood—about this stranger, that made the countess find it impossible to like him. This feeling seemed to herself so much the offspring of mere prejudice, towards one whom she had known for so short a time, that she would not allow it to bias her mind; still less would she endeavour to impart it to her husband, until she should see more of a man, of whom both he and her brother thought well. Why should she endeavour to injure him with either, until there were more sure grounds for disapproval? She thought it would be injustice, on a mere instinctive impression, to condemn him herself, or to influence others against him. She determined to be silent, and observe as impartially as might be.

Had she known where, and how her brother had met this young man, she would not have deemed it her duty to be so passive. In a brawl at a low casino, and afterwards at the gaming-table, the acquaintance had commenced and progressed. Sir Toby's sense of delicacy was not so nice or refined, his perceptions of right and wrong were not so scrupulous, as to suggest to him the impropriety of presenting one encountered amid such haunts, to his brother and sister. He could see no reason why one whom he found an agreeable companion, should not be a fit associate for them, or even for their innocent children. Accordingly, the chevalier Dorfaux's specious manners, his plausible tongue, and his artful knack of winning his way, had an opportunity of exercising their powers among the inmates of Casa Benucci. With the exception of the countess, there was not one of them, with whom he had not soon made himself a favorite.

He was respectfully facetious and jocular with the count; he behaved to the countess with implicit deference; he flattered the grave self-love of Malvolio; he drolled with Feste; and. he lent himself to all the sports and pastimes of the children. He took part in their old games, and taught them new ones; he played with the eagerness of a boy, and entered into all their pleasures with a spirit that seemed as genuine as it was vivacious. "Well done, little fellow! Bravissimo!" he exclaimed, on one occasion, as Cynthio was swinging his sister Olivia, in a large swing that their father had had erected for them between two lofty trees in the grounds. "For such a slight little chap, you have famous muscle in your arm. It must be your good-will that puts such strength into each push, or they could never send her flying that height. Well tossed! Parbleu, well done!"

His praise stimulated the boy to strain every nerve, to exert all his strength.

"Cynthio mio, you will tire yourself; do not work so hard. I have just as much pleasure in being swung less high;" said his sister.

"I am not tired ; not in the least ; " said Cynthio.

"Let me swing her, let me take my turn ; " said the chevalier, taking his place.

He continued for some time swinging Olivia, the two other children looking on. Once or twice they spoke to her ; but Olivia seemed distracted from attending to them by something or other ; uneasy, and unable to answer them.

Suddenly she said :—" Brother, I wish you would swing me ; or, stay,—no,—I have had enough. I'll get out. Help me down, Cynthio, dear."

But the chevalier stepped forward, and lifted her out of the swing. The little girl did not thank him ; but freed herself from his arms as quickly as she could, and walked away to a seat somewhat apart.

"Now let me swing! I should like to have a swing now!" said Astrella. "And toss me high! high! high! you know I love to fly up among the tree-tops, and fancy myself a bird!"

"I'll take care!" said Cynthio, as he helped her into the swing.

"Here, let me!" said the chevalier.

"No, no ; I'll swing Astrella ; I always swing Astrella ; " said Cynthio.

"I'll bet you what you will, I toss her higher than you can ; " said the chevalier, after Cynthio had gone on some time.

"I'm sure you couldn't ; though you're a tall man, and stronger than I am ; " said the boy. "I shouldn't be afraid of the wager ; but I can't let you swing Astrella."

"No! And why not, pray, my brave little fellow ? " laughed the chevalier.

"Because I never let any one swing 'my wife,' but myself ; " said Cynthio, quite gravely.

"Oho, young gentleman! you're afraid of her safety ; but I'll be very cautious, I assure you."

"I'll trust nobody but myself to take care of her ; and I can't give up the pleasure ; " said Cynthio.

"Well said! Quite a gallant little husband, I declare! You ought to be very proud, signorina Astrella, of such a lord and master."

"The beauty of my little husband is, that he never lords it over me, nor ever tries to master me;" answered Astrella. "Cynthio's too kind and good to be a tyrant."

"Quite a jewel of a little husband, indeed!" said the chevalier. "But come, if you won't trust your cara sposina out of your own hands, what say you to taking a bet that you won't be tired of swinging her before another hundred tosses."

"I'll bet you that, and welcome!" exclaimed Cynthio.

"Well then, what shall be the wager?" said the chevalier.

"All my pocket-money! I don't care how much! Any money you like!" said Cynthio, eagerly.

"Don't lay a wager about it,—your arm will ache, Cynthio; it'll be too much for you;" said Astrella.

"Not a bit of it. I'm not afraid!" said Cynthio.

"What pocket-money have you?" said the chevalier.

"I don't know exactly; but never mind,—any sum you like; I can ask my father for the rest, if it shouldn't be enough."

"No, no; let it be as much as your own money amounts to—whatever that may be. Now say, ' Done, and done'—and begin your hundred;" said the chevalier.

"Don't bet, Cynthio mio;" said his sister Olivia. "Remember, mamma did not like you to lay a wager with cousin Toby, once, when he proposed it. She said it was an idle practice, and might grow into a vicious one."

"Did she? I had forgotten;" said Cynthio.

And so the matter ended.

A few days after, the three children had been taking the chevalier Dorfaux a long walk through the grounds, to show him the spot by the sea-side where they had spent their pleasant holiday; and as they returned, it happened, that a brook, which was ordinarily so narrow as to be easily cleared by jumping, was now swollen so wide by late heavy rains, as to be almost impassable. But it was far round, to get to a bridge that crossed the stream in the direction of the house; and as the little girls were somewhat tired with their long walk, they wished to get home as quickly as possible.

"I will lift the young ladies across;" said the chevalier; and turning to Astrella, who stood nearest to him, he raised her in his arms, and bore her across the brook.

"Why did you not leave her to me? I would have carried my wife myself;" said Cynthio to the chevalier, who now returned for Olivia.

"I fear it would have been too much of a feat for the gallantry of even the gallant little husband;" laughed the chevalier. "The little husband would have been too little for that, I fancy."

"I am stronger than I look;" said Cynthio, with a bright color in his face. "I don't want to brag, but I'm sure I could have lifted her. Let me try to carry you, Olivia mia."

"Give me your hand, dear;" she answered. "I mean to step through the water, myself; it is not deep. If you let me hold by you, we shall steady each other."

"Best let me bear you across;" said the chevalier. "Your feet will be wet through, signorina."

"I can change my shoes and stockings, as soon as I reach home; we are not far from the house, now, I thank you, sir;" she replied.

When they had all safely reached the other side of the brook, the chevalier walked on, with Astrella. As the brother and sister followed a little way behind, Cynthio said :—"You did not like him to lift you in his arms, Olivia?"

"No;" she said quietly.

"You did not like him to swing you, the other day? I have noticed, that you have never let him swing you since;" said her brother, after a pause; as if musingly.

She did not answer; and presently Cynthio went on :—"I don't think you like this French gentleman so well as you did at first, do you, Olivia?"

"No;" she said.

"Why, sister?" said the young boy, looking suddenly but earnestly up in her face, as he walked by her side.

"I hardly know;" she replied; "he is as amusing, as obliging, as good-natured in his manners as ever; but——"

She stopped. After another pause, Cynthio said :—"You did quite right to ford the brook, sister. I wish I had carried Astrella across—or that she had walked through, as you did, holding by my arm. Let's step on and overtake her. I was sorry, at first, when I heard that the chevalier Dorfaux was to leave us next week; but now, I think, I am rather glad."

"Take my arm, Astrella;" said Cynthio, as he and his sister came up with her and her companion; "you are tired, sposina."

"Here is mine at the young lady's service;" said the Frenchman, offering it with such alacrity as to render acceptance almost unavoidable.

But Olivia, on seeing Astrella take it, said:—"Your little husband's arm affords excellent support; it brought me through the brook as firmly and strongly, as though it had been a giant's. Did you not see how bravely it upheld me?"

"'Tis a doughty little arm, indeed!" said the chevalier aloud; adding in a whisper that only Astrella could hear:—"pity 'tis of such dwarf-like proportions!"

In a few days time, the chevalier Dorfaux's visit at Casa Benucci came to a close. He took leave, and sir Toby went with him; as it had been agreed, that the two gentlemen would take a trip together to. Naples, during the carnival season.

Her brother had not long left them, when the countess Benucci was attacked by a mortal illness, which terminated her existence suddenly. So suddenly, indeed, that there was scarcely time to summon her brother home, ere she had breathed her last.

Sir Toby was on his way to Casa Benucci when he learned the fatal issue of his sister's disorder; but as it was then too late, he turned back and prosecuted his journey with Dorfaux, unable to encounter the spectacle of his brother-in-law's grief. He sent him an affectionate letter; but in his own bluff style: declaring that until he could hope to bring back courage enough to face home without her who had made it home to them, he should wander on, in search of as much amusement as he could now find heart to enjoy.

The count too, thought it best to travel for a time; that change of scene might work its good effect upon the young people and himself. He knew that it was precisely at their age that travel is apt to be of most advantage in forming the character. He therefore took them a tour into Greece;

which occupied a considerable period, with profit to both mind and body; restoring them to Casa Benucci in recovered peace.

The count was well-pleased to see the grace and discretion with which his young daughter filled the post of mistress, in presiding over his household. It was a proof how well she had profited by a childhood passed beneath a mother's eye; that Olivia, still so youthful, was able to acquit herself as lady of the house, in a manner to justify the joyful pride her father took in her. He sent for his tenant's daughter, Maria, and placed her as waiting-maid about the person of the young countess, knowing Olivia's liking for her; and thinking that her sprightly disposition would make her a desirable companion. Maria was the very briskest and smallest of creatures; she was like a fairy in her proportions; neat and trim in her dress as a doll; light and quick in her motions as a bird,—nay, as a bat,—but then a bat has an ugly face. Now hers was a nice little round face, with pippin cheeks, and cherry lips, and bright beady eyes. They looked as sharp and as piercing as needle-points,—darting mischief through their keen glances : merry, waggish, roguish eyes. You could not think of their prettiness for their mischievousness ; and could hardly trouble yourself about their mischievousness, for their good-temper ; and certainly, whatever you might think about when you looked at them, you couldn't keep yours off them, such bewitching little wicked eyes they were. She flitted about the house like an elf, or a sprite ; so light of foot, so airy, so quickly appearing, so swiftly vanishing, was she. You caught sight of her whisking skirts like a butterfly's wing ; they had fluttered away before she could settle—what she had come for ; or you, that you had actually seen her. She darted into your ken like a falling-star, and disappeared as abruptly. She could neither move, look, nor speak, but rapidly. She was a midge, an atomy,—anything that is lightest, brightest, and smallest.

Insensibly time crept on. The children had grown up into youth and confirmed beauty, preserving still the same characteristics which had from the first distinguished them. Sir Toby found them all wonderfully grown, when, after loitering away a long period in each different city that took his fancy, on his return from Naples, he came back at length to Illyria. He declared they were metamorphosed, from little brats,—whom he could dance on his knee, or have a good game of romps with, or pull about in any frolicsome fashion he chose,—into orderly young people, comely gentlefolks, whom he should learn to look up to, to respect, and even to consult, upon matters of moment. He said that when he looked at the loveliness of Astrella, he should feel that he must be on his guard against all the dangers that are said to lurk in the titles of 'a wit' and 'a beauty;' that when he contemplated the perfections of his niece Olivia, he should be obliged to call himself to task for all that could militate against the kindred between himself and the impersonation of so much purity, sense, and grace ; and that though Cynthio's girlish face and figure might make him seem the least formidable of the three, yet that there was something of angel mixed with mortal knowledge about the boy, that made him stand more in awe of him than of all the rest.

"Truly, a man feels ashamed to call nephew, one whose innocent face makes his uncle look to his sins,—which mayn't so well bear a reckoning ;— and feel a twinge when he thinks of his own remote acquaintance with the Latin grammar. I'll warrant, now, he knows the deeds of Alexander, Belisarius, and Cæsar, like his A. B. C; when, if I know more of them than their initials, I'm a heathen Turk, and no Christian Englishman. 'Tis so long since I have looked into a book, that I hardly know how it opens."

"You will find Cynthio and the two girls good, dutiful children, still, though grown into all but young men and women ;" said the count; "and as well-inclined for a frolic with cousin Toby as ever."

"'Tis a good hearing ; for is not mirth the spirit of existence, and jollity the wine of life ? Without mirth and jollity, man is little better than a drained flask, a stale anchovy, a musty melon ; a dry, empty husk,— fruitless, worthless, to himself or others."

"Thy metaphors, brother, remind me that we have offered thee no refreshment yet ;" said the count; "forgive us our scant hospitality, omitted in the eagerness to welcome you back. After your warm walk, a cool flask of Cypro will not be amiss. Olivia, bid them bring fruit and wine out here in the garden ; let it be placed beneath the shade of this spreading chesnut."

I

Olivia despatched her gentlewoman with the requisite orders ; and her uncle had fresh occasion to laud her grace and housewifely accomplishment.

" By my troth, they shall be my three mirabilaries ; " said he, looking upon her, Cynthio, and Astrella. " I will quote them as wonders of creation, and vaunt them to be no less than perfections of nature."

" You will risk spoiling your wonders, cousin ; and then they will be no longer perfection ; " said Olivia. " That methinks, were scarcely the deed of a good or wise kinsman."

" To be wise and good, asks more prudence than dwells in frail humanity, when there are such things to praise and enjoy, as those now before me ; " said Sir Toby, helping himself to some of the fruit and iced wine ; " Casa Benucci overflows with excellence ; from its inmates to its good cheer ; fairest creatures, and choicest fare ; what would a man have more to make him the reverse of prudent ? "

" Is not prudence just the requisite quintessential drop that gives the highest flavour to all the rest,—the truest relish to their enjoyment ? " asked the count.

" Truly, I know not but you sober. fellows may have the advantage in the long run over us roysterers ; " said sir Toby ; " but while we are running, we think wholly of the sport, nothing of its consequences. But what a keen eye to consequence have you shown, brother, in your choice of the people you have gathered about you, since last I was here. For signor Malvolio,—who is a treasure of consequentiality in himself,—you had him for a steward ere I left ; but there is that lad, Fabian, who carried hither the wine ; he hath a fund of intelligence in his face, that promises well for a helping hand at a joke, or a pleasant device ; and then there is the other lad,—Feste, I think you called him,—with a trick of eye, and a humorous twist of his lip, that speak a world of lurking jest and good fooling."

" And you shall hear him sing a song presently, brother, that shall make you call him a lark in human shape, so blithe, so airy, so melodious and untiring is his voice ; " said the count.

" With all my heart ; I love a good song as I love good wine ; it sets a man's blood spinning triumphant ; and fills me his brain with ecstatic fancies. A man is a god while he listens to music, and quaffs grape-juice."

" Good mistress Maria, bid Feste come hither ;" said the count, to his daughter's waiting-maid, who had just brought out a veil for her young lady.

" And then there is that little silver moth of a damsel, whom you have chosen for my niece's gentlewoman ; " continued sir Toby ; " can anything be better devised, than having such a grig of a girl always in sight. Her very look is enough to banish spleen from a household."

" She is indeed, merry and lightsome as a bird ; " said the count.

" A very titmouse,—a golden-crested wren ! " said sir Toby.

" And when heard you from your friend, the chevalier Dorfaux ? " asked the count.

" Odso, I had forgot ! I have a letter here in my pocket from him ; " said sir Toby. " It is dated from Paris ; but in it he talks of leaving immediately, and travelling fast, so as to meet me on my return hither ; he may, therefore, be expected, nearly as soon as his epistle."

" He was a well-graced, pleasant young man, I shall be glad to see him here again ; " said the count.

He had hardly given utterance to the words, ere a servant announced the arrival of the chevalier himself.

" We will all go into the house and give him welcome ;" said count Benucci.

As Cynthio and Olivia, with Astrella, followed their father and uncle from the garden, the youth said to his sister :—" I had almost forgotten there was such a being in the world. It seems like a dream, when he paid us a visit before. Do you remember that time ? Do you remember the evening we crossed the brook, Olivia ? Did you remember this French gentleman, Astrella ? "

A visible confusion passed over her face ; for she thought of the disparaging words the chevalier had whispered about him who now asked her the question.

" I see you do ; " he said.

He fell into a deep reverie ; from which he was awakened by their reaching the house. He heard the chevalier paying eager greeting to all, and receiving the welcome of the count and sir Toby in return. He looked up to see the young Frenchman bowing upon Astrella's hand, and

pouring forth a profusion of compliments upon the heightened charms that
time had wrought in both her and Olivia. He advanced mechanically, to
offer the usual words of salutation to the newly-arrived guest ; when the
chevalier, turning, saw him, and exclaimed :—" Ah, ' the little husband !'
How are you, mon cher ? "

At this instant, Cynthio caught sight of the group they presented, in
one of the tall mirrors near. He saw the handsome face and figure of the
Frenchman ; tall, elegant, full of that self-possession and polished air, which
knowledge of the world confers. He saw beside it, his own slight, boyish
frame, and girlish countenance ; striking him as something singularly inconsiderable, ignoble, and effeminate. He saw, or fancied he saw, a look
of embarrassment cross Astrella's face, as the chevalier, in his cool, easy,
French style, uttered the words "little husband."

For the first time in his life, Cynthio found himself wishing, that they
had never been applied to him in connection with Astrella.

He was frightened at the rush of emotion that came upon his heart, as it
followed the thoughts that suggested themselves in rapid succession upon
this idea. To deal with them freely, and unobserved ; to question their
true source ; to endeavour at the comprehension of his own feelings, so
strange, so new ; he left the saloon, and wandered forth alone into the
garden-grounds.

It was just such an evening as the one he had often heard described,
when Astrella was first brought home, an orphan babe, to his father's
house.

" She has never regarded me in any other light than as a brother,
I fancied I thought of her but as a sister, notwithstanding the idle titles
they gave us ;" he passionately mused ; " but what I have learned of my
feelings within this last hour, tells me, it is as no sister that I love her.
When I think of Olivia it is with a calm joy, an assured content, a pure,
undisturbed, unanxious happiness ; ah, how all unlike the tumultuous
rapture, the transport, the intoxicating flood of delight that agitated my
heart, when I looked upon Astrella this night, and asked myself for the
first time, what was the affection I felt for her. But is hers for me of the
same nature ? Does not she rather behold in me but the friend, the

companion, the playfellow of her childhood,—the mere boy brother? Her every easy look, her every confiding word, the very warmth and unrestraint of her manner, tell me but too plainly that what she feels for me is not love,—not the love mine is for her. She is too demonstrative, too affectionate, in her innocent unreserve towards me, too frankly tender, too open and lavish in her endearments, to give me hope that any of the passion which now burns at my heart, has found its way to hers. And shall I not hazard even those marks of her gentle affection, if I let her see the new kind of love that has taken the place of mine own old attachment towards her? Will she not shrink from any but the fraternal tokens of regard that have hitherto been mine? How will she bear to think of me as a lover,—me, a brother, a boy, as she has always considered me? And what am I better? A poor paltry boy, with a creamy face, a stripling form. I saw it—I saw it—against his, so tall, so manly. At this very moment, am I not shedding hot, childish tears, at mine own poverty of spirit, that yields to so base, so unworthy a feeling as envy? Yes, I envy him, I am jealous, jealous. Envious if he appear comely and brave in her eyes, while I seem but as a boy. Jealous, if she find in him a lover, when in me she can see but a brother. Oh Astrella! Astrella!"

The poor young fellow strove to contend with his emotion; but it would have way. He wept for some time in bitter, burning, vehemence. Then he raised his head from between his clasped hands, and said :—

"But this is not the way to render myself worthy of her,—giving way to these unmanly tears—to this weak lamentation—less than all, to this mean envy and jealousy. Never after this night will I so degrade mine own nature; which shall be deserving of her love, though it may never hope to win it. If but a boy, a poor silly youth, in appearance, let me be a man in spirit, in heart. My first task shall be to teach myself control: that I may not shock her by a premature betrayal of any other feeling than the affectionate brotherly love to which she has been accustomed; that I may patiently seek to convert the regard she has for me into the preference I would have it; and that I may gain assurance no such preference is already growing in her heart for another. But if she should learn to love another? Astrella,—my Astrella! Can I bear to yield her? She, whom I have never thought of apart from myself,—whom I love far

beyond myself,—whom I have worshipped from infancy? Ay, if I do
worship her,—if I do indeed love her beyond myself, her happiness
should be dearer to me than my own. Well then, once let me find that
she cannot give me her love,—that she can only find her happiness in
another,—and I will resolve to secure her peace at all risks. Whatever
befall, she shall see none of this boyish weakness. If her little husband
cannot gain her affections, he will at least preserve her esteem."

At breakfast next morning, Cynthio began his self-imposed task of
keeping strict guard on his every look and word. His sister Olivia, noting
in him the heavy eye, and white contracted lip, that betokened the anxious
vigils of the past night, asked him of his health. A headache, which he
might truly avow having had, formed sufficient plea. Declaring that he
now felt quite well, he exerted himself to chat with his father, and the
chevalier; and joined heartily in a plan the former was setting on foot for
an excursion to a neighbouring spot, celebrated for its fine view. The gay
manner in which he rattled on, passed completely with all the rest; but
Olivia thought she could perceive that her young brother's spirits were
forced.

It was agreed to make the excursion a riding-party. Horses were
saddled, and brought round; the young people, with the count, preparing
to set forth with all the gleeful anticipation that a suddenly-proposed
holiday of the kind is apt to inspire. Their father ever entered so warmly
into their pleasures, so entirely making himself one of themselves, that his
presence,—instead of acting as a restraint,—was always felt to be the
crowning satisfaction, without which theirs was incomplete.

The count placed his daughter on horse-back himself; and Cynthio was
preparing, as usual, to offer his assistance to Astrella in mounting, when
the chevalier advanced, in his peremptory style of officious deference, and
lifted her into the saddle. She cast a look at Cynthio, saying :—"I am
accustomed to have you for my groom, am I not? I cannot fancy any
one else. The chevalier will excuse me. But Cynthio spoils me, with his
indulgence of all my whims."

The youthful face was turned towards her, glowing with happiness, at
her affectionate words and manner.

"The little husband is doubtless only too proud and happy to be your equerry. Who would not?" said Dorfaux. "But I should have thought the little husband's stature would have scarcely fitted him for the office. It demands a tall, stout fellow. Young signor Cynthio's proportions are more page-like, than beseem a 'palfrenier.'"

"There is more knack, than strength, required, I fancy, in assisting a lady to mount her horse;" said Olivia; "Cynthio's skill and kind care more than supply whatever defect of height may be his."

"So long as my services find acceptance with my——with Astrella, I shall aspire to be her master of horse, as well as her faithful page;" said Cynthio.

"As gallant a little husband, as ever, I declare! But perchance, the little husband does not choose to trust any one with the nice task of placing his wife in her saddle. He was wont, I remember, to think no one could take such good care of her as himself;" said the chevalier, with that peculiar gay sneer, which is meant to pass for playful jesting, but which often covers deepest malice.

"Cynthio is too modest to vaunt his loving care;" said Astrella; "but I can avouch it for him; none could be more indulgent to my every wish, more tender of my every caprice. The care he has for his own sister, does not surpass that he takes of his Astrella.. When little more than an infant, I have heard my dear lady the countess say, his devotion for the baby-stranger was remarkable, and often made them all smile with its pretty shows of affection. Once, when quite a little fellow still, it was demonstrated, even at the risk of his existence; for it took him into my room to share life or death with me, at a time that I lay sick of a raging fever. Well may he think no one can be so devoted to Astrella as her kindest Cynthio." The young girl spoke and looked with enthusiasm.

Her boy-lover, as he looked at her radiant countenance, and heard her fervent words, felt his heart elated into something like hope; but she had scarcely ceased, ere he thought;—"Would she speak with this ingenuous warmth, did she love me otherwise than as a sister? Would she allude to my affection for her thus frankly, had she the slightest suspicion it were any other than a brother's? Ah, no! Surely no."

"The little husband is honoured, indeed, by so glowing an eulogium on his devotion, from the lips of his spouse;" said the chevalier.

" So, you have caught up the foolish titles we allow ourselves to use for
these two young ones, have you, chevalier ? " said the count. " Cynthio
is growing almost too big for such a baby name, and as for Astrella, she's
now so tall a girl, we shall have her a young woman in no time. I forget
how years slip by! Why, it seems but the other day, that she was
brought, a little starry-eyed thing of a few months old, into our house."
The count sighed ; the sigh that generally follows looking back into the
past.

The chevalier Dorfaux asked some question that led the count on to give
the whole history of Astrella's first appearance among them.

" No relation to the family—no friends—no name—a way-side 'trou-
vaille '—a dependant on the count's charity ; " were the thoughts that
passed through the chevalier Dorfaux's mind, as the tale concluded.

All the while the count had been speaking, Astrella's horse had shown
symptoms of uneasiness. It was a skittish, spirited creature ; and Cynthio
had always objected to Astrella's trusting herself on its back ; but she was
a good horsewoman and a fearless rider, and she would hear nothing in
disparagement of Bayardo's good qualities. But now, the heat, and the
gnats, together, tormented Bayardo beyond his patience. He pranced, and
curvetted about, and at length began rearing. Cynthio rode close in upon
the snorting beast, seized the bridle, and effectually checked him.

" Well done, ' petit palfrenier ! ' Bravissimo, master of the horse ! " exclaimed the chevalier, approaching, when the steed was quieted ; for, during
the worst, he had kept at the respectful distance usually observed by French
horsemen in emergencies of the kind. They rode on for some time after
this, quietly enough. But at a turn of the road Bayardo suddenly darted
away at full gallop.

The chevalier was mounted on a noble animal, one of the finest in the
count's stud. It instantly set off after Astrella's runaway horse.

" Stop, stop, chevalier ! Your pursuit will but endanger her ! " shouted
the count. " The sound of your horse's feet will only urge hers on the
faster ! " But it was in vain. The Frenchman's skill sufficed not to rein
in a horse bent upon a chase.

" He does not know, father ; he thinks to rescue her ! " said Olivia ;

(Cynthio could not speak.) " All we have to hope is that he may succeed. Heaven grant, his rashness may answer better than our caution."

And the three went on as quietly as their impatient fears would let them. Meantime, the two runaway horses had shot far out of sight. Bayardo dashed on at full speed. On, on, they went. The breathless rapidity of the pace she was going, the terror, the imminence of the peril, at length caused Astrella to swoon. Then she was thrown. But she fortunately alighted on a turf-bank, which broke the violence of the fall.

The chevalier's horse had stopped of his own accord, not far from the spot. The suddenness of the check had like to have pitched the rider over, head foremost. But he recovered himself, dismounted, and went towards Astrella who still lay senseless.

She revived, to find the chevalier Dorfaux bending over her, and whispering softest entreaties and enquiries.

" You have saved my life, sir ; " she said. " How can I be sufficiently grateful for your intrepidity, your presence of mind. I owe you my life."

The Frenchman made no denial. " You can more than reward any help I may have been so fortunate as to afford, sweet Astrella. It is my life that is in your hands. Dispose of it ; redeem it from misery, if you think that I have saved yours. Make it henceforth a happy one, by telling me I may win your love."

Astrella did not reply ; she looked round, as if for her accustomed friends.

" You do not answer me, lovely Astrella ; look upon me,—say you do not hate me,—say,—— "

" Hate you ! How can I hate one who has been so generously good to me ?—one who has just risked his life to save mine ? " said the young girl ingenuously.

" Say then that you will take pity on me, that you will love me, that you will let me prove my love for you ; " and the Frenchman pressed her in his arms.

Astrella withdrew from his embrace, saying ;—" But where are Cynthio and Olivia ? Where is the count ? "

" You think more of the little husband than of your unhappy lover. Can you see my misery, and not yield me one word of comfort ?. Cruel Astrella ! "

" Indeed I would not be cruel—ungrateful ; what would you have me say ? " she replied.

" Say that you will give me your love.; that you accept mine ; " said Dorfaux.

" I have never thought of love ; " the young girl answered.

" Save for your little husband ; " said the chevalier.

" Ay, for Cynthio, and for Olivia ; they have been like brother and sister to me, as the count has been a father. I could not love them all more dearly, were they indeed such relations. But the love I bear them, is not the love——" she hesitated.

" Not the love I mean,—not the love I desire from you ; " continued the chevalier eagerly. " No, charming Astrella, the love I would have of you is a supreme love, a love paramount to every other, a love capable of all generosity, of all kindness and favor ; one that will accept love in return, —mutual love, blissful love, the love of lovers."

Astrella sighed ; looked down ; then gazed about her once more, in search of her own true friends.

" Mine is a passion that has grown to full force at once ; " pursued the chevalier ; " though I loved you before,—when quite a young girl, your early promise won my heart unconsciously, and prepared it for the passion which has now taken possession of me wholly. Do not doom it to despair ; do not, in the hour, when you think you owe me a life, condemn mine to misery. Be generous, say you will not refuse the vows of your lover."

Dorfaux would have attempted to seal them upon her lips ; but Astrella timidly shrank back, and he went on :—" Or if you cannot now resolve to accept them, promise me you will think of it,—that you will take time to reflect. But let me owe all to your own free choice ; consult only your own heart ; do not refer my fate to any one else's judgment. To you—to you alone, I leave the decision of my future happiness."

" I will think,—I will consider ; I will question myself ; " she said, trembling. " If I know anything of my own heart it is neither ungenerous nor ungrateful. Now let us seek the count, Cynthio, and Olivia ; they will be very uneasy."

She had hardly finished speaking, ere they all three came in sight.

"She is safe, then! How can we thank you enough, chevalier, for your care of our dear one?" said the count, grasping the chevalier's hand, while Olivia and Cynthio threw themselves off their horses, and hastened to Astrella.

"She shall ride home on my pony, she shall not mount the vicious beast again!" exclaimed Cynthio; "old Nerino is quiet as a cardinal's pad-nag."

This incident made the chevalier a greater general favorite at Casa Benucci than ever. The service he was supposed to have rendered Astrella, gave him every opportunity of prosecuting his schemes upon her. He had marked her out for his prey from the moment he heard she was an orphan, with no kindred claim upon the family in which he found her. He dedicated the majority of his time to her, at the count's mansion; and the remainder to sir Toby, at his bachelor lodgings, where primero, and dice, were the amusements, which gave him free scope for beguiling and fleecing the knight.

Warily, stealthily, he proceeded, with all the craft and cunning of a practised sharper. It is precisely upon such unworldly people as the count, and the rest of the inmates at Casa Benucci, that such a man's art is likely to impose. They are too good, too guileless, themselves, to detect anything amiss under the specious exterior of such a man as Dorfaux. Once, indeed, Feste, the clown, whispered in the ear of Maria, a scoff at his title of chevalier; declaring that for his own part, he believed it was through industrial qualifications alone, that Dorfaux could lay claim to it.

"'Industrial!' He's said to be a man of birth and honor;" answered Maria; "such people are above being industrious, thou know'st. Their spirit won't let 'em earn their own bread. They'd rather beg it; or eat it out of other people's industry."

"You don't take me, good mistress Mary;" he replied. "Be it known unto you, that there is a certain order of chivalry in his country, that live by their brains, and such odd quirks of contrivance as the brain deviseth; knights of the fertile invention, that by the aid of quick wits, and it may be, of nimble fingers, do manage to pick up a living out of the follies and foibles of their fellow-men; and these knights, being notable workmen, ever-busy in operation, passing active in practising their art, have been distinguished by the appellation—'chevaliers of the order of industry.' Their badge is a swan ; which beareth a fair white body on the surface, and plies black legs beneath."

" Pick-pockets, pick-purses, highwaymen, and thieves, are the brothers of such an order of chivalry as thou describest ; and none other than god Mercury their Grand-master ; " answered she.

" Thou choosest ill-favored names, mistress Mary ; " replied the clown. " But the gentry I mean, might come under the category of polite pick-pockets,—robbers on the high-way of saloons and drawing-rooms."

" And such a one thou thinkest this chevalier Dorfaux ? " said she.

" Think what I may, I say nothing. 'Tis seldom safe to say half we think ; and nothing is less than half ; " he concluded, turning on his heel.

And so, this shrewd surmise of Feste's passed off but as one of the fool's jests.

Meantime, the chevalier's insinuating address, elegant person, and per-severing court were winning their way with Astrella. Above all, the claim she conceived him to have upon her gratitude, in saving her life, inclined her to return his ardently-expressed passion. She began to love him as he could wish, warmly, devotedly. Unpractised in the ways of the world, un-suspicious, unguarded, she had followed his insidious wish of keeping the avowal of his feelings a secret. It accorded best with her own timidity and indecision on being first asked whether she could love in return; and gradually,—almost insensibly, the matter had gone on thus, unac-knowledged to her friends. On a certain morning, she sat at one of the windows in the room where the family usually passed the forenoon, occupied with a drawing, which she was making of a group of flowers, for the count's approaching birthday. The chevalier was hovering near the table, under the pretence of making a sketch of the view of the grounds from the window.

Cynthio held a book in his hand, and sat reading, or appearing to read, not far from them, in the next window-seat. Olivia was turning over the leaves of some lute-music, and trying a piece or two, that she intended to sing with her brother and Astrella on the coming occasion.

Under cover of the low-struck chords, and half-hummed singing, the chevalier was pursuing a murmured conversation with Astrella, as she bent over her drawing.

Presently, Olivia approached the table, to see the progress made in the flower-group. " 'Tis finished! Surely there can be no more touches required!" said Olivia. " 'Tis lovely! 'tis perfect! That rose looks as if it breathed perfume."

" The ' rose d'amour!' The most exquisite rose that blooms ;" said the chevalier.

" Is that the name of the rose?" said Olivia. " 'Tis fitting that it should be among the flowers Astrella presents to my father on his birthday."

And she moved away ; presently leaving the room, with the intention of joining the count in the garden.

" He will have the enduring blossoms,—those fixed in imperishable beauty by the fair artist's fingers ; but who shall have the originals ? " said Dorfaux, pointing to the group of flowers in the glass before her.

" They will be good for nothing but to be thrown away; they will have faded ;" said Astrella.

" Thrown away! Their having served you for a model ought surely to exempt them from such a fate. Let me keep them. Give me at least the rose ;" said the chevalier.

Cynthio heard no answer; but as he raised his eyes from the page before him, he saw the bright blush that accompanied her silent denial.

" I will get you fresher flowers by-and-by, from the garden ;" she said, after a moment.

" The rose,—the rose, is the one I would have ;" he urged.

Yet another moment she hesitated ; then she raised her hand, as if about to draw it from among the others; but in the act, her eyes met those of Cynthio.

" The chevalier Dorfaux shows less taste than usual, Cynthio ;" she said, attempting to cover her conscious confusion, by a gay manner ; " he would fain persuade me that these half-withered flowers are better than fresh ones."

" They have acquired a value from having formed a study for my father's gift ;" said Cynthio, anxious to relieve her embarrassment. " Come, you shall distribute them ; give me one."

"And welcome;" she said, in her frank cordial manner; "choose which it shall be."

"Not the rose! I have claimed that!" said the chevalier.

"I will be contented with this little star-flower;" Cynthio said; "I know not its name, but its simple, innocent beauty is all I could wish. Is it a jessamine?"

"That! What an ignorant botanist you are, Cynthio mio;" said Astrella; "that is a humble little hedge-side blossom,—a weed. I think they call it 'stellaria;' Olivia and I met with it in one of our walks, thought it pretty, and brought home a root of it to set in our garden. It was Olivia who would have me put it in the group for the count's birthday drawing; she said the little starry thing would remind him of his Astrella. Choose some other; that's a poor weed. 'Tis not worth your having."

"Nay, if you give me any, give me the stellaria;" said Cynthio.

"If you've taken a fancy to it, you shall have it;" she said, drawing the stem of the delicate white blossom out of the water;" let me put it in the button-hole of your vest, for you; since you pay the meek little wretch the honor of choosing it, its glory shall be proclaimed to the world."

As she stuck the flower in his bosom with the playful freedom of a child; as her hands lightly hovered about him, and her gentle head with its fragrant hair bent close before him, Cynthio had need of all his resolved control, to forbear clasping her to his heart, and imploring her to show less of such loving ease, torturing in its very sweetness and familiarity. The fondling intimacy of her manner, the innocent unconstraint of her approach, the confiding tenderness of her attitude,—transporting as they were in themselves to him,—how gladly would he have exchanged them for the blushing consciousness, with which, a few moments after, she turned to comply with the chevalier's re-urged request that she would confer upon him the other flower,—the one he had chosen,—the rose d'amour.

It was no longer to be refused; denial would now have betrayed that more meaning was attached to the gift, than the mere bestowal of a flower asked in sportive gallantry. But the glowing cheek, the downcast eye, the trembling hand, with which it was presented, the eager triumph with which it was received, spoke plainly the deeper pledge it was felt to convey.

"She loves him! I can no longer doubt; she loves him!" was the thought that smote upon Cynthio's heart, as the chevalier led Astrella away, beseeching her to indulge him with a walk through the grounds to the flower-garden ; under pretext of comparing the rose he had preferred, with those she had offered to gather for him. "She loves him ! she loves him ! Oh, Astrella ! my own Astrella !"

He wrung his hands ; he clasped them together, and flung them wildly over his head. But as the boy-lover felt the anguish of his heart swelling up to his throat, and struggling to have vent, he made a strong effort, forced back the emotion, suppressed it, mastered it. His chest heaved; his nostril quivered, his lip trembled, in the vehemence of this wrestle with his feelings ; but not a sound, not a sob escaped him. He had conquered ; but the victory left him as if overpowered, vanquished. His arms fell heavily beside him, and his head drooped on his breast.

His eyes fell upon the stellaria. Its sight had well-nigh wrung from him those tears which he had so lately repressed ; but again he bade them back, and compelled his heart to be firm. It was one of those moments when the soul attains the growth of years in a single point of time. Cynthio's spirit had learned its own powers of fortitude, of endurance, and resistance ; its force of will, its energy of purpose, its strength in self-contest; he had acquired the maturity of feeling wrought by such a struggle ; and however boyish his person might remain, he had acquired a sense of internal mastery which rendered him thenceforth a man.

Olivia, when she had quitted the room, with the intention of seeking her father in the garden, knew at once the spot where she should most likely find him. It was a bowery seat, deep-shaded and cool, even in the height of noon-day ; it was formed in the heart of an old box-tree, so close, so thick of leaves, as to form an impervious wall of green. There was space enough for two or three people to ensconce themselves within, very conveniently ; and its screened snugness made it a favorite resort of the count's, who frequently brought his book there, and loitered away hour after hour in pleasant leisure. His daughter took a volume with her, that she might not disturb him ; for they both liked to sit thus together, severally occupied,

but in each other's society. There is something peculiarly delightful, to
two people fully and confidingly loving each other, in this silent communion, this mute participation, of reading or writing alone together; it is
solitude without loneliness, company without exertion. No need to speak;
the sense of the beloved presence is there in its all-sufficing charm.

When Olivia now joined the count, in the box-tree bower, she merely
peeped in, saw he was there, and crept quietly to a seat by his side; while
he, looking up, welcomed her with a smiling holding out of his hand, and
went on reading. The father and daughter sat thus for some time; the
stillness of the spot and of their employment, harmonising with the quiet
understanding between them, and producing that exquisite contentment,
that serene condition of being, which is almost more perfect than joy. It
is happiness without any exciting element. It is consummate peace of
heart and soul.

Presently, upon the silence, there came a sound of low-murmured conversation; or rather of one voice, breathing in soft pleading tones, which
were only now and then responded to by a still softer, sweeter voice,
faltering forth a few words.

The speakers were in a green alley, carpeted with turf, and canopied by
over-arching shrubs and trees,—a covert walk that led immediately at the
back of the box-tree bower,—and as they came nearer, what they said,
could be distinguished. There was something equivocal in the import of
the pleading speeches that seemed to strike upon the count's ear. He
listened; changed colour; then started up, exclaiming :—"He would not
dare be guilty of such baseness, such perfidy! He dare not mean such
villainy!"

Olivia rose also, eagerly about to question her father, but he laid his
hand on her arm with an imperative gesture.

Again he listened, his teeth hard set, his hands clenched. Then he
stepped forward, made himself a way through the branches of the box-tree,
and stood in the green alley, confronting Dorfaux and Astrella.

For a moment the count gazed earnestly upon the latter,—without
anger,—but keenly, penetratingly, as if he would read her heart. Then he
turned to the Frenchman, and said, with a stern calmness :—"You love

this young creature? You love her truly,—honorably? Your intentions are honorable? I cannot, will not doubt it."

" I am a younger brother, my lord, with but a younger brother's portion to support a wife; how can I hope to marry,—how dare I offer marriage,——" stammered the chevalier.

" Yet you dared to offer love, sir ; " said the count. " You dared seek to entangle the affections of an artless, innocent girl. But if, as I fear, they are indeed won," he added, again glancing at the trembling Astrella, " your plea of scanty fortune shall be no bar. She is my adopted daughter. As mine own daughter will I treat her. She shall have no less a dower than I destine for Olivia. If your views, therefore, are what, for your own sake I will not doubt them to be——"

" What can they be but marriage,—marriage with one I love even to the forgetfulness of aught save my rash passion; " interrupted Dorfaux. " It urged me to forget the strange appearance my secret suit might bear; it led me to forget what was due to my Astrella's protector, her guardian, her more than parent,—her adopted father."

" Come hither, my dear child; " said the count to Astrella. He took her tenderly in his arms, and said :—" Do you love this gentleman? Can you accept him for your husband?"

" He saved my life,—he loves me ; " whispered Astrella, as she hid her glowing face upon the count's bosom.

He half sighed ; but he kissed her cheek encouragingly, affectionately. Then he put her hand in Dorfaux's, saying :—" You will understand me, when I tell you, sir, that for the sake of this gentle heart, I accept your own construction of the words I overheard you speak to her. I will believe they meant no other than the declaration of an affection, sincere and honest,—seeking but her welfare, her honor, her happiness. Let your future care, prove that they were your sole object ; when she is your wife, they will be your own. Cherish them ; cherish her. She has known nought but cherishing from those among whom she has dwelt from infancy; let her find none but kindness from him who will henceforth possess the treasure of her affection,—her husband."

The chevalier replied by a profusion of acknowledgments, and grateful

VOL. III.   K

protestation ; appearing penetrated with the count's goodness, and enraptured with his promised bride. Once more, he was all his gay former self.
He rattled on with twenty amusing trifles ; he laid himself out to please
and entertain. The count's generous, open disposition, was not proof
against such an appearance of good-hearted frankness. He believed the
young Frenchman to be as inconsequent and thoughtless as he seemed;
and restored him to his full confidence again, thinking him to have been
led away by temporary error, and never dreaming that he had been prosecuting a scheme of hardened and premeditated iniquity. They returned,
with Olivia, to the house ; the count playfully talking over his projects for
settling the young couple in a charming cottage he had on the borders of
his estate, so that Astrella should be always near her old friends ; his
plans for fitting it up newly to receive the bride ; and his resolve to have
a speedy nuptial, and a gay celebration. He was still chatting on, upon
this topic, when they entered the sitting-room.

"Cynthio moping here by himself, upon one of the couches, when there
is so much lively matter toward !" exclaimed the count. "Rouse thee,
boy, for shame ! Thou look'st half asleep, I think. But we have news
that will wake ye up, I warrant. What think ye of a wedding ? "

" I think Cynthio has one of his bad headaches to-day ; " said his sister
gently.

" I ought to have burst into the room, less noisily, if so ; " said the
count. " But we have tidings that'll startle your headache away, my boy.
I can hardly believe it myself. To think of such a young creature,—why
it seems but yesterday that Toby brought her in ; and that she was
dancing and leaping in his arms, with her staring starry eyes reflecting
the brightness of the candle."

" You forget, my lord, that the little husband may not be so delighted to
hear that his wife is to be taken from him ; " said the chevalier, laughing.
"Who knows but he may be for fighting a duel with me."

" Pooh ! It's high time that foolish name should be given up ; " said
the count. " It was all very well when they were babies together.
Cynthio is a tall lad now ; and boys are apt to be so absurd as to feel
ashamed of a title like that. We'll spare his bashfulness the awkwardness

of asking us to cease calling him the 'little husband.' Eh, Cynthio? it shall be so, shall it not? And you needn't look disconcerted, or vexed, about such a trifle. Why you bite your lip, and turn as white, as though you were really angry. Come come;" continued his father;·"we all know you love Astrella nobly, and truly; as a good brother should; she is no less dear to us all, than if she were in truth our own flesh and blood. This very evening, we will all go in a body, and look at the pretty place of which she is soon to be mistress. You know the cottage I mean? The one I call the little farm; with the olive-ground and vine-yard, and the peep of the sea from the upper windows?" And thus the count chatted on, in the gaiety of his heart.

In the evening, sir Toby joined the count and the young lovers in their walk to the cottage-farm; Cynthio owning that he was indisposed, and that he would rather remain at home; and Olivia preferring to stay with her brother.

"And now, Cynthio mine, you shall not talk, and I will be as quiet as a mouse, so that you shall get rid of your headache before they return;" said his sister in her gentle voice, as she drew the couch with its back to the light for him, and took a low stool by his side. "Perhaps you will sleep, and so be better."

"I shall not sleep, but I shall be very quiet thus;" he said, as he took her hand, and laid his cheek in loving thanks upon it. "How pleasant and cool your hand is, Olivia mine, and how sweetly you minister to my comfort."

"Your cheek is hot!" she said; "and how burning your forehead! Your eyes, too, so languid and heavy. You are indeed not well, my Cynthio."

She put back the light golden locks, and kissed the white brow, and thought how fair and childish her young brother still looked.

"It is the light. Pull the blinds quite down; make the room as dark as you can;" he said. She did so. He lay quite still for a few minutes. Then he said:—"Now, tell me how it all befell."

"You mean the chevalier's proposal for Astrella. My father and I were sitting reading in the box-tree, when voices approached; they proved to be Dorfaux's and Astrella's. Something in what he overheard, seemed to offend my father extremely. He arose, as if indignant, and went straight to where they were. I followed, and saw my father standing, drawn up to his full height, with his arms folded, and speaking in the lofty tone which you know he can assume when he is displeased. Dorfaux looked as I have never seen him look before,—thoroughly abashed and confounded. Poor Astrella seemed scarce able to stand. I went to her, and made her lean upon my arm."

Cynthio moved a little, and kissed the gentle hand that lay beneath his cheek.

"Nevertheless, I could not help feeling very angry with her ;" continued Olivia. "That she should have borne what followed ! That she should have witnessed it, and yet consent ! When she must have gathered from my father's words, as I did, that——No, a woman fails in what is due to the delicacy and dignity of her sex, who can accept a man for her husband, who has once tried to obtain her on other terms ! I cannot understand it of Astrella, so good, so pure-hearted ! But, I suppose it is to be accounted for by that which reconciles all that is strange, and inconsistent, irrational and unaccountable, in a girl's conduct. It must be, that she's in love, as it's called."

A sharp quiver, that he could not restrain, shot through all Cynthio's frame.

"You are suffering ; my talking disturbs you, dear brother ?" she said.

"No, no ; 'tis nothing. You wonder that she——"

"That Astrella should fall in love ?" Olivia resumed, finishing the sentence her brother left unfinished ; "no, not so much that. She is of a gentle, affectionate nature, and it was likely that some time or other, she should love ; but I would have had her choice fall upon one whom we both could have thought worthy of her. We who know her excellence, can hardly feel contented to yield Astrella to such a man as this chevalier—this Dorfaux."

Cynthio writhed ; but recovering himself, added in a faint, inward voice :—"You do not like him, Olivia ?"

"I never liked him ; but I tried to conquer my dislike ; and I must try still more to do so, if he is to be Astrella's husband ;" she replied ; "yet

I can hardly bear to think it, even now. It is possibly my prejudice,—but he seems to me not the man to deserve such a creature as our Astrella. How she, by possibility, could come to love him, is what I cannot comprehend. Methinks it shows her less nice in judgment, less exact in taste, than I believed her."

"You must not blame her,—do not let her suffer abatement in your esteem, sister;" said Cynthio;—"that would be worse than all. Still think the best of her, however unhappily she may have bestowed her liking; nay, she the rather needs unfailing regard from those who have loved her from childhood, if he——"

"If this man should prove that my instinctive distaste has not done him injustice;" said Olivia; "then indeed, will our poor Astrella need more than ever our love, our care. All our tenderness will barely suffice to console her, if his should grow less. Unless I grievously mistake, that careless-seeming manner, and shrewd, calculating eye, combine not to make a constant-hearted man—unless it be, constancy to his own interest. It did not escape me, that his sudden change from lukewarmness to eagerness in matrimonial aims, dated from my father's mention of Astrella's dower."

"How! Her dower? Could it be other than herself, that he——"

"My father nobly, and like himself, declared that he regarded Astrella as his own daughter, and should bestow, with her, a similar portion to the one he destined for me;" said Olivia, in reply to her brother's few breathless, indignant words. "I observed that immediately upon this, Dorfaux spoke of marriage. He then spoke of it with promptness, with decision, and has ever since been most earnest, most pressing; following my dear father's motion for an early day with all a lover's eagerness."

"If indeed he be the hollow mercenary villain your interpretation of his conduct proclaims him, sister," said Cynthio, raising himself on one arm, with flashing eyes, and an energy almost wild in its startling and vehement eagerness, "she should be saved from such a man! It is not yet too late! She shall be saved! She must be saved!"

"You forget, dear brother;" said Olivia mournfully; "if Astrella love this man, as I fear she does, she will not think it saving; she will think it undoing, destruction, wreck of all her happiness!"

Cynthio sank back with a stifled groan.

" If she love him, she will believe all we could say, mere prejudice, misconstruction, misapprehension ; she will think that we do him injustice, and
therefore be inclined herself to do him more than justice. With so little
real knowledge of his character as we possess, all that we could say, would
in fact seem but injurious suspicion ; and that would naturally dispose one
so generous as Astrella, still more in his favour than before. Nay, I think
it is but too plain that her heart is already so deeply engaged, that to prevent her marriage now, would be to ensure her future misery. If so, to
express our doubts of him would be not only cruelty, but would produce
a greater evil than the one we dread,—which, after all, our anxiety for
Astrella may lead us to exaggerate."

Olivia paused ; but Cynthio made no reply ; and the gentle sister could
not hope that he shared the cheerfuller view she had striven to take of
Astrella's prospects.

" At all events, we shall have this comfort, brother ; we shall have her
near to us, thanks to my father's kind provision ; and we will pledge ourselves still to watch over Astrella's happiness, will we not, Cynthio mio ? "

Cynthio strained the sisterly hand against his heart, for all answer. But
inwardly he murmured :—" Her happiness ! Yes, her happiness ! Be
that secured, come what else may ! "

Never once did it cross Olivia's thought, that her young brother's own
happiness was involved in the question they had been discussing. He
seemed so mere a stripling, such a boy, such a child in face and form, that
the idea of a man's passion, a man's fullness and intensity of love taking
possession of his soul as it had done, seemed impossible. He had loved
Astrella from babyhood, with so entire, so unreserved an affection, that it
never for a moment struck her that it could be other than the same kind
of love with which she herself loved Astrella. Its very strength was understood ; for was she not conscious of loving both Cynthio and Astrella
with as strong, as firm, as devoted an affection ?

The walking party returned. The chevalier all gay rapture, and amiable
gallantry. He was full of the cottage-farm, of its beauties, of the para-
disaical life he looked forward to leading there, with his young bride. He

was full of himself, and of his happy prospects. He spoke in ecstacies of the vineyard, the olive-ground, the myrtle-hedge, and the trellis of roses.

"But, rich in beauty as those roses are, not even they, can ever hope to equal in my eye this one little single bud ; " said the chevalier, touching the flower that drooped from his button-hole ; " it is faded, alas, but I still wear it as a trophy of my triumph—'tis the token of my conquest—my victory—the pledge of my having won this coy little heart. Not for the universe, would I have suffered my rose d'amour to stray from this faithful breast, where the lady of my destiny vouchsafed to let it rest."

The chevalier gallantly raised Astrella's hand to his lips, as he concluded ; then glanced at Cynthio's vest, adding with his gay sneer :—" I perceive the little star-flower has not been thought worthy of equal cherishing. I shall be ready, as her devoted champion, to do battle with any one capable of slighting my mistress's favors. The stellaria has not kept its place with the same constancy as the rose d'amour ; but my lady is too gentle to resent the throwing away of her one flower-gift, though I trust she is sensible of the homage paid her in the faithful preservation of the other."

Astrella little thought that the white star-blossom had been tenderly withdrawn from its conspicuous position outside the vest, to be enshrined within ; and that at this very moment, it was lying close against the young beating heart of him who sat there so mutely, offering no word in answer to the Frenchman's light talk ; but she said in her own sweet manner, at once unaffected and affectionately trustful :—" Cynthio knows he can have as many flower-gifts as he pleases, from his Astrella ; why should he keep a withered one ? No need of love-tokens at all, between him and me ; we have known each other's hearts from childhood ; he is as sure of mine, as I am of his. In a love such as ours, what need of flowers, and tokens ?"

"Yet you gave me one,"—said the chevalier, glancing at the rose d'amour.

"Ah, *you !*" said Astrella ingenuously ; then blushed at her own emphasis, which involved so much.

The tone, the look, stabbed sharp to the heart of Cynthio ; but he was growing skilled in concealing his emotions, even if the lovers had not been too much engrossed with each other, to have leisure for observing him.

The whole order of celebration of the approaching wedding was confided by the count to his steward, Malvolio ; that grave functionary being peculiarly fitted for the appointment and careful supervision of such an occurrence. There was to be a sumptuous entertainment, to which all the count's friends were invited. The nuptial ceremony was to be performed by a priest, who filled the office of chaplain in the count's household ; and was to take place in the chantry or private chapel attached to the mansion.

All was active preparation and bustle in Casa Benucci. Maria flitted to and fro with even more than her usual vivacity, in breathless consultation upon the all-important questions of skirts, robings, and tires of every description ; now suggesting some valuable hint in the style of a trimming, or inestimable suggestion in the set of a feather ; now insisting upon the indispensable necessity of trying on a new dress for the twentieth time, now whisking a bewitching hat on to her young mistress's head that they might judge its effect, or sporting an irresistible mantle on her own shoulders, to show it off to the least advantage first, she said ; now spreading silks, and admiring velvets ; and anon holding up jewels to the light, dangling ear-drops against her own laughing cheek, contrasting them with her own bright saucy eyes, twisting chains round her fingers, coiling and uncoiling strings of pearl, and playing a thousand madcap tricks of pretended busying with the bridal finery.

Feste was on the alert with new songs and plenty of ready jests for the coming occasion ; and Fabian undertook to marshal the rustic sports, and out-of-door pastimes, that were to be arranged for the count's tenantry in the grounds.

Sir Toby proffered his services to assist the pantler and butler, in the selection of rarest dishes and choicest wines ; that all due honor might be done to the festive part of the celebration ; while the count looked on, with his usual quiet enjoyment of the gaiety and activity that were going forward.

Amidst the general pre-occupation, Cynthio's misery passed unnoticed. His father observed that the lad looked pale and thin, but thought him out of health. His sister perceived his feverish hand, his wan complexion, and his contracted lip, together with a general air of lassitude, and abstraction; but she also attributed these symptoms to indisposition of body, partly caused by his anxiety respecting the character of the man who was to become the husband of their Astrella.

As the day approached, these outward evidences of his secret sufferings were with more and more difficulty suppressed; but Cynthio's fortitude and power of self-control grew in proportion with the increasing demand upon his courage; he resolved that nothing now should force from him a betrayal of those feelings, the knowledge of which could only serve to mar the happiness of Astrella. He compelled himself to take comfort from seeing her look happy; he strove to repress all thoughts that bade him repine at not himself forming the cause of that happiness; he schooled his heart to satisfy itself with the one consolatory fact, that hers, at least, had its wish. When he was most dejected, he forced himself to look upon her sweet countenance, so expressive of innocent hope, and joy, and trust; when he was most sunk in bitterness and sadness of regret, he sought to soothe them with the aspect of modest gladness, serenity, and fulness of content that dwelt in Astrella's air.

"If she be happy, have I not a thousand times told my heart, that shall suffice? And shall I lie to my own heart,—to my own soul?" He had so bravely and steadfastly kept this truth and singleness of purpose present to his spirit, that it sustained him to the end, in his resolve. No one— Astrella least of all—had a suspicion of how it was with him. It enabled him, on the day itself of the espousals, to bear his part in the festivities, with such self-possession, that he seemed to share the general interest and animation. His spirits might have seemed forced, his cheerfulness over-strained, had there been leisure for observation; but all attention was, of course, concentrated on the chief actors of the scene,—the bride and bride-groom.

The ceremony in the chantry was performed; the banquet in the grand saloon was concluded; the sports in the grounds had been protracted to a late hour, and the dancing had continued in the saloon; when the count and his family assembled in one of the small withdrawing-rooms, to bid the young couple farewell; it having been agreed that they should at once occupy their new home,—the cottage-farm.

The count was occupied in delivering to the chevalier Dorfaux the title-deeds of the small estate he had presented to his adopted daughter, together with a casket containing her marriage-portion ; Olivia was interchanging loving assurances of constancy in their mutual sisterly affection with the new-made young wife ; sir Toby was playfully bantering her on her late-vowed duties of obedience, and honoring submission ; Maria was fluttering about, adjusting and readjusting the bride's garments ; now arranging the folds of the veil, now giving an extra twitch to the base of the skirt, now sticking an additional pin into the bodice, now admiring from a distance, now darting close up, to give still some crowning grace, some final touch of tire-woman's art.

A little apart stood Cynthio ; striving to conceal the trembling of his heart, by as marble an exterior as he could command. The restless activity, the perpetual movement, the hurried, continuous talk, with which, through the day, he had contrived to cover his agitation, could now no longer serve ; and he was compelled to the still more difficult task of remaining quiet, yet preserving hidden the tumults within.

In endeavouring to appear calm, his attitude became fixed ; in the effort to seem composed, his features became rigid. As he stood there, with his white, set face, and his slight motionless form, he seemed rather some Greek statue of boyhood, than a warm, living youth.

The count turned to where his adopted daughter stood, spoke some fervent loving words to her, embraced her tenderly, and paternally, and then was about to surrender her to the chevalier ; but Olivia took her from her father's arms, saying :—" Astrella, dear sister, remember you have two homes now ! Although you have a home of your own henceforth, yet forget not that you have, beside, the home of your childhood, where your old friends will miss you, if you do not often accord them your presence."

" Dear Olivia—my more than sister,—revered father,—kind uncle,—beloved brother,—" faltered Astrella, as she gave her hand to each in turn, " you know my heart, dear friends, you know it is not ungrateful, though unable to express its recognition of all your loving care."

Sir Toby had hugged her against his broad burly chest, with something that sounded very like a sob trying to smother itself up in a chuckling laugh ; but not succeeding altogether to his mind in his effort at mirth, he had playfully pushed her away, declaring that she should not choke up his throat, and prevent his draining the dozen bumpers he meant to quaff to the health of the bride and bridegroom after they were gone.

Astrella turned from the good-humoured knight to Cynthio, who stood next to him.

" Cynthio, dearest friend, kindest brother,—" she said, " forgive me if I have ever encroached on your unwearied tolerance of all my whims of babyhood, childhood, and girlhood. Often and often I have felt your generosity, when I have only appeared to take advantage of it. Pardon your old playmate's caprices, and think only of your own indulgence towards herself."

Cynthio, in a blissful dream of one moment, held her in his arms, where she had thrown herself with all the frank freedom of her innocent, loving heart. He held her in his arms,—for the first time since he had learned how he loved her ; he held her in his arms, close against his bosom, against the bosom that throbbed with so passionate, though so boyish, an ardour. He held her in his arms, with the desperate intensity of joy that concentrates into one transient instant the imagined bliss of years. Vague and dream-like, yet profoundly conscious, were his sensations, during that single point of time. But he could utter no articulate sound, save a murmured echo of her own last word :—" Herself! herself ! "

From the mingled ecstacy and agony of such a moment, Cynthio was recalled by hearing the chevalier's voice, saying in its tone of paraded gaiety :—" The real husband may now assert his privilege, in preference to the little husband. Come, Astrella ; in pity to the impatience of your grown spouse, limit the leave-taking of your boy spouse ; in deference to the claims of your legitimate lord and master, pray abridge the farewell of your temporary possessor. He will doubtless cede you to the wishes of our friends here, as well as to mine. See, they are all tarrying to escort us as far as the garden-gate."

Cynthio, as still in a trance, saw the chevalier advance to lead Astrella away ; he saw the train of friends, gathering round their receding figures ; he unconsciously clutched at something near him for support, which he fancied was the cushioned back of a couch by which he stood ; he watched the gradual disappearance of the crowd, while the buz of eager voices floated in his ears, and the mass of moving persons swam before his eyes, until the last had passed through the portal ; then he staggered blindly forwards, as if with some indefinite idea of following, in the hope to gain yet one more parting glimpse of her.

By his side had stood Olivia. .She had noted the rigid and deathlike aspect of her young brother as he had remained rooted there, a little apart, before the leave-taking ; she had seen his strange, wild, wrapt look, in the instant of Astrella's embrace ; she had heard his inarticulate murmur ; she had beheld the start with which he had been recalled from his momentary dream ; and she it was, who in happening to lean on the back of the couch, had received the vehement imprint of Cynthio's grasp upon her arm. She read his secret. She saw that the young boy, the stripling lad, cherished a passion strong as ever mastered man. She saw that it was with no brother's affection that Cynthio loved Astrella.

In deep sympathy with him, she would have instantly followed ; but she had her duties of hostess to perform towards those guests, whom her father had quitted, that he might attend Astrella partly on her way. For the present, therefore, Olivia returned to the saloon, joined the dancers, fulfilling her office of presider and entertainer with her usual grace. But hour after hour went by, and yet she saw nothing of Cynthio. She had hoped that he might come back with her father ; or that if not, the count's return would enable her to quit the company, and go in quest of her brother. But still some fresh delay occurred, to detain her where she was ; and still the hours passed on, bringing no relief to her anxiety respecting him. At length, the party broke up ; at length all the duties of leave-taking had been gone through ; at length she was released. As she saw the last lady-guest withdraw, leaning upon her father's arm,—for the count, with the formal politeness of the old nobility, omitted not to pay his fair guests the courtesy of leading them to their coach,—she flew out of the ball-room, to seek Cynthio. As she sped along the corridors, the soft light of the dawn, peering through the windows, told her of the lapse of time. She crept gently to her brother's sleeping-room ; though she scarcely dared to hope hat she might find him retired to rest. The chamber was empty; and the bed bore evidence that it had not been occupied that night.

With one lingering hope still left, Olivia went to her own room, knowing that Cynthio used often to come thither in old childish times, and sit with her in quiet brother-and-sister talk, after guests were gone. But her fears had whispered more truly than her hope. Neither there could she find him. She threw open the casement, and leaned out into the morning air, that its sweet freshness might calm her troubled fancy, which began to busy itself with a thousand undefined alarms for her young brother. All looked so bright yet so peaceful, that she would not allow herself to believe aught of harm could have befallen him. The trees and grass, sparkling in their dewy coolness beneath the slanting rays of the rising sun—the stillness—the pure beauty of the skies—all seemed to give her assurance of serenity and comfort. She breathed a prayer to Heaven, that they might once more be her brother's, when time should have softened to him this first bitter trial of his young heart. She besought, —if it might so be,—that a sister's love should suffice to console him for the loss of that other love, which was now denied to him.

Meantime, where should she seek him, that she might manifest the tenderness which should prove a refuge and a solace? Suddenly, a thought struck her. She snatched up her veil, and hurried forth into the grounds. There was one spot, where she instinctively felt she should find him. It was a little green knoll of sloping turf, planted thick with trees, which formed a kind of grove; and stood on the highest ground in the park. Its eminence commanded a rather extensive view. It was the one spot in the grounds, from which the cottage-farm was visible,—the roof which now held Astrella.

The sister's presage had not deceived her. Olivia, as she approached the green knoll, saw a figure stretched at length upon the turf, beneath the trees. It was there Cynthio had flung himself in his despair; it was there he had given free vent to the misery that had been so long denied expression; it was there he had abandoned himself to the full violence of the anguish until now taught to crush itself within his own heart. Alone with Nature, he had at length suffered his spirit to cry forth its agony. Olivia stole

close to him, and knelt upon the grass beside him. She raised the head
that was buried in the folded arms, and bent her own face against his, until
their cheeks touched.

"Olivia! My sister!" exclaimed Cynthio.

"Ay, dear brother ; Olivia, come to beseech you will stay no longer
here. The night-air has chilled you—the dews have soaked your hair and
linen. Imprudent!"

She laid her hand upon his chest, that had neighboured the damp earth ;
she thought of the hollow cough that had lately made itself insidiously
heard, and shuddered.

"Fear not for my health, Olivia mia ; " he said, with an attempt to speak
lightly ; " 'twill do well enough ; a night in the open air, after the fever
of a ball-room, should be refreshment not injury. These limbs are but too
puny ; I would make them hardy ; I ought to learn to rough it. How
shall I ever be a man,—fit to protect my elder sister, fit to champion her
as she should be championed ? Why, such a poor stripling as I, am meeter
to be her page, than her knight. See, here is brawny muscle, for a woman
to trust her cause to ! " he said, baring his slender boyish arm, and holding
it out, with a scoffing laugh. " Let me do what I can to put due toughness
into such giant thews and sinews."

"Night-dews will not strengthen a delicate frame, any more than a show
of lightness warrants a sound mind, or a careless exterior can hide a bruised
and bleeding heart ; " said Olivia softly.

At the tender earnestness of his sister's voice, Cynthio's face fell, from
its assumed gaiety, to an expression of deepest sadness.

"Braving out a malady, whether of mind or body, is not always the
surest means of relief ; " she said ; "it too often but skins the wound over,
leaving it to fester within, and breed more fatal evil. Not only relief, but
healing,—cure,—come of careful heed ; of soft tendance, gentle nursing,
for bodily ills ; of confidence, kindliness, and sympathy, for those of the
soul."

Cynthio looked straight into that sweet earnest face, into those soft,
loving eyes, that were regarding him with such a look of angel compassion.
They seemed to say:—"Tell your griefs to me ; cease to add to their load

by these shows of heart-ease, which are a mockery between you and me; let your sister share your weight of sorrow, she will help you to bear it; it will relieve you of half your burthen, while it will be less for her to endure, than this present pretence, this make-believe of tranquillity."

"You think I have a pain,—a sorrow, that I conceal from you;" he faltered.

"I know it;" she replied.

He shrank, as though she had touched a hurt.

"I do not ask you to reveal it, to speak of it;" she went on, in a low voice, that breathed rather than uttered the words; "but let it be understood between us, that I may aid you to endure its pangs; they will be softened to you, when you need no longer seek feints to deny their existence, or to account for the evidence they will wring from the stoutest human heart, in moments of imperious torture. To know that there is one being who perfectly comprehends and feels your inmost sufferings, who in her sisterly sympathy yearns for your every throb, is moved by your every emotion, and shares in unison your every thought, must help to sustain an over-charged spirit. Let its nature be unavowed—unalluded to, if you will, since it is now irreparable; but let it no longer be withheld, that there is this woe to be borne together. No reserve shall henceforth mar the brother and sister love between us."

Cynthio's head drooped upon Olivia's bosom. She gathered him in her arms, gently and lovingly as a young mother might have done; his fair face, and slender figure, making him look still quite a boy, and much her junior.

"You guess my secret?" He at length said, in a broken tone, just venturing to glance at her countenance, while he kept his own averted.

"I do."

He looked fixedly for an instant into her face; then started from his reclining posture on the grass. Olivia arose also. He walked a few paces from her, as if irresolute; then returned, and stood beside her, with his hands clasped in each other, and his teeth set firm. And then once more he gazed into his sister's face.

She answered the mute questioning of his look, by a silent, but eloquent gesture. She laid one hand on his arm ; and with the other she pointed to the roof just visible among the olive-trees,—the roof of the cottage-farm.

Cynthio flung his arms about his sister's neck, drew her face towards him ; kissed her on the mouth and eye-lids ; and then led her beside him, with one of her hands grasped in his, towards their own home.

He walked on in silence until they had nearly reached the house ; then he paused abruptly, and said in an under-breath :—" Now I am glad you know this."

He wrung her hand, and was turning away ; but she detained him yet one instant, to whisper :—" You will promise to take some rest ? "

He nodded, and was gone.

In an hour after, Olivia crept to his room, and found him in a profound slumber. He had flung himself upon the bed, dressed as he was ; and exhausted by his previous emotions, as well as by the immediate reaction of feeling caused by his divulged secret, he had fallen into this deep sleep. His sister, blessing Heaven for this first propitious result of the step she had taken, watched that his repose should continue undisturbed. When her father came down to breakfast, as usual asking for his children, she caused herself to be apprised by Maria, that she might join him immediately, and forestal his enquiries respecting Cynthio.

" I feared he would take cold, coming out with us into the night-air, after the heated rooms, and the exercise of dancing ; " said the count. " Boys will be thoughtless of their health. We learn better wisdom as we grow older. I did not once forget your charge to don my velvet cap, Olivia mine, each time that I left the ball-room for the hall ; while there was that young scapegrace of ours, with his bare head and throat, out in the portico ; although, could he have seen his own face, he would have known he ought not to play such tricks. We must teach him to take more care of himself ; he really looks worn and white, and has a cough that I do not like to hear."

" I mean to nurse him myself, dear father ; " said Olivia. " I shall treat him like an invalid, that I may frighten him a little, and persuade him he is worse than he thinks. I have made him lie late this morning ; and shall take heed that his rest be not broken, until he wake of his own accord."

With ceaseless vigilance, Olivia dedicated herself to the care of her young brother. She guarded his secret from suspicion, she protected him from remark, as from all that could surprise him into self-betrayal, or add poignancy to his regrets. It was touching to see the loving ingenuity with which she devised means of screening him, both from observation, and from fresh cause of pain. It was wondrous in how many ways, the instinct of her sisterly affection taught her to spare his feelings. She seemed gifted with a subtle and intuitive perception of what could most jar them, as of the best method to avert the threatened effect. She was ever near, ever watchful, to prevent, to shelter, or to soothe. Yet, with the delicacy as well as rectitude of such a love as hers, she contrived amidst all this tenderness of her brother's unhappy passion, nowise to foster it. She was gentle to its sufferings, without feeding its weakness; she was indulgent to its misery, without indulging its malady. She rather checked than encouraged, even while she was most forbearing to its waywardness. She contrived ever to strengthen and to stimulate towards a more healthful state, at the very time she was most lenient to its morbid condition. She sustained and supported, instead of yielding; she assuaged, but never enfeebled; she administered relief, but she neither ministered to the disease, nor promoted its growth.

One of the earliest occasions Olivia had for the exercise of her sisterly thought, was when Maria flew into the room where Cynthio and she were sitting together quietly, to announce the first visit of the new-married pair.

"She's come, she's come! The bride is here! The bride and her husband! I should say, the bride and bridegroom,—or, properest of all,— the chevalier and madame Dorfaux. How strange the new name sounds! Our young lady Astrella;—madame Dorfaux!"

Knowing how the new name, thus abruptly spoken, must smite upon his heart, Olivia made the most of her own startled hearing of the sound.

"And is it in this wild fashion thou bring'st me the tidings?" she said; "but, in sooth, a wedding is apt to turn the soberest of damsels' wits; and thou, Gill-o'-the- wisp as thou art, must e'en be forgiven for startling me thus. Come, lead me where she is."

L

And Olivia, anxious to afford a moment to her brother for the recovery of his composure, hastily followed the steps of Maria, who had darted out again.

He was prepared, when they all entered; but he laid down the book he had been reading to his sister, for the hand that held it, shook. It was the only thing that might have shown he was agitated. All else was outwardly calm.

"Any commands to sir Toby?" asked the chevalier, towards the conclusion of his visit. "I hope to see him this evening."

"This evening?" said the count. "Do you expect him at the cottage-farm?"

"No;" carelessly replied the chevalier; "I fancy cottage-charms hath no charms for the worthy knight; he would find it dull. No, he gives a little supper this evening to a few choice spirits, and hath done me the honor to include me among them. He had the cruelty,—you may think it the grace,—to say that perhaps I might have some scruples in leaving my wife so soon, to spend a jolly bachelor evening out; but I told him we Frenchmen are not foolishly uxorious—whatever other faults we may have."

"And what says Astrella?" said the count, drily.

"Oh, Astrella is too good a wife to deny her husband any pleasure;" said Dorfaux.

"And the pleasure of the bachelor evening at sir Toby's, outweighs that of a dull evening at home?" said the count.

"On the contrary, the charms of a domestic tête-à-tête must of course surpass those belonging to every other mode of passing the time; only, that delight we can enjoy whenever we please,—we, who have the good fortune to be married men; but, a little supper—a social meeting—an evening with choice spirits,—that is not to be refused, when it offers. Astrella was the first to entreat me to accept sir Toby's invitation."

"The 'first?'" repeated the count.

"Yes, the very first,—after I had mentioned it to her;" answered the chevalier.

"Humph;" said the count, holding his under lip pinched together, and tapping on it with his fore-finger, while he looked thoughtfully on the ground.

" Speak, Astrella ; " said her husband ; "tell the count, it was your own wish."

" Indeed it was ; I should have been sincerely grieved if Dorfaux had lost a pleasure to indulge my selfishness ; " replied she.

" Yes, yes ; she is, as I tell you, my dear sir, too good a wife not to prefer her husband's enjoyment to her own ; " said the chevalier, with the air of a man who can afford to be generous in his praise.

" 'Too good a wife! too good a wife !' " repeated the count in a musing tone. " It depends on the husband, if a woman be ' too good a wife.' "

" Exactly, my dear sir; it depends on a husband's good sense, on his own discretion and wisdom, combined with a proper tenderness and consideration for the foibles which his cara sposa shares in common with the rest of her dear sex, whether she shall be ' too good.' ' Too good ' is sometimes rather too bad, egad ! Too fond, for instance, is apt to be a little too much of a good thing ; " laughed the chevalier.

" 'Tis seldom a fault complained of, in a young bride ; " said the count.

" But the young bride is, one day or other, to settle down into the— I will not say, old—wife ; " said the chevalier, with a gay bow to her ; " and in order that she may not feel the change, she shall learn the character by degrees—rehearse it, as it were."

" Act the part in play, before she learns to play it in earnest ? " asked Olivia.

" Well, young lady, something like it. I intend to enact the judicious husband, for my part, that she may not be ' too good ' a wife. It would be quite too good, were she to let her fondness detain me at home, when I wish to be abroad. No, no ; I must not have her ' too good.' "

" Can she be too good a wife for such a husband ? " said Olivia.

" Too good a wife for my taste ; " said the chevalier ; "as I have explained how ; I mean betimes, to show my wife that I know how ' to love wisely and not too well,' as the saying goes."

" Not too well ! not too well ! " repeated the count, in his abstracted tone, still gazing on the ground, and tapping his lip. " Too good a wife ! too good a wife ! " And he rose, walked to one of the windows, looked forth with a sigh, adding to himself :—" Too good a wife for him, I fear ! "

The intimacy between sir Toby and the chevalier Dorfaux, was maintained now with greater zest than ever. Astrella's dowry formed an agreeable supply to her husband, at the very time when his previous resources had dwindled to a mere nothing. It principally found its way to the gaming-table ; but there were other resorts of so-called pleasure, where this sum quickly melted. Amusement, entertainment, sociality, were the aim of sir Toby's roystering habits ; the chevalier had other ends in view. But as is mostly the case with such objects as his, pursued through such means, they failed in their attainment. Instead of turning his gambling and licentious life to account, it gradually left him poorer and poorer,—profitless,—bankrupt in pocket as well as in morals.

After some months, scandal began to be busy about him ; it was whispered that he owed more money than he was able to pay ; his credit waned ; the tradesmen with whom his extravagant tastes and habits had involved him, grew clamorous ; while the gentlemen towards whom he had contracted debts of honor, became rather more than politely pressing.

Rumours of these things spread through the town, beyond it, and at length reached Casa Benucci.

" I have been to blame—I have been too easy—too unregardful ; " thought the count, as he sat in the box-tree bower one morning, after a visit from a town acquaintance of his, who had dropped some hints relative to the chevalier Dorfaux's spendthrift courses, not knowing the connection existing between the Frenchman and his friend ; " I have given my child—or one whom I love as though she were my child— to a stranger, a perfect stranger, in all that regards his character. I took him upon trust, because he was a pleasant companion, and had the good word of my kinsman Toby. Knowing as I did, the knight's loose notions on the score of social right, how came I to allow his choice to decide mine, in introducing a friend here—an associate, an inmate, with mine innocent children ? I have been culpably unsuspecting. I ought to have mistrusted those insidious, those equivocal advances made to my poor Astrella ; instead of which, by sparing her a temporary heartache, I have allied her with one who may break her heart. I sought to account for her late altered looks and mien, by attributing them to her prospect of becoming a mother; but I fear me, they may have been occasioned by anxiety, by unhappiness; by her husband's frequent absences, and by a suspicion of their cause. He truly said, though in his wonted sportive style, 'too good a wife.' Yes, she is too good a wife to complain of the lot her own rash choice has drawn. Poor child! It should have been the part of her adopted father, to protect her against her own inexperienced heart. Now, it may be too late to interfere; rather increasing her troubles, than mitigating them, were I to remonstrate with her husband."

The count was still communing with himself on this theme, when Fabian came to announce the chevalier and madame Dorfaux.

"At this hour! In the heat of the day!" exclaimed the count, as he entered the saloon, and saw Astrella looking pale and faint. "You should not have let her walk so far in the mid-day sun, Dorfaux; I would have sent the coach for her, had I known you were coming."

"A thousand thanks, my dear count; but not the least occasion. I like to see my wife above whimsical airs and nonsense. Astrella is too sensible a woman to give way to any such fanciful follies. She knows I despise all those contemptible tricks of pretended delicacy, and affected weakness, which her sex are too apt to give themselves, as much as I admire her for being above them. My wife cannot please me better, than by evincing her superiority to the general run of young ladies."

"The general run, meaning the majority, I presume?" said Olivia.

"Alas, my dear young lady, I am sorry to say, the majority of your sex are not too wise;" said the chevalier, with his usual bow; "you and my charming Astrella, form the beautiful minority."

"The minority are obliged to you for your limited opinion of them, and for your enlarged estimate of the rest of their sisterhood, sir;" she replied.

"I came to ask you, my dear count," Dorfaux next said, "to let us all ride over this morning to see some archery, which I hear is to take place in some grounds about five miles off; it will be capital sport; there is to be a high prize given; there will be some good betting; it will be excellent sport; the ladies will enjoy it, and——"

"You would not surely venture on horseback, Astrella?" said Olivia, putting into words of her own, the anxious thought she knew was in Cynthio's heart.

Astrella looked timidly at her husband.

"Pooh, pooh! 'twill do her good! Nothing like a good scampering gallop for health. You will go, ma chere amie ; " said the chevalier.

"Certainly ; " she said gently. Astrella's gentle voice had, for many weeks past, become more than gentle,—it was subdued, in its tone of mild resignation. There had, almost imperceptibly, stolen over Astrella's whole air and person, a great change, from the bright, elastic-spirited creature she once was. The alteration had been so gradual, it had been so carefully sought to be concealed from her friends, by the assumption of as lively a manner as might be, whenever she was with them, that it could scarcely be traced, during its progress ; but Astrella now, after some months of marriage, and residence at the cottage-farm, and Astrella the happy, light-hearted girl of Casa Benucci, contrasted with each other, were two different beings. For a long while, knowing nothing of the chevalier's course of life, little imagining that evening after evening, he left his wife alone at home, while he repaired to the capital, returning only after dawn, sleeping away the best part of each morning, her friends guessed not the cause that existed to make her less happy than she seemed ; while her own efforts to appear contented and at ease, contributed to keep them blind to the growing change in her looks ; and whatever vestiges of less blooming health than heretofore might be apparent, had an ostensible source in her condition. The thinner cheek, the hollow eye, the lassitude of frame impossible to be entirely concealed, were gladly referred by them to this cause, rather than believe them to originate in sadness, or depression of spirit. One, especially there was, who longest clung to the desperate hope that it was not unhappiness that wrought the effect he involuntarily acknowledged. Better impaired health, than sorrow,—disappointment. Better believe her ill, and suffering in body, than sick and suffering at heart. Had he not sacrificed all thought of his own happiness, that he might secure hers? And was she indeed not happy, after all ? If so, there was yet a bitterer pang for him, than all he had hitherto endured. Of late, he had reluctantly admitted this question. Now, it was forcing its truth upon him.

Olivia, with her intuitive perception of Cynthio's feelings,—though no explicit form of words had ever passed between the brother and sister upon the subject, any more than on the first morning, when she had shown him his secret was known to her,—had marked the process of his mind throughout; and saw that he had at last unwillingly arrived at the terrible conviction that his self-abnegation had failed in its aim,—that it had not purchased her happiness for whom the sacrifice had been made. She saw that he at last perceived how it was with Astrella; how she had given her heart to a man unworthy of her; a man who took advantage of her gentle nature to make her submit to all his selfish humours; a man who by superficial compliments, and parade of gallantry, covered his real indifference; a man who had married her for mere convenience, as an indispensable accompaniment to the sum of money which he could not otherwise have obtained than as her marriage-portion; that she was, in fact, a despised, a neglected wife. And this was the result of Cynthio's heroic resolve, for her sake, to bury his passion within the recesses of his own soul! He had yielded her for this! His Astrella! His beloved Astrella! Olivia knew how all these thoughts were burning at his heart, while the above conversation was passing; she saw how he had need of his most resolute control, to preserve the silence he uniformly maintained on occasions such as these. She herself was about to entreat Astrella would rescind her assent to the proposition of riding, at the risk of betraying her sense of its inconsiderate selfishness, when the count said quietly, in reply to the young wife's last complying word :—" My dear child, I will not have it so; your husband must allow me the license of an old married man and your adopted father, to forbid your mounting on horseback. I do not think it would be prudent for you to ride; and moreover, the chevalier will excuse me if I add, that I do not approve of amusements where betting, and high stakes form the chief attraction."

" But I assure you, the archery itself is expected to be very fine; that in itself will be excitement sufficient;" said Dorfaux, with his usual glib decision, and off-hand mode of turning a question to his own view of it. " I would not lose the sight for the universe; so, if your paternal care of Astrella—for which I cannot be too proudly grateful—will not let you think it safe for her to go, I beg you will have the kindness to lend me a horse for the occasion. It is too far to walk; and as a poor country gentleman like myself cannot afford to keep a nag, I must e'en be beholden to my friend."

"I am glad to learn the chevalier Dorfaux is guided by prudential considerations, even in so far as the keeping of a riding-horse is concerned;" said the count. "Rumour gives him not credit for so strict an economy."

"Oh, I assure you, my dear sir, I am the most economical of men;" said the airy Frenchman. "Were it not for the sake of my wife—your all-charming Astrella—I could be content to live upon a crust;" added he, helping himself plentifully to some of the iced wine and other refreshments that the count's attendants brought in at this juncture.

"It is the part of a fool to make wise observations," said Feste, the clown, who was pouring out a goblet of water mingled with Aleatico, for his master; "and I've observed that those people who say, 'I can do with a crust,' never find a crust do for them."

"It is the part of a fool, if he be wise, to keep his sapient remarks to himself, until they be called for;" said the chevalier, with more petulance, than his usual craft of careless gaiety allowed itself.

"That remark of yours, shows you know nothing of a fool's duty, sir chevalier;" replied Feste; "a fool should make all his remarks aloud, that his hearers may benefit: the vicious, by the wisdom contained therein, the innocent, by the wit. And as for awaiting solicitation, 'tis the essence of his vocation that his sallies be ever ready, and forthcoming, undemanded."

"Nay, it may be so, good fellow; I pretend to know nothing of the merits of a fool;" said the chevalier; "I should be wanting in modesty, were I to say other than that there is little of the fool in me."

"More knave, than fool, perhaps?" asked Feste, slily.

"You exceed your license, sirrah;" said the count; "because your over-boldness is tolerated by ourselves, in allowance for your jester's privilege, I cannot have you take liberties with our guests."

"Where there is no truth in the sarcasm, there is no offence in the jest, my lord;" said the clown. "Conscious of integrity, the chevalier can surely hear the word knavery without wincing. Even though he be taxed with it, the idle word can no more cleave to him, than breath to a mirror. His unsullied conscience doubtless, like the crystal, only shines the purer and brighter for the passing attempt to mistify it."

" A truce with thy mistifications for the present;" said the count; "bid thy fellows remove these things, when the ladies shall have had what fruit they please; and meantime, the chevalier will do me the favor to accompany me to my study, where I have a word for his private ear."

In the interview that ensued, the count spoke to the young man with the explicitness warranted by his age and character. He told the chevalier the reports that had reached Casa Benucci, of his reckless expences, his extravagance, his debts. He told him that he could forgive imprudence, thoughtlessness; but that he trusted to his sense of honor, to his sense of what was due to his wife and to his unborn child, for a promise that he would in future be more circumspect in his conduct, and not endanger the peace, as well as involve in ruin, those whom he was bound to shelter from harm. The count ended by presenting him with a sum, which he said he hoped would free him from present embarrassments, as an earnest of his own confidence that he would be more prudent in future.

The chevalier was boundless in professions of good intention, profuse in acknowledgment, and lavish of promises to reform; and the good count, willing to hope the best, and knowing none of the worst features in the young man's conduct, gave credit to assurances that he wished to believe true.

The count Benucci had lived so retired a life, had seen so little of the world and its ways, that he was singularly simple and undiscerning. Having no experience, and being by nature very unsuspicious, it was scarcely to be wondered at, that, with such a man, a specious-worded, plausible-mannered, conventional gentleman like the chevalier Dorfaux, should pass for what he wished to appear. The count, himself an upright, worthy man, had none of the severity of judgment which sometimes accompanies righteousness; nay, it must be owned he was somewhat deficient in judgment. He was rather disposed to see things kindly, than to discern them justly. It was one of the notions of this kind-hearted, but not very far-seeing gentleman, that his kinsman sir Toby, by his example, led Dorfaux into many of the irregularities which were reported of him. The count knew that the jolly English knight was prone to indulgence, and that he and the chevalier were boon companions.

He thought, therefore, that if he could persuade his brother-in-law to adopt a somewhat stricter course in his own pursuits, it might influence the younger man to follow his example.

He did not, in his easy good-natured way, like the idea of speaking to sir Toby himself; as a hint from him, he thought, might look too much like prescribing, and assuming upon the sort of right which his position gave him to interfere. But he knew that Olivia had much influence with her uncle ; and he desired her to take an opportunity of winning their kinsman to a more orderly mode of life, and to re-urge the former proposal of his coming to dwell in the house with them.

Olivia had a pleasant way with her, that made any suggestions, or even counsel, accepted willingly by her friends. She never, in what she said, had the air of lecturing, or dictating, which so often renders advice unpalateable. Playfully, or earnestly, she spoke, as the case might need ; but always affectionately,—carrying the irresistible impression that it was for love of the person addressed, and not with any thought of self-interest, self-pride, or self-display. A woman, among men-friends, she possessed their confidence, their esteem, their respect, as well as their love. They regarded her opinion, no less than they cherished her sweetness and beauty ; they consulted and valued her judgment, as much as they doted on her gentleness and grace ; they prized her good sense, while they were charmed with her modesty, and womanly bearing. Her father relied upon her ; her uncle was at once swayed by, and fond of her ; her brother felt towards her the devotion and affiance of perfect sympathy in feeling.

In pursuance of her father's wish, the next time sir Toby came to Casa Benucci, Olivia took an opportunity of sportively chiding him for letting so long a time elapse between his visits to them ; telling him that she would not allow his acquaintance to have stronger claims upon his time than his friends ; that she wished he would give up his bachelor lodgings in the capital altogether, and come and live with them ; for that she was sure, as a family-man, among those who loved him, he would be more comfortable, more happy, and it might be, more good, than among those with whom he now associated.

" ' More comfortable ? ' Why, niece mine, to your lady niceness, 'twould sound strange, were I to say, that there is, to us free hearts, a certain charm in ruffling and riot, in discomfort, disorder, and disregard of teasing proprieties, beyond all the dull smoothness of comfort. As to 'more happy,' there may be a wicked joy in pleasure, that makes happiness seem but vapid, flat, faded, colorless, worthless in the comparison; but this also is enigma to your pure sense. Let that pass. For 'more good;' all I can say, is, would I were as good as Nero."

"As Nero, cousin?" replied she, humouring his humour, and falling in with it, as was her wont.

"Ay, truly. Had he not five years of worthiness? I,——that cannot answer for myself through the four-and-twenty hours! Why, an' I could lead a good life for five years together, methinks I should have no cause to despair of my virtue. Might every man boast his 'Quinquennium Neronis,' your saintly ones need weep no more over 'this wicked world!'"

"Nay, cousin," laughed she; "we have but Seneca's word for it. He may have lied, for the honor of his pupil. Every way, the credit of those five years is due to the philosopher, rather than the emperor; for, granting their tolerable decency, it lasted but so long as Nero suffered himself to be guided by the wise counsels of his tutor. An' thou wilt take pattern from Nero, be warned by his example in this,—cast not away thy good advisers. Be ruled by me, and amend."

"Take warning from the story thyself, niece. When Seneca's advice grew unpalateable, he was bid to make an end of it and himself at once. If thou wouldst have me hearken to thee with the old pleasure, sweet lady cousin, give me no counsel but such as I can relish."

"Thou ask'st for advice after the fashion of all counsel-seekers; it must accord with thine own fantasies, or thou'lt none on't. But in sober earnest, good mine uncle, for thine own sake, and to pleasure my father,—which I know will weigh even gravelier with thy good heart,—keep more within range."

"Range, quoth'a? I will range! I will become a very ranger. Thou shalt have no cause of complaint on that score;" returned sir Toby.

"'Tis a settled thing, then, that thou accept'st the office my father would have thee fill, cousin? Thou wilt be ranger of our park-grounds? And the office implies residence, thou know'st; so I may tell my father you will become one of our household; and I'll give order that apartments be got ready for your occupancy forthwith."

"Thou dost with me e'en what thou wilt, fair niece; there is no withstanding aught thou say'st, denying what thou ask'st, refusing what thou hast set thy heart upon, or avoiding that which thou hast fixed,—more especially when thy demands square so prettily with a man's own desires. For to tell thee sooth, I have long had it in my mind to take up mine abode with you. Had it not been for a lingering scruple of independence, I had owned this before. But we learn to subdue toys of conscience, as we wax in age and sageness."

"You know how to grant a favour with the grace of letting it seem one to yourself, kinsman;" she replied.

But after sir Toby came to live with them, it soon became evident that his example was not the cause of the chevalier Dorfaux's prodigal courses. News, not only of his reckless expenditure, but of his dissolute habits, his dishonorable practises, were now perpetually coming to their ears, from sources not to be doubted; and they could no longer conceal from themselves the entire worthlessness of the man to whom their Astrella's fate was joined. The count now saw that it would be mere weakness to supply her husband with money, out of any hope of giving him an opportunity to arrange his affairs, and retrench; all he could do was to furnish her with as many personal comforts as possible, that she might not feel the destitution to which such courses as Dorfaux's would in all likelihood eventually reduce her. From discomfort of this kind, her friends could still protect her; from the bitter sense of disappointment in him to whom she had given her affections, and allied her faith, they could not preserve her. Theirs was a nice task; but with all the tact and judgment which love such as theirs inspires, they fulfilled it with truest delicacy and tenderness. They respected her wifely duty by refraining from blame or reproach towards her husband; and as their candour would not permit them to speak of him with respect, they gradually ceased to mention him save in terms of mere courtesy and requisite enquiry. When they saw him, they treated him with that polite reserve, most chilling to persons of honest feeling and right sensibility,—most agreeable to persons of his calculating selfishness, and superficial, worldly sentiments. So that they but tacitly disapproved, he cared not; provided they ostensibly received him. It mattered not to him that he was endured, tolerated, for the sake of his wife; if his presence were permitted, it was enough. It suited him to visit at the count's house; it told well for him to have his countenance; that he was an uninvited guest,—that he was there on sufferance, signified little. To such men as Dorfaux an unexpressed dissatisfaction gives no pain; a silent reprobation no inquietude. That all goes smoothly on the surface, is quite sufficient for them. That all should seem well before the world, is the utmost of their care.

The birth of Astrella's child was a joyful circumstance to those who loved her. It afforded a source of sympathy between them, unconstrained, complete. Upon this little creature, its beauties, its gifts, its perfections, they all could descant to their hearts' content. Here was a subject upon which they could dwell without fear, without consciousness, without alloy of satisfaction. To Cynthio, above all, this babe was a delight, a treasure, upon which he could lavish all the secret store of love he had cherished for its mother. He would hold it in his arms for hours, hanging over it and fondling it with those caresses which in the days of his own bygone childhood he had given to his girlish playmate. It was the restoration of those long-past happy times; it was a renewal of his old, glad, unrestrained feelings of affection, when they might pour themselves forth in kisses and embraces innocent as they were warm and free. He had his Astrella once again! His little Astrella! His darling Astrella! His own Astrella! His father would laughingly joke him for his unmasculine fancy for nursing a baby; but Cynthio was too much in earnest, too content in his new-found delight, to be laughed out of his enjoyment.

Olivia was enraptured with the advent of this source of solace to her brother. She could truly define the profound feelings with which he held it to his heart. She could estimate the sensations of relief and freedom with which he lavished on it those evidences of a love so long pent and hidden. She knew the past anguish; she could understand the present joy. When she saw Cynthio's eyes, so long conscious, and troubled, and full of inquietude, gazing in placid comfort upon the sleeping babe; or when she saw his writhing disgust beneath some selfish speech of the father's, refuge itself in tracing the pretty smiles or still prettier gravity of the infant; or when she beheld the look so often forbidden to dwell upon Astrella's face, now turned in open, unrestricted, fullness of love upon that of her child, Olivia inwardly blessed Heaven, that had vouchsafed this requital of her brother's past unhappiness.

Astrella herself, in her affectionate regard for Cynthio, saw with delight the joy he took in her little one. She rejoiced to see the power it had to interest him, to rouse him from that apathy and abstraction, that strange kind of restraint which she had with pain noted in him for some time past, and for which it had frequently given her as much concern as perplexity to account.

She was sitting leaning over the back of a low couch, upon which Cynthio lay playing with her child one morning. She watched them romping and frolicing together, and saw the gentle way in which he lent himself to the humours of the little creature, now submitting to be crawled over, and tumbled over, and pulled over; now hiding his face beneath a handkerchief, now popping it forth, that the babe might have the glory, and startled transport, of discovery; now still as a mouse, now joining in the sudden crow and giddy laugh that succeeded revealment; now letting the little open palms pat and stroke his face, now allowing the bits of fingers to poke their way in pursuit of the white, irresistible teeth, that lurked at hide-and-seek behind his lips; now suffering them to make vain clutches at his eyes, that showed so bright, so tempting, so provokingly unattainable, when he opened and closed their lids for baby's wonder; now abandoning his hair to the most ruthless of tugs, now smoothing and caressing the fair locks (that light golden brown he loved so well) of the little tugger's own head in turn. And as Astrella watched all this, and saw the tender pleasure, the absorbed enjoyment that Cynthio took in playing with her child, a feeling of contentment, partly at his happiness, partly at her own, in causing it to him, thrilled through the young mother's heart.

"Little rogue!" she said; "thou supplant'st thy mother in the indulgent love which was once hers."

"It is the same;" said Cynthio in a low voice.

The child had found out a new object of attraction; it was now plucking at a dark slender chain, espied among the folds of Cynthio's vest.

."Be good, little encroacher;" said the mother, gently trying to disengage the coil in which her babe's fingers had entwined themselves; "thou wilt break it! Be not so graceless, as return injury for indulgence. Let go, let go, naughty one!"

"She will be unlike her mother before her, if she requite loving-kindness with anything but gentleness;" said Olivia, who sat near. "Gently, gently, little one;" she added, leaning forward to help extricate the chain from its grasp; "since the toy is woven of my hair, Cynthio would not care to have it broken. Gently, gently! let go, Astrellina-Strellinetta!"

But it was too late to prevent what Olivia foresaw. The child's pertinacity had succeeded in twitching forth the chain; and at the end, hung a small crystal case. The clearness, the dangling motion of the trinket, together with the success of attainment, combined to delight the babe, and nothing could persuade it into relinquishment. No; fast, fast, the little fingers clutched; triumphantly it crowed, as it brandished the new-found gaud; and perseveringly it threatened to scream, upon the least attempt at withdrawal.

They could have laughed to see the baby wilfulness; had they not all three been possessed by secret thoughts that made their smiles but constrained. Olivia's was for her brother. She instinctively felt and knew the charm which the contents of that locket possessed for him,— though she knew not absolutely what those contents were,—and she trembled to think what Cynthio now felt, to see them hanging in the babe's grasp, close in the eyes of its mother. She dared not look at her brother's face, lest she might behold, as well as draw attention, to the confusion painted there; she directed her efforts to playfully speaking with the child, and making it a means of diversion to them all. But neither Cynthio nor Olivia need have feared. The little star-flower treasured within the crystal, though clearly visible through the transparent enclosure, was no longer recognizable. It had too surely lost all shape and color. To his eyes the fair white petals, the slender green stem, were still there in all their delicate beauty; to his eyes, the form of her who gave it, her look as she placed it in his vest, every myriad association of herself in all her loveliness and grace were there enshrined and apparent; but to all eyes else, a few faded shreds, without distinguishable substance or import, were alone perceptible. And still the child held them in its mother's sight, and still no trace of their identity reached her. But there was something,—all at once,—in the embarrassed silence which had seized Cynthio, that struck her as giving significance to the contents of the little bauble which her baby persisted in bringing forth to light, and holding up for display.

"Can it be, that he loves? Can it be, that so young, he has already loved? Can he, so young—have known disappointment?—so gifted—have loved in vain? Cynthio! He?"

This train of ideas engrossed her. She could scarcely attend to the delight of her babe, that continued unabated. She sat absently gazing at her little one, hardly seeing its leaps of ecstacy, or hearing its shrill cries of pleasure.

"I am fanciful;" she thought, smiling to herself, after a few moments, as she looked upon Cynthio's face, and saw it resume all its usual calm (a calm resumed in the conviction that his secret was safe,—that no eyes save his own, could trace aught of it beneath the withered stellaria); "I am supposing a mystery where none exists; the dark hair is the color of Olivia's; the chain is her gift; doubtless, the locket also; the thought that it might be injured, caused his momentary embarrassment; while his love for me and my baby, prevented the expression of his uneasiness. Dear Cynthio! ever kind, considerate, loving! Gentle and good,—how could he love in vain? I was mad to think it but for an instant."

As she looked upon that face, so full of earnest sweetness, so boyishly young and fair, yet so beaming with the sensibility and intelligence of a passionate nature, Astrella felt that it would indeed be a sore grief to her to think that he was doomed to know the bitterness of a fruitless affection. In the depth of her feeling, she breathed a mute prayer that he might be spared this cruellest of all pains. At the very moment of her inward aspiration in his behalf, Cynthio chanced to raise his eyes towards her; and there he read the same pure, ingenuous look of loving regard that had ever beamed upon him from his Astrella. He blessed her in his heart, while she was praying for him in hers.

The babe had at length given up its plaything, and had fallen into a quiet sleep in Cynthio's arms, when the chevalier suddenly entered.

"Desolate to break up so charming a society!" he exclaimed, bowing round; "but I am compelled to request my wife's return to the cottage-farm immediately; I have business to transact there, that cannot be effected without her presence. Desolate, I assure you! But it must be."

Astrella arose to obey her husband.

"My father has taken the coach this morning, to pay a long-deferred visit to an old friend, who lives at some distance;" said Olivia; "is it indispensable that you must return home immediately, sir?"

"Indispensable! absolutely indispensable, parole d'honneur!" he replied, laying his hand on his breast, and bowing again; "or I would not be so barbarous as to exercise my conjugal authority and prerogative."

"We will walk with you across the park-grounds, Astrella;" said Olivia; "you must not carry your baby so far."

"Do you think I should have permitted my cara sposa to bear the burthen? You do not give due credit to the gallantry of our nation, signora;" said the Frenchman.

Olivia did not say she had so little faith in it, that she knew he would only carry the babe out of sight of the house, and then let his wife bear it the rest of the way; but she said:—"The child is asleep; best not disturb it. Cynthio will carry it. And I shall contend for my turn, when it wakes."

"As you will; I always defer to a lady's proposals, and comply with her wishes, when I can;" returned the chevalier, with another bow; then turning to his wife, he said:—"Allons, ma chere amie; pray use a little of your usual complaisance, and get ready in less time than the generality of your charming sex take for the adorning of their sweet persons. Come, where is this shawl? Let me have the felicity of putting it on for you."

The chevalier was evidently in a violent hurry. His utmost blandness and politeness were in requisition, to cover his impatience. All his suavity was employed to mask the eagerness with which he hastened them along.

But Olivia, who could see the ill-suppressed tokens of Astrella's faint-ness and fatigue, and knew the slight frame and unequal strength of her brother, contrived that they should have rest. The chevalier tried to con-travene her ; but even his adroit manœuvring, was not a match for her quiet arrangement. He was working for himself ; she was acting for her friends.

It happened, that as they came to the green knoll, the chevalier, who thought he would try to laugh her out of her plans, proposed their resting there ; but Olivia, ever-mindful of Cynthio's feelings, had purposely chosen a seat a short space before they came to it, in order that her brother might be spared sitting in this spot, of all others, with his present companions ; she therefore led on, declaring that she knew of a shady nook a little farther, that would be much better for their purpose. It was often curious to see how the quiet dignity, the honest courage, the simple, straight-forward decision, with lady-like ease, of this young girl, could put aside and baffle the wily selfishness of the man of the world.

When they reached the cottage-farm, Cynthio put the child in its mother's arms ; and Olivia, knowing how unwillingly her brother entered that roof, took leave at once. The chevalier made not even the pretence of detaining them ; and his wife was too anxious to know the cause of her abrupt recall, not to acquiesce.

She learnt it but too soon. A pressing demand, had caused her husband to return and extort all that she had left. The last remnant of her money had long since vanished ; her jewels had followed ; and now the title-deeds of her estate,—the cottage-farm and land, which had been the gift of her adopted father, in an instinctive desire to endow her with a home,—were to be ceded to the rapacity of him, whose duty it was to protect her from robbery, not to rob her himself. It was to sign away these deeds, that he had summoned her ; it was to deprive herself and child, of house and home for ever, that he had fetched her to that home. She made a feeble attempt to remonstrate, to entreat that he would not strip them of this last resource ; but with his selfish inflexibility, veiled in smoothest and most amiable terms, he compelled her to sign. The instant he had obtained what he wanted, he seized the parchment, snatched up his hat, and with a smiling bow, departed.

That night Astrella's second baby was born,—dead. That night its father was spending the hours in revelry,—the king of his company, the admired of jovial men, the adored of pretty women. One of these latter,— a lady who had abandoned all the observances of her rank, save a sovereign contempt for the opinion of those whom she considered beneath her, condescended to accompany the chevalier Dorfaux to a rural breakfast at his cottage-farm; and on their arrival, the gay couple were much discomfited to learn the inconvenient incident that prevented the mistress of the house from doing the honors, and receiving them. But they did as well as they could without her; that is, they discussed an excellent repast of strawberries and cream, which the town-lady was so obliging as to declare more delicious than any she had ever eaten,—and then they went their way again; but not before the gallant husband had paid a visit to his wife's bedside, kissing her hand with the most assiduous tenderness, and beseeching she would take care of her health.

Not many hours after, the person who had now a right to call the cottage-farm his own, sent men to take possession; they were proceeding to make an inventory of the goods, with other usual forms, when the good peasant woman, who acted as nurse to madame Dorfaux, took upon herself to despatch one of the farm-boys up to the great house to inform count Benucci how matters were going on.

The count was still absent, but his son and daughter hastened to their Astrella. Her delicacy would yet have kept them in ignorance of this climax to all that she had been suffering so long, in secret; but she was now left no option. The well-meaning nurse met them at the gate, and told all. She spared no detail of Dorfaux's misconduct; she even censured Astrella's too great yielding.

Olivia saw the expression of Cynthio's face, and hastened to interpose, ere he should give utterance to the rebuke she saw trembling on his lips;

but before she could speak, the nurse added :—" Poor young thing ! She has
dealt herself her own death-blow, through her weakness; it has killed her infant, and it will kill herself. She's not long for this world, and she knows it."

Olivia saw Cynthio stagger, and turn deadly white. She hastily sent
the woman for water, that she might get her from the room, saying :—
" We are her dearest friends, you tell us this too frightfully."

Cynthio wrung his sister's hand ; turned away ; then came back with
a look set into stern composure, and said :—" We must see her ; she must
see nothing of what we feel. For her sake,—for her sake.——" His
words died away ; but the look with which his sister met his own, told
that he was understood.

The nurse returned, saying that her young mistress had heard her
friends were come, and begged that they would let her see them.

The brother and sister went to Astrella's room.

They found her sitting up in bed, propped by pillows ; with a faint
flush on her cheek at the joy of seeing them. In the arms of a young girl,
the nurse's daughter, was Astrella's child. It stretched out its little hands,
and crowed with delight, at seeing its friend Cynthio. Olivia stepped forward, took it in her arms, and sent the attendant away. The babe would
still have made advances to be taken by Cynthio ; but his sister carried it
to the window, and soon contrived to amuse it, and engage its attention
to herself.

The mother's eyes dwelt with serene delight upon her child in the arms
of her gentle friend Olivia. She signed to Cynthio to sit upon the bed's
edge beside her, and stretched forth her hand for his. She held it locked
in her own, and lay thus half reclined, with her gaze fixed upon her child,
and her two dearest friends, looking wrapt in a content and peace so deep,
as to seem like happiness.

For some time no sound, save the innocent cooings and murmurs of the
little one, broke the stillness in that hushed chamber. Each felt the presence of the others a sufficing comfort. No need of communion, where
mutual sympathy was so truly understood, so deeply felt.

At length the voice of Astrella made itself heard, low, inward, nearly
extinct ; but tranquil,—with no inquietude, no agitation.

"Dear friends," she said, "it will be your best solace to know that I am happy. Happy in the ceasing of my own weary task,—happy in the knowledge that my little Astrella will have the same guardian care that sheltered her mother. At like infant years, you took me in, a little wandering star ; and now, another. Both bereft of a parent's care ; my father perished ; hers is dead to her., You will never let her know the lack of a father—I feel, I know, you will not."

"You know us too well to doubt it ;" said the soft voice of Olivia ; while the pressure of Cynthio's hand bore testimony to his confirmation of his sister's words.

"One promise I have to entreat of you ;" Astrella went on. "It is this. Should her father's caprice ever claim her as his child, promise me that you will refuse. He is no meet parent—no fit protector, guide, for childhood—for girlhood." She shuddered ; then resumed her steadfast tone. "Hard as is the task, to deny a child to its father, this task I beseech of your friendship. I entreat you to save her, to preserve her, from a man to whom she must not belong. Pollution, soul and body, is in the guidance of such as he. And shall it be risked, in deference to a claim, nominal, conventional? Parentage consists not solely in blood. What parent could have trulier fulfilled his part, than the father I have found in yours ?"

"She shall be our child ;" said Olivia ; "my brother and I will never yield her."

"I am conscious that I ask a pledge that may involve you in difficulty, in contest. But I know the strength and constancy of your friendship ; and I tax it thus far, conscious that your best reward, as your best comfort hereafter will be, the peace which this knowledge and reliance gives me in my dying hour. It brings me peace upon the only point where inquietude could have reached me—my child, my little Astrella. In Olivia's gentle care she will become happy and worthy ; in your protection, Cynthio mio, she will be safe from her unworthy father. In this thought, I can resign my soul to the bliss of its release."

"You can leave us—leave life without a sigh ?" murmured Cynthio in

broken tones. " Your existence was then a burthen; your sufferings were
bitter; why did you not confide in those who loved you ? Why not have
let them take you from this bondage ? Why not have yielded them the
poor preference to death ? "

" It is hard to own a heart mistaken, deceived, betrayed ;" she returned;
" harder still to arraign him whom you have once loved. Cruellest of all
to know him unworthy. The humiliation of being wedded for what you
bring, not for what you are ! And oh, the misery of living unloved !"

Cynthio started. Then he said in an under-breath :—" That misery has
not been Astrella's."

" True ;" she replied, with the look of full, open, loving regard which
her face always wore, when she spoke or thought of the affection between
them ; " I do not justice to the love of my friends, when I talk of living
unloved; but ah," and her face sank to its previous sadness, " the heart will
thirst for a paramount love, an exclusive love,—love itself. There will
come a day when my Cynthio's young heart will learn this thirst—this
imperative demand."

" It has already known it ;" he said in the same tone as before.

" Then the crystal I saw—it did contain the secret of your heart,—your
love ? I thought it, and yet——"

" It contained yourself—my little star—my Astrella !" he faltered.

Her eyes were fixed upon him. They seemed as though they would
seek the truth of that wild incredible surmise which now, for the first time,
presented itself to her imagination. Her eyes were fixed upon him ; but
their other sense,—that inward sight which busies itself with by-gone
things, past scenes, deeds, words, looks, at the very time the outward sight
is occupied with a present image,—was actively employed searching for
corroborative circumstance of what she heard.

Sadly, mournfully, yet with a rapturous intensity that was akin to
transport, his eyes were bent on hers, and seemed to follow their process
of retracing remote events and objects. He saw the tender remembrance,
the gentle memories that glided upon her vision ; he saw the moistened
eyes with which she recalled certain passages in their past life ; he beheld

the soft smile which played in them, as she at length murmured :—" My little husband!"

"He loved you!" Cynthio exclaimed; and the passionate truth of the words was told upon her lips.

Olivia was at length alarmed by the silence that ensued. Approaching the bed, she saw them pale and lifeless. Her young brother was·in a deep swoon. He had bravely sustained sorrow; but joy was too mighty for him. For Astrella,—she had died in the knowledge that she was beloved by this faithful, noble heart; she had resigned life, contented, happy.

Now it was that all Olivia's tenderness, and thoughtful courage, all her womanly qualities, and gentle excellence, had scope. Her first care was to recover her brother; her next, to break to him gently the sad truth; and then to soothe and sustain him in his affliction. She controlled and suppressed her own grief, that she might minister to his. And when he, passive and unresisting, suffered her to lead him from the chamber of death, she put Astrella's child in his arms, bidding him remember that here was a part of herself left him to love and to cherish; that here was at once a source of consolation, and a bond of union with her who was now in Heaven. And seeing him shed gentle tears over the babe, as he pressed it to his heart, she left appealing innocence and helplessness to work their own kindly effect upon his loving unselfish nature; while she returned to pay the last sad duties to the remains of her friend.

With the unflinching energy which belongs to women of her sweet and gentle, yet steadfast and generous natures, Olivia took upon herself the whole of the mournful tasks which followed; she spared those she loved, from all that she could save them from, by the exertion of her own courageous forethought; and when her father returned, he found that all had been already done, which his presence could have effected.

Count Benucci warmly seconded his son and daughter in their resolve of adopting Astrella's child; and supported them in their resolution to withstand the claims of its father, should he ever think fit to urge them.

For some time, there seemed no chance of this; but after a space, the thought that his little daughter might be made a means of extorting money from those whose love for the mother had evidently been transferred to the child, induced Dorfaux to threaten the assertion of his natural and legitimate rights. He applied by letter; for even his brazen assurance failed him, at the thought of meeting face to face those whom he had so cruelly, so basely injured. The count wrote in answer; temperately, but decisively declining to give up Astrella's child.

The chevalier retorted peremptorily, violently. He declared that nothing should prevent his appealing to a tribunal that should compel submission to his legitimate plea; he should lay his cause before his friend Orsino, the reigning duke of Illyria.

This name he thought would carry weight; and force the count to a compromise. He relied upon a passing introduction he had once had to the duke, and to his own insinuating address, and plausible representation, in case he should have to carry out his menace of applying to his grace.

The count's reply was but a repetition of his former one; and the chevalier Dorfaux, exasperated by this resistance, and the disappointment of his mercenary purposes, waited upon duke Orsino.

But speciously delivered as was the tale, there was something in the bare facts of the case, that suggested other feelings than the ones sought to be produced.

The duke felt interested in the noble family who had shown this generous sympathy with orphanhood; he felt irresistibly drawn towards, and curious to see, persons who had refuged and fostered the mother, and now championed and protected the child. He secretly resolved he would enquire farther into the matter, ere he delivered his opinion; and coldly told the chevalier that he would take time personally to consider of it, before he could even encourage him that he would sanction its consideration by his council.

The duke was a man of a romantic nature, chivalrous sentiments, and a poetical and passionate sense of beauty. There was something in Dorfaux's hard, calculating eye, and shrewd smile polished into complaisance, peculiarly repulsive to Orsino's refined and delicate perceptions. He instinctively doubted a man that inspired aversion by his mere look. The idea possessed him that he would take means to see the other actors in this drama, and judge whether their appearance affected him contrariwise to the impression he had conceived of them.

He called a confidential attendant, named Curio; bade him get horses saddled, and prepare to ride with him a short distance out of town, suddenly, and quite privately. Orsino had informed himself of the whereabouts of Casa Benucci, sufficiently to know that he was approaching its precincts, when, on looking over a park paling, among some trees, he saw, seated beneath their shade, a group,—a family-party, that at once arrested his attention. It consisted of a venerable gentleman, of benign aspect, and distinguished bearing, who occupied an easy chair; near to him sat a youth, with a young child upon his knee, over whom he bent in fondling interest with its half-articulate prattle. Close beside the youth stood a lady, reading a letter. She was young, and very beautiful; there was a mingled dignity and sweetness in her countenance, both majesty and graciousness in her mien. The tidings of the letter seemed pleasant, for a smile sat upon her lips, and brought into sight an exquisite dimple that lurked in one of the most perfectly and softly rounded cheeks imaginable. As she raised her eyes, the smile shone there too, in those large, dark, lustrous orbs of transparent depth.

"And Toby writes cheerfully, and happily, does he?" said the grey-haired gentleman, as he looked up in her face, and saw its expression; "when does he talk of coming back to us? He has found Venice attractive. His stay there, this time, has been longer than ever."

The young lady did not immediately reply; her eyes had encountered those of the stranger on horseback, who was looking over the fence towards their party. He raised his hat, on perceiving that she had observed him, and rode on to the gates of the mansion; where he caused himself to be announced as duke Orsino, who requested an interview with the count Benucci.

"I have seen the venerable count, if I mistake not, seated with his family in the grounds;" said the duke. "Stay, I will not give his lordship the pains of coming to the house to receive me. I will seek him there myself."

The attendant summoned the count's seneschal, Malvolio, who ushered his grace with much ceremonial, to the spot where they sat.

Duke Orsino, with his native urbanity, introduced himself to the count, saying he had wished to make his acquaintance ; and since his lordship frequented not the court, he, as the younger man, thought fit to waive the privilege of rank, in deference to that of age, and come to see him in his retirement,—a retirement he could no longer wonder at, since he saw what inducements there were to its preservation.

The duke, as he concluded, bent courteously to Cynthio and Olivia ; asking if he were mistaken in supposing them the count's son and daughter.

They made suitable replies ; and then the duke, taking a hand of the child's into his own, led to the enquiries he wished to make, regarding her story.

The little one shrank from the strange gentleman, clinging to the bosom of her friend Cynthio ; and the duke, smiling, remarked that she proclaimed her own choice of father and protector.

"Dorfaux has then made the appeal he threatened !" exclaimed the count. "But surely your grace will not uphold him in his unjust claim."

The duke replied that he had before felt doubtful of the right contended for ; but that since what he had beheld of the loving protectors of the child, he should be more than ever inclined to contest the power of him who seemed inclined to exercise it rather in hate than in love ; that their kindliness ought to give them a superior authority to that of mere kindred ; that he could scarce conceive their affection to have less natural force than the tie of an unnatural father ; nevertheless, that being a grave question of right—it must be decided by law, and not by private judgment, if the chevalier still persisted in maintaining his claim.

With some farther expressions of his personal sympathy and interest, the duke took his leave ; entreating that the count would permit him to improve an acquaintance, so happily to himself commenced.

The count replied with the warmth which this gracious advance demanded, and they parted, mutually pleased.

More than pleased was Orsino. Enchanted, enamoured, with the rare beauty of Olivia, he could think of nothing, dream of nothing, but her, her alone. But as yet he hazarded no avowal of his admiration. For the present he contented himself with visiting the family, and forwarding their wishes as much as lay in his power relative to the trial of the cause which soon commenced between them and the chevalier. He contrived that it should be protracted, and judgment deferred, as long as might be; trusting that these silent attentions might win him a way to her liking, ere he risked a declaration of his sentiments.

It was hoped that the delay of the law's decision would tire out Dorfaux's patience, and exhaust his means, so that he should be compelled into yielding. It effected the two former; but when he found himself baffled, he took a resolution to have revenge, since he could not obtain profit.

His drained resources forced him to fly the country, and he determined to steal away his child, and carry her with him, as the most stinging cruelty he could inflict upon those who had defeated him.

He laid his plans well. He watched his opportunity. His knowledge of Casa Benucci enabled him to take his measures securely, and surely. One evening he got into the house; lay in wait; watched Olivia, her father, and brother, go out for a ride on horseback; knew that the child had just been put to bed; contrived to elude the vigilance of the nurse; took it from its cradle; made free with one of the count's horses, and rode away at full gallop. He was seen by one of the servants, just as he made his escape; and when the riding-party returned, they were told what had befallen.

Cynthio, scarcely staying to hear the direction Dorfaux had taken, set off in pursuit. He was much lighter, and a far better horseman than the Frenchman, besides being animated by feelings that urged him to the speed of the wind. Although some time had elapsed, yet he did not despair of overtaking him.

At a turn in the road, he saw him! He gained upon him! Faster spurred the chevalier! Swifter flew Cynthio! The houses of the capital were in view,—the shipping in the harbour, where Dorfaux meant to embark. To the very rowels the miscreant strove to plunge his spurs. The gallant beast reared, then bounded onwards.

What was it Cynthio beheld ? He saw a something white, like a stricken dove, fall from the saddle,—either jerked out of the chevalier's hold by the horse's curvet, or dropped by the dastard arm that preferred seizing its own last chance of safety.

Breathless, appalled, Cynthio darted on, and flung himself out of his saddle. Too truly had his foreboding heart told him the fatal truth! It was his darling! His bequeathed treasure! His only Astrella!

Bleeding, and lifeless it lay there, a white heap in the dust.

Tenderly he lifted the little mangled body, and bore it home.

From that hour Cynthio's spirit drooped. His heart died within him. His body gradually declined. His health, long undermined by secret conflicts, sank into habitual malady. He had no active disease ; but his frame, never strong, was now so enfeebled and worn, that it became reduced to a mere skeleton. He was gentle, uncomplaining, but he visibly languished and perished away.

Olivia tended him with all her wonted care, and loving assiduity. She devoted her time wholly to him ; and after their father's death,—which occurred about that period,—she had no object in life, to divide her thoughts with her beloved brother. All her study was how she might best cheer and sustain him ; all her faculties were dedicated to the devising means for his comfort, his consolation.

They lived a more quiet, secluded life than ever. Cynthio's state of health would not permit his entering into society ; and Olivia derived no enjoyment from that which fatigued and oppressed him. A few very old and intimate friends of the late count, still visited at Casa Benucci, and were always cordially received for his sake, by the orphan brother and sister ; but they made no new acquaintances, and accepted no invitations.

Among their few visitors, was duke Orsino. He came still ; but still delayed the declaration of his feelings, out of respect to Olivia's recent bereavement, promising himself that when her term of mourning for her father should have expired, he would then prefer his suit.

Sir Toby had returned from Venice, and was now permanently established at Casa Benucci. He had lately received a letter from England, from an old schoolfellow of his, one sir Abel Ague-cheek, written on his death-bed. It recommended to his friend sir Toby's notice, his son, Andrew, who was about to visit Italy, where the family possessed an estate, and where the new sir Andrew would in all probability settle. The letter spoke in high eulogium on the benefit of foreign travel in forming a young man, and ended by entreating that sir Toby would undertake the supervision and farthering of this desirable end; as all that the young man lacked, was a little forming.

"'Forming,' quoth'a?" was sir Toby's comment to himself, as he folded up the letter, and put it in his pocket; "I'll form him, I warrant. He shall be reformed altogether. Marry, he shall be no more a fellow of the same substance, 'neath my polishing."

As a first step in sir Toby's views upon the young knight, he introduced him to his niece Olivia ; and encouraged the young gentleman in the passion with which he was at once smitten for her. He promoted his amusement ; and initiated him into divers gay methods of spending his time and his money; he kept him entertained, and contrived himself to profit by his entertainment.

"What like is this young English knight?" said Maria to Feste, the clown, after sir Andrew's first visit to Casa Benucci. "Thou hast seen him, I know; for thou wert in the hall, and reached him his hat, as he took leave. Tell me what he is like."

"'Faith, he's like to the picture,—if such a one could be painted a speaking likeness,—of a born simpleton, and a grown natural ; but truly, of all living men, he is likest to himself;" replied the clown.

"Is he good-natured ? Hath he wit enough to be that?" asked she.

"Many a man may be pardoned folly, if he have but so much inkling of sense as to let good-nature shine through it."

"Well, he's what often passes for good-natured. He's a doughy loaf without any crust . And a loaf without its top crust,—its first letter,—is oaf."

" And those three letters sum his character ?   Sir Toby told me he was a monstrous eater of roast beef ; and that's the staple of character, as I've heard, where he comes from."

" Was that what sir Toby was telling thee, when I saw him whisper thee, in the box-tree, t'other day ; " asked the clown.

" None of thy rogue's questions, master Feste ; they'll get but scant answers from me, I promise thee ; " said Maria, turning away with a laugh, and a reddened cheek.

" I did but ask, for the sake of knowing what could be the parley that made a chuck under the chin meet commentary and adjunct ;" returned he.

" Be gone about thy business,—if thou hast aught of business, beside idling and trifling ; " she said, whisking away from him, and darting up-stairs to her lady's room.

Sir Toby, whose jovial habits nothing could restrain, and upon whose boisterous hilarity the society of his gentle niece and sick nephew acted a a restraint, gave them less and less of his company ; and associated almost wholly with Maria, Fabian, and Feste, whose gayer spirits assimilated better with his tastes.

While Olivia and Cynthio sat quietly enjoying a book, or music, in the saloon together, sir Toby would be luxuriating in a cool stoop of wine in the buttery-bar ; or discussing a bowl of Ipocras in the orchard, while Feste trolled him a merry song ; ever chatting, bantering, toying, drinking, joking, or singing.

" Give me more of that pickle-herring.   I'm athirst like the salt sea-sand, which never tires of sucking in ; " he would say.

" Pickle-herring !   How shall that mend your drouth ? " exclaimed Maria.

" What, wench ?   Doth it not provoke drinking,—and is not drink a quencher of thirst ? "

" 'Tis but a satisfaction once removed ; " said Feste ; " and happy is he that hath satisfaction so near at hand.   No farther out of reach than one remove off, is no intolerably deferred content, methinks, for poor humanity ; which mostly hath its cravings beyond mortal gratifying."

" Yonder is Malvolio pacing up and down the terrace-walk, stupidly sedate, like a fish going his rounds in a glass vase;" said Maria; "an' you keep up this noisy talk, he'll overhear you; and then he'll think it his duty to bid you be quiet, out of consideration to my lady. He's of so fractious a virtue, that reproof hath more relish to his palate than anchovy; and he indulges his taste, under pretence of regard for my lady's wishes. Be less loud, for the love of peace and quiet."

"Marry, when the knight is in his cups, he becometh over strepent;" said the clown. "As my lady's loving uncle, beseech you, sir Toby, be less nuncupative. Pity that your joys should not be joys unless they be audible. Emulate the mouse in his cheese, who nibbles on in plenitude of smothered satisfaction."

"Hang such hole and corner doings say I!" roared sir Toby. "Give me an honest open debauch! Come, Maria; let's have t'other flagon."

Sometimes sir Toby would meet sir Andrew at a place he called his cubiculo,—where he had sleeping quarters in the neighbourhood; and would take Feste with him to make merry, and sing to them. The clown had a trick of rhodomontade in his jesting, which mightily took the two knights; and he spared not to use it for their amusement. Sir Andrew doted on him; and lavished money on his singing, and praise on his wit.

"He's passing excellent at it;" he would say. "I know not whether I don't prefer it to mine own. Mine is more like a natural fooling—but his is a gift of art."

"And who shall say thou art not natural,—a very natural?" returned his friend sir Toby.

"Who indeed?" said the clown. "For so sure as Anaxarchus was no flincher, so Diodorus Siculus was as much a tapster as a stay-at-home; and how shalt thou prove the stars to be sparks, but by allowing that the moon is made of sea-water? Thou art no sager than cheese, if thou canst not dispute me these things scholarly and wisely."

Meantime, Cynthio grew rapidly worse. He could not now stir from the couch on which he had used occasionally to rest. His sister constantly occupied a seat near,—reading to him from some choice volume, or playing to him on her lute, some favorite air; breathing it, soft-toned and musical, in her sweet voice. She could not bear to quit him now for an instant; although she did not yet allow herself to own her fear that there was danger; she could not, would not, believe that he was so ill,—dying. He looked so fair, so young, it seemed impossible that he had lived out his life; that he had reached the end of his existence. But involuntarily she felt that she must husband her time with him, that she must treasure up every moment, for that they should not be long together. She grew miserly of each instant spent by his side, and jealous of each second that took her away.

The duke Orsino came one morning as was his frequent wont; but he saw that in the sitting-room they usually occupied, and into which he was shown, the brother and sister sat no longer. Malvolio, with his grave face, and stilted manner, was explaining to his grace how it was that the countess Olivia, in order to spare her brother the fatigue of descending a flight of stairs, had had the couch disposed for him in her own apartment, when Maria glided into the room, like the reflection of the sun in a looking-glass, flitting upon a wall, and said that her lady prayed the duke to excuse her from receiving him that morning, as she was in close attendance upon her brother. Orsino sent a message of courteous sympathy in return, saying that he would not detain her, but that he trusted she would indulge him with an interview, were it but for one moment, as he could not return, without a word of assurance from her own lips, respecting the condition of her brother. The duke awaited with a beating heart, the answer to his message. The door of the apartment opened, and to his disappointment he beheld Feste.

"Good fellow, I had hoped to have seen thy mistress; will she not accord me an instant, will she not come, think you?"

"She is coming, my lord;" replied the clown. "I announce the presence of my mistress, as the dial's gnomon shadows forth the blaze of noon."

When the young countess entered, she made the duke a graceful apology for having at first declined seeing him ; but owned that her brother's state was now so precarious as to make her unwilling to leave his side for however short a space of time.

The duke's manner of expressing his spmpathy with her anxiety, was so warm, so particular, that Olivia, for the first time perceived his attachment for herself. The embarrassment which this discovery occasioned her, told Orsino that his secret was guessed. He could no longer refrain from urging his suit. He told her that he had loved her from the first moment he beheld her ; that he had only been deterred from declaring his passion from respect to her filial grief; that he now besought her to listen favorably to his suit, which he trusted might find acceptance and sanction from both herself and brother.

There was something inauspicious in her manner, as she prepared to reply, that caused Orsino to add hurriedly that he would not urge an answer now ; that he would not detain her longer from her brother, to whom he entreated she would confide his proposals, as he trusted to Cynthio's friendship to dispose her graciously towards them ; and that he should hope, the next time he came to Casa Benucci, to receive with the news of Cynthio's better health, confirmation of his own happiness.

No sooner had the duke withdrawn, than Olivia hastened back to her brother.

There was a look of blushing confusion visible in her, as she reappeared, that confirmed a thought which had occupied Cynthio's mind while she was away. He had not been so long a passionate lover himself, without having learned to detect the symptoms of a silent passion in another. He had for some time marked the ill-concealed preference of Orsino for his sister, as well as the unconsciousness of its existence on her part. He saw that she had not the most distant suspicion of the duke's attachment ; but he could not believe but that when it should be declared, it would win for him all the regard from her, which the love of so noble, so well-graced a being as Orsino deserved. He had seen that this love could not rest much longer unavowed ; and when Orsino's second message was delivered that morning, pressing to see her but for a moment, Cynthio had felt that this was the occasion when all would be avowed. Olivia's countenance, on her return, told him how truly he had presaged.

He held out his hand to her, as she took her usual low seat beside his couch.

" I fear that you have dismissed his grace with less than your usual grace, sister mine ; " he said playfully. " Your love for your brother will make you scant in courtesy to your guests ; and this must not be, for the honor of our house. You know, by our father's will, you are left in the protection of your brother ; and he must take care that you consult the dignity of the family in every particular of your conduct."

" 'Tis for the honor of our house, and the dignity of the family, both, that love should take precedence of courtesy, that a brother should be held dearer than a guest ; " she replied in the same tone, delighted to find him able to rally into cheerfuller mood than had been his for some time.

" Than a guest, ay ; " returned her brother with smiling emphasis. " Orsino is our guest. The duke of Illyria is our honored guest."

" Our honored guest ; " she replied.

" Our welcome guest ; " Cynthio added.

" Our welcome guest ; " she repeated.

" No more ? " he asked looking into her downcast face.

She did not answer. And Cynthio reverted to what he had said before :—" By our father's will, he left Olivia in the protection of her brother. But in sooth, it should have been the brother who was left in the protection of the sister. Olivia's gentle bravery of heart, her loving strength, her constancy and care, make her the guardian—not I. What would become of me, poor, frail, puny youth, were it not for the courageous, noble woman ? But so it is, the manly prerogative is to be maintained ; and thus the young countess Olivia is left in the guardianship, the protection, of the young count, her brother,—the son, the heir of the house. Come then, let me exercise a little of this guardian authority, this right of protection. Do you acknowledge it ? "

" Entirely ; " she said, with her smiling eyes full on his.

" Orsino is not merely duke of Illyria ; " said Cynthio ; " he is a noble gentleman, high and honorable in principle; refined and pure in feeling; accomplished, well-gifted, brave, learned; young, and very handsome."

He paused. His sister's eyes had drooped from their open gaze. She thought :—"He wishes this alliance! Can I thwart him? Can I tell him how averse my own wishes are? Can I oppose them to his? Can I deny Cynthio aught he desires?"

The brother's thought was :—"She loves him! Let me not be selfish, and keep her by my side, when her heart has found it can love even more tenderly than it has done yet. Because her brother has hitherto possessed the treasure of her love, let him not grudge its bestowal when she herself would yield it to one, who, though he cannot return it more truly, may yet requite it more fully and happily to herself. Why should I bid her rest satisfied with brother-love, when she has learned that there is yet a dearer love? Why should I, because she is the most loving of sisters, limit her generous heart to sister-love, doom her to know none other than brother-love? The more deeply and fondly her brother loves her, the more it behoves him to take heed that his own love do not become a selfish love; nor preclude her from the joys of love itself."

"Well, what says my sister? My ward? What says Olivia to her brother,—her guardian?" he resumed.

"That Orsino is all you have described him;" she replied softly.

"And this noble gentleman, rich-gifted by nature as by fortune, has told my sister, that all the good gifts of nature and fortune are valueless in his eyes, unless she will give them their crowning value by accepting them?" said Cynthio.

"I cannot deny that he tendered himself to me,—that he professed love for me,—this very morning;" said Olivia.

"And he felt what he professed. Orsino loves you. I have long seen it;" said Cynthio.

"And oh, my brother, you wish that I should accept his love!" she exclaimed.

"Ay, if you love him;" Cynthio said.

"But I do not—I cannot love him! That is——" she paused.

"That is, you have only just discovered you love him; and so start

from the first avowing of your new-found secret.   But fear not to speak
frankly to your brother, my Olivia; think how often he has derived
consolation from his feelings being known to you.

"Dared I speak frankly to you, Cynthio mine,—dared I tell you all
that is in my heart, without fear of opposing your wishes——" she faltered.

"Speak frankly, honestly; there should be no shadow of reserve between
you and me;" he said.   "Tell me that you have not seen Orsino's
excellences without yielding them their due tribute; tell me that you have
not heard his love, without requital.   Be not afraid to tell your brother
that you have found one whom you love only better than himself.   Be not
afraid that he will be so selfish, so unworthy, as to repine at this most
natural impulse of a heart so rich in loving capability as yours."

As he continued to speak she looked up; and once more her eyes met
his with smiling, happy, open, fullness of regard.

"And it is in the thought that my heart is engaged in this suit, that
you urge it?   I might have known that my Cynthio's sole thought would
have been for his sister,—for her happiness, above all.   Dear brother,
know that my happiness is to remain with you; I seek no other love than
yours; I love none other than my Cynthio, my brother."

"But can it be that Orsino's fine qualities, his many excellences, have
failed in inspiring a yet more powerful affection?   I know my Olivia's
love for her brother—as genuine, as devoted, as noble a love as ever dwelt
in the heart of sister;—but has no tenderer feeling touched that gentle
heart?   May it not unconsciously have yielded to the worth and manly
beauty of Orsino?"

"Not a whit;" and she looked with so clear, so transparent a truth,
into her brother's face as she spoke, that he could not but give credence to the
entire sincerity of her smiling words.   "To tell thee sooth, my Cynthio,—
and now, remember, I am confessing in all honesty of avowal to my
guardian-brother,—to tell thee the very inmost of my heart, I will own
that it is not such a favor as Orsino's that could win my wayward fancy.
You speak of his manly beauty.   To please my fastidious taste, there
must be a delicacy, a grace, a subduing gentleness and sweetness, in the
youth I could love, which I do not find in my lord duke.   I could describe

to thee precisely the sort of being, to whom, methinks, I could give my whole heart, were it not that instead of painting thee a picture, thou wouldst say I but held up a mirror before thee."

"A sorry image, sister mine;" he said with his own sad, sweet smile; "what should so weakly, so effeminate-framed, so baby-faced a being as I, present, to win the liking of such a woman as my Olivia? Nay, nay, thy partiality would make me believe impossibilities. Thou wouldst as soon fall in love with a girl, as with such a girlish-looking youth as thy Cynthio."

"Could a girl look like the glorious creature I see before me," Olivia said, with enthusiasm, as she gazed upon her beloved young brother, and thought of all the noble qualities, the high heart and mind that were enshrined within that delicate face and slender form, "I should sooner be bewitched into losing my heart to such a semblance, than to the substantial proportions, and giant bulk of my lord duke. His grace's grace is not the grace that findeth grace with me. He is over tall and portly to please mine eye; his bearing too lofty and commanding to suit my taste. No, when I can find a youth, with eyes at once soul-appealing and sportive, brow white and smooth, yet with such intelligence as ought to bring wrinkles, mouth both sweet and serious, limbs of slender mould, and deportment gentle as sincere, giving earnest of the high spirit within, then, and then only will I love,—love as you would have me. Till then, I'll content myself with mine own love, my love for my brother, and with his for me."

"Best and dearest of sisters!" exclaimed Cynthio, as he drew her to his heart.

And when this well-beloved brother expired,—yielding his last breath in her arms, and blessing her for all that she had been to him,—what wonder that Olivia, in her first paroxysm of grief, shut herself up from the world, vowing to abjure the very face of the sun for the space of seven years, and observing well-nigh cloistral seclusion in her own apartment, that she might dedicate her thoughts wholly to his memory? Orsino sent hourly embassages of enquiry, condolence, and sympathy; but dreading a renewal of his suit, she sent coldly courteous replies. Her kinsman sir Toby, and her household, with a respectful observance of her mourning sorrow, pursued their own devices apart, and as far from her ken as might be.

Once however, the knight had been spending a roystering evening with sir Andrew Ague-cheek; he had sat up, the night through, roaring songs and catches with Feste, the clown, and, with him, had reeled home to the mansion at day-break. This disorderly, and ill-timed conduct, had much offended the lady Olivia; and when, some hours later, the jester came into her presence trying to disarm her anger, and make his peace, by a few of his usual sallies, she turned from him in displeasure, saying:—

"*Take the fool away.*"

How the fool was pardoned; how the wiseacre was befooled; how the lady found her ideal embodied; how the waiting-maid married the knight; and how the duke wedded a damsel-page in lieu of the countess; with "each circumstance of place, time, fortune," may now be known, since "golden time convents," and "Twelfth-night, or what you will," awaits you.

FINIS

THE

GIRLHOOD

OF

SHAKESPEARE'S HEROINES;

IN

A SERIES OF FIFTEEN TALES,

BY

MARY COWDEN CLARKE,

Author of the Concordance to Shakespeare.

"as petty to his ends,
As is the morn-dew on the myrtle leaf
To his grand sea."
Shakespeare.

TALE XIII.

HERMIONE; THE RUSSIAN PRINCESS.

LONDON:

W. H. SMITH & SON, 136, STRAND; AND SIMPKIN, MARSHALL, & CO.,
STATIONERS' HALL COURT.

1851.

TALE XIII.

HERMIONE; THE RUSSIAN PRINCESS.*

"A gracious innocent soul;"
Winter's Tale.

THICKER aud thicker fell the snow. Fiercely keen blew the Northern wind, heaping the drifts into crannies and gullies, then whirling them far and wide, as if in disdainful caprice. The gloomy fir-trees were all be-hung with mocking wreaths of sheeted white, that the next blast flung abroad in scattered showers. The murky sky lowered sullenly above all, grey, and cheerless, and hopeless; as a man,—setting his teeth hard, and facing the rough inclemency as he best might,—cast his eyes up towards the heavens' unpromising aspect, and then looked around him, with an air that plainly bespoke his having lost his way amid the solitudes of this primæval pine-forest. A bleak and desolate monotony met his view on all sides; the same endless rows of tall straight black boles, crowned by funereal branches; the same blank, trackless waste of snow under-foot; the same grey veil of mist, and lead-colored uniformity of sky, and falling flakes, overhead.

Something very like a muttered curse upon his own folly, broke from the lips of the man, as he turned in bewildered uncertainty from each new attempt to retrace the path by which he had entered the forest.

He might have been a denizen of the place, for the coarseness and even

---

* In extenuation of whatever discrepancies, or anachronisms, may be discovered in this story, the reader is requested to bear in mind, that it belongs to a play so intentionally romantic in its license of time and place, as to contain a reference to the decision of the Delphic Oracle, an allusion to Judas Iscariot, and a compliment to the works of "that rare Italian master," Julio Romano; besides a pedlar that talks of "one mistress Taleporter," and a clown that mentions "a Puritan, who sings psalms to hornpipes."

squalor of his clothing. The rough tunic and cloak of commonest sheep-skin, the bear-hide gloves, and wolf-skin cap, befitted the meanest serf,—wood-cutter, hunter, or herdsman; but his evident unacquaintance with the spot, showed him to be no inhabitant of any neighbouring hamlet. For all his peasant-garb, it was clear he was a stranger in this part of the country.

With one more perplexed look about him, he suddenly shouted aloud. The sound seemed dulled and deadened, by the damp frozen air, and the curtained canopy of overhanging trees. It seemed as though it could not penetrate through the sullen atmosphere, or make its way beyond the dense enclosure of fir-trunks. His voice, like himself, seemed pent and shut in, within the confines of this dreary wood-prison. Yet once again he shouted —once again sent forth an appealing cry for aid—if it might be that human aid was near. And then,—amid the gloom and silence,—there came an answering sound,—a cry high-pitched, but dulled by distance, and by seeming lack of power in the shouter.

The man turned his steps in the direction of the response he had heard, calling loudly and lustily himself, as he made towards the sound. It was repeated; and evidently drew nearer. Just then, he perceived that he emerged from among the thickest of the trees, into a more open space, a sort of track, or cleared pathway, leading through the forest.

Along this track, he could now see, coming towards him, a small dark figure, muffled in fur. It looked like a black bundle, more than a human being; the head was enveloped in a dark sheep-skin cap, that fitted so closely round the face, as to show only a circular nucleus containing eyes, nose, and mouth; the body was wrapped in a cloak of the like sombre, woolly wear; and the lower limbs were encased in thick leggings and boots of the same. Excepting that the head and shoulders were plentifully besprent with flakes of snow, and the small patch of face that was to be seen, looked bright and rosy, the whole seemed a moving mass, or ball, of coarse, dark, furry stuff. But the rosy patch looked cheerily; the dark leggings stumped along with an alert, assured step; and it was evident that from this small muffled individual came the high-pitched cry that had answered the man's call for help. The childish voice piped shrill and chirping, and carried with it an inexpressible sound of hope and encouragement. There was a look of resolution, of indomptable will, about this little creature, that inspired an irresistible feeling of reliance and security. She looked as if nothing would turn her from a purpose on which she had set her mind; as if her determination would surely win her purpose ; and as if whatever purpose she made her aim, it would as certainly be a right one, as a pursued and attained one.

Something of this impression was felt by the man from her look and voice, as he hastened to meet the child, saying :—" Well met, little one! You are come to me in happy time, to direct me how I may best get out of this confounded wood. Be my guide. You doubtless know every tree, every winding of the forest-path. You live hereabouts ? "

" I am a stranger in these parts ;" the child answered. " I came from the capital. I live in Kief—that is, I did live there—I am going to find a home with my father."

" And where is your father ? " said the man.

" They banished him—he's in exile—I am going to him ;" she replied.

" Going to him ! Do you know how far it is to the frozen regions whither culprits are banished, little one ? " asked the man.

" Yes ; I know it is a long way off—but I have managed to come nearly a fourth of my journey, and I shall get through the rest, never fear."

" ' Never fear ! ' But don't you fear ? It's a fearful way, and a fearful place when you get there."

" I know it is ; but if it's bad for me, it's bad for my father—and it will make the place better for him if he have his little Paulina with him, to help him bear its fearfulness."

" I am not speaking of what it is to him ; it would be more tolerable to him, I dare say, with his child to keep him company there ; but 'what I mean is, that it will be a terrible place for you—you don't know its horrors."

" Oh yes I do ; they told me of them when he was banished ; they tried to prevent my going after him; but I got away; I made my escape— I crept out of the house—I watched my opportunity—I managed to get past the sentinels at the city-gates—I have made my way on, by little and little, and I have got over a fourth of the distance. I shall reach there,

never fear." And she nodded with an assured air, as she repeated the last
words.

The man shook his head. " You don't know the place you are so eager
to reach, my little maid ;" he said.

" I dare say it's very dreadful ; but however bad it may be, home is
worse now,—without my father."

" And who is your father ? " said the man.

The child was just about to answer in her prompt, straightforward way ;
but she caught the earnest, scrutinizing look, of the stranger, as his eye
rested upon her, while he asked the question. She checked herself, and
said :—" Didn't you say you had lost your way in this forest ? Let me
see if I can't help you ; though I'm a stranger here, I seem to be more at
home than you. Do you live far from here ? "

An odd smile passed over the man's face, as he answered :—" Yes ; very
far. I have wandered among the depths of this confounded forest, till I'm
perishing with cold, and starving with hunger. I wish I could get food
and shelter. How far distant is the next village ? "

" They told me it was some miles on ;" said the child. " But I'll tell
you what I'll do for you. Instead of taking you on with me there, I'll turn
back with you, to the good woman, at whose ·hut on the borders of the
forest I slept last night. She gave me a night's lodging, and I dare say
she'll do as much for you. She has a kind heart ; and won't refuse a meal,
and a seat by her hearth, to a poor wayfarer."

The same smile passed over his face, as the man replied :—" If you
present me to her as your friend—an unfortunate fellow who has lost his
way—a poor wanderer—I have no doubt she will take me under her roof.
And truly, in this snow-storm, the sooner food and warmth may be had,
the better. But in securing them for me, you are hindering your journey,
little one. Shall you not grudge the delay ? "

" It will be but a few hours ; you need my help ; if I turn out of my
way to give it you, my journey afterwards will prosper the better ;" she
said cheerfully. " My father would rather give up seeing his little Paulina
until a few hours later, than that she should omit doing a good turn to
a poor man who wants her assistance."

" Your father is a worthy man, then ? "

"You seem to doubt it!" said the child, turning a flashing eye up towards the speaker.

"If he be so—and his teaching his child charity and kindliness of conduct, speaks in his favor—how comes it that the emperor banished him?" returned the man.

"The emperor was made to believe unjustly of my father. Enemies misrepresented his actions; his very devotion and attachment were misconstrued. My father was too proud to vindicate himself to his sovereign, even had he had the opportunity of pleading his own cause. But he was condemned unheard,—on mere calumnious report. He was banished; sent into solitary exile. I determined that at least one part of the sentence shouldn't be carried out; I determined he shouldn't live alone; so I came to join him. It was all I could do. If I could only have hoped to get at the emperor himself, I would have told him all my father's noble heart disdained to urge in his own justification. But I knew there was no hope of such a little girl as I am, making my way to court; so I gave that up, and tried to make my way to my father."

"A journey through forest and snow-storm, over frozen rivers, across tracts of barren land, easier than palace access!" exclaimed the man.

"You see I'm a fourth of my way, already, and I shall manage the rest, never fear!" said the child, with her assured nod.

Again the man smiled; and then fell into a reverie, which held him for some time silent; while his young conductress took him by the hand, and led him along the path by which she had come, retracing her way in search of the hut she had left that morning. After a time, she looked up into his face, and seeing its dreamy expression, said :—"You are feeling sleepy, are you not? Beware of that!"

"I do find myself drowsily inclined;" said the man; "the cold—the long fast—the many hours' wandering—I own I shall be glad of a moment's rest, little one; let us stop here, a few minutes." And he would have leaned against the trunk of one of the nearest trees skirting the forest-track; but the child exclaimed vehemently,—tugging at his hand, and plucking at his skirts, and pulling him onwards,—"No, no! you must not rest! Anything but stop and rest! Rouse yourself! Come on, come on!

Here, take me up in your arms, and carry me for a little way; the exertion
will do you good, and the warmth of my body will help to unnumb you.
Lift me up; be quick!"

The man laughed; but obeyed her peremptory order. There was such
an air of decision in all she said and did,—as if it were the only right thing
to be said or done,—that it was difficult to resist her commands. In the
present instance, the course she had appointed was certainly the best that
could have been hit upon for averting the threatened danger. The effort
of raising her, helped the man to throw off the immediate overpowering
sensation of drowsiness that was fast seizing upon him; and when she was
in his arms, she nestled close to him, and hugged him round the neck, and
put her bright, glowing, rosy cheek against his, in such a frank, kindly
way,—the sweet, confiding, ingenuous manner of a child brought up to
meet with nothing but gentleness from others, and to mean nothing but
gentleness herself,—that he found his burthen anything but an unpleasant
one. She was a slight child of her age, so that she was not inconveniently
heavy; yet had she been even heavier, the man, though unaccustomed to
bear such weights, would have willingly gone on carrying her, for the sake
of prolonging the amicable companionship and proximity which was thus
established between them.

"Do you know, I have just such a little girl of my own—a little daughter—perhaps a year or two younger than yourself;" said the man. "She
would have been very unhappy had anything fatal befallen me, from giving
way to an untimely nap, or from losing my way inextricably and irretrievably in this dismal forest; against both these chances you have been
my preserver; I should like my little girl to thank you for your care of
her father. I wish she could see you. What say you to coming with me
to my home, and making friends with her?"

"I should like it very much; but you live far from here, and I must
not let anything interfere with my journey to my father."

"But my home—at least, the place where my little girl now is—lies all
in your way; you must pass it, going to your father in his exile. We'll
journey together, as far as we can. I was on my way to my daughter,
when I happened to stray out of my road, and lose myself. The first con-

cern is, to get back to your friendly peasant-woman's hut, recruit our strength, and, afterwards, to devise some means of getting on. Perhaps, she can provide us with a guide."

"Trust to me, I'll guide you;" said the child, in her prompt, assured tone, and with her little satisfied nod. " I've found my way hitherto, for a fourth of my journey, and I'll find the rest, never fear. I don't suffer myself to be tempted into straying out of my path; I keep the beaten track; I have no fancy for peering into woods, and losing my way among the pines and firs of the forest."

He laughed at her sarcasm; but she looked quite grave; as if being diverted from a resolved course were much too serious a matter for a smile.

"Now you've got over your drowsiness, you can set me down again;" she resumed.

"But you'll be glad of the lift—you must be tired;" said the man; " and I don't mind carrying you, if it rests you."

"O, I'm not at all tired; I've learned to walk a good long way, now, without wanting to rest. When I lived at Kief, I used to be tired with quite a little walk, and used to make my nurse carry me; but since I've begun my journey, I've become quite a stout walker. You see it's all for the best—it was very hard at first—but it has taught me to depend on myself, and to use my legs, and my wits; so that I shall be much stronger, and thoughtfuller, and more able to be of use to my father, than before our misfortunes happened. Then, I was a poor little helpless child, only fit to be pampered, and spoiled, and waited upon; now I'm a stout, big girl, able to wait on my father. It seems as if I had grown much older all of a sudden; I can hardly believe it was so short a time ago, since it all began. But set me down, 'please. It will do us both good to be in sharper exercise. Here, let's set off at a good run ! It'll warm us—put us in a glow. Come ! One, two, three, and away !"

The man hesitated :—" I'm not in the humour to run ; " he said, laughing.

"Nonsense ! It'll do you good ! You must !" she replied. " The less you feel inclined to stir quickly, the more necessary it is you should exert yourself. It's only the numbing effect of this bleak air. It is bitter ; you feel cold quite through you,—chilled inside, don't you ? But never mind !

Nothing like a race to cure you. Now then! Give me your hand! Let's start for that clump of low bushes, yonder!"

The man yielded to her imperative manner, as he had done all along; amused by the child's dictatorial urgency, and by her evident confidence in her own right to dictate, as the wiser and more practically-experienced personage of the two.

She planned several of these running-matches, fixing the starting-posts, appointing the goals, arranging and deciding all the particulars, with her own eagerness and authority of prescription. And when they had been successively achieved, she turned to the man, and said with her little assured nod, and an air of satisfied triumph :—"Well! wasn't I right? You feel warmer now, don't you?"

He returned her nod with another; smiling, and highly entertained. But she, quite gravely, rejoined :—"Of course; and yet if I had not made you take a good run, you'd have kept creep-creep-creeping along, till your blood had become as stagnant as the surface of our Dnieper, when it's frozen into ice a foot thick. Besides, the race has not only made you warm, it has beguiled the way; for here is the good woman's hut close at hand. Now, one more stout run, and you're arrived. Give me this much start, and I'll beat you!"

The good peasant-woman received her little guest of over-night with much hearty kindness; extending her hospitality to the child's companion, and commending her for her having taken care of the poor man, who had lost his way in the forest.

"'Tis a wild place;" she said; "and when one of these sudden snow-storms come on, 'tis hard for us,—let alone a stranger,—to find the way out. Well, if a body's not lost, for good and all."

"For bad and all, rather;" said the child with her decisive nod; "and as for letting alone a stranger,—if we did that, he'd not have a chance. I've given him a helping hand as far as I can; it's now for you to do your share, and kindly to give him a meal, as you did to me last night. Your charity won't be misbestowed; for if ever my father should be restored to his own again, he'll prove to you that his little Paulina has a grateful heart, and that he is thankful to you for your care of his child. As for this poor man," she added in a low tone, " your own good deed by him must reward itself ; for he seems to be quite destitute. But the more miserable he is, the greater need for help and charity, you know."

" What I have, · he shall be welcome to ; " said the woman, half in answer, half to the man, who had overheard the child's whisper.

" Thanks, mistress ; " replied the man. " I shan't forget you ; and one day or other——" he paused ; and little Paulina finished his sentence for him. " One day or other," she said, " it may be your chance to meet ·with some poor body even worse off than yourself. Do what you can for them ; that will be the best way of returning this good woman's kindness to us. My father used to tell me,—I often find myself thinking over what he used to say, since he has been taken away from me,—that very few people have the opportunity of returning a service in equal kind, to the individual who has rendered it ; but that we can all requite a kindness received, by doing one to the next person who needs it from us."

The child said this while she was bustling about, helping the woman to spread the table, and prepare the meal. She trotted about diligently and assiduously ; making herself quite at home ; seeming to know the places where everything was kept ; and taking the lead in all useful and active proceedings.

She still kept the poor stranger under her immediate protection ;—under her wing, as it were ; providing for his accommodation and comfort, pointing a seat out for him near to the hearth ; relieving him of his outer cloak, and hanging it up on a nail ; lifting the fur cap from his head, and beating the snow out of it, before she replaced it ; hovering about him, and perpetually paying him one or other of those little fondling attentions, half cherishing, half deferential, which mark the conduct of a child towards an indulgent parent. They seemed greatly to touch and interest the man, even while their air of guardianship and familiar patronage amused him ; he was pleased with the liking they evinced, at the same time that this assumption of superiority in a child towards a grown man, tickled him immensely. He had partaken of the coarse fare set before him, and had once more drawn towards the fire, when the little girl, sitting on a low stool by his side, took one of his hands between both hers, and began chafing it,

saying :—" For all you have eaten, you are still cold ; let me rub your
fingers for you ; I'll soon get warmth into them, I'll engage."

" You take excellent care of me, my little protectress.   I am sure
I ought to be very much obliged to you.   You are as good as a little
mother to me.   What makes you take such a fancy to a poor fellow, for
whom you have done so much, and who has been able to do nothing for
you ? "

" That's the very reason, perhaps ; we generally take a liking to those
whom we have been able to help ; " answered she.   " But, I think, the
principal thing that makes me like you, is, that you told me you had a
little girl about my age, and it makes me think of my own father, when
I am doing what I can for hers."

" You long to see your father very much, then ? " said the man.

The child did not answer ; but she bent her head more closely over the
hand she was chafing, and the man could feel, after a moment or two, a few
warm drops fall upon it.   She brushed them off, however ; saying softly,
yet as if she were trying to steady her voice :—" Crying's of no use ! How
foolish to cry ! crying wont help me ! yet sometimes, when I think of
him———"

She broke off ; presently she resumed in a cheerful tone :—" What a
curious ring you have upon this finger.   It's something like one that my
father used to wear.   But his was an emerald ; and this is, of course, a bit
of green glass.   Still, it's very pretty,—it looks almost as well.   Indeed,
it's larger ; and here are some curious characters engraved upon it.   Who
gave it you ? "

" It was my father's ; " said the man.

" Then, of course, not in the worst poverty could you part with it ;" said
she.   " That would make it precious to you, though it were of less worth
than it is.   It is a false stone, isn't it ? "

" Having passed from father to son, for many generations, and from my
own father's hands into mine, it possesses a value for me beyond the most
priceless gem ; " answered he.

" And it really is pretty in itself," said the child, " and very curious.
These characters are like those I have heard my father describe upon the

Imperial signet; he said his own ring was very like the emperor's, only smaller, and quite plain. Yours is about the size,—and with just such characters. Perhaps it was made in imitation; but though it's an imitation jewel, it's very bright and pretty. It's just as good as if it were real."

" Just;" said the man. " I'm quite satisfied with it. The emperor's own signet-ring couldn't content me better."

"Ah, but it would me;" said the child. " If I had that, I'd soon use it to some purpose. I'd affix it to the deed which should repeal my father's sentence of banishment."

She turned the ring round and round upon the man's finger, as his hand still lay in hers; sighed thoughtfully; then looked up towards the still-falling snow out-of-doors, saying :—" But I am dreaming of what I should like to happen, when I ought to be working at what I can do; there is no hope of my father's recall from exile, though there is good hope of my joining him in his banishment. We stay too long. Come, let us be going."

" The afternoon is set in for a continued fall of snow;" said the peasant-woman. " Best not to venture into the forest now. Nightfall will over-take you before you can reach the village on the other side of the wood. Abide another night here; and set out to-morrow early, with the morning before you. You will be all the better for the rest—you will proceed the faster on your journey, afterwards, depend on't."

" But even if you are so kind as to let me sleep here again, and share your eldest child's cot, as I did before, how can you manage for our poor friend here ? " said the little girl, pointing to the stranger.

"The good man can lie upon this settle, by the side of the hearth; 'twill be a warm, snug berth for him; and if it be a little rough, or hard, he has lain upon many a rougher and harder, I'll warrant; eh, master ? " said the woman with a good-humoured smile.

" The field of battle is a harder couch,—stretched wounded upon the earth in the open air, is rougher lying, than upon this good settle ; " replied the man.

" You are warm now, hands and all ; " said the child. "I will leave you for a little while, that I may help our kind hostess to scrub the plat-ters and trenchers we have used for our meal, and to put them on their proper shelves. While she and I are about it, you can rock the cradle with your foot, yet still cower over the fire, and keep yourself warm, you poor chilly mortal. A soldier's life should have taught you to brave our Russian cold better than you do. By-the-by, take care and call us, if the baby should cry, while its mother and I are away. We shall not be gone long." She nodded, and vanished into an inner room, where she was soon actively employed helping the good woman of the hut in her housewifery.

While they were thus busied, the peasant chatted with the little girl, telling her of her husband, of her children, of the difficulty they had sometimes had in scraping a living, but how that they were better off this year, since her husband had got employment in one of the great timber-yards in the nearest town. That he was expected home shortly, and that then there would be feasting and rejoicing in the hut among them all.

While the woman was gossiping on, the little Paulina was struck by a sound in the outer room, as of talking. It did not reach the ear of her who was speaking at the highest pitch of her own voice ; but it was distinctly heard by the child. She listened ; she could not distinguish the words, but she felt certain that she heard another man's voice in reply to that of the stranger. The talking was carried on in a low whispered tone, but talking she assuredly heard.

She presently made a pretext to leave the woman, and return into the room she had left. The stranger was alone, and sitting in precisely the same attitude as she had left him ; bending over the wood embers, spreading his hands to catch their welcome warmth, and with one foot resting on the rocker of the cradle.

" You see, I am scrupulously obeying your commands in your absence, my little protectress ; " he said, glancing with a smile towards the cradle ; " I'm nearly as watchful to guard the babe's slumbers, as you were to prevent mine in the wood."

" I'm glad to see you can profit by good example ; " she said. " Never too old to learn a lesson,—even of a child. I fancied you were neglecting your duty ; and so, came to remind you of it. But it's all right ; I made a mistake, I see."

The next morning, at day-break, little Paulina was astir, and preparing to set out. She went to rouse the stranger, whom she found still fast asleep on the settle.

"Awake, awake! It is time we were off;" she said, as she shook him by the shoulder.

"How now!" exclaimed the man angrily, as he half started up, half opened his eyes, and looked around him in the surprise of finding himself in an unaccustomed place.

"It is a fine morning—the snow has ceased—we ought to be on our way. Come! up with you!" said the child.

"It is too early,—by-and-by—another hour's rest;" muttered the man, as he let himself fall back upon the settle, and seemed about to compose himself again to sleep.

"I can't afford to wait an hour longer—'twill throw us too late;" said little Paulina. "If you prefer another hour's sleep to having my guidance, stay behind. But, take my word; you had much better go in company through the wood. Remember how you lost yourself yesterday. Well, what say you? Decide at once; for I am in a hurry to be off."

"Since you will have it so,—I suppose I must;" said the man, yawning, stretching, and rising reluctantly. "But what a terrible tyrant you are, with your guidance, and your guardianship, my little protectress."

"It's all for your good;" returned she. "I press our setting out early, in order that we may reach the village on the other side of the wood before evening. It's well to have daylight for passing through that wild gloomy forest. I persuade you to shake off your sleep, and come with me, because I think safe conduct is better than a sound nap—that is, a prolonged nap; for you have had a good long sleep, and a good night's rest—and you don't want any more—it's only laziness. Depend on it, you'll be glad enough, yourself, by-and-by, that I forced you to your good. I shouldn't wonder if you were to thank me, when you've had time to recover."

The man laughed; while she alertly set before him the hunk of black bread, and the draught of warm milk-and-water, which the good woman had provided for their breakfast, and brought him his sheep-skin cloak, and helped to fasten it under his chin.

"You laugh;" she said, with her grave little nod; "but it's quite true. I know, myself, we're very apt to feel cross on being first awakened, and to be vexed at any proposal that is made for our good, then; but if we're given time to recover,—to think it over,—to see the right,—and to shake off our sleepiness, we're sure to come to ourselves, and do what's proper."

"Very true, little one;" said the man. "I own you're in the right; I own you have a care of my interest; I own you act for the best for me, —and I thank you, heartily."

"Very well; you can't do better than acknowledge yourself in the wrong, and another in the right, when you are convinced of the truth;" replied she. "Now let us bid our kind hostess good-bye, and set forth without delay. We can eat our breakfast as we walk along."

The weather had quite cleared up; for a Russian climate, the day was fine; and the two wanderers made their way across the forest with such good speed, that it was still early in the afternoon when they reached the village that lay immediately beyond. It was an inconsiderable hamlet, consisting of a few wood-cutters' huts. At the door of the most important looking among them,—which served as a sort of post-house, or place of public entertainment,—there stood a sledge-equipage, surrounded by a small retinue of attendants, as if awaiting the advent of the master. Little Paulina lingered a moment to admire the pretty trappings, and adornments of the vehicle, its soft cushions, its fur and velvet linings, the bright harness, and the elegant shape of the coach itself.

"It looks like a fairy car;" said she. "How pleasant it would be, if some kind spirit were to offer us a seat in it, and convey us to our journey's end; you, to see your little girl,—me, to my father! I wonder where it is going."

Her companion asked one of the men standing near, whither the sledge was bound.

"We are going to take it for our master to Igorhof;" replied the attendant.

"The very place where my daughter is;" exclaimed Paulina's friend.

"That would do exactly for us!" said she.

"As the equipage is going empty to Igorhof, I wonder whether these people would allow us to ride in it;" said the man. "I can but ask them. I'll tell them I'm not so poor as I seem; and that if they'll trust my word, I'll pay them for their courtesy when we arrive at Igorhof, where I have friends and money."

"But is that true?" asked the child.

"Perfectly true;" answered the man.

"We can but try, then;" said Paulina. "It would help us on our way delightfully. · But I'm afraid they won't believe such shabbily-dressed people as you and I; and perhaps they'll object to our riding in the fine coach, lest we should soil it, and they get into disgrace with their master. Still, we can but try. After all, if they refuse, we are but where we were."

"To be sure;" said the man. "Besides, I can offer them my ring as a pledge for the money I promise them, until we reach Igorhof."

"But as it's a false stone, they won't care to take it;" said the child. "And if they believe it real, and accept it for such, that would be deceiving them."

"Never mind, I can but try;" repeated the man.

"Well, you can try if they'll take it, when you have owned it to be false; but tell the truth. Better walk on as well as we can, than get a ride by a deception. My father wouldn't like it; I shouldn't like it. Mind you tell the truth."

"Never fear; I'll say nothing but the truth,—the exact truth;" said the man, as he advanced towards one of the attendants, to parley with him.

Paulina could not hear exactly what passed between them; but she saw the stranger show the groom his ring,—she saw that there was an explanation—a request made—and, at length, acquiescence given.

The man returned to her side. "He has consented;" said he; "and has undertaken for his fellows to agree that we shall occupy the empty carriage as far as Igorhof."

"That will be charming!" exclaimed the child. "I hope they'll not be long before they set out."

"Well done, eagerness!" exclaimed the man. "But you forget that I've fasted since day-break, and I must have something to eat. I'll go into the house, and see what's to be got."

"Well, be quick ;" said Paulina. "You can bring out your ration, and eat it here, ready to start, the moment the sledge is ready."

"Won't you come in, and have some too ?" asked the man. "You must be hungry."

"Yes, I'm hungry ; but I don't want to come into the house ; it'll only take up time. You can bring me out something to eat, here. Stay," she added, "take this ; perhaps they won't give you any food for charity ; sometimes they're very good-natured, but sometimes I've found the people at inns very harsh and grudging. If so, they'll make you pay for what you want—and I suppose you've no money. I, luckily, have enough to serve us both. See here."

The child showed a handsome embroidered purse ; and when the man expressed surprise at seeing such a thing in her possession, she told him that very fortunately her father had given her this purse full of gold for a plaything one day ; that she had rattled it, and emptied the coin in and out upon the floor, and amused herself with it as long as she liked ; that it had been thrown by, a forgotten toy, until the day when she left her father's house, to follow him into exile, when the purse had been discovered and thankfully brought with her, as a provision for her journey.

"Will not your father be displeased that you should squander your money on a stranger ?" said the man, as she held out one of the coins towards him.

"My father has always taught me, that the best use I can make of money is to bestow it on those who need it ; and though you say you are not so poor as you seem, and can command money when you get to Igorhof, yet you need it now, for present food ; so here it is ; take it."

"I must know more of your father ;" said the man, hastily. "He must be worthy himself, to teach his daughter so worthily. What is his name ?"

The child looked steadily into the man's face :—"I must know more of you," she said, "before I trust you with my father's name. He has already been undone by too generous trusting of those who proved themselves traitors."

"Traitors !" exclaimed the man.

"Don't be hurt,—or offended ;" she said quietly and gravely. "I don't say you are a traitor ; I only say I don't know enough of you to trust you with my father's secrets. If you know yourself to be no traitor, it's of little consequence even were you called so ; but since you are not called so, and since you would have me believe that you mean us kindly instead of treacherously, you will rather approve than blame me for being strictly careful of my father's safety."

" Well pleaded, little one ; quite right ; " said the man. " It is curious how often I've been constrained to own you're ' quite right,' since we have met."

" I don't know whether it isn't more honorable to be able to own another in the right, than to be in the right ourselves ; " said Paulina, with her usual grave look ; but more reflectively than usual. Her gravity was generally that of earnestness and eagerness of conviction, with the desire to impress upon those she spoke to, the truth of what she uttered.

By the time the two wanderers had partaken of some refreshment, the equipage and retinue were prepared to start. The man helped the little girl into the luxurious coach, took his place beside her, and the next instant, they were off at a smart pace. As the sledged carriage glided smoothly over the frozen snow, and the dark objects that skirted the way seemed to be flying past, and the road to be melting before them,—as she felt herself borne swiftly and easily along, Paulina could have believed herself in some pleasant dream, so delicious, so wondrous, did it all appear. She sat breathless, fixed, and perfectly upright ; unable as yet to yield herself to the full luxury of her position, in the bewilderment of its novelty.

The man, noticing her constrained attitude, and state of excitement, asked her if she would not like to lean back among the cushions, and enjoy in perfection the warm, soft, snugness and ease, of this fairy car.

" Presently ; " she said. " I can hardly yet make myself believe that it is all real ; that I am actually flying on thus, speedily, and delightfully, instead of toiling along on foot. It is like magic. It must be a fairy car, as you call it."

" Nay, 'twas your own word ; " said the man. " But, in truth, it does seem a marvellously well-contrived sort of affair, this sledge coach. See here, what commodious pouches in the side ! Well-stored, I dare swear, with comforts of all kinds. Ay, here is a shawl for the throat ; and here, a flask of some kind of good liquor. Neither exterior nor interior solace is neglected, I perceive, in this fairy car. Truly, the owner must be a fellow of some taste and ingenuity to provide thus for his accommodation in travelling."

"The credit of the arrangements may perhaps be said to belong rather to his coach-maker, or his servants, than to himself;" said Paulina. "But at any rate, I should think he would not be best pleased to see his private comforts peered into, and meddled with, and appropriated by a stranger;" she added, as she observed the man, to her great vexation, twisting the shawl round his neck, and preparing to help himself to some of the contents of the flask, by means of a small silver cup, which he found in the pouch with it.

"I dare say he wouldn't be very angry with me,—I dare say he and I shouldn't quarrel about it, even were I ever to meet him face to face; which, by-the-by, is one of the most improbable things in the world;" said the man. "How should a poor fellow like me, come across a rich great lord, such as the master of this equipage must needs be?" he added.

"You say you are not so poor as you seem;" said the child quietly. "Who knows? Perhaps you may meet him, some day or other."

"Not likely;" returned the man.

"At any rate, you ought to behave in such a way, that, whether you meet him or no, you shouldn't feel afraid to do so;" said the child.

"How do you mean?" returned the man.

"I mean that when you have been allowed to ride in his coach, when you have been suffered to enter it notwithstanding your shabby, dirty clothes, you should be careful that your conduct is neither shabby nor dirty; and certainly, taking the liberty, to wear his travelling-shawl, and drink his wine, is not the way to prove your delicacy. If you wish to be worthy the privilege accorded to you,—if you wish to show yourself grateful,—if you wish to be not ashamed to look him in the face, should you ever chance to meet the owner of this coach, I would advise you to forbear taking such unseemly freedoms with his property."

"By Jove, you are right again, little one!" exclaimed the man, laughing. "Though you do rate me so sharply, and in a style I'm little accustomed to, yet I confess you have reason in what you say."

"You think so?"

"Yes, I say so."

"Then show that you mean what you say, by following my advice. Let the things alone. Take off the shawl; put back the flask and cup. You won't wish for the wine when you don't see it. Best keep temptation out of sight. Give them to me; I'll put them away, on this side, out of your reach."

The man laughed; but did as she bade him.

"You think I'm not proof against temptation, little one;" he said. "Do you doubt my honesty? What sort of man do you take me for?"

"It is difficult to make you out exactly;" said the child, ingenuously. "You said something this morning, that made me think you had been a soldier; yet you didn't say so, absolutely. You may be an honest man enough,—but I don't know. You say you are not so poor as you seem. What is your profession?"

"Profession? I don't profess anything—I—make no professions;" he said, smiling.

"You are evading my question;" she said, gravely. "I mean, what is your trade,—your calling?"

"I am no tradesman,—and as for my calling——"

He hesitated; and the child looking steadily into his face, said:— "You avoid answering me directly about-yourself, yet you wonder that I don't tell you at once all about my father. Let us each keep our own secrets, and be as good friends, on all other points, as may be. Come, tell me a little about your daughter. How tall is she? Is she pretty? And is she very fond of you?"

"You will see her soon, I hope, and judge for yourself;" answered the man. "But in my eyes she is very pretty; and she is certainly very fond of her father."

"That may be one reason why he fancies her pretty;" said the child. "I remember I used to think my nurse pretty, because she was fond of me; but once I heard somebody say she was ugly, for that no one could be good-looking with that flat nose, and red hair, and squinting eye; so I suppose she was."

"Had your nurse all those beauties you mention?" asked the man, laughing.

" Yes ;" answered Paulina, gravely. " But," continued she, " I dare say your daughter is not so plain, as to seem pretty to you only because she has a kind and loving face, like my nurse. I can believe that she is really pretty, as well as pretty from affectionate looks, and from being fond of her father."

" And pray what may be your reason for believing this ?" rejoined he.

" Because you have rather a nice face yourself;" she said; " and children are apt to take after their fathers."

" Rather a nice face !" echoed the man, still laughing; " is that all the praise you can find for me ?   I assure you, I am accounted passing handsome ; nay, I have been told a thousand times that I am the handsomest man in all my —— in all these dominions."

Paulina looked him straight in the face, with a serious, considering air, and then said :—" No, not handsome ; good-looking, pleasant,—very good-natured,—but not handsome.   Your nose is too little,—you've got a wart upon your eyelid,—and one of your teeth rather sticks out.   They were flattering you.   But it's a nice face ;   I like it."

" I'm glad of that, however ;" said the man.   "After all, I shouldn't be surprised but you're right about those people being flatterers, who tried to persuade me I was handsome."

" Absurd !" said Paulina.

" The handsomest man in all Russia—the handsomest man of my time—they have actually said, over and over again !"

" Ridiculous !" exclaimed she.   " And impudent !   They were either joking,—laughing at you in their sleeve,—or trying to wheedle you."

" I shouldn't wonder ;" said the man, drily.

" Either way, an insult.   I wonder you didn't resent it.   Yet you were wiser to let it pass.   Only, of course, you didn't believe them."

" Humph ;" responded the man in the tone of one who half assents, half feels posed.   " But, here we are at Igorhof," he added, as the sledge drew up at the gates of a large mansion but indistinctly seen, now, through the grey twilight of a Russian evening.

" You are getting out, here ?" said the child.   " Have you much farther to go, before you reach the place where your daughter is ?"

"No; 'tis close by. Give me your hand, little one;" said the man, as she stepped out of the sledge after him; "'tis my turn to guide you, now."

He led her on,—she could not see exactly where, by reason of the deepening darkness; but it seemed to her, as though they crossed a spacious area or courtyard, in the direction of the grand mansion indistinctly seen. There was an imposing flight of steps, and a lofty entrance in front, towards which the man was making his way. But as he approached nearer, and seemed about to ascend the marble steps, he paused, and turned short to the right, as if he had changed his purpose, and led on, until he came to an angle of the building, which abutted upon a garden with terraces and trees. He stopped at a small side door, which he opened, and entered. Within, was a kind of vestibule, lighted by the softened light of a lamp, that hung at the foot of a winding staircase.

"Have you a right here? Are you not making your way into a strange house?" said Paulina, hanging back, as the man prepared to mount the stairs, still holding her by the hand.

"Trust to me—as I trusted you, in the forest;" said the man, smiling. "Trust to me, and,—to use your own word,—never fear!"

"I don't;" she replied. "That is, I don't fear you would lead me into harm, in return for my helping you when you were in danger; but I do fear doing wrong—and I shouldn't choose to go with you any farther, if you are stealing into a place where you've no business to be."

"I assure you, I am neither committing a trespass, nor leading you into any mischief, little scrupulous;" said the man. "I know the master of this house; and it is here I expect to meet my daughter. Trust me; trust my word."

"I will, though you are a stranger, and I don't like some of your ways; yet you've a true-looking face, and I'll trust that. Besides, I think for the sake of your own little girl,—whom you would not like to have led astray,—you would not willingly mislead a daughter who is in search of her father."

"Right, little one;" said the man; "I would not have it upon my conscience to swerve one inch from her path of duty, so honest, so rightminded, albeit so blunt, a little soul as thyself, for the wealth of all Europe."

As he finished speaking, they reached the top of the staircase; and throwing open a door which stood opposite to them on the landing-place, the man led her forward into a spacious room, richly furnished, hung with tapestry, and lighted by a large silver lamp suspended from the ceiling.

The man threw a hasty glance around, as if in search of some one; then, muttering :—"She will be here anon;" threw himself upon one of the cushioned couches, as if thoroughly wearied. He sat, beating his foot a little, impatiently, at first; then he fell into a fit of thought, as his eye rested upon some papers that lay piled upon the table. Presently, he drew the heap towards him, and began turning them over, when his hand was arrested by Paulina's exclaiming :—"How can you? Don't you know it is dishonorable to peer into papers that belong to others?"

"Humph! You keep a strict eye upon me, my little guardian. You don't like some of my ways? You said so, just now, you know. This is one of my doings, I suppose, that you don't approve of?"

"It is;" said Paulina.

"And the others, pray? What may they be?" he rejoined.

"I didn't like your meddling with the articles in the sledge-pockets; I didn't like your creeping into this house without announcing yourself; I don't like your fingering those papers, and prying into them, without leave. It makes me sometimes suspect—in spite of your miserable condition, which made me pity you at first—and in spite of your face, that made me like you, and think you an honest man,—that you are, after all,——"

"Well?" said the man.

"That you are,——in short, that you are——"

"Well; what?" smiled the man.

"A thief!"

The man was still laughing at this uncompromising reply, when the door of the apartment opened, and a little girl entered. She was very young, but there was such ease, grace, and high-breeding, in her air, that she seemed older than she really was. There was a refinement, a gentle dignity, a sweet sedateness of aspect, singular in so mere a child; and which bespoke her exalted rank, even more unmistakeably than the costly apparel she wore. There was a noble frankness that looked out of her eyes, a pure serenity and candour that dwelt upon her clear brows, which adorned and distinguished her far more than the rich furs and jewel-clasped velvet, that formed her attire. Her look proclaimed her a right royal child. Honor and majesty sat enthroned on that fair young face, in the midst of all its transparent innocence. She looked the fit descendant of an imperial race.

As she advanced into the room, she gazed with a quiet wonder at the two strange figures there; but looking more intently at the man,—whose coarse, rude garments at first prevented her recognizing him,—she sprang forward, and threw herself into his arms, exclaiming :—" Father ! dear father !"

He embraced her fondly in return; and for a few moments they were wholly engrossed with each other. Presently, he turned to where Paulina stood in mute astonishment at this scene, and said :—" But I must not forget my little preserver. Thank her, Hermione. I owe her my life. She helped me out of that confounded wood, where I might have wandered on till now,—or perished, starving of cold and hunger; she saved me from the snow-sleep, in which I might have been frozen to death. She guided me through all these mortal dangers; to say nothing of her keeping guard upon my morals, as well as my perils."

He was laughing heartily as he concluded; but Paulina never altered from the serious look with which she regarded him. She kept her eyes steadily upon his face, with the grave, enquiring scrutiny with which from time to time she had observed him, ever since she had had doubts of his being the poor destitute creature he had seemed at first.

" Well, little one, have you made up your mind yet about me ?" he said. " Are your notions as to what my vocation may be, still of the same favorable nature as you hinted—nay, told me plump,—just now ?"

" I have heard of robbers going out prowling in poor shabby clothes, and having a rich home, with plenty of luxuries to come to ; " she said, with her composed, straightforward way; " so you may still be what I took you for,—a thief. But somehow I don't think you are, now."

" And pray what may have altered your opinion ?" said he.

" Your daughter ; " she replied. " Since I have seen her, I think you must be an honest man ; an honorable man, a gentleman,—for all you are meanly dressed. Perhaps that may have been from some chance—some accident ; and that you are, in fact, some great lord."

" Well done ! Well aimed ! " he exclaimed. " Come," added he, " I'll make a bargain with you. If you'll tell me your father's name, I'll tell you who I am."

" As I believe you to be honorable, and that therefore my trusting you will not injure him," she said, keeping her eyes fixed upon his face, " I will tell you his name. It is Vladimir Betzkoi."

The man's brow darkened for an instant ; it contracted into a frown. But after the pause of a few seconds, it cleared, and he muttered :—" I will not believe it ; he must have been calumniated. His child's artless speeches and conduct bear incontestible proof that he must be a man of worth and probity ; I will rather credit their involuntary testimony, than those hostile allegations. At all events, I will have it looked to." Then he added aloud :—" You did me no less than justice, little one, in believing me a man of honor. So far from betraying a child's innocent confidence, and suffering it to prejudice her father, I will do what I can to make it the means of aiding him. Now that you have trusted me with his name, I will use all my power to have his case inquired into, that if wrong has been done, it may be redressed."

" You will interest your friends ! you will use your influence with them to have my father's case properly represented to the emperor ! you will do what you can for us ! " exclaimed little Paulina, her eyes sparkling with joy, and fixed eagerly and hopefully upon the man's face. He nodded, with his usual amused manner, when he looked at her, and talked with her ; and she went on :—" I remember ; you said you knew the master of this house. He must be a rich man—a powerful lord—you will interest him ? You will speak to him in my father's behalf ? "

Again the man nodded ; and again Paulina went eagerly on :—" Mind you speak earnestly ; or stay, if you will let me speak to him, I will tell him, I will explain, I will make him understand and feel, how cruelly my father has been wronged ; how deeply he has ever been attached to his sovereign's cause and person; how faithful, how loyal, how devoted he is! Will you let me see your friend, and tell him all this myself, that he may the better represent it to the emperor, and plead our cause? The master of the house! Perhaps he's at home now! Come, let us go to him at once!" she exclaimed, starting up, seizing the man's arm, and pressing it between both hers, in her eagerness.

"Softly, softly, little one;" answered he, smiling; "you forget how tired I am with my wanderings; you in your loving zeal for your father, feel no fatigue, need no rest, care for neither food nor drink; but I own I'm worn out; I must have some of all these, before I can stir a step in any matter,—even in that which my little preserver has so much at heart, and which I have so much at heart now, for her sake."

"I am thoughtless, selfish,—I forget all, in my one concern for my father; but you will forgive his daughter for her sake, won't you?" said Paulina pointing to Hermione, and then proceeding to bustle about, as she had done at the peasant's hut, lifting his cap from his head, drawing his gloves from his hands, and helping him off with his cloak.

His daughter joined her in her ministry, with her own quiet, gentle, yet decided manner; a graceful, dignified self-possession marking her air, in all she did. She moved, less with the vivacity of a child of her age, than with the elegance and staid composure of a woman grown. There was not a particle of stiffness in her bearing; but there was a remarkable placidity, and repose, in face, person, and gesture. She was, for the most part, sparing in speech; and had, throughout this scene, offered no word of her own upon what passed, though her countenance had more than once expressed surprise, with constant interest. She had stood by her father's side, the whole time, with one arm upon his shoulder, as he sat; while he held her in one of his, passed round her waist.

"You have fasted, then?—you have been delayed on your journey?—some accident?—these clothes?" she now said, in her tender voice; full of affectionate interest, though so gentle and low. "Dear father, tell me what has happened. But first you must need refreshment; I will give orders that some be brought hither, that you may not have to leave this couch; you know you like to have a snug little meal in your Hermione's room. They shall bring supper here."

"Ay, let it be so;" he answered. "And Hermione," he went on, beckoning her to lean down and listen to something that he whispered in her ear, in addition. She looked in his face with a smile of amusement reflected from his own, as he concluded; and then glided swiftly from the room to give her orders.

"Your hands are very different now, from the poor, numbed, frozen things, they were in the forest hut;" said little Paulina, as she laid one of hers on the back of his; "they are in a nice glow, arn't they."

"Ay, but my feet are not so warm; they are very cold,—cold as stone;" said the man.

"That mustn't be;" replied she. "Stay, let me draw off your boots, and chafe them for you; I used often to do this for my father, when he came home cold-footed; and he always said no one chafed his feet so comfortably, and made them so cosy, as his little Paulina. Here, hold out your foot;" and she knelt down beside him; "I'll soon have the boot off. Now the other! That's it! And then I'll sit upon this little stool, and you can pop both feet upon my lap—and I'll have them warm as a toast in a trice."

"You've taken up all your first liking to me again, since you've found out for certain I'm not a thief?" he said laughing. "You pet me, and make as much of me, now, as you did in the hut, when you told me you liked me because you had been able to help me."

"Yes;" she answered, with her quiet gravity. "By-the-by," she added with sudden animation, "you have never kept your part of the bargain! You were to have told me who you were, you know."

"Patience, patience; all in good time;" said he laughing.

"'Patience!' I think I have been very patient;" she said. "If I had not been very uncurious,—my father used to say I was the least inquisitive child he ever knew,—I should have tormented you long since to keep your word and tell me."

"Well, I'll tell you soon,—presently."

"'Soon!' 'Presently!' Oh, that's very unfair! I told you at once my secret—and now you put me off about yours. That's very unfair!"

Just then, Hermione returned, followed by a train of servants, with preparations for the meal. Some spread the table; while others drew near to the couch where the man sat, bearing a furred dressing-gown, and slippers.

Paulina put out her hand for the latter.

The attendant would have withheld them; but, at a sign from the man, gave them to her. She put them carefully on his feet, saying :—" They're as warm as your hands now, arn't they ? Now for your wrapping-gown." The other attendant stepped forward, about to hold it ready ; but Paulina took that also from his hands, with " No, no ; give it me ; I'll put it on. I'll step on the stool, on tiptoe; and I shall be able to reach."

" Let her do it ; " said the man quietly, and with his amused smile.

" You've never answered my accusation, you know; " she resumed. " I said it was very unfair, and so it is, not to keep your bargain with me. If you're not a thief, you break your promises, and that's nearly as bad."

There was a stir, and a look of amazement among the attendants ; but the next moment it subsided.

" Is not that rather a rude way of reminding a person of his promise ? " asked Hermione, with her calm smile.

" I don't mean to be rude, but I speak the truth ; " said Paulina, in her grave way, which was too sincere, earnest, and straightforward, to be insolent, though it was often startlingly vehement. " I observed my part of the bargain at once ; I put myself in your father's power by trusting him with the name he asked, and I expected he would keep his word with me in return."

" He will do so, be sure ; " said Hermione, smiling, and looking at her father.

He nodded, laughingly saying :—" But let us have some supper first. You say you are not of a curious nature ; so it will be no pain to you to suspend the cravings of your curiosity, while I satisfy those of my hunger ; which are urgent, I can tell you."

He chatted gaily, and seemed in high spirits, and very happy, as he sat between the two little girls ; his daughter Hermione on one side of him, Paulina on the other,—both waiting on him, with those affectionate, familiar, half-playful, half-tender attentions, that belong to the intercourse between children and a grown person whom they like.

" How came you to tell me such a fib about your daughter ? " said Paulina suddenly.

" How do you mean ? " was the reply.

" You told me she was pretty, didn't you ? "

" Yes ; don't you think her so ? "

" No ; she's very different from pretty. She has the most beautiful face I ever saw. It's like what I fancy a queen's must be. It looks as if a crown would sit well upon it. Her temples are so white, so high, and so noble ; her eyes are like the deep blue of the summer heavens, and look as still, and as clear ; her mouth is firm, yet kind. Yes, even when it smiles, as it does now, it looks as if it half disdained to hear its mistress's beauty praised to her face."

" You hear how whimsically plain-spoken she is ; " said the father of Hermione to her. " She told me just as openly,—but far·less complimentarily,—what she thought of my face."

" Of course ; why shouldn't I ? " said Paulina. " I dare say, now, " continued she to Hermione, " your love for your father makes you think him handsome. He says he is accounted to be so. But surely you must own, if you look at him soberly and impartially,—without thinking of him as your father, you know—that he is anything but handsome ; rather plain than otherwise."

There was the same stir, and tokens of amazement among the attendants as before ; but as before, it subsided, at a glance from Hermione's father. Paulina saw neither the amazement, nor the glance ; but went on, intent upon what she was saying.

" You see he has a very little nose—almost a snub ; and though his eyes are fine, yet there is a wart near the left one ; and then he has an odd tooth that projects just there, and gives a queer, droll effect, to his mouth, which is otherwise very well shaped, and has full, red,—indeed very beautiful— lips. He has just that sort of face which might be handsome, but which isn't handsome ; it is much better than handsome, I think. It's a face one likes to look at again and again, instead of admiring it like a picture, and then have done with. It's a face pleasant to welcome, unpleasant to bid good-bye to. It's a kind of face one's always glad to see, and always sorry to part with."

Hermione gazed fondly upon the face in question, and smiled acquiescence with the truth of what was last said of it.

" Then you wouldn't like to know you were never to look upon it again,
—for all its ugliness ; eh, little one ? " said the owner laughing.

" ' Like to know ! ' " she repeated, with more than even her usual gravity ;
" it would make me very unhappy ; I have taken a great fancy to your face
—to you—I should be very very miserable if I thought——"

The child stopped ; with a break in her voice that was even more eloquent than speech.

The man was touched with the artless evidence of liking in this sincere-
spoken little creature. After the pause of a minute, he said :—" Come, give
me a kiss upon this ugly cheek of mine ; or, if you like better, upon these
lips that you are pleased to think not so poorly of ; I'll promise you, that
you shall hereafter see as much of this homely face that you've taken a fancy
to, as you could wish. You and I are friends for life ; for you saved mine,
remember."

" If she don't remember it, we ever will, will we not, my father ? " said
Hermione, as Paulina stood on tiptoe beside him, and gave him the kiss he
had asked, heartily, and affectionately ; saying at the same time, with playfulness :—" I trust to this promise, though you broke the other. I'll
believe you will keep your word, that we shall be always friends, though
you have not yet kept your word, and told me who you are. I ought to
have held back my kiss, till I knew who claimed it."

" I have a father's right to it ; " answered he. " I am your father, while
your own is away."

" My father ! " she exclaimed.

" Your father ! " he repeated ; the father of all my subjects,—the father
of my people. I am the emperor of Russia."

Paulina stood gazing at him fixedly, in utter astonishment. Her face
worked eagerly ; her breath went and came. Then she dropped upon her
knees, flung her head on his, and clasped them round, as she exclaimed :—
" My father ! My own father ! Think of him ! Grant him his freedom !
Pardon him ! "

The emperor kindly bent over her, and spoke soothingly.

Presently she started up. " Yet why do I say, ' Pardon him.' He has
done nothing that needs pardon. He has been ever loyal and faithful.

VOL. III.

Do him justice ! Search into the truth. Redress the wrong that has been
done him ; and restore to yourself a devoted officer and servant !"

" If only for his child's sake——" the emperor began.

But Paulina vehemently interrupted him with :—" Not for mine ! Not
because I happened to do you a service ! But because he himself deserves
to be freed—he who has been punished as a traitor, when he was none."

" Never fear, little Conscientious !" said the monarch laughing. " Entire
justice shall be done. Your father shall have the benefit (as I fully believe
it will prove to him) of a close investigation into his case. Will that satisfy
you ? "

" Quite ; " she said in her grave way.

" And moreover, perfectly to content your scrupulous jealousy for your
father's honor, I will tell you, that I was about to say, when you interrupted
me just now, in that blunt style peculiar to your sincere little self—showing,
by the way, how completely your little ladyship is unaccustomed to a court
—that it was for his child's sake I felt inclined to recall him from exile ;
not because she was the means of saving my life ; but because, from what
I learned of her mode of acting, feeling, and speaking, I am convinced that
he who instilled such principles must be a man of probity, of truth, and of
honor ; and therefore had been wrongfully banished."

Paulina said nothing ; but she took the emperor's hand in both hers, and
hugged it against her full heart, while she looked him straight in the eyes,
with her own brimming over.

" And now, you will satisfy my longing to know all your adventures,
my father, will you not ? " said the calm sweet voice of Hermione.

" I will tell you the whole story ; " said the emperor, drawing her within
his arm, as before ; while he left his other hand in the grasp of Paulina.
" I was on my road hither from Kief to see thee, when the sledge was by
accident overturned, just on the borders of the forest. My people helped
me into a sort of miserable cabin,—the nearest at hand ; and as my clothes
had become wet with the snow, even in the short distance I had to traverse
between the overturned vehicle and the hut, when I arrived there, I donned
some of the good man's dry apparel in lieu of mine own, until they could
be rendered fit for me to resume. To this end, they were hung near the

embers ; and while the process went on, I, to beguile the time, and feeling stifled with the smoky, close-pent atmosphere of the cabin, strolled forth into the open air. The snow-storm had abated ; besides, the peasant's coarse, but impenetrable garb, kept me well protected against the weather. I wandered on, striking into the forest ; and, interested with a scene so wild, and to me so unwonted in its near aspect, I unconsciously proceeded farther than I was aware ; until, at length, the snow beginning to fall thickly again, I woke up to a sense of danger,—that I was losing my way,—that I should be unable to retrace it,—that I should find difficulty in making my people aware of my situation. I shouted ; but in vain. I plunged desperately on ; but felt that I only involved myself farther, and that each step but diminished the chances of rescue. In this perplexity, I encountered my little friend here ; who kindly took me in hand, and managed for me, when I could not have helped myself—emperor of all the Russias as I was— and bit of a thing as she was. I was immensely entertained at the utter unsuspicion she evinced of our relative situations—or rather at the peculiar view she took of them ; conceiving herself to be the protectress, and I the helpless dependant,—as indeed I was, under the circumstances. I resolved to maintain this state of things between us, as long as I could ; and chance befriended my determination. While we were housed at her friendly peasant-woman's hut,—whither she had conducted me for present shelter, food, and rest,—it happened that my faithful equerry, Ivan, joined me, having found where I had taken refuge. He had set out in search of me, the instant he learned I was missing, and had succeeded in tracking me thither. It was while Paulina was in the inner room, with our good hostess, that he entered the outer one where I sat. He could hardly restrain an exclamation of joy, when he discovered me ; but I made him a signal of silence, and in a low voice, rapidly explained my desire that he should go back to his fellows, bid them meet me on the following day with the carriage at the village post-house, and observe, with them, the utmost care in avoiding any betrayal of my identity."

" Ah, I thought I heard voices !" exclaimed Paulina, who had been listening breathlessly to this account ; " low as you spoke, I heard you ! "

" You're a terribly vigilant little guardian, as I know ;" said the emperor laughing ; " shrewd, observant, penetrating ; and as strict a monitress, as watchful a guardian. You will protect the unfortunate, helpless stranger, carefully, nay tenderly ; but you will not be unmindful of his slightest deviation from uprightness, or overlook his most trivial approach to error."

" Your instructions were obeyed, my dear father, and you were able to remain unknown for any other than the poor man you seemed ? " said Hermione.

" All went well ; " replied her father. " The sledge met us at the place appointed ; and the men played their parts to perfection. Little Scrupulous here, had not a suspicion but that she obtained a flight in a fairy car, by the most singular piece of good fortune—although quite honestly, or she would not have had it. If she had known there was the least spice of deception in the matter, she would have disdained acceptance."

" The carriage was your own—what better right could you have had to a ride in it, or to give me one ? " said Paulina.

" You have me there, little one ; " said he. " Well, when we arrived here," he resumed, turning to his daughter, " she must needs take it into her head that I was a burglar, stealing into a strange dwelling-house, and roundly she took me to task for my evil deeds, and for endeavouring to make her an accomplice. But I found means to pacify her suspicions, until your appearance did them all away, teaching her to confide in the belief that your father was an honest man ; as I have come to the same conclusion, respecting her's, through a like guarantee. Well is it for a parent, when his child's ingenuous face vouches for his own integrity."

Paulina's father was recalled from exile ; his innocence triumphantly proved, while he himself was reinstated in all his former possessions ; the emperor graciously and distinctly signifying that it was a simple act of justice, and that he himself rejoiced to have a faithful subject restored to his service. Vladimir Betzkoi was an officer in the Imperial guard ; had been traduced, and, too proud to vindicate himself to a master, who he thought should have known his worth and loyalty, had submitted mutely to his sentence. On his return, he found his little daughter in high favor at court. She was encouraged and indulged by the emperor, who took a strange fancy to that familiarity and blunt sincerity in her, the least approach to which, he would have so strongly resented in any other being. They were natural to her, a part of her character, and had become known to him under such singular circumstances as had given them a certain charm and interest. There was the freedom of childhood in them, all unconscious of the conventional observances due to rank and majesty; there was the unreserve of strong personal liking in them, peculiarly winning to one accustomed only to professions and displays of attachment, of which there could be no genuine test, and which were open to the suspicion of originating in self-interested motives. Next to his own child Hermione, the emperor best loved the little Paulina. In the first he took a fond pride ; he felt an affectionate admiration for her noble character, her pure beauty, her high-minded excellence. With the latter he was amused ; he was entertained by her steady gravity when she spoke of things that seemed to her serious and important ; and was excited by her frank and spirited mode of speech at all times. He was glad to have a girl of her sterling principles, and strong sense of rectitude, as a companion for his young daughter. Hermione,—herself of a noble disposition, exalted in spirit, as well as in birth, grand-hearted, lofty-natured,—took a great liking to Paulina ; and had for her that firmest and most enduring of regards, an attachment founded on confidence, esteem, and respect. They grew up together, less like princess and dependant, than friends. There was little of expressed affection between them ; for neither of their natures was formed for giving outward tokens of preference. Hermione's was concentrated, steadfast, undemonstrative ; her feelings rather profound, than apparent. Paulina's nature was full of ardour, and her feelings powerful ; but she was apter to be vehement in indignation, and more frequently roused to energy and warmth in denouncement, than moved to evidences of fondness or partiality. Each knew she could rely upon the other's faith, constancy, devotion, if need were ; but in the ordinary course, there was little question of either existing between them. The military duties of Paulina's father, necessarily detaining him much from home, Hermione made it a point that whenever he was absent, his daughter should sojourn

with her; and as the princess attained more years, Paulina was enrolled
among her ladies of honor. The indulgence of the emperor, and his confidence in his daughter's prudence and discretion, left Hermione almost
uncontrolled mistress of her pursuits, and pleasures; while his fond
munificence delighted in surrounding her with all the luxuries and refinements belonging to her station.

She spent a large portion of her time at Igorhof,—a delightful summer
palace which the emperor possessed at some distance from the capital. It
had extensive grounds and gardens, and had been fitted up for a beloved
wife, by an ancestor of the emperor's, in a style of great magnificence, and
exquisite taste. Here, the young Hermione, and her four favorite ladies,
Paulina, Emilia, Olga, and Rogneda, passed the hours in the studies and
recreations proper to their season of life ; and when the emperor could be
lured from Kief to make one of the rural party, his daughter's satisfaction
was complete. At other times, the princess and her train accompanied
the emperor to court ; where the highest intellectual society that could be
commanded, was drawn together ; foreigners renowned for their attainments
being won to join the Imperial circle whenever they visited the Russian
metropolis ; men of genius and learning from whatever quarter they
presented themselves, being eagerly welcomed by a father's anxiety to
secure for his child all the opportunities of culture, so fair, and so
naturally-gifted a young creature, alone required to make her a paragon.

The fame of her beauties and excellence, had already extended far and
wide. Embassies from numerous foreign courts brought offers of alliance.
Wherever these was a kingdom possessing a prince of a marriageable age,
—an heir to a crown requiring a consort,—straightway an emissary was
sent, treating for the hand of the incomparable Hermione.

Hitherto the emperor had turned a deaf ear to all these proposals,
affirming that as yet his daughter was too young, and that he could not
bear to think of parting with her. But at length a proffer came on the
part of the king of Sicily, in behalf of his son,· prince Leontes, so
advantageous to Russia, so conformable to the emperor's views, so tempting
to him in every particular of its proposals, that he hesitated ere he sent
a negative in reply, as he had till now promptly and immediately done.

He bade the two embassadors, Camillo and Antigonus, do him the favor to abide his consideration of their master's suit; and meanwhile to make themselves assured of a warm welcome, and a desired sojourn in his good city of Kief.

There was another reason, besides the political advantages presented by this alliance, which induced the emperor to think of it; this was, a doubt he had entertained latterly concerning a certain youth, named Alexis. He was an orphan; the child of a younger sister of the emperor's who, when a mere girl, had fled from the palace, and united herself with a man of neither fortune nor birth. This marriage, which, in its clandestine circumstances, and its inequality of match, he held a disgrace and a degradation, so deeply wounded the monarch, that he never forgave, or beheld his sister, after. The name of the princess Eudoxia was banished from courtly lips, in imitation of the silence observed by Imperial ones. The emperor seemed to have forgotten that such a being had ever existed; but when, on her widowed death-bed, she sent him her orphan son, he showed that he was true to the memory of the early love that had been between him and his sister, by adopting the boy, and having him brought up beneath his own eye. The young Alexis had shared the tuition, with which a father's care had supplied Hermione; and the two cousins had grown up in all the intimacy and affection of their mutual relationship. He was a remarkably handsome, vivacious youth; and it was only lately that the emperor had perceived he was fast becoming a remarkably handsome, vivacious, and attractive young man. He was lively-mannered, accomplished, and peculiarly deferential in his manner towards women. He had passed so much of his time in the society of the princess and her ladies, that he possessed that softened manner and refined address, which belongs only to men accustomed to the company of women—to a man habitually domesticated among them.

It struck the father, that when he had proposed to Alexis remaining with him at Kief, instead of accompanying Hermione and her train to Igorhof, when last the princess repaired thither, the young man had discovered not only eagerness, but embarrassment and confusion, in the impetuosity with which he had urged his wish to go with her. The emperor had not particularly remarked this, at the time; but it had since recurred to him with significance.

"Can it be," thought he, "that the boy has dared to look upon my daughter with other eyes than those of the reverence and humble devotion befitting the child of his protector, his patron? Is there to be another misplaced affection? Another unsuited inclination?—more shame—more misery? Is my noble child to be drawn into unworthy liking, by a mean insinuator, the parallel and son of the man who betrayed a previous victim,—high-born, innocent, inexperienced, as herself? If so, I cannot too soon withdraw her from even the chance of such destruction. What better means than to affiance her to a noble, a royal husband? Once betrothed—once given her plighted word—and I know my Hermione's high nature too surely to fear that she would suffer her eye to be betrayed, her heart to be lured from honor, from duty. It would be a safeguard to preserve her from a moment's thought of this pretty squire,—this lady's page and plaything, this youth, this boy, Alexis,—should he have dared to play the man, and fancy himself a lover."

The emperor lost no time in repairing to Igorhof, that he might see and question his daughter, determining at once to resolve his doubt. He knew too well the candour, the pure, and perfect ingenuousness of her character, to fear for an instant, but that he should learn the truth from herself.

He found her, seated amidst her ladies, embroidering; while her young cousin read aloud, from a scroll,—a Greek poem, that had lately reached the Russian court.

The suddenness, the unexpectedness of her father's arrival and entrance, caused a bright color to mount into the cheek of Hermione,—generally rather pale than otherwise; but it was the blush of joy, the glow of open animation and delight, with no one mingling of consciousness or confusion, which heightened her complexion, and sparkled in honest pleasure from her eyes. Almost in that one look, her father was satisfied. Almost by that look, he felt her heart was solely occupied with a daughter's happy, untroubled, assured love. He cast a hasty glance at Alexis; who had made a somewhat abrupt withdrawal from his close vicinity to the ladies' embroidery-frame, near to which he was seated, at the moment of the emperor's entrance. The youth's face did not exhibit quite so un-embarrassed an expression as the princess's; but he seemed no less glad than herself to see the emperor; and came forward, and bade him welcome, with the wonted graceful mixture of affection and deference, that marked his manner towards his uncle and benefactor.

The emperor, signifying his desire to be left alone with his daughter, her ladies, and Alexis, withdrew.

In the conversation which ensued, her father showed the reliance he had upon Hermione's truth, honor, and good sense. He spoke gently, kindly; but simply, and plainly. He told her the views he had for her; the intention he had formed, that her marriage,—whenever she might wed,—should reflect honor on herself, by the worth and honor of him she wedded; should give assurance to her father of her future welfare, by the unblemished lineage, and personal merit, of the man who was to become her husband; and should at the same time promote the interests of her native land, by securing for it, through her means, advantageous con-nection and union with some other nation, whose friendship as an ally it was essential to gain. He told her, that as a royal princess, it was her duty, no less than it doubtless would be her pride and preference, to make such a choice, as should prove that her country's welfare, her ancestors fame, and her own honor, were her dearest considerations.

Hermione echoed the word 'choice' with so light,—so almost gay a tone, as she playfully asked her father whether it might ever be a princess's fate to 'choose' in marriage; that he felt reassured—at ease—with respect to her entirely disengaged heart.

He replied, in her own tone, that a princess had sometimes so much of the right of choice as belonged to womanhood generally, in these matters; the right to choose among her offers, which she should accept, which she should reject,—among her suitors, whom she should encourage, whom she should dismiss.

"Then dismissal, refusal, denial, to one and all, shall be my choice, for the present, dear father!" she exclaimed gaily. "I care for neither suitor nor offer,—marriage nor alliance, just now; that is, inasmuch as regards myself. For, you must know, I have another match in my head, and so nearly at heart, to bring about, that I have neither head to dream with, nor heart to give away, in love affairs of mine own."

"And pray for what, and for whom may your highness be plotting, and taking up the unsatisfactory office of match-maker?" said the emperor, pleased at finding more and more confirmation of relief from his suspicions. "Beware you are not disappointed. Match-making is seldom profitable, either to the promoter, or the objects, of the proposed match. But who are they?"

"Alexis and Paulina;" replied his daughter. "I suspect he is beyond plummet's depth in love with her; and I am much mistaken if she be not brought to return his attachment. He is never happy but in company with me and my ladies; and I know who is by far the most admirable among them,—Paulina. It must needs be her. But I shall keep strict watch upon them both; and when I have discovered their secret, I shall pray you, my father, to give him that commission in the army which you have always promised shall be his, when he is of age; and which will ensure him fortune sufficient to maintain such a wife in the position she deserves."

The emperor, smiling at her warmth of zeal, yet well contented that it should be friendship, and not love, which had called it forth, promised her that all should be as she wished, regarding the provision for Alexis, in case she discovered that he desired to marry Paulina.

"She has been summoned to Kief by her father, who is at present in the capital, and wishes to have her with him;" said Hermione; "but when she returns hither, I shall not fail to aid Alexis in bringing her to a discovery of the preference with which I am sure she returns the one he feels for her."

"Meantime," said the emperor, "try and withdraw your unselfish thoughts for your friends' happiness, from them for a time; and see if you cannot bring your mind to bear calmly and seriously upon what I have to propose for your own, my child."

He spoke gravely and impressively, yet very tenderly. He told Hermione of the embassage from the king of Sicily, suing for her hand in the name of his son, Leontes. He told her how fair a renown the young prince enjoyed, as a scholar, and a gentleman; as being well-graced, well-accomplished, generous-tempered, and handsome. He told her how well a father's pride and affection would be contented, in having her united to one who bore such a reputation; he told her how entirely his kingdom's interest would be consulted, by the fulfilment of this proposed alliance.

Hermione listened calmly, seriously. Then she placed her hand in his, and said :—" I have no will but yours. Dispose of me as best seems to you. I have no wish, but to fulfil your desires. They, I know, are for both our good. Be it as you think fit."

Her father pressed her to his heart, proudly, fondly.

On the emperor's return to his capital, he called a council, and stated his determination to bestow his daughter, the princess Hermione, in marriage with the heir-apparent to the crown of Sicily, prince Leontes. He then convened an assembly, in which he received the Sicilian embassadors, Camillo and Antigonus; and signified to them his willingness to accede to the proposals of their royal master. They were to return to Sicily, bearing with them the emperor's consent; and when all conditions on either side were finally agreed, the embassadors were to come once again to Russia, and, the ceremony of solemn betrothal concluded, to carry back the princess Hermione as the bride of the prince of Sicily,—where the nuptials themselves were to be celebrated.

The appointment of these particulars occupied some considerable space of time; so that several weeks elapsed between the arrival of the Sicilian embassadors in the Imperial city of Keif, bringing their king's proposal for the hand of the Russian princess, and the period of their departure, when they carried back with them the emperor's pledged and written word of compliance.

These weeks had been spent by Camillo and Antigonus, and their suite, in a succession of visits, at the houses of the various noblemen who formed the Imperial court. Each of these latter had vied with the other, who should most hospitably receive and welcome, personages distinguished by

the emperor's express recommendation, and countenance. It soon became
bruited about, that there was every probability of the Sicilian king's proffer
being acceded to ; and every one was eager to show attention to, and form
amicable relations with the members of a state shortly to become allied
with their own. Among those who strove most to make his house acceptable
to the distinguished strangers during their sojourn, was Vladimir Betzkoi.
He pressed the two embassadors to make his mansion their home ; and sent
for his daughter Paulina to come thither, that its comfort and attraction
might be secured, by having so fair and so competent a mistress of his
household to preside over its arrangements.

The domestic party thus formed, became mutually pleased with each
other. General Betzkoi was a man of quick observation, and intelligence,
had profited much by the extensive travel, which his military life had procured him, and was an agreeable, conversational companion. He was proud,
sensitive, and the very soul of honor. The lord Antigonus was a shrewd
worldly man ; a complete courtier, versed in the intrigues and manœuvres
of a diplomatic life, and accustomed to the expediency, and unscrupulous-
ness in exigence, of a statesman. He had the air of being extremely yielding, full of concession and agreement, in colloquy ; but he was a man who
made up his mind secretly, and followed out his own convictions and intentions quietly, but implicitly. He never contradicted ; he never showed
that he dissented from any expressed opinion, however he might internally
disagree with it; but he entertained a private judgment, and acted in con-
sonance with that. He was a general favorite, from his complaisant demeanour, and his appearance of coinciding with those who conversed with him ;
his company was liked, his intercourse sought, and his friendship prized, as
a kindly, good-hearted, obliging man ; but in fact, his kindliness originated
in love of ease, his good heart consisted in self-love, and his obligingness
never took a more active form than obliging words, and never went beyond
an assiduous care of his own interest.

Camillo, his colleague, was a man of sterling honesty, sound sense, and
generous feeling. He was a man of no distinguished rank ; but of gentle,
though not noble birth. He had made his way from obscurity, by his own
talent and integrity ; tokens of both had come to the knowledge of the young

prince Leontes, and he, with the judgment which was generally and deservedly attributed to him, brought Camillo forward, advanced his fortunes, allowed him scope for his abilities, enabled him to prove his desert, and finally made him his own friend and counsellor. It was owing to the young prince, that Camillo was appointed envoy to Russia in conjunction with the lord Antigonus, on the occasion of the king of Sicily's treaty of marriage between his heir and the emperor's daughter, Hermione.

Camillo was considerably the junior of his brother embassador ; but while the years, and experience of lord Antigonus obtained him general ascendancy, the known favor of the prince, and his own obvious merits, gave the younger great influence, and caused him to be regarded with universal favor and respect.

During their stay with General Betzkoi, the frank graces, the sensible conversation, and spirited beauty of his daughter Paulina, had made a powerful effect upon both the visitors. But Camillo, with the strict uprightness, and singleness of purpose that distinguished him, resolved to suppress his incipient passion, and to defer all consideration of its interests, until those of his royal master's wishes had been fulfilled. He determined neither by word or look to betray his feelings to Paulina or her father, until he should have returned from Sicily with the mutual agreement of the two courts respecting the projected royal marriage ; and then he would endeavour to effect his own with the woman whom above all her sex, he desired to call his wife. The lord Antigonus was withheld by no such nice scruples from endeavouring at once to secure the prize he had in view ; he thought he could not too early make sure of so beautiful a girl, who moreover, was the favorite of her who in all probability was destined to become his future queen ; he therefore immediately, although privately, declared his love to the father of Paulina, and asked her hand of him ; but, with a prudent eye to appearance, and judging that it would not tell well, that he should be attending to his own concerns, whilst those of the king were yet unsettled, he made it his request that the engagement should remain secret, until he could come to claim the hand of his betrothed bride, at the same time that he returned to fetch the future consort of his prince.

Vladimir Betzkoi eagerly closed with the proposal ; pleased with the

prospect it afforded, of providing his child with a permanent home beside
her to whom he knew she was so strongly attached ; and he told Paulina
of the consent he had given, confident of her glad acquiescence with an arrangement that promised so happily.

"I knew a husband must be my fate, at some time or other ;" was her
answer to her father's intimation; "I have long made up my mind to endure
the impending evil, when its time shall arrive.   Let me thank my stars for
the reprieve.   Who knows what may happen in the interval ?   My future
lord and master may repent of the engagement, and never come back to claim
his betrothed spouse.   Meantime, I have several good months of freedom."

Her father could not discover, from her light tone, what were her precise
feelings with regard to the engagement he had made for her : but he saw
she offered no objection ; and that was, he thought, all he had to expect,
from a young girl accepting a suitor for her hand.

Her friend and mistress, Hermione, had a nearer view of what her sentiments were upon the subject ; when, a few days after the departure of the
embassadors, Paulina had returned to Igorhof, and the princess sat with her
favorite lady,—the embroidery-frame furnishing a pleasant occupation for
hands and eyes, while they were engaged in interesting talk.

"And now tell me, Paulina,—now that we are alone, (Alexis would
fain have stayed, but I bade him escort Emilia, Olga, and Rogneda, through
the gardens, to see if my little friends in the aviary are well cared for)—tell
me if thou bring'st back the same heart, thou bor'st with thee to Kief.
A capital, and a court, are sore places for the beguiling and losing of
hearts.   Hast thou thine safe yet ? "

" Safe and sound ; safe in mine own keeping, and sound from any scratch
of the blindfold archer-boy's shafts ;" said Paulina, laughing—though
a little constrainedly.   "But though my heart's free, my hand's fettered.
Fathers have a right to forge a golden link for our finger, that is apt to
set an iron one upon the wrist ; and we find ourselves bound hand and foot
for life, before we've tried the use of our limbs, or found out whether
we've a heart or not, to wish to guide them after our own fashion."

"'Fettered! bound!'   How mean'st thou ?" exclaimed Hermione.

"My hand's fettered by a promise ; I'm bound to become a wife, whenever my husband comes to fetch me;" said Paulina. "I'm engaged,— betrothed. My father has accepted the offer with which lord Antigonus honored me; and has passed his word that I shall become his wife, when he shall come to claim me."

"And when is that?" said Hermione.

"When he returns from Sicily to escort you thither, madam, as the bride of his prince;" answered Paulina. "There is this bright point in my lot; I am not to be separated from her I love better than any man of them all."

"Then thou lov'st not this lord Antigonus?" said Hermione, after a pause.

"I love him not; neither do I hate him; he is too venerable a gentleman to be hated,—his years, if nothing else, secure him too much respect for hatred;" said Paulina. "In sober earnest, he is a man to be both esteemed and liked; and I should have probably both liked and esteemed him more, had he not taken it into his head to like me—and to ask for me for a wife, before I had time to think whether I liked him better than any other man in the world,—which is what a wife should do, to be a good wife and a happy wife. What ailed him to be so troublesomely ready, I should like to know?"

"So ready to step in with his suit, before some one else could propose, whom you might have preferred, do you mean?" asked Hermione.

Paulina started; then fell into a reverie, during which another pause ensued. After a few minutes she resumed, with a sort of half sigh :— "Whatever might have been, it is useless now to consider. My father's word of honor is pledged; and it shall not be forfeited by fault of mine."

"Poor Alexis!" thought the princess. "He has been too tardy in speaking his love; its discovery might have revealed to her her own for him, which I fear is lurking within her heart unknown to herself. Best as it is; her honor to her affianced husband, will preserve her from a knowledge of the secret,—which could now only produce pain. All that remains to be done, is gently to awaken him from his dream; and contrive to withdraw him from her continued society, which would endanger his future peace, by confirming a passion that is now, I will hope, only in its dawn."

It happened the next day, Hermione was walking in the gardens, surrounded by her ladies; when Alexis joined them, bearing a beautiful exotic, which the emperor had sent to his daughter for her conservatory. After the princess had admired it, and dwelt with delight on her father's goodness,—ever watchful to provide fresh gratification for his indulged. child, Paulina observed that the latter cause indeed, gave it a charm; else, it possessed not, to her thinking, superior beauty to some of their own native flowers she could name. Emilia, Olga, and Rogneda, confirmed her opinion, by citing, each in turn, a favorite flower; which, they avouched, far surpassed the stranger blossom, in shape, scent, and hue. Hermione, zealous for the honor of her father's gift, insisted that they should all four go seek the flower which they severally averred outshone the one she had just received; and as they withdrew, laughing, talking, and eagerly discussing the merits of the one they championed, Alexis, in allusion to the musical mingling of their voices, said :—"Discord skilfully touched, marreth not harmony, as the best musicians know. Hark how their dissension makes a blended sound sweeter than concord; the melodious tones of your ladies' voices, render even wrangling tuneable. How it comes wafted towards us beneath the trees! more delicious than ring-dove's cooings, or warblings of ouzel's throat. That thrilling, joyous laugh above all!" he exclaimed; "I should know it among a thousand!"

"You have a distinguishing ear, cousin;" she said.

"The dullest would single out that tone!" he rejoined with enthusiasm. "Liquid, clear, penetrating, the artless gaiety of her soul rings out through her voice, like the carol of a bird in Spring-time."

"Her voice is generally low;" said the princess. "Earnest, full, impassioned, it is, I allow; but I should never have thought of attributing the qualities you mention, to her voice; it would require a lover's partiality, methinks, to discover the liveliness of a lark's singing in Paulina's grave and impressive tones."

"Paulina's! I was thinking of Emilia's! I was speaking of hers! Whose could be heard or instanced, when hers was near?" The rapture in his own voice, and in his look, spoke unmistakeably.

"You love Emilia, then?" said Hermione, with a deep-drawn breath.

"More than life;" he returned. "You must have seen it; my secret could not have escaped your penetration; but I have striven to conceal it from herself, and still would do so. I dread to startle that young, shy heart; I fear to alarm that innocent, artless, child-like nature, by a premature discovery of the passionate feelings she inspires; I would have her remain in ignorance of the ardour with which I regard her, until, instead of shrinking from it, she shall have learned to look upon me with something like interest,—with something akin to the warmth and love with which I adore her. Meanwhile, I endeavour to guard my preference from suspicion, by maintaining an appearance of equal courtesy and liking for all your ladies; and I have flattered myself that hitherto no idea of the truth has reached her. I know I can depend upon your prudence, that she shall never know of it, other than through the quiet, gradual attentions, by which I hope to make my approach to her heart."

"I leave it to your own good discretion, to plan your advances, as best they may appear to you likely to win that heart;" said the princess. "You need fear no injudicious interference from me. My father once warned me against the quicksands of match-making."

"Yet I shall hope for your good offices in my behalf, when I shall have dared to avow my passion;" he replied; "and meanwhile, I trust I have your good wishes?"

"They attend yours to a successful issue;" she answered, as she left him to join the flower-seekers, while she herself returned to the house, musingly.

"It is indeed a hazardous thing to plan the assorting and bringing together of hearts;" she thought. "They have a wayward mode of their own,—discovering and deciding of themselves, their mutual fitness and bestowal; sometimes involuntarily, unconsciously, — but ever best unprompted, by the suggestions or whisperings of others. Had I betrayed Paulina into a vain preference for Alexis, by misleading her as to his sentiments,—had I inspired her with the false notion I entertained of his attachment for herself, and fatally induced a corresponding feeling on her part towards him, I should have had the remorse of knowing the pangs of a hopeless passion were hers to struggle with, through my means, instead of, as now, seeing her submit to her father's will, with merely the in-

difference natural to one who has thought little about love or marriage,
and who knows even less of her future husband. And yet that half sigh !
that start, when I spoke of his having anticipated another, who might have
been preferred, had he proposed in time. Yes, it must be so. She might
have learned to love Alexis, had he shown love for her, and asked her of
her father, before this Sicilian nobleman stepped in, and secured her. But
fate has assigned her his ; and it is well that her regrets at what might
have been, are vague, and insufficient to disturb her peace."

Her generous concern for her friend's happiness, led to reflections
touching her own lot. The Sicilian nobleman had brought to her mind
the Sicilian prince ; and she fell into a train of thought, having for its
object the qualities of person, temper, and mind, attributed by report to
her future husband. He was said to be handsome. Should she think him
so ? He was reputed to be of generous nature, strong impulse, and quick
affections. She had heard that he was an obedient son, implicit in duty to
his father ; and that his attachment for the young Polixenes, prince of
Bohemia,—with whom he had been brought up on terms of the tenderest
intimacy and brotherhood,—had grown and strengthened with their years
into the firmest and most affectionate friendship. This argued well, she
thought, for the excellence of his heart, and for its capability of constancy
and fervour in love. As for his mind, she knew that he was accounted
one of the most accomplished scholars of his time ; intellectually gifted
beyond the average mental endowment of princes, and cultivated by
study,—for which he was said to have an unusual thirst,—into a well-
learned, and highly-accomplished gentleman.

The time now approached for the ratifying of the promise which her
father had made, on her behalf The embassadors from Sicily were
daily expected to arrive in Kief; and at the emperor's desire, the princess
Hermione, with her train, repaired from Igorhof to the capital, to be
present at the state reception. It took place in a spacious hall of audience,
in the Imperial palace. The Russian monarch occupied a gorgeous throne,
raised upon a dais, on which there was a seat near him for the princess,
his daughter. They were surrounded by their court, in robes of state :
the counsellors, noblemen, and officers, near their sovereign ; her ladies

beside the chair occupied by Hermione. She was attired in white and gold; a drapery at once simple yet magnificent, falling in massive folds to her feet. Her white temples were surmounted by her closely braided hair, and by a plain circlet of gold, from which depended a transparent, but ample veil,—shading, but not concealing her matchless face. Her look was the perfection of queenly self-possession and dignity, together with chaste, maidenly purity.

The rest of the hall was occupied by soldiers of the Imperial guard, pages, gentlemen, and other members of the household; in the centre, a space or alley being preserved for the approach of the embassadors and their train.

Camillo and Antigonus entered, followed by their suite; and presented the king their master's credentials, on one knee, to the emperor. While he graciously advanced a step, in honor of his royal brother's missive, and took it from the embassadors' hands, and proceeded to open and peruse it, his daughter could not resist the impulse of interest and curiosity which led her to scan the countenance of him, whom she knew by his superiority of years, to be the lord Antigonus, her friend Paulina's destined husband. The examination did not result altogether unfavorably; she thought he seemed a good-natured, pliant, well-bred kind of man, likely to make an indulgent husband; but she could not avoid the thought that in point of age, if in no other, his brother envoy, looked by far the more suited to her beautiful, spirited, young companion. She had gone on to think that the sensible, intelligent countenance of Camillo evinced yet farther claims to have entitled him to the prize which fate had awarded to his elder colleague; when her attention was attracted by a face immediately behind the one which had previously engaged her consideration. It was regarding her with a serious expression; not admiration,—rather curiosity,—a grave, not to say cold, scrutiny. At first she felt somewhat offended at this look, bent on her with so little of ceremonial regard in its deliberate investigation. Gradually, she took an interest in what was so singularly different from the usual style in which she was gazed at, —neither awe to propitiate her high station, nor admiration to gratify her womanly feelings; besides this kind of interest, there arose another,—

that of liking to look upon a face so beautiful in itself, in its shape and features. The head was classically formed, set on to the shoulders with manly firmness, yet with grace and ease; the hair in rich clusters, but disclosing the white, high, polished forehead; the eyes dark, liquid, and lustrous, seeming capable of the most sparkling intelligence, and animated expression, but now resting upon her with that calm, grave, thoughtful composure, as if scanning her, estimating her,—not paying her the homage of unquestioning admiration. The mouth looked capable of all-eloquent praise,—both of smiles and words; but it was now motionless; the lips lay in that quiet half-compression, which betokens inward reflection and consideration, not an active and irrepressible approbation. But the shape of the mouth was very beautiful; the colour of the lips was opulent in youth and health, and their every line seemed formed for persuasive appeal. Of his figure she could judge but little, hemmed in and concealed as it was, by the crowd which pressed on all sides; but it seemed manly, easy, and gracefully proportioned; although clad in a suit of simplest material, and quietest colour. Indeed the habit he wore, from its plain fashion, among so much that was costliest and gayest, would have rendered him conspicuous, had he not been distinguished by the marked beauty of his person. But in that large assemblage, occupied as it was with the principal actors in the scene, and with what was passing immediately near to the dais and throne, the youthful stranger passed unobserved, save as forming one in the suite of the Sicilian embassage.

The ceremonial concluded. The king's formal agreement to the conditions proposed by the emperor, was read aloud to the council; and a day appointed for the solemn betrothal of the contracting parties, at a sufficient distance of time to admit of all pomp and pageant of preparation.

During this interval, the princess was to retire to her favorite residence—the summer-palace of Igorhof; its country seclusion best according with her desire for quiet and meditation. Since the morning of the state-reception, she had found herself thinking frequently of the face that had then so powerfully arrested her attention. A something she had scarce defined,—of which she was scarce conscious, had deterred her from enquiring who this young man was; she knew he was one of the train accompanying the Sicilian envoys, and she chose to ask no farther. She was provoked to find how incessantly, and involuntarily her mind reverted to his image; how pertinaciously and unexpectedly it recurred to her fancy, how it clung to her thoughts, and how they busied themselves perpetually, and without any spontaneous action of her will, with the looks, and expression of that grave, considering, but handsome face. Vexed to find this uncontrolled exercise of her imagination, gaining ground upon her, and forcing her to obey its impulse in spite of herself; her better judgment roused her to an attempt of casting off this spell, and prompted her to a method of abstracting her thoughts from a subject which she felt occupied them too much. This was, by fixing them resolutely and exclusively upon another; and to this end, and that she might concentrate them upon one accordant with the duties before her, she begged her father would procure for her a competent master, with whom she might study the Sicilian language, as henceforth the subject of Sicily, its dialect, and its literature, should be the dearest object of her interest, and endeavoured attainment.

Her father,—ever anxious to promote her wishes, so invariably had he found them tending but to her own honor and dignity,—readily promised to grant her desire. He consulted Camillo; who replied that he was happy to have it in his power to second the views of the emperor, since in the suite of the embassy there was a man precisely fitted to fill the office of tutor to her highness the princess. The person in question was his own secretary it was true; but this subordinate situation,—which he at present held, in consequence of his desire to avail himself of the opportunity it afforded of visiting and advantageously seeing the Russian court and capital,—did not prevent his being in reality a deeply-read scholar, a profoundly-learned student, a perfect sage in knowledge and wisdom, in research and erudition. Camillo ended by saying he would himself follow the princess to Igorhof, when she repaired thither; and have the pleasure of presenting his secretary to the princess as her instructor, if she would graciously permit his services in that capacity.

This point thus settled, Hermione sent to summon Paulina from her father's house, that she might accompany her to her country retirement;

but to the princess's surprise, the messenger brought back a humble
entreaty for her highness's pardon, that duty of a yet more imperative
kind than her mistress's command demanded her obedience, and bade her
pray to be excused from waiting upon her this time to Igorhof.

"There is matter in this;" thought the princess. "Paulina is not one
lightly to refuse behest of mine. Her duty to her father supersedes all
other duty, doubtless; but she owes it to her friend, to say why we cannot
be together at this juncture."

Hermione sent the messenger once again, with a paper bearing the
words :—" Come to me now."

Paulina's reply was her appearance before her friend and mistress;
who received her alone.

"Tell me, dear friend; what is this?" Hermione began, in her benign
voice. "You have been in trouble,—in sorrow? The tokens of grief are
yet in your red eyes and swollen cheeks. 'Tis not a little makes you
weep; you are no more easily moved to tears than myself. It must have
been something of moment to shake you thus. You are trembling still.
Is it alarm,—anxiety,—or fatal certainty of evil?"

"Certainty should bring firmness; it is only suspense that ought to
know agitation;" said Paulina, striving for her usual steadfastness of tone
and manner, and as if in disdain of her present perturbed condition. "But
I am still beneath the influence of the scene that has taken place this
morning,—but now,—just before your messenger brought your highness's
first summons."

"What scene? Forgive my urgency—forgive my seeming indiscretion
in pressing you to speak of what so moves you;" said the princess; "but
I cannot help longing to share your uneasiness, that I may seek to relieve
it, if it is to be relieved, to soothe it by my sympathy if it is past relief.
Confide in me; confide in your friend ;—your Hermione."

Paulina pressed her mistress's hand to her lips, to her bosom; then
with an effort, spoke :—" I ask no better than to confide to you the truth,
—to reveal all,—to you. But it is difficult—it is well-nigh impossible, to
utter some things." She paused, then resumed. "You remember, I once
hinted to you, that, had not lord Antigonus been so premature in his pro-

posal to my father, he might have been forestalled by,—— there might have been one who,—had he spoken earlier,—— that, in short, there was a man, whom I——"

"Whom you could have preferred?" said Hermione, finishing the sentence that died upon her friend's lips.

"Whom I could have preferred,—whom I did prefer; whom I liked better than I myself knew I did;" she returned; "for whom my liking would have been love, had I known he loved me,—had I known he so much as thought of me. But he gave me no reason to suppose he cared for me one jot beyond ordinary courtesy and kindness of regard,—then. Now however,—now,—this very morning,—he,—that man——"

"Yes; Alexis,——" rejoined Hermione.

"Alexis?" echoed Paulina, in amazement. But the next moment she recovered from her surprise, saying:—"True, you knew him not,—you knew nothing of him,—never saw him, save on that single occasion,—at the state-reception. In a crowd, in a public room, fulfilling a ceremonial office, how could you discern aught of the good sense, the right thinking, the nobility of mind that distinguish him in private,—in daily converse,—in hourly intercourse. You knew not, as I did, the—— but enough of this;" she said, checking herself. "It is for the last time I yield to the worse than folly of dwelling on this theme. It is because I would not let a shadow of reserve rest between myself and her who has been my royal mistress and tender friend in one,—it is because I will not have anything unexplained, or mysterious, in my conduct towards you, madam, that I tell you, at whatever cost, the whole of my secret. That man whom I could have—that man whom I now must resolutely put from my thoughts,— he, who this morning avowed his love for me, and asked mine in return— too late,—is no other than Camillo."

Paulina's usually full, round, firm voice, sank to a whisper as she pronounced the last word.

Hermione clasped her hand in one of hers, and passed the other arm round her, saying gently:—"Why too late? Why need it be too late?"

"My hand is promised; my father's faith is pledged. His daughter's weakness shall not cause it to be impugned;" she said, with more of firmness than she had yet shown.

"You shall come with me to Igorhof, dear friend ; we will together try for courage to meet this cross in your fate, since you resolve to submit to its award ;" said the princess.

"Not there ! Not there, of all places, now !" Paulina exclaimed vehemently. "He is to be there; he is going thither, to introduce your grace's Sicilian tutor. You forget, madam ; Igorhof I must shun, as I would shun betrayal of future peace and honor." And she knelt before her young mistress, beseeching her to aid her in her strength of resolution, by leave to stay at Kief.

"Be it as you will, dear friend ;" said Hermione. "I honor your virtuous purpose too sincerely, to seek to shake it. Remain here ; but let me have your news from time to time. And may they be of such restored serenity and comfort, as so true and noble a spirit deserves."

The day after the princess reached Igorhof, Camillo was announced ; praying leave to wait upon her highness, and to present the gentleman who was to have the honor of superintending her Sicilian studies.

"Bid them approach ;" she said. "My mind has been so engrossed with thoughts of Paulina," she added, to herself, "that I had well-nigh forgotten my proposed pursuit. It will be welcome ; it will serve to distract me from fruitless reveries. No leisure for vagrant fancies, or vain repinings at what might be, and what cannot be, with a sober book before me, and a soberer monitor beside me."

From what her father had repeated to her of Camillo's words, concerning the person who was to be her instructor, Hermione had pictured to herself, a grave, elderly man, robed in black, with silver hairs,—a complete impersonation of a sage, a philosopher. What then was her surprise, when Camillo made his appearance, followed by a young man, clad in a simple grey suit, bearing a portfolio of papers and some books, whom he presented as his secretary, Leon ; and in whose face she at once recognized the one which had so arrested her attention in the audience-hall, and had since so haunted her imagination.

She learned this at a glance ; for she was immediately occupied in receiving Camillo with a benignant grace all her own ; now enhanced, by associations with the idea of her friend, as she looked in his face, and beheld traces of the deep disappointment he had endured.

"You are welcome at Igorhof, sir ;" she said. "I trust you will make it your sojourn, so long as it may be agreeable to you. Its gardens, and vicinity, are well worthy a stranger's inspection, and my cousin will have much pleasure in escorting you to those spots best deserving your notice."

As she concluded, she turned to her cousin Alexis, who, with her ladies, was in the apartment, and presented the two gentlemen to each other. Camillo acknowledged her gracious courtesy; and that he might show himself sensible of it, withdrew shortly after, to pay the visit to the grounds, which she had recommended.

As he retired, accompanied by her cousin, the princess addressed the young secretary :—"You have been so good as to anticipate my wish, sir, I perceive, and have brought with you the means of commencing our lessons at once. I cannot too soon begin the task I have before me; I fear me, the time will be but short, for its accomplishment. But I will refer me to your skill in teaching, rather than rely upon mine own poor powers of learning."

"Such as it is, it shall be at your highness's command in all devoted zeal ;" replied Leon, as he spread the books and papers on the table, and placed a chair for the princess ; taking his own station quietly behind it.

She had expected a grave, staid, elderly personage ; and here was one in the prime of youthful manhood. In years, then, her new tutor was the total opposite of the picture she had represented to herself; but in the two former particulars, it was impossible to be more exactly fulfilled by the fact. The young secretary might have been a stoic, a cynic, for the measured sobriety, and cold severity of his deportment. He might have been Mentor himself, for the rigid calm, the dispassionate, senile composure of his bearing. Had his face seen seventy winters, in lieu of the hardly more than twenty summers which it seemed to have witnessed, it could scarce have worn a more frozen composure of aspect.

There was something in this look of his, that made it seem unfit he should be standing, beside her, or rather behind her,—at the back of her chair ; his character of instructor, too, no less than his air, warranted greater respect ; and she accordingly said :—"Be seated, sir, I pray you."

The secretary quietly placed himself in the chair she pointed to, over against her, and drawing one of the books between them, commenced the lesson.

Day after day, the studies thus proceeded; the princess and her tutor occupying a table in one of the windows, while her ladies sat at the embroidery-frame in another. These latter were frequently joined by young Alexis; who, finding that Camillo's melancholy more frequently led him to prefer solitude in his walks, than company, gradually left him to himself, and sought the society of those who possessed more congenial charms for him. Sometimes he would hang over the embroidery-frame, trifling and chatting with the ladies of honor; watching Emilia, and flattering himself that he discerned tokens of her increasing affection. At other times, he would approach his cousin's writing-table, playfully tax her with too close an attention to her studies, and lure her forth into the flower-garden to idle with him and her ladies, as fitter pursuit, than leaning over musty books and papers. The cold, stern looks with which the young tutor regarded him on such occasions, passed unheeded. A secretary, a teacher, was too insignificant a person to be observed,—his opinions of vastly too little importance to be even perceived, by Alexis. It was not from contempt, or pride, or haughty disdain of an inferior; but simply that supreme indifference, that perfect disregard, with which a man in his station is apt to treat one in that of Leon.

The manners of this latter were not such as to conciliate a gay youth like Alexis. They were too taciturn, too grave and reserved, for his taste; he found him a silent, abstracted scholar; one, who, in his silence and abstraction, no less than in his inferior station, was better left unnoticed. This seemed best suited to his mood; for, save with the princess, his pupil, and with Camillo, his master, the secretary held little communion with any one.

It was during the lessons, that he gradually evinced an animation and interest, the reverse of his habitual frigid quietude. By degrees the coldness, and distance of his original manner wore off; by degrees the lofty composure with which he had stood aloof, in the commencement of their intercourse, yielded to a warmth and energy of assiduity, while conveying his instructions to his scholar, very different from the measured, unmoved air with which he had entered upon his office. He no longer regarded her with that grave, considering look, that chilling, deliberate investigation, with which he had at first contemplated her. His face, now, was eager, lighted with interest, full of intelligence, sparkling and glowing with sympathy, as he imparted each new precept, and watched the quickness and activity of faculty with which his pupil seized each new idea, and appreciated and retained every freshly-explained principle. His delight in instructing, evidently grew with his discovery of her capacity for acquiring; and in return, her pleasure in the lessons as evidently increased in proportion to the interest and sympathy with which they were now given.

The hours spent in her Sicilian studies, were the happiest Hermione had ever known; they seemed like the opening of a new existence to her; in addition to the zest of attaining knowledge, was a new charm, that she had never felt before, even in the like intellectual pursuits. She resolved the question as to whence this added charm arose, by believing that it was because Sicily,—which was to become her adopted country,— its language, its history, its people, its laws, its customs, its scenery, formed the themes of discussion between herself and her instructor. When he dwelt with fervour upon the poetical traditions of his native isle, upon the classic stories of its shores; when he painted to her the golden glories of its climate, the purple hues of its mountains, the fertile luxuriance of its plains; when he described the bee-haunted, odoriferous Hybla, or the majestic, fire-vomiting Ætna; when he spoke of the ice-cold streams of the transformed Acis, of the lovely fields of Enna, where lovelier Proserpina and her nymphs gathered heaps of wild-flowers; when he told her of piping shepherd-gods, and enamoured nereids, those earlier denizens of the island, still haunting its remoter shades, to the eye of poesy, whilst mortals of noble mould and action peopled its towns and cities,—the princess deemed it was interest in his subject, that caused the enthralled attention, the wrapt fascination with which she listened to his words. She would sit entranced, unconscious of the lapse of time, drinking in each syllable; and dreamed it was because Sicily and Sicilian lore were his theme, that she was thus spell-bound.

He was once relating to her a legend of a mountain castle, built when god Saturn reigned in Sicilia, and Ceres was presiding genius of its teeming prosperity ; he told her how the island was then known by the names of Sicania, or Trinacria ; how it had ever enjoyed the especial favor of the gods ; and how, in deference thereto, its highest legislative decisions were still regulated by appeal to the oracle, in Apollo's temple, at sacred Delphos. He spoke of the wondrous strength of this castle ; and how it had held out, impregnable, against all hostile attempts. He told her of its romantic site, its picturesque environments ; of the abrupt and almost inaccessible crags, amid which it reared its giant front. In the midst of this narration, one of her ladies approached, to remind the princess that it was her highness's usual hour for exercise ; and prayed to know whether Rogneda and herself should accompany her to the gardens. Hermione looked up, as if suddenly awakened from a vision, in which her whole soul was absorbed ; then said, gently :—" Go you, good Olga, with Rogneda ; I will follow anon with Emilia, who, I think, is engaged upon a silken group she would fain finish."

But Emilia embroidered on ; and still the princess offered not to quit the study-table. She sat, with thoughts rivetted to his words, and eyes fastened on his face ; devouring each syllable that fell from his lips. She seemed a statue ; so motionless, so breathless, she remained.

Presently, Alexis, impatient at Emilia's not coming forth with the other ladies, came in from the grounds to seek her ; and finding what detained her,—for one or other of the princess's ladies always sat in the chamber, during the tutor's attendance,—went towards his cousin, and urged her not to lose so fair a morning in-doors, when open air, and bright sun, and sweet-scented flowers, wooed her abroad.

" Remember, fair cousin, the sullen season will be here shortly ; and then adieu to walks, and gardening, and out-door amusements ; time enough for poring over dry scrolls, like a book-worm, when fog, and snow, and dreary weather, curtain the heavens. Cheerless tasks befit a murky day ; but while the sun lends us his glorious countenance, let not us Russians neglect to profit by so rare a favor."

Hermione's imagination had been steeped in the fervid rays and azure depth of Sicilian skies; while she gazed upon a Sicilian face lighted by intellectual fire, and glowing with beauty of feature and expression, scarce less than those of the pictured Phœbus himself. And she absently echoed the word;—" Cheerless ? "

"Ay, cousin; to a poor idle scapegrace like myself, study does, I own, appear cheerless, in comparison with sprightly talk. I know I speak heresy; but what are books, to conversing,—in the fresh air, amid the breath of flowers,—with the voices and looks of fair women ? "

The angry flush which sprang into the cheek of the young tutor, at these words, was not perceived by the speaker. The secretary's general demeanour was so cold and staid, that his face alone betrayed his feelings. Towards this, the eyes of Alexis never so much as glanced. He no more thought of looking at the quiet student, than he would have looked at the chair he occupied.

" You paint yourself more graceless than you are, cousin mine ; " she said; " do you not remember the time when you would read to me, yourself, by the hour together, regardless of rain or shine ? "

" I could have done more than that to pleasure you, fair cousin ; though sooth to say, books never possessed the charm for me, that they have for you—especially since you seek in them how to answer, in his own language, the Sicilian prince who is to whisper a lover's and a husband's vows."

The crimson mounted to Hermione's brow. She rose hastily; but spoke no word; and stood looking down, with a sedate dignity,—yet something proudly,—her hand resting upon the back of the chair from which she had risen.

Alexis gently took the white hand, and said :—" You will forgive me, if in playful thoughtlessness, I hurt your delicacy. I but alluded to an engagement known to all,—sanctioned by your father,—spoken of by all his subjects. Come ; if you will not leave your beloved studies for the sake of the sunshine, and the flowers, come to pleasure me. See, Emilia is ready to attend you."

As her cousin, drawing the princess's arm within his, and offering the other to Emilia, led the two ladies from the apartment, the young secretary started up, with a wrath that had only been controlled by an imperative effort till then; and paced up and down, rapidly and perturbedly. Presently, he returned to the study-table, sat himself down before it, and took pen and paper, as if about to write. Then, pushed them from him, arose, and hurried from the room. He went straight to the suite of chambers appropriated to Camillo and himself during their stay at Igorhof; but found no one there. Camillo was gone upon one of his solitary rambles through the grounds.

Leon, with a hasty exclamation at his absence, threw himself into a chair, and sat for some time, with his face buried in his hands. There were writing-materials before him; and, after a space, he drew them towards him, and began a letter, as follows :—

" Best friend and brother,

" As of yore, in boyhood, we were wont to share each other's childish joys and griefs, so, now, arrived at man's estate, continue we to interchange our mutual cares and confidences. Sympathy of spirit, and written words, may still unite us ; though communion of speech be beyond our reach. Thou art not ignorant, my Polixenes, that my father's wishes in this Russian alliance guided mine own ; and that no sooner had I, in obedience to his will, yielded my consent that the treaty should go forward, than a desire to behold this princess, ere fate had bound her irrevocably mine, engendered a resolve that I would hazard all to effect my desire. Camillo's report strengthened my purpose. His description of her beauty, bore testimony that fame had not magnified the truth in this respect ; but I could not resist a misgiving that one so perfect in person, might possibly be less gifted in qualities of heart and understanding ; that her charms might have blinded public judgment to defects of disposition and temper ; or that, to a faultless face and form, might be joined a feeble character, or a silly, vacant mind. In order to satisfy my growing anxiety to see and judge for myself, I determined to accompany him, on his return to Russia ; and, that I might have the better opportunity of carrying out my intention, I confided to him my plan, and went, not in my own person, but in the character and guise of his private secretary.

" I saw her. Dispassionately as I strove to scan her beauty, I could not but own its supremacy. In figure, as in feature, admirable. Her deportment was dignity itself. There was a still majesty in her attitude, more nearly allied to the repose of sculptured marble, than to living womanhood. Even from this, she struck me as too statue-like, too coldly passive. She seemed to lack the warmth, the vitality of feeling, which should course through the veins of a youthful beauty,—to render her a perfect beauty. But the scene was a public one; and the apparent insensibility, might be but the reticence of modesty.

"Fortune favored me in my hope of forming a nearer judgment, by giving me the opportunity of beholding her in private,—in daily, domestic converse and communion. I became, by a happy chance, her instructor; I was to verse her in our Sicilian tongue, to familiarize her with Sicily and its history. Guess, dear friend, with what eagerness I accepted an occasion so favorable to my purpose! But I preserved my adopted sage demeanour, that I might the better maintain my character of quiet, unassuming secretary; and the more opportunely pursue my project of observation. Calmly, temperately, have I endeavoured to form my opinion. But ah! my best Polixenes, your friend, in watching the sweet perfections of her nature, and in the gradual discovery how truly they match with those of her person, is subdued heart and soul to the witchery of their influence, and has scarce control of faculty or discrimination left him, beyond the single, and all-engrossing perception of her consummate excellence. Beneath that still exterior, she hath a susceptible spirit, keenly alive to all great and gracious sentiments. Under that royalty of countenance and gesture, lieth womanliest delicacy and goodness. With all her outward composure, she is capable of profound emotion, and generous ardour. To see her countenance beam with enthusiasm, at the recital of a worthy deed, or a magnanimous act,—to see her eyes kindle at the image of injustice or tyranny, is to feel that her intelligence of mind, her nobleness of soul, outshine even the graces of her person. But in the very process of attaining this conviction,—of simultaneously perceiving that her chaste dignity was that of purity and depth of feeling, not of coldness, and of finding how entirely my own heart did homage to the truth, by unreserved acknowledgment and worship of her worth,—I came to dread that it might be my fate never to

call so incomparable a creature mine, as I could wish her to be mine. In
learning to recognize her beauty of heart and mind, as well as of shape and
face, I learned to desire that I might possess her by the voluntary gift of
that heart and mind, and not by mere deed of contract ; I felt that I could
not be satisfied, unless I owed her hand to preference, and not to state
alliance ; I would have such a woman my wife by her own wish ;—and
become her husband upon no other claim than that of love,—mutual love.

"And now,—how shall I tell it thee ?   There is a young fellow,—
a cousin,—one Alexis,—who by reason of his kindred, and of the emperor's
kindness, is admitted here on terms of such nearness and frequency of intercourse with the princess, that he obtains more of her notice and favor
than any other being. The intimacy, the familiarity of his manner with
her,—warranted as it is, in a measure, by the relationship between them,—
offends and revolts me almost beyond my powers of concealment. In vain
I tell myself that he is her cousin,—that as a poor relation he is entitled
to her regard and consideration ; that her own tender benignity and
graciousness prompt her to the tokens of interest she evinces ; and
occasion the kindness and attention with which she treats him. I cannot
endure to behold the freedom of his address—the ease of her replies ;
I cannot endure to see her follow his suggestions, or fulfil his wishes.
This morning he dared to take her hand ; and, though she was evidently
disinclined to quit the discourse in which we were engaged, he must
needs urge her to walk, against her wish. And she yielded her will to
his ! She obliged him in his desire to have her accompany him. She
left the subject we were discussing,—left her tutor with a bow of courteous
dismissal for that day's studies ; and suffered herself to be led away, her
arm resting upon the audacious, triumphant cousin's ! And the tutor
stood there ; the humble secretary, as in duty bound, stood mutely there !
What claim had he to offer word or look of objection ? The princess and
her kinsman had undoubted right to dispose of themselves and their time
as best they thought fit, without consulting the opinion or pleasure of so
insignificant a person as Leon. The teacher's morning task was fulfilled.
He was done with. He and his books might be put away together. In
that moment I felt that I could have cursed mine egregious folly which had

placed it out of my own power to assert myself—to confront this minion of royal blood on equal terms. He was not insolent towards me—let me do him this justice—he thought not of me,—that was all. For her, neither insolence, nor arrogance, nor other unwholesome emotion, ever casts its shadow upon that fair serenity of countenance. Her nature,— stainless and transparent as her complexion, clear and lustrous as her eyes, beams pure, and candid, and radiant, in her face. But should her heart have already spoken in favor of another,—all unconsciously as it may have been,—can I bear that her hand, in mere cold fulfilment of an international bargain,—in obedience to a state compact, shall be conferred . . . I am interrupted. I hastily close this letter, and despatch it by our trusty messenger, Demetrius ; and will write you farther ere long. Meanwhile, as ever,

Thine, in truest and dearest friendship,

LEONTES."

To Polixenes, prince of Bohemia ;
greeting : these, with secrecy and dispatch."

Next day, the princess sat at her frame, among her ladies, when letters arrived from the capital. They brought intelligence of the lady Paulina's marriage. It had taken place at her father's house, privately, without much of ceremonial, and in some haste, in consequence of a summons to join the army, which took him away abruptly ; he desiring to see her in safe and honorable protection ere he left her. In Paulina's letter to her friend and mistress, briefly stating this, Hermione could perceive the strict adherence to duty, the firm abiding by a resolved course, the prompt fulfilment of what she had once acknowledged to be right, which marked Paulina's conduct. While the princess mused upon the energy of rectitude that distinguished her favorite's character, her other ladies were engaged in discussing the news, with all that flutter of interest usually evinced on such occasions. Olga and Rogneda were expatiating on the unlucky necessity for hurry, which prevented due preparation in dress, jewels, equipages, and other particulars that formed, in their opinion, the most important incidents of a wedding. Alexis was whispering Emilia something that grew out of the tidings of these nuptials,—something that brought no reply ;

but, instead, a blushing silence that served better than speech, and that
caused him who addressed her, to feel no lack of conversation. Camillo,
on the very first opening of the letters, had quitted the apartment; his
secretary, soon after, following him.

The princess had noted the withdrawal : in sorrowful comprehension of
the feelings which caused Camillo's ; and in cordial approval of the motives
which drew Leon after him. She understood the desire to attempt consolation, the hope to soften his friend's anguish, which had prompted the
secretary to follow. She accompanied them with her gentlest wishes, her
deepest sympathy ; and, presently, she went towards the conservatory,
which adjoined her sitting-room, that she might uninterruptedly pursue
the train of reverie into which she had fallen.

She was still here,—standing in a motionless posture, her eyes looking
forth, but fixed, and lost in thought ; one arm drooping at her side, the
other leaning upon a marble ledge that supported some flowers ; scarcely
seeming to breathe, so wrapt was her abstraction ; whilst the ceaseless
plash of the fountain near, appeared rather to chime than to jar with her
musings,—when a quick footstep approached, and roused her from her
waking dream. It was Alexis, who, radiant with joy, came to tell her the
prosperous issue of his suit ; how he had ventured to declare his love to
Emilia, in consequence of what they had that morning heard ; how—out
of the interest she had expressed in her sister lady-of-honor's fate, and the
hope she had uttered that Paulina's happiness was secured by this match,—
his courage had risen to speak to her of her own fate in wedlock, her own
future happiness ; how he had learned the joyful truth, that he himself was
concerned in both,—that unless he were the bridegroom she would never
wed, unless he were the lover she could never know happiness in love.

Hermione with her usual warmth and generosity of interest in that which
concerned her friends, listened to her cousin's raptures, encouraged his hopes,
and promised to use her intercession with the emperor, for their speedy
crowning, by entreating his sanction to the union, and his permission that
Alexis should at once enter the army, as a means of honorable and in-
dependant support for himself and his young wife.

Alexis, in a transport of gratitude, was in the act of raising the princess's hand to his lips, when the shadow of two figures darkened the entrance. They were those of Camillo and Leon.

The face of Camillo was pale, but composed; as if set in that resolved calm which is the result of a severe struggle between feeling and will,— a struggle wherein the latter, by dint of sense and reason, triumphs. The countenance of his companion was agitated; and worked in uncontrollable evidence of secret emotion.

While Camillo advanced,—and courteously offered a few words of apology to the princess, for having intruded on her privacy; saying that he knew not she was there, or he would have sought his apartments by other access than the one through the conservatory,—Leon merely bowed, and passed on, towards the door leading to their own rooms.

Hermione, with deepened color, but with all her own quiet dignity and self-possession, assured Camillo that he had not entered unseasonably; that her young cousin had concluded the communication he had been making to her; and that she was now free to welcome the approach of others, whose society, from its intellectual worth, and genial qualities, must ever be esteemed a privilege. As she concluded, the princess made a gracious motion towards a seat near to the one she had taken, that Camillo should remain beside her; and then gently drawing him into conversation, in kindly, womanly-wise, she won him to other sources of thought than the one she knew was gnawing and throbbing at his heart.

After a time, Alexis left them; impatient to rejoin Emilia. And then Hermione said, with a smile:—"My young cousin thinks to keep his secret hidden, because he speaks it not; but let his lips be shut ne'er so close, an' if his eyes blab his exultation, all who look on him may behold it. However, his cause of joy will be known to the whole court soon, so there is no indiscretion in revealing it, either by involuntary look, or explicit word, to surrounding friends."

"May I be considered near enough in friendship, by reason of the liking I bear him, to learn this secret, which your highness says is soon to be told to all?" said Camillo.

"He has gained the love of one of my ladies,—the youngest,—Emilia; he hopes shortly to wed her; and it was in the happiness of this hope, as he confided it to me, that my cousin was saluting my hand with so much fervour, when you approached, just now;" said Hermione. "'Tis a gay, good-hearted youth; and his natural high spirits have risen to exuberance, and into even more than their wonted enthusiasm of expression. It joys me to see him so happy. And now sir," she added, rising, "if it suit the leisure of your friend, I will gladly pass an hour or two in the saloon with our Sicilian books."

Camillo withdrew to summon Leon.

He found him pacing the apartment with rapid strides. On Camillo's entrance, he turned, and exclaimed :—"Thou saw'st it! Thou saw'st it, Camillo! Thou saw'st how, with tender gallantry, with all a lover's eagerness and devotion, he——"

"I saw his thanks, his gratitude, imprinted on her hand, for the sister's part she had played—for the friendship with which she had advocated his suit—for the affectionate interest with which she heard he was plighted to his mistress,—Emilia;" interrupted Camillo, in a distinct, impressive manner.

Leon gazed into his face. "Emilia! His choice! His plighted mistress!"

"His affianced wife;" answered Camillo. "They are shortly to be united. But her highness, the princess, awaits her tutor in the saloon; and bade me summon him thither. It is not fitting that my secretary— her teacher—should detain her;" he added with a sad smile.

Leon grasped his hand warmly; and ejaculating " My good Camillo!" hastened away.

As he entered the sitting-room, to attend the princess, the secretary beheld confirmation of what he had just heard. Alexis was leaning over the back of Emilia's chair; and one glance at the countenances of the lovers, sufficed. The studies proceeded, that day, with a zest, an animation, they had never known before. Never had Leon been so earnest, so assiduous; never had Hermione listened and learned with greater intelligence. Never had the teacher been so eloquent, so eager; never had his pupil hung upon his words with more of interest and devotion. For several successive days, the lessons went on with the same engrossing delight to both master and scholar; mutually, they became absorbed in each other and their pursuit. Minutes melted into hours, morning into afternoon, afternoon into evening; and still the princess and her tutor would sit at the study-table, as time crept on unperceived by either. They were no more interrupted by the solicitations of Hermione's young cousin, that she would leave her books, and stroll forth with him and her ladies. He was contented to lead away Emilia; and although the advance of winter now prevented the gardens from being the scene of their rambles, yet the sheltered conservatory afforded pleasant resort for the lovers' arm-in-arm walks, and whispered colloquies.

A second letter that Leon wrote, best pictures his state of feeling at this juncture.

"Dear friend and brother,

"Thy love for Leontes will rejoice to know that the cloud of doubt which then darkened his dawning hope, is now dispersed. I have had proof that my fears concerning this young cousin were groundless. Indeed, I now wonder how I could for a moment imagine that one so peerless, should abase her thoughts to an object unworthy her excellence— a·paltry, frivolous boy, a dependant on her father's favor for his very education and maintenance. But then,—I know not,—what am I, to all appearance, but a dependant, a mere hireling in the suite of the embassage, an officed appendage, a serviced scribe,—a secretary? And yet, upon this secretary, this poor dependant, I think she casts an eye of favorable regard. Is it that she discerns beneath his humble exterior, something that wins her esteem, something that involuntarily claims her respect, and bids her feel that he is not all unworthy her regard,—not altogether the poor, abject thing he seems? Or is it that her own pure and righteous mind sees nothing base in a man's exercise of those talents, those faculties and endowments with which nature and education have gifted him? She treats her instructor with all that delicacy, that deference of haviour, which bespeaks respect for his office, recognition of his intellectual superiority, and reverence for the wisdom that puts to use its advantages, and confers them upon those who need enlightenment. 'Tis true, I read all this, of noble thinking, of genuine estimation, in the feeling with which she regards her tutor. But is there nothing more, of nearer, dearer interest

in the attention, the devotion, with which she observes his words, and
hearkens to his precepts? Sometimes I would fain flatter myself there
is; that there is a deeper meaning in those entranced looks, in that
suspended breath, and motionless attitude. Sometimes, when that downcast face, fixed in silent gaze upon the book before us, gives me opportunity
to watch its beauties, and divine the secrets its expressive lines reveal,—
I dream I read a gentle delight, a tender pleasure in the inward listening
soul, such as no ordinary teaching inspires. Sometimes, when those full
eyes of hers—so soft, yet so starlike lustrous, are turned upon me in
eloquent enquiry of some passage or sentence I have ill explained, I ask
myself,—amidst the pulsing confusion into which my every sense is
thrown, when her eyes thus meet mine,—can it be, I really see within
their translucent depths, an enthusiasm, a gladness, beyond even that of
drinking in knowledge? Can it be that their look of tranquil joy, of
confiding happiness, owes its origin to a thought of him through whom
she gains this knowledge? Can it spring from any complacent idea of her
poor tutor? May I believe that the teaching is more welcome by reason of
the teacher? I know not what to think; or what to wish. At times,
when I am beneath the influence of these gentle looks, and swayed by
the tender hope they inspire, I am all given up to the desire of beholding
her softened and won into compassionate regard for the being before her.
At others, my heart swells to think her capable of yielding to a sentiment
which must needs degrade her,—a preference for a stranger—an obscure
person—one who, for aught she knows, may be of mean birth, of base
origin—one whose highest recognized position is that of secretary—
amanuensis to the envoy at her father's court. Yet, on the other hand,
should she feel no preference for him,—for any one;—should her untouched heart leave her at liberty to fulfil her father's engagement, and
bestow her hand upon this unknown Sicilian prince, can I endure to have
found her inaccessible to any emotion of liking for him, so long as he was
known to her but as the poor secretary, the humble tutor? Can I care
for her consent to become the future queen of Sicily, when I shall have
learned that she cared not to be the wife of the obscure and penniless
scholar? Can I desire to possess her—all beautiful as she is—when
I have never been able to touch her heart? Can Leontes accept of

herself, when Leon could not win her love ? I am torn by a thousand wild and passionate mistrusts. I could wish to be loved for myself alone ; yet dare not hazard the test. I dare not attempt to gain her affection for Leon, at the expense of her faith to Leontes. Yet if she remain true to her own and her father's plighted word, how may I be sure, that it is not from indifference, and in cold obedience to a parent's will ? After all, I am sorely inclined to rival myself. It suits best with my present distraction. I cannot much longer maintain my controul, or conceal from her the passion that is beating at my heart. I would fain try whether my hope whispers truly ; and learn if that gentle feeling indeed exists, which shall in the end prove too strong for mere prudence and duty. Either way I must triumph. Should she be faithful to her contract with the prince of Sicily, I gain proof of her steadfastness in virtue, her firmness and nobility of principle ; if she yield to love for Leon, I have the glory of finding that I am beloved for mine own sake. Could I have your counsel in reply, my Polixenes, you would doubtless ask me whether I be not about to tempt her unfairly and unwisely ; trifling with my own happiness ; and by all these refinements preparing future tortures for myself,—deeming her light of faith if she yield to her affection, or wanting in love, if she prove constant to her plighted word. I answer by owning myself a lover,—a passionate lover ; and in this title,—as I feel,—are comprised a thousand inconsistencies of misgiving, assurance, doubt, surmise, confidence, hope, fear, conjecture. To one of my temper and susceptibility, to love is to be on the rack, so long as my wishes are in suspense, my desires unfulfilled. But once certainly accomplished, they can know no farther distrust, no jealous alarms. Once possessed of Hermione,—heart and soul, my own, as in name, my wife,—and farewell, for ever, to a thought of assay or proof. It would be a wrong to one, matchless in purity as in beauty. I could as soon entertain a doubt of thee, my Polixenes,—whose tried friendship is beyond all suspicion,—as of this noble creature, once assured mine. That she may become so, is the sole and devout hope of

thy bounden brother-in-affection,

LEONTES."

The next morning's study chanced to be upon Sicilian poetry. Leon
spoke of the Syracusan Theocritus; who, although writing pure Greek,
was Sicilian in his tastes and subjects, no less than by birth; he spoke of
the pastoral grace of his poesy,—the sylvan coloring, and rustic charm,
that pervaded so much of his verse,—showing how it was an offspring of
the national shepherd songs of Sicily, primitive in their simplicity, classic
in their association. The tone in which he cited some of the Poet's idyls,
and especially dwelt on the words :—

> " Ah, those
> Were golden times, when the belov'd loved too.
> Would it were so again, oh father Saturn,
> Oh ye immortal gods, who grow not old ! "

had an earnestness, a passionate warmth, that vibrated on the heart of
Hermione, and caused it to thrill with a sensation it had never till then
known. It was as if some remote chord had been struck, whose strange
harmony sounded sweet answering music within her own soul. She sat,
lulled, and still; listening, as it were, to the soft echoes of this gracious
melody. The next theme was a verse—not from a named poet—or read
from any set scroll; but simply, a few lines, written on a loose sheet,
which the tutor drew from among some other papers, and laid before the
princess, as he was wont to do by whatever book or paper might be the
subject of discussion. The verses were in the Sicilian language,—a dialect
comprising features of both Greek and Italian. They were full of fire, and
poetic fervour; they described in glowing words, the tumults of a passion
nourished towards an object hopelessly superior in station, as in excellence,
to the writer.

Hermione waited, until her instructor should read them through to her,
and then render them into her own tongue; but Leon merely said, in
a somewhat lower voice than usual :—" They are for your highness to
construe."

The princess bent over the lines, in silence; and began to read. She
had dipped a pen in the ink, and held it ready to note down her translation; but after a moment, she replaced the pen, and continued her perusal.
Leon could not be sure that the hand had trembled. The frame was

motionless, and the face seemed calm, as,—slightly averted,—it remained fixed upon the paper,—while he watched, and she read on. Presently, with a perfectly steady hand, she retook the pen, and wrote out a Russian version of the lines, saying quietly :—" I have translated them as nearly as I may ; you will correct what I have failed in comprehending."

" It is literally rendered ; " he said, as he glanced over the writing ; " but it might be interpreted—— there is a force, and meaning, in the original, which,——" He hesitated.

" I am yet but an unpractised scholar ; " she said, with an air of mingled modesty and dignity ; " I shall hope to profit by your revision of my un-skilled attempt to do justice to the poem. Is the author known ? Is he held in repute ? "

" He hath no name,—no celebrity ; " stammered Leon. It was he who colored, whose hand shook ; awed by her manner, which was the more impressive from its very quietude.

At this moment, a messenger from Kief was announced. He brought letters for the princess from her father. The emperor had been suddenly taken ill (dangerously ill, the messenger added, according to the report that flew from mouth to mouth in the capital,) ; and wrote to beg his child to come to him, as speedily as might be.

" This instant ! Without delay ! " said the princess. " You, Alexis, can take charge of my ladies ; and the rest of our suite will follow, as soon as may be. Good sir," she added, to Camillo, " you will excuse this brief leave-taking ; I return to my father. The sledge that brought the messenger shall bear me back, without a moment's loss of time. All fitting preparation can be made for yourself, and your friend, who can travel in company with my cousin and ladies ; and I shall hope to welcome you together, kind friends, when you arrive in Kief, with happier tidings of my dear father's health."

There was a controul, a willed composure, in her speech, that showed the power she had over her strongest feelings. It might have told Leon, had he been still there to mark her, that little could be judged of her emotions, from what she permitted to be seen of them, even in moments when they most claimed empire. To have seen her, the tidings of her father's danger, might not have been supposed to affect her as powerfully as they really did; but her actions spoke her sentiments. The promptitude of her decision to return on the instant, waiting for no preparation, no retinue, proclaimed how sharp was her anxiety.

As she left the room, she cast an involuntary glance towards the study-table, that she might include Leon in the hasty farewell she took of all. But he was no longer there. He had vanished.

Thoughts of him,—of the last words that had passed between them—of all the incidents of their last interview,—mingled with her solicitude respecting her father, and thronged upon her as she flew along, commencing her journey. Swiftly as the sledge that bore her glided on, did her fancy busy itself with reviewing the various images that presented themselves. His looks, his tone of voice, swam before her eyes, and rang in her ears. The sound of that delicious inward music seemed again to play voluptuously upon her senses, and recall the beatitude into which it had plunged her. But scarcely had she yielded herself to the influence of these ideas, as she reclined in the fast-flying vehicle, ere they were jarred, and put to flight by fears for her father. These again were crossed and chequered by the intolerable inquietude of suspense; and the fancy that the sledge was moving slowly in comparison with her wishes. Then her thoughts recurred to Leon—to the lesson of that morning—the Sicilian poem—the Russian translation; and she asked herself, had she been too chilling, too haughty? And then her heart whispered:—"Ah, it was because I had then first discovered that I could haply feel too warmly, speak too softly." She started at her own thought; and resolutely put it from her; and forced it to take some other shape. She brought the image of Paulina before her; she revolved her courage and constancy; and took the example home to her own bosom. She ruminated upon the nature of her father's attack, and exhausted herself in longings to arrive at his bedside.

She told herself she was thinking of these things,—she was *trying* strenuously and honestly to do so,—yet behind them all lurked an image that would not be banished, but kept pertinacious possession of the background of the picture, confounding itself with the other figures, blurring, and confusing, and occasionally blotting them all out.

She roused herself, and looked forth. The scene was cheerless enough. A sullen grey sky; a gathering fog, which, more than the advancing afternoon, threw a darkening gloom upon all around; heavy clouds, threatening snow; with a general air of oppression, and murky, lowering menace.

They were approaching the banks of a river; it was frozen over; and when the driver stopped to enquire of the princess, whether her highness chose to go round by the bridge, or venture over the ice, she exclaimed:—"Go straight across! No going round! The shortest, nearest way, by all means."

The rapidity of the stream, in ordinary weather, together with its sudden and recent freezing, caused the surface to be much broken up into inequalities, and large irregular lumps; and the man added something of the "roughness of the road." But Hermione rejoined:—"No matter! 'Twill save a good half hour! Cross the ice!"

There had been no time, since the setting in of the frost, for passengers to have worn a track across, even tolerably smooth. The ice lay rugged, and uneven; here cracked, and split, in thin, crisp slabs; farther on, in small crumbled pieces; and,—where the current beneath set most strongly,—in huge blocks, and swelling, projecting masses. Towards the opposite bank, these impediments lay thickest; but the sledge had almost surmounted them, and gained the other side, when it came suddenly in contact with a rough-jutting wedge, and was overturned. The shock unseated the driver; and the princess was thrown violently out. She was stunned by her fall; and lay among the blocks and splinters of ice, powerless, and almost senseless.

She imagined that her senses had indeed left her, when she felt herself tenderly raised; and a voice that she knew but too well, called upon her name in agonized, passionate accents, beseeching her to speak if she yet lived.

"Leon! you here!" she faintly exclaimed, in the utmost amazement; and looking up, to assure herself by sight, that her hearing was not playing her false.

"The gods be praised!" was the deep-breathed response, as his eyes beheld hers unclose, and he heard the murmured tone. "Speak no farther

word—you will but exhaust yourself, beloved lady;" he added, as he saw
her make another effort to speak. "I have the blest assurance of your
safety,—no more need of words. Soft! I will bear you to the sledge; it
is replaced, and ready to proceed. I know you are eager to be on your
way again."

He lifted her in his arms, and placed her in the coach; but seeing that
she sank languidly and feebly down; he said:—"You are not able to support yourself—I fear I must presume on my privilege of master, and
beseech my pupil to let me sit beside her. I would not otherwise dare,—
I would else have returned to my former seat,—I would not ask to enter
your coach,—but you are still weak, and——"

His manner expressed such unfeigned reverence, and respectful distance,
—a deference of courtesy never shown in the same degree, when she was
in her height of state, and surrounded by all the appurtenances of her
rank,—that the princess would have extended her hand, frankly and
kindly; but her strength failing her, she gently bowed her head, in token
of consent.

Leon sprang into the sledge; and, signing to the driver to proceed,
addressed himself to the assistance and revival of Hermione. He sustained
her with a firm yet gentle arm; he supported her with all that care and
delicacy, so welcome from man to woman, when her weakness demands
help from his strength, and when his manly conduct gives no less reassurance to her feelings, than to her frame, his masculine aid.

"By what miracle, came you to be there,—on the spot, to succour me?"
she at length said. "I cannot yet comprehend how you, of all the world,
should——"

She stopped; there was a tremulous emphasis on the word 'you,' that
caused her to falter consciously; and that made Leon eagerly rejoin:—
"Who but I should be there,—at hand—to help you, if need were?
When I heard your sudden resolve to return at once,—to set forth to the
capital alone, unattended,—that your filial eagerness made you forgetful of
all risk, all possible peril in this hurried journey,—I determined that you
should have at least one faithful guardian by your side, in case of need.
I hastened to the courtyard, where the sledge stood ready, and got the

equerry or groom, who occupied the seat in the rear, to yield me his place, on the plea that by the princess's orders, her preceptor was to attend her to Kief in his room."

"And you submitted to occupy the post of a lackey,—a menial,—for my sake! A scholar! A gentleman! You!"

"Thanked be the sacred gods, I was there, when the accident happened! No matter what seat in the sledge I occupied, so that I was with it!" he returned.

"And could you believe that I would allow you to return to a groom's seat, when there was a place in my carriage? Think your scholar knows better what is due to her master,—her tutor,—her kind protector."

The very aid he had afforded her, the very exclusiveness with which she was thrown upon him for help and care, together with the generous frankness of her acknowledgment, caused Leon to abstain from responding to her words, otherwise than by a continuance of the deferential respect he had observed towards her. He would not now betray to her the feelings that he cherished—he would not now seek to learn hers,—he would not agitate her by a confession of his love, or an avowal of his identity; but would wait until they should be arrived at Kief, where, in her own home, and in the calm of finding,—as he trusted,—her father better, she should confirm the hope to which her present manner gave birth. Meantime, he wrapped himself in the content it engendered, and in the sufficing joy of finding himself side-by-side with her; together speaking, or together silent, communing with each other in word, or in thought, but mutually, solely, entirely.

The sledge sped on. Evening was drawing in, as they entered a thick forest. It was wild and desolate; with scattered pine-trees, and dark, spiring firs. The driver knew the track perfectly, so there was no impediment to their swift progress; but the air was cold and bleak; the sky was leaden and dreary; the pendant snow and icicles upon branch and bough, looked dripping, drooping, and cheerless, and added to the cutting sharpness of the frozen atmosphere. As the blast swept by, keen and piercing, Leon drew the fur mantle more closely round his charge, endeavouring effectually to screen her.

The wind howled dismally and fiercely. During one of its wildest gusts, Leon thought he perceived Hermione shiver.

"You tremble—you are chilled,—this open sledge ill shelters you;" he said.

"I am warm,—quite warm;" she replied. But her face grew paler as she spoke. There was a look of secret horror in her eyes; and her lip blanched, though she held it firm from quivering.

"You are alarmed,—you dread something,—what have you to fear?" he urged.

Hermione seemed striving to master her terror, ere she trusted herself with another word. At that moment, a louder, fiercer, wilder howl than before, came upon the blast. And then, through the rush and roar of the air, Leon heard the dismayed voice of the driver, shouting:—"The wolves! The wolves are upon us!"

An instant after, he saw something dart across the track,—dark, shadowy, gaunt; then another, and another; presently, two and three together, and then five or six. He could discern the shape of the rough, coarse-haired creatures; he could see their lank, famine-starved sides, their pointed muzzles, their small, ferocious eyes. He could see them savage, and sinister,—now leaping forward, now bounding among the bushes and low trees, now gathering thicker and thicker, and faster and faster,—until a huge drove of them had collected, and maintained a rapid race almost parallel with the sledge, as if in steady pursuit of their hoped-for prey. They looked like some spectral pack of hounds, galloping on with sharp yells and growls, mingled with prolonged howling cries,—ravenous, fierce, rapacious, unrelenting.

This appalling sight, the sense of imminent danger, the chance of becoming the victim of these fanged devils, only seemed to nerve the heart of Leon into sterner courage, and excite him into higher and braver resolve. He held Hermione, firmly sustained, with one arm; whispered encouragement and inspiriting words to her; and called to the man to drive swiftly and boldly on, as their best chance of safety. "We may keep them yet at bay!" he shouted. "They cannot outstrip us, while we keep this pace! Do thy best, good fellow! Thine own and thy mistress's life are in thy hands! Spare not speed! On! on!"

He turned to Hermione. She had conquered her first overwhelming fears. She was herself in her self-controul, her noble firmness, her high-souled dignity. He looked at her beautiful face,—elevated as it was with an expression fine, and intense, beyond all usual beauty.

" You look radiant,—as though you exulted, not feared ! " he said.

"I do exult ! I shall never live to be queen of Sicily ! I die, as I could wish ! " was her answer.

In her words, in her eyes, was the confession that it was because with him she should die, she rejoiced. The passionate response of his heart flew to his lips, and would have found utterance ; when a huge wolf sprang from the herd ; with a bound leaped upon the side of the sledge ; and, as it clung there, made a snap at Leon's disengaged arm. Instinctively he struck at it with his dagger, which he held ready. The blood gushed from the creature's throat; it quitted its hold, and fell. For an instant, its fate seemed to act as a check upon the rest ; with the cowardice that equals their ferocity, the panic seemed to spread through the pack, and a general halt ensued. It was but for a few seconds ; and again they were racing onward, in eager, bloody pursuit, with their howling, ravening throats, galloping open-mouthed to rend and devour.

At the sight of his near peril, Hermione gave way. She would have dropped, had he not caught her in his arms. " It is slain ! They give back ! " he cried ; but she had swooned, and heard him not. As she remained there, fainting,—she whom he had never seen otherwise than in the serenity, security, and majesty of her position—with all the distance which the difference of rank established between them,—he the humble secretary,—she the imperial princess,—now lying within his arms, helpless, senseless, wholly dependant on him for support and safety,—Leon's emotions grew into a strange delirious kind of rapture. There was something that singularly appealed to the chivalrous romance which formed part of his character, in this wild moment. The scene, the lonely pine-forest, the gathering darkness, the bleak and roaring wind. He felt an intoxication and excitement in the very peril of their situation ; the fleet motion of the horses, the swift rushing through the keen Northern air, the blind onward speed,—the advancing wolves—all had a strange bewildering charm for

him, as he clasped her nearer to his heart, and echoed her words, "I die
as I could wish!"

He took no farther heed of the howling, raging, ever-approaching
fiends. He had fixed his eyes upon that marble-pale face, that he might
look upon it to the last; when, suddenly, a piercing cry from the driver
struck upon his ear.

"A light! A light!" it cried. "They are coming! We are saved!"

In effect, a large troop of horsemen, bearing torches, and accompanying
a travelling sledge, might be perceived in motion towards them, among
the trees. The light, the noise, the approach, scared away the wolves,
who fled precipitately. In a few moments more, the cavalcade came up;
enquiries were interchanged; and while the rescuing company proved to
be the lady Paulina and her retinue, come to meet that of the princess, on
its progress to Kief,—the sledge with which they had so timely encountered, was discovered to contain Hermione herself.

Leon lost no time in committing the princess to the care of her friend,
that immediate means might be taken for her recovery from the fainting-
fit in which she still lay. Hermione,—like many women who either
suppress their feelings, forbidding them the usual vent of tears and sobs;
or who, by nature, cannot find relief in such outward demonstrations,—
was subject to swoon away, upon a strong, overpowering emotion.
Hitherto, her young life had known few such fearful extremities; but
now, the anxiety concerning her father, the agitation of her newly-
discovered passion for Leon, the consciousness of its variance with the
ties already formed for her by duty, together with the terror of the recent
scene, combined to throw her into the deep swoon, from which she was
with difficulty restored. When Paulina had at length succeeded in bringing her to herself, the princess was eager to know by what good fortune
she found herself safe in the arms of her friend. A sense of double
security, of escape from more than one threatened danger,—from two
imminent perils, made her throw herself upon the bosom of Paulina, as
a sure refuge; while she besought her to explain, by what happy chance
it was there to shelter and preserve.

Her friend told her, that knowing her filial solicitude would be awakened by the news of the emperor's attack, and finding that report greatly exaggerated its severity, she determined to set out as soon as possible after the courier to Igorhof, that she might soften the tidings she feared he would bring; and thus, not only allay the princess's immediate anxiety, but be ready to accompany her back to Kief, when she should repair thither to attend her father.

While the two ladies were thus interchanging comfort and reassurance, as they journeyed forward together, Leon followed in the other sledge, alone, wrapped in his thoughts. The whole seemed a vision, a fleeting delusion, a trick of the imagination, a vanished dream. Had she indeed been there, close within his arms, passive, unresisting, held against his heart? Had those fierce-mawed deaths really raced side-by-side with them, threatening immediate doom? Had he in fact swept through that wild forest, pierced by the night air, pressed by ravenous beasts, while, fast clasped in his embrace, she, with him, rushed to meet impending destruction? It seemed a wondrous, impossible fable; something that he had read or heard of,—ages ago,—in some remote country; not that which had happened even here,—scarce two hours since,—to himself. But beneath all this vague, insubstantial, though vivid dream, there lay one blest piece of certainty, one tangible, palpable, actual reality. Those words she had uttered, in the crisis of their menaced fate,—nothing could deprive him of those. They at least, had transpired; were positive, absolute, and true. Like a secret treasure, he could hug them, hoard them, possess them. They sat beside him in the dark, empty sledge; they kept close to him through the lonely night; they travelled with him to the end of his solitary journey, and made him feel no lack of companionship. " On my arrival, I shall see her, and draw from her their sweet import!" was his constant thought.

But when he had reached Kief, and found himself again in the capital,— again at court—once more surrounded by the order, and observance, and ceremonial of a palace; when, upon his requesting an interview with the princess Hermione, he found himself shown into a state apartment, and bidden to wait until her highness's farther pleasure should be known as to his reception, he felt how entirely the scene had changed, and how completely the old formalities, and limits, and cold prescribed distance, had been reestablished between them. Again she was the emperor's daughter; he, the secretary, the preceptor, the humble dependant. All his conflicting doubts and wishes came back confusedly upon him, and made him pause in his impulse to avow all.

He thought she wronged his impatience by letting him expect her so long; he accused her of indifference, of forgetfulness, of neglect, that she could thus keep waiting, one, between whom and herself such momentous passages had taken place. He felt jealously alive to the fear, that if she could observe this ceremonial delay in receiving the man who shared with her the perils of that night, he must be mistaken in supposing she had ever entertained a thought of tender regard towards him. Thus did he torture himself with perplexing surmises, and painful conjectures, until the words —those words he had deemed beyond all else real, amid the visions of that eventful night—became now the shadows—the insubstantial, delusive, vanished dreams.

Little did he think,—as he paced there, racking himself with jealous fears, and restlessly awaiting her coming—that her delay was owing to her own want of courage at the approaching interview. How little did he guess, that it was because she dreaded to meet him,—lest she should be unable to maintain the adherence to her own and her father's vowed word, which she had firmly resolved upon, yet which the sight of him might shake,—that she did not come. How little did he imagine, that so far from indifference, or forgetfulness, causing her to tarry, it was only from a too keen sense of his presence, and of its influence upon her feelings, that she still hesitated to encounter their effect.

But at length, schooling herself to firmness, and fortifying her resolution, by all her most imperative considerations of honor and duty, she appeared. Her aspect was serene, gracious, gentle.

She advanced to where Leon stood, gave him her hand with kindness,— with even a bounteous and cordial effusion of manner, yet with all her native self-possession, and tranquil dignity; and in a voice calm and

collected, yet full of a breathing earnestness and sincerity, she said :—
" My grateful thanks to him whose courage and devotion enabled me to
carry through my wish of coming to my father without delay ! I can
never forget that I owe it to you, kindest preceptor and friend, that
I reached home alive, and in time to see my father recover. You will
rejoice to learn, that he is now out of danger,—all but quite restored."

Leon bowed upon the hand he raised to his lips, unable to utter more
than a murmured gratulation.

" The emperor's first care, when able to receive his loyal friends," she
went on, " will be to join the expression of his gratitude to that of his
child. He bids me say he is eager to acknowledge his obligation to the
man, whose intellectual resources, inestimably dedicated to her advantage,
are equalled by a bravery and intrepidity which risked life for her
protection."

" Such risk is privilege !" he exclaimed. " The best blood in my veins
should be freely poured forth for such another grace of fortune as that
night's hazard—that night's events—that night's words !"

The beautiful face maintained its expression of calm resolve, though it
visibly crimsoned beneath the ardent gaze with which he regarded it, as
he spoke.

" The gods vouchsafe but seldom such blest chance ;" he continued.
" Still, once to have owed to them the accident of your rescue, together
with the memory of those words,—words extorted by the terrors of that
night, yet words so priceless in their gentle significance,——"

" Let them be forgotten !" said the voice of Hermione, vainly striving
to steady its tremulous sadness, as she interrupted Leon's eager speech.

" They are treasured in my heart—never to be driven thence—never to
be expelled, or effaced !" he said impetuously.

" Then hold them buried there !" she said firmly. " I will neither deny
them nor retract them. I will rather consign them to your keeping,—
to your honor ; I will rather refer me to your generosity, your strength,
your help, to aid me against myself, and the consequences of my words.
They were fatally, rashly, weakly uttered,—in the moment of extremest

mortal excitement,—in the face of death itself,—when I believed that life
and I had done with each other,—when I thought that life's duties, life's
incumbencies had ceased for me, and that I was free to rejoice at my
enfranchisement. But I was restored to life; and, with it, to life's demands upon my faith and truth. I abide by them; and I ask you, my
tutor, my guardian, my friend, to aid me in mine intent."

She stood with such a majesty of virtuous determination, yet with an
air so full of feminine gentleness and feeling, that Leon, no longer able to
contain his transport, cast his arm about her, and drew her towards him, as
he whispered:—"And what if faith and truth were not opposed to freedom? What if they were one? What if they sanctioned avowal of the
sweet meaning of those words which only the agony of death could force
from that noble, faithful, true heart? What if tenderness for Leon, plight
to Leontes, were one? What if Leon himself, and Leontes, were one?"

Hermione, in utter wonderment, gazed at him; withdrawing from his
arm, and raising herself to full height of erect and dignified posture.
Never had she looked so cold, so marble still, so statue-like in her lofty
quietude.

The prince threw himself at her feet with a diffidence, a humility—
unknown to him in his character of secretary.

"Leontes,—your lover, — your promised husband,—your suitor for
a confirmation of the gracious hope accorded to the honored, happy Leon."

"The prince of Sicily! Leontes!" she at length exclaimed. "Your
highness wrongs yourself by this attitude. Rise my lord!" She spoke
with a haughty composure and condescension, which she had never
observed towards the poor student. "You wrong your greatness by this
lowly posture, no less than by the disguise, the deception, with which it
pleased you first to approach me."

Leon stung by her manner, no less than by her words, started from his
knee, echoing the word, "Deception!"

"Was it not a deception, my lord? One that might have compromised
her who was to be your wife? One unworthy yourself and me? Yet
can I better forgive that, than my own weakness,—mine own self-
delusion." And she turned from him, as if proudly abashed.

"Let us exchange forgiveness;" he said. "Hermione shall forgive me, that I ventured hither to behold with mine own eyes the truth of those virtues and beauties which fame extolled as so surpassing; and I will forgive her that she should own to a softness of heart, which in my mind, but adds another charm to her character."

"May not soft-heartedness become a defect rather than a charm, if it mislead its mistress into unworthy yielding and self-forgetfulness?" asked Hermione with a smile which had more of her old ease and warmth of manner in its sweet seriousness, than she had yet shown. "Come, my lord, since you are resolved to throw off austerity with your character of preceptor, and commence suitor, as in duty bound, by flattering my errors, and persuading me they are but so many merits and excellences, I will abate no jot of my rightful courtship; but will be wooed in all set form, and proper observance. Since your grace hath honored me by the compliment of coming so far, to play the wooer yourself instead of by proxy, I mean to enjoy all the glory of so princely a suitor; and shall hope to bid your highness welcome in your own proper person, among my company this evening."

She curtsied with gay graciousness, and withdrew; leaving Leontes perplexed, fascinated, chagrined, pleased, provoked, charmed, dissatisfied, —all at once; yet more enamoured than ever.

This playful manner she maintained towards him. With livelier grace than she had ever before deported herself, she enacted the courted beauty, and behaved to the prince as to her admitted admirer. She received his visits; she accepted his attentions, his assiduities; she allowed him to compliment her, to offer her gallantries of adulation and homage,—nay, seemed to expect them from him; she granted him her ear and her society, but it was when surrounded with others, by her ladies, her court; and always in such sprightly sort, and with so much of easy vivacity and gaiety, that he felt less gratified than annoyed by these interviews. He could never obtain a serious word from her; all allusions to love were turned off as mere gallant speeches, as matter-of-course courting, and protestation. All endeavour to draw her into particular conversation

was avoided; all attempts to win her apart, or to see her alone, failed.
He bitterly regretted the old pleasant times of preceptor and scholar, of
master and pupil, when side by side he sat with her, undisturbed, at the
quiet study-table, in the window-nook, at Igorhof. They then had seemed
to understand each other perfectly, although so silent, so still, so abstracted.
Now they met constantly, talked openly, communicated freely, yet were
they more than ever widely asunder; he felt more removed from her,
more estranged from her, now that he saw her and conversed with her
daily, as her avowed suitor, than formerly, when he approached her but at
humble distance, as her tutor, her instructor.

He fretted beneath this change. He arraigned her of trifling, of heartlessness; yet one look from her beaming, gracious eyes, sufficed to convince
him of the tenderness, the truth of that pure nature. He was incensed at
her reserve, resenting it as caprice and tyranny; but the music of her
voice, the gentleness and softness of her most sportive manner, bespoke
the womanly sweetness of heart, the innocence of soul, which forbade him
to believe her wanting in warmth of generosity.

Weeks crept by; and weeks merged into months; until three had
passed, since things had gone thus between Hermione and Leontes. She,
sensitively alive to the fear that she had been on the verge of yielding to
an inclination which might have vanquished her sense of right, and anxious
to prove, both to herself, and her lover, that she was not to be lightly won;
he, tortured by the desire to know whether he really possessed that power
over her heart, which he had once dreamed was his.

He had sent her a few rare flowers; accompanied by some verses. He
had written them with a full heart, thinking of those he had once before
ventured to offer her,—the poem,—the Sicilian theme,—which were to
form the medium of his love-confession. " Will they move her to a kindly
recollection of that old by-gone time," he mused, " or will they encounter
a like wilful misconstruction ? She interpreted the first as a mere meaning-
less theme,—coldly, calmly ; yet, let me own, like a right noble and royal
lady, as became her. But will she now treat my poor lines,—writ, Heaven
knoweth, in all truth of heart-sincerity,—as mere idle gallantry, pretty
words, frothy compliment ? "

As he had dreaded, so the event proved. The princess no sooner saw him, after she had received his verses, than she rallied him upon their hyperbole, their exalted strain. "It is impossible I can merit this eulogium,—this high-flown panegyric, my lord;" she said gaily. "But it is the privilege of you lovers to deal in flatteries, and the part of us ladies to affect to believe them. See here, my father!" she said, appealing to him, "see what my lord the prince hath set down, of my being 'unequalled in worth as in beauty;' and I know not what else of impossible fictions, permitted only to poets and lovers,—the licensed falsehood-mongers of all time."

"Thou art ungrateful, child; and like a spoiled beauty, know'st not how, properly, to estimate the homage of love and poesy. But I leave thee to thank this poetical lover of thine as he should be thanked; and that is, by promising him an early day for the betrothal which has been too long delayed for my good will; and for his too, I'll warrant me, though he is too generous to urge us. Sue her, prince; thou hast her father's sanction for a little pressing."

And the emperor good-humouredly left the lovers to themselves.

It was the first time Leontes had found himself alone with Hermione since the interview in which he had avowed his identity. For an instant he hesitated, overpowered by mingled sensations of joy, hurt feeling, eagerness, hope, bitterness, dread, delight. But the latter prevailed, as he saw her change colour, rise abruptly, and then stand irresolutely, consciously, looking down upon the ground. He hurried towards her; and poured out imploring words that she would yield to her father's wishes, and crown his own.

Hermione tried to rally; to recall some of her playful ease, her sportive grace, as she replied. But her voice faltered; and she concluded with gentle gravity :—"I am ready to fulfil my father's will,—to redeem his pledged word."

"I will not claim you upon that contract;" he answered, impetuously; "the cold fulfilment of a vow cannot content me; my passionate heart cannot starve upon distrust and misgiving,—upon mere compliance, and

conformity with duty. Give me such bounty of love as I used to dream
I read in your eyes for the poor secretary."

" Let me look upon him again,—knowing him for naught else,—and
haply I might learn to regard him as you could wish;" she said.

" I cannot bear this trifling;" he returned. " My love is too deeply
in earnest, to endure a doubt. I can better resolve to yield you altogether,
than to owe your possession to a bargain—a compact—a poor formality.
Be mine from the promptings of your own heart; or I will renounce the
privilege of claiming you at all. If you cannot grant me the assurance,
the blissful certainty, that I am dear to you for mine own sake, I shall
return to Sicily,—contend with my regrets as I best may,—and—leave
you free."

" You cannot do that, my lord."

Her altered voice,—altered from the light ease it had endeavoured to
assume, to a low tone, serious, and tender,—made him start, and look into
her eyes. They met his for a moment with their own sweet composure;
then fell, as she went on, in reply to his eager look :—" You cannot do
that ; I am no longer free."

" Hermione !"

" No ; for I,——" she let the white hand he had seized, clasp palms
with his,—" for I,——' I am yours for ever.' "

He held her to him. " With full love mine ? I am greedy of assurance."

" With full love. I could have died with Leon ; I would live till death
with Leontes."

He folded her to his satisfied heart.

And now the preparations for the public ceremonial of solemn betrothal
went forward in good earnest. Meantime, the lovers passed their time
together, with unclouded joy. Hermione, once her love revealed, was
above the affectation of coyness or reserve, and permitted its genuine
warmth of feeling to flow unchecked. She was tender, confiding ; full of
cordial sympathy, and ingenuous affection. Leontes, his heart at ease, his

doubts at rest, his hope confirmed, became animated, vivacious, happy. Never had he looked to so much advantage; never had he shown so attractive in person, so winning in manner, as now, that his fine features shone elate and joyous, and his words sprang forth, copious, and spirited, and eloquent. Now indeed, he stood confessed, the handsome, the accomplished prince; the well-graced gentleman, the high-bred scholar, the noble Leontes,—Sicilia's hope and pride. Now, at length, the emperor, the whole court, saw in him that vaunted prince of Sicily, worthy in fact, as in report, to be the husband of their beloved Hermione; whilst she herself felt, that in him, was fully embodied her ideal of manly beauty, honor, and excellence.

The royal lovers had taken a mutual pleasure in witnessing the marriage of Alexis and Emilia; and in establishing the worldly prospects of the young couple. After a brief period of wedded happiness, the bridegroom had quitted the capital, to join the army, leaving his bride in the charge of her friend and mistress, Hermione, with whom she still remained, as one of her ladies-of-honor.

Camillo returned to Sicily; that he might precede the prince his master, and have all things in readiness for the immediate solemnization of the nuptials, (which, in deference to the wish of the king, were to be celebrated there) on the arrival of Leontes with his betrothed consort.

So long a time had insensibly crept away, that Paulina's first child was born, ere the ceremony of her royal mistress's troth-plight took place. Hermione had made a point that her friend, and favorite lady-of-honor, should be present on the occasion; and this had again deferred the day. But so soon as Paulina recovered sufficiently to go abroad, the public rite was performed; and Hermione, the imperial princess of Russia, was solemnly contracted to Leontes, prince of Sicily.

Some short time afterward, Hermione and Paulina happened to be alone together. The latter had brought her new-born little one to the palace; and the two ladies were engaged in affectionate comment on its pretty baby looks, and infant ways, when Paulina said:—" But in hearing you praise my babe, my motherly delight,—which is apt to be selfish and forgetful,—

makes me lose sight of your grace's new demands on your time ; they may require your presence. In all likelihood, the prince is expecting you. I must not let a thoughtless mother's raptures—which are inexhaustible— detain your highness from more important claims on your attention."

" From more agreeable,—more interesting,—more welcome,—as well as more wise raptures than a mother's, wouldst thou say ? Those of a lover, eh ?" said the princess smiling. " But in sooth, Paulina, I am thine, and thine urchin's, for as long as thou wilt, to-day. My lord hath received letters from Sicily, and he is busy writing answers to them ; together with despatches for his bosom friend, Polixenes, prince of Bohemia, which are to be forwarded by the same messenger, who is now waiting for the rest. This will occupy Leontes for some time ; so e'en let us have our nursery-chat out, in full comfort and length of gossipry."

" Letters from Sicily ?" said Paulina in a grave, enquiring tone.

" Ay, from his royal father ; and from his confidential friend, and counsellor ; " said Hermione.

" Camillo ; " repeated Paulina firmly. " Fear not to speak the name, lady. I can both hear it, and utter it, without a thought that shrinks from scrutiny. I am glad to have the opportunity of telling you this. I were unworthy of the name I bear, as of the title of your friend, could I not honestly say as much. What might have been, is as it had never been, even in possibility. I can honor, revere, admire, the high qualities of Camillo ; I can take delight in hearing of them, even with the added deeper, and prouder interest which, in a woman's heart, must always cleave to the idea of a man who has once preferred her to all other women ; but, for a shadow of the feelings with which I once could have regarded him—there is no trace—no faintest vestige remaining. I believe that with a right-hearted, right-minded woman, the image of the man to whom she is married,—the father of her children,—will always supersede that of any other. If she herself be hearty and sincere in her desire to obliterate the idea of that other,—however he may have succeeded in attracting her imagination, and touching her feelings, in the first instance,—if she be in earnest, and if her husband be kind and good, her love will in the end become his. And my lord, Antigonus, is both good and kind; he is lenient, indulgent. He bears with my somewhat peremptory disposition. He hath toleration for my warmth of speech; for my hasty, and, I fear, sometimes, over-urgent manner. Not only reconciled, have I for some time been, to the union I once looked forward to with repugnance, and with the sole intention of fulfilling a duty; but I have come to believe that such an indulgent husband as Antigonus is better suited to an inflexible temper like mine, than a less yielding man might have been. Your Paulina now owns herself, an entirely happy wife and mother."

Hermione pressed her friend's hand in both hers, as she said :—" Thanks my Paulina, for this picture of your heart. It strengthens mine. Yours has been an ennobling example for me; but at one time, I fear me, my wayward affections ran a chance of profiting less by it, than they might and ought."

When the time came for Leontes and Hermione to set forth for Sicily, they were attended by a numerous train of friends and followers; among whom were not only the lord Antigonus, and his wife and child, but the lady Emilia. Alexis had fallen in his very first campaign; and the young widow, without a tie to bind her to her native country, followed her royal mistress to her new home.

This grief, and the parting with her father, were the only shadows upon the happiness of Hermione, when she prepared to accompany her betrothed husband to the land of his birth. The journey southward; the visiting new scenes, in the spring of the year, and of her own young life; the introduction to all the glories of a sunny clime, after the chill and gloom of a northern one; were each so many fresh delights to the princess, enhanced by the supreme charm of enjoying them in the society of her lover,—of him she loved. They would have been content, both of them, thus to have travelled on together, ever; had it not been that at their journey's end, awaited them the crowning joy, that was to give them to each other,—to make them one for ever.

Immediately on their arrival, the marriage was celebrated. The whole
island rang with rejoicing and festivity ; and all Sicily joined their king,
in his delight to see his son wedded to a princess whom he found as
charming as fame had represented her.

This was the final satisfaction of the good old man's life ; for scarcely
had many months elapsed after the event, when, full of years and honor,
the king died, leaving Leontes to succeed him. Heartily then, did his son
take comfort from the thought that he had always been filially obedient :
that he had never crossed his parent's will, or thwarted his decrees. He
reflected with pleasure, that in the matter of the Russian alliance, which
now formed his best happiness, he had implicitly followed the wishes of
his father.

On the day of coronation, when they received the homage of their people,
and were jointly hailed by their new titles, Leontes whispered Hermione :—
" How say you, sweet wife ?   Would you now, that you had never lived
to be queen of Sicily ? "

" You taught me to prize that title for the sake of him who confers it ; "
she answered.   " I am afraid I should have been graceless enough to care
little for the name of queen, had it not comprised another, and a dearer
one—that of wife to a certain rogue secretary, who had the presumption to
aspire to a princess ; ay, and who moreover had well-nigh perverted her
faith, as certainly as he stole her heart."

Time went on.   Another child had been born to Paulina and Antigonus,
ere hopes were entertained of an heir to the crown of Sicily.   But at length
the joyful tidings were sent to Russia, that the emperor might now expect
to hear of his daughter's presenting her husband with the son he had so
ardently hoped for.   This intelligence gave great delight to the affectionate
parent ; but he was destined never to have it confirmed ; for before the
birth of his grand-child was announced, he himself expired.

The news of her father's death brought mourning to the hearts of
Hermione and Leontes ; and they were still in the first bitterness of
their grief, when their boy was born.   They could not have had a
sweeter source of comfort and consolation, than the little Mamillius.

He was a gentle-tempered fondling child, with a fund of quiet spirits, and imaginative fancy. He would laugh softly, and take pleasure in jesting plays, and frolickings; but they must be of a quiet kind. He liked no turbulent games, no rough sports. He shrank from abrupt, or boisterous amusements. He could not bear noise, or violent action. He was very merry, but it was in a placid, under-toned way of his own. He had plenty of courage, and nobility of feeling, but he never showed it by loud, or active demonstration. He had some timidity of manner; but none of heart. He was a sensitive, impressionable child. He was fond of stories that excited his imagination; and used to tell them, or listen to them, with a kind of breathless awe, in a low voice, and with his features working, and his eyes fixed upon the hearer or narrator. He would stand at his mother's knee, and relate his wonders, charmed to note in her grave, sympathetic countenance, the sort of interest he felt, and delighted to inspire. With his father,—who was less patient, and who rather bantered him, and amused himself with him, than attended to him,— he would bandy playful speeches, and strive to exchange railleries. With the ladies-of-honor, he was whimsically humorous; and returned their petting jests, with a little quiet sarcasm of his own peculiar kind,—childish and innocent, yet full of a fanciful, though staid sprightliness. He was very fond of Paulina's youngest child,—her third daughter, born some time after himself; for her, he would invent long histories, and relate them by the hour together, watching her face, and marking their effect upon her. She was a good listener; as fond of wonders, and sprites, and ghost-stories, and tales of magic, and hobgoblins, as himself. These two little creatures would sit in some corner by themselves, absorbed, and happy, lost in a marvel-world of their own, heedless of time, and caring not to join in the livelier gambols of their companions.

Paulina was dotingly fond of the little prince; and would often beg him of his mother, that he might come to spend a day with herself, and her children, at a quiet country house she had, somewhat removed from the court.

It was a retreat fitted up by the indulgence of her husband perfectly in her own taste. Paulina was a woman of an earnest nature. She was de-

vout ; and she had an intense love of art. These two paramount feelings
of her soul and mind were combinedly consulted by the manner in which
this retired spot was adorned. There were usual sitting-rooms ; but adjoining them was a gallery, filled with treasures of art,—pictures, sculpture,
and many curiosities in gems and medals. At the end of this gallery, was
a chapel built entirely of white marble, lighted from the ceiling, and containing a curtained recess, intended for a group of statuary, whenever Paulina
should have met with one of sufficient merit to occupy this particular niche.
To this gallery and chapel, Paulina would often lead the young Mamillius, and her own girls, pleased with the entertainment of the children,
who crowded round her, holding her skirts, and drinking in her words, as
she explained to them some of the beauties and curious valuables of the
gallery, or endeavour to make them understand some of the glories and
mysteries belonging to the chapel. In this latter spot, the little prince
delighted to linger ; his eyes fastened upon her lips, as, with grave, simple,
earnest words, she spoke of some of those high and sacred themes in terms
she thought best suited to his childish comprehension.

Once as he stood there, grasping her hand tight, and nestling close at her
side, and looking earnestly at the curtained recess, opposite to which they
had paused,—Paulina thought she felt the boy tremble. She asked him if
he feared or ailed anything.

"No I am not afraid,—I feel very well—very happy."

"What makes you whisper ?" she enquired.

"I don't know. In this room I never can help speaking low." He
shifted restlessly from one foot to the other ; but kept his eyes fixed upon
the thick folds of the curtain.

"Do you see anything ?" she added.

"I thought I saw the curtain move. I was thinking, if the folds were
suddenly to draw back, and show us a grand, gracious form, standing there.
It would be beautiful, would it not ? "

"Yes ; but there is nothing there. I will show you there is nothing."
And Paulina would have advanced to draw back the drapery, that he might
be convinced the recess was empty ; when the boy exclaimed :—"Don't

think that I am afraid! I will go to it myself! I'll pull it back myself. Only that while it's undrawn, I can fancy that it moves; and believe that perhaps there's something beautiful standing there, behind it."

Leontes had often spoken with enthusiasm to his wife of his dear friend and brother-in-affection, Polixenes. He, like himself, had lately succeeded to his father's throne, and was now king of Bohemia. Polixenes had married shortly after his friend; and about the same time that the birth of Mamillius had gladdened the heart of his parents, the queen of Polixenes had also brought her lord a son. Leontes would frequently tell Hermione of the happy boyhood times that he and his brother-friend had spent together; and dwelt with delight upon the hope of seeing him one day in Sicily. He said what charming companions the two little princes would make for each other; and longed that Florizel and Mamillius could enjoy the same schoolfellow intimacy which had been their fathers', at their age. At length, after many a pressing entreaty and invitation on the part of the king of Sicily, his friend Polixenes consented to come and spend some time with him, on the express condition that on the following summer Leontes should return his visit, and make some stay in Bohemia. Nothing could exceed the enthusiastic delight with which Leontes prepared to receive his friend. He appointed an especial retinue and establishment for him; he placed at his disposal all comforts, conveniences, and luxuries, he could desire; he entrusted his own faithful Camillo with the especial care of Polixenes' safety; placed this tried and confidential servant in the office nearest to his person, and made him his cup-bearer.

For some time before his friend's arrival, Leontes could speak to Hermione of nothing else; and she, with her usual cordiality and warmth of sympathy in all that interested him, evinced as anxious a desire to see this dear brother-in-love of her husband's, as her husband himself. From the same cause,—after Polixenes had landed, and had been their guest some time, and had lengthened, and yet again prolonged his visit, at the instance of his friend,—Hermione would play the kind and affectionate hostess, with no less earnestness, than her husband played the part of host. And thus they still urged, and Polixenes still yielded, until many months had flown by in the continued visit of Bohemia, to his brother king and friend, Sicilia. At last, Polixenes withstood all farther solicitations of his kind entertainers, by fixing a certain day for his departure—the morrow, the very morrow, of the one on which Leontes again pressed him to remain, and called upon Hermione to second his entreaty; when she playfully replied :— *" I had thought, sir, to have held my peace, until you had drawn oaths from him, not to stay."*

Thus far the spring of Hermione's fortunes. " What to her adheres, which follows after, is the argument of" a ' Winter's Tale.'

FINIS.

THE

GIRLHOOD

OF

SHAKESPEARE'S HEROINES;

IN

A SERIES OF FIFTEEN TALES,

BY

MARY COWDEN CLARKE,

Author of the Concordance to Shakespeare.

"as petty to his ends,
. As is the morn-dew on the myrtle leaf
To his grand sea."

Shakespeare.

TALE XIV.

VIOLA; THE TWIN.

LONDON:

W. H. SMITH & SON, 136, STRAND; AND SIMPKIN, MARSHALL, & CO.,
STATIONERS' HALL COURT.
1851.

TO

J. PAYNE COLLIER, ESQ.,

WHOSE SHAKESPEAREAN ZEAL AND PRIVATE COURTESY

CLAIM HER ESPECIAL ACKNOWLEDGEMENT,

THIS TALE IS

GRATEFULLY INSCRIBED

BY

MARY COWDEN CLARKE.

TALE XIV.

VIOLA; THE TWIN.

Seb. " A lady, sir, though it was said that she much resembled me, was yet of many accounted beautiful : but, though I could not, with such estimable wonder, overfar believe that, yet thus far I will boldly publish her, she bore a mind that envy could not but call fair."

" One face, one voice, one habit, and two persons ;
A natural perspective, that is, and is not.
* * * * * *
An apple, cleft in two, is not more twin
Than these two creatures."
Twelfth Night.

On the Eastern shores of the Adriatic, is a place called Messaline. It will not be found in the map. But we have great (poetical,—not geographical) authority for its being there—somewhere on those shores—not far down beyond the coast of Illyria. It is,—or rather was,—a fine stately place ; with noble shipping, and handsome buildings. It had a goodly harbour, and commanded a grand expansive view of the broad, blue, sparkling sea. Its inhabitants were of Greek origin, and maintained many of their Grecian peculiarities of custom, speech, and dress; although they had become much Italianized by their vicinity and association with their neighbours on the opposite shores of Italy. There were many beautiful islands clustered close about ; fertile, luxuriant green spots, embosomed in the glittering azure of the waters ; looking like portions of the shore, parted in some giant freak of Nature's, from the parent land, which wound in deep undulating indentations, forming lovely bays, and sheltered recesses, along the edge of the sea.

In this Messaline, dwelt a young man, named Sebastian. He was a scion of a noble house ; but it had many scions, and there was not enough of the vital sap,—money—in the whole of the parent tree, to nourish its multitudinous branches. This one, therefore, resolved to cut himself away from the parent stock ; to engraft himself upon a more vigorous one ; to be no longer a sprig of nobility ; but to try if he could not support himself, and flourish, as an individual independent plant. In other words, he determined,—much to the chagrin of his noble brethren, who were all far too proud, and too conscious of what was due to their own honor, and the honor of their house, to think of working,—to adopt a profession, which he thought calculated to afford him the means of earning *his own* bread. He availed himself of the offer of a humble connection of his family's,—a wealthy merchant, who could boast no noble, (.but some very good) blood in his veins,—to enter his house as a junior partner ; to take an active part in the business, to travel for them, to conduct their transactions, superintend their concerns, and effect their sales and purchases, in those foreign places with which they had dealings. At the death of this rich friend, and humble connection of his family's, the young Sebastian found himself the head of the mercantile house to which he now belonged ; and his noble brethren were so far reconciled to him,—for they could never entirely forgive him,—as to accept at his hands, sundry pecuniary accommodations and assistances ; merely temporary, of course ; loans, not gifts. This arrangement pleased all parties. The noble gentlemen preserved their complacent feelings of having done nothing derogatory to the dignity and honor of their house ; and the merchant-brother rejoiced that his was in a condition to spare from its industry and wealth, sufficient to keep his relations from starving.

But Sebastian nearly forfeited even this last claim to his family's countenance and support ; by marrying a poor girl, with no name,—but an honest one. They were highly incensed ; vowed they would never see him more ; and declared that all communications, henceforth, must be limited to writing. It is recorded, this limitation was so strictly observed, that several cash-orders passed between the two houses, but no instance was ever known of either acknowledgment or acquittal finding its way from one to the other. The noble house was rigid in holding as little intercourse as possible with the commercial one. It would not be guilty of sanctioning its degraded member, by farther notice than was absolutely necessary. Its inmates would not utterly cast off and renounce their unworthy brother; they received his letters, they opened them, and made themselves masters of their contents, but they never replied. They did not refuse his notes; but they answered none.

The young merchant bore this neglect very philosophically; he was over head and ears in love with his wife; and her society consoled him for the loss he had sustained in that of his relations; indeed, it is a question whether he ever missed it.

But he had not been many months married, ere Sebastian found that his affairs abroad required his personal supervision. So long as he had travelled, and inspected the foreign transactions himself, they had flourished; but since he had left them more to themselves, or committed them to the care of agents, they languished, and the prosperity of the concern was in danger of decreasing. He resolved, therefore, to use no delay, but to set sail at once. The reluctance he felt to leave his wife,—whose present situation formed a new claim on his love, and his desire to remain by her side,—was counterbalanced by the thought, that it was now more than ever his duty to provide for their future comfort and maintenance. Taking a tender leave of her, therefore, and bidding her keep a stout heart, for that his absence was but to ensure a fortune for the little creature whom he hoped to find happily born by the time he returned, he went on board one of his goodly vessels that lay in the harbour, and bent his course southward.

His voyage included an expedition to the Coast of Barbary, whence he was to bring away a cargo of fine ivory. In his way back he touched at Trapani, in Sicily, famous for its coral fisheries, and for the skill and beauty with which its inhabitants wrought the native produce into ornaments of rare device. Laden with these costly wares, he determined to proceed at once with them to Venice, where he was sure of a ready mart for his merchandise, and where he had other business that required his presence. These objects necessarily occupied a considerable space of time; and several months had elapsed, ere the prow of the vessel pointed northward. As Sebastian neared his native shores, on his return up the Adriatic, his heart sickened with impatience, and he felt sorely tempted to land at Messaline, to behold his home, his wife, and as he hoped,—his child, before proceeding farther. But resisting the impulse, he manfully pursued his passage up the Venetian gulf, resolved to complete all he had to do, ere he permitted himself to enjoy the happiness which he should then so justly have earned. He fortified all his prudent resolutions, by telling himself, how enhanced would be his delight at returning, when he should bear with him the profitable results of his long voyage, and compensate the lengthened absence, by the rich reward.

But the affairs that demanded his attention at Venice, occupied much longer than he had anticipated; and having already devoted so much time to their due arrangement, he would not be deterred from seeing them finally and decidedly settled. Thus, many more months crept by, and still his return home was protracted. While he was detained at Venice, he met with a dear and esteemed friend of his father's house,—the reigning duke of Illyria. The duke was spending some time on a visit to the doge, accompanied by his young son, Orsino, a handsome intelligent boy, of about seven or eight years old. The duke had always entertained a great respect and liking for Sebastian. He admired his independent character; he knew him to be sensible, enlightened, and of high principles. The two young men maintained a strong friendship for each other,—nowise interrupted by the circumstance of the one being at the head of a dukedom, the other at the head of a mercantile house. The merchant loved the duke for his superiority to the prejudices which swayed so many of the old Italian nobility, teaching them to scorn commerce as beneath the dignity of their birth, and to believe that begging or starvation was preferable to the dishonor of labor; while the duke loved the merchant for his noble way of thinking, his probity, his industry, his courageous rejection of that pride of blood which would have prevented his being the architect of his own fortunes.

At length the whole of the important transactions which had held him prisoner at Venice so long, were prosperously concluded, and Sebastian was free to return home. He bade farewell to his friend; the duke drawing from him a promise, that at no very distant period, he would make it in his way, during some of his future voyages, to come and see him at his capital of Illyria. The merchant gladly consented; and once more set sail. But contrary winds delayed him; until he began to think there was a spell against his return home. He had been absent now, more than twenty months; and from the time he had left its port, no tidings had reached him from Messaline. The little communication by letter that then prevailed, the infrequency, the uncertainty of intelligence, caused it to be no unusual occurrence with travellers long abroad, to hear neither from, nor of, their friends, until they themselves returned. Absence, in those times, had redoubled pangs and terrors. But Sebastian would not let himself give way to fear. As valiantly as he could, he determined to persevere in hope; and to look steadily forward to the unclouded happiness which he trusted was so soon to be his.

Stress of weather had compelled him to put into harbour, at one of the islands that lay scattered in his course. He remembered, when he landed, that in this island, on her own estate, resided a certain maiden aunt of his, —an old lady, very precise in her notions, very demure in her manners, and very particular in all her ways. She had a pale, faded face; a pinched, wiry figure; thin, transparent hands, with their veins very prominent; and a dabby voice, with which she dab—dab—dabbed on, in a perpetual, ever-flowing, complacent tattle.

But she had been very kind to Sebastian when a boy (she owned to a strong partiality for boys), and he had a pleasant recollection of the little old lady, who used to bring him toys and sweetmeats, and beg holidays for him, and beg off scoldings for him, and treat him with a petting kind of patronage, very agreeable to a lad who was not a great favorite in his own home. He resolved, therefore, to pay a visit to this maiden aunt, now he was so near her demesne; and he accordingly mounted the rather steep rise on which it was situated, and making his way to the mansion, enquired for the lady Annuccia.

He was shown into the large plainly-furnished apartment; in which, at one end, he found her sitting, with one or two of her woman attendants, spinning.

When he had announced himself, calling himself to her remembrance as the nephew to whom she had formerly been so kind, at the time of a visit she had paid to his father, at Messaline, the old lady extended her slender fingers to him in an affable kind of flurry, and said :—" Dear me! Well!

And so it's you, Sebastian! Well! Dear me! Only think! How you've grown! Dear me! Ay, you're married, since, I recollect. Dear me! it seems impossible! Only think; married! Well, well! I declare it quite flutters me, to think of it, and to see you! Dear me!"

She took up her large green fan, that lay beside her, and fanned herself in a sort of mild agitation; looking at him approvingly, at intervals; and, between whiles, hemming softly behind her pocket-handkerchief, as if to gain breath.

"I ventured to believe you would be glad to see me, aunt Annuccia," he said; "and being so near you, I would not miss the pleasure of a visit."

"Dear me! You're very good, I'm sure, my dear boy! that is, my dear young man—my good nephew! Dear me! yes, well, it's quite an unexpected treat, I'm sure, a visit from you, my dear nephew! Who should have thought of seeing you enter the room, of all beings in the world? Ay, well, yes; strange things do happen! Dear me! I had a visit a day or two since—a visitation, I may say,—Dear me, well!—a visit from your uncle,—you remember your uncle, don Ignazio? Well, ay, he, who but he, should make his appearance here!" The old lady gasped, and played her fan so impressively, and fluttered so perceptibly; and taking her kerchief from her lips, laid it on her heart, so pantingly, that Sebastian felt called upon to echo :—"Dear me!"

"Yes, indeed! Well! He, and none but he, I'll assure you! He came, he said, to spend a few days with me;" (here the thin fingers found their way to the lips again, and the soft hems were repeated, interspersed with a gentle simpering sound;) "to spend a few days here, since it was so long since we had seen each other. So strange, you know, my dear boy,—my good nephew!"

As she paused, evidently expecting that he should respond to the surprise she expressed, Sebastian said :—"Yes; that is,—is it so remarkable that uncle Ignazio should come to visit you? I thought you and he were cousins."

"Precisely; my dear boy—my dear nephew—that's it! Dear me! That's it, which makes it so strange."

"Oh!" assented Sebastian ; not seeing at all how the matter was cleared.

His tone was so obviously unconvinced,—he was evidently still so much abroad, that his aunt condescended to be more explanatory.

"Why you see,—dear me,—well,—it's difficult to—it's awkward to know how to—dear me! How shall I——? Yet you're an old married man, quite a steady old married man,—yes,—dear me,—to be sure, well, there can be no hesitation, with an old married man like you, in——"

Her dab—dab—dabby voice had quavered off; and came to a full stop. Sebastian looked at her; more at a loss than ever.

The maiden lady caught up her handkerchief again, hemmed; laid it down, and took up her fan; fanned herself; then waved it towards the door, saying to her women:—"There can be no harm,—no impropriety; —you may go, girls; well, yes, you may,—yes, you had better, go."

Seeing that none of her women could boast fewer years than herself, the title by which she had addressed them seemed something misapplied; but she had so long been accustomed to use it, that she never dreamed of its absurdity.

"You must know, my dear good nephew, I am very particular,—dear me,—very much so—and very properly too,—yes,—very particular in having my maids in the room with me, when I have company. A maiden lady cannot be too punctilious,—too regardful,—dear me, certainly not,—of her reputation. Well, I should never,—dear me, no,—have thought of sending them away,—when a stranger—that is—a visitor—was here. But I will consider you, my dear boy—ahem—my excellent nephew—as a friend—quite as a confidential friend, I may say. Your character for steadiness—good sense,—sobriety,—dear me! it's really very embarrassing, —but,—ahem—your character as a married man—and—a—a father of a family,—by-the-bye, any family?"

Sebastian contrived to insinuate a word to the effect that he hoped to find himself a father on his return; that he had been long absent from home; that he had received no tidings since his departure; but that when he had left Messaline there was a prospect of his becoming long ere this, a family man.

"Dear me! ah! well! That's a comfort! A perfectly respectable character! In virtue of which, my worthy nephew, I may confide to you,

—I am warranted in speaking openly to you,—I may tell you—ahem—
that this visit of your uncle Ignazio's, very much perplexes me—in fact,
distresses me. He bears a character that,—a character which—well, dear
me,—a character, in short, the very reverse of correct. He is quite an
unfit visitor for a lone maiden lady—a lady of nice conduct—of delicate
notions—as, I may say,—dear me, I hope, without vanity,—I am."

She fanned here with such solemn, dignified wafts of her broad green
fan, that it created wind enough to lift the hair from her nephew's temples,
and give him the aghast look which her communication demanded.

"Ever since my earliest childhood," said lady Annuccia, coughing
softly, and looking down, "I have been made aware of my cousin Ignazio's
unhappy defect of character. My father used to warn me against him as
'a sad dog;' and although—dear me,—I was too innocent then, to understand all the frightful meaning of that name, yet I am wiser now,—I know
too well all the appalling things, the atrocities, the villanies, involved in
that title, as applied by one man to another. 'A sad dog!' I shudder to
think of it! And my mother also, early set me on my guard. 'Your
cousin, my dear,' she would say, 'is a dangerous man; he's not a marrying
man; he declares as much; he has had the effrontery, the brazen audacity
to proclaim it. He owns he never means to enter the holy state of
matrimony, but to live a jolly bachelor life (as he terms it), all his days!
The profligate! I've no patience with him! But beware, my dear'
Annuccia,' she would continue, 'you are forewarned, duly cautioned!
Beware then, my child, how you suffer your innocent heart to be beguiled
by this monster, this deceiver!' My mother's words are ever present to
me;" pursued the maiden lady; "and I am anxious that not the remotest
chance shall exist, of my name being compromised, or my reputation for
strict decorum hazarded, by the visits of a man whose character is but too
well known."

"As how, my dear madam?" said her nephew. "Too well known
for what?"

"For gallantry;" whispered she. "It has been said—dear me—well,
—you know that pretty 'campagna' he has in one of the neighbouring
islands—well,—dear me—between you and me,—it is said, that he kept

a bachelor establishment there—quite a harem—a seraglio—dear me,—a positive harem!"

"I remember now, I heard something of that scandal!" said Sebastian, scarcely able to restrain a laugh; "but, my dear madam, that was a tale of ages ago! Don Ignazio can be no chicken, by this time! Why he must be an old man, now.

"'Old!' by no means;" said lady Annuccia; "he can't be above five years older than myself."

There was nothing to answer to this, of course; and Sebastian held his peace. Presently, he enquired:—"And so, don Ignazio is on a visit here? Where is he, my dear aunt? Did you not say he was at this house?"

"He would come—dear me,—he was not invited,—but he would come;" said the maiden lady, using the green fan again with a meek vehemence of protestation. "He came the day before yesterday—dear me,—I couldn't be denied to him. Yes, he came; and said he was come to stay a week or two,—dear me, well, I couldn't turn him out, you know."

"Of course not;" said Sebastian.

"Certainly not;" said lady Annuccia, with a decisive wave of her fan, and putting it down on the table, resignedly. "I accordingly gave orders for an apartment to be got ready for him—the green chamber—which is on the opposite wing of the house,—farthest removed from the one containing the sleeping-rooms of myself and my maids; for I would not on any account expose them, poor things,—dear me,—well, I wouldn't for any consideration, that he should have any opportunity of turning their heads with his idle talk,—he's a gay man, and, there's no knowing—girls will be girls; and, in short, my dear. boy, my good nephew—he's a dangerous man, a very dangerous man."

"And where is he at present? Where is don Ignazio this morning, aunt? Do you not permit him to be with you in your sitting-room. It is hardly a visit, if you keep him at such a terrible distance. Does he occupy the green chamber by day, as well as by night?" said Sebastian.

"Oh, dear no, he's welcome to be with me here in the saloon, whenever he pleases—at proper hours; but this morning, he left me under pretence of strolling down to the beach, to look at the sea, which is fine, they say,

this morning, after the storm of last night. But I do suspect—well,—dear
me——" she hesitated; took up the fan; fidgeted with it against the tips
of her thin fingers; cleared her voice; and then dabbed on again :—
" I have heard that there's a certain fisherman's daughter down there among
the rocks, who's reckoned good-looking; and my peasants are prettyish
girls, some of them. Now his ramble on the beach may be all a pretence,—
a sham,—dear me! He may be gone to look after,—to talk nonsense,—
to play up some mischief or other, with—— Ah," she concluded with
a flutter, between a simper and a sigh, " my mother truly said, he's a
dangerous man ! "

The next moment, a stout, short, ruddy-cheeked, ruby-nosed, scarlet-
lipped, red-throated, crimson-eared, little gentleman came bustling into the
room. ran up to Sebastian, hugged him, and exclaimed :—" My dear fellow,
my dear nephew, glad to see you ! Corpo di Diana ! glad to see you !
I heard the news, down below there, on the sea-shore, that your vessel had
put in here, in the gale, last night ! Corpo di santissima Diana ! Delighted
to see you, my dear fellow ! "

Sebastian returned the old gentleman's warm greeting ; and recognized
him at once for the same don Ignazio, whom he remembered some years
since at a general re-union of the various members of his family at his
father's mansion near Messaline. There were the same deep-set, twinkling,
grey eyes ; the same sprinkled, grey hair ; only rather more thickly
sprinkled, and a little less curly than formerly. But still, upon the whole,
very much the exact person he could recall, as his uncle, don Ignazio.

" And so you're married, my dear fellow ! " continued the brisk little
gentleman ; " Corpo di Diana, give you joy ! Never had the good fortune
to get married, myself ! But I'm quite ready to give every body else joy,
who's so fortunate as to get a wife. Corpo di Diana ! Nothing like
woman, lovely woman, for making home happy ! "

" Now, cousin Ignazio, if you are going to broach any of your improper
sentiments,—dear me,—I must really——" said lady Annuccia, rising, as
if about to leave the room.

" My dear madam, pray sit still. Corpo di Diana ! You needn't be
alarmed. I was merely congratulating my nephew—our nephew, here,

upon his marriage. Any little folks, eh?" He continued, turning to the young merchant, with a facetious poke in the ribs.

Sebastian smilingly explained his domestic prospects; adding, that it was rather late, he feared, to ask them, otherwise he would have requested his aunt and uncle to stand godfather and godmother to his child.

" My good nephew," said lady Annuccia, " it is too late as you say,— dear me,—well,—to offer my services as sponsor; otherwise it would have been my pride,—I'm sure. It has always been a wish of mine, you must know, to be godmother,—since it is not likely——well, dear me,—never mind,—but I have always had a longing, I say, to be godmother to a boy. I confess to a liking, an affection for boys—I own my fondness, my doting for boys,—a partiality, a predilection, a preference,—I may say, a perfect mania for boys. I ought perhaps to blush to avow such a weakness, but I do own, I'm fond of boys. Boys are my passion! Now, my dear nephew, for all it is too late to be godmother to your child, if you should find on your return home, that a boy has been born to you, I promise to give him a gold mug, richly chased; and moreover, will set him down in my will for something handsome."

" A boy? Pshaw!" exclaimed don Ignazio. " A girl for my money! give me girls, *I* say!"

"Now really, cousin Ignazio, I must request,—I must insist——" said lady Annuccia; " if you are going to make any of your unpleasant remarks, your free speeches,—I shall be compelled, however unwillingly, to retire."

" Bless the woman! I'm not saying anything wrong, am I? I'm only saying that girls are my delight, my passion! Corpo di santissima Diana! I've a right to say that, I suppose? I'll tell you what, nephew;" he added; " if you find, when you get home, that you have a little girl, I'll give the pretty moppet just such another gold goblet, as my lady here has promised your child, if it should be a boy. If it's a son, she's welcome to him; if it's a daughter, I'll give her a dower, as if she were my own. Come, is it a bargain, my dear fellow?"

Sebastian expressed suitable acknowledgements to both aunt and uncle; saying, he hoped it would not be long before they each favored him with a visit, to see the little creature in whom they had now an interest; and then, observing that the wind had changed, and the weather quite cleared, he took leave of lady Annuccia, saying he was anxious to lose no time in getting aboard, and taking advantage of the favorable homeward breeze."

Don Ignazio, accompanying him down to the harbour, said, as they walked on :—" Cousin Annuccia is an excellent soul, a worthy, good-meaning creature, but what a pity she's such an old simpleton ! Corpo di Diana ! She keeps such a fidgety look-out for wicked meanings in a man's words, that she won't let him be decent. She puts mischief into his head, with her nicety. And then those scarecrows of women, of hers ! Her maids, as she calls them ! A tribe of wrinkled, withered witches ! I wonder she isn't ashamed of keeping such frights about a house ! She needn't be alarmed. Corpo di Diana ! A man would as soon think of toying with Tisiphone, Alecto, or Megæra, as playing the fool with one of them."

It was evening,—late evening, when the young merchant's ship sailed into the harbour of Messaline. Sebastian left all to the care of his people, and hurried away ; pulling his cap over his brows, and folding his cloak close about him, that he might not be recognised by any of his friends, and detained. There was a moon up ; and as he walked on at a rapid pace, by the quietest streets he could find, he heard in the distance, the voices of revellers, and the sound of guitars, and singing, and resonant talk,—all the stir and animation of an Italian evening ; when the inhabitants come abroad after the heat of the day, to throng the public places, to meet, and chat, and loiter, and take ice, and flirt, and idle away the cool hours together. His house lay in one of the broad, handsome off-streets of the town ; a substantial mansion, with a court-yard, set round with oranges, and oleanders, in stone vases, somewhat formally ; and leading into a spacious garden. At the back of the house, overlooking the garden, there was a sort of projecting balcony, or terrace, of white marble, with a flight of steps at one end. Over this balcony was stretched a sloping, striped awning, of bright stuff, to screen off the heat and glare of the sun from the windows. In the balcony sat a lady. As the fresher breeze of coming night slightly stirred the valanced edge of the awning above her head, the lady looked up, smilingly. On the broad marble ledge of the balcony, near her, stood a vase and goblet, with iced water; and as the movement caught her eye, she dipped one finger in the water, and held it, thus moistened, up into the air. "It blows from Venice!" he could hear her say. For Sebastian had stolen close beneath the balcony, knowing where he should probably find her. He dreaded to startle her by his too sudden appearance; and thought for some means of announcing his presence. He took the jewel from his cap, and rolling it into his handkerchief to give it weight, pitched it up with so true an aim, that it fell into her lap.

She rose hastily, shook out the token, recognised it for her husband's, and looked round with eager joy. In another moment, he sprang up the balcony-steps, and had caught her to his heart.

"The child! Our child! Let me see it!" were among some of his earliest words.

His wife looked into his face; and then said:—"Come!" They stepped through the window that opened from the balcony, into a room where stood a small bronze hand-lamp. She took it, and led him up-stairs. They entered a sleeping-room, where there were two little beds, side by side. She went towards one of them, and lifting the snow-white insect-net which completely curtained it, disclosed within, nestled upon the pillow, a cherub face. Then, turning, with the other hand, she lifted the net of the second little bed; and there, close nestled, lay another angel face.

"Amazement! Two? The same! The one the counterpart of the other,—as if reflected in a mirror!" said the young husband in hushed wonder.

"Born both in one hour! Our twin boy and girl! Our twin-children!" answered his wife, with her glad eyes fixed on his.

"You greet me with riches, indeed, sweet wife, to match those I bring you! I return a wealthy man, in atonement for my long absence, to find my home treasures increased beyond all hope. Prosperous merchant! Happy Sebastian!"

"My rover must needs be returned rich;" she said, smiling; "since he hath jewels enough to toss into the lap of the first woman he meets."

" Ay ; since the first woman I meet, chances to be my first of women ! "
he replied.

Next morning came the delight of seeing the little ones, awake ; up and
stirring, and trotting about, for they could walk now, and prattle some few
words ; of seeing their beauty of limb, their grace and activity ; above all,
of noting their wondrous and complete resemblance.   So perfect was it,—
heightened too, by the fancy their mother had for dressing both the
children precisely alike,—that it was with difficulty they could be known
apart.   Their native costume admitted of this similarity, even between
a boy's and a girl's garb ; for the dress of a female differed but little from
that worn by the men.   It consisted of a snowy tunic, or short, ample skirt,
gathered in close-set folds, from the waist, which was girt with a rich sash ;
a loose jacket of some bright color, thickly embroidered, with sleeves open
from the wrist to the elbow, showing beneath the full white sleeves of the
shirt, which closed in plaits upon the bosom to the throat.   The limbs
were cased in shapely leggings, or greaves, of the same color and fabric with
the jacket ; and like it, embroidered, either in gold, silver, or silken braid.
Upon the head, set amid the clusters of hair,—for it was not large enough
to cover much space,—was worn a cap of correspondent texture and hue
with the jacket, or vest ; either fastened by a pendant jewel, or gemmed
clasp, or ornamented with a long thick tassel of gold, silver, or silk,
according to the material of the embroidery.

It was in a suit of this kind, that the two little creatures made their
appearance before their father, the morning after his return.   He could not
cease from admiring,—as much at their extreme loveliness, as at their
singular likeness ; as much at their extraordinary similarity, as at their
striking beauty.   He could do nothing but praise them, fondle them, use
them like toys,—like playthings ; so pretty, so curious, so odd, so amusing,
they seemed to him.   His wife's delight equalled his, at the spectacle of
his entertainment.   She had pictured to herself all his joy, his wonder,
when he should behold these little twin beings for the first time ; and the
actual scene fulfilled,—almost surpassed,—what she had imagined it would
be.   He never seemed tired of watching them ; of looking at them together,
then alternately, then side by side, then apart ; of puzzling himself about

their identity, and mistaking one for the other, and trying to distinguish them, and again bewildering himself, and laughing at his own blunders. They were a merry party, the father still playing tricks with them, the mother looking smilingly on, the children joining in the frolic, and enchanted with their new companion,—when don Ignazio was announced.

Sebastian had but just time to whisper his wife that she should say nothing about the children, whatever she might hear remarked; when in bustled the old gentleman. He looked as ruddy and as brisk as ever; hugging Sebastian as warmly as before, and greeting him as heartily.

"My dear fellow! Glad to see you! Knew you'd be glad to see me, so came straight here, instead of going home. Got myself into sad disgrace yonder! Corpo di Diana! I don't know how it happened, exactly, but it seems I gave some unpardonable offence to cousin Annuccia. Worthy woman, but sickeningly nice! And, santissima Diana! so sinfully skinny! —Well, my dear fellow, and so you're cosily nestled at home? Soft bosomed in domestic joys, eh? Charming wife, lovely babe,—ah, how's this, two? Or, egad, is it one cut in half?"

"Twins, my dear sir;" said the smiling Sebastian.

"Twins, eh? Corpo di Diana! What little beauties! The havoc they'll make among the men, by-and-by, eh? 'Gad, the young fellows had best look about them, when these little Hebes grow up. However, there are luckily two of them, and not a pin to choose, which is prettiest! Santissima Diana! The dear little blooming rogues! Who would have boys, who could have such sweet moppets as these? No, as I say,—give me girls! By the way, I owe you two golden cups, and two dowries, since you've two daughters! Corpo di Diana! What two-fold beauty! What double loveliness! But I say, my dear fellow," added the lively old gentleman, dropping his voice, and drawing his nephew away by the button, "egad, it's lucky for you, the chits are so alike—so perfectly twins! Corpo di Diana! It's an awkward thing for a husband to come home after a long absence, and find his wife with *two* children, instead of the expected *one!* Santissima Diana! It's well your girls carry their twinship in every look! There's no mistaking that they were born at the same time, egad!" concluded he, with his favorite jocose poke in the ribs, and a twinkle of his merry grey eyes.

"As you say, it's impossible to doubt their being twins;" said Sebastian. "I find it myself, very difficult, even yet, to know one from another."

"Never saw such a wonderful resemblance in my days!" returned his uncle. "Corpo di Diana! Their lovers will have enough to do, to learn them asunder by heart! Whoever takes a fancy to the one, can hardly fail of falling in love with her sister; and whenever they marry, their husbands must mind what they're about, to make no mistakes with each other's wives! Pretty confusion, egad, there'll be! Santissima Diana! 'Twill be fortunate if there's no bloodshed and duelling!"

The brisk little gentleman, soon after, took a bustling leave; declaring he had some visits to pay to some old acquaintances in the town, whom he would not miss seeing before he left Messaline.

Not long after the uncle departed, the aunt arrived. Lady Annuccia came in great pomp; having sailed from her island estate in her own barge, and being attended by a numerous train of servants, male and female.

"Dear me, well,—and so that is your young wife, my dear boy,—my worthy nephew? Dear me! She looks an excellent, amiable young woman, indeed. Dear me! Well, I'm sure, I'm happy to make your acquaintance my dear,—my dear niece. And where is your little one? Dear me, I shall be delighted to see it, of course, I'm sure. I hope it's a boy!"

"You do not know, aunt Annuccia, that a double happiness awaited me on my return home;" said Sebastian. "I found twins born to me."

"Twins! Dear me,—well,—it quite flutters me to hear it—to think of it;—well, dear me,—you must have been very much pleased, of course. Is it possible! Twins! I shouldn't have thought it! Dear me, well! Indeed! I should never have thought of such a thing."

"My love," said Sebastian, to his wife, "will you bring the little ones hither?"

The young mother, to whom her husband had explained the old maiden lady's peculiarities, as well as the circumstance of her and don Ignazio's several prepossessions regarding the children, went to fetch them; and returned, leading one in each hand.

The old lady sat, lost in admiration, gazing from one to the other. At length she exclaimed:—"Dear little fellows! I never beheld two such loves! Absolute cupids! Only—dear me—well, it's a shame to make such a comparison—so beautifully dressed as these two darlings are—while cupids,—well, dear me,—never mind! But was there ever such a perfect pair! They're certainly the most lovely boys I ever set eyes on! Dear me,—well,—partial as I am to boys, I never beheld any to equal these! I shall be only too proud,—too happy, I'm sure, to send the gold mug I promised,—one a-piece,—to these beautiful little fellows. What a glory, what an honor, I should have felt it, to have been, well,—dear me, yes,—god-mother, to either, or both, of these darling boys! My dear good nephew,—my excellent young niece,—what a pride it must be to you, to be the parents of these two darling sons!"

"I own, we are not a little delighted with our pretty twins;" said Sebastian.

"Pretty! Dear me! They are handsome as angels! But you will excuse me, my dear children,—that is,—ahem,—my dear nephew and niece,—if I leave you so soon; but I have a commission to execute in the neighbourhood, which I would fain see to, without delay; I shall not be absent long. I will return forthwith,—immediately."

The old maiden lady went straight to a goldsmith's, close at hand. "I want two golden drinking-mugs, my good sir;" said she to the master of the shop; "they must be very handsome,—fit for a,—dear me, well,—fit for a christening present."

She had scarcely thus announced her wish, when who should bustle into the goldsmith's shop, but don Ignazio.

"Ah, cousin Annuccia! Well met. To what do I owe this fortunate chance? What brings you here?"

"Dear me! Well!—to make a purchase, cousin Ignazio."

"Just what brings me here;" returned he. "I am come to order the golden mug I promised to our nephew's bantling. You've heard the news, I suppose. Corpo di Diana! Lucky dog! Twins! And as beautiful as Venus! You never saw such a couple of young charmers!"

"I have seen them, cousin: and it is that very errand brings me here,—the golden mug I promised. I shall make it a pair, of course."

"So you've given up your mania for boys, have you?" said don Ignazio. "Corpo di Diana! I honor your better taste."

"Not at all, cousin Ignazio; it is because I find our nephew has two such beautiful boys, that I ——"

"Boys! Girls you mean!" exclaimed don Ignazio. "Two blooming girls!"

"Girls! Boys you mean!" echoed lady Annuccia.

"Don't tell me, my dear madam;" said the brisk old gentleman. "Corpo di Diana! I ought to understand something of these matters; I consider myself a judge of female beauty; and if ever I set eyes on two lovely girls,——"

"A truce with your libertine observations, sir!" said the maiden lady, with a wave of her fan, sternly supercilious. "To show you how entirely *my* mind is made up, on the point, I shall proceed with my purchase. Two gold mugs, if you please, my good sir;" continued she, turning to the goldsmith.

The goldsmith bowed.

"My dear madam," said don Ignazio, "since we're both convinced, and both mean to make our respective presents, suppose, instead of letting them be of the same kind, you were to give——"

"Two gold mugs, if you please, my good sir;" repeated the maiden lady.

Again the goldsmith bowed.

"Cousin Ignazio, you'll excuse my not attending to what you say. Too well I know you to be a dangerous man,—a very dangerous man. That it is dangerous to listen to you, and——"

"Corpo di Diana!" burst forth the indignant little old gentleman. But lady Annuccia interrupted him; reiterating in precisely the same tone of dabby obstinacy, as before:—"Two gold mugs, if you please, my good sir."

"Certainly, madam;" replied the goldsmith. "I think I have two articles lately sent me, that will just suit your ladyship's purpose. They are a pair of golden goblets of rare workmanship, by a renowned Florentine artist. The chasing is admirable; its design,—the exploits of Castor and Pollux."

"Couldn't be more appropriate! Leda's twin *sons*!" exclaimed lady Annuccia, with a triumphant glance at don Ignazio. "Dear me! yes; of course! And though the story of their origin is not altogether what I,—well,—never mind. Since the chasing represents their adventures, not their mother's, why,——"

"Exactly, madam;" assented the goldsmith.

"I think I may venture to decide upon them, as gifts for my dear little boys;—that is,—not mine,—but, dear me,—well,——"

"I understand, madam;" said the goldsmith.

"They're very beautiful;" said don Ignazio, who had been examining the goblets. "But I should like to vary my present. You haven't anything ornamented with the stories of their sisters, now, have you? Anything representing Helena, or Clytemnestra? Corpo di Diana! Helena, the world's beauty!"

"Now positively, cousin Ignazio, I must entreat you will not dwell upon the historical particulars of any member of that family; they were extremely disreputable people,—all of them,—the females especially. As for the mother,——"

"Who, madam?"

"Leda, sir; she was a wanton, good-for-nothing hussy, who carried her bird-fancying scandalously too far. Dear me! We won't talk of her. Let her drop, I beg."

"By all means, madam;" said the goldsmith. "But my dear sir;" he added, turning to don Ignazio; "if you want something very tasteful, and choice, to present to your two little friends, what think you of these newly invented articles from Piacenza? They are wrought in silver, and are very dainty and seemly, for eating with; quite a luxury. They are called forks. But just introduced. Only used at the tables of the first Italian nobility. Now, one of these forks, with a silver spoon to match, would make a very elegant gift."

"Be it so;" said don Ignazio. "Give me two of each, for my brace of infant graces. Corpo di Diana! I may say Venuses."

"So you persist in speaking of them as girls?" said lady Annuccia, scornfully.

"Of course, I do. As I said before, I ought to know something of girls, and——"

"Oh, doubtless, doubtless! But we won't trouble you for any repetition of your ribald remarks, if you please, cousin Ignazio. I shall take my gold mugs, and return at once to our nephew's ; where we shall soon find who's right."

"We shall !" said don Ignazio confidently ; as he attended her back to the merchant's house.

"We have brought your little ones our promised gifts, my dear fellow !" he exclaimed, as he entered the room, where Sebastian, his wife, and their two children, were together ; the former, seated side by side, watching the latter, who were rolling, and tumbling with one another, on the floor.

"Already !" exclaimed the young merchant. "They are unfairly won ; they mustn't be bestowed ; you mustn't be beguiled of them by a trick. In jest, we allowed you to think, that you both had your wish. So you have, in some sort ; I have luckily, a child to please each of your several fancies. Yours for a boy, my dear madam ; yours, for a girl, my dear sir. But there's only one a-piece. Come hither, children !" he added, laughing.

The little ones ran to him. "I'm puzzled myself ;" said the smiling father, as they both stood at his knee, looking up in his face, with their full, blue eyes, their ripe, round, pulpy cheeks, and rosebud mouths, so perfectly in fac-simile ; "I declare I know not which is which, myself !"

"Ask them ;" said the mother.

"Who's this ?" he said, gently pinching the cheek of the one who stood nearest.

"Viola ; papa's little girl ;" lisped the little creature.

"Then here is your pet, uncle Ignazio ;" said the young merchant, passing her over to the old gentleman ; who took her up upon his knee, and began making acquaintance with her.

"And this ?" continued the father.

"Sebastian, papa's-namesake ;" said the little fellow, using, as his sister had done, the fondling answer taught them by their mother, to beguile the time of her husband's absence.

"Then here is your favorite, my dear aunt ;" said the merchant ; leading his little son towards her. As the maiden lady seated the young boy on her lap, and gave him the glittering present she had brought for him, and smoothed the fair locks,—scarcely less bright and golden than her gift; she said :—"Well, dear me! I don't know but it's happiest as it is! I shouldn't have known which to love best! And now, I'm quite sure,— of course,—dear me,—of course, I like this one best! I'm so fond of boys! I have an affection for boys, I own! I ought perhaps,—to feel a delicacy in confessing such a preference,—but,—I avow it—I am passionately fond of boys!"

"My dear madam, on the contrary, it does you honour!" said don Ignazio. "Corpo di Diana! your liking for boys, is the best point about you!"

"Now, cousin Ignazio,—I beg,—instead of making such personal, and particular allusions,—dear me, well,—you will oblige me, by giving to your little favorite, this other golden cup, like her brother's; and if you please, you may hand me over your duplicate gift, and I will present it, in your name, to mine,—ahem,—well, dear me,—to him."

Some very happy time was spent by our young merchant, at this period, in his own home. He would sit with his wife, when evening brought in cool repose, after the daily fatigues, and anxieties of business, watching their children from the balcony, as they gambolled in the garden. It was a favorite seat with them both. It had been the scene of many an hour of early wedded happiness; it had been the scene of their meeting after long absence; it was where they now by preference sat to watch their twin boy and girl, frolicking in the sweet air, and shady quiet of sun-down. Here they saw their little ones run races beneath the trelliced vines; or thread the narrow paths between the flower-beds; or chase one another down the grassy slopes: and then the father would track his little Viola by her less-assured pace, as she tottered along, and bundled over; and his boy Sebastian by his quicker pace, and firmer footing, with which he would run to help her. And the mother would note the care with which her young boy supported his sister up the marble steps; and smiled to see how the little masculine frame, though no stouter or stronger to look at than the girlish one, yet gave indisputable token of its superior power. The boyish limbs were no less softly rounded, no less delicately moulded, and gracefully proportioned, than those of the girl ; yet their alert vigour, and the command he had over them, attested the force which hers lacked.   In action, the two children could be readily distinguished ; at rest, it was no easy matter to tell one from the other.   Their father still found the same diverting perplexity, in trying to know them apart ; but the mother's instincts were more unerring.   She never failed.   He would often smilingly refer to her, when he was at a loss ; for he found she could always name them aright.   Sometimes, he would affect to disbelieve her, and appeal to the child itself ; but the laughing answer always came in accordance with what she had said :—" Mamma guessed ; I'm Viola, papa ; "   or :—" Mamma's right ; it's Sebastian, papa."

His wife at last pretended to declare she could not submit to such insulting doubt of her word ; and that in order to make sure of them for himself, he had best tie something about the neck of one of the children, that he might at once distinguish it from its twin brother or sister.

The merchant agreed ; and that evening, when his little Viola came to wish him good-night, he fastened a string of coral round her throat, saying she was his pretty pet fawn, with her red collar on.

The child was pleased with the gawd ; but it could not make her forget or omit, a certain little ceremonial which always took place between her father and herself, every night, before she went to bed.

This was, to climb up upon the balcony-seat by his side, saying :— " I must bid good-night to my mole !   Viola can't sleep, if she don't kiss her mole, and say ' Felice notte,' to it."   Then she would stand on tip-toe, beside him ; and her father would bend down his forehead ; and she would put back the locks of hair from his white, polished temple ; and precisely on one particular spot, she would press her lips against his brow, where lurked a small brown mole ; saying a thousand, murmured, fondling words to it."

This was the little Viola's delight ; just one of those sportive fancies, those whimsies of affection, in which a parent indulges a caressing, gentle-natured child ; and which form bonds—in addition to the natural one that unites them,—slight as threads of gossamer, yet subtly potent as the magnet-link.

In after years, when sailing on the lonely sea, far from home, a wanderer in search of wealth to store for his children, the merchant, thinking of this fanciful baby caress, would find his eyes moisten, and his heart swell, with an emotion that many a graver thought would fail to excite.

And in yet other subsequent years, Viola, recalling the image of her father, found no point more vivid, than this same little mole upon his brow.

While Viola was wishing 'good-night' after her fashion, her brother Sebastian would be performing it after his. He would mount up upon the marble ledge of the balcony, run along its whole length, swing himself round the iron supports of the awning, and play off other such boyish antics, to get rid of some of his superfluous vivacity, before going to rest ; always ending by catching his mother round the neck, and giving her half-a-dozen hearty kisses : while she, suppressing her involuntary alarm, forbore to repeat the caution she had once given him about the height and risk, lest she should make a coward of her boy, and damp that brave, fearless spirit, which she loved to note in him.

Sometimes, Viola, tired with play before the hour of bed-time came, would leave her brother to finish out his romps, or his ramble, in the garden, by himself; and then she came toddling up the steps, into the balcony, to lean against her father's knee, while he talked with her mother ; preferring the quiet, and the rest, and the cool shade, with them,—to the ever-enacting, never-ceasing game with Sebastian. Her father would pass his arm round her, draw her near to him, and show by his manner, that he loved to have his little girl in her favorite position, close at his knee ; and she understood these silent tokens,—she felt that she was welcome,— though no word was spoken to her, he continuing his conversation.

The merchant would relate to his wife various things he had seen in his travels, likely to interest her ; he would describe curious scenes, and strange places ; he would tell her of odd people, or pleasant people, that he had met with ; he would paint to her secluded nooks, and grottos, on beautiful Sicilian shores ; or depict the animated St. Mark's place, and crouded Rialto of Venice. He would speak to her of his dearest and most esteemed friend, the duke of Illyria ; and of his son, Orsino. He would describe the distinguished bearing of the boy; his frank, yet refined beauty; the poetical look that beamed in his earnest eyes, and animated his handsome intelligent countenance.

"He is a noble lad!" the merchant exclaimed; "and would make a charming companion for our children, as they grow older. Would that I might ever realize my dream of bringing them together! He would make an admirable friend for our Sebastian; and,—who knows?—for our Viola, he might become——"

His wife laid her hand upon his arm. "I guess what you would say, love;" she observed. "But it is best unuttered. Were our little girl some years older, I should fear such words inadvertently spoken before her, lest they produced unthought-of mischief. Out of slighter matter, have grown hopeless affection, wasted energies, blighted lives. Yet even at her age, there is no knowing how soon an impression is conveyed, that is not dreamed of by the speaker. We are too apt, I think, to imagine that little children are blind, deaf, senseless, because they do not give apparent token of seeing, hearing, or marking, what passes around them. Far from being unobservant, children are often the most keen noticers of their elders' sayings and doings; and although seemingly careless and disregardful at the time, the silent comments they make, shall be none the less acute, because made to themselves, instead of being spoken aloud, or betrayed by looks. Not only do we find this, by casual remarks that drop from children at subsequent periods, relative to words and events supposed to have passed unperceived by them at the time; but we can recollect, all of us, on looking back to childhood, many scenes, persons, incidents, speeches, or circumstances, that then were believed to flit by unheeded, but which since recur in all vividness of impression. Pardon me, dear husband, that I speak thus eagerly, upon a theme, which must have struck you with equal force. My foolish, anxious, mother's heart, makes me prate; and to one who knows all more wisely than itself."

"You cannot speak too earnestly, or too frankly with me, upon such a subject, sweet wife;" said the merchant. "With whom should we confer, but with each other, as to the best means of securing our children's happiness? Let it be in all candour, all sincerity, ever. Were you to commit an error, as it seemed to me, in respect to them, I should frankly remonstrate with you; why therefore should not a wife point out, with equal freedom, to her husband, what she believes he has done mistakenly. But thy pretty wifely modesty teaches thee to pray forgiveness of thy lord and master, lest his manly prerogative take alarm at being preached to, or chidden. Is't not so? Never fear; I trust it hath less coxcombry of pride, than belongs to such husbands as dread its impugning, each time a wife utters an opinion beyond the boiling of polenta, or the set of a feather. Thine own gentle discretion, and unassuming good sense, have taught me to love nothing better than to hear thee speak openly upon all our mutual concerns; and what concern, so near, or so dear, as our children? May I ever have thy counsel at hand, to aid in their guidance towards good,—to secure their virtue and happiness."

Too soon, alas, was the young merchant's aspiration defeated by the event. This gentle wife, this tender mother, this faithful partner of his joys and cares, was snatched from him by a fever. Within a few hours, he learned to fear for her life, and to mourn her death. Distracted by his loss, he thought of nothing but of flying from the spot where he had sustained it. He resolved to travel, as the readiest means of escaping from a scene fraught with so much bitterness of recollection. He thought that by plunging into the bustle and stir of the world, he might the better deaden the poignant regret which tortured his solitary moments; as he might also devote himself to the sole object that now remained for him in life,—the providing a future competence for his children. He hastily formed his plans for the present, for them; he determined to leave them in the care of a certain Marcella, the widow of one of his former clerks; a woman of whom he had heard a good character for prudence, notableness, and housewifely accomplishment. She was said to have been a good mother, when her own children were alive; and had a name for extreme neatness and economy in her domestic management.

Her house was scrupulously clean and orderly; an air of decent parsimony reigned throughout, as though poverty were not permitted to bring squalor with it. Some such impression struck the merchant, as he brought his motherless children there, to consign them to Marcella's care. He thought they would be at least wholesomely, and comfortably lodged, during his absence ; and that the sum he paid for their maintenance would supply additional luxuries.

She was volubly assuring him of something of the kind, while the young merchant stood there, in his deep mourning habit, and with his pale face, holding one of his children in each hand, and gazing at them, deep in thought, hearing not one word she said ; dreaming of how and when he might look upon them again, and seeking for courage to part from them now, without betrayal of such emotion as might sadden their innocent hearts.

"You look very white, dear papa;" said little Viola, with her soft eyes raised to his. "Are you going to fetch some of the roses on your cheeks, that you bid me fetch for mine from the fresh air, when I go out walking. There's a fine fresh air blows from the sea, sometimes; and you told us you were going to sail upon the seas, didn't you?"

"Ay, my little Viola ; and what shall I fetch from beyond the sea for thee ? From the grand, brave cities across the sea, where there are stores of gay things, to bring home?"

"For me, papa ? Why, bring me that nice boy you were telling of, one evening, that would make such a good play-fellow for Sebastian and me. You said he was 'a noble lad.' I should like to have him here with us."

The artless words of his child, brought to the merchant's mind, with a pang, the conversation they referred to ; the impression received by the little silent hearer, so truly then foretold,—and by whom foretold. The very expression he had used, was repeated by his little girl ; thus confirming her mother's idea. He turned hastily to his young son :—" And what shall I bring home for my Sebastian?" he said.

"My mother;" answered the boy, in a low voice. "They took her away,—she is gone. Bring her back; bring her home. I want to see her. I want her with us again."

The father turned away.

"Papa!" said Viola, "don't go without bidding us good-bye. I want to say good-bye to my mole. Lift me up, that I may kiss it, and bid it not stay away too long, and tell it, I shall think of it every night when I go to bed, and send a hundred times 'felicissima notte' after it!"

He took her up in his arms; and hugged her to the heart that had so much ado to hide its anguish. Then, with another embrace to her little brother, he tore himself away.

The woman with whom the merchant had left his children, was what is called a good manager; that is, a hard manager, a close manager; what might rather be called a bad, than a good manager; for nothing good was in her management; all was disagreeable, pinched, and comfortless; the very reverse of cosy, pleasant, commodious, or attractive. That which might, by really good management, have been done quite as economically, though with more taste; was, by her kind of good management, made intolerably hateful. She had been called a good mother; that is, she clothed her children decently, and fed them sufficingly, upon an incredibly small sum; but she was a hard mother, a close mother, hard in her measure of affection, close in her allowance of tenderness. Such things as endearments, or loving words, were never bestowed; they were looked upon as so much waste of time, profitless expenditure. Indulgence was an idle luxury; kindness a useless extravagance. She had enough to do to 'make both ends meet;' and all that tended not to this conjuncture, was deemed worthless; while whatever feelings were crushed, or ideas cramped, or tastes violated, in the process, passed unheeded. Her children might grow up with contracted hearts, stunted intellects, undeveloped faculties, and common-place, grovelling minds; but she would have brought them up 'with an eye to the main chance,' and very creditably in the eyes of the neighbours,—in short, like 'a good mother.' They never did grow up, however, to prove the merits or demerits of her system; they all died in their infancy,—unluckily, or luckily, for them.

The sum that Marcella received from the merchant, for·the maintenance of his children, so far from being applied to increase the comforts and accommodation of the household, was devoted to increase the small hoard which had slowly accumulated beneath this excellent contriver's care. It was the result of many a carking hour stolen from heart's ease and mirth; it was the result of many a nipping, penurious shift; of many a sparing

meal ; of many a darned, or patched garment ; of many a saving snatched
out of something that 'would do just as well,'—that 'wouldn't find it out,
or miss it ;' it had been the product of many a difference with her husband, of many a severity towards her children ; but it was her dearest-
prized treasure. It had originally sprung out of a thought for them ; it
had been begun with a hope of 'putting by' something which should help
them, and prosper them ; something that should be ready 'against a rainy
day' to benefit them. But it had gone on, in spite of them, as a counterbalance to their thoughtlessness, as a protection against their improvidence.
When they had all died, it went on from habit ; no habitual usage gaining
more confirmed ground with age, than the habit of saving. And when the
merchant's motherless children were placed in the charge of this good mother
and manager, the money he paid, was scrupulously, or rather unscrupu-
lously, added to her beloved hoard : so fatally may deeds, having their
source in virtue, end in becoming vices, if unwatched and undirected
aright.

"I don't like this place—I wish we were in our own nice house, our
own home, again ;" said little Viola, in a low voice, to her brother, the
first time they were alone together ; Marcella having gone to attend to
some household affair in the kitchen. "There's no garden here ; it's so
dull,—only looks out upon streets, and houses. I wish we could go back
to our own pleasant home."

"So do I ;" sighed Sebastian. "But this is to be our home now, since
papa left us here, and told monna Marcella to take care of us. What
a dismal, ugly house it is, as you say, Viola !"

"Look at this floor, like the ground ; and these straight chairs and
tables ; and these grim, grey, wooden blinds ;" she said. "Do you
remember our pretty inlaid floors, and carved chairs, and the soft, cool
light from the green blinds, in the sitting-room at home ? And worse
than all, that close square yard, yonder, instead of our dear, beautiful
garden, where we used to play so happily ?"

"I feel as if I could hardly breathe here, sometimes ; and my legs and
arms seem quite cramped with want of room, in this miserable pent-up
place ;" said Sebastian. "But it's of no use complaining ; it only makes

us feel the disagreeables more. I oughtn't to make it worse, by grumbling. Come, let's have a game of play, together."

"What can we play at? What is there to play with, in this dull, empty place?" said Viola dolefully, as she looked round upon the plain chairs and tables, set formally against the bare walls, in forlorn neatness, and cheerless ugliness of shape and arrangement.

"Stay, we'll pile up the chairs, one upon another, and make a high, high tower; and you shall get up on the top, and be the princess; and I'll be the invading army; and you shall defend the walls bravely; and I'll scale them; and you shall knock me over into the moat. Won't that be good fun? eh, Viola?"

"Well, suppose we make the table my castle; it'll be stronger and safer;" she said; "and if you like, you can be a giant on the tower of chairs; and we'll shoot arrows at one another, and have a siege at a distance; eh?"

"Yes, that'll be capital!" answered he. "Here, I'll help you up on to the table. And now for my fortress!"

The two children were in the full glory of their game, when in came Marcella.

"Why what in the name of all the saints in paradise, is here to do!" exclaimed she. "Santa Rosa! what have you two brats been about? Knocking the furniture to pieces, breaking the legs of my chairs off, scratching my table, destroying my property. Come down this instant, you young urchins! Pretty mischief, indeed, may be done in no time, when one's back's turned, and a couple of troublesome children are playing up their tricks."

The two belligerent forces came meekly down from their respective citadels, in silence.

"And you might have broken your necks too! And there'd be doctor's stuff to pay for, and a surgeon, and I don't know what. To say nothing of the taking your Pa' would be in, and the scolding he'd give me, when he came back. Come, the dinner's ready. Set the chairs in order, do; and then help me to lay the table; and then sit down to your victuals, like christians; and let's have no more such untidy, disorderly doings."

Y

Monna Marcella had a harsh, snappish voice; not so much proceeding from unkindliness, as from mere rigid, dry performance of duty, the succinct enunciation of what was right and proper to be done, without superfluous gentleness, or softness. It mostly sounded as if she were cross, or peevish; when, in fact, she was only exercising her ordinary discipline.

"What's the matter with that soup, pray?" she said to little Viola, seeing that the child did not eat it, but kept spooning it up, and letting it dribble down into the plate again, with disconsolate looks. "It's good, wholesome soup. Are you too dainty to fancy it?"

"The soup's very well; but I don't like the spoon;" said little Viola. "It's all colours, and ugly. It's wood. I like my pretty bright spoon, that I had at home, to eat my soup with."

"Oho! you like that one, do you? You're mighty particular. But that one's silver; and it's too good for every day. I've locked it up, against high days and holidays. You shall have it out, for a treat, the first festa-day that comes."

"But I like to have it every day. I had it every day at home;" said the child.

"So had I, mine;" said Sebastian.

"You're a pretty pair of spoiled brats, upon my word;" answered monna Marcella. "And so you can't eat with an honest, wholesome wooden spoon, can't you? But we mustn't have such fine fantastical airs here, I promise you."

"Why is one spoon more fantastical than another?" said Sebastian. "If we've got pretty spoons, why shouldn't we use them?"

"Because it's extravagant to have them out every day; they wear out, with the constant fretting and rubbing."

"I don't think they'll wear out; they're very hard;" said the boy.

"What a hideous, clumsy, brown mug this is!" said little Viola. "I don't like drinking water out of this. It used to look so clear, and so sparkling, in my mug at home. I want my golden mug, 'please."

"Oh, you do, do you? But I can't let you have it. Isn't plain excellent earthenware, good enough? If it's extravagant to use silver every

day, what is it to have gold ? I shall allow no such absurd goings on here,
I assure you ; " said monna Marcella.

" But since they're ours, why mayn't we use them ? " persisted Sebastian ;
for he saw that his little sister's liking for everything pretty, and distaste
for everything that was ugly, made it a serious annoyance to her to be
deprived of their accustomed luxuries. Besides, the boy wished for them
himself.

" I tell you it's extravagant ; what thrifty housewife would allow gold
and silver to be in use every day ? There's the danger,—the temptation to
thieves, in the first place ; and next, there's the wear and tear ; and
moreover, there's the time and trouble they'll take to keep bright and
cleaned. No, no, I'll have no such wasteful doings in my house, I can
tell you."

The children gave up the point.

The elegant home, in which this young boy and girl had been reared,
caused the penurious, niggardly appointments of the one to which they
were now removed, to be a source of constant misery to them, and gave
rise to perpetual offence on the part of its mistress. She thought them
dainty, whimsical, fastidious ; whereas, they were only accustomed to
refinement and indulgence, and severely felt their loss. She could not
comprehend the little ones' inbred desire for all that was tasteful and
beautiful ; while they could yet less understand the necessity and preference she felt for all that was plainest, coarsest, and meanest. There
was a ceaseless disagreement going on ; and as monna Marcella had the
power in her hands, it followed as a matter of course, that she obtained
her way. She was not conscious of doing anything beyond her duty,—
her strict duty. So far from thinking that the merchant would object to
the manner in which she treated his children ; she imagined that he would
highly approve, could he know how judiciously, how properly she managed
them. So far from believing that she was frequently harsh, tyrannical,
unjust, she fancied she was but exercising that due authority, beneath
which a father would be best pleased to have his children brought up.

When she scolded them for veriest trifles, and punished them for merest
childish scrapes, she thought herself most worthily fulfilling the charge
she had undertaken.

Little Viola was a timid, sensitive child; she shrank from the shadow of blame, and felt keenly the smallest approach to unkindness or severity. She had been accustomed to much petting from her father; and had never received other treatment from her wise and tender mother, than the gentlest reasoning, when rebuke was needed. Upon her, therefore, the harsh-toned reproofs, and strict penances, of monna Marcella, produced a strong effect. She grew dull, dispirited, unhappy; she lost her appetite for meals, and her relish for play. She slunk about as if in constant dread of something,—she scarcely knew what; of being chidden, or punished, for some offence she might have unconsciously committed.

"What makes you look so scared, Viola mia?" said her brother, coming in, one evening, and finding her with trembling lips, and tears in her eyes. "Has monna Marcella been finding fault with you again?"

"Oh yes! And I don't know what for,—I didn't mean to do wrong; but she's very angry; and says that while she goes to market to-morrow morning, she'll lock me up in the yard."

"Well if she does, never mind!" said Sebastian. "We play there every day, you know. What does it signify whether the door's locked, or not?"

"Oh, I don't mind being there with you. But she'll lock me there alone; and I'm afraid of that big, snarling dog, by myself! He jumps to the end of his chain, and makes at me, and comes so close; oh, much closer,—at least it seems so,—than when you're by, to take care of me."

Viola looked so pale, and so piteous, as she let her imagination picture all the horrors of being shut into the yard, alone with the fierce dog, that her brother hastened to comfort her.

"Don't be afraid! I'll take good care you shan't be there by yourself. I'll come with you, and keep off Lupo."

"But you won't be able to come; monna Marcella will set you to do something here, the meantime, as she did the other day, when she wanted to punish me, by locking me into the yard alone with the dog. She knows I'm afraid of him."

"But I'm not;" said Sebastian. "Stay, I've thought of something. Trust to me, Viola mia; and I'll engage you shan't be locked in with Lupo." He began to talk of something else; and invented a new game, to withdraw her thoughts if possible from the subject that haunted them; but he could see that it recurred, and hung heavily on her spirits. Sebastian knew that monna Marcella scarcely ever distinguished himself and his twin-sister apart. She generally spoke of them, as "the children," or "those urchins;" and addressed them, either as "you two," or "you brats." She rarely gave herself the trouble to individualize them, or think of them separately; she treated them as the couple, the pair, the two children, whom she had in charge. The boy determined, therefore, to preserve his sister from the penance she so much dreaded, by personating her, and performing it in her stead. For the better effecting of his purpose, he crept, that night, to the bedside of Viola, took the string of coral,—which she always wore,—from her throat, while she slept, and fastened it round his own neck; in order that when he encountered monna Marcella next morning, there might be no chance of her not taking him for his sister.

Exactly as he had hoped, it fell out. He was locked into the yard; while Viola was given some task to do, in the house. She thought she had been forgotten; that by some happy, extraordinary chance, monna Marcella had overlooked the delinquency of the past evening, and with it, the delinquent. After a time, she wondered where Sebastian was; and went to seek him. She was still searching all over the house, when, from one of the windows, she saw Marcella returning from market; green fan in hand, basket on arm, come plodding up the shady side of the street.

Presently she heard he rshrill, grating tones, calling to the servant-girl:—

"Here, Menicuccia! Come hither! Take the basket from me, while I go to unlock the yard-door, and let that troublesome chit out.

The whole light flashed upon Viola at once. Her brother had saved her from punishment by bearing it himself! In a tremor of excitement and gratitude, she watched for him, as he came from durance.

"Dear Sebastian! You have been locked in! You have borne the punishment! It isn't right! It isn't fair!"

"But it was no punishment to me; I don't care for the dog; you do. It was better that I should be locked in the yard;" he said.

"Still, it isn't right;" said Viola. "Though you're brave, and not afraid of Lupo, yet it's a penance, a disgrace, to be locked in ; and it isn't fair that you should bear it."

"Since I didn't deserve it, it's no disgrace ;" said Sebastian. "We neither of us deserved it."

"But she thought I did ; and if any one bore it, I ought ;" said Viola. "I shall go and tell monna Marcella the truth."

The child went, in all the warmth of honest feeling, straight to the woman.

"Monna Marcella, you locked up Sebastian in mistake. It's very unjust. He oughtn't to have been punished. If any one, it was I."

"What do you mean, child ? Santa Rosa ! What plagues these brats are !"

"I mean, that you took him for me, when you locked him in with the dog, this morning."

"So, it was the other one, was it ?" returned monna Marcella, eyeing Sebastian, who had followed his sister to her presence.

Sebastian nodded.

"I've a great notion you're deceiving me ; and that I punished the right one, after all ;" said she, looking keenly at them both alternately. "And yes,—to be sure ! There's the coral necklace ! That must be the simpleton of a girl, who's afraid of Lupo ! It's a trick of her brother's,—of yours, sirrah, to deceive me, and screen her !" said monna Marcella, turning sharply round upon Viola.

"She came to tell you the truth !" said Sebastian indignantly ; "and you accuse her of deception. I took Viola's coral beads, that you might mistake me for her ; as I don't care for the dog, and she does. More shame of you to frighten her with him, and to punish her so cruelly ! It's too cruel for anything she did."

"Upon my word, master malapert ! And so you're to judge what's too cruel, and what's not ? A pretty pass, truly, when chits like you are to decide upon what's proper punishment, and what's not ! What's just, and what's unjust, forsooth ! It's enough to provoke all the saints in paradise, to have to deal with such a couple of tormenting urchins. But mind, I'll match you the next time, you artful little toads !"

This threat did not make much impression on the boy ; but on the little girl it weighed sadly. With her, a vague terror was almost worse than a defined one ; it appealed to her imagination, and filled her with a nameless dread of she knew not what, which might happen she knew not when. She often repeated to herself :—" I'll match you, the next time !" wondering what might be the fearful device, which was to equal any amount of enormity that could be committed by her brother or herself.

At length the impending evil came,—as unexpectedly, as suddenly.

It was a saint's-day, and monna Marcella had promised to take the children out with her to spend the evening at a friend's house, which was a little way out of the town. This prospect of a country holiday was charming to the two little ones ; who had felt the confinement, and close-pent air of a town dwelling, inexpressibly wearisome. They had dined at the usual hour of mid-day, and were beguiling the seemingly interminable afternoon, by a game of play together in the little stony yard at the back of the house,—keeping at a respectfully safe distance from Lupo,—while the good manager, monna Marcella, was helping the servant girl to wash up the utensils that had served at the noon-tide meal. Presently the careful housewife missed the children's gold drinking-mugs, and their silver spoons and forks ; which, in virtue of its being a festa-day, they had been permitted to use.

"How's this, Menicuccia !" said monna Marcella, with more than its usual asperity in her acrimonious voice. " How's this ! I don't see the plate. It was had out to-day, to please those whimsical brats ! Where is it ? Santa Rosa ! How the wench stands ! Where in the name of all the saints, is it, girl ? Where have you put it ? "

" I haven't put it nowhere, ma'am ;" answered Menicuccia, in trepidation. " I an't so much as touched it. Santa Madonna di Loretto forbid !—I see the twins take the cups and things out with 'em into the yard, to play with ! "

" You did !" screamed monna Marcella. " Well, this beats all ! They must make play-things of their property, must they ! and such valuables as those, for toys ! Nothing less, I'll assure you, than gold and silver, will serve the turn of my young master and mistress to batter about, and spoil.

It's enough to make the hair of all the ' Beati ' in Paradise stand on end, to think of such tricks ! "

Monna Marcella muttered this, in a shrill growl, as she hastened to the scene of these reckless proceedings,—not the crinose feats, but the tricks; not paradise, but the stony back-yard.

She found the children busily employed, raking up the pebbles and dust, filling the gold cups to the brim, and preparing to make dirt-pies, by the addition of water from the dog's pan, which Sebastian was adventurously bringing, by spoons-full at a time, from under Lupo's very nose.

" Upon my word ! " exclaimed monna Marcella, in a tone likest to a peacock's cry before rain, as she stood looking at the twin culprits. " Pretty doings, truly ! Who began this ? Who set the example ? But I said I'd match you, and I will ! I'll punish you *both* this time ; and then there can be no mistake.   You shall both be locked up."

" I shan't mind that ; we shan't mind being locked up together ; " said Viola, suddenly relieved.

" I know who says that ! It must be the coward of a *girl !* " said monna Marcella. " But no, child ; I mean no such thing. You are not to have the comfort of being together ; that would be no punishment, I know. Besides, you'd amuse yourselves ; and I intend you shall be miserable the whole evening, to teach you how to get into mischief another time.   You shall both be locked up ; but separately,—in your separate rooms ; while I go to spend the evening at messer Gervasio's ' campagna,' without you."

It is possible that even this ' good manager ' might have shrunk from inflicting so much of what she thought salutary misery, could she have guessed its amount.   As it was, she was struck with its effects, when she returned home.   It happened, that the weather, which was superb when she left her house, turned out unfavourably.   A violent rain-storm, with thunder and lightning, had come on ; and she was detained at her friend Gervasio's until a late hour of the night.   She went at once up to Viola's room, with a sensation of misgiving upon her.

She found the child lying upon the bed.   Its bright hair was in disorder ; its cheeks very pale ; its eyelids swollen and stained with tears, and the long lashes matted together ; while the lips lay parted, and almost colorless. Upon even the hard, unobservant Marcella, these tokens of the distress and agony which the little creature must have gone through, did not fail of producing an impression. She thought she might possibly have carried her strictness a little too far; and she half resolved that in future, she would be more lenient,—or at all events, more careful that the punishment should not exceed a prudent proportion. She felt that the best thing which could now be done, would be to prolong as much as possible the deep sleep into which the child had fallen; drawing, therefore, the bed-clothes smoothly about her, and composing the little limbs, as gently as might be, Marcella crept out of the room again.

It was not at all in such a woman's nature, or system of management, to speak to the child the next morning, either soothingly, as regarded what had passed, or promisingly, with respect to the future. That would have been too much like an apologetic tone; which was the last thing monna Marcella would have dreamed of, as expedient in bringing up children. Therefore little Viola had no idea that there was anything softened in the state of affairs between herself and the harsh-voiced, harsh-visaged personage, who sat watching her and her brother next morning, as they took their breakfast meal beneath her eye.

"What ails ye, child? What's amiss? Why don't you eat your polenta, and drink your milk?"

"I'm not hungry, thank you;" said Viola.

"Not hungry? nonsense, child! Eat your victuals, when they're set before you, or we shall have you getting ill; and that'll never do. Come, they're excellent good victuals, I'm sure. Nice fresh polenta of chesnuts; which you like, you know. And milk! Sweet milk! Come, drink it off, there's a good child."

Viola obediently put the cup to her lips; but she felt as if she couldn't swallow; and set it down again, with an incapable look, and a timid, deprecating glance towards monna Marcella.

"You make it seem like medicine to her, monna Marcella, by saying 'drink it off;'" said Sebastian.

"Grant me patience with such a couple of fanciful, whimsical children!" exclaimed she. "But come; to humour you, I'll get you your gold cup to drink out of,—as I don't think you are quite the thing, and I don't want you to fall sick,—if you'll promise to drink your milk, like a good child."

" I can't; I would if I could; but indeed I can't get it down ;" said poor Viola, trembling with her own feeling of incapacity, and still more at monna Marcella's rising ire.

This ire was fast reaching a high pitch.   Not so much from anger at the child, as at her own sense of the difficulty in managing it properly.   She felt it was unwell, feverish, from the effects, probably, of overnight's agitation, and therefore required tender treatment; and at the same time she felt the repugnance, the almost impossibility, which existed in herself to deal thus yieldingly with one under her controul.   How many, too many, of those charged with the care of young children, are subject to this complication of feeling in their management; and resenting the difficulty they know not how to overcome, vent their angry emotion upon the objects of their perplexed solicitude.

" Obstinate, perverse little toad !" exclaimed monna Marcella ; " I've a great mind to give you a good shaking, and see if that wouldn't shake the naughtiness out of you.   But I'll tell you what; I'm going to market.   I'll leave you that time to recover yourself; and if I find, on my return, you've been a good child, and thought better of it, and have drunk up your milk, I'll give you a lump of sugar.   There now !   Won't that be nice ? "

When monna Marcella was gone, Viola said :—" I don't mean to be obstinate, but I can't eat or drink ; I don't know how it is,—but I feel as if it would choke me, every time I try."

" Then don't try ; " said Sebastian.   " Why should you ? "

" Oh, she'll be so angry if she comes back, and finds it not gone !   She'll think me perverse ; and perhaps stand over me, and make me take it. And I can't; indeed I can't."

" Then you shan't ; " said Sebastian stoutly.   " Here, give it me."

He snatched up the trencher of polenta, and the mug of milk ; hurried out with them to the yard, and flung them to Lupo, who licked them up in a trice of grateful gobble.

" What a good thought !" exclaimed Viola, with a sigh of relief, as her brother returned.

"But you're not well, Viola mia;" said the boy, as he saw how languid her eyes looked, and how white her cheeks and lips were.

"I feel stifled;" said she. "I wish I could have some sweet, fresh, open air; I wish we could have one of those pleasant walks, down by the sea-shore, that we used to take long ago, when we lived at our happy home."

"Let's go!" said Sebastian. "I'm sure I could find the way. Let's go, Viola!"

A bright smile crossed her face as she started up to go with him; but the next moment it fell, as she said :—"But monna Marcella won't give us leave to go out by ourselves."

"Why need she be asked?" said Sebastian. "Her marketing will keep her a long while; we shall have time to take our walk and be back again, long before she returns."

Viola joyfully gave him her hand, and the two children left the house together.

It lay in one of the narrow, suburban streets of the city; so that they had soon got out of the town, and reached the outskirts, where there was a path, which they knew led down to the sea-side. The children had often been brought this walk, and remembered it well. It lay among olive-grounds, fenced by low, stone walls, from the path-way; which was a torrent in the winter season, but dry and rubbly in the summer, and used as a passage down to the beach, by the people of the country, on mule-back, or on foot. The sun's rays beat down hot and scorching, and were reflected by the rough white stones beneath their feet; but the two little ones trudged merrily on, hand-in-hand, looking up at the silvery olive-boughs, which overhung the walls, and at the glorious blue sky above.

"How bright and beautiful all looks now again!" said Viola in a happy voice to her brother. "Who could think last night was so terrible!"

"Ay, there was a thunder-storm, was there not? But I slept soundly, and heard little of it;" said Sebastian.

"Slept soundly! Is it possible you could go to sleep at all, last night?" said Viola. "I couldn't, till the storm ceased. Oh, what a miserable, terrible night it was!" She shuddered. "Let us sit down here, in this pleasant place, and I shall have courage to tell you all I suffered."

"There is a better seat, down among the rocks, close upon the sea;" said Sebastian ; " let us wait till we reach it. There is shade there."

They soon reached the spot he meant. It was a recess in the cliff,— worthy to be a nereid's haunt, so cool, so secluded, so deep in shadow. It lay in a small bay, or cove ; where, along the margin, a few fishermen had built their huts, and, in its shallow water, kept their boats moored. The two children seated themselves upon one of the fragments of rock, scattered in the recess ; and, as they talked, feasted their eyes upon the beauty of the scene before them.

"Yes, it was very dreadful ;" whispered Viola ; "she took me up stairs in silence,—I should have been glad to hear her cross voice then, better than to have her lead me so sternly, without a single word,—and put me into the room, and locked the door, and walked away. As I heard her step going off in the distance, as if it said no ! no ! no ! angrily, at every stamp, I felt quite a pain here ; it seemed to tread upon my chest, and hurt me, and crush down all the hope I had. Then I couldn't hear anything going on in the house. Everything sounded so still, and so lonely. And then it grew dark,—not so much the evening drawing in, as the sky growing blacker and blacker. All the blue dulled into grey ; all the sunshine blotted out of the sky ; and still it grew darker and darker ; and everything was so frightfully silent. It seemed as if I had never known so long, so dreary, so dismal an evening. At last the silence was broken by the distant rolling of the thunder ; then it came nearer, and nearer, and the darkness was interrupted by the flashes of lightning ; and they made the darkness seem doubly dark the instant they were gone. I could only see the black sky out of the high window ; if I could but have looked out at the street, or at the houses opposite, or caught a glimpse of anybody, or anything ; but I could only see the black sky, and hear the roaring of the rain, and the bursts of thunder. I knelt down by the side of the bed, and buried my face in the clothes, that I mightn't see or hear the terror. I tried to think of what Mamma used to tell us of the goodness and power of God, that can protect us through all danger, and keep us safe. The words of those prayers that monna Marcella makes us repeat every night and morning, came into my mind too ; but they brought the sound of the sour, snappish voice, in which she teaches them to us, (just as if she were biting the words, and spitting them out),—so they did me no good,—only confused me ; therefore I put them out of my head, and thought of Mamma's words, and of her soft, gentle voice, and of the hopeful things it had told me. And then I fancied that the thunder had meantime grown less loud, and less frequent ; and I listened, and so it had ; and then I took courage to look at the sky. And it had cleared ; the dark veil of clouds was drawn away ; and the deep, beautiful blue was to be seen ; and some dear, twinkling stars were looking out at me, like kind eyes ; as if some of the little angels were peeping out of heaven to cheer me ; and the sky which had been my terror, was now my comfort. And so I kept looking up at it, till my eyelids felt heavy, and I suppose I fell asleep ; for it was bright morning, and the sun was up, when I awoke."

" And how sparkling and beautiful the morning looks now, here, out in this lovely place, with the open air about us, and the fresh clear sea, and the rocks with those feathery olive-trees above them, and those snug little cottages nestled yonder among the green vines and maize-grounds, and those boats lying in the water, scarcely moving, the sea is so glassy and still ; " said Sebastian.

" I'm so glad we came ; " said Viola ; " it has made me feel quite well, —quite hungry. All my choking, sick feeling is gone ; and I should be glad of my breakfast, now, that I couldn't swallow before ; " she added laughing.

" I oughtn't to have been in such a hurry to throw it away ; " said Sebastian, in the same tone ; " it would be very welcome, if we had it here ; eating in the open air is so pleasant."

" Never mind ; the pain of being hungry isn't half so bad, as being forced to eat when you can't swallow ; " said Viola cheerfully. " I had rather twenty times be here, in this beautiful place, and a little hungry, than shut up in that stifling house, with plenty of food before me that I can't get down."

" You enjoy being out here, Viola ? So do I ; " said Sebastian. " As you say, I'm glad we came."

" I suppose it's time for us to be thinking of going back ; " said she, with a sigh ; and a timid look crossing her face, as she thought of monna Marcella.

"Not yet;" said Sebastian. "We can't have been out an hour; not half an hour. Let us go and see what those men are doing in that boat yonder, which has just come ashore. They are landing, and bringing something with them."

"It's a basket of fish; and a heap of nets, I think;" said Viola; as she followed her brother towards the spot.

The children stood watching the proceedings of the fishermen, much amused; they saw the men land their haul, divide it, and separate in the direction of their several huts; while some stayed on the beach to spread the nets in the sun; and another drew up the boat, mooring her alongside of the other small craft that lay there.

The last man that lingered, took up his share of fish, and went into the nearest hut, that stood just at hand, close down upon the sea-brink. The two children, half unconsciously, followed, interested in his doings. The door of the hut stood open, as usual; and the children, hanging about the threshold, could see what went on inside. It showed the interior of a kitchen, which opened at once from the outer entrance. Near the doorway was a table, or dresser, beneath the latticed window; in the farther corner was a rude stone stove, over which hung knots of garlick, bunches of onions, of herbs, and of maize; the room was flanked at the back by another dresser, on which were strewed some vegetables, and coarse bread, with several bowls and pipkins of earthenware. At the table stood a woman, busily employed in preparing the fish, which her husband had just brought in; while he went and lay in the shade, on a wooden bench, beneath a trellice covered with passion-flower, at the side of the house. Beside the woman, stood a boy, crunching a raw tomata, having one hand in his pocket, and looking with lazy interest at his mother's proceedings. The two children, in the doorway, watched also. They saw her take the fish, which she could hardly hold, they were so slippery, and so leaping alive; (Viola thought it cruel; and Sebastian, almost a pity, to kill such beautiful creatures; they were mottled blue, on the back, like porcelain, and silvery beneath, with a vivid scarlet mark along their side;) and holding them on the dresser, she cut their heads and tails off, scraped and cleaned them, and dropped them into a bowl of fresh water one by one. When they were all thus far prepared, she drained them out of the water, and put them into a pipkin with some oil, pepper, salt, and onion; then she reached down a garlick, crushed it with her fist, on the dresser, into cloves, which she added to the contents of the pipkin; then she fetched some dried bay-leaves, and a fresh lemon, which she sliced and put with the rest. Then she covered over the pipkin, and set it on to the wood fire, that crackled and glowed on the top of the stove, between two stone rests. While it simmered, she cut some sippets of bread into a large bowl; and when it was done, she poured the hot savoury mess, upon the thin layers of bread, and her dish of fish was ready. It smelt so relishing, and looked so delicious, and seemed so like the crowning of the whole dainty preparation they had been watching, that, joined to their previous appetites, the two children could scarce resist the urgent promptings they felt to ask if they might not partake of the feast.

The expression of their faces so markedly painted this feeling, that,— on the good woman's raising her eyes and catching theirs, as she lifted the smoking bowl from the dresser, preparatory to taking it out under the trellice, for domestic discussion,—she could not help exclaiming to herself:— "What two pretty creatures! They're as like as two almonds in one shell! They look mortal hungry. I've a good mind to ask 'em if they'll have some fish with us. Rocco's had a good haul to day; we can well spare some. Hé, Piccinini! What say ye to coming under the trellice with us, and eating a bit? You shall be right welcome, for the sake of your pretty little twin 'visetti'!"

The two children joyfully followed the good woman into the shade of the arbour; where, with true Italian rustic taste, the fisherman and his family were wont to take their meals. The benches and table were rudely hewn, it is true; the bowls and trenchers were of the commonest kind; but the thick-trained passion-flower over-head, the glorious view of the sea and rocks of the bay, seen through the supports of the trellice, together with the kind, hearty manners of their entertainers, combined to make this one of the most exquisite repasts the children had ever enjoyed. They expressed their grateful pleasure in innocent words of delight, better than the most elaborate thanks; and took leave of the good-natured people,

with mutual liking. The fisherman resumed his lolling on the bench, and
dozed off into a 'siesta'; his wife betook herself to her household duties;
and their son Giorgio (the boy who had beguiled the tedious half-hour before
dinner by munching a crude tomata) lounged down on the beach, to join
some companions of his own age, who were capering in the shallow water,
and scrambling into the boats, and rocking themselves to and fro, and
pulling about the boat-hooks and the oars, and making a great show of
seamanship.

The two children had followed Giorgio, and stood watching him and
the other boys, as they pursued their evolutions in the boats.

It was one of those brilliant afternoons in a southern climate; where
the air seems saturated with the sun's rays; where azure and gold seem
the pervading blended hues; where the undulating cliffs crowned with
rich foliage, look soft, yet defined, in harmonious outline, as they lie
bathed in the glowing light; where the sea shows as a vast resplendent
mirror, clear, tranquil, lustrous, where all-beauteous Nature looks, perhaps,
most beautiful.

Viola had been gazing at the effect of the sunshine under the keel of
one of the nearest boats. The sea-water, with the light thus through it,
looked like liquid emerald, so bright, so translucent, did it shimmer, buoying
up the bark, and showing within its own depths, the shelving shingle
beneath; every pebble and shell distinctly visible. Sebastian had been as
earnestly engaged, observing the movements of two lads, who had unmoored
one of the small vessels; had pushed from the shore; and were now slowly
paddling themselves across the bay.

"How I should like to be with them!" exclaimed Sebastian, half to
himself, half to his sister.

Viola looked in the direction of his eyes, and saw the two young
boatmen making their way, out upon the smooth surface of the water,
towards the farther point. "It looks very pleasant;" she said, as she
shaded her eyes with her hand, and stood watching them, with her brother.

Presently, a woman passing along the strand, called out to one of the
boys idling in the near boats, to come from his play, for it was late, and
she wanted him.

"Late!" echoed Viola, with a start, and a tone of alarm. "Oh, what shall we do? What will monna Marcella say? I never thought of the hour! The morning must be passed; and we not returned! Oh, what shall we do, Sebastian?"

"I suppose there is nothing to be done, but to make the best of our way back;" said he, ruefully. "But we were so happy here; and that dull house is so hateful."

"And then she will be so angry—oh, so angry! All she has ever done to punish us, will be nothing to what she will invent now;" said Viola. "I daren't go back; oh, I daren't go back!"

"Then don't let us go back;" said Sebastian. "The place is detestable. She is detestable. Why should we go back to either? It's more like a prison than a home. It's no home to us. Let's find one of our own."

"That would be delightful;" said Viola. "But where shall we find it?"

"I'll tell you what I've been thinking, Viola;" said her young brother. "Why shouldn't we do as those boys did? Get into a boat, and push ourselves away from the shore, and go and look for some of those beautiful lands beyond sea; where there must be plenty of pleasant homes to choose from."

"Papa talked of brave countries abroad; and perhaps we may meet him! Wouldn't that be joyful? He sailed away upon the sea, you know. If we were to meet his ship! Eh, Sebastian?" And Viola's soft eyes brightened with childish glee.

"Who knows? We might. We can but try;" he answered. "Here, give me your hand; I'll help you into the boat, and I can leap in after."

"Do you think you shall be able to manage the boat?" said Viola, as she obeyed his directions, and stepped in.

"Oh yes; I've been watching those boys all this time; and I'm sure I can do what I saw them do;" he replied confidently.

"How pleasantly it glides along;" said Viola, charmed with the smooth motion of the boat; "and how safely it is taking us away from the chance of that cruel monna Marcella's finding us.".

Luckily for the two children, the sea had not a ripple. Sebastian soon found that his strength was insufficient to lift, far less to use, the large oars which lay in the boat; but there was a long pole, or boat-hook, much lighter, with which he contrived to push off the craft, and to guide it through the shallower portion of the bay. As the water deepened, he found no resistance at the end of his implement; yet still he wielded it manfully, flattering himself he was propelling their bark like a veritable able mariner. The truth was, what slight current there was, drifted them gently out to sea, and bore them along independent of any effort on the part of the young boatman.

So long as the shores of the bay were near at hand, seeming to close them round, and protect them by their placid green beauty, the children went on happily enough, delighted with their adventure, with the motion of the boat, and with a sense of escape and safety. But as they got farther from land, and the expanse of waters seemed to spread widening out on all sides of them, without offering any prospect of haven or refuge, Viola began to cast anxious looks at her brother's face, to see whether she could detect any glimpse of uncertainty, or misgiving, as to their position. He strove to preserve a cheerful, courageous countenance, as if he perceived nothing that should abate their enjoyment of the voyage; but secretly, he began to have doubts of its being quite so pleasant as it had appeared at first. He had been trying,—without saying a word to Viola,—to turn the head of the boat back again, but he found he had not the least power over it,—that in fact, it proceeded entirely of its own head, without consulting his will or liking, or being in the least guided by either his opinion or his strength. He did not communicate this discovery to his sister; first, because it was somewhat mortifying to his newly-assayed seamanship; secondly, because he did not wish to alarm her.

She, not wishing to disconcert him, or trouble him, by anything which might sound like a fear, or a complaint, determined to repress her anxiety, as much as possible; and tried to keep chatting on about the clearness of the water, the delicious sea air, the glad feeling of liberty that was theirs, as they glided along, far, far away from monna Marcella, and her sharp voice, and her close, dull house, and her snarling, fierce dog.

"We are so free, and so safe, are we not, Sebastian. So safe; an't we, caro?" she said, with another peep at the expression of his face.

"Yes; safe, quite safe,—from her, from them;" said her young brother; "at any rate, we're safe away from all that misery. You don't wish yourself back again, do you, Viola?"

"Back again! Oh, if you knew what I suffered last night, locked up in that lonely room, you wouldn't ask me. I am only too glad to be out here, in this pleasant boat, happily, by ourselves; instead of in that dreary place, with that ill-natured woman."

"Viola," said the boy, "come here, and help me to push with this pole; I don't know how it is, but it don't seem to make the boat mind what I want it to do."

"The boat seems to go on very nicely, I think;" said Viola, in a dubious tone.

"Yes, it *goes on* very well;" said her brother, with his eyes fixed on the fast-fading shore.

Viola came and placed herself by her brother's side, trying to understand all his directions for the proper swaying of the boat-hook, which he used in manner of a scull, at the stern. She strove with all her little strength to aid him in his efforts, and with all her young intelligence, to comprehend and second his intentions. The two children showed the native gentleness of their tempers, the genuine goodness of their dispositions, in this moment of trial. Not one word of impatience or fretfulness, fell from either; he directed her energetically, strenuously, but with nothing of dictatorial haste, or boyish petulance; and she obeyed him without a syllable of murmur, or utterance of teazing fear. He endeavoured to make himself understood clearly, and rapidly; while she tried to catch his meaning promptly, and to execute it implicitly. Left to the impulses of their own sweet natures, these two young creatures proved that neither harshness, nor authority, were requisite to make them act rightly. Out upon the open sea, with no human eye to controul or observe them, they behaved with loving, mutual help, and kindliness.

What little added impetus their joint slender force was able to afford, in moving the boat-hook to and fro at the stern of the vessel, assisted the effect of the current in the boat's onward progress; and it drifted farther and farther away from the main-land.

After a time, Viola ventured to cast one anxious look round upon the wide-spreading world of waters on every side ; and the tone of relief and exultation with which she exclaimed :—" Sebastian ! we're coming to some land !" showed how keen in reality had been her previous solicitude. As much was confessed in the voice with which he echoed :—" Land, Viola !" and by the eager look he cast over his shoulder.

It was true. They were approaching the shore of one of those numerous islands which lie dotted along that coast, rising out of the serene waters of the Adriatic, verdant and fruitful,—exuberant in vegetation and in beauty.

The children exerted all their strength and skill, to push vigorously, and to guide the boat right against the shelving beach, as they had seen the boys do in the bay, when they wanted to land. Their manœuvre was crowned with success ; and their little bark came with a kind of smooth crunching, right on to the shingly sand.

Sebastian assisted Viola out ; and as he sprang out himself, after her, he couldn't help giving her a hug, which she returned, for joy to find themselves safe on dry land again.

" I wonder what place this is !" said Viola, as she and her brother began to look around them, after a moment or two.

" A very pleasant place, seemingly ;" said Sebastian, in all the recovered spirits of a prosperous coming ashore.

" If it should be a desert island !" exclaimed Viola ; " or inhabited only by savages ! What an adventure that would be, after all our day of adventures, wouldn't it ? "

" Yes, but it don't look like a wild, or desert place, such as the stories tell of ; " answered he, looking about. " See ! yonder's a vine-yard, and farther on there's an olive-ground ; and here,—between the trees,—look Viola ! there's a peasant's house."

" I see it ;" she returned. " And Sebastian, just peep through this aloe fence ; do you see those people ? " she added, in a whisper.

He stooped a little, beside her, and looked in the direction she pointed. Seated on the grass, in the shade of some tall cane plants, and beneath the peach and fig trees of an orchard, that were hung with flaunting festoons of vines, was a group of some four or five persons. They seemed to be peasants; young men and women, of scarcely twenty; eating their supper, and resting after their day's work. They had a large bottle-gourd of wine, and some food spread on the ground beside them; while they eat and drank, laughed, talked and sang, all at once, after their noisy, gay, careless fashion. They looked a very merry party in their bowery nook; and the children remained watching them for some time, before rambling on.

The path they took led upwards from the sea-shore, among green enclosures; olive-grounds, maize-grounds, orchards, and vine-yards. Sometimes the road was skirted by plantations of high, broomy-topped canes, next by terrace rises, studded with olive-trees; anon by a row of cypress-trees, upright, straight, and slenderly tapering,—strangely graceful in formality; again, by banks covered with low-spreading caper-plants, with their stretching stalks like green feelers, and their pale, delicate, white and lilac blossoms; these were succeeded by the narrow, flaggy leaves, and bursting ears, of the Indian corn, or maize; and farther on, by a tangle of fruit trees, vines, and vegetables,—an Italian orchard.

Near to one of these, little Viola lingered. "Let us sit down to rest;" she said; "we have walked a long while. An't you tired, Sebastian?"

"No;" he said; "but I should like something to eat. An't you hungry, Viola?"

"Yes;" said she, laughing. "But there's no good fisherman's wife near here, to give us some of her nice dish. I'm afraid we must go without supper. No more such delicious hot fish."

"But though there's no hot fish, there's something better still, for supper;" said Sebastian. "What think you of some delicious cool fruit, Viola? on some cool, green leaves?"

"I think it would be only too dainty;" she said. "But where are we to get it?"

"Stay; you sit there, where you are, on that slope of turf;" returned he; "while I creep in here, and pick up some of the fruit I see scattered on the ground under these orchard-trees, just above, here. It will not be stealing; for you know nobody thinks anything of the wind-falls. I shall not gather any, only take those that have dropped of themselves."

Presently he returned with a lap-full of pears, peaches, and ripe figs;

and he sat down beside her, while she arranged them temptingly on dishes
of vine-leaves, which he had not forgotten to bring, and the two children
enjoyed their supper together, like ' making a feast.'

They sat thus, munching, and chatting, very happily ; amusing themselves by watching the different people that passed ; for they chanced to be
in a road much frequented by the peasant inhabitants ; so that they had
abundant token, as Sebastian had said, that it was no desert island.

First came by a tall lad, bearing on his head a basket, from which
depended drooping leaves, and straggling sprays of the verdure with which
it was filled.   Then a girl, with a distaff and spindle in her hand, spinning,
while she tended a flock of mingled sheep and goats, that strayed along the
sloping turf sides of the road, and nibbled their fugitive supper as they
passed.   Next came two boys seated astride on a mule ; or rather, on the
top of the animal's high-piled load of fir cones, packed into bales, by
a lattice-work of string, for fuel.   Then a girl with a bright crimson
kerchief round her sun-browned face, and over her shoulders ; with one
arm stuck in her side, as she balanced on her head a huge bundle of
luxuriant green fodder, and stepped along with a firm, smart pace ; looking
out slantwise from her large dark eyes, at the two little ones seated by the
road-side, as she passed them, humming a rustic song.

"Hark, Viola !   Don't you hear the sound of running water ?   There
must be some brook, or rill, near here, and I should like a draught of fresh
spring water, shouldn't you ? "   Sebastian presently said.

"That I should !   And care for no gold mug to drink it from, or to dip
it with ; " she answered, laughing.   "This pleasant out-of-door life makes
me forget to have any 'fine whimsies,' as monna Marcella calls them.
The hollow of our hand will do quite as well for a cup, won't it, Sebastian ? "

He replied with a smiling nod ; and then added :—" Don't you feel as if it
were an immense time ago, Viola, since we were living in that dismal
house, with that dismal woman ?   To me it seems as if it were,—oh,
I don't know how long,—years ago ! "

"Yes ; I can hardly believe it was only this very morning, that we came
away ; " said she.   "But then we have seen so many new things, and
people, and places, and have gone through such adventures, and made

a sea-voyage, you know! So that it isn't wonderful it should seem a long while since."

They had been proceeding, as they talked, in the direction whence the sound of water seemed to come; they entered among some low trees and underwood, that grew on the opposite side of the road, like a copse, or thicket, of less cultivated ground; it was covered with brambles, and wild roses, and nut bushes, and climbing honeysuckles, and interwoven shrubs, and flowering weeds, leaving no trace of pathway, and scarcely any passage between the close-pleached foliage; but the two children crept underneath, and made their way through, still pursuing the alluring noise, until they came to its source. It was a small natural fountain; formed by a silvery stream, which made its way from some of the higher ground about, and fell through a rocky fissure, green, and moss-grown, and profusely hung with the slender sprays of the plant, popularly named maiden's hair.*

This spring flowed on, and emptied itself into the bed of a torrent, which skirted the copse; and which now, in the summer season, was dry, and empty; save where the small stream intersected its stony centre, a mere slender brooklet. After the children had refreshed themselves with a hearty draught at the fountain, they wandered on, along the edge of the broad water-course, beneath the shady, green-fringed banks of the wood; now stopping to watch some lumbering beetle, or quick-darting lizard; now some light, satin-winged moth, or burrowing water-rat; now a bird, glancing overhead among the twigs and boughs of the coppice, or a flitting, shadowy-wheeling bat. The glow of the day was subsiding into a gorgeous-hued evening, when the two young wanderers came to a spot, where they at once made a halt. It was a deep hollow, or cave, beneath the banks; overhung by the trees, and underwood, and trailing plants, of the copse. Its floor was strewn with a thick layer of dried leaves, that had drifted in, and lodged there, for many successive autumns; while its low roof was over-arched with a verdant screen of clustering myrtles, hazels, and flaunting briony.

" What a pleasant seat! What a soft delicious bed, this would make!"

* In Botanical parlance, Adiantum Capillus Veneris; a green-house beauty with us, —a weed in the South.

exclaimed Viola, letting herself sink upon the springy, elastic heap of leaves. "What a snug, charming nook, altogether!"

"What a delightful home it would make for us!" said her brother, couching beside her. "Where could we find any place we should like better,—to live in; eh, Viola? Why need we seek any farther for a home? Why not fix, at once, on this one?"

"Why not?" she replied, in a triumphantly assenting tone.

The two little householders took possession of their new abode by ensconcing and settling themselves comfortably in two huge, high-piled beds of leaves; and by continuing to note the beauties and conveniences of their chosen dwelling, while they congratulated each other upon their good fortune in having at once met with one so precisely suited to their taste.

"There is even a view of the sea from our window;" said Viola, gleefully, as she pointed to the horizon, visible from the mouth of the cave; where the torrent, slightly deviating, and declining towards the beach, in the distance, showed a brilliant blue line of water, almost of the same hue with the azure of the firmament, surrounding it.

Gradually, the deepening light of evening blended the two tints into one harmonious color; until they could only be distinguished by the one being studded with stars, and the other by its uniform surface. The eyes of the two children were fixed upon the calm beauty of sky and sea; their thoughts took that shape of devout gratitude and reliance, which is the natural and spontaneous form of prayer, arising untaught and unbidden in innocent hearts; and their last uttered words,—in a happy, restful, going-to-sleep tone,—were, "Good night, Viola!" "Good night, Sebastian!"

The next morning, with the dawn, they were up and stirring; making their house tidy; sweeping all the stray leaves into the heaped beds, so as to leave an unscattered floor between. Sebastian made Viola a broom for this purpose, with some gathered twigs, bound by fibrous grasses and withes; and while she was performing her part of housemaid, he consulted with her about a garden, which he proposed fencing in, and planting, in front of their domicile.

"You see, Viola, I mean to clear off all the stones from a space of ground, down in the bed of the torrent, just beneath our cave; and then, round this plot of good earth, we'll stick twigs of cane and willow, and intertwine them, as I've noticed in such garden enclosures ; and then we'll get some seeds of beans, and peas, and melons, and gourds, and tomatas ; and set them ; and when they grow, we'll train them up; and they'll not only look pretty, and green, and blooming, but we shall have vegetables, as well as flowers from our garden ; which will be useful, you know, for our housekeeping ; " said Sebastian, with all the sanguine vision of his age, which beholds a flourishing plenty, where not a germ is formed,—not a seed yet sown.

"Very ;" said Viola, hopefully. Certain questions arose in the mind of the young housekeeper, touching the 'where' they should get these seeds, and the 'how' they should cook these vegetables ; supposing the seeds were obtained, and had actually grown into available, edible plants; but she was not only so prudent as to foresee and to speculate upon these chances, she also had the prudence to keep her foresight and her speculation to herself, lest they should damp the ardour of her co-partner in providing. Well, if all young housekeepers possessed the same sageness of discretion on such points, as this child's love for her twin-brother inspired her with. They made their breakfast of some nuts and berries from the wood, and a draught from the limpid fountain-rill ; and then they climbed to a neighbouring rise, which commanded a beautiful prospect of land and sea. They sat beneath the shade of some trees ; and looked out upon the vivid glare beyond, where all lay in the sunny intensity of an Italian forenoon. The bright green of cresting orange-trees, and luxuriant vines, contrasted with the hoary sheen of olives, in their sloping, terraced grounds ; here and there the white corner of a peasant's stone hut, gleamed among the tufted foliage ; beyond, lay the glittering, sparkling sea, while above, spanned the glowing, cloudless sky. Abroad, all was a resplendent dazzle of light, that made the cool, deep shadow in which they sat, doubly grateful.

When they at length quitted their umbrageous resting-place, they rambled down, through the covert, until they came upon a rural dwelling, situated just at its foot. The two children were lingering near the open door, when a girl came out, with a pitcher of green glazed earthenware on her head, a basket full of bright scarlet love-apples in her hand, an orange-colored handkerchief on her neck, and a sprig of jessamine tucked into her hair, behind her ear. She cast a wondering look at the two little strangers, and then called to her mother, who was busy inside the cottage, to come and look at these two pretty creatures,—'Maraviglosamente simili! Ma similissimi!'

The mother came, and exclaimed with equál delight and wonder at the 'gentilissimi gemelli,' as she called them; and then, fancying that they looked as if they had been wandering far, she asked them to come in and rest. The two children accepted her offer with alacrity, and sat watching her, as she bustled about her household affairs. She was making 'ricotta,' and 'maccaroni.' Seeing that the little ones took an interest in what she was about, she chatted to them, and explained, as she went on. They saw her rake forward some charred wood, and place upon it a red earthenware pipkin, which she filled with sheep's milk; covering it up, and putting a folded white cloth over all, to make the 'ricotta,' or sheep's-milk curds. Then she took some wheaten flour, passed it through two sieves, a coarse and a fine one, till it was what she called ' ben stacciato.' She sifted it on to the top of a bread-trough, that stood there; and into the middle of the flour she broke some eggs, and added a little water; saying, as she made it into a paste :—"I am going to make six eggs of maccaroni to day." Then she took a rolling-pin ; and as she made the paste into what she called 'panelle,' or sheets, the children admired the dexterity she showed in rolling them out wide and thin. Then she put the sheets of paste to dry, on spread bread-cloths, on the bed, as the largest space near at hand; the culinary and dormitive accommodation, being here, as in most peasant households of the kind, on the same spot. Then she took the opportunity of looking meanwhile to her 'ricotta;' putting it on a plate to cool.

When the warm air had sufficiently dried them, she folded the 'panelle,' —as a modern dandy would his starched cravat,—and began to cut them ; slicing them as fine as possible with a very broad and sharp knife, which she took from the side of the table ; where it stuck ready for use, in a piece of nailed-on wood, like a scabbard. Instead of slicing them all alike, she made some fine, which she called 'tagliolini ; ' and others broader, called 'lasagne.'

Finding how pleased the children were with her cookery, closely noting her proceedings, and admiringly observing her skill, the peasant woman gossiped at great length on the subject of nice dishes ; and told them of two spring dainties she especially favored,—broad beans with new cheese, ('fava, con cacio fresco,' as she called it); and a plate of thinly-cut raw ham, eaten with 'fallecciani,' or early figs.

Talking of figs reminded her of a particular kind now in season,— 'fichi cori,' little green figs with red hearts ; and she went and took some out of a large round basket, filled with fruit ; on one side, grapes, divided by vine leaves from the other side, in which were melons, and some of these delicious little figs, of which she gave a handful to the children to taste. She told them that this basket was packed ready to go up to the great house ; that she was a tenant of the lady who lived there ; and that she regularly sent some of her choicest fruit for the 'padrona's' table.

Of this great house, and this lady, the children heard a great deal, in their daily intercourse with the neighbouring peasantry ; who seemed to be all more or less connected with her, either as tenants, or as dependants on her bounty or influence. She was never spoken of by her name, but always as the 'padrona,' the mistress, or presiding great lady. She seemed, by all accounts, to be a kind woman, charitable and good, but very particular. Her estate was large, and gave her almost universal sway over the island and its peasant inhabitants, of which and of whom, she seemed to be a sort of queen.

In this way the children now lived : housing in their cave at night; and rambling about the neighbourhood by day, picking up a living, in the way of food and nourishment, as they best might, from the kindliness of the peasants round about. Their pretty twin figures and faces won them general favor ; and not a dweller there, however poor, but was glad to afford a bit or a sup to the 'gentilissimi gemelli,' as they were called among these good-hearted simple people. One day, it was but a handful of lupin-seeds, nuts, walnuts, or 'pignoli ;' another time it was a lapful of fruit ; sometimes a bowl of soup, with cheese and maccaroni, or bread, in it. When they were in better luck, it was perhaps a trencher of 'umido di polli,' or of 'frittata.' But half the enjoyment and relish of these good things, was derived from seeing them made, and watching the cookery. The children would particularly like seeing the slices of bacon, and pieces of fowl, put into a stew-pan with cloves, and a little water, and salt, and pepper, for the highly-seasoned, savoury 'umido di polli;' or admire the promising frizzle of the morsels of bacon, and the hissing dash of the eggs, as they were broken into the pan, before the hot, crisp 'frittata' was turned into the dish, ready to be eaten, in tempting perfection.

Sometimes their only meal would be a hunk of 'pan-pepato,' or pepper-bread,—a sort of coarse ginger-bread, made of the strongest pepper, and flour, sweetened with wine boiled down, or honey gone winy, 'mosto cotto,' which is the sugar of the peasants. They would get this given to them in the harvest-fields by the reapers ; to whom it was sent out, with other snacks of the kind, provocative of drinking, together with old wine, kept on purpose for harvest-time, in order to maintain the labourers' strength through the heat of the day. The harvest-people would have spared some of their wine, also, to the 'gentilissimi gemelli ;' but the children cared for no drink but spring-water, of which they could get as much as they liked from their own clear fountain-rill, near their cave-home. They liked, however, to chat with the good-natured, sun-burned reapers ; and to help them to make up the little bunches of wheat formed of one ear from each sheaf, that the quality and number of sheaves, might be shown ; which it was customary to take to the proprietor of the field. Many of these fields belonged to the 'padrona,' at the great house ; and thus again, Viola and Sebastian heard of her.

They were much entertained, likewise, to see the bell-ringer of the village cathedral come into the field, with his 'bisaccia,' or double sack, slung over his shoulder, or across his mare's back, going his rounds among the peasants to collect toll for tolling against bad weather ; and sometimes the peasants would refuse ; and reproach him with not having rung strenuously enough to keep off the last hail-storm ; and make him promise that he would set to in good earnest, with better vigour, and heartier good will, the next time any threatening clouds should make their appearance,—grey, or whitish clouds, always portending unfavorably.

Then they were interested with the large carts, in celebration of the harvest-season, containing chairs fastened in by cords ; with four props at the corners, and canes arched across, the whole covered with coarse sheets for an awning, and drawn by white, or dove-colored oxen.

Then there was the ' Bovaro,' or ox-driver ; a fellow of considerable dignity ; and the ' Caporale di Bovi,' his eldest son, who had the charge of the oxen in the field.

This 'Caporale di Bovi' was called Jacò,—short for Giacomo, in peasant dialect. He had three sisters ; Annù, Terè, and Rò,—short for Annuccia, Teresa, and Rosa. And these little country-folks used to make a prodigious noise, screaming out, at the top of their loud, bawling, unrestrained voices to each other, as they pursued their several field avocations, one marshalling his oxen ; another her herd of pigs, a second her sheep, or calves, and the third her flock of turkeys ; all the three girls spinning, the while; and all the four raving, screaming, scolding, and even swearing, at their respective charges.

The ' gentilissimi gemelli ' instinctively shrank from the companionship of these young boors; and when the prolonged yelling call of " O Rò !" or " O Terè !" resounded in the vicinity, Viola and Sebastian would hastily make their retreat from the spot. But they were very civil when they chanced to meet ; and were very thankful for any kindness shown them by these peasant children ; who were only rough and ill-bred, not ill-natured, and could not help their unpolished manners—knowing no better.

Viola was essentially sweet-tempered, gentle, and graceful-minded ; the two latter qualities made her involuntarily recoil from the coarseness of the little rustics, as the former led her to forbear from showing any dislike towards them ; she only avoided them as much as possible. The same refinement and grace of mind, it was, that had caused her to feel so unhappy amidst the sordid, untasteful environments, and monotonous, commonplace existence, of monna Marcella's house,—street-enclosed without, bare, and dull, and unsightly within. But this native refinement was not shocked by the rudeness and privations of her present out-door life ; they were scarcely felt as disagreeables ; and when they did present themselves a little hardly, —from a scant meal, or a protracted fast, she was the first to make light of them, and to join her brother in bearing them laughingly and good-temperedly. She was his cheerful, industrious, affectionate little house-keeper; and he was her glad, eager, active helper and purveyor. They enjoyed some very happy time together, in their cave-home; and often spoke of their good fortune in having discovered it. But the rainy season was approaching; and even their sanguine little heads perceived the difficulty they would have to remain there, in the ill-sufficing shelter of the cave, open to the air as it was, when the bad weather should set in.

They were sitting, silently, each half admitting some such thoughts to themselves, one afternoon, in their cave, side-by-side; and watching the advance of a thunder-shower, that was lowering over the hills, on the opposite side of the torrent.

As the sky blackened, and the landscape faded, and the birds became hushed, and that gradual, portentous stillness crept upon all things,—the suspensive silence, and gathering gloom, which precede the bursting of a storm,—the two children sat with held breath, and beating hearts, in that condition of admiring awe which such a scene inspires. Then came the large heavy drops: spare and at intervals, first; sounding among the leaves overhead, distinct, and separate, in single, splashing spots, forming muddy, dotted lumps on the dry and dusty earth before the mouth of the cave; then thicker, and faster, driving and pelting down, in a wilful, determined slant of wet; then a closer and more violent vehemence, pouring down in sheeted continuity; while the electric wind sprang up, tossing the branches and boughs above, to and fro in wild agitation; and the sharp thunder-claps pealed forth; and the sudden lightning-flashes seemed to shatter the air in abrupt concussion.

" It is very grand, brother, is it not?" whispered Viola, in an under tone.

Sebastian nodded, and tightened his grasp; for they had unconsciously taken each others' hands, and sat together with clasped palms.

Presently he said :—" You are not afraid to look out at the storm, now, Viola; though you were so alarmed that night at monna Marcella's, when there was thunder and lightning, and rain."

" I was alone then;" she said. " I am with you, now."

There was another pause; and then she added :—" I could only see the terror, then; now I can see the beauty. I'm not miserable about other things; I have you safe at my side; so my attention is not distracted, I suppose, from the grandeur. I don't know how to express it; but I feel as if there was nothing to make me see the ugliness, and frightfulness of the storm, and everything to make me see the wonder and the beautiful grandness of it."

"I understand;" said Sebastian, quietly.

They sat, in silence, watching on; until the heavens, by degrees, grew clearer; the rain ceased; the thunder rolled away in the distance; the clouds dispersed, and drew off; light gleamed through the grey veil; patches of blue sky appeared; and presently, the sun darting the splendour of his beams athwart the scene, turned the raindrops which trembled upon leaf and spray into a thousand glittering diamonds, and gave to view a majestic rainbow. The gorgeous colors grew out of the murkiness, and painted themselves on the sombre back-ground of the leaden-hued horizon, in Nature's own magic mastery; and the children sat gazing upon them, in charmed delight.

Out of their heart-gladness at the beauteous sight, and the happy feeling of peace and safety, on the return of fair weather, sprang to their lips a little tune, that they often sang together. It was some light popular air, graceful and melodious, in its Italian character, which had been taught by their mother to her twin boy and girl before they could well speak. The words they then lisped to it, had been forgotten; but the tune remained, vibrating in their memory, with a pleasant echo of the old by-gone home-life at their parent's knee. They had put words of their own to it; and used to chant it in manner of a childish duet; Viola singing the main air and words, while Sebastian repeated the burthen, as a sort of accompaniment, in a fanciful independent measure, that nevertheless chimed harmoniously with the key and rhythm of the tune.

Viola had an exquisite voice; both speaking-voice, and singing-voice; she had, among other peculiarities of her delicate organization, an admirable ear; and she possessed a natural taste for music. It had been a delight to her, to invent the words for this song, and to sing it with her brother, in their moments of light-hearted joy and sense of freedom, since they had lived out here in their sylvan liberty. They frequently sang it, in return for the hospitable entertainment they received at cottage-doors; and these kindly peasant-people deemed themselves well repaid, when they could get the 'gentilissimi gemelli' to carol their childish roundelay.

One evening, shortly after this time, as the two children were preparing to return home to their cave, and thinking that the air of latter autumn was beginning to be chill,—on crossing the road that skirted the copse, they beheld a coach, or litter, rumbling along; and presently they saw Jacò, the 'Caporale di Bovi,' tearing across the field, where his charge roamed; and heard him shouting to them to come and be harnessed to the 'padrona's' coach, that they might help the horses to drag it up the steep rise on which her house lay. The twins loitered, that they might see the interesting ceremony of fastening the milk-white oxen into the traces; and likewise in the hope that they might catch a glimpse of the stately 'padrona' of whom they had heard so much.

As the coach halted, to await the coming of the assistant team, Viola and Sebastian could see withinside, the slight, diminutive figure of a little old lady; who leaned forward, looked out of the coach-window, peered about impatiently, and exclaimed with dabby irritation :—"Dear me! I wonder what ails them that they don't bring these cattle. What can the people be about?   Bless me! why an't they ready?"

"'Cause they an't, I s'pose;" was the somewhat unsatisfactory reply, that proceeded from a loutish youth, seated beside her in the coach.

The two children could see that this companion of the little old lady was deedily employed, peeling a long cane, which stuck its spiring length out of the opposite coach-window, while he scattered the shreds and fragments on the coach-floor, as he stripped them off.

"Dear me! What if you were to get out, and hasten these people, with their cattle, my dear boy?" said the lady.

"What if I wasn't?" retorted the lad.

"Well,—I don't know,—dear me—it might hurry their movements a little;" meekly dabbed the little old lady.

"It might, or it mightn'tsh ye see;" rejoined the lout. "Anyways,

I can't see what's the odds, whether they hurry or no ; it can't signify for a minute more or less." And he whistled ; and continued to strip his cane ; showing how perfectly immaterial it was to him.

" Dear me, quite true ; certainly, as you say, my dear boy, it is not of much moment, if I reach home a few minutes sooner or later. Still, I'm fond of early hours, and—— "

" Ah ! minutes an't, hours, ye see ; " observed the youth, sententiously.

" But minutes make up hours, my dear boy ; " returned the little old lady, with dabby deprecation ; " and if we neglect the minutes, we lose the hours."

" What's the use of argufying and prosing ? " he said, stretching himself, and flirting off the remainder scraps of pith and rind from his knees.

" Perhaps, my dear boy, you could manage to prevent those shreds from littering and making a mess in the coach ; " said the old lady, eyeing the morsels as they scattered down.

" P'rhaps I couldn't ; " he replied bluntly. " What's the fun o' ridin' out, if there's to be such a fussin' and pheesin' about everything ? "

" Dear me ! well,—it's very true, my dear boy ; it's hard to check all your innocent amusements ; young people will be young people ; boys, above all, will be boys, I know ; " said she, with a little sigh, and in a tone of dabby resignation.

" O'course they will ; " assented he. " Oh, here come the oxes ! Come, you sir ! look sharp, will you ? " he added, addressing the ' Caporale di Bovi,' with a startling shout from the coach-window. " Hallo ! Jacò ! Be alive, young chap ! Don't'sh ye see my lady's in a mortal hurry and flustration to get home."

" In three seconds, ' padrona ! ' " said the ' Caporale,' touching his cap to his lady mistress.

" Ah, she'll ' padrona ' you, if you don't bustle your bones a little quicker, master ! " said the lout, hanging out of the window, and touching up the ear of one of the white oxen, with the tip of his cane ; while the ' Caporale di Bovi ' solaced his disgust at the upstart young gentleman's insolence, by stealthily making one of his expressive Italian gesticulations, indicating measureless contempt.

While these amenities were going on at one side of the coach, on the other, lady Annuccia happened to catch sight of the two children, who stood there, side-by-side, hand-in-hand, looking on.

"Dear me!" she exclaimed; "well I never thought to see such another pair,—so singular a couple,—so perfectly twin—so alike—so—dear me! well! It's extraordinary, I'm sure!"

"What now?" cried her boy companion, drawing his head leisurely into the coach.

"Dear me! well,—the most wonderful resemblance! Not only to each other,—but, dear me,—to my nephew's little boy and girl in Messaline. They were mere babies when I saw them; but still, I can remember, they were as like those two children yonder, as anything can be. Two cherries on a stalk, are not more alike, than these young things are to one another, and to my nephew's twins! Dear me!"

The little old lady leaned back, and gasped; fanned herself faintly; and then stooped forward once more, and called, with more than her usual dabby feebleness of tone :—"Come hither, children! Dear me! Come hither, I say!"

Viola and Sebastian seeing the 'padrona' beckon with her fan, advanced towards the coach-window.

"My dears! Bless me! Well,—dear me,—I never! The nearer they come, the more striking the likeness! Dear me! Well,—ahem,— my dears, tell me; what are your names?"

"Sebastian, madam;" }
"Viola, madam;"   } they simultaneously replied.

"It is they themselves!" ejaculated the little old lady, sinking back into the coach, with another gasp. Then jerking forward again :—"Bless me! I never knew anything so amazing! So you are actually your own selves, are you? Dear me! I should never have thought it! I should never have dreamed it possible,—dear me,—that you should have left home, —that I should see you here,—alone, ragged; all your pretty clothes faded and torn. My poor young dears! Bless me; pray come in; come into my coach. I shall be delighted,—of course—to take you home; to hear all about you, why you are here, and so forth. Dear me, to be sure!"

And the 'padrona,'—who was no other than lady Annuccia herself, —made the children get in, seating them on the opposite seat to her, and went dab-dab-dabbing on, in a strain of complacent wonder and welcome, while the lad beside her, sat staring at them, with what would have been an open mouth, had it not been partially closed into the utterance of a low whistle, signifying mingled astonishment and admiration.

At the top of the steep and long hill, the coach turned into a pair of lofty iron gates, which formed the entrance to lady Annuccia's grounds. The drive up to the house was beneath a trellice of vines, supported on each side by square stone pillars; between which, were small cypresses, and rose bushes, planted upon violet-beds, growing on a low ridge, or parapet, that skirted the trelliced pathway. Beyond this, lay, on each side, a profusion of pomegranate trees, orange and lemon trees, fig and peach trees, mingled with flowers and vegetables growing beneath; and where the latter were newly dug and trenched, the warm, rich, brown earth, added yet another hue to all this wealth of color.

The little old lady was gratified at the admiration which the two children ingenuously expressed at her beautiful place; and when they alighted, she led them into her own sitting-room, and pointed out the best views of the garden from the windows, and welcomed them affectionately, and again assured them that she was :—" Dear me, of course, delighted to see you both ! "

While the owner of the cane was lolling out of window, and exchanging a few farewell compliments with the 'Caporale di Bovi,' lady Annuccia gave orders for the appointment of certain rooms for her young visitors, and desired one of her women,—a grave-faced, but kind-looking person, named Annunziata, to make it her care that the twin brother and sister should want for nothing; and to consider them, in short, as her special charge.

That night, a violent tempest arose. The wind blew a perfect hurricane ; and as Viola lay and listened to its howling gusts, she congratulated herself that she and her brother were safely housed, beneath better shelter and protection, than their cave-home could have afforded.

Next morning, the sun shone out again brightly, and the blue sky was

apparent in all its Italian vividness, though the wind still raged ; and as
Viola was talking with Sebastian before lady Annuccia came down,
rejoicing that they had met with their kind relation in time to save them
from encountering such weather in the open air, they overheard the servants speaking of the rough night ; and of several fishing vessels having
foundered during the gale ; and of a large vessel, which had been wrecked
off the coast, and gone down, with all her crew.

After breakfast, the proprietor of the cane flung off to see his tame
rabbits ; saying to lady Annuccia,—who asked him whether he wouldn't
take the young visitors to see them :—" Oh, I da' say ! If they want to
come, let'em."

" Shouldn't you like to go and see Gabino's rabbits, my dears ? " said
the little old lady. "He'll show them to you,—dear me,—I've no doubt,
—if you'll follow and ask him."

" Thank you, madam ; " said Viola ; " I don't want to go with him ; I
don't wish to see the rabbits, thank you."

" Viola and I would like to take a walk together, if you please, madam ; "
said Sebastian. " We should like to go down to the beach, and see the high
waves, this morning ; and the torrent,—whether it is full ; and our cave,
whether it has been washed into."

" Well,—dear me,—though I don't approve, in general, of solitary walks
for young ladies ; of their going out alone,—unattended ; yet with their
brothers, there can be no impropriety. Go, my dears ; but be back by noon
to dinner. I like punctuality in my hours."

The children promised ; and went off in their usual, happy, hand-in-
hand fashion.

They loitered on the beach, some time ; watching the dashing of the spray,
and the ponderous frolics of the billows, roaring, tumbling, and rolling over
one another. Then they rambled down to the side of the torrent ; which
they found, swelled by the rain to a wide and rapid river, nearly filling its
broad bed. But they contrived to creep down along the banks, as far as
their cave. At the entrance they paused, and peeped in. It was still high
and dry ; untouched by the advance of the waters, which had not reached
its mouth. Upon one of the heaps of unwetted leaves, lay a man, in a fast

sleep. He seemed, by his dress, a mariner; its torn condition, and his attitude, bespoke fatigue, and struggle with the waves and rocks. He looked flung there,—spent, bruised, and dead weary. The children stood gazing at him, with sympathy and commiseration in their faces.

"He is one of the shipwrecked men, from the vessel we heard of, that went down, last night;" whispered Sebastian.

"Look there, brother!" said she, in the same low pitch; but her tone and her excited manner, caught his attention; and instead of following the direction of her pointing finger, his eyes turned towards her own face. It was agitated with surprise, and peculiar interest.

"Look there, upon his forehead!" she repeated.

She stepped softly nearer; and leaned, breathless, over the sleeping man. She put back the locks of sea-stained hair, very gently; and then whispered :—"It must be, brother! It must be our father! Do you not see the little brown mole? My own dear little mole! I should know it, wherever I saw it!"

She could not refrain; but bent down, and touched it with her lips. However light the contact, it was felt. The sleeper stirred; and unclosed his eyes. As they met the soft, violet ones, that peered above him,—and as his scarce awakened senses inhaled the fragrance of the child's breath, and of her balmy hair, falling on either side her sweet face, and hanging over his,—he let them close again, murmuring :—"Still dreaming! My little Viola! My pretty one!"

"I am here, papa!" she said; "Sebastian too! Look at us, dear papa!"

Her brother stood by her side; and when the happy father again raised his eyes, it was to encounter, with his waking sight, the living, actual faces, of his twin boy and girl; while he clasped in his eager, glad embrace, their veritable selves.

"It is predestined, that you shall never cease to have strange guests, coming, and taking you by storm, aunt Annuccia;" said the merchant, as they all sat, a happy party, at the old lady's noon-tide table. "Here have my children been claiming your hospitable kindness, no farther back than yesterday. And this morning, when they go out for a couple of hours' stroll, they return, punctually, indeed, as you bade them, to dinner; but bringing with them a wandering father, who has been for some time missing, strayed, or stolen, and who now comes back a penniless beggar. But though he has lost his all, he does not intend remaining a dependant on your bounty. Present food and lodging I receive most gratefully, at your kind hands, for myself; and will be farther beholden to you for the maintenance and care of my children, until such season as I can re-claim them of you, and support them myself. It is true, the bulk of my fortune has perished by this shipwreck. The largest of my ventures, and a considerable sum, the result of my last voyage, were embarked in the foundered vessel, but I have my merchant-house at Messaline ; and, thanks to the care of the trustworthy Raimondo, my confidential clerk, affairs still keep their head above water there. I shall set sail again immediately ; work hard to retrieve my losses ; and hope, within less time than we now think, to be once more the prosperous merchant I was yesterday. I have industry, and energy ; I have gratitude towards you, and love for my children ; and with these spurs to aid me, I do not despair of winning the race."

"Dear me, well,—I hope so ; I'm sure I trust so, my dear boy—my dear nephew. And as for taking charge of these little darlings during your absence,—I'm sure I shall be delighted,—of course ;" replied his aunt.

The young merchant spoke thus cheerfully and hopefully, to keep his spirit firm to the resolve he had formed of quitting his children without delay. He felt the duty, the necessity of this measure ; and however his heart might yearn to spend some time with these newly-recovered dear ones ; he would not let his inclination supersede his sense of right. He accordingly took his passage in the first vessel leaving the island, and bent, his course towards one of the principal foreign ports with which he traded; promising his aunt, that it should not be long ere he sent her tidings of his improving prospects.

The issue justified his hope. Not many months elapsed, ere he was able to send lady Annuccia accounts of his numerous successes, together with a large sum of money ; begging her to appropriate it for the behoof of his children, and to accept his loving thanks for her care of them.

The father's gratitude was honestly due. Lady Annuccia was most kind to the twin boy and girl. The old maiden lady, as she grew in years, grew in indulgence. With her age, increased her kindness, her toleration, her forbearance. She even abated somewhat of her particularity, and rigid notions. This greater leniency owed its origin to a shock she had received, in hearing suddenly of the danger of a very dear friend,—no other than her cousin, don Ignazio. On his death-bed, he had addressed a letter to her ; while reading which, she for the first time discovered, in its full extent, the regard she had for him. She had never herself suspected, how, beneath all her virtuous indignation at his improprieties of speech and conduct, had lurked a fondness for the man, which gave a double edge to the expression of her wrath. No greater proof could have been given of the strength of this secret partiality, than by her compliance with the request contained in don Ignazio's dying letter. It besought her to adopt a boy, a reputed god-son, the child of a peasant-woman, widow to one of his tenants ; it alluded, with a kind of mournful playfulness, to her known partiality for boys ; and concluded in these words :—" I might tell you of other claims he has to your kindness,—your compassion (for his mother, poor thing, is a weak silly woman, whose pretty face is her sole thought ; and who is as unfit,—God help her !—to take care of, and bring up, a boy, as I am,— Heaven forgive me,—to meet the saints in paradise !) But I know your nice punctilio, and will not tax its delicacy by farther explanation. Suffice it, that I take a strong interest in the boy ; that I am dying, and have no means of providing for his future welfare, otherwise than by beseeching you, cousin Annuccia, to take charge of him ; and that I entreat this at your hands, out of the love I think you bear your

graceless, but affectionate cousin,

IGNAZIO."

This boy was Gabino ; the loutish youth, who was with lady Annuccia, in the coach, on the evening she met Viola and Sebastian. She had sent for him ; taken him into her house ; and not only had virtually adopted him, but petted him, indulged him, and in short made just such a favorite out of him, as many maiden ladies—who have outlived what should seem the natural season for judicious choice in the objects of their liking,—find in the shape of other uncomely brutes,—snarling cur, mischievous monkey, sly and treacherous cat, or vicious parrot. It was wonderful to see the patience with which she would submit to the bearish behaviour, and humour the lubberly caprices of this lad; and how blindly she would allow him to commit perpetual breaches of good manners, while she was so scrupulously observant of the slightest indecorum in others. She originally tried to think the best of him, and to fancy she discovered something pleasant in the lout, for the sake of him who had bequeathed him to her; and she succeeded so far, as to bring herself to overlook his disagreeable qualities, and to believe that they were mere superficial defects of manner; until, in time, she became so accustomed to them, as not even to perceive their existence.

The presence of this boy, Gabino, was a source of inexpressible annoyance to Viola. His rude, uncouth bluntness of speech; his ungain bearing; his gruff, grating voice, his lumbering gait, his vulgar habits, all revolted her. The little girl's innate sense of beauty, her constitutional affinity with whatever was gracious, graceful, elegant, and refined, were perpetually repugned by his coarseness. Above all, his propensity to stare, most disturbed her.

He would sit gloring at her; whistling, or sucking his teeth, with a smacking noise, that had the effect of proclaiming his indifference to the opinion of the world in general, and to the feelings of his company in particular. This trick, joined to his fixed gaze, was peculiarly offensive to the little girl. She had the greatest difficulty in suppressing the evidence of disgust and abomination, when beneath the infliction. It was only her own good breeding and delicacy, which prevented the expression of her abhorrence; and which enabled her to endure silently, rather than risk giving offence in return by a distasteful speech.

Once, after undergoing a long twenty minutes' endurance of this kind, biting her lip, and swallowing her repugnance, as she best might, Gabino suddenly relieved her by taking his departure from the room, on lady Annuccia asking him to do some trifling service for her that interfered with his plans,—saying :—" Don't'sh you think it, my lady ! I've other fish to fry ! "

" Hateful, ill-conditioned cub ! " thought Viola. Her feeling was so visibly painted on her face, that,—as lady Annuccia left the room to execute herself, what she had requested her favorite to do,—Sebastian said :—" I don't think you like Gabino, do you, Viola ? "

" Like him ? I loathe him ! " she exclaimed.

" Come, that's a tolerably strong expression of dislike ; " replied her brother, laughing ; " or rather intolerably strong,—intolerant. You are too fastidious, Viola mia. He's an odd beast,—an ill-bred animal, to be sure ; but it's only manner. He's very good-natured."

" Good-natured ! Yet so rude and uncomplying to lady Annuccia ? " returned Viola.

" She doesn't mind it, you see ; " he answered. " You should learn of her to be more tolerant."

" I'll try ; " she said, in her own mild way, ever open to reproof, to the candour of belief that she might possibly be in the wrong, and to the desire of amendment, if it were so. To the end that she might the better learn to tolerate master Gabino's behaviour with indifference, if not with favor, Viola resolved to abstract herself as much as she could, from noticing it, or dwelling upon it; indeed, if possible, to divest herself of any influence from his presence, by forgetting it, and ignoring it utterly. She tried never to look at him ; and considering how odious he was to her, there was no difficulty in that. She turned a deaf ear to his tone of voice, and withdrew her attention from what he said, whenever he spoke ; if he were not absolutely addressing her. By these means she contrived gradually more and more to disengage herself from the annoyance he had occasioned her ; and she was still farther freed, by the pursuit, which she was now able to enjoy, of her favorite taste,—music.

Lady Annuccia used to sing to her mandolin, in a tremulous, querulous voice, certain old-fashioned love-songs and pastoral ditties, such as were supposed to have ' no offence in them ; ' insipidity, and fatuity, counting as none ; offence to the understanding, or injury to the intellect, never entering into the maiden lady's category of evils to be derived thence. However, Viola's good sense, and good taste, saved her from any of the harms by possibility accruing from these foolish old platitudes. Through their means, she gained a competent knowledge of the instrument ; and when she had mastered all the fingering requisite for the execution of these tunes, it taught her to pick out others for herself, to discover better harmonies, to invent gratefuller combinations, and to fashion out airs and accompaniments that had truer accordance with her own musical perception.

Meanwhile Gabino pursued his own devices with Sebastian. This lad had a good deal of wily craft, beneath his loutish exterior. He was sly, mean, and selfish. He had seen with instinctive vexation, the entry of the twin children into the house of their aged relative, lady Annuccia. His mother, a vain, artful, mercenary woman, had not failed to instil into her son the interested hopes which lady Annuccia's design of adopting Gabino had inspired. They trusted it would result in the old maiden lady's making the boy, whom her cousin had commended to her protection, her sole heir ; and it was because the introduction of the twins into her household offered some chance of interference with this scheme, that Gabino beheld their advent with a jealous eye. His cunning taught him to conceal this emotion ; or at any rate, to let only so much of it appear, to lady Annuccia alone, as should advance him in her favor, and give her the idea of his dread that any one else should divide or weaken her affection for himself. He always contrived to insinuate the profound attachment he had for her, in spite of his bluff manner ; and the old lady, in the very weakness with which she submitted to the latter's rude demonstration, evinced the faith she had in the existence of the former.

To the twin brother and sister, he showed outward liking, after his own peculiar loutish fashion. He glored at the beautiful face of Viola ; and he lugged about Sebastian to join him in his various diversions. He would show the boy how to climb trees ; to find wasps' nests, and bees' hoards ; to make bows and arrows for shooting game ; and how to dam brooks for fish.

He was sleepless in his contrivances to keep Sebastian away ; dreading lest lady Annuccia, in her strong predilection for boys, should acquire a liking for this handsome, gentle-mannered one, which might eventually frustrate his own favorite scheme. Of the little girl, he entertained no such dread. He allowed her to be as much with her protectress as she pleased ;

confiding in the notion, that, however, she might gain ground in the old lady's good graces, it could never be to any dangerous extent.

Time thus passed on. Year succeeded year; and yet the only intelligence they had of the merchant, was either by letter or by message; for still he eagerly pursued his purpose of achieving wealth for his children, that he and they should enjoy in luxurious leisure, the period when he should have gained enough to cease from toil. Ah, that vision of 'gaining enough!' How many men does it delude into sacrificing the best years of their life, divided from those they love; until the time comes, when eternal separation steps in and crowns all, in lieu of the hoped-for rich and happy consociation.

Viola had grown, from a child, into a beautiful girl of twelve years old. Her face had still that sweet ingenuous charm,—that purity and innocence of look, which beamed from her soft, appealing, confiding eyes of darkest blue. Her figure was eminently graceful; and rather slenderly than fully proportioned. Her brother had shot up into a tall stripling, slight, and agile. He was more robust in force, than in muscular development; and was more firmly knit, than strongly made. Between himself and his sister, there was still the same remarkable similarity of frame and feature; and, although, as they grew up, their suits varied more, yet when dressed precisely alike, the resemblance was no less striking than ever.

With the young girl's increasing loveliness, had waxed the inveteracy of Gabino's stare. But she had by this time so inured herself to its inconvenience, that it scarcely moved her; and were it not, that latterly it had been accompanied by more active denotements of brutish admiration, she might probably have learned to disregard it altogether.

Once, she happened to be clipping and trimming the branches of an arboured alcove, where lady Annuccia and she were wont to prosecute their mandolin studies. It was a favorite seat of the old lady's; and it was the pride and pleasure of Viola to keep it in perfect order for her reception. As the young girl stood on tiptoe, with her arms upstretched, to reduce some of the stray branches above her head to order, Gabino chanced to lounge by, and saw her in the bowery corner, her graceful shape shown to peculiar advantage by her attitude and employment. After a moment's stolid gaze, the lout bounced into the arbour ; and, laying hold of a bough on each side, with his arms spread out, kept her close prisoner, as in a cage.

"Caught'sh ye, my bird!" he exclaimed. "It's o' no use your fluttering! I've got you fast; and I don't mean to let'sh ye fly, till ye've given me a kiss!"

His face came so horribly near to hers, pent in the angle as she was, that she instinctively thrust at him with the pointed implement she had in her hand, to keep him off. The next instant, making a sudden dive, she ran under one of his arms, and darted away.

Viola half determined to tell lady Annuccia of this insolence on the part of Gabino ; but knowing the old lady's particularity, she thought she should get him into too deep a disgrace ; besides, she felt that she had already taken her revenge into her own hands. She afterwards, still farther rejoiced having forborne to make any complaint, when she found that he,—not ungenerously, as she thought,—made a point of screening her, for her share of the encounter. His face bore the mark of the cut she had given him in her own defence ; and when lady Annuccia, peering into her favorite's blatter countenance, and discerning the scar, said :—"Dear me,—my dear boy—what's the matter with your cheek? There's quite a gash—dear me, what can it be?" Gabino answered :—"That young kitten of yours, my lady! She was up among the trees of the arbour ; and gave me a pat with her claw. I took her for a bird, but found she was a spiteful cat!" Here he leered at Viola. "But it was only her play; I forgive her, though she did give me this ugly scratch."

"Suppose you were to clip her claws, or give her a good beating,—dear me, not too hard, you know,—to teach her better manners."

"'Spose I wasn't;" was the ungracious reply. "I'd rather give her a good—— 'Well, never mind,' as you say, my lady."

The ascendancy which her uncouth favorite had gained over the little old lady, became greater and greater. He lost no opportunity of cajoling her in private ; while outwardly he continued his overbearing bluffness ; thus maintaining, at once a smooth hold upon her affection, and a tight hand over her habitual submission to his will. He made no secret, *to her*, of his. dread that Sebastian should rival him in her favor ; and even paraded his jealousy of any show of liking testified towards another boy than himself. He got her to call him ' my boy,' or ' my dear boy ; ' and never failed to express his displeasure, whenever she chanced to call Viola's brother by the same title. He chose to be her pet boy, her own boy, her only boy. By this kind of wheedling when alone, and by his rough blunt rudeness, before others, he not only succeeded in his plans with her ; but he guarded them from being suspected either by herself, or any one else. As lady Annuccia advanced in years, and grew more and more childish, and weak, he ' got her completely under his thumb,'—to use his own vulgar term, wherewith, in thought, he brutally exulted.

A whimsy, which the old lady's silly fondness prompted her with, in order to please her lout, was, to get up a feast unknown to him, at which she resolved that the twin brother and sister should attend as young lady guests. She determined that they should both be dressed as girls ; and took an imbecile delight in knowing how perfectly Sebastian's slight figure, and youthful beauty of face, would enable her to carry out her design of deceiving Gabino, while she pictured his approbation at seeing no boys present but himself.

Sebastian, of course, made no hesitation in humoring this freak of the old lady's ; and with the help of one of Viola's dresses, he transformed himself into such a precise counterpart of his sister, that lady Annuccia was in an ecstasy.

After admiring, and exclaiming, to her heart's content, at the marvellous beauty and likeness of the two charming young ladies, as she called them, she dismissed Sebastian to the sitting-room, where she promised to join him with Viola, so soon as the last finishing touch to her own dress (which was to be extra fine on this festal occasion, to do honor to her favorite), should have been added.

While Sebastian was awaiting them, Gabino entered the room. He saw, as he thought, the figure of Viola, standing at the window half hidden among the drapery of the muslin curtains, half screened by the stand of flowers which stood near. He stole behind her, exclaiming as he

seized her in his arms, and strove to snatch a kiss :—" Limed at last, my
pretty dear !"

To his infinite surprise, he received a sound box on the ear ; and the
young lady twisted herself out of his embrace with a vigour that staggered
him.

" Young vixen !" he muttered ; " and how confounded strong !"

At that moment, in came lady Annuccia, with the real Viola ; and while
her lubberly favorite stood rubbing his discomfited cheek, and staring in
oafish bewilderment from one Viola to the other ; the little old lady enjoyed
her dabby triumph at his perplexity.

" I knew, my dear boy, that you would be surprised ! Well, dear me,—
it's a little treat I've contrived for you. You are to have nobody but young
ladies to dine with you to-day ; so you must mind and be very gallant, and
attentive to us all."

" S'prised ! I think I am, indeed ! What made'ge you go and hit upon
such a fool's trick as this, my lady ? Dressing up, and mummery, and
nonsense ! But come ; don't'sh you look grum, and sorry, and ashamed.
I an't angry ; I know you did it to please me ; and, 'pon my life, they
look very pretty, both of 'em. There an't a ha'porth o' choice betwixt 'em,
which is prettiest, or which is most like t'other !"

Sebastian had some very ireful feelings rising within him, and glowing
into a red spot upon his cheek ; but he did not like to spoil the old lady's
glee, or mar her little festivity by any quarrellings and ill-temper. He
therefore struggled with his vexation, and suppressed all token of it, though
it still rankled inwardly ; for he had now some inkling of the source of his
sister's particular dislike to this low-bred lad.

" Brute ! No wonder she finds him odious !" thought Viola's brother,
as he watched the fellow gormandizing at table ; gorging the dainties
provided by lady Annuccia ; gobbling till he choked ; strangling himself
with the wine he swilled, and coughing in his glass ; winking jocularly at
the young ladies ; noisily toasting the elder one ; getting into violent
spirits, and growing perfectly uproarious ; while lady Annuccia encouraged his sallies, by her laughter, and her dabby commendation.

As soon as they could, Viola and Sebastian made their escape from the orgy, and went to take a cool walk in the open air, among the shrubberies adjoining the house.

They had been there about an hour, when Annunziata came hurrying towards them, with dismay in her usually quiet face. "My lady! My poor lady! Oh, come in quickly to her, signorina!", she exclaimed, to Viola. "She has been taken ill, very ill; a surfeit—a fever—I hardly know what! I fear she has eaten too many of them sweetmeats, and almond mischiefs, that she would have cook make for this feast. It's all owing to that Gabino. Ah, there's never been any good for my poor mistress, since that bumpkin of a boy came here to be made a favorite of. A pretty object for a favorite, forsooth! As well make a pet out of a roaring bull! Which he is; a great, lumbering bull-calf!"

They were hastening towards the house, all the while the good serving-woman poured forth this, for her, most unwonted exhibition of wrath. Ordinarily, she was one of the gravest, and kindliest of personages. But now she seemed excited by her mistress's danger into irrepressible vituperation.

"A sly, artful cub, he is, too; for all he's such a looby. If anything happens to the 'padrona;' it'll be found so, I know;" she went on. "If mistress should die, it'll be found, for all his awkward, hobbedehoy, dolt's ways, he's had shrewdness to play his game well. Thick-head as he is, he knows fast enough, which side his bread's buttered."

The event fulfilled Annunziata's hint. That night lady Annuccia died; and when her will was opened, it was discovered that Gabino had been named her sole heir. The document contained an affectionate mention of her nephew the merchant, and of his children; but she distinctly excluded them from any portion of what she had to bequeath; giving as her reason, that she knew they needed nothing, while 'her dear boy' Gabino was entirely dependant on her bounty.

Viola was sitting mournfully in lady Annuccia's parlour, recalling the little old lady's many acts of kindness towards her brother and herself, and lamenting, with tears, her loss, when Gabino flung into the room, exclaiming in a loud voice :—"Where's Sebastian? Where's your brother? I want him."

Viola raised her weeping eyes; but could not immediately speak.

"What you're cryin', are you, pretty one?" he said, coming near her; "but ye mustn't cry. No use o' cryin', you know. It makes your eyes red ; and it'd be a pity to spoil 'em. Cheer up! What though the old lady's gone? She lasted her time, ye know ; and there's the more room for us young 'uns."

"She was very kind and good to us;" faltered Viola; "and we are very unhappy to lose her."

"Don't'sh ye sob so! Don't take on so! If you've lost one friend, you've got another! I'll be a friend to you. I'm master here now. Master of the house, and of everything in it. But'sh you know, that needn't make any difference to you ; you may stay here, if you like. You may live with me, and be mistress of the house ; and only pay me in kisses. But'sh you mustn't refuse me them, you know ; and as many of 'em as I choose!"

In a clumsy sort of half sleepish, half bold way, Gabino sat down in the chair beside her, and would have taken the hand that held her handkerchief to her eyes, from before her face ; but she drew away, and muttering something about going to seek Annunziata, she started from her seat and flew out of the parlour. After that, the young girl never left the side of the good serving-woman ; she remained with her, hour by hour, and at night slept in her room. She would have begged Sebastian to take her at once from the house ; but she dreaded having to explain her reasons for wishing this immediate withdrawal, lest she should embroil her brother with the bearish Gabino.

The young 'padrone' was highly affronted at Viola's keeping thus aloof from him ; and tried to circumvent her avoidance by hanging about her vicinity as perseveringly as possible ; but the constant presence of Annunziata vexing him, and making him feel shy, awkward, and constrained, instead of able to give free vent to his naturally blunt, overbearing style, he suddenly said to her,—as he lounged into the room where she was employed about some household work, Viola standing by, watching her :—"Come, mistress Annunziata, you begone! We want none of your duenna-ship here. I've got something to talk to the signorina Viola about ; and we don't want'sh you listenin', and spyin', and pryin' there!"

Viola cast a beseeching look at Annunziata ; which the latter showed she understood, by replying, in a quiet composed way, to Gabino :—" *We* don't want you, sir, here ! "

" You don't, don't'sh ye ? " he returned. ".But as I'm master here,— in this room, as in all t'other rooms, in the house,—my wants are to be attended to, before yours, d'ye see, mistress Annunziata. I want'sh you away ; so, away with you ! Troop ! Be off ! "

" But I'm not going ; " she answered, coolly. " These fine things have got to be ironed ; and so I shall stay to iron them. I can't be hindered in my work."

" But your work must give way to my pleasure, mistress ; " said Gabino. " Besides, I have but to say the word, and your work here's at an end altogether. As I'm master now, I shall bundle you out of the house, at a minute's warning, if you don't obey my orders."

" But I shall take neither orders, nor warning, from——" the serving-woman had it on her tongue to say, " a base-born brat like you," but she prudently curbed herself for the sake of Viola, substituting, " such a young gentleman as you."

"Young as I am, you'll find I know how to make myself minded ; " he retorted. " So do as I bid you, mistress Annunziata, or you'll lose your place. Signorina Viola and I, want to have some chat together; therefore take yourself out of the way, d'ye hear ? "

" I don't see that the signorina wants to have any talk with you, sir ; " she said drily. " She seems quite well amused, watching my ironing and plaiting."

Whatever Gabino might have been about to rejoin, was interrupted by Sebastian's bursting into the room, exclaiming :—Viola ! Viola ! Where are you ? Who do you think is here ? Papa's come ! Papa's arrived ! "

" Papa ! " was her joyful ejaculation. And away they both ran to meet him.

It was a happy return, of the merchant and his children to Messaline. As they sat together on the deck of the vessel, during their short sea-passage, from the island homeward, the father indulged in happy prospects for the future; of retirement, of uninterrupted domestic pleasures with his son and daughter, of providing them with masters that they might make up for lost time, and of superintending, or rather joining them in their intellectual culture. "We have all three of us, led such vagabondizing lives, hitherto," said he, smiling, "that we are in equal need of study and polish, to render us fit for civilized society. I am well nigh as ill-informed and unformed a youth,—notwithstanding the elderly gentleman I am, alas, growing,—as any school-boy of them all! And I shall be glad of the opportunity to begin from the beginning, with my two dear young fellow-pupils; who are also becoming of a venerable age to commence schooling. Why you will be thirteen, soon, I declare. To-morrow is your birth-day, my Viola!"

"And Sebastian's, dear father;" she replied, in her gentle, musical tone. "We shall have you with us, to spend it in all due joyful celebration!"

He went on to tell them of his prosperous voyages; of his profitable speculations; of the wealth he had amassed; and of the delight with which it was dedicated to their use and enjoyment. He told them of the valuable connections he had formed; and dwelt with pride and pleasure on the friendships he had acquired. He spoke with peculiar fervour and exultation of the intimate affection that had subsisted between himself and the late duke of Illyria; and of the one (in which it was renewed and maintained) that still existed between the duke's son, Orsino, and himself. He expatiated on the many virtues and excellences that adorned this noble young man; and said he had admirably fulfilled the promise of his boyhood.

"I remember;" said the melodious voice of Viola, as her soft eyes looked out musingly across the sea; "when I was quite a little girl, I heard you speak of that noble, handsome boy! I could wish to see him."

"It has long been a favorite dream of mine, to take my children with me to Illyria, that they may learn to esteem and love him as I do!" said the father. "The dukedom is happy in being ruled by so well-governed a youth! Some day or other, when those same studies you wot of, shall have enabled us to appear with credit among our fellows, and have graced us for a court-life, we will first visit Venice, and, on our return, present ourselves at Orsino's capital, as his friends and guests."

On their arrival in their native city, the wanderers found all nearly as they had left it. The merchant's dwelling-house had been kept in habitable order by the care of Raimondo, the worthy head-clerk; who had never ceased cherishing the hope, that, one time or other, his beloved master would return with his family, to take up their abode in the old home.

With delight, Viola and Sebastian found themselves among the well-remembered scenes of their infancy; the suite of lofty sitting-rooms, so tasteful in their unostentatious elegance; the marble balcony, with its terrace-steps; the spacious and umbrageous gardens; all were visited and surveyed with the eagerness of happy retrospection, each recalling some childish pleasure, some fond association.

As the brother and sister returned from their ramble through the grounds, and ascended into the balcony, they found their father sitting there, in a thoughtful attitude. His head was bent forward upon the broad ledge; his face hidden in his hand. As he raised it, on their approach, they could see that it was very pale, and that he had been weeping; but his children respected his emotion too much, to notice it. His daughter Viola seated herself beside him, and began speaking, in her low, sweet voice, of the preparations, she, as his young housekeeper, had been making for the morrow's festival; and telling him how she had determined to make it a doubly brilliant one, in honor of his twin-children's birth-day, and of their happy home-return and re-union.

Cheered by her gentle, winning tone, he was able to answer in her own hopeful strain; and before retiring for the night, the old sportive ceremonial of kissing the little mole on his brow, and of bidding it a 'felice notte,' was gone through; and Viola and Sebastian had the comfort of seeing the pale face revive, and the trace of tears quite vanish, ere they took leave of their father.

Next morning, with earliest dawn, the twin son and daughter were at their parent's chamber door, to greet his awakening ears, and to usher in the birth-day of his children, with a little dual song, which they had prepared together, on the previous evening, for the occasion.

As their mingled voices died away at the close, he came forth from his room, with loving smiles, and a cordial blessing.

The morning passed serenely, and happily ; and their festive meal was brought out into the balcony, that an additional air of holiday entertainment, and ' al fresco' enjoyment, might be given to their banquet.

The father's spirits were in a mood of contented, placid joy ; he saw himself united once more with his beloved children, in a home, where tranquillity of heart, and peace of soul, awaited them, together with active mental pursuits,—perhaps the most perfect combination in enjoyment, that can fall to the lot of humanity. He was about to quaff a goblet of Cyprus wine to the health and happiness of the twin monarchs of the day ; when he started up, declaring that the cup should be crowned with roses, to do fitting honor to his pledge, and leaned over the marble coping, to gather some of the clustering half-blown blossoms of his favorite flower, which grew in profusion, trained in front of the high balcony.

He had plucked several ; when, stretching imprudently far, in eagerness to reach a peculiarly beautiful bud, which he destined to adorn his Viola's hair, the father unhappily lost his balance, fell forward, and came with the whole weight of his body to the ground. The head being bent beneath, the neck was dislocated ; and death was instantaneous.

When his agonized children reached the spot they found him lifeless.

The period of mourning for their father, was spent by the orphan brother and sister, in strict seclusion, and in carrying out those plans for their mental culture and improvement, which he had suggested. They had a sad pleasure, in thus obeying his wishes, and following his instructions. They felt, while fulfilling his designs for them, as though they still preserved him by their side in protective care and approval. They had brought the good-hearted Annunziata away with them from the island; and she now superintended their domestic concerns, as housekeeper.

They subsequently made some enquiries about their former guardianess, monna Marcella : and found, that after becoming an inveterate miser, she had died in want of the commonest necessaries of existence, although possessing a sum capable of procuring her its choicest luxuries ; that her treasured hoard had grown into a considerable sum, but that she still converted it into a hard wretchedness, by using it as a pillow, lest it should be stolen; that this precaution had availed her nothing; for that the half-starved servant-girl, Menicuccia, had purloined it, drawing it from beneath her mistress's head in her very death-agony, and had made off with it, together with the golden mugs, and silver articles, which had belonged to the twin-children, and which it was supposed had long been objects of her cupidity.

After some years devoted to study, and to the perfecting of Viola's taste for music, in which art she attained an exquisite proficiency, Sebastian and his twin-sister resolved to pay the visit to Venice, which their father had projected for them. Leaving Annunziata in charge of their Messaline home, they set sail for the Queen-city of the Adriatic.

Gentlest breezes prospered their voyage: and kindly greetings awaited their arrival, from several persons, with whom the probity, and upright dealing of the merchant, had brought him into honorable knowledge; and who were pleased to have the opportunity of showing, by the cordiality and warmth of their reception to his children, the credit and respect in which their father was held.

Sebastian had heard, from his father's confidential clerk, Raimondo, of a certain poor man in Venice, who owed the house money, and whom his father had been anxious to release from his obligations. The merchant had permitted these to remain in force for a time, knowing that his debtor was weak, easily led, and dissolutely inclined; and thinking that his liabilities might act as a salutary restraint, until such season as he should see fit to acquit him of them. Latterly, tidings had reached the mercantile house in Messaline, concerning this young man's conduct, which led Raimondo to believe that his master's hope had been fulfilled; that the man was reformed, and deserved the intended immunity. With the view of signifying his deceased father's purposed clemency to its object, Sebastian lost no time in endeavouring to trace him out; and to this end, as he had to search through some of the lowest alleys in Venice, he confided the care of escorting his sister to see one of those beautiful churches with which the city abounds, to the woman of the house where they lodged.

Viola, rather than oppose the arrangement of her brother, acquiesced; but she felt indisposed to go out without him, more especially with a stranger; who, though a decent worthy-seeming person, was more an attendant than a companion.

The chastely-majestic fane of Santa Maria della Salute, with its marble dome, and its stately approach,—a broad flight of terrace steps rising, sheer from the waters of the canal grande,—was thronged with gaily-dressed people, hastening thither to celebrate one of the highest festivals of the church. The sprightly Venetians, ever eager to give a holiday-air to even their gravest, and most solemn ceremonials, were on this occasion not wanting in splendour of apparel, richly appointed retinues, and as much of blazonry in the scutcheons of their gondolas, as the Republic's law for preserving one uniform black equipment would permit.

There was a dense crowd in the church ; and on the conclusion of the service, Viola found herself,—she scarcely knew how,—separated from her conductress. She looked in vain around ; on all sides, none but faces utterly unknown to her, met her view. In her distress, she was accosted by a beautiful, and very richly-dressed lady, who begged to know if she could in any way assist the young stranger.

Viola explained her dilemma ; and the lady responded, by entreating she would favor her by permitting her own gondola to convey her home ; adding that the favor would be greatly enhanced, were Viola to accompany her to her own house first, and, by spending the morning with her, commence an acquaintance which promised to be very agreeable.

Won by her prepossessing appearance, and by her attractive manners,—which had all that subtly flattering charm of apparently involuntary liking towards the person addressed,—Viola accepted the gracefully-made invitation ; and stepped into the lady's gondola. It was luxuriantly furnished with velvet cushions, and silken curtains ; its rowers were in sumptuous liveries ; all bespoke its owner's magnificence of taste, and superiority of station.

As the lady reclined beneath the shade of the awning, and partially drew the curtains to exclude the sun's glare, Viola noticed that she often had to bend forward and acknowledge the courtesies of salutation and recognition, which were made to her almost unceasingly, from the numerous gondolas gliding by, or darting past, in quick succession.

The rowers halted at the landing-place of a noble-looking palace residence. The lady, leading the way with an air of graceful assiduity, and hospitable eagerness, as one receiving an evidently welcome guest, took Viola's hand, and, with her, entered a spacious hall, from which branched a marble staircase, conducting to the upper range of apartments. There was a profusion of gilding, and of rich color on the walls and ceilings; and the spacious sitting-room into which the lady introduced her, was hung with choice pictures, mirrors, and costly silken hangings. The windows looked out upon the canal; and from between the green screen of plants, and lowered blinds, might be discerned the sparkle, and animation, and ever-moving, ever-shifting scene, of the watery thoroughfare. In one of these recessed windows, the lady took her station; placing Viola upon one of the commodious couches, with which the nook was provided, and taking her own seat opposite to her; and then fell into a pleasant flowing strain of conversation, which while it exhibited interest and admiration for her young guest, was peculiarly calculated to set her at her ease by its mingled courtesy and familiarity. She seemed much struck with the surpassing loveliness of the young lady stranger; while Viola, in her turn, was as much absorbed in admiring the luxuriant beauty, and charm of deportment, which distinguished her entertainer. The lady was tall, and lustrously fair. She had full, expressive eyes, that seemed capable by turns, of the most brilliant animation, as of the most languishing suavity. Her figure was large, and rounded in its proportions; but shapely, and moulded in the perfection of womanly softness. On entering the room she had thrown back the mantle with which, out-of-doors, she had been clad; and the apparel in which she now appeared, was so fashioned and adjusted, as to show her grace of person to its utmost advantage.

Viola thought she had never seen so beautiful a living human picture, as this Venetian lady presented, leaning back in her chair, in a half indolent, half voluptuous attitude, as if enjoying the tempered heat of the air, that breathed in through the window among the flowers; one hand lying in her lap, idling with a fan of feathers; the other, (the white arm to which it belonged, clustered with jewels, resting on the window-ledge) employed in responding languidly to some passing salute from the gondolas beneath; while her throat and bosom, of dazzling hue, and much displayed by the closely-fitting dress, were more set off, than hidden, by the long golden curls that fell nearly to her waist, from the net-work of pearls which partly restrained their profusion.

Presently a visitor was announced ; and a gentleman,—whose distinguished look and bearing would have proclaimed his high rank, even had
not the servant ushered him into the room by name, as the marchese
Fontana,—advanced to the lady of the house, and saluting her fair
hand, paid her his compliments, with an air at once of homage and of
freedom. There was a gay carelessness, not to say levity, in his mode of
speech, which belied the first impression he conveyed by his appearance.
The one proclaimed refinement and finished behaviour ; but when he spoke,
there was a mixture of impertinence, of trifling combined with insolence, which destroyed the idea of his good manners. He seemed at once
haughty and obsequious ; disdainfully contemptuous, and full of adulation.
His compliments conveyed a notion of scorn for the understanding and
sense of the woman he addressed, even while .paying her the most pro-
fessedly deferential observance. All this Viola had an opportunity of
concluding from his farther conversation and conduct ; for other visitors
being announced in succession, and forming a group around the mistress of
the mansion, the marquis addressed his attentions, and his vivacious talk
exclusively to the young lady stranger ; although from time to time her
entertainer, by appealing to her, included her as much as possible in the
topics that were being discussed by the company in general.

Gradually an uneasy sensation crept over Viola. A feeling of discomfort, of doubt, of dread, which she could hardly define, assailed her. She
felt profoundly melancholy ; sad and sick at heart ; disturbed, agitated,
and beset with a sinister impression as of something insecure, unstable,
hollow, wrong. She felt, as one mysteriously warned of a danger ; near
at hand, yet unseen, uncomprehended.

She now for the first time observed that of all the visitors assembled,
there were none but gentlemen ; and Viola suddenly remembered that
those who had saluted the lady from the passing gondolas, both when seated
in her own gondola, and at her window, had invariably been cavaliers and
noblemen. Not one person of her own sex had interchanged a single token
of recognition.

She looked at the fair face and figure of her lady-hostess ; and their
beauty all at once seemed to strike her, as with a shadowed brightness.
There was something in her alluring tones that now sounded unreal,

untrue ; as but the mockery of good feeling. The gay, loud voices, and laughter of the guests, vibrated unpleasantly, nay mournfully, rather than cheerfully upon her spirit ; they had an echo of strained mirth and forced vivacity; and above all, of a heartless, hard, disrespect of good. It was altogether joyless ; though so much of light ease and freedom, in both conversation and conduct, were going forward.

Viola arose ; and going to the side of the chair where her beautiful entertainer sat, as if enthroned, surrounded by her admirers, said, in a simple, quiet voice :—" I thank you heartily for the kindness you have shown me. Will you add to it, by letting your gondola take me home ? "

The lady of the house made a graceful demur at parting with her already, which was echoed by a murmur of polite objection from the gentlemen. But Viola rejoined with the same steady simplicity as before:— " You will do me a favor, if you will permit me to take my leave at once. My brother will wonder at my lengthened absence."

" I will escort the young lady to her home ; my gondola is in waiting ;" said the marquis, advancing, with his air of mingled arrogant decision, and polished offer.

Viola curtsied slightly ; replying :—" I will not tax your lordship's leisure." Then turning again to the lady, she added :—" I will be beholden to your goodness, to give orders that one of your servants shall attend me home. Let me bid you farewell, with gratitude for all your courtesy."

" Since you are resolved to quit us so soon, we cannot urge our claim against your brother's ; but remember that you have friends here, who hope speedily to see you again ; " said the lady ; " and meantime my own woman shall attend you."

Viola repeated her adieu to her entertainer ; and with a general obeisance to the company, withdrew. She had scarcely attained the antechamber, on her way to the grand staircase, ere she was overtaken by the marquis, who offered his hand to conduct her to the gondola. She could not without discourtesy, decline it ; and he led her to the landing. She there found awaiting her, the lady's female servant, who advanced towards her to assist her into the boat. But the marquis put the woman aside, by leading Viola forward to the edge of the gondola, and handing her in himself ; then turning to the attendant, he did as much for her ; and lastly, just as the gondola was pushing off, he leaped into it also, and took his place by Viola's side.

She started at this intrusion, and at the pertinacity with which he followed up his proffer of accompanying her home, in spite of its having been declined. But she marked her displeasure no otherwise than by silence; until his words, proceeding from compliment into open flattery, and from flattery, into undisguised insult of admiration, forced her to speak.

"My lord, you presume upon my forbearance. Let it obtain me yours. Forbear this insolence—this outrage."

"Call you insolence the simple expression of the effect produced by your beauty, fair one? Outrage, the but just tribute to your charms?" he said, with even more of impertinence in his eyes and tone, than in his words.

"My lord, I am a lady,—unprotected,—a stranger in your city; any one of these claims should entitle me to the respect and consideration of a gentleman,—if such you be."

"By mine honor, a fair challenge! I will prove myself a gentleman, sweet one, in the magnificence of my offers,—of my treaty; in the noble, —nay, regal—style, in which I will evince my gratitude to my charming foe, if she will consent to lay aside her enmity, and become my friend,— my ally—my worshipped mistress,—my queen."

Viola could not find words to answer, in the depth of her wounded feeling. But the indignation swelling in her heart, gave her strength to fix her sincere eyes upon his; while the clear, honest truth of genuine modesty looked through their springing tears.

Even the obtused sense of the libertine marquis, could perceive something of the eloquence of innocent appeal, in this mute reply. But its influence was soon lost, in the one produced upon him by her heightened beauty. Those gentle, confiding, violet eyes, showed still more beaming and lovely, against her raised complexion; animated as they were, too, by honest emotion, and swimming in glistening drops of diamond brightness. He could not see the moral beauty of her look, for its physical beauty; which found quicker comprehension from his gross perceptions.

Blinded by these, no less than by his pre-conceived notion of what was her real character and condition, the marquis was proceeding with still plainer and more offensive terms of adulation and proposal; when the gondola, arriving at the landing-place near to the house where she and her brother lodged, gave Viola an opportunity of springing out of the boat, to certain refuge.

On seeing Sebastian, she could not help throwing herself into his arms, and weeping out her agitation, her relief, her sense of insult, escape, and safety. The feeling of shame, so natural to outraged delicacy,—when it should of right torment only the outrager,—overwhelmed her; and for some time, sobs were the only reply she could make to his eager, anxious questions. At length he drew from her the whole of her morning adventure; and it was not until he bade her repeat the name of the nobleman who had offered her these indignities, that she half regretted having been betrayed into the imprudence of mentioning them to her brother at all. But it was now too late; and her only consolation was to perceive that Sebastian dwelt no farther on the circumstance; but turned his enquiries to what could have become of their hostess, the mistress of the lodging-house. Alarmed at missing her young lady charge, the poor woman had not yet returned home; but went seeking, in distracted bewilderment, through all the places she thought it likely Viola could have strayed to. At length, the bright thought struck her, that possibly the young lady might have found her way back alone; and when she at length hastened thither, she found her safely and happily housed.

Sebastian had preserved a calm exterior, so long as he was in presence of his sister; but at night, when she had retired to the rest she so much needed after her day of excitement, he wrote the following letter :—

"My lord,

She whom you this morning so, unworthily, and injuriously affronted, is a lady of birth and honor. The insult you offered, reflects more disgrace upon yourself than upon her; yet it shall nevertheless not pass unresented by her brother. He arraigns you as the cowardly aggriever of a defenceless woman; and summons you,—if one spark of manliness exist in a nature capable of such base offence,—to meet him an hour before sun-down, to-morrow, on the Lido; there to answer your transgression at point of sword. The seclusion of the spot will secure us from interruption, and the presence of our respective gondoliers will suffice for the purpose of

witnesses to fair play ; since, stranger as I am in Venice, I have no friend
here, of whom I should choose to ask his offices for my second.

SEBASTIAN GIUSTINIANI."

The remainder of the night was dedicated to putting his papers in order;
to securing the acquittal of his father's poor debtor; and to the making
such written provision for his sister, in case of his death, as should ensure
her pecuniary comfort. He forgot that all comfort for her would henceforth be destroyed by the very casualty in question ; the risk of which was
increased by the deed he himself contemplated.

Confiding his missive to the care of the gondolier he usually employed,
and upon whose fidelity he knew he could rely, Sebastian charged him to
take means that it should reach the hands of the marchese Fontana himself, without delay ; and farther desired him to have his boat in readiness,
to convey him that evening, to the shore of the Lido.

All day, the brother devoted himself to talking playfully and cheerfully
with Viola, so as to prevent her from entertaining by possibility, suspicion
of his harbouring a resentful recollection of what had passed. He succeeded so well, that his sister believed he felt, as she did, content to let the
event be forgotten, in like manner with any other distasteful occurrence,
which had brought no ill consequences.

He had a harder task in controlling his emotion, and in taking no
tenderer leave of her than usual, when he quitted her that afternoon on the
pretext of renewing his search after the poor debtor. As he framed the
subterfuge, it gave him a pang to feel that he was parting with something
like an untruth from the sister, with whom he had ever lived in open, unreserved confidence and affection. He felt it to be a kind of treason to
such love as theirs had been, that he should bid her farewell thus ; when
it might be for ever, in this life. And then, at last, came the thought,
that if he fell, what would be the despairful agony of this young creature—
his twin sister—his orphan sister—his beloved Viola. But not daring to
trust himself with the idea, he forced it from him ; and compelled himself
to utter only light, hopeful words to her, and to jump into his gondola
with a gay air, as she waved her hand to him from the window of their
lodging.

Aloud, he said :—" Keep safe within doors, my Viola ! No more wandering abroad, unguarded by your faithful squire-brother. Be careful of yourself, for his sake!" In his inmost heart, he added :—"To our father in heaven, and to his and our Heavenly Father, I commit thee, my Viola! In case I am denied to come back to thee, Heaven will afford its guardian care, protection and comfort."

In the strengthening confidence which such thoughts conferred, Sebastian found himself pacing up and down the flat, sandy level, of the Lido strand. His impatience had made him forestal the appointed hour ; and it wanted yet five quarters, ere the sun should set.

Sebastian was an excellent swordsman. He had applied himself of late years, with great diligence, to attain skill in fencing ; as an accomplishment of all others calculated to supply the requisite command of limb, and grace of carriage, needful for a gentleman, which might have been defective, from his wandering, unschooled youth. He was slight of make ; but possessed considerable strength of wrist, and vigour of sinew. He had great personal bravery ; and a lion's spirit, with a heart affectionate, generous, and modest. He was tender and considerate as a woman, towards women : at the same time that he was loyal and chivalrous on their behalf ; not only in his own commerce with themselves, but in his championship of their cause with others. While he was gentle as a young maiden, with women, in his conduct towards them, and in his thoughts of them ; he was fearless and undaunted as the boldest of his sex, when it was a question of a woman's right or honor, among men. Though so delicately formed as to be well-nigh girlish in figure, and so beautiful of feature and complexion, as to look almost femininely handsome in face, Sebastian was essentially manly. His loyalty of feeling with regard to women, his spirited resentment of injury or injustice committed towards them, his high-hearted courage, were all man-liness itself.

At length, another gondola approached. From beneath its black awning, a solitary cavalier emerged ; who, from the expectant look he cast around as he landed, Sebastian at once knew must be the marchese Fontana.

The gentlemen had hardly accosted each other with interchange of enquired name, when the marquis exclaimed :—"Herself in disguise, by all that's propitious !"

He hurried forward, adding :—"How may I thank my sweet foe for appointing me this meeting—for granting me this occasion to tell her——"

He had eagerly snatched a hand to raise it to his lips ; when Sebastian flung him off, threw back his cloak, and drew his sword, crying :—" Betake yourself to your defence, my lord ! "

The action, attitude, and whole air of the youth, were so unmistakeably masculine, that the marquis gazed upon him in dumb wonder. He could scarcely credit his senses. The countenance and figure before him were so perfectly identical with those of the lady he had encountered yesterday, yet so strongly contrasted in their present demeanour, with the feminine gentleness of hers in their previous bearing ; that he stood as in a dream, unable to reconcile images so perplexingly at variance, yet so singularly the same.

" If you are indeed not herself—but some sprite who has assumed her form——" he at length said, hesitatingly ; " if you are not she, but some arch-fiend who has had power to take the semblance of an angel——"

" I am her twin-brother, my lord ; " said Sebastian ; " and have been, by many, accounted like her. I am no shadow,—no mockery,—but a sober reality ; here to call you to earnest account for your ruffian behaviour towards a virtuous lady. Once more, my lord, betake yourself to your defence ! "

" If this be so," said the marquis, still looking steadfastly at him, and showing no intention of drawing his sword, though the youth appeared about to press forward upon him, " I have indeed to bethink me of my defence ; though I fear me it can be but a sorry one. The defence I should offer is not with my sword, but with my tongue ; and ought to be a vindication of my conduct ; which, in all candour be it confessed, is certainly neither to be vindicated nor defended. But it can be explained, and explanation is due ; it can be apologized for, and apology is due. To her brother I owe explanation, rather than the added injury of fighting him, after having offered indignity to his sister ; and to her I owe apology, —sincerest apology, as the only reparation for my most unwitting offence against virtue, delicacy, and innocence, in her person."

The marquis then told Sebastian that he had, on the receipt of his letter, been convinced of the unhappy mistake he had committed, from having met Viola in companionship with one of the most noted courtezans in Venice ; that he had resolved to attend him at his own appointed time and place, in order to have any opportunity of frankly acknowledging his error, and of craving the forgiveness of himself and sister ; that the marvellous resemblance between them, had at first bewildered him, and rendered him incapable of the avowal he meditated ; but that he now besought him to accept this explanation as the true origin of his unintentional insult.

"You will perceive," he concluded, "that I was misled altogether in my belief of her quality and character, when the house where she was, and the society in which I found her, gave me to suppose——"

"You should have judged her from herself, my lord;" interrupted Sebastian. "Methinks, in that clear face, in that pure look, you might have read the truth."

"My eyes were dazzled by the sun of her beauty, and could see naught but false colors;" answered the marquis. "I am confounded at mine own dullness of vision, which could not discern the whiteness of modesty and innocence, beneath the gorgeous hues that invested it."

"Would you deem it a recognition of that in your character which makes me regret you should abase it by indulging unworthy tastes, and not take it as an impertinence of unsought advice from so young a man as myself, my lord," said Sebastian,—won by the nobleman's behaviour, which was by nature ingenuous and honorable,—"I would reply, by asking you whether you might not restore the clearness of your impaired sight, by restraining it from the contemplation of a meretricious glare, to which heretofore, you have haply too much accustomed it."

The marquis returned the young man's frank smile, with one as open ; while he said :—"I believe you are right. I have hitherto been a traitor to whatever there may be of good in me, by listening to the worser portion. I have associated too much with the worthless and the profligate ; which has fed my splenetic inclination to think lightly of my species. Henceforth, it shall be my ambition to obtain the friendship of my superiors in worth ; in the faith that they will teach me how to cultivate that lurking better tendency, until it grows into something akin to their own excellence. Meantime, let me thank you for the hope you have inspired, by your kindly

recognition of that lurking good ; as well as for the generosity with which
you have dealt with my error."

Sebastian returned the warm grasp of the marquis's hand, with a
cordiality equal to his own ; and,—in his eagerness to prove this,—with
so vice-like a grip, that Fontana said with a laugh :—" That was no
lady's pressure ! Its undoubted manhood tells me I have had a fortunate
escape from the encounter of your sword. Yet even with that strong
testimony, I can scarcely now separate your identity from that most
womanly creature, whose face has haunted me ever since like a madness,
and seems at this instant to look upon me." He gazed upon Sebastian as
he spoke ; concluding in a tone of almost wildness, and with a fixed look.
Then, suddenly passing his hand across his eyes, he said :—" You will
think me mad, indeed ; but I have gone through so many powerful emotions
in the last few hours, that my nature seems to have undergone a total
revolution, and I feel scarcely master of myself or of my own mind. But
that I feel I have scarcely a right to speak thus of her, and to you, I should
tell you that that gentle, beauteous creature, made an impression upon my
inmost soul which no woman ever touched me with before. It has wrought
a change upon my spirit, my heart, every fibre of my frame. Bear with
me, while I venture to speak to you of this."

The marquis even shook with the feeling that inwardly stirred him.

" Even before the receipt of your letter, I had a vague idea of the mistake I had committed ; although my idea took no definite shape. I felt
that I had not paid sufficing homage to her, when she was present, yet
how, I understood not. The desire to behold her again, absorbed me
wholly. Her image pursued me through the night unceasingly. With
the pertinacity of a delirious fancy, it kept my eyes from closing,—there,
palpably before me, to claim my sleepless regard. In the morning, your
letter reached me. It cleared my mental sight upon at least one point. It
showed me distinctly the nature of the injury I had done her, and in what
way my homage had been insufficient. I now discovered that I loved her,
—with no passing liking, no mere casual personal admiration,—but with
a fervour, a passionate intensity and purity, of which I had never thought
my nature capable. The first purpose that my newly-awakened better
judgment taught me to form, was to see her brother, that I might seek to ap-

pease his just resentment, by honest confession; my second, and which now claims fulfilment with paramount urgency, is to implore pardon of her."

Sebastian could not have better shown the impression which the marquis's candour had made, than by the promptitude with which he replied:— "We will go to her at once, my lord. I will myself conduct you to her."

There was something peculiarly winning about Fontana's manner. It evinced so genuine a regret for what had passed, at the same time that it showed so cheerful a hope that his present altered feeling and conduct might be permitted to expiate his former error; that the young man felt he had not only forgiven him, but that he already liked and esteemed him. As the gondola bore them back to Venice, Sebastian found himself speculating whether his sister would equally concede, first pardon, then liking. He knew her delicacy, her refinement of feeling and sentiment; and he doubted whether even the subsequent favorable impression could by possibility efface the obnoxious one which had been first given. He felt, that to a woman like Viola, the having once encountered offensive admiration and proposals from a man, would in all probability act as an effectual bar to her ever considering him in a pleasant light; far less, to her receiving him as a suitor for her hand.

Each of the gentlemen had been engaged in silent thought; when, as they neared the Rialto,—not far from which branched the canal where they were to land,—the marquis broke from his musing, with:—"By the lion of St. Mark! the nearer the moment draws on for tendering my apology, the harder do I feel the difficulty of finding an excuse for my misdeed. When I think of meeting that face, and remember the wrong I did its gentle innocence, in believing it could be any other than that of a pure and virtuous lady, I have no courage to supplicate its mercy. I refer me to her brother's advocacy. In that I put my hope."

"You shall have its intercession, my lord, in all sincerity;" replied Sebastian.

"Call me Fontana, dear friend;" said the marquis, as he once more exchanged a hearty grasp of the hand with the young man. "I know from your letter, the name of her brother; and that the noble blood of the Giustiniani family runs in his veins: while from his own nobleness, I have learned his best claim to nobility."

" His proudest title is the honorable name derived from his father,—
Sebastian of Messaline, the merchant;" replied the youth; "I will not
leave you the task of enquiring another name, which you are doubtless
thirsting to hear. It is Viola."

Fontana repeated it murmuringly, caressingly, as if its very sound reflected the beauty of her image to his thought; while he kept his eyes fixed
on her brother's face,—so strongly resembling the one he beheld in fancy.

" You are very like her ;" at length fell from his lips. " Yet when
I first saw you, I could think it was she come to meet me! Alone! Disguised! An appointment! An assignation! Traitor that I was to her
sweet perfection, to dream it but for one moment !"

" We are here ;" said Sebastian, as he stepped from the gondola, and led
the way to the house. "Be of good cheer! Viola is as gentle and for-
giving, as she is innocent and true-hearted."

Viola proved her brother's word. She was most gentle in her reception
of the penitent marquis ; accepting his apologies frankly and generously ;
and according him her forgiveness freely and fully. But she could not
like him. She could not patiently listen to him, when he laid his rank
and fortune at her feet, and besought her to become his wife. She could
not hear him speak of love ; or feel any pleasure from his society. It
embarrassed her with a painful sense of her own inability to forget,
although she forgave, his past conduct ; and it also oppressed her with
a generous dislike to witness the proofs of a passion which she could not
return. She permitted his visits for some time, because she would not
distress him by refusal ; and because she feared that if she denied herself,
he might misconstrue the cause of her avoidance, and think that she had
not cordially forgiven him ; and moreover, because these visits gave
pleasure to her brother. But they became more and more distasteful to
herself ; since she felt that they only kept alive hopes, which she could
never fulfil.

At length she resolved to ask Sebastian to leave Venice, and return with
her home to Messaline.

" And can you really not find in your heart one spark of pity for poor
Fontana ?" said Sebastian in reply to her request. " Is it possible you
can meditate abandoning him without a hope ; without the most distant

prospect of one day winning your regard. Have you no compassion for the misery, the despair you will occasion ? "

" Despair from thwarted ambition,—from unsuccessful aims in fortune, intellectual renown, artist fame, military glory—or even from baffled will, might perchance be the death of a man, brother mine ; " said Viola, smiling. " But for despair from disappointed love, I have no faith in its power to kill any one of your strong sex."

" I am speaking seriously, Viola mia ; " said her brother. " Fontana loves you with no common affection. It is deeply in earnest ; and perhaps all the more profound, from his feeling that it once took a shape injurious to the womanly perfection which he now recognises and worships in truest faith. Can you not indeed grant him hope ? "

" Since Sebastian asks me seriously, I will answer him as gravely, and as honestly ; " she replied with her soft, sincere eyes full on his :—" What hope should I give ? That I will learn to esteem, respect, regard, and love, one, who at our first meeting, did his utmost to root out all such emotions from my heart ? That I should end in taking for a husband, one who commenced his wooing as a seducer ? That I should give him for honorable and honored wife, the woman whom he would have dishonored ? I cannot give such hope. And if I could, I would not. I can pardon, from my heart, the offence that was given : but I can neither sanction it, as I should do, were I to admit the offender within my heart ; nor reward it, by preferring him to all other men."

" You are right, my Viola ; " her brother said. ".Though I grieve for my friend, and deplore the rigour of his sentence ; yet in justice to my sister's delicacy and nice sense of honor, I must confess she has decided wisely. It is not every lady, however," he added more playfully, " who could have exercised so cold a prudence where so handsome a culprit was in question. Fontana is a gallant gentleman, in person, as in heart. The latter was perverted for a while, by an over-indulged and unrestricted youth ; but by nature it is noble, and it has lately learned to be true to its nature. A less pure and exalted regard for unblemished virtue than my Viola's, might have found it difficult to withstand so much that was attractive,—to refuse so much that was excellent,—for principle's sake."

Viola, afterwards, had a little secret remorse of conscience at this fond encomium from her brother. She felt that she did not altogether so entirely deserve his praise for magnanimity in remaining firm to her principle of honor in this case. She felt that had her imagination been perfectly free when she first met Fontana, and that he had succeeded in touching her heart, she might then indeed have found a difficulty in abiding by her virtuous resolve not to accept of him as an honorable lover, who had begun by dishonorable advances; but in her inmost soul she knew that her fancy had long been pre-occupied by a certain image which effectually prevented any other from producing an impression. Her father's mention of that noble youth,—that princely son of his old Illyrian friend,—that handsome, generous-hearted, generous-minded Orsino, had insensibly obtained so strong a hold upon her thoughts, that it had assumed a positive form and substance; which became the object of her fond contemplation, her romantic regard, and filled her mind to the exclusion of any other man's idea as a lover. Her candour might have led her to avow this scruple of conscience to Sebastian; had it not involved the confession of feelings, which she scarce yet confessed to herself. They were rather entertained than understood; hoarded, not analysed. Delightful shadows; sweet, involuntary visions; insubstantial, but dearly-cherished soul-dreams.

The twin brother and sister set sail from Venice. But they had not proceeded far on their voyage, when a terrific storm arose. The ship struck upon a rock; split, and went to pieces. In the confusion of that fatal moment, Viola was separated from Sebastian, and hastily lifted by the captain into a small boat; which some of the crew had lowered over the side of the fast-sinking vessel. With the captain, and this poor remnant of his men, she suddenly found herself cast upon a strange shore, alone, desolate, almost despairing of ever again beholding in life that beloved brother, with whom every hour of her previous existence had been spent. Heart-forlorn, and well-nigh hopeless, she turned to her companions, saying :—" *What country, friends, is this?* "

For the rest, " My lord would speak, my duty hushes me."

FINIS.

THE

GIRLHOOD

OF

SHAKESPEARE'S HEROINES;

IN

A SERIES OF FIFTEEN TALES,

BY

MARY COWDEN CLARKE,

Author of the Concordance to Shakespeare.

"as petty to his ends,
As is the morn-dew on the myrtle leaf
To his grand sea."
                          Shakespeare.

TALE XV.

IMOGEN ; THE PEERLESS.

LONDON:

W. H. SMITH & SON, 136, STRAND; AND SIMPKIN, MARSHALL, & CO.,
STATIONERS' HALL COURT.
1852.

TO

THE SHAKESPEARE SOCIETY,

IN HONOR OF THE PRINCIPLE OF ITS INSTITUTION,

THIS TALE

IS RESPECTFULLY DEDICATED

BY

MARY COWDEN CLARKE.

TALE XV.

IMOGEN; THE PEERLESS.

"She's fair and royal;
And she hath all courtly parts more exquisite
Than lady, ladies, woman; from every one
The best she hath, and she, of all compounded,
Outsells them all."

Cymbeline.

BRITAIN triumphed. Her hardy sons had repulsed the invading Roman, and forced mightiest Cæsar himself to give back. But victory,—as ever with such victories,—came hand-in-hand with mourning. The royal Cassibelan, while rejoicing at his people's brave achievement, had to deplore the loss of him who had mainly aided its success. His brother Nennius lay at point of death. Fifteen days he languished beneath his mortal wounds; and before the day fixed for the celebration of the victory, arrived, he had ceased to breathe.

The king had published a decree, summoning all the nobility of Britain, with their wives, to his capital of Trinovantum, in order to render, with sacrificial rites and offerings, solemn thanks to their tutelary gods; who had granted them conquest over so great a commander as renowned Julius. He had also called the companions of his victory together, that he might amply reward them, every one, accordingly as they had severally distinguished themselves; and now, this appointed solemn rejoicing, for which the chief of his realm were convened together, he resolved should be mingled with the sad but honoring tribute of a national celebration, in his brother's funeral exequies. He appointed them to be performed with regal pomp; and decreed that they should take place on the first day of the general assemblage; that,—the mournful observances fulfilled,—the rest of the time might be devoted to its original object of triumph and thanksgiving.

The procession took its way to the North gate of the city, as the ordained place of sepulture. Cassibelan would have chosen the one built by his predecessor and elder brother, Lud ; but that it bore its builder's name, and he wished no other fame to overshadow his, who was now to be consigned to immortality. For the same reason, he forbore to have the body of Nennius deposited near that gate of noble structure, which had been erected by his royal ancestor Belinus, upon the bank of the Thames. This goodly edifice consisted of a large tower, which had beneath, a fine haven, or quay, for ships ; but on the summit of the tower, was a golden urn, in which lay the ashes of king Belinus, causing the edifice to be known ever after as Belin's gate.

To the end that exclusive and impressive honors might be paid to the memory of his valiant brother, Cassibelan decided that in the tomb should be placed, and buried with him, that sword he had mastered ; Cæsar's sword, known by the name of terrible significance, 'Crocea mors,'—as being mortal to every body that was wounded with it. He also determined, himself to pronounce the funeral oration over his beloved brother's remains ; that the people might learn the full extent of Nennius's heroic deeds, which should thus be treasured in their hearts while they lived, and be transmitted, in trumpet eulogy of tradition, to their posterity.

In sad and solemn pomp, the funeral train proceeded. First came a troop of virgins, clad in white, with long mourning veils, two and two, hand-in-hand, bearing each a cypress branch. Immediately following, were the venerable forms of the Druids, and Bards, with flowing white beards, and close-shorn snowy hairs, crowned with oak ; the former carried, every one, a wand or staff, emblematical of their magician power ; and wore, hung about their necks, inclosed in gold, the charmed serpent's egg ; the latter, to their harps decked with mistletoe, chanted dirges, and lamenting strains, interspersed with hymnal eulogies, and elegiac songs, recording the exploits of the brave deceased. At their head was the Arch-Druid, clothed in sacerdotal robes ; wearing on his head a resplendent diadem of burnished gold, figuring the rays of the meridian sun. Next, came a number of British matrons in sable garments, with garlands of yew, and cypress ; and in their hands, wreaths of rue, and rosemary, with green boughs of shining laurel. Then, a band of warriors, whose rugged features and stern-set looks had hard ado to maintain a firm countenance beneath their manly grief for the brother-in-arms they had lost. After them, came, high-raised; upon a war-chariot, the body of Nennius, exposed to reverent view; around him were ranged his victorious arms, his shield, his spear, and his heavy battle-axe, each of which in turn he had used with success against the invaders of his country; while upon his breast lay his last and proudest trophy, that which had cost him his life,—Cæsar's sword.

Behind the car came the king. Bare-headed, in simplest mourning garment, with brotherly sorrow and brotherly pride contending for the mastery in his face, he walked alone ; followed at a few paces distance by his body-page, bearing the golden circlet, symbol of rule and sovereignty; which, in this moment of humility and heart-dejection, Cassibelan had put off. Next in order, came his two nephews, Androgeus and Tenantius, sons of the late king ; and after them, the procession was closed by a long train of the nobility, soldiery, and populace.

Arrived at the place of burial, the train formed into a broad-spreading circle round the car, while their monarch ascended into it, and taking his stand beside the dead body of his brother, addressed the people in a voice that gained power and steadiness as he proceeded :—

" You have learned, that it hath pleased the sacred gods to grant us victory over the most redoubted conqueror of the earth; to grant to us few Island men, resolute in the defence of our Island liberty, will to resist, force to repel, and might to subdue, the insolent invasion of Rome and her imperial Cæsar. You have learned,—for such glorious tidings spread with winged speed to the uttermost corners of a country threatened with hostile subjection,—that the arrogant Roman's boast of advent, view, and conquest, at a breath, has been, in our happy Island case, rendered vain and empty; that the lion hearts and iron sinews of our Island men,— whom he dared to despise as a handful of barbarians, a paltry brood of savages, whom it was just worth while to assail in their remote sea-nest, and despoil of their few pearls and their freedom,——have been able to defeat his haughty vaunt, to vanquish his all-conquering strength, and to beat him back to his ships, glad that he had the sea for his camp."

" He left our shore, its mould drenched with the blood of the slain, as though washed by the sudden ebb of the retiring tide ; but that encrimsoned strand not only bears witness to the vengeance taken by our Island lions upon those who venture in their lair with purpose to rob them of their liberty, but to the zeal with which they are ready to pour forth the best contents of their own veins in its defence. Mingled with that sanguine pool, is the blood of him who lies here, lifeless. He spared not to shed it, as water, when his country needed its sacrifice. Nay, he seized, as a boon of Fortune, the occasion to hazard its last drop, when the chance of the field brought him into actual encounter with Cæsar himself. He boldly made up to him, in martial joy to think he should gain so much as one blow at so great a man. Cæsar seeing him advance, and reading the hope painted in his face, stretched out his shield to receive him, and with all his might, struck him upon the helmet with his drawn sword ; then lifted it again with intent to finish his first blow, and make it mortal. But our brave Nennius, nowise losing self-command, dexterously prevented him with his shield ; into which Cæsar's sword, gliding with great force from the helmet, came to be so hard wedged and fastened, that when by the breaking in of the troops, they could no longer continue the encounter, the Roman was not able to draw it out again, and recover it. Nennius thus became master of Cæsar's sword ; and throwing away his own, plucked the other forth, and made haste to employ it against those whom it had before led. Whomsoever he struck with it, he either killed, or left wounded past hope of recovery. That its blows are mortal, my brother's death, after receiving a wound from it, too surely and fatally bears testimony. Not only is it superior in its temper, and quality of hard polished steel, to our weapons of copper, welded with tin ; not only is it superior in its pointed, shapely, compact finish, to our long, unwieldy, pointless swords ; (which owe their prevailing virtue to the valiant hearts, and nervous arms of their owners ;) but it is gifted, by sorcery and necromancy, with invincible powers, and well deserves its ominous name of ' Yellow Death.' Above all, it is Cæsar's sword ; or, was Cæsar's ; has been won into the keeping of us Britons, through a Briton's undaunted spirit ; and shall now be consecrated to the undying possession of him who purchased its mastery, at the expense of his own life. It shall lie beside him in his grave, as an eternal monument of British courage, honor, and victory."

At the conclusion of their king's speech, the people sent up a shout, such as Britons' lungs have been famous for, from time immemorial ; one of those hearty sounds so impressively proclaiming the impulse, the feeling, and the will of the multitude, put into a single potent roar of sympathy.

As it died away, Androgeus whispered to his brother Tenantius :— "Our uncle is now so fortune-swollen, that our claims will stand less chance than ever of obtaining justice at his hands."

"Steep thy thoughts in patience and in silence, the only things at present left us ;" returned his younger brother in the same tone. "We will speak farther of this, when we are alone."

So soon as the rites of sepulture had been performed, and the body of Nennius committed to its glorious tomb, the sacrificial offerings to the gods were commenced. For the due celebration of so important a victory, there was a vast slaughter and destruction. As a votive tribute to Jove, sovereign of gods and men, (who could only be propitiated for the sacrificed lives of those who had fallen in battle by the immolation of additional lives,—so the people were told, on the best authority; that is, the best they had, that of their Pagan priests,) the Druids had had constructed, a gigantic image of wicker-work ; which was filled with living men, and then set fire to. The beings who thus perished, were criminals, reserved for the purpose; as (so stated, on the same authority) peculiarly acceptable. To Mars were sacrificed all the prisoners left alive ; and the chief of the spoil taken in fight, was, by order of the sacrificing priests, gathered together, and carried to an appointed spot. Heaps of valuables thus collected, were put aside, in certain consecrated places ; and rarely was any one so regardless of religion, or so hardy, as to dare secretly to retain any portion, or to take it away when thus stored ; since for such a sin there was adjudged a very severe punishment, accompanied with torture. Various sacrifices of cattle were offered up at this solemnity ; several thousand cows, sheep, and fowls of several kinds, besides wild beasts of divers description.

After all these sacred rites, in honor and thanksgiving to their gods, had been performed, they feasted themselves with the remainder, as was their wont on such occasions; and spent the successive day and night in various national sports.

Cassibelan's two nephews, at the conclusion of the orgy, secretly communed together concerning their joint prospects. They were the sons of Lud, the late king; who, dying when they were in their minority, had been succeeded by his brother, Cassibelan. Their uncle had found little difficulty in causing himself to be nominated to the throne of Britain in their stead; and he had since made some show of considering their claims to the whole, by assigning them each a portion of the kingdom. Upon Androgeus, the elder, he conferred the district of Kent; and upon Tenantius, that of Cornwall; but reserved to himself chief sovereignty over them, as over the whole of the realm, in his title of king of Britain.

In the heart of Androgeus had long rankled resentment against his uncle's interference with his birthright; not so much from love of sway in himself, as from a hatred of submitting to injustice. He could not endure to live beneath the dictates and government of a man, who he felt had stepped in between him and his just claim. He fretted under the necessity there was for attending his convocations, for appealing to his authority, for abiding by his decisions, and especially for wearing a countenance of amity and deference, when all within was disapproval and resistance. This last compliance with his uncle's summons, to celebrate the victory over Cæsar, had put the crowning sum to his long accumulating sources of discontent. It happened that, in his quality of ruler in Kent, he had had occasions of communication with the great Roman, which wrought anything but a feeling of personal enmity against him. On the contrary, as a man, as an able general, as a noble commander, as a fine intellect,—in short,—in every respect, but as the enemy of his country, he both admired and esteemed Julius Cæsar. Moreover, during the period of the late invasion, there had been a serious difference between himself and his uncle, regarding a certain youth called Hirlas, a relation and friend of his own, whom one of Cassibelan's officers had wounded in a quarrel; and the injurer of whom, the king had refused to give up to Androgeus's wrath. These reasons, joined to the original cause he had to deem himself ill-used by his uncle, made Androgeus resolve that he would no longer remain in Britain; but would pass over into Gaul,—whither Cæsar, after his defeat, had retired,—and follow the future fortunes of that renowned leader, in preference to wearing out his existence in subjection to a man who had both offended and injured him.

"And is it possible, you can consent thus to abandon your native land; to forego all your hopes of succeeding to its throne?" said Tenantius, in amazement at this suddenly-announced determination of his brother's.

"For my native land, I am not permitted to evince my devotion to it as I could wish; and for any hope of succession to its throne, I bequeath all such slender chance to my younger brother;" replied Androgeus. "Thy patient disposition, thy peaceful nature, and sound good sense, my Tenantius, will render thee far fitter to await such hope, and to fulfil with honor its successful issue, should haply such arrive, than I. If ever one of our father's sons succeed, as of right, to his great office, it is thou, good brother, who will make best king of Britain. I cede all my elder claims to thee."

"Nay, thou art too sudden-rash in thy resolve; take time to consider whether thou art acting prudently—acting rightly, thus to resign——"

"I have little right judgment, and less prudence, dear brother;" replied Androgeus, interrupting him impetuously, though with an affectionate smile; "I leave such better wisdom to thyself. I have but just so much of wise foresight, as to show me that if I remain in Britain, I shall not long keep myself unembroiled with our right royal and usurping uncle; now more than ever arrogant in his pride of victory and success. See you not how he maintains the name and style of Trinovantum in the capital, to the setting aside of the title our father justly bestowed on it, in commemoration of the goodly improvements he effected? Did not our royal father enlarge it, and wall it about, and form of it a noble city, calling it by his own name,—Lud's town? And was not this resented by both our uncles,—the insolent Cassibelan, and more especially by him who, since he is now inhumed, let his faults be buried with him,—Nennius? Did they not both take it heinously, that our father should strive to perpetuate his worthy deeds, when their own ambitious pretensions were insatiate? No;

if you would have me avoid open revolt, and disclosure of how in my
heart I rebel against this man's tyranny, let me show myself prudent and
wise, in the only way I can ; by withdrawing from beneath an ascendancy
to which I can no longer tamely submit."

" Perchance you think that I show too tame a spirit, in preferring to
remain here, and to go on yielding passive obedience, and dwelling in
meek dependance, on our lordly uncle ? " returned Tenantius. " But
I hold my own quiet hope ; and am content to abide its period of fulfilment. Meantime, I have, to sustain this hope, complete faith in our
British proverb,—' The country is more mighty than the lord.' "

" And you think the voice of the country would be for us, in the event
of aught occurring to shake Cassibelan in his royal seat ? " said Androgeus.

" I am sure of it ; " answered Tenantius. " The people of Britain are
ever just and right in the side they take, when freedom of choice is theirs."

" You who esteem them thus highly should be their king ; " replied his
brother. " Once more, if ever such chance of kingship should revert
to us, be its advantage all yours. I have made up my mind to depart from
Britain, and resort to Rome. There, lies a field for wider and nobler
ambition. There, knowledge, civilization, arts, letters, flourish ; and there
will I endeavour to attain a peace of spirit, which here may not be mine.
You shall let me take with me your young boy, Cymbeline ; that he may
have the advantage of Roman education and polish. If ever thou set'st
thy foot on Britain's throne, send to me for him ; and I will return him to
thee a more accomplished prince, yet a no less loving son."

Thus it was finally arranged between them ; and the brothers bade each
other farewell, Androgeus taking his young nephew Cymbeline with him
abroad, while Tenantius remained in his native country, awaiting patiently
any propitious turn that affairs might take.

Julius Cæsar welcomed Androgeus with much of courtesy and cordiality ; he was glad to have this seceder to his side from among
the sturdy Islanders. But the Briton although he accepted the friendship of this great man, and allied himself to his fortunes, was no traitor to
his legitimate connections. On the contrary, he served his native Britain
still, by watching her interests with Cæsar ; by advancing her cause, and

farthering her advantage wherever he could. He so far overcame his sense of injury from Cassibelan, as to obtain a considerable remission of the sum of tribute, which was paid by agreement to Cæsar; and when subsequently, the restless ambition of Julius prompted a second attempt to conquer Britain, Androgeus avoided accompanying the expedition, by joining that portion of the Roman army which was sent against the Salassians, about this time. Nor could he help rejoicing in the depth of his British heart, when he found that Cassibelan, having intelligence of the Roman's design, everywhere fortified his cities, repaired his walls, placed armed men at all the ports; and, in the Thames, on which Cæsar intended to sail up to Trinovantum, caused iron and leaden stakes, each as thick as a man's thigh, to be fixed under the surface of the water, for Cæsar to split his ships upon; that he assembled all the forces of the Island, and took up his quarters with them near the sea-coast, to be ready for the enemy's coming; and that in fine, the result of these brave preparations, was another encounter, another repulse, and another victory.

Androgeus was a generous, noble hearted-man. When once removed from the sphere of his uncle's presence,—which irritated and kept alive the recollection of those various wrongs he conceived he had sustained from him,—he cherished no animosity, nursed no revengful feelings. With such a nature as his, injuries and the injurer, once out of sight, were out of mind. Freely to forgive was no difficulty to him; the only difficulty was to forget, so long as he was compelled to a perpetual consociation, communication, and pretence of friendship with the aggriever. But, asunder, all offence died away; and was both forgotten and forgiven, as though it had never been. To be apart, is sometimes the only thing wanting, to bring about mutual toleration, between two people, whom a mistaken idea of kindred and kindliness, forces to live together.

Androgeus had never felt so inclined to remember his uncle's good qualities, and even to like him, as when half a continent, and the British channel, lay between them.

Sometimes he was ready to reproach himself, that he had, for so long a period, separated the young Cymbeline from his father, Tenantius; but the boy was so happy with him,—who amply fulfilled a loving father's part,—and he himself was so fondly attached to the lad, that he could not find it in his heart to regret having brought his nephew abroad. The advantages he had foreseen from the youth's residence and breeding in so polished a court as that of Rome, were undoubted. Cymbeline had an opportunity of attaining cultivation and refinement, of forming enlarged views, and of gaining extended information and experience, which could never by possibility have been his, had he not been taken from his Island home. There, his heart might have been nurtured in right feeling, in simplicity, in goodness, in true honor, in both moral and physical courage ; but had he never seen aught beyond the circle of his native place, he would have lacked the teaching of much that was high and noble in mental accomplishment. How he profited by this teaching is yet to be seen. So far as martial discipline, proficiency in the art of war, and enthusiasm in military glory and achievement went, the young Cymbeline became an adept in the advanced degree of excellence to which such matters attained in Imperial Rome.

After Octavius had succeeded Julius, under the title of Augustus Cæsar, the youthful Briton became a great favorite with the new emperor. He received the honor of knighthood from his hand ; and was always foremost, when promotion, and gracious notice were bestowed. He served several campaigns under Augustus, in his continental wars, and not only distinguished himself, but obtained military distinction among his fellow-soldiers, and from his commander.

Among other advantages gained by this imperial regard for Androgeus, and his nephew Cymbeline, was the farther exemption and immunity in the matter of the tribute paid to Cæsar by their native country. Cassibelan had availed himself of the favor enjoyed by his two relations, at the court of Rome, by gradually permitting the annual amount of the tribute to lessen, and then to be unpunctually sent ; until by insensible degrees it fell into desuetude, and became merely nominal. Augustus had been content to wink at this ; partly for the sake of the liking he entertained for the two Britons, and partly because otherwise occupied,—at one time, engaged in settling the state of things in Gaul, at another, passing into Spain, and appeasing certain rebellious stirs in the Asturias, besides being in frequent warfare against the Pannonians and the Dalmatians.

One of the most esteemed friendships Androgeus had made in Rome, was with a gentleman of the name of Philario. He was of patrician blood, and had been a soldier in his youth : but was not more honorable by birth, than by nature ; or more exact in martial virtue, than in moral excellence. He was a perfect gentleman ; by birth, by breeding, and in spirit. This Philario often told his British friends of a dear Roman friend of his youth ; who had been a fellow-soldier with him, who had more than once saved his life ; and whom he esteemed as the very exemplar of all that was brave and skilful in warriorship. His name was Sicilius. He had early left his native Italy, with his fellow-Romans, on the occasion of their first expedition into Britain ; and had taken so strong a liking to the warlike courage, and inborn hardihood, which he found there among her Island sons, that he had abandoned the service of Julius Cæsar, and taken military office under Cassibelan, one of whose ablest, and most trusted generals, he had long been. He had since married, and settled there ; having fallen in love with one of the fair British virgins, and espoused her. By her he had two goodly boys ; whom he was training up to follow in the steps of their father, that they might become brave and able leaders in the cause he had adopted.

Upon the death of Cassibelan, the services of this experienced general, were of notable service in the secure establishing of Tenantius as successor to the throne of Britain. He and his two youthful sons performed prodigies of valour, in the many internal contests that ensued, during the first few years of the new king's reign ; while his faithful devotion to the royal cause, and his military skill and tact, rendered his counsel and support invaluable.

The young Cymbeline, on hearing of these merits of Sicilius, through his friend Philario,—who still maintained by correspondence, the old amity that had existed between them,—learned to esteem the noble warrior, as a staunch adherent, and powerful abettor of his own and his father's rights. He determined that whenever he should return to Britain, the first person whose value he would show he fully estimated, and whose regard he would take every means to cherish and preserve, should be Sicilius. A Roman born, and a Briton self-naturalized, was one above all others to inspire an instinctive attachment in the Briton-born and Roman-bred Cymbeline. The young prince felt, that whenever the time should come to proclaim his title to succeed his father Tenantius, as king of Britain, there was not a man so fitted to aid him in the inevitable divisions and dissensions that would then arise among all the rulers of the various petty states in the island kingdom, as the able military commander, Sicilius; and he accordingly resolved to omit no pains to win the same devotion to himself, that had been so advantageously evinced towards his father and predecessor.

These schemes of incipient royal policy, were soon to be put into action. Androgeus died; and his nephew, the young prince Cymbeline, no longer detained in Rome, took leave of the emperor Augustus, bade farewell to his friends and companions-in-arms, and set sail for Britain.

Tenantius, during the time that he ruled, fulfilled the prediction of his brother Androgeus. He made a good and worthy king. His chief endeavour was to preserve his realm in peace and tranquillity; and he was a strict observer and enforcer of justice. So that when his reign came to a close, his son Cymbeline found that he had less opposition to encounter, in his succession to his father's throne, than from the contentious spirit which then prevailed, might have been anticipated. In the course of those unavoidable struggles that had taken place during the generally peaceful period of Tenantius's reign, Sicilius had served with great glory to himself, and abundant advantage to his royal master. He had achieved highest military distinction; and had gained the honorable surname of Leonatus. Cymbeline had compassed the purpose which he had proposed to himself, in attaching this veteran general to his own person, with no less firmness of fidelity, than had been displayed towards the late king; and when occasion broke forth, for calling Sicilius Leonatus's martial skill once more into play, it was exercised with the same enthusiastic devotion, and admirable judgment, as before. But though it won conquest and victory to the young king, it brought despair and death to the old faithful servant.

The two sons of Sicilius fell, sword in hand; and their father, stout in battle, but sensitive in affection, took their fate so bitterly to heart, that he did not long survive them. His widow, left in the most distressful plight that can befall woman, but lived to give birth to the child who should have comforted his parents for those children they had lost, and then yielded her last breath.

The young king Cymbeline took this poor orphaned babe to his own care ; and, to commemorate the sad circumstance of his birth, no less than to perpetuate his brave father's honorably achieved title, had him named Posthumus Leonatus.

About this time, proposals were made to Cymbeline, by the father of Flur,—a princess of Cambrian descent, who claimed to have royal blood in her veins,—that some ancient differences and feuds which had existed, should now be adjusted by the espousal of his daughter with the young king ; while, at the same period, advances were made, of the like nature, from the father of Estrildis, a descendant from another kingly race.

Cymbeline, by nature an admirer of female beauty, and by his residence in Italy, a judge of its perfection, gave no rashly premature reply to these two proffered alliances. He resolved to ascertain first, whether the two princesses in question, were handsome ; and secondly, which of them was the handsomer of the two. He devised an answer sufficiently vague to each of the fathers ; and meantime, gave instructions to his envoys, to bring him particular information on the subject of the charms respectively possessed by the daughters. The intelligence brought back to him was anything but satisfactory. When pressed to be candid, both the envoys confessed, that among the whole race of British virgins,—famed for their preeminent fairness,—seldom had been seen plainer-faced, harder-featured, more graceless, or more utterly ordinary-looking maidens than these two damsels. Nay the deputed judge of the princess Estrildis, declared that he thought it was a piece of malice, a deliberate and wilful cheat, devised to entrap and inveigle the unwary, to have given this particular name to one so utterly devoid of any pretension to personal charms. He considered it little less than a sin, he said, to give the same name as that of the renowned beauty of beauties, Estrildis, Locrine's queen,—celebrated in the history of their island for her passing loveliness—to a lady so extremely forbidding as this princess, whose father had the audacity to offer her as a bride to his royal master.

In consequence of this very decisive report, Cymbeline sent back equally decisive, although carefully courteous replies, to the several proposals ; and for some time, no farther treaties of the kind were made. But marriage had become the theme of the young king's thoughts; and he began

VOL. III.   2 E seriously to wish that he knew of some lady whom he could prefer for a wife.

Chance brought about that for him, which set plans had failed to effect.

It happened, that as he was repairing from Lud's town to the place which he made his chief seat, and favorite abode,—Camalodunum; on crossing through a thick wood, in order to avoid some plashy, undrained marsh-ground, that lay in its vicinity, the king heard the sound of a woman's voice, uttering cries of distress. He rode forward, and found a young girl in the hands of some straggling soldiery belonging to a neighbouring insurgent state. At sight of the advancing king and his retinue, the ruffians quitted their intended prey, and fled; while she, pale, and ready to swoon, stood trembling, with affrighted looks, sinking limbs, and stricken face, gazing mutely up at that of her deliverer.

The young king dismounted, went towards her, and said a few words in a gentle voice, while he supported her from falling; for he could see that with grief and agitation, she was scarcely mistress of herself.

She kept gazing in his face, with a dumb look of misery and bewilderment the most appealing; but she could not speak.

Her hair was disheveled, her garments smirched and torn, her cheeks white, her lips colorless; but through all shone so rare a beauty, that the king thought he had never looked upon its equal.

Again he spoke a few words of kindly encouragement; and then, at length, she found voice to falter brokenly:—"They killed him! Oh, they killed him!"

A feeling he could scarcely define, made the king start, and half withdraw his sustaining arm; but the sound of her own voice had broken the spell which before held her in speechless grief, and as she burst forth into a passion of lamenting tears, he could not refuse the support she so sorely needed.

As she wept there, her frame shaking and panting with emotion, she seemed some frightened bird, fled for refuge to his bosom; her whole manner betokening a self-abandonment of terror and grief, throwing itself upon him for comfort and protection.

"Speak to me as your king,—your friend, maiden; one both able, and willing, to protect you; tell me your grievance, and I shall know how best to redress and console."

"They killed him! My brother! They murdered him, and dragged me hither! Oh, my brother! My beloved, unhappy brother! My young, my innocent brother!"

Some of Cymbeline's escort had meantime scoured the wood; one party going in pursuit of the rebel soldiers, the other beating the thicket in search of ambush. These latter had discovered the dead body of a youth, flung hastily among the leaves and brushwood; and now returned to inform their royal master, that they had recognised it for that of a young Briton, who had dwelt in his father's house near the borders of the wood, with his sister, both having lately been left orphans; and who, probably, in venturing to walk abroad unprotected, had fallen into the hands of a marauding party of the enemy,—for whom no deed was too lawless.

Cymbeline gave orders to his attendants that the body of the youth should be borne in their train; and turning to the unhappy sister, he once more addressed himself to her consolation.

"Let me fill the place of your lost friends; be it mine to supply to you, father, brother, guardian, in one;" he said gently. "Come with me; confide yourself to my care."

The young maiden looked into his face for one moment; then meekly bent her head, saying :—"I have no will but yours; deal with me as you list."

The soft reliance which from the first she placed in him who had rescued her from a fate worse than death, was never altered. She cast herself simply and unreservedly upon his good-faith and kindliness; seeming to have sufficient pledge of their existence, from the manner in which they had once been exercised in her behalf. She was of a gentle nature; utterly guileless, and innocent; and so void of self-confidence, or self-assertion, that her modesty amounted to an absolute distrust of any merits of her own. It rendered her timid beneath reproach; passive beneath oppression. She could more readily conceive herself unconsciously to blame, than that another should blame her unjustly. She was proner to believe that she might have unwittingly erred, than that others should wrong her by a groundless suspicion, or injure her by a falsely imputed charge. She could easily fancy herself in fault ; but tardily imagine wilful harm or intended cruelty from those about her.

There was something in this character of hers, joined to her extreme beauty, which had peculiar attractions for such a man as Cymbeline. He was selfish, weak, and obstinate ; and while his inclinations would be fully gratified by possessing a woman of such rare graces of person, his foibles would be equally ministered to, by her yielding disposition.

He made her his wife. He delighted in having her treated as his queen, —as the consort of his throne and greatness, by others ; and in treating her, himself, as his adored mistress, his worshipped idol. He took pride and pleasure in surrounding her with observances, and in providing her with luxuries,—very unusual in those rude early times of Britain,—but which his communion with Rome, and his encouragement of those Phœnician merchants who traded with the remote sea-girt island, enabled him to procure. But while he thus ostensibly and superficially ministered to her, his chief secret delight lay in knowing that he had not a more obsequious ministrant to his pleasure, a more absolute slave to his will, than his adored mistress, wife, and queen. The very extent of the personal worship he paid her himself, and the implicitness of the homage he exacted for her from others, was in fact but one subtlest medium by which he fed his own weak love of power. While he exalted her outwardly, he subjugated her the more entirely in herself ; and while he idolized her beauty, he played the despot with her nature. He took advantage of her timidity ; practised on her meekness ; and tyrannized over her passive spirit.

But she loved him ; and perceived nothing of all this, during the first year or two of wedded happiness, while all yet went on smoothly and prosperously between them.

She brought him two fair sons. The elder was named Guiderius ; the younger Arviragus. They had their mother's beauty ; and their father was both fond and proud of them.

For some time past, Cymbeline had heard rumours of muttered threats rom Rome. Question of the old covenant of yearly tribute was revived ; and there was a talk of re-levying it, as well as of enforcing arrearage. In order to be prepared for the worst, the king mustered his forces, strengthened his defences, and put himself at the head of his army. The post of Sicilius Leonatus had been supplied by another able commander, named Belarius; whom Cymbeline had made general in his stead, and in whom he placed great trust. The measures of the Britons had not been taken in vain. The Roman host poured in upon them; but they were ready to receive its assault, and after a bloody engagement, were left conquerors. Belarius enacted marvels of military prowess, and rose still higher in the esteem and favor of his sovereign. Cymbeline loaded him with honors; and gave him as large a share of his confidence, as one so self-seeking and so little generous by nature, could bestow. Like many weak people, the king was apt to misplace his trust from want of judgment; and then to become mistrustful. He would lavish his reliance upon unsound persons, who had the craft to deceive him into a credulous idea of their worth; and endeavour to redeem his error when he discovered it, by suspecting and doubting those in whom he should have had unshaken faith. After the many proofs he had had of his general's fidelity, Cymbeline permitted himself to be led into a belief of his perfidy; and actually gave credit to the calumnies of two of Belarius' enemies, who accused him of treacherous confederacy with the Romans. In a flame of wrath at the supposition of his having been deceived by one he had so esteemed and trusted, Cymbeline pronounced immediate sentence of banishment upon Belarius; not even affording him the justice of a hearing.

The choleric and impetuous soldier, indignant at this summary condemnation, without so much as having been allowed to plead one word in extenuation, or rather refutation of the charge brought against him, determined to take deep revenge.

The favor he had hitherto enjoyed near his royal master, together with the high position to which his military services had raised him, had often brought him as an honored and welcome guest to Cymbeline's palace. Here, he had been much struck with the beauty of Euriphile, one of the queen's women, who acted as nurse to the two young princes. He knew that Euriphile regarded him with an eye of favor; and he believed that were he to offer marriage, he was secure of her.

Carefully he laid his plans.   On setting forth to the appointed place of
exile,—which was Cambria,—he secretly struck across the country ; held
himself concealed in the wildest, and most unfrequented spots ; and finally
made his way by night into the king's palace ; procured an interview with
Euriphile, won her over to his wishes, persuading her to escape with him,
and to carry away the two princely babes, as the fearfullest penalty he
could inflict upon their father, who had so cruelly punished him.

Cymbeline's grief and rage on the discovery of his loss, were tempestuous.
He gave way to a torrent of lamentations for his sons, mingled with
thunders of invective against the unknown destroyers of his peace who had
borne them away.   No clue as to who these robbers might be, could be
obtained.   That some one had suborned the nurse, and bribed her to steal
away her charge, was the utmost that could be known.   The king's
suspicions wavered between the Romans, and some of the neighbouring
insurgent states, either of whom might have hit upon this device for
obtaining a valuable hostage, or for dealing a secret wound at an adver-
sary, whom they could not otherwise injure.   But no certainty of conviction
was found ; and no suspicion attached to Belarius.   The king's mind never
so much as glanced towards his late general.   He had banished him ; he
was gone ; and was believed to have been put away,—utterly quelled.

Cymbeline's wife, Guendolen, had been witness to her husband's storm
of fury and despair, when he had first learned the tidings of their cruel
loss.   While her own heart had been wholly given up to anguish, his had
been divided between grief and anger.   He had shown as much wrath
against the purloiners of his children, as mourning for the bereavement of
themselves.   He had expressed fully as much ire as sorrow.   His agony
had betrayed quite as deep a sense of the wrong his pride, as his affection,
had sustained.   He seemed to feel as acutely and bitterly the injury
inflicted on his right, his power, as upon his love.   He resented that
king's sons should be thus filched away ; that all his royal might should
have been insufficient to preserve him from this treacherous blow.   Above
all, the mother was struck to perceive, that while she deplored her babes,
while her heart was torn with the sole misery of losing her children, he
passionately lamented his boys, his princes, the inheritors of his throne.

For some time after their loss, and when every effort to trace its origin, or to recover them, had proved unavailing, the king fell into a state of sullen, despondent wrath. He was morose with those about him; and even his wife was not unfrequently the recipient of his moody humours. He was not exactly harsh towards her, but he was sour and sarcastic; and to have witnessed his behaviour, it might have been supposed that she had in some way or other caused their calamity, instead of being, with himself, its chief victim. It was not until she had given birth to a third child,—a little daughter,—that her husband resumed his wonted kindness of manner, and his natural cheerfulness, and good-humour. But when once they were resumed, they returned in all,—nay, in more than their former force. He was gay, animated, delighted with his home, his wife, his child; and seemed so wrapped in the joy of possessing this new little one, as to have lost sight of his regret for the loss of the others. His wife, charmed to see him restored to his old serenity, took every pains to minister to its continuance, by fostering the present sunshine, and carefully avoiding all allusion to the bygone shadow.

She learned this precautionary wisdom, from a slight incident that occurred: for Guendolen, like most timid wives wedded to capricious husbands, learned to be observant of apparently the most immaterial trifles which could indicate her lord's temper; not with a view of amending the evil itself, but of avoiding and evading its consequences.

When the little Imogen was first born, and her mother had the joy of placing her in her father's arms, with the timidly-conceived hope that she might prove a solace for his former bereavement, Guendolen had fondly pointed out to her husband that the infant bore upon its breast a mark precisely similar to one which had existed on the neck of their eldest-born child, Guiderius.

"See, dear husband, this little crimson-specked mole, like the velvet touches in the cup of a flower! Just such a flecked carnation spot,—in shape, a bright and glowing star,—had our boy, Guiderius! She is sent to replace him to us, in baby beauty, as in love."

The cloud that came athwart Cymbeline's face at her words, warned his wife, that the revival of the thought of his first-born whom he had lost, outweighed in bitterness, the pleasure of the image of happy substitution, which she would fain have conveyed. From that moment, she secretly resolved never to revive the names of their sons; but to devote all her endeavours to the centring of his affections upon their little daughter. In this she succeeded. The king had never been so fond, so indulgent. He lavished the most profuse tokens of affection upon both mother and child. He redoubled his attention to his wife's comfort and gratification, in the luxurious appointments with which he surrounded her, and in the presents he made her. He was more than ever sedulous to please her, and to procure for her all that could minister to her taste or convenience. He had never been more prodigal of caresses; more full of endearment and show of tenderness. He passed every moment he could spare from his state duties, with her and her baby daughter. He took a proud pleasure in abandoning himself to the most familiar intercourse with them; of making himself their companion, their playfellow, their sportive intimate. He gloried in throwing off his sovereign grandeur with them; yet was never more profoundly conscious of it, than when he most seemed to cast it aside. He would fling himself on a couch beside his wife, and watch her in simplest maternal offices,—bathing or dressing her child,—which she took delight to do herself; and while he affected to aid her, would bid her notice how well a monarch could play the nurse. He would yield himself to all the sportive whims of the child, lying with it on the floor; allowing it to roll, and tumble, and crawl over him; to tug his hair, to pat his face; to play every kind of baby trick with him; and amidst all, would betray how keen a sense he had of his own condescension, by calling on his wife to look at the low-laid head of the king who had held a successful struggle with Cæsar, now pulled about at the mercy of an infant girl.

The little Imogen grew very fond of this indulgent, playfellow father. She learned to look for his advent as the signal of frolic; to look for his approach as the sure precursor of a game of romps. Long before she could talk, she knew him, and could welcome him by her own inarticulate, but significant, language of welcome; by happy crows, and bright, expressive looks. She had found him ever cheerful, ever complacent, ever good-natured and kind.

She had another playmate, in the young boy whom her father had taken under his protection, Posthumus Leonatus. He was sufficiently near to her own age, to make a more conformable partner in the childish sports which the little girl pursued ; but not greater favor did even he find in Imogen's eyes as a companion, than her royal playfellow father. She gambolled with the one as her equal; with the other as her pet and plaything. She shared her games with the one, and joined in his pastimes ; but with the other she frolicked, as with something under her controul,—subject to her will. She treated the young boy as her superior, her instructor in all the mysteries and devices of play ; as her preceptor, and leader ; the planner and projector of all their schemes of amusement ; but her father she looked upon as her property, her toy, the instrument of her pleasures and entertainment.

Imogen was still quite a baby, when Cymbeline was called into the western district of his kingdom, to march against a rebellious force that had mustered there, against him. Although he was nominally sovereign of Britain, his realm was perpetually disturbed by internal divisions. In parting from his wife and child, for an indefinite period, and for the purpose of engaging in a desperate battle, Cymbeline had an access of his late bad humour. He was loath to leave his home, loath to encounter all the fatigues, anxieties, and perils, of a civil war ; and he submitted with a very ill grace to the necessity, which he felt existed, for assuming in person the command of his army. But there was no one to whom he could with safety trust the charge of heading his men, and leading them against the insurgents ; and he accordingly decided upon doing so himself.

When he bade farewell to his queen, Cymbeline gave her the option of remaining at Camalodunum, or of sojourning at another palace he had in Lud's town, during his absence.

Guendolen,—partly from her passive disposition, which rendered her averse to removal, or change of any kind ; partly from habitual deference to her husband's choice, which seemed to her to be indicated by his having named Camalodunum in the first instance ; and partly from the indifference she felt as to what place she dwelt in, when he was away,— answered absently that she would prefer staying where she was.

Cymbeline, who had hoped she would have chosen otherwise, as then he should have had her accompany him partly on his way westward, gave his assent in a tone that showed he was vexed at her decision.

His wife hastened to retrieve her error, by assuring him that she had no preference in the matter ; and begged he would determine for her.

"Nay, I care not ; it is not I who have to remain. It is thou; and I should have thought that,——but no matter ;" he added, interrupting himself, and biting his lip. He could not help feeling hurt that she had not humoured his wish, forgetting that he had never so much as hinted it. He was so accustomed to have her anticipate his desires, almost divine his likings, that he resented her not having discerned this unexpressed one.

"I have offended you — most unwittingly, believe me ;" she said. "Forgive me !"

"'Offended ?' I have taken no offence ;" he said, with that cold manner which strives to conceal a swelling pride. "'Forgive !' What should I have to forgive ? I offered you a choice. You made one. I have no cause to be offended,—no need to forgive."

"Dear my lord, yet pardon me ! I have no will but yours. Signify it to me ; and my pleasure, as my duty, shall be to obey. Show me that you have taken no offence, by choosing for me my abode while you are absent."

"'Tis a favorite sentence with you, meek lady mine, to assure me that you have no will of your own ;" he said, with that tone of half sarcasm, half bitter sportiveness, in which he was wont to give vent to his temper, fancying he cloaked it, whilst he most surely betrayed it. "Do you know that you are well-nigh wilful in your will-lessness ; resolute in your absolute negation ; all but active in your positive passiveness ? There may be such a thing as will in the very spirit with which you will to have no will ; can you conceive this, my most humble, most unresisting, most obedient lady-wife ?"

"Put my obedience to what severity of proof it shall seem well to you, my lord," she replied with gentle earnestness, "and it shall abide the proof. To you I owe life and honor ; to you they have been, and evermore are consecrated. Deal with them,—with me, as you list. I am yours wholly."

He could not withstand so much of softness and sweetness,—so utter a self-abandonment to his mercy ; he embraced her with a sort of remorse at his own wayward exercise of power towards one so mild and inoffensive.

"Convince me that I am restored to your favor, dear my lord," she said, " by appointing where I shall dwell. All places will be alike to me, when deprived of that which gives them their charm,—your presence."

"Then be this your home, and our child's, while I am away;" he returned; like a true victim of temper, punishing himself for a former petulance, by choosing what was most distasteful, instead of frankly avowing his original error.

The western insurrection was more speedily and thoroughly quelled, than Cymbeline could have hoped. But its field of action was far removed; and in those times, crossing from one extremity of the island to the other was a work of time. The king's return was attended with considerable delay; and he was still on the borders of Cambria, when he was entering a thick forest, after having made his way across an extensive morass. Suddenly from among the densest of the underwood, darted a form that seemed like some wild animal; so agile its motion, so bright and restless, and almost fierce, its eyes, so matted and tangled, its elf-locks of hair, and so bare its limbs, as it sprang to the rein of Cymbeline's horse, and clung there, crying :—" Good-morrow, cousin king!" Cymbeline started, and recoiled, as at something unearthly; for scarce human did this strange, lithe, gaunt, yet dwarfish being seem. The attendant soldiers crowded round their royal master, offering to strike the creature off.

But the king raised his hand.

"I'll not leave my cousin king!" exclaimed this curious being, in a voice singularly at variance with his uncouth exterior. It was as harmonious and beautiful, as all else was rugged, wild, and incongruous.

One of the king's guards made a feigned blow at him with his partisan, whirling it close round his head, and letting it fall heavily on the ground· within an inch of him; but no flinching, not so much as the stir of a limb, or the quiver of an eyelid, betokened fear.

The king was interested; his soldierly instincts were aroused; his despotic humour amused. He called to one of his officers, and whispered him. The men were led off, and stationed apart.

"Wilt not quit me, sirrah?" he said to the strange creature that still clung to his bridle-rein.

"Not with life, cousin king!" was the reply.

"And thou'rt not afraid to brave my displeasure?" continued Cymbeline.

"Not a whit, cousin king!"

"Bind him!" exclaimed Cymbeline.

Two of the guards seized hold of the young savage, wrenched him from the vice-like grasp he had on the horse's bit, and bound him fast, his arms behind him. He had struggled fiercely, at first; but once mastered, he remained motionless.

The rest of the soldiers drew up in line, awaiting the king's farther command.

"Archers, take aim at his heart!" cried the king in a stern voice.

The bows of the men were all bent in direction of the pinioned culprit; a lad in seeming years, a man in dauntless bearing.

"Wilt thou now promise to leave me in peace?" asked Cymbeline.

"I promise nothing; not even to cousin king;" was the answer.

"No sign of blanching in cheek, or blenching in heart;" said the king, looking keenly at him. "Hast no thought of thyself? No dread?"

"I care little for life, and fear naught of death; but have ta'en a whim for cousin king!" returned the young savage.

"Let fly, then, archers! And be sure you hit the *hart*!" cried the king, with a loud laugh.

The bowmen, as previously instructed, through the whispered order to their officer, sent a flight of arrows right over the lad's head, into the thicket immediately behind him.

"Cut his bonds; and go see if there be not a wild deer in the covert; methought I marked one lurking there;" said the king, still laughing, to the soldiers; "better make quarry of a hart that will roast, and furnish good eating, than of a heart that is too tough to yield, and therefore promises but sorry fare."

"That should be a morsel for a monarch!" said the lad, in the same tone; and flinging his freed arms about joyfully. "Make it yours, cousin king! Reserve it for thine own especial tooth and keeping. It yields itself to thy good liking; secure that thou wilt neither gnaw it with ill-usage, nor grind it with hardship, nor bite it with cruelty, nor, worse than all, spit it out with rejection. Do but chew it patiently and tolerantly; and thou shalt find it a sweet kernel, within a rough husk. 'Tis like the fruit that grows upon this hazel-twig;" he continued, drawing a small rod from his girdle, and switching it smartly to and fro; it hath a poor, unpromising exterior; a dry, fibrous rind, and a hard shell to crack; but within lies a milky centre, pleasant and wholesome to the taste."

"What if I find thee hollow, empty, rotten, like some light nuts?" said the king. "If so, best chuck thee away at once; and not lose time trying my teeth, while I try thee."

"Nay, I pretend not to be more sound than is good;" returned the stripling, with his bright, quick, gleaming eyes,—which had a strange wild light in them,—looking up into those of the king; "the nut that the worm affects, is oft the daintiest; and few men are the worse for those odd maggots of the brain, with which mine abounds. All I say is, try me, cousin king; and if I prove not worth the cracking, set thy heel on me, and crush me into nothingness for ever."

"I take thee at thy word, good fellow;" replied Cymbeline. "And now tell me who thou art, and what made thee seek me, and stick to me, and claim cousinship with me."

"Thou remember'st that Corineus of Cornwall, who overcame the hugest of the giants, that lurked in rocks and caves on the Cornish coast? In their mortal wrestle, the monster, with a terrible hug broke three of the hero's ribs; whereat Corineus enraged, heaved him up by main force, and hurled him headlong from the cliff into the sea. These Island giants were not the only ones overthrown by his might; for before he came to Britain, Corineus had made war against the Tyrrhen giants, and with his irresitible battle-axe had mown them down like blades of wheat. This rod is a slip from the staff of that invincible weapon, when it lost its head, and its master used it as a club;" said the lad, bending, and caressingly handling the hazel-twig he held, with a look of wistful pride and fondness; "and that renowned Corineus, who bequeathed me the relic of his might, was my father."

"Thy father, was he?" said Cymbeline, laughing at the whimsical gravity of the lad, as he told the legend. "Seeing that Corineus flourished some centuries since, at the lightest computation, thou must be a son of giant growth in years, though not in bulk and stature."

"If Corineus were not my father, I know not who was;" said the young savage, with his vaguely-eager, gleaming eyes. "But of my mother I am sure;" he continued, lowering his voice, and creeping nearer to Cymbeline, as he walked close beside him at his bridle-rein, the king riding at a foot-pace, to accommodate his strange young companion, in whom he began to take much interest. "'Tis a sad history, but I will tell it to cousin king. She was one of the nine vestal priestesses, vowed to the service of our Druid temple, in the sacred grove adjoining this wood. She expiated her crime with her life; but I, its unhappy fruit, was saved from perishing with her, by the interference of one whose word was not to be gainsaid. He was among the highest of the consecrated order; a Druid revered by his brethren for peculiar sanctity, wisdom, and knowledge. He took charge of me from infancy, till lately, when he died, full of years and honor. He trained me with a view to make me one of themselves—a Druid. But whether it be that my brain hath too many vagrant fancies of its own, to be able to store soberer truths; or whether it be that it is somewhat crazed and leaky for the holding of so many curiously massive marvels, as the Druid doctrine contains, certain it is, that I could never master the multitudinous lore it behoved me as a neophyte to retain; and since I have lost my protector, I have had reason to believe, that when once it should be discovered that I am unfit to become one of themselves, they would make no scruple of devoting me to the flames, the first time a human sacrifice was wanted."

"But it needs the taint of crime, to render a victim qualified for a sacrificial offering;" said the king, more gravely; "nurtured as thou say'st thou wert, thou couldst hardly have had opportunity for misdeed."

"When they can find none entitled by guilt to the privilege of burning, when they are out of those requisitely stained for their purpose," said the lad, with a quaint sort of dryness in his manner, half light, half earnest, "they e'en content themselves with plain virtue; when nigritude fails, they make shift with simple purity; and when no acceptable blackness is at hand, they will put up with spotless and immaculate whiteness, rather than want a victim; and thus should poor innocent I have stood a chance of honorable ashes."

The king looked at the figure of the young savage, as it stepped along, alert, vigorous, sinewy; but although of such short stature as to be almost dwarf-like, it was neither stunted, nor disproportioned. It was lean, and meagre; seemingly compounded solely of bone and bronzed skin. Very little of flesh and muscle was apparent; but the ribs were plainly to be counted, and the joints of the limbs showed knobbed and prominent, his only covering being the skin of some beast, wrapped about his lank loins. His face was a strange mixture of thought and wandering; of intelligence and inanity. At one moment his restless eyes would brighten with a look of almost supernatural comprehension; at another assume a dreamy, lost expression, as though their sense lacked distinction and understanding. The chief characteristic of his whole appearance, however, was that of a fearless, sincere erectness, of spirit and body.

"And thy name, boy? Thou hast not yet told me how I am to call thee;" said Cymbeline.

"I am called Bergion;" returned the lad. "They named me after that noble warrior, brother to the famed Albian, Neptune's giant son; who gave his own name to this white-cliffed isle, when he first subdued it to his power, and after ruled it for well-nigh half a century. When I think of cousin king, I call it Britain; when I think of itself,—as mine own fair, white-browed island, set amidst the spray of the sea, and free as the bounding, high-crested surges themselves,—as mine own by right of descent from heroic Corineus, and by title from the blood of its first ruler, then I name it Albion."

"And thou art content to share its sovereignty with me, cousin Bergion?" said Cymbeline, willing to humour the stripling's oddity, which amused him.

"More than content; I gladly yield thee all my claims to royalty, cousin king, provided thou wilt let me abide with thee, under thy protection. For mine own mystic right in the beauty, and freedom, and natural qualities of the isle,—that is inalienably mine, neither for me to give up, nor any one to take from me, so long as I keep possession of this hazel-wand, bequeathed to me from father Corineus. So long as a single fibre of it exists, and I retain it within mine own power, so long am I lord of the white-cliffed isle,—of that portion of it for which I care,—and of mine own life and being."

"And hath that slight rod such magic virtue?" said Cymbeline smiling, and extending his hand for the hazel-twig, which the young savage bore.

"Nay, cousin king, all else I will give thee; all else I have, thou may'st command; but for this, an' thou demand'st it, or destroy'st it, thou destroy'st me. My existence, and all that makes existence of worth,— the love of fresh air, the joy in the green woods, the gladness of sunshine, the calm of the moon's soft light, the hopeful happiness of the bright stars and the blue sky,—would all pass from me, an' thou wert to insist on my yielding thee this slight wand of hazel."

"Far be it from me to exact so vast a sacrifice;" said the king laughing. "Keep thy rod of might; and give me thy fealty, and thy loyal love."

"They are thine already, cousin king;" said the lad, fixing his eyes with a clear frank look of pure sincerity, upon the face of Cymbeline. "I sought thee at first for the sake of thy powerful protection; I have since attached myself to thee by the infrangible bonds of liking."

A deep-laid scheme of craft and villainy awaited the return of Cymbeline, to undermine his best peace and happiness There was a certain lord, named Mempricius, who was one of Cymbeline's court, at the time when the king had wedded his wife Guendolen. This sleek courtier, unable to conquer the powerful impression made upon him by the surpassing beauty of the young queen, had, in one desperate moment, lost sight of his interests in the dominance of his passion, and had dared to avow it to her. Guendolen's innocence and virtue made her profoundly resent this insult; but hers was not a nature to rebuke it by open reproof and dismissal. She contented herself with a silent but complete repulse of the man, letting him see the extent of her own contempt and aversion, while she permitted him to retain his place and favor in the court of her husband; thus giving another proof of the many evils arising from timidity, and want of encouraged confidence, on the part of a wife. The crafty Mempricius had only too gladly availed himself of this tacit reprehension. He withdrew his attempts upon her virtue; but he devoted all his energies to destroy her fame and honor. He set himself secretly, but surely and sleeplessly, to the collecting together of such circumstances and facts, as, joined with unscrupulous fabrications, misrepresentation, and false testimonies, should combine to form a mass of evidence against her, which should indubitably work her downfall.

With a weak, obstinate, and selfishly credulous man like her husband, this was not so hopeless a scheme. The wily Mempricius well knew the vulnerable points of his royal master's character; and what favorable ground they afforded, for being acted upon by his agency. At that period of time, previous to the abduction of the young princes, and not many months before the birth of Imogen, it chanced that the young king of a neighbouring state,—for although Cymbeline was reckoned general monarch of the island realm, yet several of the rulers of the several districts into which it was divided, chose to assume the title of king,— had come to settle a treaty of peace, with his sovereign, in person, and had sojourned some time at the palace of Camalodunum, as an honored and distinguished guest. This young king of the Coritani was a remarkably handsome man, of courteous address, and winning manners. Him, Mempricius fixed upon, as a fitting object of his accusation, for the supposed partner of queen Guendolen's imputed crime. With patient cunning, with wary progress, Mempricius accumulated and matured the several ramifications of his plot; until at length, they were all fully formed, and ripe for fruition, just as the king returned from his western expedition.

He was met by the hypocrite courtier with a well-dissembled honest grief, and warmth of devotion to his person and cause, which trampled on all considerations of discretion, where the peace and honor of a king and husband were concerned. He disclosed the ficticious tale, unveiled the supposed truths, brought forward and laid bare the alledged facts. By an artful train of falsehoods and forgeries, he succeeded in persuading Cymbeline that the queen had been false to his bed, had conspired with the king of the Coritani to deprive him of his throne, had aided in the nocturnal theft of the two young princes, and that, finally, the infant princess was the offspring of an adulterous commerce, and not his own child.

" As one crowning proof of my most unhappy, but alas, too true, allegation, my lord," concluded Mempricius, " ask her majesty but the simple question, whether the two princely babes were not wrapped in a mantle belonging to herself at the very time they were stolen; and see if her looks do not convict her of her treasonous criminality."

" If criminal in that, criminal in all else ; " muttered the king through his ground teeth ; with true feebleness of soul, admitting at once the possibility of guilt in one whom he ought to have believed incapable of belying that good which he *knew* was part of her character. " If she could have found it in her heart to wound me through that tenderest point,— my children, I can give credit to aught of wild and improbable that she may have committed."

The king buried his face in his hands, giving way to a passionate burst of grief and self-pity ; while Mempricius continued to pour into his ears corroborative point after point ; until at length Cymbeline, raising his head, and drawing himself up to his full height, said :—" No more need be added. Too fatally am I convinced of her perfidy, her falsehood. And could she— she whom I so idolized, have thus——but this is my last weakness. Henceforth, I am calm ; I am firm."

Set firm indeed, in the steadfastness of obstinacy, in that inflexibility,— which is the fancied strength of principle and right,—but which is in fact the refuge of a weak nature, Cymbeline went straight to the apartments of his wife. She flew to welcome him, and the little Imogen clung to his knees, in all the fond ecstacy of recovering him who had been so long,— or seemed so long,—absent ; but the king held himself stiff and unmoved, and with a stern cold tone bade the women attendants leave the room.

" Take this child with you ! " he said, holding himself upright and apart, while he pointed to the little Imogen still hanging about his knees ; neither venturing to look towards her, nor his wife, but keeping his eyes fixed upon nothing,—upon the blank space in the middle of the room.

"My good lord,—dear husband,"—faltered the trembling Guendolen, "are you well, that you speak thus, look thus? You are pale,—your lips are quivering—these cold, averted eyes—are you indeed ill?"

"Sick at heart,—poisoned in very soul;" he returned. "Poisoned, Guendolen!" he added with emphasis, as he turned his eyes upon her face, gathering courage to do so, from finding her so agitated.

The proposed means of ridding herself of him, to be at liberty to wed with her paramour, were alledged to have been poison; therefore, when Cymbeline uttered the word thus emphatically, he secretly made it a kind of test upon the expression of her countenance.

The timid Guendolen of course changed color at the fearful word, and still more at her husband's manner.

Cymbeline proceeded to try her by the mention of the mantle, as artfully prompted by the wily Mempricius; who had built much on this single point of truth, wryed by him to his purpose, through misrepresentation.

Her demeanour on this allusion, confirmed all. The circumstance of the missing mantle had struck Guendolen at the time; but her dread of dwelling upon any point that recalled the loss of his boys to her husband, had acted as a check to her telling him of the only incident by which they might perhaps have been traced. It was the consciousness of the suppression of this fact, and the reason that had influenced her, which now held the queen mute, shaking from head to foot, her weeping eyes cast upon the ground, while her face flushed, now crimson, now white, with alternate shame and fear.

But when her husband went on to reproach her with her infamy, to accuse her of falsehood, treachery, dishonor, she found courage to raise her eyes to his with one silent, but eloquent look of refutal.

When he came to a pause, she still stood there motionless, as if unable to speak. But at length she said, in a low, but distinct voice:—

"Can you believe this?"

"Too surely, alas, am I compelled to believe it;" returned he. "Not lightly, oh, not lightly, could I have credited the tale. But proofs, most damnatory proofs——"

" I am innocent ; " she said simply.

" I may not trust my own heart to listen to thy false tongue, thy witchery of seeming virtue. I will not hear thee plead ; " he said hurriedly, as if in misgiving of his own weakness—not the weakness he should have mistrusted,—but the weakness which he fancied was his, in favor of her beauty, her candour, her gentleness.

" I plead nothing ; " she said ; " if you can but for an instant think thus of me, I would not urge one word in my defence.   If your own soul does not acquit me, I am content to submit to its award."

" You are all submission, all obedience, I know ; " he said with a fierce sneer, as the thought arose within him, that in spite of all this meekness of hers, she had secretly revolted against his power, his love, and his honor. " Prove it now, by yielding implicitly to my will."

" I can but repeat, what I have many times said ; " she replied.   " I have no will but yours ; deal with me as you list."

" Then hear me pronounce your sentence ; " he said ; " and let it be fulfilled without a question.   I have resolved, for the sake of mine own bleeding peace and honor,—which well deserve this single piece of tenderness and consideration, that no public trial shall ensue.   For the sake of what has once been between us, I will have no examination into charges and countercharges, accusations and proofs.   I will have no prying into facts that are all-sufficing in their own misery of knowledge to me, without the torture of their reproduction, and open ripping up before all eyes.   I take upon myself to be sole judge in this, mine own particular grief.   As your condemnation is private, so shall be your penance.   You shall neither be publicly shamed, nor publicly punished.   Your imprisonment shall be merely imposed by my will, observed by yours.   Neither bolts nor bars shall confine you ; but simply my commands shall restrain you.   By this, I test your professed obedience and submission.   You know that retired lodge, built for the chase, on the borders of the forest near here.   To that betake yourself and your child ; and if you wish to show that you really have no will but mine, remain there, shut up, apart from allo ther human being.   I will take means that you shall be supplied with food, and all necessaries for life ; but hold no intercourse with any one ; keep yourself secluded, strictly alone in the world, henceforth."

She had stood while he spoke, her head bent upon her bosom ; without movement, without tear, or sob.

As he concluded, he trusted himself to look for one instant at the statue of meek, unresisting hopelessness, which her attitude presented ; but feeling in spite of himself, touched by its involuntary and affecting appeal, he hardened himself in his resolve not to be moved from his purpose, by adding, as he turned away :—" And nevermore will I look upon your face, or that of your child, in this life !"

As he precipitately left the room, with these words, his wife dropped to the earth, as if felled by a heavy blow.

Not a voice was upraised, not a question was mooted against the proceeding of the king. He had despotic power, and he used it. The courtiers each made their several and secret comments, but outwardly all acquiesced. The queen took her child in her arms, and in a simple garment, quietly, wholly unattended, left the palace for her appointed lone retreat. She had uttered no word ; neither of complaint nor of explanation The king had spoken no word ; neither of comment, nor of command. All passed in silence ; the subordinate actors in the scene taking their cue from their principals. The only person,—one other excepted,—who had breathed a syllable upon the subject, was the boy Posthumus, who with the artless out-speaking of his age, had asked why his little playmate Imogen was taken away. But the heavy frown, and stern voice of the king, when he had answered this question of the boy's, by desiring him never again to mention either the child's name, or her mother's, on pain of being banished for ever from his presence, had effectually silenced him.

The other sole exception was Bergion.

There was something in this lad's fearless sincerity, his wild quaintness of speech, and his air of half-witted yet blunt boldness, that peculiarly hit the king's humour. He took a strange fancy to him, and permitted him to use a tone of freedom and intimacy towards himself, that he would not have borne from a living creature beside.

Cymbeline concealed the depth of his anguish at his wife's supposed defection, beneath an exterior of marble indifference. While his soul was

torn with conflicting feelings, of wrecked love, of passionate regrets, and of
torturing doubts about the child's filiation,—for there were certain instincts
of paternity that perpetually arose within him, to sting and goad him into
remorseful uncertainty, when he thought of that innocent face, and its
guiltless expression of love towards himself,—he would hide, and attempt
to stifle all, by indulging in a saturnine humour, a bitter, moody, scoffing
levity. He would bandy words with Bergion, and encourage him in his
wild sallies ; while in the forced, sardonic laugh, with which he himself
replied, could alone be traced how hollow was the mirth which he affected.

" What a whimsical brain thou hast, boy ; " he would say, in return for
one of Bergion's fantastic flights.

" 'Tis a very whirlbat of a brain, I thank it ! " answered he. " It hums
like a sling at full circle. At night my brain sings to me. In the dark,
I hear it throbbing its strange music. At times, some glad tune that thrills
me with a sharp, quick joy, and sends a sudden quiver through my feet.
At others, wildest and saddest sounds, like wind lamenting. Now and
then, soft, sweet stops, like shepherds' oaten pipes by river side. Often,
brave, wise things, that tell me more than earthly truths. Oftest, whirling
nonsense, that circles round and round, and shoots forth gleams of false yet
starry light, like those I see flitting before mine eyes through the gloom."

" The wise things thy brain sings to thee, must needs be the most
humoursome of all, boy. Let us hear some of thy madcap wisdom, for the
love of laughter and oddity."

" Last night of all, then, cousin king, I heard my brain whisper a queer,
sighing song, of a lady with none to help her ; who threw herself upon her
judge's mercy, and said :—' I have no will but yours ; deal with me as you
list.' Tush ! 'Twas a silly saying."

The king's brow darkened for an instant ; but the next, he said, with
a constrained laugh :—" ' A silly saying ? ' I find naught amiss with it.
What wouldst thou have had her say, pry'thee ? "

" Marry, this. She should have said :—' I have no will but yours ; let
it be a kind one. Deal with me as you list that I should deal by you.'
'Twould have reminded the judge of his duty—forbearance ; while she
fulfilled hers—submission."

" Go to, thou'rt a foolish wiseling,—a most ignorant sage ; " replied the king, still laughing as before. " An' thy brains whisper thee no better wisdom than this, we'll have them taken from thy scull, buttered, and served up instead of the next calf's slaughtered for the royal table. Let's have no more of thy brain's sapience, cousin Bergion ; but as much as thou wilt of its nonsense."

While at the palace, all went on at the king's good pleasure, at the retired lodge in the forest, dwelt Guendolen and her child. To her stunned and bruised spirit, this solitude was not altogether unwelcome,— especially at first. But its effect upon her child, taught her to perceive its weary wretchedness. The little creature moped ; missed the luxury and brightness of its old home,—above all, missed the kindly companionship to which it had been accustomed. It missed its playfellow father, with his indulgent frolics, and gay romps ; it missed its constant playmate, the young Posthumus, with his gentle care, his petting protection, his ready prevention of every wish, his boyish invention in their games. The little one missed the smiles from her mother's face ; and wondered to find ever-falling tears, and sad looks imprinted there, in their stead. Cheerfulness, —that heart-nourishment of a child,—seemed faded and gone from the little Imogen's existence, and in the blank shadow that had now fallen around her, she drooped, and her spirits dulled. The mother awoke from her trance of sorrow, at the sight of her child's altered mien ; she accused herself of selfish absorption in her own grief, and strove her best to suppress its outward tokens, that she might not add to the forlornness which crept upon the little one in its changed life. She found courage to dress her face in smiles, to force back her tears ; and though she could not alter its ghastly pallor, she constrained it to wear a calmer aspect, and to control the betrayal of its quivering lip, and heavy swollen eyelids. She exerted herself to play with her child, to fashion amusements for it, to plan sports for it ; she twisted garlands from the weeds and wild-flowers, plaited curious playthings from the reeds, and rushy flags of the brook, built toy houses, and fences, from the twigs, and sticks, and fallen branches, of the forest trees ; and,—hardest effort of all,—compelled herself to talk cheerfully, hopefully, to her child, that she might win it from its dullness, and lure it into interest and energy.

But at night,—when she had lulled her little one into happy rest, and she could leave it fast wrapped in that sound sweet sleep of childhood, which knows no waking till morning sun appears,—the poor mother would get up, steal forth, and in the silence and the darkness, give free vent to her anguish. In the dim shrouded light of the wood, when the moon shed its beauty through the thick boughs of the lofty oaks, she would indulge her misery by a passion of sobs and tears,—or by those short acute cries, that burst from an overcharged heart alone with its agony, and are its uttered throes.

Had it not been for these respites of relief to her aching heart, it must have broken beneath its struggle to suppress its pangs. Guendolen passionately loved her husband ; and to be deprived of his presence and affection, was even a sorer grief to her, than the loss of fame and good name. She knew herself innocent, therefore could bear the stigma attached to guilt ; but what she could not endure, was the being out of his sight,— banished from his society. Had she but the hope of looking upon him, she thought, for ever so short a space of time, at ever so rare an interval, or at ever so protracted a period hence, she could have fed her courage upon that slight comfort, and so have learned to sustain the present misery ; but he had expressly bereft her of this very hope, and she felt utterly abandoned to despairful affliction.

One day, when she had succeeded in engaging the attention of her child towards a large, broad-spread web, which a speckled spider was industriously weaving, across the outlet which served for the only window to their dwelling, she suffered herself to lapse into a brooding silence, while the little Imogen watched, with baby interest, the movements of the spinner, in his airy circle.

Suddenly, the mother was startled by a loud cry of joy, and spring of delight, from her child, as she sat upon her knee. Guendolen looked forth, to see the cause ; and there, among the trees, just in front of the house, she saw, rapidly approaching, the young boy, Posthumus Leonatus. He had seen the child, and was running hastily towards her.

"I have found you! I have found you!" he exclaimed as he bounded into the place. "I knew you must be hereabouts, and I have never ceased hunting, till I found the exact spot."

The boy threw his arm round Guendolen's neck, and pressed his face against her bosom, to hide the tears which his manliness forbade him to give way to; then embraced his little playmate Imogen, who leaned from her mother's lap to hug him heartily in return.

"My dear boy, how came you here? How did you find your way? You must go—you must not stay—it is forbidden——"

"I set out from the palace early, I made my way right across the wood —I knew the lodge must lie in this direction. I would not ask much about it; for they all pretend to know nothing, and besides, I didn't care to speak to any there of my wish;" said the boy, in honest confusion; "but I was determined to see you; so I never rested till I found you out for myself."

Guendolen kissed his glowing cheek, at a loss how to explain the reason that he must neither come nor stay; and pained to check his generous sympathy.

"An't you glad, mamma, to see Natus? Natus is come! Natus is here!" said Imogen, with joy sparkling in her eyes, and gladness in every tone, as she welcomed him by the baby name she had invented for Leonatus.

The young boy returned the child's caresses, and her looks and words of delight, with no less eagerness than her own; while the mother struggled for firmness to put an end to what gave them all so much happiness,—the only happiness they had known since they had been parted from each other.

"My dear boy, listen to me;" said Guendolen at length, in her own low, gentle voice. "Try and understand me, without my explaining more than I can well utter."

She paused; then went on, as the boy stood, very gravely, and with a varying cheek, looking at her:—"You have found that they do not speak of me yonder,—that I have fallen into disgrace,—and that my name is no longer mentioned? Is it not so?"

The boy with a bright color flashing into his face, and with a sparkling eye, looked the assent he could not speak.

" I have fallen into the displeasure of——the king ; " Guendolen's voice faltered here ; but she resumed. " We all owe him duty and obedience. He has willed that I shall dwell here apart—alone—with my little Imogen ; that we shall see no one, speak to no one. You will help us to observe his wishes, will you not ? "

" If you wish it,——" he began, but could get no farther.

" I do wish you to fulfil his commands. It is on this account, and not because I do not feel the full force of your generous love and affection in coming hither to seek us, dear boy, that I beg you not to stay, not to come hither again."

" Never to see you—to see her ! " exclaimed the boy. " I don't understand the cause of your——" he could not utter the word ' disgrace ; ' but hurried on :—" I can't make out why my lord the king is displeased ; but surely this is too cruel—too unjust—to send you hither ; no one to attend you, to see you, to speak to you——"

" Hush, dear boy ; " said the gentle queen, drawing him towards her affectionately and soothingly, yet in spite of herself charmed with his honest indignation ; " we must not murmur against a will that hath a right to controul us. If you would indeed pleasure me, learn to subdue all feeling, as all word, of remonstrance, against the dictates of him who has not only a right to dictate, but who hath a claim upon your especial love and gratitude, for the paternal care he hath bestowed on yourself."

" To me he has been ever good, ever kind ; " said the boy ; " but why to you, to her, should he show himself so harsh ? "

" Question not, but submit in silence, dear boy ; trusting that all is wisely and justly ordered, though thou canst not fathom its meaning. I told you there was much I must ask you to take upon trust, without my explanation. This much, understand, and believe. However the sentence that decrees my banishment hither may be undeserved, it is thought to be fully merited,—to be even a lenient one, compared with my desert ; and therefore, he that pronounces it, must be freed from blame. All we may do, is to pray that the time may come, when he shall see mine innocence as clearly as I know it."

" But in the meantime——" said the boy eagerly.

"In the meantime, I am content to abide my lord's pleasure, until his heart shall speak in my favor, or his eyes be unsealed to the truth;" said Guendolen.

"Come, Natus; come and play;" said little Imogen, who had not comprehended one word of the grave talk going on between her young companion and her mother; and who now thought it had lasted quite long enough, and that her claim upon him had some right to be attended to.

The way in which the young boy leant down to his little friend, and entered into her views, and listened to her proposals for a game, and contrived to evade their immediate fulfilment, without thwarting them, and to please and pacify her, all the while he was reconciling her, and bringing her by degrees, to the necessity for his leaving her, showed the impression the gentle queen's words had made upon him. He had won Imogen into seeing him prepare to depart, without a murmur; and as he turned to bid her mother farewell, Guendolen pressed the noble boy to her bosom with an affectionate, approving warmth, which told him how fully his behaviour was appreciated. Taking one parting hug of the child, he turned away with a swelling heart, and left the lodge.

Imogen sat watching him from the window, as he disappeared among the trees of the forest; and when she could see him no longer, gave a deep sigh,—a strange sigh for one so young.

"My Imogen must not be vexed;" said her mother's low, sweet voice, when her child had remained thus for some time, lost in thought, silent, and grave.

"I am not vexed—only sorry;" said little Imogen, with another deep-breathed sigh.

Her dejection did not pass off. It clung to her with a constancy rarely seen in a child of such tender years. She would often, after that, climb up into the window, and sit in its wide-ledged recess, looking out into the wood, in the direction that she had seen Leonatus disappear.

"He won't come again;" her mother heard her once say.

Guendolen redoubled her endeavours to amuse, and distract the child's thoughts from dwelling on this source of regret. But the sight of her favorite young companion, had powerfully revived all Imogen's desire for

his society, and she was with difficulty won from brooding over this second
loss of its pleasant, cheerful influences.

The only relic of her former prosperous existence that Guendolen had
brought with her, was a certain ring. It was a diamond,—of great worth ;
but that which gave it its priceless value in her eyes, was, that it had been
her husband's first gift, when he had spoken his love, and asked her to
become his wife. All else that was costly, with which his approving
affection had since loaded her, she had left behind her, with her happiness ;
but this one object she had not been able to part with, linked as it was, in
association with all that had been dearest and most blest in her fate. This
ring she would fondle, and hold to her lips and her heart, while she
breathed loving murmurs of regret, and yielded her spirit to a thousand
passionate memories connected with it. The little Imogen had many times
seen her do this ; and with a child's innocent, imitative fancy, would ask to
kiss it too, and talk to it, and pass it on her finger, and admire, and cherish
it, in a half playful, half affectionate manner.

Finding how the trinket pleased her little one, the mother gladly
availed herself of this source of delight and interest,—as she would of any
that might procure even a moment's amusement to one whose strange sad
fate had shut it out from all the natural diversions of its age ; and in her
own pure, self-denying gentleness of nature, she gave up even this last
treasured possession, to the promotion of her child's gratification. In
putting it on and off her baby finger, Imogen had once risked losing it ;
and to prevent this, as well as that her child might have it at hand, whenever her fancy chose to make it a plaything, Guendolen fastened it
securely by a string round the little one's neck, and consoled herself for
her sacrifice, by the sight of her child's pleasure.

Meanwhile, with creeping time, came no diminution of her heart's thirst
to behold her husband. It ever grew more feverishly, and more imperatively, until it seemed to prey upon her like an inward fire, drying up and
consuming her very life-blood.

Rumours of the king's being again engaged in war, reached her, by means
of a wandering mendicant, who had asked a draught of water one evening
at the forest lodge.

Cymbeline had never rested until he had succeeded in re-opening former hostilities between himself and the king of the Coritani; so that without having to avow the secret cause of his hatred, he might have an opportunity of revenging the wrongs he conceived had been .perpetrated. The engagement was a desperate one; many officers of rank had fallen; and hundreds of men on either side had been left mortally wounded, dead, or dying on the field. In the course of the battle, Cymbeline had obtained his sanguinary wish. He had met the young chief of the Coritani hand to hand; and had slain him on the spot.

In double joy at the victory to his arms and the consummation of his revenge, Cymbeline resolved to celebrate this conquest with especial splendour and rejoicing. He appointed a day,—sufficiently deferred to allow of adequate preparation,—for the meeting of his nobles and people, and for the attendance of the sacrificial priests who were to give sanction and importance to the ceremonial by their august presence, and by the performance of their imposing rites. Among the sports devised for the occasion, there were to be gladiatorial exhibitions, and human encounters with wild beasts, after the manner of the Romans, as Cymbeline had witnessed, when a young man, at the Imperial court. An arena was being enclosed for the purpose, by means of felled trees, and firmly-driven stakes, near to the temple of Jupiter, in Lud's town, where the celebration was decreed to take place.

All this, Guendolen learned of the mendicant traveller; who gossiped of his own accord, while he rested, and took the refreshment, which she could not refuse to his need.

" Tis very well for the conquerors to rejoice,—those few miserable survivors,—to make merry, and offer thanks to the gods, and laud themselves, and cry ' well done'! as though a grand and happy deed had been performed. But methinks, 'twould be better after the mournful necessity of a battle is over, were men to devote their thoughts to succouring those wretched beings, widowed and orphaned by the dire event, and to repairing those unavoidable mischiefs that follow in the train of war; instead of indulging in senseless and wicked rejoicings, and in blood-polluted thanksgivings that would offend an earthly king tender of his human brethren, yet are supposed to be acceptable in the nostrils of the gods who have the care of human-kind. Here are these rejoicings appointed, and

for men who call themselves brave, true-hearted Britons, while hundreds
of their fellow-creatures are languishing from the effects of their act. Not
only are scores of wounded still lying uncured, perishing by inches; not
only are their wretched relatives, and those of the already dead, cast into
affliction and mourning; but pestilence is spreading through the land from
the heaps of unburied carcases left upon the field, and famine is following the
destruction of the many who should have been gathering in the harvest,
instead of mowing down their fellow men. Well-a-day! I am old, and
feeble, and mayhap foolish ; and moreover, having been naught all my life
but a poor herdsman, never been bred a soldier, know nothing of the mysterious so-said sweet taste of glory. Thus, I cannot but wonder to see men
make such strange perverted use of life, and energy ; and then after all to
plume themselves on their sad mistakes !"

Guendolen had heard no word of the old man's muttered reflections ; all
her thoughts were engrossed by the tidings he had first spoken.

Long after he had wandered on, and departed, she revolved what he had
told concerning the appointed royal celebration and public triumph. The
idea, that here was an opportunity of beholding her husband, of looking
upon him unsuspected, undistinguished amongst this vast assemblage, of
seeing him, herself unseen, had suddenly come upon her. It recurred
again and again ; haunted her ; took possession of her imagination, as a
thing possible, feasible, within her power to accomplish. Next came the
question, should she attempt it ? Had she not tacitly agreed to observe
her husband's will, which had decreed this spot as her perpetual prison ?
Should she break the spirit of their mutual compact, by leaving the lodge,
to go look upon his face, who had vowed never more to behold her ? In
the very bitterness of the recollection of those cruel words, she found
strength to resolve upon for once acting on her own responsibility :—
"I ask him not to break his determination. He need not see this poor
offending face and form,—but I feel that I die, if I see not his ; and look
pon them I will, e'en though I die the next succeeding moment." With
this sole wilful decision of her whole life, whispered to her heart in its
desperate agony, Guendolen took her child in her arms, and set forth upon
her pilgrimage that same day.

Painfully, on foot, now resting by the way, now toiling onwards, through fens, and woods, and across bleak, open commons, now by uncleared copses and coverts, now by wide, swampy wastes, anon, by a few straggling huts, and again by rougher and opener ground, did this gentle lady perform her tedious journey ; lifting her little one up, and bearing her slowly forward, when Imogen's slender strength failed her, and she grew too weary to walk by her side. At length the whole tedious distance was surmounted ; and the mother and child, on the very eve of the celebration, entered the eastern gate of Lud's town. In a house of the humblest description, Guendolen obtained a night's shelter and food, of a charitable widow, who, standing at her porch, and seeing the spent condition of the wayfarer, as she passed, with her child in her arms, asked her under her poor roof, with kindly earnestness, little thinking who she was harbouring.

The sadness and dejection of the mother, together with her sweet voice, and mild manners, won upon the tender heart of the widow, while the innocent beauty of the young Imogen, completed the interest she felt for the two wanderers. She bathed Guendolen's toil-worn feet, she made her rest in her own bed, she warmed a wholesome mess of pottage for her and her child, and watched them eating it, with words of simple, cheerful sympathy. She could not have waited on the gentle queen with more cordial zeal, or ministered to the child's comfort with kindlier earnestness, had she known the rank of her guests ; nay, it is not unlikely that the flutter of receiving the queen of Britain, and the infant princess-royal, might have rather impeded than aided her hospitable care.

Next morning,—shrouded in her long, dark garments, and her face completely concealed by the sagum, or cloak, then usually worn, which could be drawn at will over the head, as well as shoulders,—Guendolen, with her child in her arms, took her station among the crowd that thronged the arena ; and by degrees, made her way close to where the king and his court were to be seated.

It chanced, that while the crowd were awaiting the coming forth of the king from the temple, the press increased so much, that Guendolen, alarmed for the safety of her child, crouched near to one of the guards, who was keeping the limits of the space appointed for the reception of the royal party ; and the man, noting her distress, and struck with the beauty of the

child, favored them a little by hedging them in, and contriving to afford
them the shelter of his brawny person, saying, as he did so :—" What
a plague made you bring that pretty bantling hither, mistress, into all this
bustle and hubbub ? But since you're here, and going back's as dangerous
as staying, e'en stand where you are for a bit ; and when you see the royal
train coming, just creep in here, under my arm, and sit ye down snug and
close, and nobody'll be a bit the wiser, and pretty moppet there'll be safe."

She followed the man's directions to the letter ; and amidst the stir, and
swell, and heaving of the crowd, and the roar of its acclamations, and the
general turmoil and confusion, she found herself seated within a few paces
of him, whom she had come to look upon. The moment her eyes caught
sight of his face, they fastened upon it ; and from that moment, among all
the multitude, she saw, she heard, but him alone.

The child, tired by the noise, and dust, and glare, sat quietly upon her
lap, leaning against her bosom, half asleep ; so that Guendolen had nothing
to withdraw her thoughts from the object that absorbed her every sense.
She saw him speaking to those around him ; she saw him look haughtily
triumphant ; she saw him wear an aspect of proud consciousness, of assured
conquest and mastery ; and she exulted in his exultation. She watched
his affable words to his courtiers, his approving ones to his officers ; and
she could have envied them. She saw him lay his hand upon the arm of
one of his generals, in the familiarity of address ; and she felt as though she
could have given worlds to be the object of even such a token of intimacy
and good-will. She heard him utter one of his short, sarcastic laughs, that⁻
had now become habitual with him ; and while her wifely, unselfish heart,
rejoiced that he could be gay and happy, the sound involuntarily smote
upon her womanly sensitiveness, with wonder to think he could laugh at
all. And then, gradually, she discerned,—beneath the triumphant look, the
proud aspect, the haughty bearing,—one latent expression of care and inward
thought, that told her all was not so well at ease within, as the surface
seemed to proclaim. The more she gazed, the more conviction grew upon
her that there was much of acted content, of simulated ease and self-command. Nay, she could almost have fancied, as she continued to observe
him, that some subtle sense of her presence, some occult consciousness

of her being so near, beset him, and secretly embarrassed him, through all his apparent self-possession. She could have believed that he was resolving to prove his strength of purpose, in willing thus to wear an exterior calm, and to evince how firmly he was capable of maintaining it. This impression gained upon her, in spite of her reason. She knew how wildly improbable it was that he should suspect her proximity. She was muffled close in her plain, coarse raiment, and sat there crouched and motionless ; and it was impossible that he could have distinguished her. Yet, nevertheless, the more she watched his looks, his manner, the more it seemed to her, that his indifference and unconsciousness were assumed. She knew one of his prevailing prides was to be thought potent in self-command ; and were it as she fancied, he had now an occasion for its perfect display.

Presently a pause in the performances of the arena, gave an interval of conversation and repose to the spectators. There took place a bandying of comment and light talk among the courtiers ; and some change of place ensued ; many stood up, lounged, and rested by an altered attitude. The king, among others, quitted his seat ; and, surrounded by a group of his favorite gentlemen, came nearer towards the spot occupied by the trembling Guendolen. She sat like a statue, perfectly still, clasping her child to her throbbing heart, as her husband approached,—so near at last, that she could almost have touched his robe, as he stood, with his back towards her, still engaged in smiling, easy, gracious speech, with those about him. While her breath seemed suspended, and she could have heard the beating of her pulses, the king talked on.

His voice, so near, and so loud, raised as it was in the animation of gay, free talk, caught the ear of the half-slumbering little one. She lifted her head, listened, looked about, and at last exclaimed :—"I hear papa ! "

Her mother drew her close within the folds of her cloak, and attempted to hush her into silence ; but the child was not to be restrained.

"Don't you hear papa, mama ? " she said, looking up eagerly into Guendolen's face. "He is here ; he is near to us ! " Again she looked forth earnestly; all around her. "See there ! There he is ! Papa ! Papa ! " she exclaimed in a transport of joy, as she recognized his figure, standing at a few paces from them.

But the figure never moved; the back was still turned towards them; the loud, smiling talk was proceeded with, as though nothing had occurred to interrupt it.

"Papa! Papa! Look at us! We are here! Papa! Papa!" again exclaimed the glad clear tones of the child.

And still the unmoved position was maintained; still the ease and self-possession of the king's speech was preserved; and the courtiers, dressing their features in the royal mirror of exampled unconsciousness, took no notice of the young voice, that broke in with such guileless unreserve of claim.

So long as their royal master chose to act perfect ignorance of his wife and child's being there, so long as he chose to exhibit his stoicism of indifference, and sternness of inflexible will, his obsequious train were bound to second him, by affecting to ignore any such presence, even though they saw the outstretched arms, and sweet ingenuous face of Imogen, heard her joyous cries, and guessed at the identity of the muffled figure upon whose knee she sat.

Without a hint that could betray his having heard the voice, or so much as a glance towards the spot where sat the shrouded woman, Cymbeline was about to move away, and return to his former seat; when suddenly, a fearful roar was heard, and through the midst of the press, came ramping a large lion, that had broken loose from one of the dens of the arena, immediately towards the spot where the king stood. In a trice, the flying crowd cleared a space; and right onward sprang the ferocious beast, with wild leaps, mane erect, eyes glaring, and loud, fierce, angry roars.

With that rapidity of thought, and instinctive action, that love alone knows, Guendolen had cast her child into the arms of the nearest person, and thrown herself immediately before her husband. The impulse had been carried into effect with the speed of light. In far less time than it takes to tell it, the wife's body had interposed, and received the whole shock of the animal's assault. Mangled and bleeding she sank upon the earth, while a look of heavenly content irradiated her face. Cries of horror and pity burst forth on all sides; a hundred weapons were turned upon the lion by the rallying crowd, to despatch him; while the whole confused scene swam and receded before the eyes of the dying queen.

Her husband hung over her in a paroxysm of remorseful anguish.

"My wife! My Guendolen! Dear injured patience! Can you forgive me?"

"Have I aught to forgive?" she murmured. "You believed that I deserved your rigour."

"Such belief in itself, was worst injury. Too late, I feel this now;" cried he. "But must it be, indeed, too late? Must I lose thee, noblest, truest, best? Can nothing avail, to save thee from dying for me unworthy?" He wrung his hands in bitter, helpless agony.

"Grieve not for my death, oh most best beloved!" she said, faintly, but happily; "it has been vouchsafed me, to prove that I could not have practised against thy life."

He writhed in self-reproach, and in speechless misery.

"Suddenly, the fast-dimming eyes of the gentle queen re-lumed with an eager expression, and her half-extinct voice revived with the force of mother's affection, as she murmured:—"Our child—for that she is *our* child, I take yon Heaven, whose judgment I soon must meet, to witness,— you will not suffer her to languish, severed from your love? You will take her to your heart as before?"

"Solemnly, as I trust one day to join you there with her, I too, take Heaven to witness that I will henceforth be to her a father in kindness and in love, as surely as I believe myself to be her father in the truth of thy white and spotless faith, mine innocent, injured wife!" he said.

With a smile of more than mortal happiness, Guendolen expired.

The person into whose arms the little Imogen had been hastily placed by her mother, was no other than Posthumus Leonatus. The boy had seen the child, had recognised the shrouded figure in whose lap it sat, and had kept his station close behind them, to watch over their safety, and if possible to gain an opportunity of following them, after the public show was over, and learn where they sojourned, and how they came to be away from their forest retreat. He had thus been at hand to receive the little one, at the moment its mother started up to rush to her husband's side. Imogen,

delighted to find herself with her favorite, had been so happily engaged
recognising him, and prattling to him, that she had escaped the terrible
sight of her mother's death. Her young friend had withdrawn from the
crowd with her, and borne her safely home to the palace ; but too thankful
that he had been able to preserve her from witnessing so fearful a scene.
With innate good feeling and tact he kept the child amused and happy,
until her father should enquire for her.

The king evinced his gratitude for the boy's kindly thought towards his
little daughter, by an increased liking and confidence. He had always
been fond of the lad ; and now he favored him, and took pride in distinguishing him more than ever. He encouraged him in his care and protective liking for the young princess ; and permitted him to be her constant
companion and playfellow. He appointed ladies of known discretion, good
sense, and good temper, for her women-attendants ; surrounded her with all
the appurtenances of her birth and station ; and took every pains to show
that she was reinstated as his beloved daughter, and the acknowledged
heiress of his throne and kingdom.

The conviction of his wife's innocence had struck Cymbeline with indisputable self-evidence in the scene of her death ; the testimony of her
constant love had reached him with affecting force, in the discovery of the
ring, his first gift, fastened about the neck of their child ; and the crowning
proof of her purity and faith, came in the shape of a dying message, from
him who had been her traducer.

Mempricius had taken arms in the service of his sovereign, in the late
expedition against the king of the Coritani. In the heat of the engagement, the false lord had fallen. But in his death hour, the remembrance of
his perfidy hung its heavy weight upon his soul, and made the burthen of
his wounds seem light in the comparison. He whispered his nephew,—
who had accompanied him to the war as his squire and disciple-in-arms,
and was now leaning over him, and tending his hurts,—to hearken his
last words, and bear them faithfully and literally to the king.

" Tell his majesty," said the dying courtier, " that she whom I maligned,
is innocent ; and that her child is lawfully born. He will understand the
truth ; and will recompense thee for bringing it to him, as the most wel-

come news he could hear. You, nephew, will profit more from his favor, by the repetition of these few words, than I have gained by a whole life of lies. Let my speaking honestly at last, expiate!"

The nephew of Mempricius lost no time in hasting to fulfil his uncle's last behest. Leaving one of his officers to perform the last duties towards the remains, he set forth without delay to Cymbeline's court, that he might either overtake the king on his return thither, or arrive there as soon after him as might be. But his eagerness defeated its own object. He fell ill on his way, took the pestilential fever that was then raging, and lay for some time, at the point of death, in the cottage of a poor wood-cutter, whose wife charitably nursed him till he recovered.

It was therefore not until the queen was dead, and her child restored to its father's heart and home, that this last testimony of her unblemished honor reached her husband. But it was welcomed by him as the conclusive proof of her worth ; and he heaped rewards and honors upon him who brought it.

The nephew of Mempricius was named Cloten. His parents were alive ; but he had been brought up by his uncle, for the sake of the advantages, which the latter's position in the court of the king of Britain, afforded. His father was king of the Brigantes ; a tribe, and territory, on the north of the Humber. This father was a feeble-minded, ignorant, sensual man ; given up to the pleasures of the table, and completely under the ascendancy of his wife,—an artful, designing, ambitious woman, of great personal beauty, but of unscrupulous character. She had sent her son to his uncle's care, that his fortunes might be more securely pushed, than they could be in the obscure petty court of his father ; and they had not only hitherto prospered, but the incident of his uncle's death-message, transmitted through himself, had confirmed him in royal favor and state preferment.

He was a swaggering, pretentious young fellow, with about equal shares of vulgar cunning, self-conceit, and obtuseness. His mother's craft, his uncle's wiliness, in him took the shape of a selfish perception of his own interest ; while the ignorance of his animal father, was in him boorish insolence, brutal humour, and a clod-like self-sufficiency, with contempt of others.

The king, not too clear-seeing, thought him good-natured, for all his coarseness ; and frank, because of his bluff bluntness. He had a certain kind of unreserved license of speech and manner about him, which passed with Cymbeline for openness and goodness of disposition ; but which was in fact nothing more than a callous indifference to the feelings of those he addressed, a total blindness to his own deficiencies, and the free-and-easy expression of his likings and dislikings, his inclinations, his aversions, and in short, his opinions, of whatever kind they might chance to be.

Between this young gentleman, Cloten, and the lad, Bergion, there was a perpetual word-sparring going forward. Each enjoying the favor of the king, the one as a rising courtier, the other as a sort of privileged page-jester, they were frequently in collision and encounter. There was not more dissimilarity in their persons, than in their several natures. While the tall, brawny proportions of the Northern youth, strikingly contrasted with the lithe, spare figure of the young Cambrian, their minds and words were equally at variance.

As the boy, Posthumus Leonatus, advanced in years, and became more of a companionable age with the two others, he often amused himself by noting the instinctive antipathy, and constant war of speech that went on between them ; and took pleasure in drawing them out.

"Yonder servile lackey-lord," said Bergion, nodding contemptuously towards a young courtier, who had been enquiring after Cloten, and hurried away to seek him, "makes a god of this insolent boor ; who repays him by making a dishclout of him,—wipes up his filth with him, and then chucks away the clout. When this fellow hath served Cloten's turn, he treats him like reptiles' excrement. But, in sooth he deserves no better that can cringe to such a thing as Cloten."

"Thou hast no liking for my lord Cloten ?" said Posthumus, smiling.

"What is there to like in him ? Hath he not an ugly, morphewed nature ; all distorted and crusted with self-conceit ? Is he not a burly bully, ever vapouring, and talking big, and doing battle with shadows of his own creating ? Hath he not a malignant tongue ; a ribald contempt for good ? Is he not hebete, and dull of brain ? Doth he not swear, when he is at a loss for words ; and heap abuse, when he cannot find retort? What he lacks in wit and argument, he makes up in bluster, and violence of gesture. He lays down the law, like a man sowing broad-cast; and when he would carry a point, he flings about him like a thrasher."

" 'Tis a fair picture of my gentleman, indeed;" laughed Posthumus.

Just then, in came Cloten, fretting and fuming, blurting out his words by fits and starts, as was his wont.

"Paltry, scurvy fellow!" he exclaimed; "I won't abuse my sword, by crossing it with him. But I'll use it to fustigate him, as with a cudgel."

"Hath some one offended your lordship?" asked Posthumus.

"Yonder slavish scoundrel dared to reason with me, and oppose what I had to say;" replied Cloten.

"A superabundant folly in him!" said Posthumus.

"But such resistance rather whets than damps the flame of my courage, I can promise him;" said Cloten.

"Let him beware he wet it not, to its extinguishing;" said Bergion; whose singularly beautiful voice, against the harsh, abrupt one of Cloten, formed yet another contrast, between the two.

"Art thou there?" said Cloten, looking over his shoulder, at the lad, who sat quietly in a corner, twisting his hazel-switch into various forms of coil and circle. "But know, that my bravery is beyond suspicion. A man that hath done what I have, need fight no more to prove his valour. Certain feats achieved, as they have been, methinks I have done enough."

"Done enough! No man hath done enough, until he have done the last thing he can do,—died;" said Bergion.

"A marvellous silly elench! And altogether worthless sophism!" cried Cloten.

"And when do you propose to punish this offending lord?" asked Posthumus.

"Forthwith,—immediately,—this very afternoon;" answered Cloten. "No time like the present."

"Save the past and future, which are wonderfully semblant with it;" said Bergion drily.

"I know thou liv'st altogether in the past, like a poor dreaming losel as thou art. Thou content'st thyself with the deeds of thy Cambrian ancestry,

in lieu of valour of thine own.   Thine only courage is intrepidity of belief;
gravely crediting the feats of the cow, Camdoga, who filled all the
dairy-pans in thy native mountains, in one night;" said Cloten, with a
horse-laugh.

It was a favorite amusement with him, to taunt the lad with his Welsh
origin, and to scoff at the legends of his country.

"For me, I'm neither soldier, nor civilian;" said Bergion quietly;
"your lordship's a military man, therefore I can't expect you to be civil."

"A civilian, quoth'a?   Thou'rt scarce civilized, fellow.   A half-re-
claimed savage; barely better than a brute,—untamed, untaught, save in
those foolish traditions and tales, flogged into thee by thy masters, the
Druids.   Do I not know that thou'rt only learned in fables, wise in
figments?"

"Well if a man be learned and wise in aught; even in the holding of
his tongue, and refraining from empty or scurril talk;" replied Bergion.

"Pshaw; I know that thy bravest maxims have been no better than such
as thine old Cymry proverb, 'Pawb wrth gynffon ei henfon;' in plain
parlance, 'Let each betake himself to the tail of his cow;" Cloten went on.

"A goodly saying, truly, and a safe!"

"As safe confiding in his cow's tail, as in his calf's tongue;" returned
Bergion.

"I know 'tis flat heresy to laugh at thy worshipful Cambrian sayings,
and thy Druids' stories.   To doubt, is as hateful in Druid faith, as hen,
hare, goose, or fish, to Druid scruple.   But come, if thou'rt as cool as thou
wouldst fain have me believe, under the lash of my wit, tell us some
of these same Cymry legends."

"Whom does your lordship mean by 'us?'" asked Bergion.   "Doth
the young prince of the Brigantes already affect the royal style, ere his
father be dead?"

"'Us' may signify Posthumus Leonatus, and myself, to play audience
to thy fantastic leasings;" replied Cloten.

"Hast thou any wish to hear them?" said Bergion, quietly, turning to
Posthumus.

"I would gladly hear some of thy quaint histories, good Bergion;"
answered he.

"And a man may do worse, than store his memory with the high actions of those who have gone before him;" returned Bergion, with the thoughtful look settling upon his face, that it usually wore, when he spoke upon such themes. "They teach him how he should himself act and live, so as to earn self-respect; and to command, or at all events, deserve, both good-will and honor from his fellow-men. Where is the idleness of learning to reverence Hu the mighty, who came from those sunny lands of the South, called by our bards 'the Summer country;' and settled in our water-guarded island; and became famous for making Poesy the vehicle of Memory and Record? Wherefore should we not feed our fancy by hearing of Gwrgant Grim-beard, whose squadron encountered a tower of glass, in the midst of the Irish seas, and all but one vessel rashly attacking it, perished; while the king's ship, bearing on board sagacity, caution, and experience, warily surmised it to be an iceberg floated down from the remote Northern ocean; and so steering clear, avoided destruction? And may we not be the better for musing of Hyfaidd, the tall, whose deeds were applauded by men, and blessed by Heaven?"

"If he were so tall a man, would he were alive, that I might lower some of his lofty pride, and abate somewhat of his giant might;" said Cloten. "I cannot abide to hear of fellows of such towering pretensions, without a desire to bring them down from their presumed height."

"To level them to an equality of baseness with those who envy them?" replied Bergion; then turning to Posthumus again, he continued :— "Surely, 'tis a pregnant lesson, to ponder on the doings of Bladud; how he discovered med'cinable waters in a certain spot in the West; and built a town and temple there, consecrating them to Minerva; and how, afterwards, growing rash in conceit of his own powers of invention, he made him wings to fly; which upbore him but just above the height of the temple, whereon he fell, and was killed. And we may find worse study, than the memory and example of Dunwallo Mulmutius, great and good, worthy first to wear a golden crown; who framed wise laws, promoted the welfare and protection of his subjects, and, in memory of peace restored, built the temple of Concord, within our goodly city of Lud's Town, erst called Trinovant. Then, for those who have neither kingly ambition, nor kingly power to enact kingly deeds, there are the fames of such men as

Idris, the far-eyed, Gwydion, the son of Don, and Gwyn, the son of Nudd, the three sagest astronomers in Britain; whose knowledge of the stars and their influences was so great, that,—as our Bards have sung,—it were to be wished it could have been preserved till the day of doom. But," added Bergion, with the wild light gleaming from his eyes, "'tis the only drawback I find in the godlike gift of knowledge; that it cannot be bequeathed. A man stores up sumless treasures of learning and science in his own mind, but he cannot transmit them to his posterity. They perish with their storehouse, his brain; they rot and are buried, with the carcase wherein they were hatched."

"As such mouldy, maggotty rubbish should be!" exclaimed Cloten.

"Since they cannot be willed after a man's decease, with the rest of his valuables," said Posthumus to Bergion, "it behoves every one so gifted, to impart as much of them to his fellow-man, while he himself lives, as may be. And when the art of writing shall encrease, men will be better able, both to acquire and to diffuse learning."

"Let me but note my will with my sword, I care not for knowing how to do more than note my name by a mark;" cried Cloten, with his overbearing laugh.

"Writing is a glorious science!" said Bergion. "Yet at best, it is but a limited means for the soaring range that thought might take, in its conception and in its extension. Methinks I would have knowledge command a power of spreading and multiplying itself over all the universal mind of man, when once it hath been engendered in a single human brain. What if, in after ages, men should discover some mystic art that should communicate thought as widely and as beneficently as the very air itself, spanning the habitable earth?"

"Here is a brainsick madman that would fain blow a bubble big as the globe!" exclaimed Cloten.

"And here is a prince content to pen his brains within the compass of a millet-grain!" said Bergion. "Meekest and humblest of princes!"

"Taunt not me, thou son of a sainted,—or rather, tainted,—vestal!" cried Cloten.

In one second, Bergion sprang upon the burly braggart, caught him by the throat, and, for all his superior bulk and weight, shook him to and fro like a reed. The young savage was agile of limb, strong of sinew, and possessed of a grasp like a vice, for all his slight make; and moreover his spirit when roused, was fierce as a wild beast's. The scoff at his mother, had done what no insolence to himself could effect; it had stung him into resentment.

Leonatus stepped forward to interfere, and make peace; but Bergion, having slaked his rage by treating Cloten as a mastiff might have used a mongrel cur, loosed his hold, flung him off, and walked leisurely away.

"White-livered rascal!" exclaimed Cloten, looking after him; "he knows, that for the sake of my lord the king, who favors him, I shall not disgrace the royal precincts by a stir, and a quarrel, and a contention. He takes advantage of his jester's privilege to attack me, knowing it would be beneath the dignity of my weapon to challenge such a peasant slave and churl as he!"

"You do well and wisely to forbear him, my lord;" said Posthumus.

"Ay, I think so; but let him beware how he overtaxes my magnanimity;" said Cloten.

"He will not tempt it too largely; he hath a due sense of its extent;" answered Posthumus.

"He's a coward, and a traitor both! A poltroon, a dastardly sneak and villain!" exclaimed Cloten. "But I take care not to trust him too far with my mind."

"You do right still, my lord;" replied Posthumus. "Yet after all, 'twould be no such vast risk, considering the object."

"Nay, I fear not risk; but I dread compromise."

"Of yourself? Or of your principles?" asked Posthumus, quietly.

"I dread compromising the good-will and favor I enjoy with his majesty;" returned Cloten. "I would not have my devotion and fidelity brought in question, by the misrepresentations of such an artful, pitiful knave as yonder Bergion."

"Take no thought of him, my lord;" answered Posthumus. "He hath no malice; he hath already forgotten all cause of anger between you, believe it well."

"Well, for this time, I forgive the varlet;" said Cloten.

Meanwhile, the young princess grew in intelligence and beauty. She was of an affectionate disposition, capable of strong preferences, and stead-fast attachments. Her nature was both loving, and constant; and even during her childish years, it manifested itself in singular warmth and energy of denotement. Although she had lost her mother when still so mere an infant, she had felt the bereavement more sensibly than is usual at such an early age. But she had transferred the chief strength of the affection she had borne her mother, to her young companion, Leonatus, who had been early associated in her mind with that mother; and who had since, by his boyish assiduity, and tenderness of care towards herself, won her dearest liking.

While she was yet quite a little girl, her father made her and her young companion, a present of a gold piece each, as a keepsake, and rare gift. Cymbeline, from his early connection with the Romans, had introduced the art of coining into his kingdom of Britain; and two of the first coins struck, were those which he gave to his little daughter, and his favorite, young Posthumus Leonatus. They were much prized by the children; not only for their rarity and beauty, but for their bearing a head of the king himself, encircled by his fillet of pearls, and by his name.

Once, it chanced, that as her royal father was playing with her on his knee, and fondling her, and admiring his little girl's beauty, while he was pretending to notice her dress, and asking her about its fashion and stuff, and promising her some new girdle, or other ornament, that should be likely to please her childish fancy, she began to tell him with great glee about a certain pocket, that her lady-attendants had had put into her last new garment. She was evidently very proud of this lately-acquired curiosity, and she kept extolling its usefulness, and vaunting its many excellences to her playfellow father.

He, humouring her, affected great interest in this pocket; and began guessing what she had in it, and begging for a peep, and enumerating its probable contents.

" Come hither, Posthumus, and help me to guess! " said the father. " I'll wager now," continued he, " I hit upon the very first thing you've got in this wonderful pocket. I remember telling you, when I gave it you, to keep safely, and always about you, the gold piece with your father's picture graven on it. I know my little Imogen's loving heart too well, not to believe that she hath ever done so. Is't not so? Thou hast it about thee now. Hast thou not? In this very pocket?"

At first the child's face had worn a delighted, triumphant expression; but gradually it grew graver, and thoughtfuller; and the smile with which she had looked into her father's face, subsided, and the playful hold she had kept over the opening of her pocket, tightened with a firm clutch.

"Come, let me have a peep;" her father continued, not noting her change of countenance and manner; "I know thou hast it about thee, hast thou not? Come, let me look into the pocket, aud see it snugly lying there."

But Imogen drew back, and guarded the opening of her pocket from his advances.

"So, so! Thou dread'st my discovering that thou hast not so fond a regard for my gold portrait, or so strict a care of it, as I supposed;" said Cymbeline, laughing. "But never fear! I shall not be angered, even should thou not have it there. I love my little girl too well to chide her, for even a grosser piece of thoughtlessness than this. One, of her childish years, may well be allowed a little giddiness and forgetfulness. Let's speak no more of it."

Just then, one of the king's pages coming in to announce that his council board had assembled, and awaited his commands, Cymbeline kissed his daughter's forehead, set her down, and left the room, saying he should come soon, and spend another hour with her, when state affairs would give him leisure.

"I thought I saw your highness put the gold coin in your pocket, not long since;" said Imogen's chief lady; who was both friend and instructress to the young princess; and who had narrowly watched the whole scene between the little girl and her father.

"Yes; I did;" said Imogen. "It is there now."

"Then why, when his majesty asked to see it, did you not say so? Why did you let him think you had it not about you? If it were not for his indulgence, and leniency, he might have thought you wanting in affection, so to slight his gift,—and moreover, his picture."

" I did not slight it; I had it safe; I always keep it near me;" answered Imogen.

" Then why should you let him suppose otherwise?" persisted the lady.

" I should be sorry, if he thought I did not prize it, as I do, very dearly;" said Imogen.

"Then why not show him that you had it at this very time, about you?" said the lady.

" If I had shown him my gold piece, he would have next asked to see Leonatus's;" answered Imogen.

" Well?" said the lady; "what then?"

" I do not think Leonatus has his about him; and if my father had found out that, he might have been displeased with him;" said Imogen. " Therefore I risked letting him suppose I had not mine, knowing that I had it, rather than let him ask Posthumus for his, when I believed that he had it not. It was better to be fancied neglectful, when I was really careful; than for him to be discovered in want of thought, that might have been taken seriously amiss."

As she grew into womanhood, Imogen's peculiar characteristics strengthened. In her nature were combined the inherited elements of both her parents' dispositions; but modified, and elevated, into finer qualities. In her, her mother's passive timidity became gentleness,— resignation, with spiritual fortitude,—brave, uncomplaining endurance; while her father's wilfulness, and obstinacy, took the shape of steadfastness, constancy, and moral courage. The concomitants of each, formed a certain quiet energy,—the perfection of a womanly, an English womanly character.

His daughter's beauty of face, and symmetry of form, together with the expression of the one, and the grace of the other, had informed her father somewhat of her sweet perfection; but it was not in the nature of such a character as his to estimate the full excellence of hers. He could perceive that she was unrivalled in person; but he had little idea of the consummate charm of her moral being. He knew he possessed a treasure of beauty and goodness; a daughter worthy to be his heiress and successor; but even he, in all the proud delight he took in her, knew not the whole hidden worth of this virgin soul,—lustrously white in purity and innocence, radiantly bright in virtue, charity, and loving faith.

She was so genuinely modest, so essentially true,—contented ever to be, rather than to seem, that few superficial observers could have properly estimated her supreme merits. But even the least discriminating, could perceive that in all external graces the princess Imogen was preeminent among her sex. She had a graciousness of aspect, and a gentle benignity of manner, the most winning. The tone of her voice, was music, in itself; and her speech breathed candour, and kindness, in one.

Among Cymbeline's Gaulish connections, was one, who had been more than commonly allied in acquaintance with him, in former years. This was a chief of the tribe of the Averni, a man of bold and aspiring disposition; and possessed of considerable repute for sagacity and skill in policy. He had an only daughter, about Imogen's age; and he proposed to his old associate, that in their children should be renewed the friendship which had at one time subsisted between themselves. To this end, he invited Cymbeline's daughter to his court; and when this was declined, on the plea that the British king could not part with her for so long a period as this visit would occupy, the prince of the Averni proposed that his own daughter should come over to the British court, and spend some time with a princess of whom he had heard the most advantageous reports. Cymbeline, unable farther to refuse amicable advances so urged, returned a courteous assent; and despatched a band of chosen gentlemen from his own court, to escort the French princess to Britain. At the head of this convoy of honor, the king appointed Posthumus Leonatus, as a young man of birth and breeding, one near to his person in favor and consideration, and one in whom he could confide for the scrupulous fulfilment of his every wish. He instructed him to show especial attention to the princess; to devote himself entirely to her person; to make it his peculiar duty to protect and watch over her safety; and charged him to omit no opportunity of pleasing her, of propitiating her good-will, and of winning as much as possible her confidence and trust.

Upon the princess's arrival, these instructions were renewed. The king impressed upon Posthumus his desire that no pains should be omitted to evince respect, and honoring care, towards their distinguished guest. That in order to ensure this, he deputed him her knight, her especial champion and protector, the constant attendant and guardian of her person, so long as she should remain in Britain. That he should address himself to obtain her esteem and liking, to the end that she might feel safely and confidingly at ease, during her sojourn in a foreign court. That in short, he was to do all in his power, to make the princess's stay among them pleasant to herself, and agreeable to her father, so as to render the relations between the two courts more than ever amicable.

Posthumus Leonatus, bound both in gratitude and affection towards his royal master, promised to second to the utmost of his power, Cymbeline's views ; and undertook the delicate charge entrusted to him, with zeal and perfect good faith.

Cymbeline, true to his character of weakly distrustful, and selfishly reserved, did not reveal to his agent all the motives, or all the intentions, he had in the matter which he wished effected through his means. He did not tell Posthumus that through all his courtesy and hospitality, there lurked self-defence. He did not tell him, that beneath all the professed amity and outward cordiality there were suspicion and dread. He did not say, that unwilling to show open dislike of the Gaulish prince's proffer, he had acceded to it, determining to take such precautionary measures, as should defeat the surmised object. He did not mention that he thought the French princess's visit to the British court was a mere pretext of her politic father's, for sending an unsuspected spy thither. Cymbeline thought it far better to make of his own young friend and favorite an unconscious spy in return, upon her and her actions; instead of showing an unwillingness to receive her, or betraying any part of his scheme to him who was to carry it out. He contented himself with setting Leonatus to play the part, without unveiling to him any of the features of its office, which might deter him from undertaking it, or from enacting it with spirit and effect.

The princess Eponine was handsome, gay, and vain. She was accustomed to a profusion of compliment, of gallant adulation and observance; she both expected and encouraged it, from all who came near her. She had lively, off-hand manners, and seemed even more thoughtless and frivolous than she was. She won general liking, for she was good-humoured, and accessible; and seemed pleased with everything and every body that approached her. She had a laugh for all that was said, a smile for each that spoke.

" Thou seem'st not to share the general admiration for this lady guest of our king's ; " said Posthumus to Bergion, one evening, when the two princesses had retired to their several apartments, after a gay, unwearied chat had been maintained by the foreigner amidst a circle of gentlemen, who had formed a little court about her ; " thou kept'st aloof the whole time, lounging in this window-seat ; never once unbending thy brow to all her playful sallies, or yielding to her manifest condescension, when she would have included thee among her hearers."

" Mine ears were otherwise employed than listening to a lady's prattle, alluring as it might be ; " returned Bergion. " I was hearkening the caw of yonder rooks, in the high trees that tower above the palace roof. They told me many an odd tale of busy home-toil and parent care for nestlings ; and of sly pilferings, and loud squabbles with their neighbours for twigs and straws."

" 'Tis the churl's jealousy, which affects a liking for croaking crows rather than admire this brilliant, French fairy, whose sprightly talk will soon eclipse his dull jests and dreaming wit ; " sneered Cloten, as he turned away.

" Tell me what in truth thou think'st of her ; " pursued Leonatus, to Bergion, when Cloten was gone. For there was a fund of shrewdness, and quiet perspicacity, beneath the wild, restless mood, and gleaming look of the lad, that would now and then utter itself in dry, quaint observations, which Leonatus liked to draw forth.

" I think that for all her noble descent, she is more bright than noble ; and for all her honorable lineage, she is more accomplished than honorable. Her cleverness is adroitness ; her gaity, part trifling, part trick."

" Bright, accomplished, gay, clever ! Summed up, the attributes thou accord'st her, should form a tolerable encomium ; " said Posthumus. " Yet withal, thou seem'st not cordially to admire."

" Nor do I. This French lady is not wisely clever, but cunningly

VOL. III.   2 H

clever, as I interpret her. And Cunning is but a left-handed, bastard kind
of Wisdom. In the misbegotten imp, the sire's straight, clear eye, is
turned to a shortsighted squint. He hath but a trick of his father's favor ;
while he's all over ugly, like his mother—Selfishness."

" But this fair princess ; I cannot think she is other than the sportive,
guileless creature she seems ; " said Posthumus. " I am her knight, thou
know'st, and bound to defend her against foul aspersion,—even against
unhandsome inference."

"Being a descendant, as she is, of that brave and noble Vercingetorix,—
who led his countrymen against the usurping Roman ; who held him at
bay, and stoutly resisted him, until even the proud Cæsar, in that lordly
book he wrote, recording his own deeds in Gaul, was fain to confess himself baffled and perplexed by his patriot perseverence,—she should be
right noble, and virtuous, and true. But in despite of her lineage, I cannot help suspecting that this French princess hath an appetite for intrigue,
a turn for dissembling and double-dealing. Above all, I like not to see her
in too close intimacy with our white-souled lady, the British princess,
Imogen."

Leonatus, who had before questioned the lad, half in idleness, and for
the mere entertainment of a passing moment, grew earnest and interested.

" Dost thou mean that this Gaulish visit portends ill to our sovereign
lady, the king's daughter ? " he asked warmly.

" I have no farther guide than mine own wild fancy ; " said Bergion,
seeing that he had succeeded in awakening Posthumus's solicitude. " All
I have to say, is, thou art nearest in vigilance to both the ladies. Be it
your care to see that no evil befall our own Island treasure, from this fair-
seeming guest. Her father speaks of old friendship between himself and
our king ; but that warmth hath had time to grow cold ; and a cooled friend
is your hottest enemy. The daughter professes dearest liking for our
royal lady ; but professions are oft but shadows of the substances they
represent. Be watchful that they darken not, nor endanger not, the path of
our clear star."

" The thought of her, shall keep me wary and watchful ; " said Leonatus,
grasping Bergion's hand as they parted.

The princess Eponine was extremely proud of her appointed knight, Posthumus Leonatus. He was by far the handsomest and most accomplished man of all Cymbeline's court; he carried away the palm in all personal feats of skill ; such as mastery in fence, and dexterity in athletic games, where command of limb, grace, and agile ease, were requisite ; and beyond this, he was intellectually endowed, and by education refined, to an unusual degree for those times. His royal benefactor had taken a pride in supplying him with those opportunities of mental culture whereby he so well profited, and did such high credit to him who had in a manner adopted him.

The young knight was no less preeminent in manly gifts, than in manly beauty ; and the French princess was peculiarly flattered by having this gentleman, of all the British court, selected for her especial guardian and protector. She seemed never better pleased than when she could exhibit him in this light,—proclaim her right to his services, enlist them in her behalf, and manifest at once her power over him, and her approval of him.

In one of the sprightly conversations that were now perpetually taking place among the courtiers in presence of the two princesses, since the advent of the lively French guest, who by her own untiring gaiety set the example, and elicited it from others, there arose an eager dispute, whether Gaul or Britain had produced the greater number of eulogists of their several native lands ; which country the better merited eulogy, contained the larger subject for it, and afforded truer and nobler themes of glorious desert. The debate was warmly maintained on either side ; and voices grew high in verbal warfare, each one advancing some strengthening evidence, or some conclusive argument in favor of the cause they espoused. At length it was agreed that a day should be fixed for the ultimate settlement of the question ; which was to be proved by the preponderating written evidence that could be collected in the meantime, by each of the fair champions, who were to represent their several nations ; Imogen, her island Britain ; Eponine, her bright France.

The two princesses had no sooner acceded to this compact, than Eponine turned to Posthumus Leonatus :—" I engage your aid, my faithful knight, expressly on my behalf. I have a host of verses in my memory, that only want reducing in battle array upon paper. I know your renown as a scribe ; you shall be the generalissimo of my forces, and muster them for me, so as to ensure victory. And you, and you, and you ; " she added turning to some gentleman of her train, whom she knew skilled in the then rare accomplishment of writing. " I shall want you all, for the next intervening space of time, solely and wholly devoted to my pleasure, to transcribe whatsoever my own recollection, and your own, can supply to do fitting honor to our fair Gallia ! "

Cloten, and some other of the British courtiers, lounged away as unconcernedly as they could, from the scene of discussion ; while the one or two who were left, offered their services to the princess Imogen, who accepted them with her own gracious smile, saying :—" I will add mine own slender help ; and we will do our best, my lords, for the glory of Britain."

" If your highness would grace my poor endeavour, by allowing it a place among those of your scribes," said Bergion, "it might assist the good cause. Though I have no ready pen, yet my memory is not ill stuffed with odd scraps of verse, which might serve to swell the heap in due laudation of our own white-rocked isle."

" Nay, if thou afford'st me thy help, good fellow, 'tis a host in itself. I know, thy bringing-up furnished thee with store of such poetic lore ; and with this, our side is sure of victory."

" Not so sure ! " exclaimed the French princess. " I have made up my mind to win ; and win, I must, and shall ! This bright carnation for him who enables me to gain the day ! " she added, pointing to a cluster of those flowers that stood in a vase, near ; " carnation is mine own especial color ; and he shall wear it as a favor, whose pen wins for me ! "

" And this white rose shall be the meed of him who shall conquer for Britain ! " said Imogen, looking kindly at Bergion. The combatants set to in earnest. Tables were ranged, scrolls were spread, and hour after hour, nothing was seen or heard but busy tongues, and busy pens, quoting and noting, citing and inscribing. On the evening of the first day, however, the French princess declared that there was too much confusion, for much to be achieved by this mode of progress; she therefore withdrew her troop of gentlemen scribes into the quiet of her own range of apartments, declaring that they should not stir from thence, till the appointed period of trial.

Eponine had a secret motive for this arrangement; she feared that Posthumus Leonatus, from his natural leaning towards the British cause, might lend the aid of his pen to transcribe the verses supplied by Bergion. She saw the importance attached to this supply by the British party; and her chief hope rested in the tardiness with which the lad could write them down, to counterbalance the advantage from the number he could cite.

While Leonatus, therefore, was immediately beneath her own eye, together with the rest of those she had enlisted in her service, she felt better secure; and she bound them all by a playful oath, to devote themselves entirely to her dictation for the following three days.

The destined one arrived. The two princesses, and their respective allies met in the presence of the king; who had entered into the spirit of this match between his daughter and her young guest in support of the fame of their several native lands. He had been appointed umpire on the occasion; and prepared to give his decision with all the gravity and impartiality which so important a case demanded.

The mere first aspect of the written papers brought forward, gave the princess Eponine a forboding of triumph; and she gaily clapped her hands as she saw the pile produced on her own side. But on farther inspection, it proved that the preponderance of bulk was mainly in appearance; for Imogen's hand being small and neat, and she having supplied by far the larger quantity on the British side, while, on the contrary, most of the French gentlemen and Posthumus had written in a bold, free hand, the number of verses in the honor of Britain were not so inferior in number, really, as they seemed.

Still, on comparing them, they were found fewer; and Cymbeline was about to give judgment in favor of France, when Bergion stepped forward, bent his knee to Imogen, and delivered to her several additional scrolls. She opened them with a look of surprise; then smiled, and handed them to her father.

"They are higher testimonies than aught yet, in honor of our island realm;" said the king, as he looked into them; "and their number assigns the victory to Britain. Daughter, the white rose is fairly due to Bergion."

Imogen took the flower from the hands of one of her ladies who held it ready; and bestowed it upon the lad, as he stood there, in his usual quiet way.

He received it with a natural, simple grace. But, taking off one of the snowy petals, and putting it reverently to his lips, and then into his bosom, he placed the rose itself in the hands of Posthumus, saying :— "To him, of right, belongs the British prize! He penned down the verses; not I."

"'Tis the hand of Leonatus, indeed;" said the king.

"I engaged you as my scribe! You are my knight! I bound you to write for no other, during three days!" exclaimed the French princess vehemently.

"Your grace bound me for three days; but there was no mention of nights!" returned Posthumus, smiling. "I worked at night for mine own white rose of Britain; by day, as in duty bound, for your highness."

"Fairly caught, I own!" she replied. "But your good pen won for Gaul the chief portion of her chance of victory. To you, therefore, is the carnation justly due. But it shall be in more enduring form than a perishable blossom;" added she, taking the bright scarf she wore, from her shoulders, and knotting it round his left arm. "I hereby invest my faithful knight with mine own colors, and bid him wear them in honor of Gaul and myself."

As Leonatus knelt to receive the French princess's favor, and raised her hand chivalrously to his lips, Cymbeline gaily applauded her for the grace and good-humour with which she had borne her defeat, or rather turned it into a triumph :—"The hero of the verse-conquest, shall rank above the king to-day;" he went on. "Leonatus shall lead your highness to the banquet, while I give mine arm to my daughter. It is fitting, that he who won the victory to Britain, should enjoy even higher privilege than her monarch."

Eponine, always lively and talkative, had never been in gayer spirits.

She rattled on in a ceaseless strain of smiling nothings, that passed well enough for conversation, uttered by such lips, and illustrated by such eyes. She seemed brilliant in speech, for she was brilliant in look; and she had never commanded more general admiration. But the one whose attention she most desired to attract, was the least apparently influenced. He was courteous in listening, assiduous in answering, when she directly called upon him; but otherwise he was absent, thoughtful, and silent. He ministered to her wants at table, he omitted no duty of observance, or attention, which, as a gentleman, and her own appointed knight, he was bound to pay her; but whenever she turned to others, either addressing them, or dispensing her smiles, he fell into a reverie, and seemed to forget her presence. Piqued at length, by this constantly recurring abstraction on his part, the French princess assailed him by such a series of direct attacks upon his notice, that he was compelled to rouse himself from his thoughtful mood, and respond to her despotically gay one.

"I am used to have all my own way;" she exclaimed, laughing; "and I am not going to yield it now, I can assure you."

"Who would deny it you? Your highness has but to announce your will and pleasure, for it to be instantly obeyed;" replied Posthumus, with as much answering vivacity as he could exert. "Have you not your elected knight at hand,—elected by the king's command, and your own gracious sanction,—to perform your every bidding. But speak your behest, it shall be fulfilled."

"Is it so indeed?" she replied. "Have I but to express my wish, to see it complied with."

"Undoubtedly;" he returned.

"What if I were to ask for that white rose, the trophy of your late victory?" she said; "have you the generosity to make the sacrifice, and surrender it to me?"

He started; and involuntarily drew back, looking his denial.

"So much for my knight's acquiescence with my wishes;" she said, with a forced laugh.

"What is that?" enquired the king, who had overheard her words, and detected the vexation in her tone.

"Nothing, my lord; " she replied. "Merely a hundredth lesson I am taking, in the difference between protestations and performance, where gallant speeches cost nothing, and pledges of their truth are unexpectedly demanded."

"How is this? How is this?" pursued the king. "It is not possible you can demand aught of your vowed knight that he can refuse;" and Cymbeline cast an expressive glance at Posthumus, to remind him of his instructions, that all should be made to conform to the pleasure of the French princess.

"But he can refuse, and does refuse, my lord;" said the spoiled beauty. "The sacrifice I ask at his hands, is certainly of some weight; but then, the greater his generosity, and the higher my triumph, if he consent."

"Assuredly;" said the king. "Come, Leonatus, I will not do thy knightly duty to thy lady's will the injury, to add thy sovereign's desire to her expressed wish."

"Her highness hath asked for no less than the victor rose; and I may not cede to another, that which I derived from the award of my born liege lady, your majesty's daughter;" replied Posthumus. "When it is remembered from whose hand I received it, its cession can scarcely be expected."

"Pshaw, my daughter willingly yields the preference of right, to our fair guest;" said the king.

"Hear my title to speak in this matter, cousin king!" interposed the melodious voice of Bergion, who stood behind his royal master's chair. "Few are greedier of power than those who oft mis-use it; and none are more jealous of authority than those unfit to hold it. By which token, I claim my right to decide. From *my* hand was the rose received; be it mine to accord permission for its re-bestowal."

"Thou art right, good fellow;" said Leonatus, drawing forth the rose, and presenting it to the French princess; "I was wrong to hesitate an instant, when her highness condescended to urge her request."

That day's events had taught a secret to two people. Posthumus's grave abstraction had proceeded from the momentous questions he was asking himself, the strange discoveries he was making, touching the true source of certain powerful emotions that arose within him, consciously, for the first time. He had been brought up in so perfect a brotherhood of intimacy with the princess Imogen, he had been so accustomed to consider her as under his loving care and protection, tenderly and confidingly as though she had been a younger sister, that he had never dreamed of asking himself what was the nature of the feeling with which he regarded her. That she dwelt apart in his imagination as something far beyond all other human beings dear, that she was worshipped by him as something more beautiful, more pure, more excellent than any other living creature, he knew; but he now for the first time learned, that co-existent with this almost reverential tenderness of affection towards her, was a sentiment of equal force, or rather one which gave redoubled force to the other. He felt that this gentle being who lived in his thought as an angel of innocence and goodness, was no less passionately beloved as a woman; and that while he had hitherto believed he cherished her as a child, respected her as the daughter of his sovereign and benefactor, and venerated her for her own beauty of nature, he now found he was enamoured of her as man loves the one woman in the world whom he would make his other self,—the sharer of his own existence.

The way in which the British princess had been contrasted with her Gaulish guest, as ladies, and as women; the way in which the one had maintained her modest dignity, and the other had made her forward claim to his fealty, while it was secretly devoted heart and soul to his own liege lady, had forcibly revealed to him the extent and nature of that secret devotion. The more the gaily wilful Eponine pressed herself upon his notice, and demanded his admiration, the more did he discover of the true admiration he felt for the high-souled Imogen.

But, even while making this discovery, came a sense of the fidelity he owed to the compact between himself and his king, with regard to this Gaulish princess. He remembered that Cymbeline had made a point of her being held in good-humour during her sojourn in the British court; that he had confided to him the especial charge of ministering to her will and pleasure; and therefore he resolved that no personal feeling of growing distaste towards her, should lead him to forget his sovereign's wish. He determined, that while she remained in Britain, he would strictly fulfil the part of her devoted knight; and that no circumstances however annoying to himself, which such a position might entail, should induce him to betray a reluctance to comply with her lightest wish.

This resolution was severely tested; but he maintained it faithfully. Meantime, the king told him that whenever the French princess should announce her intention of returning to Gaul, it was to be, with all due courtesy, acquiesced in; and Cymbeline farthermore enjoined him to hold himself in readiness to accompany her back to her father's capital of Gergovia, in quality of her knightly protector, and in order that she might be safely and surely escorted out of the British kingdom into her own.

It has been said, that to two people, did the events of that day of the verse-contest, reveal a secret. While Posthumus Leonatus was questioning himself as to the source of his feelings towards Imogen, she herself was no less earnestly examining her own heart upon the unwonted agitation it had experienced, at sight of Leonatus kneeling at the feet of the French princess; at beholding him salute her hand, while she fastened the scarf upon his arm, and bent over him with gracious encouragement; and at seeing the sedulous way in which Eponine took pains to manifest her own pride in her knight, and to attract his attention and admiration in return.

"Shame on me!" was her thought; "am I grown so narrow-hearted as to grudge the attentions of Leonatus towards any other than myself? To put an ill construction on a lady's show of favor towards him; when who can look on his grace of manhood, and not approve? Am I so poor in generosity as to feel jealous that my friend and companion should show courtesy and observance towards one, who as my guest, no less than a sister princess and lady, I am bound to treat with all kindliness and consideration?"

Then she started to find how deeply she had felt interested, in the bestowal of the white rose; in Posthumus's persistive refusal to yield it up, until reminded by Bergion's timely words, that it had been received from his hand, and not from hers. She recollected the thrill of satisfaction with which she had recognized his handwriting in the scroll which had enabled her to win the verse-victory; the glow of delight with which she had found that to his ingeniously exercised, and perseveringly executed labor, she owed the triumph of her native island's cause. But then, with the diffidence of newly discoved love, and of her own modest spirit, she thought :—"That might have been his zeal for the honor of Britain." Unable to come to any conclusion as to the nature of his feeling towards her; she only too certainly became aware of the quality of her own affection for him. She felt that however he might regard her, whether merely as the young girl whose playmate and favorite he had been from infancy, or whether with a more tender and passionate preference, she herself had undoubtedly given him her whole heart, exclusively, devotedly, and for ever.

On one occasion, Posthumus, having been detained near the king for a time, to hear somewhat he had to tell him of an expected rising in the North, hastened to join the princess Eponine, whom, in consequence of the king's instructions, and of Bergion's hints, he rarely lost sight of. He found, on enquiring for the French princess, that having expressed a wish to see somewhat of the grounds environing the palace, her young hostess had accompanied her forth for an exploring long walk ; and that when some of the ladies and courtiers had offered to attend them, Eponine had with her usual gay peremptoriness, forbidden their following, declaring that she had a mind for a quiet ramble alone with Imogen.

As Leonatus turned abruptly away, Cloten called after him that it was no use attempting to overtake them ; that they had been gone some time ; that as they had taken the path through the grove, the thickness of the trees would effectually prevent his discovering them ; and that moreover attendance had been expressly declined. But Posthumus paid no heed to what he said, excepting to note the direction which the princesses had taken ; and then, lost no time in pursuing the clue thus obtained.

He had traversed a considerable extent of the close oak wood, or grove, which lay in the vicinity of the palace, before he could perceive any trace of the two ladies ; but at length he discerned the white garments of Imogen, and the bright, many-colored robe of the French princess, among the distant trees. He hurried after them ; and as his footstep caught the quick ear of Imogen, she turned, and the expression of her face was the usual ingenuous look of welcome, which it ever involuntarily wore at his approach. As the

French princess also looked back, she exclaimed joyously :—"Ah! here is my own knight come in quest of us ! Happily arrived, good sir ; for my walk has tired me, and your support will be right grateful."

She took his arm as she spoke, and leaned upon it with her usual easy freedom, and air of pleased confidence, when his services were in question of acceptance by her ; and then went on with her wonted light volubility, showing how little she was really fatigued.

Imogen was silent, partly because there was little opportunity for reply, where speech was so incessantly maintained on the other side ; partly from her being struck to perceive that Eponine had abruptly changed the subject of conversation,—which till then had been occupied by an urgent request on the part of the French princess, that Imogen would promise to correspond with her, minutely, after her return to Gaul ; and partly from a feeling of lassitude, occasioned by the extent of her ramble.

Leonatus, perceiving that *she* was weary, led the French princess towards a green mound, or bank, that afforded a pleasant seat, and begged that she would take some rest ; while he placed Imogen beside her.

"Just one of your admirable pieces of thought for me, my kind, good knight !" said Eponine ; "this repose is most welcome ; and this seat a most charming one ! How grand and solemn the thick verdure of these Druid oaks above our head ; and how imposing the effect of yonder simple stone altar ; and what a dizzy depth of ravine beside us !" she exclaimed, as she peeped over into the sheer rift or chasm, on the brink of which the mound was situated. "'Tis a fearful pit ; dark, and well-nigh fathomless, as it looks from here, to us above. It might be the lair of some wild beast ; or lurking-place of monster, giant, or wood-demon. A fit abode for anything savage and strange. It gives one a pleasant shudder to peer down into the murky abyss."

"Your grace's imagination lends the place a dread character ;" said Posthumus ; "'tis a tangled dell, all wild, and overgrown with brambles aud thorny briars ; its steep descent makes it appear deeper than it probably is."

"I have heard it said to be of perilous depth ;" said Imogen. "None have been known hardy enough to sound its extent. Even Bergion, who hath prowled over every inch of ground through these woods, has never attempted to penetrate its mysteries."

"Yet methinks an expert woodsman or cragsman might climb its rugged sides. 'Twould be a fit adventure for a bold spirit, and an active frame;" said the French princess. "'Twould be a feat worthy his daring and dexterity, for a man who possessed both."

"'Twould surely be waste of both, were a man to expend them upon so objectless an exploit;" returned Imogen.

Eponine turned away from gazing down into the abyss; and with her usual inconsequent way of flying from subject to subject, said, as she looked at a string of pearls of great value, which Imogen wore about her throat :— "I used often to hear of the orient beauty of your British pearls. Those are of matchless size and hue. Let me examine them more nearly. They are the finest I ever beheld."

The French princess held out her hand, as she spoke; and Imogen could do no less than untwine them from about her neck, saying, as she did so :—"I value them beyond their worth as gems; they were the gift of a dear friend,—my best friend."

"Your father;" said Eponine in a decisive tone.

Imogen made no reply. But the pearls were really the gift of Posthumus Leonatus.

"They are priceless;" said the French princess, admiringly; "so marvellously clear, large, and even. I must win my father's consent to bring away with me from Britain, just such necklace, as his present, and as a remembrance of my happy sojourn here, ere I return to Gaul;" said Eponine. "Ah, that return! I almost dread it. Though I love mine own home, yet I have been made so much of, been so humoured, so indulged, as a guest in your good father's court, that I know not how I shall bear to take my leave."

While she said this, thoughtfully, and almost sadly, for her, the French princess had been absently whirling the string of pearls in airy circles round and round one of her fingers; when suddenly it spun from her hold, and dropped sheer down into the chasm.

She made a vehement exclamation; and a hurried apology to Imogen.

The latter abruptly arose, with a look of concern ; then as suddenly reseated herself, saying as calmly as she could :—" 'Tis no matter ; they are gone. You could not help it. Let us not grieve for what is past recall."

" How can you take the loss of such priceless gems so coolly ? " exclaimed Eponine, angrily. " They are finer pearls than any I have ever seen ; besides, being your father's gift, methinks, might make you show a warmer regret for them."

" They were not my father's gift ; " replied Imogen quietly.

" No ? " retorted the French princess, with a piercing glance. " Yet you owned they were the gift of a dear friend, your best friend ! A lover, then ? " she added with a gay laugh. " So, so, sweet lady Gravity ! We have found that you have a favored wooer, for all your shy discretion, and quiet moods."

" Since the pearls are gone past recovery ; " said Imogen, returning Eponine's laugh with a smile, though her cheek crimsoned, and she answered with her own simple dignity,—" 'tis of little consequence whence I had them. Believe me, I am well contented to bear their loss ; think no more of them."

Posthumus could not help feeling a pang, at hearing her treat thus lightly, as he thought, the loss of his gift.

" Think no more of them ! But I must think of them ! I do think of them ! " exclaimed the French princess. " Since you care for them so little,—if indeed, you set no more store by them, than you would have us suppose,—how say you to yielding what right you had in them, to me ? A match ! If I can recover them, they are to be mine ! It shall be so ! "

" I said not so ; I agree to no such match ; " said Imogen with more of eagerness than she had yet shown.

" Nay, but I will at all events assay my hope to redeem them ! " cried Eponine, with her usual vivacity of manner. " On you, I rely, my good knight, for the carrying out of my hope ; on you I rely, to regain them for me. To such prowess as yours, the plunging into yonder rocky gulph is nothing redoubtable. You will venture it for me, will you not ? " she said with a sparkling eye, and eager voice.

"Most willingly;" replied Leonatus, as he stepped upon the bank, and prepared to descend.

"Do not think of it! Indeed, I care not for the trinket! Leonatus! Do not attempt so perilous a descent!" cried Imogen, her sweet voice raised in earnestness and entreaty.

But there was something in the very plea she used, that gave him a reckless, desperate feeling, which urged him onward. "Though you prize not the bauble;" he said, "yet I will do my best to recover it. I may not refuse her highness's challenge to my knightly duty."

He scaled the brink of the precipice, and made his way downwards; holding fast by the straggling sprays and twigs that presented themselves; clinging to the rugged inequalities of the rock; and breaking his fall, as he leaped from point to point, by the small trees and underwood which grew among its interstices; and which formed a rough tangle of foliage covering the sides of the narrow chasm.

He had got nearly out of sight, when the two ladies, who were breathlessly watching his progress, heard a crash among the boughs, and saw him sink suddenly down, far beyond their ken.

The French princess uttered a piercing shriek, which rang loud, and shrill, through the echoing rift. Imogen, clasping her hands high above her head, stood fixed in mute heart-terror.

A death-like pause of a few moments; and then the voice of Leonatus, called out in a cheerful, resonant shout:—"I have them! I have them!" Shortly afterwards they could discern him again; clinging, climbing, straining, and toiling, on his upward path; until at length he reached the spot where they stood.

"Here is the string of pearls;" he said. "To whom am I to tender it?"

"It is mine,—fairly mine! Won by the courageous daring of mine own faithful knight!" exclaimed the French princess, exultingly.

"I cannot yield them;" said Imogen with warmth. "Yet,"—she hesitated, seeing the promptitude with which Leonatus placed the gems in Eponine's hand; "Yet, if your grace insist,—if your knight think you entitled to them,——He shall decide;" she concluded; "be it as he thinks fit."

"You regained them for me! I cannot forego them! I have set my heart on having them! My brave knight imperilled his safety to get them for me! They nearly cost you your life!" cried the French princess, rapidly. "I must have them! Give your verdict in my favor, like a true and faithful knight."

Posthumus, remembering the king's injunction, was about to speak as she wished; when Imogen calmly said :—"They are yours. Do me the favor to accept them as my willing gift. That which hath enhanced their value in your highness's eyes, hath stripped them of it in mine. That they nearly cost a brave man's life to regain, would henceforth mar their beauty, rather than endear them to me. I am well pleased that your grace hath a fancy for them; since I can gladly and freely present them to you."

"And I as gladly and freely receive them ;" said the French princess, gazing at them delightedly, and passing them round her neck. "They are beautiful as gems ; dear to me, as coming from my sweet princess of Britain's hand ; and precious for the testimony they afford of a gentleman's gallant conduct. This is one of those very instances of flattering attention to my wishes, which I spoke of erewhile, as making me so loath to quit your Britain ;" continued Eponine, as they turned to walk homeward. "Where,—even in my own fair Gaul, where all the men are brave and assiduous in the performance of a lady's wish,—where shall I find a knight more prompt to fulfil my behests, than your British gallants, of whom this gentleman is a preeminent example? But I must leave you all; alas! My father has written to urge my return ; and I fear it must be speedy. By the way, sweet lady ;" said the French princess, breaking off in the fitful style common to her; "how hath your woman Dorothy sped in the matter of that swain of hers, who was wounded in the last great battle, and who she heard was lingering in penury and misery out yonder, in the island of Mona ? I heard her speaking of it to your grace this morning."

"I propose sending to his relief ;" said Imogen ; "and count upon your kindly assistance, Leonatus, to this end. You will not grudge the long and toilsome journey so far, to see him, and carry him comfort ?"

Posthumus was pouring forth his eager assent ; when Epinone interrupted him, with :—"You forget, my knight; your good services are engaged to me. The journey to Mona, would occupy you beyond the period when I must return to Gaul; and I cannot forego the pleasure of your company and attendance thither."

In good time, Posthumus remembered his pledge to the king, and his resolution to abide by it, at whatever sacrifice to himself; but it cost him a struggle to obey the French princess's will in this instance, where it crossed an expressed request from Imogen.

However, he bowed his consent to Eponine; while she could scarcely conceal her triumph at his prompt acquiescence. As she rattled on, in her sprightliest strain, Posthumus found means to say in an earnest undertone to Imogen :—" I may not refuse; but you will do me the justice to believe I would fain have performed *your* behest."

"I know it, kind friend;" she said in her own simple, sincere way. "But be not concerned; the poor fellow shall not lack help. The trusty Bergion shall be my messenger. He shall take succour from us both. I will send in our joint names; yours, and mine own."

A look of bright and happy gratitude flashed from the eyes of Posthumus, at this gentle, gracious speech; while the French princess, with the air of half pouting jealousy with which she always perceived him looking at, or speaking to, any one else than herself, recalled his attention, by some exacting and urgent, yet trivial and unimportant words pointedly addressed to him.

Upon that little speech of Imogen's Posthumus lived. In it, she had linked herself and himself in that little word so precious to a lover,—' us.' In it she had shown her own frank, generous, true spirit; harbouring not one spark of resentment, for his apparent defection, and denial of her wish. On the contrary, she had associated him with herself in her deed of charity and compassion; evincing how entirely she would have him feel that she knew his refusal arose from no unwillingness to perform it for her.

Great need had Posthumus Leonatus of this secret sustaining comfort; for after that occasion, he had none other, of exchanging either word or look with his beloved lady, so entirely did his appointed lady engross him to herself, until the period fixed for her departure.

Vol. III. 2 I

She occupied him incessantly on her behalf; employing his time, and setting him perpetual tasks to accomplish in the way of purchases, and superintendence of equipments, which she declared no one but himself could perform to her taste.

Posthumus, faithful to his accepted trust, dedicated himself entirely to her whims, humored all her caprices, and observed, nay, prevented, her slightest wishes; and on the very eve of setting out to accompany the Gaulish princess on her homeward journey, he had the reward of Cymbeline's private praise and acknowledgment, for the scrupulous fidelity and zeal with which he had carried out his intentions.

"You have been all I could wish, my Leonatus;" said the king. "You have kept faithful watch on this tricksome French lady; and have indulged her gay wilfulness to their topmost bent. When you have seen her once safely housed in her father's court, return with dearest welcome to Britain. I have had good reason to believe that the chief aim of her visit, was to establish a secret correspondence here, sinister to our interest. But if this were so, your good vigilance, and constant humoring of the pretty trifler's whims,—has happily prevented her thinking of,—far less carrying into effect,—more serious mischief. Fare thee well, my dear youth! Let us see thee back, as speedily, and as prosperously as may be!"

The princess Eponine and her train were to take ship from the port of Lud's town; and there, just before embarkation, Leonatus had an opportunity of going to the principal pearl merchant's in Britain, in the hope of obtaining another string of equal beauty, with those he had before procured. It chanced that the most valuable set the merchant had by him, were at that very moment being bid for by a gentleman, evidently a foreigner, who was examining the pearls, when Leonatus made his enquiry. Some few words of mutual courtesy were interchanged respecting the cession of the respective purchase; when the foreigner declared himself ready to yield the string of pearls, and take a torque of gold, together with a girdle wrought in pearls, instead; as his principal desire was to obtain something peculiarly British in its fashion, as a present for his brother's wife on his return to Italy. Leonatus returned words of suitable acknowledgement; and while he was settling for the string of pearls,—the Italian gentleman moving away to conclude his purchase for the ornaments he had chosen,—the merchant mentioned that the foreigner was an Italian nobleman named Iachimo, brother to the duke of Sienna.

Leonatus, whose mind was full of something else, paid slight regard to this piece of information, as one nowise interesting to him ; and shortly after took his leave, rejoiced to have secured the pearls.

But it seems, that his courteous demeanour had so far won the attention of the foreigner, as to lead him to ask who was the British gentleman just gone ; and he obtained the intelligence in return, that he was Posthumus Leonatus, a young man of distinguished birth and breeding, high in court favor, and enjoying the peculiar countenance and esteem of the king himself.

Posthumus, meanwhile, hurried home, enclosed the string of pearls in the but two lines which he trusted himself to write ; confided the packet to a faithful attendant he had, named Pisanio, with strict charge to deliver it into the hands of the princess Imogen ; and then set sail for Gaul.

Pisanio staid but to witness the departure of his master, ere he made the best of his way to Camalodunum. He had little difficulty in procuring access to the British princess, whose charity and beneficence towards all claimants on her bounty or sympathy, rendered her graciously open to general advent.

The mere sight of this messenger, whom she knew to be a trusted servant of Posthumus Leonatus, caused Imogen a thrill of delight. That he should have been expressly sent to bring word of his master's departure, was in itself a kind of comfort for that departure, which had caused her many an involuntary bitter feeling, unrelieved as it had necessarily been by word or token of leave-taking. He had, then, sent to bid her farewell, since he had been unable to do so in person ; and Imogen, in her unexacting, unselfseeking nature, made fullest allowance for this inability, rather than tax him for an instant, even in thought, with wilful neglect or unkindness.

Her bitterness had been the bitterness of regret ; never of resentment, or unkind construction. Her gentle patience was duly recompensed, by the joy she experienced, when Pisanio placed in her hands the packet his master had enjoined him to deliver. Leonatus had, then, written ! He had sent her under his own hand, words of remembrance and valediction !

He had sent her his farewell in penned substance ; a tangible, palpable, charactered shape ; something that she could hold to her heart, and press to her lips, and weep over in mingled sadness and comfort.

She could scarcely conceal her happy exultation, as she framed words of kindly thanks, and bestowed liberal acknowledgement on the bringer of the packet ; and then hastened away to her own chamber, to read her treasure in the full luxury of solitude.

The string of pearls fell well-nigh unheeded into her lap, while her eyes fastened on the few words in his hand-writing, inscribed on the paper that enclosed the gems :—

"To replace those so nobly yielded.

Yours (in all the loyalty and truth of that word)

LEONATUS."

Her first emotion was one of pure, unalloyed rapture,—a transport of conviction. "He loves me! He loves me! 'Yours'! My Leonatus! Mine! Mine own Leonatus!" And the paper was bathed with a flood of passionate tears and kisses.

Then came the reaction of heart-humility, and self-doubt; the magnifying of his merits, and dread of her own insufficiency and unequal worth, to deserve so glorious a preference; and all the thousand and one generous misgivings with which genuine love torments itself. "Hath he not been evermore loyal and true in friendship, in kindliness, in all loving care and thought, towards the poor motherless girl?" mused she. "Has he not been loyally and truly mine in fullness of brotherly love and affection? And shall I be less than contented with this? Shall I aspire to be to him among women, what he is to me of all men? What am I, that I should be the heart-chosen, the soul-selected of this paragon of mankind? Doth not my inmost spirit approve him and avouch him sole worthy to be ranked above his sex, first of men? How am I graced in gifts of person or of mind, that I should hope to hold the place in his esteem which he holds in mine, knowing him matchless in both? How may I, weak lady, indulge so flattering, so fond a belief, as that Leonatus' love for me, can be what mine is for him? And do I indeed love so intensely and entirely, one, of whose passion for me I am yet uncertain! Alas, poor Imogen! The unasked surrender of thy heart can alone be excused by the sovereign excellence of him who hath unwittingly made it his conquest."

In the restless, pensive mood, which became Imogen's, after the departure of Leonatus, she frequently wandered forth into the oak grove; there, alone, in the thickest of its green shades, to indulge, unseen, her involuntary melancholy. She had so long been habituated to his companionship, that even in this single respect, his loss was deeply felt. But beyond this, were all the anxieties and solicitudes respecting his safety, which beset a feminine heart, when the beloved one is far away; there was the aching void of absence; the dreary blank of separation; there were the perpetually recurring questions which could obtain no answer, of what was then his pursuit? Of whom was he now thinking? Where was he actually sojourning? When would he return? Above all, was the ever-suggestive, never-allayed suspense, with regard to the feeling he entertained towards herself. This woody scene, with its canopy of trees, its Druid altar, its grassy mound, its bramble-grown chasm, peculiarly fostered these suspenseful reveries. It revived those manifestations of Posthumus's most marked interest, and deference, towards the French princess; it recalled her animated looks of encouragement and approval, his tokens of submission to her lightest wish, his acquiescence, his compliance, his devoted manner. And then arose the thought, was there not a probability that this bright, beautiful being, had possessed peculiar fascination for a man like Posthumus, well fitted to judge of brilliancy, and sprightliness, and sparkling grace. Was he not her appointed knight? Did not this afford peculiar opportunity for becoming acquainted with each other's most attractive qualities? Was it not most likely that this would end in their becoming mutually enamoured? Were they not now together? And was it not probable that they would find, in this protracted intercommunion, how necessary to each other's happiness they had become? And finding this, would they not discover to one another their mutual thought? Were it so indeed, that Posthumus loved Eponine, Imogen felt she could prefer his happiness to her own, and bear to see him united to the woman of his choice; but if it were merely that the French princess distinguished his preeminence, and loved him, then Imogen could not consent that the force of her own affection should yield to that of any other human being.

All these contending emotions of anxiety, dread, and hope, of passionate wishes, fears, regrets, of prolonged absence and suspense, preyed upon the sensitive nature of Imogen, and rendered her more and more dejected. Her lonely walks and musings grew into habitual indulgence ; and she began to give herself up to them with a mingled feeling of mournful enjoyment, and voluptuous sadness. But the sense and strength of her spirit, which came not short of its softness and sensibility, interposed in time to save her from the morbid condition of soul into which this indulgence might have ultimately thrown her.

Imogen was as high-minded, as she was gentle-hearted. She had a certain vigour of nature, — nowise inconsistent with the tenderest sensitiveness,—which in her supplied the teaching that is in most instances the offspring of exalted intellect. Imogen was not distinguished by marked intellectual endowments ; neither her inherited qualifications, nor the age in which she lived, made her extraordinarily gifted in mental accomplishment. But she possessed a nobility of character, a superiority of spiritual perception, that stood her in stead of the more strictly intelligential faculty. She had a fine understanding ; but it rather manifested itself in quiet sense, than in exercise of imagination. It directed her feeling aright ; it formed and strengthened her principles ; it refined and matured her judgment ; instead of employing itself upon active acquirement and thirst of learning. She read such rare books as her father's indulgence procured for her, with pleasure and interest, but it was rather with enjoyment, than with any more direct operation of her reasoning faculties. Justice of sentiment, from innate rectitude of character, was Imogen's prevailing power. She felt justly, she acted rightly, not because she argued upon true or false, right or wrong ; but because she was herself pure and good. Her motives and impulses being pure and good, they inspired pure thoughts and good deeds ; and from originally virtuous motives and impulses springing into virtuous thoughts and deeds, they eventually resulted in the firmest and strongest of virtuous wisdom.

It was thus, that unguided by aught save her own inborn sense of right, Imogen learned to discern that she was acting unworthily of her own character, and risking injury to its best strength, by continuing to indulge in these morally enervating solitary walks and reveries. She had just attained to a vague perception of this, when her idea was confirmed by a strong and singular impression, that came upon her like a direct vouchsafement from Heaven.

It was one of those clear, bright, December days, that sometimes occur in the depth of a winter season; and although the year wanted but a single week to its close, no sign of frost, or snow, was upon the earth. The oak grove was wrapt in that solemn silence which forms one of the chief charms of forest scenery; the glossy leaves and red clusters of the holly underwood, looked full of vital cheerfulness; the lofty trees reared their giant heads, and gnarled trunks, and spreading arms, in sylvan majesty; the pearly berries, and small, green, rounded leaves of the mistletoe, clung to the branches in beautiful abundance, adorning the venerable parent stock with their fresh vivacity; the sky was blue and serene; and the sun shone warm and brilliant, to enliven and to gladden all.

Imogen felt that it was an ingratitude to Nature, to shut her heart against the invigorating influences of such a scene. She felt reproached by the brightness of such a day accorded in the midst of the sullen season, for yielding feebly to the mistrusts and fruitless solicitudes of uncertainty. The hopefulness of the day seemed to rebuke her despondency; and to accuse her of weakness, thus to encourage idle dreams of conjectural evil, when all might be well. Was it not a kind of treason to the faith of her own love, to allow it to spend itself in vain anxieties, and uneasy surmises? Why should it not rather seek to fortify itself with a noble trust, a patient, constant hope? Out of meekest and humblest endurance, came strength and courage; as out of lowliest weeds, and least observed herbs, balm and healing were extracted.

As these thoughts passed through her mind, Imogen sat on the grassy bank, her chin resting on her clasped hands, her eyes bent on the slanting rays that penetrated the woody depths before her; when, as she gazed, the flood of sunshine seemed insensibly to expand and dilate into a pervading light—soft, yet vivid; serene, yet intense. It seemed compounded of all that was tranquil and hopeful, at the same time that it was penetrating and refulgent. It seemed to fill the air, as with a universal benignant promise; the shining forth of a manifest Peace, and Joy, and Comfort to all men. It seemed to stream forth enlightenment and revival to the whole world; to bring sustaining help, and exalted trust; to teach mercy, forbearance, kindliness; to show the folly and wickedness of strife, the iniquity of uncharitableness. Calm and healing for the wounded spirit seemed to flow from this mystic radiance, as it shed its beams upon all around.

The Druid oaks in their sturdy bulk, the rude altar of solid stone, dedicated to pagan worship, all the substantial evidences of the real scene that environed her, were blotted out from the sight of Imogen, as she steeped her senses in the pure effulgence that poured its mild lustre upon every object, and seemed to absorb their materiality into its own prevailing light. It seemed to have the power of casting into shadow and nothingness all that was grossly palpable and actual; while it shone forth with its own irresistible force of clearness and purity, declaring the one true and divine Essence.

After that day, Imogen felt as though she had acquired a tranquillity of spirit until then unknown. It seemed beyond her comprehension; but she sought not to analyse its source, she was contented to feel its effects. It brought a wisdom of its own, which taught her to restrain her former tendency to indulge in solitary musing, with vain revolving of thoughts she could not bring to satisfactory issue; and until Posthumus should return, she determined to occupy herself with deeds of charity and active usefulness, instead of enfeebling her mind and body with profitless dwelling upon one round of ideas.

She had soon additional need of all that could inspire courage and patient endurance.

The threatened rising in the North, of which Cymbeline had had some previous warning, broke into open rebellion, on the occasion of the death of the chief of one of the Northern tribes. The king of the Brigantes, dying suddenly of a surfeit at table, his subjects took the opportunity of joining the other malcontents, and an extensive insurrection was the consequence. The widow queen hastened up to the British court that she might engage Cymbeline's aid in her cause, and in the recovery of her son Cloten's rights, as his father's successor.

Cymbeline not only levied a large force of his own brave Iceni and Trinobantes, (the two tribes most especially under his governance,) and sent it without delay to the scene of the disturbances; but he was so struck by the great personal beauty of the widow queen, that he fell almost immediately into the snare which her wily perception of his peculiarities enabled her to lay for him. She saw the impression produced upon the king by her beauty; she quickly discovered the dominant foibles of his disposition; and combinedly she made them conduce to her scheme of becoming future queen of Britain. With artful allurement she contrived to heighten the effect of the former; while she unceasingly flattered and ministered to the latter,—his defects of pride, obstinacy, selfishness, and wilful love of power. So rapidly and so effectively did she conduct her plans, that she had brought Cymbeline to woo her into second marriage with himself ere she had been much more than a sennight in his court. Her success in this project, inspired her with another, as bold in its ambition. She determined to exchange her son Cloten's hope of the petty chieftain-ship of the Brigantes, for no less than the succession to the throne of Britain, by bringing about his marriage with the king's only daughter and heiress apparent, the princess Imogen.

When Bergion returned from the charitable mission on which his young mistress had sent him to Mona, he heard the news of the royal nuptials.

"How is this? Cousin king going to enter the unholy state of second matrimony? About to commit himself to the unblest condition of digamy? Can this be true? Can cousin king have so far forgot what he owes to his own hope of happiness?" he said.

"I'll tell thee what, Druid-dregs!" exclaimed Cloten; "for thine own sake, I counsel thee to keep that babbling tongue of thine within range. Thoud'st best, I can tell thee. Cousin king, as thou call'st him, is not one to be offended, without bale to the offender. Witness, a certain soldier fellow, I knew of, when I came first to court, that was general to king Cymbeline. His name was Belarius. And for all his previous favor, he was cast into the slough of exile, on the first anger he gave his royal master."

" Nay, but is this news indeed sooth ? " asked Bergion eagerly of another courtier, without attending to Cloten.

" It is as the prince says ; " replied the gentleman. " His majesty is about to espouse the queen of the Brigantes forthwith."

" Cousin king is mad ! He must have lost his wits more absolutely than I ever lacked mine ! " exclaimed Bergion vehemently. " It cannot be that cousin king is so fatally given o'er to folly ! "

" How say'st thou, fellow ? Is it thus thou presum'st on the too great license my favor allows thee ? " said the voice of Cymbeline in a wrathful tone. He had entered unperceived by Bergion, who was strangely moved and excited. " Dost thou speak disrespectfully of me in mine absence ? 'Tis enough if I permit thee the jester's privilege of slighting words in my presence. But methinks, to others, thou might'st use some discretion in talking of thy royal master."

" I know not the discretion of a hypocrite's speech, which will gloze at one time, that which it denounceth at another ; " said Bergion. " And as to cousin king, I have never said that, behind his back, which I would not say to his face."

" Then what was it thou said'st erewhile ? Hast thou the audacity to repeat it ? " said Cymbeline. " Methought it was an imputation on my judgment ; and that is scarce a reproach for a king to hear with patience."

" Yet cousin king must hear it, if he ask me the truth ; " said Bergion firmly, as he switched the hazel-rod he always bore about him, with a vehement cut through the air. Then he added, with a wild eagerness of look and tone :—" Oh, cousin king ! Listen to me ! Wed not with this widow-witch ! This snake-queen ! Give not to her that place in your bosom, where lay the white innocence and patience whom you once called wife, lest you be thought the blinded madman I spoke of ere now."

" This passes our forbearance, sirrah ! " exclaimed the king. " Away with him to the stocks ! and see if the stool of penance will bring him to a sense of his duty."

" By this token of our first meeting, cousin king," said Bergion, holding forth the hazel-wand, " think if it befit thine honor, that for a light word, far more for an earnest word, after the many of both that have passed between us, thou shouldst condemn thy faithful Bergion to an ignominious punishment."

"Pshaw!" said the king, wrathfully, as he snatched the wand from the hand that held it forth; " away with him, I say!"

"Hold, cousin king!" exclaimed Bergion with a loud cry, that amounted to a scream.

But it was soo late; the hazel-rod was twisted and rent in two, and thrown into a large fire that blazed upon the hearth, near which the king stood.

As the flames caught the slight rod, and consumed it rapidly, Bergion's frame quivered from head to foot; he turned ghastly pale; his arms fell at his side; his head dropped upon his bosom; and he stood like one bereft of sense and life.

Cymbeline turned away, repeating,—in a somewhat lowered, though scarcely less determined tone,—" See that my orders be obeyed. Let him be set in the stocks for the rest of the day. 'Twill teach him we are not to be trifled with. 'Tis fit all should learn this, who are about our person."

The next day was the one appointed for the ceremonial of the royal espousals. It took place with great magnificence; and while the new-made wife was in the height of her bridal influence, she broached to her enslaved bridegroom her desire for a union between her son Cloten, and his daughter Imogen. The royal consent was well-nigh as readily yielded as she could have wished; and the princess was informed of her father's intention to bestow her in marriage on Cloten, who had long made clumsy suit to her.

This intimation fell like a warning of death upon the heart of Imogen. It was conveyed to her by Cymbeline in his most peremptory style, just on the eve of his departure for the North, whither he was compelled to repair, for the purpose of heading his army in person against the insurgents; whom it was found less easy to quell than had been at first expected.

As the king was about to leave his capital, he suddenly bethought him of Bergion, whom he had never seen,—and never missed, during the engrossing period of his own nuptials,—since the day he had so harshly dismissed him from his presence.

"The lad lies in a languishing state, at the old forest-lodge, my liege ; " replied one of the courtiers. "On your grace's displeasure, he betook himself thither ; and hath not returned since. It is thought he hath refused all food—and so, starved into this condition ; but others, who have seen him, report that he is stricken to the heart, by the grief he hath conceived of your majesty's anger against him, and thus pined away."

Cymbeline started at these tidings of his whilom favorite. He questioned the gentleman no farther ; but as the forest-lodge lay in his road Northward, he resolved to visit the place himself, and gain personal assurance of Bergion's state.

.The king could not avoid a remorseful remembrance of another former victim to his obduracy, as he approached the old dismantled lodge in the forest. It was hither that his innocent wife Guendolen, and their infant daughter, had been banished, when they had fallen into his suspicion and wrath.

The wind sighed among the trees and blew the dark masses of the ivy that hung about the decaying walls, in sweeping, dreary gusts ; as the king, bidding his retinue await him, proceeded alone to the ruined building.

He pushed open the remnant of a door which scarcely protected the entrance, and found himself in the single room which formed the interior of the dwelling. On a low wooden settle, or pallet, lay stretched the figure of Bergion. Always lean and meagre, it now seemed a mere skeleton.

The king approached, and laid his hand kindly upon the shoulder, calling the lad by his name.

"The voice of cousin king !" exclaimed Bergion, as the old wild light gleamed in his eyes ; and he would have sprung up, but his frame had lost its pristine vigour,—and it fell back nerveless.

"How is this, my poor fellow ? " said Cymbeline, with a voice that bespoke his sympathy. "You are wasted to a shadow ; you have taken no nourishment ; you have killed yourself."

"I had no heart to eat !" said Bergion.

"How came you not to let me know this ? How fell you into this despairful state,—and made no attempt to move me to its relief ? " said the king.

"I had no hope to move you;" replied Bergion; the soft tones of his voice now peculiarly touching, in its wild and mournful cadence; "You had destroyed my last hope, when you destroyed my hazel-rod. Did I not tell you that my very life was bound up in that wand? And so it was; my trust in kindness, my reliance on all-loving, all-bounteous Nature, my faith in bonds of natural protection and sympathy, were unbroken, so long as that slender twig remained unbroken. So long as it remained mine, by the allowance and kindliness of cousin king, so long was I happy in mine existence, so long had I a hold, and a strong one, upon life. But when I saw it riven by his hand, hurled into the burning embers, and consuming beneath my very eyes by his voluntary act, I felt that I had no more to do with life; that I cared not for it. I resolved to make no farther struggle; to speak no word again; to touch no morsel more. But the voice of cousin king awoke mine own in spite of myself, to make me break my resolution to utter no word again; as the sight of him beside me, brings a joy I never more thought to feel."

Bergion fixed his gleaming eyes upon the moistened ones of Cymbeline, as a faithful dying hound might have done; then making a motion for the king's hand with his own, he drew it beneath his lips, which closed upon it, as they sighed forth their last, faint, expiring breath.

While these events were passing in Britain, Posthumus Leonatus was fulfilling the mandate of his king, by conducting the princess Eponine with all honor and observance to the court of Gergovia. This was the chief town of the Averni; over which tribe her father reigned, as a kind of petty prince. He was an intriguing man; who thought himself astute and profound, when he was but an adept in manœuvring. If he had entertained any sinister views in sending his daughter on a visit to Britain, they came to naught; for she returned to Gaul with her head full only of her own engrossing partiality for the young Briton who had been appointed her knight. It had grown from a vanity, into a fancy; from a fancy, into an infatuation; and, by the time she reached her Gallian home, she had no other thought than how she might, with least compromise of her own dignity, acquaint him with the favorable sentiments he had inspired, and retain him there evermore with her. She was possessed with the notion, that he was only restrained by a sense of the inequality of their relative positions, from declaring the passion which he really felt. She never doubted, for a moment, but that he fully partook the preference with which she regarded him ; attributing his reserve in declaring his feelings, solely to awe of her superior rank. All therefore that was left for her to do, was to assure him of the sacrifice love had taught a princess willingness to make in his favor, with the best saving of her own delicacy, and the best compliment to his honor and merit.

Accordingly, when the prince of the Averni, rendering the young British knight warmest thanks for having brought his child home in safety to her father's arms, overwhelmed him with courtesies, and hospitable urgings for a protracted sojourn in their court of Gergovia, the princess Eponine smilingly joined her entreaties to her father's, secure that one word from her to this effect, would be only too gladly complied with.

But to her amazement, Posthumus Leonatus courteously but firmly declined ; alledging, that his duty to his king now performed, his return to Britain must be made without delay.

The French princess indulged in a little pretty pouting, on hearing this reply ; but on second thoughts, she reconciled it with her previous notions, and resumed her smiles to think how soon she should bring him to retract this resolution (the effect doubtless of despair) by declaring fully her desire that he should remain.

" You have hitherto been wont to obey my lightest command, as a true, and faithful knight should do ; " she said in a tone of gay reproach ; as the train of ladies and gentlemen in attendance, obeying her highness's evident wish for more exclusive parlance, left the princess and Posthumus to walk on in advance of them, through the gardens adjoining the palace ; " you have accustomed me to so implicit a submission to my lady will, from your knightly devotion, that I cannot but expect a continuance of the like obedience. I may not believe that our air of Gallia, renowned for blithe gallantry, shall have lessened a warmth of zeal, which in colder Britain glowed with so steady a fire."

"In Britain, your knight's attention to your grace's commands were prompted by the hospitality for which our island hath some fame;" replied Posthumus in as sportive a tone as her own. "Its king desired that no observance might be wanting, to show due donor to his fair guest. That your highness should condescend to own you have perceived no lack of this observance, is best meed for the agent of his sovereign's will."

"But why should the observance cease? Is the knight weary of his allegiance?" said the princess, with her most winning smile.

"In what hath he proved recreant, madam? Please it your grace, inform me wherein I have failed in any point of knightly duty;" returned Posthumus.

"Is it not a breach of fidelity to your sovereign mistress's wishes, to refuse compliance with her express request that you should tarry here awhile longer? Is it so hard a task she sets you?"

"It is but too alluring. But I must on that very account take heed that it draw me not into the forgetting of the fealty which I owe, above all, to my rightful sovereign, the king of Britain."

"Paramount above all sovereignty, is the sovereignty of a good knight's lady-mistress—the lady of his thoughts—the lady of his heart;" said Eponine, her voice involuntarily dropping to a lower and graver tone. "She who guides his aspirations, who rules his actions, who forms the loadstar of his hopes. She, who not only is the cynosure of his wishes, but who, in turn——"

The French princess paused for a moment; then finding that he either could not, or would not reply, resumed in her tone of pouting petulance:—
"Can you not conceive what I would say? Must I speak yet more plainly?"

"Nay, rather speak no word farther, lady;" said Posthumus with earnestness; "but hear me, and understand me, in the full delicacy of my meaning, by what I will instead say to you. I have been your appointed knight; I have done mine endeavour honestly and scrupulously to fulfil all the requirements of that character. But my hope has been bounded here. I have had no higher-reaching presumption than the proud desire worthily and honorably to perform my royal master's bidding, and faith-

fully to obey yours. These, concluded by my seeing you happily restored
to your father's care, mine own wishes are crowned to their utmost scope ;
and I take leave of Gallia and her fairest princess, with all respect and
reverence."

Eponine snatched from him the hand he would have saluted, as he bent
before her on one knee ; suddenly leaned forward, and plucked from his
arm the carnation scarf which she had formerly bound there as her favor ;
burst into a flood of spoiled child's tears, as she pressed it to her lips for an
instant ; and the next, tore it into ribbands, flung it to the earth, and set
her foot upon it, grinding it into the soil, with sparkling eyes, and flushing
cheek. Then, turning on her heel, she flung away, without a syllable.

Next morning when Leonatus took his leave of the prince, and left
parting compliments of respectful farewell for his daughter, the princess,
one of her ladies brought a haughty message from her ; that she desired to
be excused seeing him, that she wished him a prosperous journey, and that
she had no farther commands.

There was something in this childish petulance, that almost provoked
a smile, as Posthumus set forth on his homeward journey. A sense of
relief mingled with the hope that beat high at his heart, as he felt himself
absolved from the duty of attending the caprices of this Gaulish princess,
and free to return to her who was the queen of his chosen homage. Now
he could yield himself to the full indulgence of contemplating her manifold
excellences ; now he could permit his thoughts to occupy themselves un-
disturbedly with her gentle image ; now he could allow himself to shape
those sweet blissful dreams, with which it was henceforth connected.
While he had been vowed to the discharge of a prescribed office, and was
bound to the whims and fantasies of a humoured lady, he had felt it a sort
of perpetual tantalization to himself, and almost a sacrilege to his own
lady's perfection, to attempt the dwelling upon her idea among so much
that was trivial, and exacting, and contradictory ; but now that he was at
liberty to entertain it solely, he gave himself luxuriously up to the pictur-
ings of his happy fancy. He painted her to himself, as he had always
beheld her, fair, gentle, modest ; peerless in beauty, as in chaste dignity,
and wise virtue. He saw, in thought, her serene eyes, beaming with loving-

kindness, and the tranquil expression of a constant soul. He saw her, gracious of aspect, as supreme in loveliness of face; beyond all women beautiful in spirit, as in person. In her, the inner nature shone forth, and gave the consummate charm.

He had been secretly meditating on this ever-fruitful theme of his delighted thought, when, it chanced, that passing through Orleans, then styled Gebanum, he fell into company with some gentlemen, who were loudly extolling the matchless qualities of the French ladies as mistresses; declaring all others to be fickle, inconstant, frail, perjured, faithless, light-hearted, and perfidious, in comparison.

Posthumus, young, ardent, zealous for the honor of Britain's women, and of his own pure lady in particular, contended warmly for the unimpeachable virtue of his countrywomen; and declared that the one among them to whom he had devoted his deathless love, was first among her sex, in immaculacy.

One of the French gentlemen present, thought fit hotly to contest the point; and from vehement assertion, the words exchanged, grew into fierce rejoinder, and then into mutual defiance, with proposal to refer the matter to the arbitrement of the sword.

Another of the gentlemen present, of maturer years, and cooler judgment, interfered between the two disputants, and represented to his own country-men, that it was scarcely courteous, or just, to resent upon a stranger his very natural defence of his island beauties, whom it was fair to believe un-blemished in innocence, until they had been proved otherwise; and that since no testimony could be alledged against them by any gentleman present, he claimed for the young Briton the privilege of having his word taken upon trust, provided he would allow as much on behalf of the fair ladies of Gallia.

In short, he spoke so frankly and good-humouredly, that the two younger men could not withstand his manner; and while the French gentleman withdrew the intemperate words he had uttered, Posthumus gallantly declared that he was willing to believe all honorably and ad-miringly of the bright fame, as of the bright faces, which France might truly boast.

For Imogen, the return of Posthumus to Britain was fresh life, fresh hope; renewal of being, revival of comfort, and trust, and happiness. Hemmed in on all sides as she was, by a designing step-mother, a hateful suitor, and a father's despotic will, she had felt well-nigh faint of spirit, and as if bereft of future joy in existence. But with his return came confidence, courage, cheer of heart, and love itself. At their very first meeting their mutual secret was disclosed ; and with its knowledge came abounding gladness, and solace for all past discomforts of doubt and suspense.

Only too well aware of her father's absolute disposition, Imogen chose rather to give herself to the man of her soul's choice without consulting the king's decision, than by awaiting his sanction, to hazard an express prohibition. She accordingly consented to plight her wedded vows to Posthumus Leonatus in Jove's high temple ; with the stipulation that her husband would there quit her for a season, until she could meet him where they should bè less subject to curious eyes. She was now sojourning in Lud's town, surrounded by the court ; hourly beset by the fawning assiduities of the queen step-mother, and the coarse siege of her wooing son ; hedged in by espial and animadversion of all kinds. She therefore besought Leonatus,—to the end that their marriage might remain unsuspected, and incur no risk of being reported to her father until such time as his return should enable them to make their own avowal while they sued for grace—that he would undertake a beneficent commission for her at some distance from the capital ; and that meanwhile she would repair to a rural palace which Cymbeline possessed in a romantic part of the island. Here her husband would be able to rejoin her, with little chance of observation ; as she intended to go thither, attended only by her own women, on whom shè could implicitly rely. It was situated in a beautiful, secluded spot ; had been adorned with great luxury and taste by Cymbeline, and was a favorite place of retirement with both himself and his daughter.

In all privacy the espousals were performed ; and at the very gate of the temple, Posthumus Leonatus took leave of his bride, his Imogen, sustaining his courage under this needful temporary separation, by the exultant thought that she was pledged his, beyond the power of fate to divide them.

The charitable deed on which he was departing, in fulfilment of his lady's wish, was the liberation of a poor prisoner, who had fallen into the enemy's hands; and, unable to pay the sum demanded for his ransom, was detained in one of the damp, unwholesome dungeons, of a neighbouring border-castle.

In witnessing the joy of this poor fellow on regaining his freedom, and on being restored to his wife and young children, who dwelt in a rude hut not far from the place of his imprisonment, although they had no hope of ever beholding him redeemed thence, Posthumus Leonatus was repaid for whatever reluctance he might have originally felt to undertake this journey. As he beheld the transports of joy with which the husband and father was welcomed to the humble home of which he was the sole stay and delight, and as he saw the honest rapture with which the freed man once more embraced his wife and little ones, Leonatus owned that to be the means of conferring so much happiness, was to receive happiness; and now that he was about to return to a still nearer and dearer happiness of his own, he felt that even this intensity and fulness of self-happiness might yet be enhanced by ministering to that of another.

In the proud delight with which a lover glories in attributing every fresh spring of joy to her who is the source of all to him, Leonatus beguiled his journey back, with thinking how he owed the heightening pleasure he had just savoured, to his Imogen's kindly sympathy with the unhappy; how he owed to her active charity, an additional feeling of complacency and gratified reflection; how, in giving him an opportunity of promoting another man's domestic beatitude, she had prepared his heart for a higher and truer enjoyment of their own. And then came the thought of how wisely and tenderly she had provided, in appointing their wedded meeting amid the quiet and seclusion of this retired spot, whither he was now wending his way, rather than among the turmoil, and the prying eyes, and the cold observance, or perhaps malignant observation, of a court.

While such ideas as these were coursing through his brain and heart, he

was urging his horse on at no slack speed, when, as he crossed an open
moor, and approached a woody covert, four men rushed from ambush,
closed round him, and dragged him to the ground. They struck no blow;
they spoke no word, and their faces were so completely muffled from view,
that Leonatus could recognize nothing by which he could identify them.
They gave him no opportunity for enquiry or expostulation; but blind-
folded him, gagged him, and led him away between them.

A long and painful journey on foot,—in what direction he could form
no idea,—terminated in an entrance beneath some kind of roof. Then he
felt himself being conducted down some steps; and at length, the folds
were withdrawn from his eyes, and the gag removed from his mouth.
But though he was at liberty to look, he could see nothing; and the
questions he poured forth the moment he was free to speak, were followed
by naught but silence. His captors retired as mutely as they had performed all else; and he only heard the heavy fastenings of the door,
which proclaimed that he was left a close and solitary prisoner. He groped
his way round the space in which he was immured, that he might endeavour
to form some idea of the kind of place in which he was. Rough stone walls,
of confined limit, with a rude settle, were the only objects he could make
out; but in making the round of his cell, a second time, his feet stumbled
against something in one corner, that proved to be a coarse loaf and
a pitcher of water. Gradually his eyes became better habituated to the
gloom, and he could distinguish objects which at first had appeared to him
a confused mass of obscurity. He perceived that his dungeon was not
totally rayless; but that a small chink towards the top, opened to the outer
air, and admitted just sufficient glimpse of light to show that he was not
entirely underground. The steps he had descended, seemed to betoken
that he was partially so, and the dank, earthy smell, bore a like testimony;
but the peep of sky, however slight, was welcome proof that he was not
wholly beneath the earth. He kept his eyes raised towards this sole point
that seemed like hope, and strove to keep his heart strong; and his courage
unshaken, that he might reason upon the probabilities of whence arose the
blow that had fallen upon him. He was unconscious of having provoked

the enmity of any one; he knew not of a single soul who could have been likely to conceive hatred against him. He had offended no one, injured no one. Who then could have inflicted this injury upon him? In vain he revolved the question. All was mystery. Perhaps he was mistaken for some one else, and might be abiding the penalty intended for another. He resolved that whenever his jailers should reappear, he would loudly proclaim his identity, and demand his freedom. He sustained his resolution, by dwelling upon these ideas, rather than risk its defeat, by suffering his thought to revert to one image that for all his bravery of struggle to keep it from vanquishing him, arose evermore in spite of himself to overwhelm and unman him. Whenever *her* image obtained the mastery, he felt prompted, to wild, ungovernable transports; he felt as though he must have madly beaten against the door of his dungeon, and shrieked to be let forth. Therefore he contained himself, forced his rage and grief to be smothered, compelled the trembling of his heart to be still, and the hot tears which would fain have sprung to his eyes, to hold back; that, for her sake, he might maintain his courage and his presence of mind unimpaired. As he wore away the hours in such attempts, the last glimmer faded from the crevice, and he was plunged in darkness. And thus the night had come on; the time when he had hoped to have arrived at the appointed place of meeting; the time when he had hoped to be welcomed by his wife, his Imogen. He cast himself on the settle, wrestling with his emotions as he best might. Then started up, choking, to swallow a large draught of water from the pitcher; then attempted restlessly to pace to and fro in his narrow cell; and at length blindly staggered once more to the settle, upon which he threw himself, headlong, worn out, despairing.

An uneasy slumber fell heavily upon him. He dreamed that he was in the temple of Jupiter; that Imogen stood by his side; that the rites which made her his were being repeated; that as he attempted to approach, her figure seemed to recede, as if wafted from him by some invisible hand. And then a branch of Jove's own oak seemed to detatch itself from among the boughs upon the altar, and point to the pavement of the temple beneath his feet, on the space that lay between himself and Imogen,

severing him from her. And then the whole pageant seemed to flicker
and vanish ; and a chaos of confused images,—wherein the released soldier
amid his wife and children, and the four disguised men, played their parts
in perplexing intermixture,—took its place with ceaselessly recurring
bewilderment, and undistinguishable lines and colors of all possible shape
and hue.

When Leonatus awoke, he could discern from the light through the
chink, that it must be broad day ; and on feverishly turning to the pitcher,
for means of moistening his parched lips, he found that it had been re-
plenished. He reproached himself for having yielded to sleep, and thus lost
the occasion of making the appeal he meditated, to his jailer. He found
also that another loaf of bread had been added ; and he now resolved to
eat some of it, that he might neglect no means of supporting his strength
of endurance, with his strength of body.

The hours of light—such as could be traced by the glimmer through the
chink,—wore away with no other visit from his jailer ; which made
Posthumus conclude that his daily ration was to be brought only once in
the twenty-four hours. He resolved that he would maintain better watch
this night ; but with the long darkness, his eyes insensibly drooped ; and
in his sleep he beheld the bird of Jupiter,—the lordly eagle, with spread
wings, and down-bent head, and close-drawn claws, make a sudden stoop
from out the sky, and point with his curved beak towards a flat slab of
granite, which looked like a cromlech, or altar-stone, on the farther side of
which, he saw the figure of Imogen, standing, with her smile of tender
welcome. The eagerness with which he stretched forth his arms towards
her, awoke him with a start. He could not restrain a groan, as he found
himself in his murky dungeon, alone, forlorn, in darkness of spirit as
of sight. He buried his face in his hands, as though to shut out the
oppressive sense of the gloom that surrounded him, and to woo again the
bright visions of his closed eyes. But he suddenly remembered his resolve
to keep awake, that he might watch the coming of his jailer. He busied
himself with trying to discern the earliest break of dawn from the glim-
mering forth of the crevice amid the sable uniformity around ; and he had

scarcely perceived the first feeble streak, which denoted the corner near the roof where it was situated, ere he heard a bolt undrawn; then another, and another; and then, through the opening door, he saw the rays of a lamp. This was borne by a muffled figure, who in his other hand held a loaf and a pitcher, which he placed on the floor in lieu of the empty one. Posthumus Leonatus sprang up, uttered a torrent of explanations, as to who he himself was, and demanded as to wherefore and by whom he had been thus outraged. But the muffled man only shrugged his shoulders, returned no answer, and retreated as he had entered.

Baffled, helpless, and despoiled of his last hope, Posthumus sank into a stupor of patient impatience; he sat collapsed, in a brooding attitude; listless, dejected, motionless; bereft of all will, as of all power to move. He remained, staring at the blank wall opposite, or rather at the intervening space of naught,—the void that was a reflex of his stunned thought. The operation of his mind seemed suspended, arrested; rendered inactive, and powerless, like his body. He seemed incapable of exertion, either of faculty or limb. His ideas, as his muscles, seemed stricken stagnant and impotent. A horrible feeling of vacancy seemed to take posession of his brain; as though it were paralysed, and empty of resource.

How long he sat thus he knew not; but suddenly, he shook off this unnatural stupor, as if he would have roused himself from coming madness; strode rapidly about his cell, striking forth his arms, and stamping energetically with his feet; pushed with vigour at the thickly stapled door, and shouldered stoutly against the rough stone walls, more to exercise his physical powers of resistance, and thereby to stimulate and excite his mental faculties from becoming weakly torpid, than from any more palpable object. The door and walls of his prison were far too solid, to have inspired the idea of trying their strength; but presently another thought struck Posthumus. He looked up at the chink, whence the only ray of light that penetrated his dungeon proceeded; and a sudden desire to reach it if possible, and to look forth from it, seized him. He heaved at the ponderous settle, that served him for a couch, trying to remove it from its corner to the one in which the crevice was; but although made of wood, it was of great bulk and weight,—almost a mere scarce-hewn block of timber.

However, here was an object on which to expend some of the superfluous activity that he thought it right to exercise. He believed that since his jailer had hitherto made his periodical visit about the same time, no interruption need be feared from him for many hours, and therefore that there could hardly occur a better opportunity for making this trial than the present. He accordingly, by main strength, tried to drag the settle inch by inch to the spot, where it could avail him to stand upon, and aid his endeavour to reach the chink above his head. By dint of perseverance, he effected his purpose of bringing the settle over ; but when he stepped upon it, his head was still some distance beneath the outlet. He attempted to gain some additional height by means of the earthenware jar or pitcher that held his allowance of water ; and doubled his cloak into a thick roll, which he placed above it ; but all was of no avail, he could not contrive to get near enough, to look forth.

Foiled in this endeavour, Leonatus would not suffer himself to be fretted by it into a forgetfulness of the precaution of moving back the settle into its former place, lest the jailer's attention might be roused to his efforts at escape ; and he laboured now as hard to reinstate the ponderous block, as he had before done to heave it forward. By the time uninterrupted darkness had again settled on the dungeon, Posthumus was glad to throw himself on his rude bed ; and, spent with his fruitless, tedious task, it was not long ere he fell into a deep sleep.

In his dreams, he enacted it all over again ; he toiled at the slow, profitless, process, he strained every sinew to move the dull weight, he expended his breath in panting, painful exertion, he wiped the drops from his forehead, and once more addressed himself with fresh and strenuous energy to the wearisome, struggling, futile work. In fancy, he again mounted upon the settle, again to be foiled in his attempt to reach the crevice ; and yet again all seemed vain, toilsome, troublous mockery and uselessness. He thought he sank down, despondent aud heartsick ; when suddenly a soft radiance seemed to penetrate the recesses of his dungeon.

At the small outlet, he discerned, high in the sky, yet as it were close to the aperture, the bright planet Jupiter,—the star said to have shined propitious at his birth. The pure rays streamed full into the narrow chasm, and fell upon the pavement of the cell, in a flood of concentrated light. The spot upon which it peculiarly shone, was a broad, flat stone, immediately beneath the settle on which he actually lay, in the corner to which he had brought it back; but which spot, by the circumstances of his dream, seemed unoccupied, and exposed to view.

The impression produced on the mind of the sleeper was so strong, that it acted upon his body; and with the impulse to rise, and examine the stone thus singularly pointed out, Leonatus awoke. The cell was pitch dark; but immediately he re-closed his eyes, the same vivid scene presented itself before them. As he lay thus, alternately beholding nothing when he opened his eyes, and seeing all clearly and distinctly recur, each time he shut them, the door of his dungeon was unfastened, and the same muffled figure entered as before, left fresh food and water, and again retired in perfect silence.

Leonatus then perceived that day was breaking; and as he arose, and partook of some of the newly-brought fare, his dream so forcibly haunted him, that he could not help forming a resolution once more to drag away the settle from the spot where it stood. His reason told him that it would be labour in vain; but his imagination operated yet more powerfully, and urged him to undertake the deed, that he might at any rate look upon the place so markedly indicated. What had he else to do? was the argument by which he finally resolved the point. At least, it would afford an object to beguile the tedious hours, and employ the activity which was better thus bestowed, than in ceaseless turmoil of thought.

He had no sooner achieved his self-imposed task, and that portion of the pavement left bare by the removal of the settle, became open to his view, than Posthumus perceived a flat, broad stone, similar to the one he had beheld in his dream; and upon farther inspection, he found it to be loose at the edges. He raised it with some difficulty; and underneath, discovered a deep declivity, as into a cavern, or subterranean way. He was about eagerly to descend ; when he reflected, that if, happily, it led to any egress from the castle or fortress, in which he was probably imprisoned, he should be less able to effect his escape now, in broad daylight, than were he to postpone his attempt until favored by darkness. He determined therefore to defer his purposed exploring ; and await as patiently as he could, the coming of nightfall. Meantime, he busied himself with vain conjectures as to the origin of this excavation ; whether it might be some underground communication between the range of dungeons, known to its guardians, and dug by them purposely ; or whether it might be the work of some desperate prisoner, who had endeavoured to burrow himself a way out from this very cell. If so, how came it left thus ? Why had there been no permanent refixure of the stone which formed its entrance ? Perhaps they had concluded that the ponderous settle, of itself, sufficiently concealed the spot ; since no ordinary man's strength would have attempted the removal of so dead a weight.

At length the last glimmer of daylight paled from the narrow chink ; evening deepened into night ; and Leonatus, recommending himself to Heaven, warily commenced his descent. There were no traces of steps, or of any regular way ; yet the decline was not so steep, but that Posthumus could proceed without peril to life or limb. He groped onward slowly, cautiously ; and at length he felt that the loose earth, and clay, along which he had hitherto made his way, changed all at once to a stony surface, rough, but uniform, as though he were entering a regular gallery, or built passage. At the end of this, he felt that he came to an iron-studded door ; but as he passed his hand carefully over it in search of fastenings, he heard voices from the other side, as of men carousing, and soldiers in a guard-room.

He turned swiftly round, attempting to retrace his way ; and as he reached about half the distance back, through the stone gallery he encountered a sharp turning, which, following, he found that it led him to the foot of a stair-case. He ascended, and discovered that it wound up through a turret ; from noting that the stone steps were wider at one end than the other. He kept close to the wall at the edge where they widened ; and when he reached the summit, he stood upon level ground. This seemed to be an insolated gallery crossing from the turret to the main-building, for along one side of its length, there were loopholes, that gave to view the night-sky, and commanded a prospect of the landscape beneath, though all was so dark that Posthumus could discern no object which might aid him to define in what part of the country he was. At the end of this gallery was a door; which, when he pressed against it, yielded, though with some creaking and stiffness, as if from rust and disuse. He now found himself in a wide corridor. There was a lamp suspended near to one of the many chamber-doors that opened from this corridor; and there were rushes strewed on the floor; and farther on, there was a wider staircase leading downwards; and altogether, signs of this being the frequented and inhabited portion of the edifice. Posthumus felt it behoved him to be more than ever on his guard; and yet a certain secret encouragement urged him onward. He went straight towards the door near to which the lamp hung. It opened, and he found himself in a small ante-room, but partially lighted. The light proceeded from an inner entrance, screened by heavy folds of tapestry. He looked between the hangings into a large apartment, and felt his secret thoughts confirmed; he was in the neighbourhood of woman, and in her gentle protection he could not but be secure of help and refuge. This must be some lady's room, of high wealth and station, so richly, so tastefully was it adorned. Few in all the island, could command such magnificent, such rare luxury. And as he gazed, something that he had heard of the particulars of these costly fittings, smote upon his memory, and caused his heart to beat with peculiar emotion. Had he not heard that the king's indulgence had caused his daughter's apartment in their favorite country palace to be adorned with just such rarity of luxuriance as this which he now looked upon? There were the rich silken hangings of Tyre, wrought in silver, with the story of that Egyptian queen who had lately filled the world with her fame of witchery; the golden-fretted roof; the marble-sculptured chimney, with its figures so life-like moulded in grace and beauty, of Dian and her attendant nymphs; the silver andirons on the hearth, two winged boys poised delicately, as though but newly

alighted. All this he had surely heard described; but he felt as if in
a bewildering dream, unable to think or to remember clearly. He might
have heard these things spoken of, yet how should he be now gazing on
them in Imogen's room. He felt certain,—that is, as certainly as he could
feel or reason upon anything,—that he was far away from her; had been
dragged miles in another direction, to be inexplicably plunged into a dark,
dismal dungeon. As he continued to look dreamily on, leaning against
the entrance, and still screened among its tapestry-folds, the hangings on
the opposite side of the room were raised, and two persons entered.
Leonatus at once recognised them for Imogen's tire-women, Helen and
Dorothy. No longer any doubt ! It was his own lady's apartment that
he had thus miraculously and unknowingly approached.

The two attendants busied themselves with preparations for their mistress's
retiring to rest; and Leonatus could hear one of them bid the other lay
the book and the taper near, as she knew the princess would read for some
time, since she slept but scantly of late. . Another moment, and Imogen
herself entered, dismissed her women, and then went towards the hearth,
standing pensively for awhile, with her eyes fixed upon the embers, lost
in thought.

She breathed a soft sigh, as she murmured :—"He should be returned
ere this."

"He is returned ;" said a voice beside her.

"Leonatus ! Husband ! "

"By what miracle came you hither ?" she said, when he left her lips at
liberty to speak.

Rapidly he told her the circumstances of his mysterious imprisonment.

Broken exclamations of indignant feeling at this outrage upon the
liberty and comfort of him she loved, burst from Imogen :—"Alone,—in
that miserable cell,—deprived of light and food ! But thou art here,
heart ! Soft; I can trust my women. They shall bring you food, love.
I will go bid them seek some."

"If you will ; go then ;" he said.

"When you release me."

"How ! " Release you ? "

For all reply, she glanced smilingly at her position. He had held her, close prisoner, folded in his arms, since he had been there.

"No matter for the food ; stay where thou art."

But even his caresses could not smother Imogen's wifely anxiety. It would not let her rest, even where she was. She recurred to the circumstances of his seizure ; marvelling who might have been the daring instigators, and how they should have had him conveyed hither for incarceration. Suddenly her thoughts glanced towards the queen. She alone had sufficient power to have ordered such a deed in this place. She had insisted on accompanying her step-daughter to her retirement. She had, by the king's will, authority enough to have enabled her to carry out her wishes did they point to such a course. And that they were averse to her own, Imogen could not but suspect, for all her cajolery of profession. Something of these hurried fears and suspicions, did Imogen breathe to her husband.

His rejoinder was a mute one. Leonatus had no room in his heart for aught save his fulness of happiness to find himself with her.

"You stop my mouth, dear my lord. But you cannot allay my fears. They will assail me, even here—in my husband's very embrace. You have enemies. Powerful ones. They will seek you in your dungeon, and find you gone. They will hunt you to the death. My father's return will be your best safety. Till he come back, let us carry all quietly. Either escape now at once ; or let them not miss you from your cell. 'Twill discover all.

"They will not seek me there till day-break ; and, till day-break, I stay here, my life, my wife, my Imogen !"

With morning-sun came fresh resolution. It was agreed between the married lovers that Leonatus should neither return to his prison, nor make his escape ; but simply that he should present himself in the course of the day, as if just returned from the expedition on which he had lately been absent. That he should neither advert to the circumstance of his recent capture, nor take any means to enquire into its origin, until the king's return.   That he should appear at the palace, on the old footing of Cymbeline and his daughter's favorite friend and companion ; but that no public avowal of their marriage should be made until the same period.

That very morning, the queen sat in her bower, writing to her royal husband. She told Cymbeline that in her zeal to promote his wishes, she had kept closely loving watch upon his daughter; and observing that when Posthumus Leonatus was in the capital, he had seemed too nearly to affection the princess, nay, to have carried his presumptuous' hope to the height of daring to think of luring her into return of liking, she had, for the better prevention of fatal consequences, caused him to be put under secret arrest and restraint.   That, she had taken this decisive measure, knowing the king's intention of bestowing his daughter's hand upon Cloten, and fearing lest the rashness of Posthumus Leonatus might prompt him to take advantage of Cymbeline's absence, by urging Imogen into an immediate union, which would frustrate all her royal husband's known designs.   But she had just learned all her precautions were so far unavailing, that Leonatus had contrived to effect his escape ; and in order to prevent any irretrievable mischief from the suspected lovers' marrying before it was too late to interfere, she prayed Cymbeline to lose no time in returning home, that a father's and a king's authority might effectually protect his daughter from so unworthy a match.   The letter was artfully worded, so as at once to inflame her husband's wrath against Posthumus Leonatus ; to inspire the king with an idea of her own subservience to his will, her anxiety to execute his wishes ; and to strengthen his intention of wedding Imogen to Cloten.

She despatched a trusty messenger with this missive to the king; and resolved to maintain a stricter watch than ever upon his daughter.

She was sitting with Imogen that same evening, in pertinacious companionship, when to her unspeakable amazement, Posthumus Leonatus was announced by one of the attendants, as having arrived from his journey, and requesting to know whether it accorded with the princess's leisure and pleasure to receive him.

" You use too ceremonious an observance, dear my lord, with your old playmate ; " Imogen said, as she rose to welcome him with her own smile of gentleness and affection ; " My father's young friend and favorite, and mine own esteemed companion, must know he is ever right gladly received, whenever, and wherever he may present himself to us. I trust my father will soon return, and join his welcome to mine. Meantime, here is my lady, his queen, who will greet you in her royal husband's name ; and aid me hospitably to make you feel at home during his absence."

Imogen spoke with so gay an ease, and Posthumus joined her with so perfect an echo of her sprightly tone, that the queen was compelled, as her only policy, to fall into their complacent mood, and take all unconcernedly as they did.

They were presently joined by Cloten ; who, unconscious of his wily mother's plots, and stratagems, and suspicions, and contrivances, knew nothing of Leonatus's late capture, and therefore had no difficulty in falling naturally into the conversation, and speaking to him as if nothing had happened, but that he had just returned from the journey on which he had been known to depart, after his return from France.

Things went on thus smoothly for some little time. The queen's messenger returned with an answer from her royal husband, which commended her good care and zeal for his interests ; but begged her not to concern herself on account of Posthumus Leonatus, as his affection for Imogen had been a childhood love, an intimacy and regard since infancy. That Cymbeline had perfect reliance on his young favorite's entertaining no thought, save of honoring loyalty towards his own person and that of the princess his daughter ; and that he knew Posthumus Leonatus would as soon meditate treason, as dream of daring to love, far less aspiring to marry, one whom the king had already destined to another husband.

The confident tone in which Cymbeline wrote, partly reassured the queen ; and the simple dignity and quietude, with smiling ease of heart, which appeared in Imogen's manner, contributed to lull her suspicions asleep. She could not think the anxieties of a mutual passion, and of a projected secret marriage, while still the king's approbation was matter of suspense, would permit of the two lovers' wearing so serene an air of perfect content, if they really were lovers. She began to think she must have been misinformed by her spies, who had conveyed to her the intelligence of Posthumus Leonatus having been seen in such closely interesting conversation, and secret inter-communion with the princess Imogen, at the court of Lud's town, when he had first returned from Gaul. She fancied there must have been some misconception on the part of her informants, or some mistake on her own, when she saw the clear countenance of Imogen, and heard her tender voice, every tone of which was musical with happiness. And then, Posthumus, there was a triumphant light in his face, an exultant harmony in his speech, that seemed rather those of a spirit rejoicing in possessed and treasured delight, than the solicitude of an ardent suitor.

When she saw them easy, animated, almost careless in their gay, light-hearted talk ; now interchanging playful words with each other, now bandying jests with Cloten, and now retorting railleries and sportive sentences with herself, she felt half inclined to believe that they had no more serious feelings towards one another than belonged to the old childish liking that had always subsisted between them.

Once, Cloten, in his blurting, abrupt way, suddenly attacked Posthumus Leonatus with :—"Pretty license have you imported from Gaul, sir Posthumus ! I have heard that morals there, are ruled by each man's sense of virtue ; and that there are as many shades of right and wrong among Frenchmen, as there are French consciences—which is perhaps, after all, limiting them to a few."

"How mean you ?" said Leonatus.

"Nay ; look not so innocent. Not that I pretend to more innocence in these matters than becomes a gentleman. But when do you mean to give up your amorous follies, turn sober, and marry ?"

"Whenever I marry, I intend no such injury to myself and my wife, as to commence a sobriety that shall discard love as a folly ;" answered Posthumus. "Who should be amorous, if not a husband ?"

"Pshaw ! This is a turn, to turn off my question ; you know well enough what I would say ;" returned Cloten.

"Nay, not I;" laughed Leonatus. "That were perhaps to presume upon knowing more than you do yourself."

"Oh, I know, and so do you, that I would ask you when you mean to give up sowing bachelor wild oats, and sit down to matrimonial daily bread."

"You speak of matrimony as no feast, but as of a dull round of dry crusts;" smiled Posthumus. "Encouraging to the lady who shall sit down to table with you! She'll hardly care to share such board."

"My son regards wedded life as a high duty, a solemn contract, a holy covenant, rather than a light toy of pleasure, an idle gratification;" said the queen. "Happy she who commits her happiness to such a husband!"

"Solemn joys are oft stupid joys—no joys at all;" said Imogen laughingly. A solemn face checks mirth, and solemnity ill ushers in a banquet. A sad brow, and a grim, formal voice, commend but poorly the richest entertainment. Nothing like a smiling cheer, for the inciting to cheerful, smiling enjoyment."

"You might not wear that smiling cheer of your own, lady, did you know the tricks yonder squire hath been playing in his Gaulish-acquired style, with one of your own women of late. 'Tis not for naught, I suppose, that I see him whispering, and meeting with her, each evening, among the laurels, in the palace-garden, just by the entrance to the women's range of apartments. But enough; I should have tattled nothing of this, had he answered my question openly at once."

"What question?" said Leonatus, drawing Cloten's attention from Imogen, whose cheek had become crimson with the consciousness that her woman was an emissary from herself on these occasions.

"'Tis not so long since I asked it, that you should forget;" returned Cloten. "I am about to turn married man myself soon, and I want to know when you are going to keep me in countenance."

"When I can find a lady who will give me so much countenance by the bestowal of herself, that I shall think I require no other countenancing;" replied Leonatus.

The queen had marked Imogen's confusion at the allusion to Posthumus's reported gallantry; and wishing to improve this hint of jealous

2 L

displeasure, as she thought it, she sought to revive and fix it on a definite object, by enquiring of her son, the name of the silly wench who compromised her reputation, and brought scandal on herself and others, by encouraging idle talk.

"Nay,—it was dark, I could scarcely distinguish her; but I know it was the same, each evening. Helen, I think they call her. But I know not,—indeed, I care not."

"If you care not, how came you to descend to watch her, my lord?" asked Posthumus. "Methinks it was unworthy your princely dignity to abase your high calling to such an office. The task of keeping an eye on the proceedings of a waiting-gentlewoman, might have better befitted a guard on duty—a hireling soldier—a paid sentinel—than so lordly a gentleman as your highness."

"It was no degradation for me. I am above lessening mine esteem with the world by any act that I think fit to do. Detraction dare not assault me. I am beyond its reach. My exalted rank preserves me from the possibility of debasement. It hath its privileges. I cannot degrade myself, or diminish mine importance, by whatever I may choose to think, say, or act."

"Undoubtedly;" replied Posthumus. "The infallibility of great ones, is as sure, as that the meanest and smallest of created things cannot become meaner or less."

"Wherefore, we great ones, hear the sneers of envious little ones, unheeded," said Cloten.

"And, well contented, deem bulk to be strength, power, and largest wisdom;" returned Leonatus. "Your lordship's philosophy is a satisfactory one."

"Nay, I never lacked philosophy enough to satisfy myself;" said Cloten.

The king returned. Posthumus Leonatus made dignified avowal. But Cymbeline's rage knew no bounds. He pronounced instant sentence of banishment against Leonatus, and ordered Imogen into strict confinement, appointing the queen her safe-guard. This wily step-mother affected

great sympathy with her victim, and even permitted the young couple
a parting interview ; but it was with the secret design of still farther exciting Cymbeline's wrath against them, so as to preclude any chance of
ultimate forgiveness. Imogen was not the dupe of this pretended interest ;
for even amidst the anguish of leave-taking, she exclaimed :—" *O*

Dissembling courtesy! How fine this tyrant
Can tickle where she wounds !—My dearest husband,
I something fear my father's wrath ; but nothing,
(Always reserv'd my holy duty,) what
His rage can do on me : You must be gone ;
And I shall here abide the hourly shot
Of angry eyes ; not comforted to live,
But that there is this jewel in the world,
That I may see again."

" Thus far ; and so farewell.
My Emperor hath wrote; I must from hence."

L'ENVOY.

" 'Beseech you all, my lords,
With thoughts so qualified as your charities
Shall best instruct you, measure me."

FINIS.

PASSAGES IN THE PLAYS

(As Illustrative Notes to Vol. III.)

IN RELATION TO

FACTS, NAMES, AND SENTIMENTS,

WITH WHICH IT WAS REQUISITE THE TALES SHOULD ACCORD.

TALE XI.

Page 6, line 31.

The warrant for Gaetano's existence, lies in the words of Leonato to Antonio : "How now, brother? Where is my cousin, your son?"

MUCH ADO ABOUT NOTHING, Act i., s. 2.

Page 7, line 26.

Leonato when he is affecting to commiserate Beatrice's supposed hopeless passion, says of her:—"I am sorry for her, as I have just cause, being *her uncle and her guardian.*"—*Ibid,* Act ii., s. 3.

Page 18, line 15.

The Greek legend was, that the sickle of Saturn falling on this spot, gave the harbour its form.

Page 18, line 28.

We are told that Sicilian manna is an exudation of the sweet sap of the ormus, a species of ash which grows in the mountainous parts of the island.

Page 75, line 21.

Leon. "Niece, will you look to those things I told you of?"

Ibid, Act ii., s. 2.

Page 77, line 13.

"bid her steal into the pleached bower,
Where honey-suckles, ripen'd by the sun,
Forbid the sun to enter."—*Ibid,* Act iii., s. 1.

Page 80, line 3.

"I saw *the duchess of Milan's* gown, that they praise so."

Ibid, Act iii., s. 4.

Page 83, line 3.

D. Pedro. "She cannot endure to hear tell of a husband.
Leon. O, by no means ; she mocks all her woers out of suit."

Ibid, Act ii., s. 2.

Page 86, line 17.

Leonato says, after hearing the high report of the messenger concerning Claudio :—"*He hath an uncle here in Messina* will be very much glad of it."

Page 88,   *Urs.* " I know you well enough ; you are signor Antonio.
line 12.   *Ant.* At a word, I am not.
              Urs. I knew you by *the waggling of your head.*"—*Ibid*, Act ii., s. 1.

Page 89,   The hints for this attachment of Balthazar's, are taken from a few
line 24.   words of his to Margaret in the masquerade scene ; and from those he
              utters just before his song, in a subsequent scene :—
              " Many a wooer doth commence his suit
              To her he thinks not worthy ; yet he wooes."—*Ibid*, Act ii., s. 3.

Page 93,   Benedick's first greeting to Beatrice in the play, is:—" What, my dear
line 20.   *lady Disdain!* are you yet living ? "—*Ibid*, Act i., s. 1.

Page 93,   ' Bella donna,'—the botanical name for the deadly nightshade.
line 30.

Page last,   Vide Ariosto,—for lost wits sought in the moon.
line 5.

Page last,   That don Pedro's last visit to Messina took place about a twelvemonth
line 12.   before the play begins, may be inferred from Borachio's words:—" I think
              I told your lordship, *a year since*, how much I am in the favor of Mar-
              garet, the waiting gentlewoman to Hero."—*Ibid*, Act ii., s. 2.

                            TALE XII.

Page 116,   The clown's name is ascertained, where the duke asks for " that old
line 14.   and antique song," his attendant answering:—" He is not here, so please
              your lordship, that should sing it.
              Duke. Who was it?
              Cur. *Feste*, the jester, my lord ; a fool, that the lady Olivia's father
              took much delight in.—TWELFTH NIGHT, Act ii., s. 4."

Page 126,   Maria's diminutive stature is clearly denoted in several passages of the
line 11.   play; among others, sir Toby's exclamation on her approach :—" Look
              where the youngest wren of nine comes."—*Ibid*, Act iii., s. 2.

Page 141,   Maria,—when her confederates in the plot against Malvolio are placed
line 25.   by her where they may watch and overhear him,—says:—" Get ye
              all three into the *box-tree.*"—*Ibid*, Act ii., s. 5.

Page 150,   The chantry belonging to the household, is mentioned by Olivia in the
line 7.   third scene of the fourth Act, as the place where her betrothal with
              Sebastian can be immediately solemnized.

Page 150,   Fabian owes Malvolio a grudge, for having " brought me out of favor
line 23.   with my lady, about *a bear-baiting.*"—*Ibid*, Act ii., s. 5.

Page 173,
line 11.

Mr. Leigh Hunt, in those delightful notes to his translation of Redi's *Bacchus in Tuscany*, tells us that Redi says :—" Our language makes use not only of diminutives, but of the diminutives of diminutives, even unto the third and fourth generation." And he himself adds :—" An Italian nurse will *piccininino* a little baby till there seems no end."

Page 187,
line 23.

Fabian says of sir Andrew :—" This is a dear manakin to you, sir Toby.

Sir Toby. I have been dear to him, lad ; some two thousand strong, or so."—*Ibid*, Act iii., s. 2.

Page 188,
line 2.

"I am a great eater of beef, and, I believe that does harm to my wit."
Ibid, Act i., s. 3.

Page 188,
line 8.

Of sir Toby's intimacy with Maria, we have hints, from the clown's speech to her in the fifth scene of the first Act ; from the knight's boast of her "adoring him," in the third scene of the second Act ; from the tone of his raptures at her " device" against Malvolio in the fifth scene of the same act ; and from Fabian's report of their marriage at the conclusion of the play.

Page 199,
line 15.

Sir And. " Where shall I find you ?
Sir Toby. We'll call thee at the *cubiculo.*"—*Ibid,* Act iii., s. 2.

TALE XIII.

Page 203,
line 14.

Kief—the ancient capital of Russia ; called, in some of the histories, " la mere des villes russes."

Page 240,
line 33.

Leontes says to Camillo :—" thou,
His cup-bearer,—whom I *from meaner form*
Have bench'd and rear'd to worship ; "—WINTER'S TALE, Act i., s. 2.

Page 241,
line 9.

That Antigonus is older than Camillo, we may infer from more than one passage in the play.

Page 241,
line 22.

The hint for Camillo's attachment to Paulina, is taken from the concluding speech of the play.

Page 250,
line 16.

We learn this characteristic touch from Hermione's own beautiful words :—   " Good, my lords,
I am not prone to weeping, as our sex
Commonly are ; the want of which vain dew,
Perchance shall dry your pities : but I have
That honorable grief lodg'd here, which burns
Worse than tears drown."—*Ibid*, Act ii, s. 1.

Page 258,
line 13.

See the first scene of the play for an account of the correspondence maintained between Leontes and Polixenes ; and the first scene of the fifth act for the title of ' brother' used between them.

Page 266,
line 9.

Leontes speaks of his "queen's full eyes;" and passionately exclaims:—"Stars, very stars,
And all eyes else dead coals!"—*Ibid*, Act v., s. 1.

Page 269,
line 31.

As one proof of the power of self-controul that belongs to Hermione, witness her preserving, unmoved, the personation of the statue, in presence of her husband and daughter whom she has not beheld for years.

Page 280,
line 17.

"O, thus she stood,
Even with such life of majesty (warm life,
As now it coldly stands,) when first I woo'd her!"—*Ibid*, Act v., s. 3.

Page 281,
line 22.

That Hermione is capable of the extreme of playful gaiety in manner, behold her in her first scene of the play.

Page 282.
line 25.

Paulina reminds Leontes :—" Sir, you yourself
Have said, and writ so, (but your writing now
Is colder than that theme,) 'She had not been,
Nor was not to be equall'd ;"—thus your verse
Flow'd with her beauty once."—*Ibid*, Act v., s. 1.

Page 284,
line 20.

Leon.				" Why, that was when
Three crabbed mouths had sour'd themselves to death,
Ere I could make thee open thy white hand,
And clap thyself my love; then didst thou utter,
' I am yours for ever.' "—*Ibid*, Act i., s. 2.

Page 289.
line 21.

Antigonus says in the first scene of the second act :—
" I have three daughters ; the eldest is eleven ;
The second, and the third, nine, and some five."
Thus, Mamillius is supposed to be about seven or eight years old at the time of the play.

Page 289,
line 31.

We hear of Paulina's "removed house" in the second scene of the fifth act; and of the "gallery" and "chapel" in the closing scene of the play.

TALE XIV.

Page 297,
line 1.

Sebastian speaks of his father as "Sebastian of *Messaline*," in the first scene of Act ii., and Viola, in the last scene of the play. Some suppose Messaline to be Mitylene ; but the story takes the license of giving it merely the poetical " local habitation and name" which Shakespeare has vaguely assigned.

Page 298,
line 17.

The duke says of Sebastian :—" right noble is his blood."
						TWELFTH NIGHT, Act v., s. 1.

Page 309,
line 27.

Sebastian says his father left behind him, myself, and a sister, *both born in an hour*."—*Ibid*, Act ii., s. 1.

Page 310,
line 8.

The Dramatist has ingeniously drawn the attention of the spectators to the similarity of dress worn by the twins, as well as accounted for it, easily and naturally, by making Viola say :—

"I my brother know
Yet living in my glass; even such, and so,
In favor was my brother; *and he went*
Still in this fashion, color, ornament,
For him I imitate."

Page 315,
line 25.

Forks are mentioned by a writer of the early part of the fifteenth century, as one of the luxuries recently introduced and used by the people of Piacenza.

Page 318,
line 21.

In page 21 of Holmes's Life of Mozart—a model of biography—there is a charming childish trait told of the boy Mozart, similar to the one narrated in this tale. It is precisely by recording such touches of infantine nature, that a clue is furnished to the power, which some of the after Artist's passages have, of creating profound emotions for which we have no expression ; but which Shakespeare has put into words for us in a speech of this very Viola's, where she says of a certain tune :—"It gives a very echo to the seat where Love is thron'd." Glorious musician to have given us such strains ! Glorious Poet to have so interpreted the unutterable ecstacy to which they give rise !

Page 319,
line 6.

Viola. "My father had a mole upon his brow.
Seb. And so had mine."—*Ibid*, Act v., s. 1.

Page 322,
line 18.

For the vivid impression and prepossession which Viola is made to entertain concerning Orsino throughout the Tale, owing to her father's mention of him, the hint has been taken from her words :—" Orsino ! I have heard my father name him. He was a bachelor then."

Ibid, Act i., s. 2.

Page 350.
line 19.

An Italian idiom ; a certain number of eggs always indicating the quantity of maccaroni made at one time.

Page 351,
line 30.

Italian peasants eat lupin seeds, put to swell in water; they peel them, and call them 'lupini.'

Page 355,
line 33.

When Viola proposes to engage herself to the duke, as his page, she says :—   "for I can sing,
And speak to him in many sorts of music,
That will allow me very worth his service."—*Ibid*, Act i., s. 2.

Page 376,
line 19.

When the twin brother and sister are recalling circumstances which shall identify them to each other, and Viola speaks of her father's death, Sebastian replies :—

"O, that record is lively in my soul !
He finished, indeed, his mortal act,
That day that made my sister thirteen years."—*Ibid*, Act v., s. 1.

TALE XV.

Page 398,   " A kind of conquest
line 14.   Cæsar made here; but made not here his brag
            Of ' came,' and ' saw,' and ' overcame': with shame
            ('The first that ever touch'd him,) he was carried
            From off our coast twice beaten; and his shipping
            (Poor ignorant baubles!) on our terrible seas,
            Like egg-shells mov'd upon their surges, crack'd
            As easily 'gainst our rocks: For joy whereof,
            The fam'd Cassibelan, who was once at point
            (O giglot fortune!) to master Cæsar's sword,
            Made Lud's town with rejoicing fires bright,
            And Britons strut with courage."—CYMBELINE, Act iii., s. 1.

Page 406,   *Cym.*   " Thou art welcome, Caius.
line 18.   Thy Cæsar knighted me; my youth I spent
            Much under him; of him I gather'd honor."—*Ibid*, Act iii., s. 1.

Page 407,   Philario, speaking of Posthumus, says:—" His father and I were
line 6.   soldiers together; to whom I have been often bound for no less than
            my life."—*Ibid*, Act i., s. 5.

Page 407,   Posthumus says:—
line 27.   " My residence in Rome at one Philario's;
            Who to my father was a friend, to me
            Known but by letter."—*Ibid*, Act i., s. 2.

Page 408,   See the first scene of the play for the history of Sicilius, Posthumus
line 21.   Leonatus's father.

Page 413,   *Bel.* " My fault being nothing (as I have told you oft,)
line 19.   But that two villains, whose false oaths prevail'd
            Before my perfect honor, swore to Cymbeline,
            I was confederate with the Romans: so,
            Follow'd my banishment."—*Ibid*, Act iii., s. 3.

Page 414,   Belarius says:—" Their nurse, Euriphile,
line 5.   Whom for the theft I wedded, stole these children
            Upon my banishment."—*Ibid*, Act v., s. 5.

Page 415,   The reader will remark the exquisite taste in the Dramatist, who has
line 26.   given, as it were, *a family-likeness* in the peculiar marks on the person of
            Imogen and her brother. He cannot fail to recollect the notedly lovely
            passage in the second act:—
                            " On her left breast
            A mole cinque-spotted, like crimson drops
            I' the bottom of a cowslip."

            And in the fifth act we hear that:—
                            " Guiderius had
            Upon his neck a mole, a sanguine star."

Page 426,
line 8.

Belarius says :—
" This gentleman, my Cadwal, Arviragus,
Your younger princely son ; he, sir, was lapp'd
In a most curious mantle, wrought by the hands
Of his queen mother ;"—*Ibid*, Act v., s. 5.

Page 436,
line 4.

Imogen, parting with her husband, says :—
" This diamond was my mother's : take it, heart ;"—*Ibid*, Act. i., s. 2.

Page 444,
line 13.

Imogen says to her father :—" Sir,
It is your fault that I have lov'd Posthumus.
You bred him as my playfellow ;"—*Ibid*, Act i., s. 2.

Page 449,
line 30.

The king says :—
" Our ancestor was that Mulmutius, which
Ordain'd our laws ; * * Mulmutius,
Who was the first of Britain, which did put
His brows within a golden crown, and call'd
Himself a king."—*Ibid*, Act iii., s. 1.

Page 475,
line 3.

" they come
Under the conduct of bold *Iachimo*,
Sienna's brother."—*Ibid*, Act iv., s. 2.

Page 479,
line 34.

Christ was born during Cymbeline's reign. And it is remarkable,
that Shakespeare's Imogen, in the spirit in which he has drawn her
character, is the most Christian of his heroines.

Page 481,
line 14.

See the account which Cornelius, the physician, gives of the queen's
previous motives, in the last scene, when he brings the tidings of
her death.

Page 489,
line 6.

For a reference to this encounter at Orleans, see the conversation
between the French gentleman and Posthumus, in the fifth scene of the
first act.

Page 490,
line 24.

We have historical authority for Camalodunum (the ancient name for
Colchester — others say, Maldon,) being Cymbeline's chief seat and
residence ; but there are several reasons against assigning this as the site
of the palace mentioned in the play. There seems to be evidence in the
third act, of its being not so far removed from Milford-Haven, but to
afford time for Pisanio's going thither and back, within the space of
" two days ; " which at that remote period would of course have been
insufficient for the travelling between Essex and Wales. Lucius desires
of Cymbeline " a conduct overland, to Milford-Haven ; " and the king
commands the escort not to leave the Roman envoy " till he have crossed
the Severn." At the commencement of the play, we find that it is
situated near to the " haven " whence Posthumus embarks for his exile
in Italy. But since it is idle endeavouring to square by matter-of-fact
rule and measure, the position of a spot, which the requirements of
dramatic fitness demanded should be left in indecision, the precise
whereabout of this palace has been purposely unstated in the Tale.

Page 490,   In the stately vision which occurs in the fourth scene of the fifth act,
line 13.   Jupiter says:—" in our temple was he married."

Page 497,   In the same speech and scene cited above, we find these words:—
line 2.   "Our Jovial star reign'd at his birth."

Page 499,   The reader need scarcely be referred to the graphic description of this
line 18.   room in the second scene of the fourth act.   It dwells in our imagination
               as a paragon of bed-chambers—a very shrine of beauty and purity.

Page 500,   The names of Imogen's attendants are indicated in the following two
line 10.   passages in the second act:—

Imo.   "Who's there?   My woman *Helen ?* "

Imo.   " To *Dorothy* my woman hie thee presently."

LaVergne, TN USA
29 December 2009

168433LV00001B/48/P